WHAT THE EYE HEARS

WHAT THE EYE HEARS

A HISTORY of TAP DANCING

BRIAN SEIBERT

FARRAR, STRAUS AND GIROUX

NEW YORK

Farrar, Straus and Giroux
18 West 18th Street, New York 10011

Grateful acknowledgment is made for permission to reprint
the following illustrations and photographs: page 18, Courtesy of
the Library of Congress; page 112, Photograph by Vandam Studio © Billy
Rose Theatre Division, New York Public Library for the Performing Arts;
page 174, Photofest; page 332, Allan Grant/Getty Images; page 374,
Photofest; page 486, Makoto Ebi.

Library of Congress Cataloging-in-Publication Data
Seibert, Brian.
    What the eye hears : a history of tap dancing / Brian Seibert.
        pages   cm
    Includes index.
    ISBN 978-0-86547-953-1 (hardback) — ISBN 978-1-4299-4761-9 (e-book)
    1. Tap dancing—History.   I. Title.

GV1794 .S44 2015
792.7'809—dc23

                                                          2015005010

Designed by Abby Kagan

Our books may be purchased in bulk for promotional, educational, or
business use. Please contact your local bookseller or the Macmillan Corporate
and Premium Sales Department at 1-800-221-7945, extension 5442,
or by e-mail at MacmillanSpecialMarkets@macmillan.com.

www.fsgbooks.com
www.twitter.com/fsgbooks • www.facebook.com/fsgbooks

1   3   5   7   9   10   8   6   4   2

CONTENTS

PART IV: OUT OF STEP

PART V: PUTTING THE SHOES BACK ON

PART VI: AN AMERICAN TRADITION, A GLOBAL ART

WHAT THE EYE HEARS

OPENING ACT

On a Sunday afternoon at the beginning of this century, if you walked by a certain small club in midtown Manhattan, you would hear tap dancing. And if you went inside, you might discover, as the source of that sound, a man nearly ninety years old. Snug in a stylish suit, his shirt unbuttoned halfway down his bony chest, he tapped out rhythms that swung hard. Age might have robbed him of the elasticity to perform the scissoring kicks and jive splits he'd been whipping off less than twenty years before, but he had learned to execute his steps with minimal effort. As long as he was dancing, he was buoyant, indefatigable, still moving with the speed of youth, and prone to revolving his hips like a stripper. Then suddenly he would stop, flatly declare he was tired, and break the spell, deflating into a fragile old man who had to be helped offstage. The transformation was poignant. He made it a joke. "I'm sure happy to be here," he would say. "At my age, I'm happy to be *anywhere*."

His name was Buster Brown, and this was his Crazy Tap Jam. Squinting, he would scan the tables of Swing 46 for a dancer ready to perform, asking in his high, throaty voice, "Who's got their shoes on?" In response, Frankie Clemente, a four-year-old with a buzz cut, might escape his family, slide into the raised stage with a thud, and scramble over the lip. "Lay it on me," Buster would say, and Frankie, stamping his feet arhymthmically, would swing his arms and spin and stand on his toes in rough approximations of steps he'd seen older dancers do. The control that Buster was slowly losing, Frankie had yet to acquire. If Buster's dancing was spare and suggestive like Chinese painting, Frankie's was coloring outside the lines. People cheered for both.

The more they applauded, the more difficult it became to convince Frankie to surrender the stage. Whichever moves provoked the loudest response, those he would shamelessly repeat. Otherwise, his movements appeared random, as did the occasions when he stumbled upon a coherent rhythm. Then his body seemed to express a different satisfaction. When he first started dancing at Swing 46, Frankie was two, and he clearly apprehended the joy of making noise. But at four, perhaps he also felt an intimation of the subtler pleasure of making music.

As haphazard as Frankie's attempts seemed, they aimed toward the models he witnessed each week. He swung his arms while he stamped his feet, because he realized that both were part of the game. His actions suggested an understanding of a defining feature of tap dance: that it falls between categories, or across them; that it is dance *and* music, sound *and* movement. Tap makes music visible, matching aural patterns with shapes in space. You can watch a film of a dancer like Buster Brown, turn the volume off, and still nearly hear the beats. It's music for the deaf. Yet tap also makes movement audible. Close your eyes and you can almost see weight shifting. Call it dance for the blind.

Most dance arises from an interaction between music and movement. But because tap can be both dancing *to* music and dancing *as* music, it's especially concerned with the combination. As the tap dancer Paul Draper once explained, "What the eye sees is sharpened by what the ear hears, and the ear hears more clearly that which sight enhances." A dancer jumps up at a tilt with bent knees, shaping his legs into a bell; when, still in the air, he brings his heels together, that bell rings. The motion that propels a trainlike step is what makes it sound like a train. The relation can be that blatant, but also highly subtle, as in the minute calibrations of force and weight with which a heel is dropped. There's also pleasure in *not* seeing the sound, in not being able to discern the source. At top speeds, a tap dancer can articulate a dozen or more discrete sounds per second. You hear a flurry of beats and can't account for them all—something has been slipped in, a bonus. It's sleight of hand, made by foot.

In practice, dancers tend to lean toward one pole or the other, emphasizing sound over movement or the reverse. The two are in tension, one often working at the bidding, or the expense, of the other. The pursuit of rhythmic intricacy and gradations of timbre pools action in the feet, so that tap dance becomes a standing drum solo in a jazz club where your view of the dancer is partial, or an audio recording in which you can't see the dancer at all. Or the dancer's attention moves to figures in space, to body parts upon which we're more accustomed to reading emotion, and to gestures, which, however eloquent, make no sound.

To put it another way, all music begins in movement: hands on keys, breath on reeds. But a musician dances incidentally—twisting to reach for a note, keeping the beat—while for a tap dancer, the motions that make the music are to be developed for their own sake. This fact locates tap between the potential abstraction of music and the unavoidable humanity of dance, in which the instrument is the body, the person. Tap similarly falls between two sides in the centuries-old debate about what dance should be, a form of storytelling or a nonrepresentational art. As music, tap has access to pure form. And yet, in its most popular manifestations, tap has been all about personality. It has been situated, not always comfortably, in narrative genres such as musical comedy. Tap can be comic, with comedy as physical as a clown's, but here, too, it is most distinctive in musical interplay, in the wit of how a rhythm is parceled out across parts of the feet.

I have one more theory about tap's appeal. Perhaps the most powerful part of our response to any kind of dance is kinesthetic: the way we seem to feel in our own muscles and bones what we see in the muscles and bones of the bodies we're watching. Tap combines this with what I think of as the kinesthetics of hearing: the way that hearing is a kind of touch, blasts of air knocking against the eardrum. We sense this most obviously in low, rumbling frequencies—in music that you feel, rolling through you like thunder—but it's operating all the time. Add to that our primal reaction to rhythm, and tap dancers have a potent set of kinesthetic responses to work upon.

In any case, Frankie Clemente's banging pointed toward the ideal, the dynamic equilibrium of sound and motion, just as his habit of making things up on the spot served as a crude version of improvisation. He was, after all, participating in a jam session in the jazz tradition, what Ralph Ellison famously called "the jazzman's true academy," a site of "apprenticeship, ordeals, initiation ceremonies," where the musician must "achieve, in short, his self-determined identity." That's a lofty description of what went down at Swing 46, but most dancers there fulfilled the tacit expectation that they test themselves in the moment. For many, improvising was an excuse to shirk the effort of putting together a routine. Yet for more serious dancers, improvising could be the harder road—requiring both a lightning-quick, fertile imagination and the technique to realize their ideas without hesitation. In a sense, the goal of improvisation is unreachable: to take the shock of invention and make it constant. Nevertheless, for jazz musicians, including the tap dancing kind, it's the ultimate measure of prowess.

Pure improvisation is rare, of course. Like other jazz musicians, like artists of all kinds, tap dancers develop habits, cling to pet maneuvers, vary formulas. Somewhere in those tendencies, just shy of mannerism, lies style: a musician's individual way of phrasing a rhythm, a dancer's unique interpretation of a step expressed through the equally unique instrument of his body, the movements he adopts and the ones he fashions and how he puts them together. Style: always some mixture of strengths accentuated and weaknesses disguised, of weaknesses converted into strengths, always some amalgam of artifice and what comes naturally, of dogged practice and of grace—that gift from who knows where. Through improvising, dancers both discover and create themselves, commonly in public.

If Frankie had the desire and discipline to follow the tradition honored at Swing 46, he might move through imitation to his own style. The high value tap dancers place on individuation helps explain why, even though what they do is seldom narrative, they like to call it "story dancing." Each time Buster danced, he was telling us who he was, what he had to say. And when he was improvising, that story, and hence that self, was open-ended. Perhaps that is why, within the partly self-determined limits of style, tap dancers so often claim to feel free. That kind of freedom is earned.

When I started attending Buster's jams, the first thing that surprised me was the variety of participants—four-year-olds and octogenarians, men and women, blacks and whites. In that room, tap cut across many of the lines that divide Americans. And not only Americans. Swing 46 regulars came from Europe, Asia, South America, Australia. What drew these people together?

Gregory Hines had an answer. "There are no judgments in tap," I would later hear him say. "Put on a pair of tap shoes and you're in." That last sentence could have been posted as the entry requirement at Swing 46. The inclusive policy attracted an eclectic assortment of types and styles—flirtatious, belligerent, sophisticated, goofy. The open invitation also blurred another dividing line, the one between amateur and professional. It wasn't uncommon for a total beginner to be followed by a vaudeville veteran, or for a fiercely dedicated yet talentless enthusiast to share the stage with a prodigiously gifted yet cavalier wunderkind. The mix was absurd, exasperating, and, if you were open to the spirit of it, fun.

It could, however, be difficult to take seriously. There's a reason that when people say someone is "tap-dancing around" a subject, they mean that the figurative tap dancer is all flash and little substance. In the popular imagination, tap has long been associated with amateurs. In movie musicals from the 1930s, some ingenue from the sticks, suitcase in hand, fills in at the last moment for an experienced professional, parlaying a few tap steps into instant fame. The most popular tap dancing star of that era—the apogee of tap's popularity—was a child: Shirley Temple. Aspiring Shirleys stocked a thousand dancing schools, and even today, tap's most common image remains that of a horde of prepubescent girls with pasted-on smiles in a recital that only a parent could bear.

Even the best tap dancers deflect serious appraisal. Racial attitudes figure in—primitivist notions of "natural" rhythm. Closely related and even more instrumental is the way that great tap dancers work very hard to create an illusion of ease and the impression that even when they're not improvising they're making things up in the moment. The strongest appeal of tap dancers can be the way they make you feel that they're not doing

much—that you could do what they're doing, if you only tried—and, at
the same time, that they're accomplishing nearly impossible feats, things
you could never do. "If you can walk, you can tap," Buster liked to say,
which is about as true as saying that if you can cry out you can sing.
Anyone who's walked to a rhythm or drummed one with his toes has tap-
danced, but only in the most elementary sense. Buster's comment, a motto
among his colleagues, might invite a dismissal of tap as no more a discipline than Frankie Clemente's flopping around. Buster said it because his
sense of theatrical etiquette was centered in such distance-diminishing
gestures. Also, after eighty-some years of doing it, tap dancing for Buster
was like walking.

A Sunday session at Swing 46 felt like a family picnic because that
was how Buster wanted it. Though he would consistently forget names
or mangle them, he seemed to know everybody who came in. And if he
didn't know you, he would soon. "Have you got your shoes?" he'd ask,
encouraging anyone who wanted to dance, making sure no one was left
out. Soon enough, Buster had me choosing a song and taking off into the
unknown. And so it was that Brian Seibert, a bespectacled white guy in
khakis and a button-down shirt, entered the Swing 46 mix. As I hopped
onstage, Buster announced, "Ladies and gentlemen, here's Duane!"

Buster would ask a new dancer to tell a bit about himself. Here's a bit
about me and tap. I've danced all my life, formally and informally. I
took my first class in 1981, when I was six, at a dance studio in a suburb
of Los Angeles. It was a studio similar to thousands of others across the
country. My teacher was Miss Thea, an archetypal small-time dance
instructor: fishnet stockings, a cane in one hand, a cigarette dangling
from the other. I had been playing soccer and was lousy at it; my mother
figured that dance classes might improve my coordination. My sister was
already attending Miss Thea's, and so, like almost every other American
male dancer with a sister, I followed mine into class.

Soon enough, I dropped soccer in favor of dance, even though (or
because) I was usually the only boy. I graduated to another studio, where
I took tap along with ballet and something misleadingly named "jazz
dance." ("Broadway dance" or "music video" dance would've been

more accurate.) By my studio's standards, I was advanced; my classmates were professional adults. But compared with the tap I would encounter in Buster, the tap I acquired as a child was like a signal that had lost strength by straying too far from its source. The tap I learned was the kind taught in most dancing schools: simplified, standardized. I felt the relation between the rhythms of the routines and the sounds from the stereo, but I don't think I ever conceived of what I was doing as playing music. I associated tap with Fred Astaire and Gene Kelly. They were hard to miss: you flipped a channel and there they were, dancing on the ceiling, trading steps with a cartoon mouse. Later, I saw Gregory Hines tap in the film *White Nights* and was more enchanted by Mikhail Baryshnikov and his eleven pirouettes. Buster and his dancing came from a world I knew little about as a child. I knew little about it as an adult, even though I was an avid jazz fan, and Buster had performed with musicians I held in great esteem. For someone who thought of himself—at least some of the time—as a tap dancer, there was a lot I didn't know.

Take Buster, for example. He was born in Baltimore, in 1913. His father shucked oysters. His mother was a maid. With seven sisters and no brothers, he was always the star. Though his given name was James, his aunt once remarked that he seemed "just like a little Buster"—a reference perhaps to the mischievous comic-book character—and the name stuck. When Buster was six, his father died, and he was brought up not only by his mother but by his sisters, who took jobs after school to keep the family afloat.

"I started to dance," Buster liked to say, "when I started to walk." By the time he was five, his favorite activity was attending vaudeville shows. He fell in love with the comedians first and didn't notice the dancers much until junior high, when a troupe called the Whitman Sisters came through town. On the bill was Pops Whitman, a dancer a few years younger than Buster: "He was a little guy that could really dance. He could do everything. A no-hand flip like nobody in the world. That and the way that he was dressed. He had on long pants. I wasn't even wearing long pants then. He was wearing long pants and this man's suit. Fit him perfectly. I knew right then this is what I wanted to do."

Buster and his friends taught themselves. "We would look at a step," he said, "and we'd spend some time learning it from the guy who did the step. This is what we called trading. There was no problem getting a guy to teach you a step, because he would be learning a step from you." They practiced on the street, in the schoolyard, down in the basement. When acts came through town—and in those days, acts were always coming through—Buster and his friends would study the dancing until they could imitate it. "You didn't need to go to no school and learn how to dance if you wanted to do a little stealing." Trading, stealing—there wasn't much difference, at least among friends.

Each year, the students at Frederick Douglass High School put on a show. Buster and two of his buddies danced as the Three Little Dots. At night, the boys would sneak out to clubs and dance for coins. "Good money," he remembered. "We thought four and five dollars a night was good money then." Compared with what his mother made, it was. Dancing wasn't like doing laundry; it was "easy living. You could do what you loved and get paid for it."

In 1932, Buster went pro. Tap was everywhere—vaudeville theaters, nightclubs, movie screens. If that meant that opportunity abounded, it also meant that competition was keen. Buster and the gang called themselves the Three Aces now, and their style emphasized speed. Even their soft shoe, a dance usually taken at a relaxed tempo, was sped up. An emcee at Baltimore's Plantation Club suggested they change their name to the Speed Kings. (This was not just an improvement in specificity; people had been mishearing Aces as Asses.) A touring show took the boys to Columbus, Cleveland, Philadelphia; another show carried them home. They modeled themselves after the trio of Pete, Peaches, and Duke, one of the most influential groups in the "class act" tradition. "We had tried to imitate them," Buster remembered, "but we had never seen them." (That's some fancy step stealing.) Once, when the Speed Kings were playing in the same town as their idols, Buster finally caught their act. "Everything they did was together. And they were the best-dressed tap dancing act ever." By comparison, the Speed Kings were average, similar in approach and execution to dozens of tap teams.

In 1938, they joined Irvin C. Miller's Brownskin Models, an all-black revue that had been touring, in annual editions, for more than a decade. Along with its famed line of beauties, the show carried singers, comedians, and dancers, accompanied by a jazz band. Most cities had a few theaters that hosted such revues, often in combination with a movie, a new one passing through every week or so. It was with the Brownskin Models that Buster first visited the Deep South and first performed in a show blacks weren't welcome to attend. Some theaters were blacks-only but would set aside a night for curious whites, and Buster would remember how the management sprayed the theater with disinfectant. Between the fear of contamination and the desire to be entertained was a space; black entertainers could squeeze in like a wedge. In the South, Buster became more aware of the peculiar role he had danced himself into. "They had certain places that the average black couldn't go in, but we were allowed." Performers were granted greater freedoms, and with them came greater exposure.

Later in life, when someone asked Buster why he got into show business, he said it was because of the girls. He signed with the Brownskin Models before a salary had been discussed. The ladies were incentive enough. When he got one pregnant, he married her, right there in a theater. The family settled in Cleveland, but Buster had to get back on the road. Though his partner John had died in a boating accident, and Sammy had gone off on his own as "Clogging Campbell," Buster continued the Speed Kings with Sylvester Luke and Emmet McClure, the brand name abiding through substitutions in the roster. It was this version of the Speed Kings that made it to Harlem, just in time to trade steps at the Hoofers' Club before that legendary hangout closed for good. It was this version that played the Apollo Theater. In 1943, the group appeared in *Something to Shout About*, one of countless movie musicals that were then being cranked out. Buster's part in the film's big finish offers the only extant footage of him as a young dancer, ten seconds long. (The dog act gets four minutes.) He also landed a role in a "soundie," a musical short made for coin-operated film jukeboxes. In it, he looks cute but doesn't dance. There would be no Hollywood breaks for him. Only a very few black tap dancers made it into that club.

The Second World War was ongoing, and though Buster wasn't drafted, his partners were. It took him six months to work up new material, but he fit it into the same mold: soft shoe, rhythm dance, flash-dance finish. The main difference now was that he had to carry the act by himself, no rest. He met Ernest Cathy, better known as "Pippy," and formed a duo called Brown and Beige. They appeared a few times on *The Kate Smith Show*, one of many television variety programs that were offering tap dancers occasional jobs. After five or six years, Buster began to tire of Pippy's unreliability. The careers of many people Buster knew were hobbled by addiction to heroin, including that of his hero, Baby Laurence, whom Buster wasn't alone in rating as the best tap dancer ever.

Buster went single again, gravitating to Chicago and its thriving nightspots, such as the mob-owned Club DeLisa. "Money burned my pocket. I could be paid that night and three days later be broke." He toured the country with the big bands of Count Basie, Jimmie Lunceford, and others. Buster didn't realize it then, but he was witnessing an end. The turning point, as he later saw it, was the death, in 1949, of Bill "Bojangles" Robinson, the most famous black tap dancer of the time, the one with movie roles. "After that, everything just fell. Bang. No more jobs." Venues closed. Tastes shifted. "By the time I got to the age when I could do some of the things I had rehearsed, show business was gone."

During the fifties and sixties, Buster worked for a record company, served as a clerk in a hotel, managed a restaurant, and cleaned office buildings. People would come to talk of these years as the time tap was dead, and many younger blacks were eager to relegate the dance to a shameful past, yet Buster and his friends never stopped dancing. He made sure to dance every day, if only to the record player at home. He and his pals would meet after work and convince bar owners to let them perform for free. From 1951 through the mid-eighties, the Copasetics, a fraternity of swing-era entertainers that Buster joined, put on an annual charity benefit attended by the Harlem elite. "You could dance," Buster remembered. "You just couldn't make any money dancing."

In 1966, touring European jazz festivals with a quartet of hoofing old-timers, Buster was surprised by standing ovations, proof that his art hadn't lost its appeal when it fell out of fashion in his home country. "In New York, we were just dancers. In Europe, we were celebrities." (Film exists of Buster dancing in Germany and France—about thirty seconds' worth.) In 1968, he joined a tour of Africa sponsored by the State

Department. The anti-Communist cultural-diplomacy effort found tap dancers valuable, images of American racial harmony to counter images of riots in the streets. The Ethiopian emperor Haile Selassie hung gold medals on their necks, and in trading steps with Africans, they discovered evidence of shared roots that both sides greeted eagerly. While Buster was away, he missed out on the *Tap Happening*, when a group of hoofers of his vintage took over Monday nights in an off-Broadway theater and caused critics to exclaim, Where have these amazing artists been hiding? He toured South America with Cab Calloway and returned to the American South with the Ink Spots—"not the original Ink Spots. There were about eight or ten Ink Spot acts working everywhere." Copying persisted while other seemingly never-changing facts of life did change. "The same people who had seemed to resent us before— looking at their wives—were kissing us."

When a generation emerged ready to appreciate tap more self-consciously as an art, Buster was well placed to take on the mantle of an old master, mentoring, teaching, receiving grants. He was perfect for revues resurrecting the past and for cameos in period films. His fun-loving manner and ancient jokes warmed tap documentaries, and he presided among the elders on Gregory Hines's landmark *Dance in America* special on PBS in 1989. This stage of Buster's career was recorded in hours upon hours of video. In the mid-nineties, when Hines and the national press anointed Savion Glover as the savior of tap, the twenty-something dancer included an homage to Buster in his Broadway show *Bring in 'da Noise, Bring in 'da Funk* and included Buster himself in concert tours. Never quite famous, Buster was now more widely known than he had ever been known before. In 2002, Oklahoma City University conferred upon him and seven other hoofers the honorary degree of Doctor of Performing Arts in American Dance. Tears filled his eyes as, standing in his cap and gown, he told those assembled that receiving the doctorate was "the biggest highlight in my life and the greatest feeling I've ever had."

Through it all, Buster never stopped dancing. He danced walking down the street, danced while drinking at the bar. He was as much a swing dancer as a hoofer, tiring out partners a quarter his age. At get-togethers in the eighties and nineties, he would sometimes nod off, and friends would gather around to watch the moving feet of the sleeping man, undoubtedly dreaming up some new step.

Such was Buster's story, or part of it, his part in the larger story of tap. That larger story is what this book strives to tell. As Buster's tale indicates in miniature, it is a story of several braided traditions, of dancers famous and forgotten, and of the times in which they lived. It is a story about the aesthetic and technical development of an art, and about America, and, unavoidably, about blacks and whites and the back-and-forth between them. Once the Swing 46 sessions had piqued my interest, I went looking for the past. I found it in libraries and on the Internet, but also in the homes of dancers, in photos on their walls, in video footage guarded like sacred relics and sometimes shared or traded, like steps. I found the past in the present: in dancers whose life experience spanned almost a century, but also in younger tappers to whom the tradition had been passed, body to body. Through them and through the historical record, I grew to know dancers I'd never meet, people who had died well before I was born and people who had lived just up to the moment before I started searching.

Again and again, I was made aware of my timing. For more than a year of Sundays at Swing 46, I tried to talk to Buster. Some weeks, I wouldn't make it. Others, he would be too sick to attend. When we were both there, I'd ask him if he would like to talk, and he'd say, We'll see. I knew he wasn't very busy. Maybe he had reason to be suspicious of a white guy asking questions. Maybe he was just tired. I didn't press him. I thought I had time. I didn't have enough. In May 2002, ten days before his eighty-ninth birthday, Buster died. What I know of him, I know partly from Swing 46, but mostly from talking to other dancers, from interviews in tap newsletters, and from video footage. His death shouldn't have come as a shock—Buster had been in and out of the hospital for years—yet it did shock me. As I was trying to understand the past, Buster's death exposed for me the impermanence of the present. The man was gone, which was sad enough, but his departure made his art seem more ephemeral, too. Some part could be preserved on film,

some smaller part in writing, but because the tradition out of which
he came so stressed individual style, his dancing, it seemed, would die
with him.

Tap dancers had an answer for this. Over and over, I heard variations
on the same idea. At Buster's funeral, the tap dancer Jimmy Slyde told
the crowd of mourners, "Buster didn't leave, he left something for us."
Gregory Hines liked to say, about himself, that when he was dancing,
you could see all the dancers who came before him. Then, as if to tell us
whom to watch for, he would invoke their names—the men he grew up
studying in the fifties as he stood in the wings of the Apollo Theater, the
men who would show him a step or two in the back alley, those surrogate fathers and uncles in whom Hines, as a boy, imagined himself as a
man. What he knew, he learned from them, including the idea that imitating them was not enough. "You can't be a great artist by copying,"
they told him. You watch and you listen and then you do it your own
way. So young Hines observed his heroes carefully—"I could close my
eyes and listen to them and know who is who." And by paying close-
enough attention, he discovered himself.

The scene at Swing 46 was as different from the Apollo's as the year
2000 was from 1950. And yet it wasn't. "Do your own thing," Buster
would tell the young dancers. "Don't copy me." But also: "When you're
dancing, I'm dancing with you." There was an idea in all of this—an
idea about the relationship between the collective past and the individual artist—that was familiar to me from jazz history and from T. S.
Eliot's essay "Tradition and the Individual Talent" and from older
sources Eliot was rephrasing. But at Swing 46, it was not just an idea.
Frequently, near the end of a jam, Savion Glover would walk in. "Ladies
and Gentlemen," Buster announced more than once, "here is the elev-
enth wonder of the world." And this wonder of the world, hailed both
in the press and among his peers as a genius, would kneel down and kiss
Buster's feet. As his skinny body bent over, the tap shoes half-tucked into
the seat of his pants stood up like bunny ears. When Buster handed him
the microphone, he mumbled, as if he had little to say. With his dreadlocks, his waistband several sizes too large, Glover seemed worlds away
from Buster and the adult elegance that Buster had admired in Pops
Whitman's long pants and man's suit. ("They look like they're coming

off digging ditches," Buster once remarked of Glover and his friends.) Then Glover began to dance, and, just as frailty fell off Buster as he slipped into a groove, so would Glover's reticence vanish as he drew inward in search of rhythms. Suddenly, he had a great deal to say, and he said it all intensely, squeezing Buster's ease into a more compressed flow, trading the illusion of effortlessness for the illusion of raw force.

If you knew the signs, you could sense dozens of dancers in Glover. And he had certainly taken their art and made it his own, reinterpreting the tradition so strongly that most tap dancers his age and younger seemed unable to do anything other than copy him. Imitating his power, if not his knowledge and subtlety, Glover's followers beat the Swing 46 floor hard enough that the management had to keep replacing it. When Glover did steps that other dancers did, the fat burned away. Much of the time, he didn't do steps at all—just rhythms, sounds. He would repeat one sequence over and over, dissatisfied, or skip from groove to groove with such frequency that it sometimes looked to me as if he were trying to evade the burden of his gift. Buster, watching the same process, once asked, "Do you think the devil's out yet?" Glover would dance for two minutes or twenty, then abruptly walk off. He rarely paid attention to the audience. And still his phrases, like stray bullets, could pierce.

Clearly, Glover was exceptional. Yet he wasn't the only evidence of continuity. At the end of each jam, all the dancers would crowd the stage for the Shim Sham, a routine from the 1920s, designed to be easy enough for anybody to do. Buster meant no harm, but he always counted it off at his speed: fast. What ensued was a fine mess. Each dancer did it his or her own way, yet the group was held together, just barely, by routine and rhythm. Everyone stopped in the right places. Everyone made it to the ending—a tag rhythm that got stuck on somewhere along the line: *Shave and a haircut, two bits!* So corny, so American. Two bits make a quarter, a coin with a motto—*E pluribus unum*—and that two-bit vision was also part of the tradition. For almost as long as Buster had lived, people had been doing the Shim Sham, passing it down. The dance had spread across the country, and across the globe. All the tap dancers at Swing 46, different in so many other ways, had it in common.

PART I

FIRST STEPS

Imitation is suicide.
—RALPH WALDO EMERSON

Only an innovator knows how to borrow.
—RALPH WALDO EMERSON

1

STEALING STEPS

Whenever there's a mixed bill of tappers, you can bet that all the dancers in the show will cram onstage at the end for the Shim Sham. Often the dancers in the *audience* will join in, too. Lingua franca and lowest common denominator, it's the one routine that everybody knows, even if the versions they know aren't exactly the same. Sixty years ago, when a top-rated TV program such as *The Ed Sullivan Show* might feature two tap acts in one episode, if the host decided, impromptu, to ask the acts to do a little something together, the dancers needed only a shared glance to break into the Shim Sham. A version without taps was even more common, a dance for performers who weren't dancers.

Where did it come from? Was it some folk tradition, its authorship shared by an anonymous collective? Or was it actually invented by someone? Up until his death in 2004, Leonard Reed claimed to have devised it; at the end of his life, when he was in his nineties, there were few people with firsthand knowledge left to contradict him. As Reed

Opposite page: "Dancing for Eels," from *New York As It Is*, 1848 told the story, he and his partner, Willie Bryant, put together the Shim Sham in the late twenties when they were touring with the Whitman Sisters.

"It was a simple thing to do for the finale," Reed remembered. Willie Bryant told the jazz historian Marshall Stearns that the dance evolved from something called the Old Man Shuffle: "We used to do it at a very fast rhythm and it was a comedy dance." They named their new routine the Goofus after a hillbilly song they set it to; later, they used "Turkey in the Straw." There were four parts (an in-place shuffling, a crossover step, a side-to-side and in-and-out bit, and a twisting, hopping finish; one motif, the break, repeated at the ends of some steps and in the middle of others). They would teach audience members one part per night. If you wanted the whole thing, you had to keep coming back.

Also performing with the Whitman Sisters was Jo Jones, who was soon fired. In New York, Jones joined up with Billie Yates, whom the Whitman Sisters had also let go. Along with a third dancer, Jones and Yates formed a tap trio called the Three Little Words, and at a Harlem nightclub they soon introduced a closing number with the catchy title of the Shim Sham. As Reed tells it, the number wasn't new; it was a slowed-down Goofus. The nightclub may have been Connie's Inn or Dickie Wells's Theatrical Grill; the routine spread fast. "The whole club would join us, including the waiters," recalled Jones, who informed Stearns that *he* had invented the dance. "For a while, people were doing the Shim Sham up and down Seventh Avenue all night long." On Fridays, a spotlight would scan the audience, and whichever celebrity was caught in the beam was expected to do his or her own version.

"I never got any money for saying I originated the Shim Sham," Reed said. "If I were to get some money, then there'd be a fight. But I don't care what they say. I know I did it." He said this in an interview with a tap dancer in 1997, by which time he was being lauded as the creator of the routine, and few people remembered Billie Yates or Jo Jones. Twenty years earlier, while being interviewed for Redd Foxx's *Encyclopedia of Black Humor*, Reed had offered a long list of his accomplishments as a producer, songwriter, and performer without including the Shim Sham. Among tap dancers, though, the routine was Reed's number one claim to fame. In 2000, when he was honored with a lifetime achievement award by the New York Committee to Celebrate Tap Dance Day, all the dancers on the program gathered to join him for the inevitable Shim Sham. A few measures into the song, Reed stopped the band, stopped the show. "No, no, no," he said. "You're doing it wrong. It's always been done wrong." The problem was in the second step, where the dancers came in half a beat earlier than he wanted. Reed demonstrated how to do it his way and expected all of the performers to fall in line. Many had been doing the Shim Sham their own way for twenty, forty, sixty years. Some followed Reed's command, some didn't. Regardless, Reed had made his point, and he went on making it whenever he saw the Shim Sham performed. Reed's Shim Sham is now official, though many dancers persist in whichever variation they learned first.

When asked to account for the longevity of the dance, Reed gave a clear answer: "Simplicity." But just as important is the answer he gave in frustration: the dance had always been done wrong. It was flexible enough to change while remaining itself. Reed couldn't have been too aggrieved about credit, because he knew that he and Bryant had cobbled together the Shim Sham from popular steps of the day. In one of his last interviews, he admitted how he and his partner had lifted "excerpts" from the older dancers Jack Wiggins and King Rastus Brown, from "old films of kids shuffling their feet," then "switched them around." Reed understood the game. "I knew how to come up with an idea," he said. "If I didn't, I would steal an idea from somebody. I didn't care who. I would steal it and change it around a bit. I watched everybody and I stole from everybody."

He grew up in Kansas City, and when he first arrived in New York, around 1925, one of the first places he visited was a gambling den two doors down from Harlem's Lafayette Theatre. A room in the back, furnished with a bench, an old upright piano, and a good floor, served as an informal rehearsal space for tap dancers—hoofers, in the parlance of the time. This was the Hoofers' Club, a small space that would grow in memory into the epicenter of twentieth-century tap. Reed, a relentless debunker, would insist that more dancers came to gamble than to practice. Even so, he remembered, "There was always dancin' going on, known dancers and unknown dancers"—so much dancing that the floor had to be replaced every six months or so. (As at Swing 46, tap would always rely on permissive property owners.)

"All the dancers would hang out," Reed recalled, "and they would trade ideas." The scene resembled the trading sessions that Buster Brown would find in Baltimore, and the gatherings on the street corners of Philadelphia, Chicago, Boston, and Omaha. But this was New York, Harlem in its heyday, where the most ambitious black dancers came to prove themselves. Reed learned his own specialty, the set of tap steps called "wings," from a guy everyone called Piano. ("I don't know his real name, and I don't know if anyone ever did.") Using the upright as a ballerina might use a barre, Piano would jump, and as he slowed his descent with his arms, he would fit in a flurry of ground-striking sounds before his weight settled. Take the piano away, and he couldn't do a thing. Not all the dancers at the Hoofers' Club were ready for the stage. But even those who weren't contributed ideas. "He invented all sorts of things and we would do them"—figure out how to accomplish the feats unassisted. A guy like Piano stretched the conception of what was worth trying.

That conception was stretched further when a known dancer came in, a master. Then the place went quiet, all eyes and ears fixed on the informal demonstration. Once the master was satisfied that he'd confirmed his mastery, he left, and only then did the younger dancers take to the floor and try to reconstruct what they had just witnessed. ("He did this." "No, he did *this*.") By such means, a solo likely improvised became set, duplicated, and distributed. Other aspiring kids around the country were memorizing the improvised solos of jazz musicians, captured on records and shipped all over, but very few of the tap dancers at the Hoofers' Club, or anywhere else, would appear on records. Just a handful made it into films. Most of the time, dancers studied their betters and rivals live. They came to the theater in packs, soaking up as much as they could. Stealing took a sharp eye and an ear that could recognize and retain rhythms. A step was a rhythmic phrase and also the movements to make it: you had to catch both. Canny dancers frustrated stealing by changing their act frequently or, through improvisation, constantly.

At the Hoofers' Club, the exposure was at its most direct and intense.

Dancers would vie for prominence in battles that might last for hours or even days. These matches were called cutting contests, carving contests—violent terms that suggest how fierce competition could get. Between bouts, a few experienced dancers might be willing to share their knowledge openly and break down steps for upstarts. One of those novices remembered King Rastus Brown, legendary and past his prime, not merely demonstrating a step but tracing its genealogy: the steps that came before it and the steps that branched off. Most masters, however, guarded their treasures closely. You had to be clever to pry anything out of them. John Bubbles, one of the greatest hoofers, became infamous for his espionage. Noticing a step he liked, Bubbles would shake his head sadly, informing the dancer that he'd missed a beat and had better try again. Taking the lure, the dancer would repeat the step, and Bubbles would say something like, "Now, that's not what you did the first time," which would prompt the dancer to repeat himself again and give Bubbles all he needed. "That reminds me of a step I used to do," Bubbles would finally say, rendering the newly acquired step and topping it with variations. If the first part of his method was devious, the last part was crucial. It followed the lesson that King Rastus Brown taught: the variations made the step yours.

Ralph Brown, a younger Hoofers' Club member unrelated to King Rastus, put it this way: "You can take whatever you stole. Because you never learned the complete step anyway. You learned how to do part of it, so you take that part and put something else with it. Then you made your own step."

"That was affectionately called 'stealing steps,'" Leonard Reed remembered, stressing the affection. "Everybody did it. That's how you learned. You would do something, and you'd say to the other dancers, 'You tryin' to steal it? All right, do it!' And they'd try it. Of course, when they did it, it was slightly different."

A challenge. An imitation. Something slightly different. Essentially, that's how tap was handed down. It was, in this way, similar to the children's game called Telephone or Operator or Pass-the-Whisper: kids confiding a phrase to each other that mutates as it travels from mouth to ear to mouth, until, through a mix of mishearing and invention, it becomes something new. So it was with the techniques, styles, and traditions of tap. Part of the change was accidental: someone misremembered a step or couldn't do what the first guy had done. Part of it was inevitable: steps just come out different on different dancers. Much of the change was willed, dancers striving to stand out, to express their individuality through the tradition. Competition pushed technical advancement, yet restyling in a more general sense was valued and encouraged. Steal It and Change It was integral to a professional code, and a way of life.

That code had rules. You could mimic somebody else's moves, among other dancers, as a tribute, a witty allusion, or a jibe. But doing it in public, for pay—that was theft. As much as there were steps that everyone shared, a dancer's specialties were part of his livelihood, distinctive goods he could offer employers and audiences. The packs of dancers in certain theaters were also inspectors, and if you tried to pass off someone else's stuff as your own, they might stand up and call you out. You could be humiliated, ostracized, maybe even roughed up. The best defense was to claim variation and try to prove it. One-upmanship was the ladder to respect.

And so if a cocky youngster was laughed out of the Hoofers' Club, as John Bubbles was on his first visit ("You're hurting the floor," the experts told him), he went away and practiced hard. "One night I started practicing about eleven o'clock," Bubbles remembered. "At three a.m. I took off my shoes and danced barefoot"—in consideration of his neighbors—"and around six a.m. I finished working out the step." By the time the shamed dancer returned to the club, he would be prepared, "fortified," in Bubbles's words, "like a fellow with a double-barreled shotgun." Then a relative old-timer like Toots Davis might be forced to swallow his laughter, saying, as one witness recalled, "I invented that step, but I never knew there were so many ways to do it." When the transformation was thorough, credit was easily granted. When the something extra was less obvious, arguments could grow hot. Disputes were unavoidable, since private creations were continually entering the public domain. The truth was, as the highly original, influential, and now nearly forgotten hoofer Eddie Rector said, "You can't copyright no steps."

Within black show business, however, the code basically held. Early newspaper reports announced the Hoofers' Club as a membership organization with a board of directors, but this was likely no more than a front for illegal gaming and liquor. Most dancers would recall the club less formally, as just the room in which steps were traded. Still, a club's a club. Anybody could walk in—anybody who was male, that is—but not everybody belonged. Some described tests and trials. For one, a would-be member danced to the clapping of everyone else. Instructed to remember that tempo, the aspirant was escorted out and walked around the block, distracted by street noises and the chatter of his guide. Meanwhile, inside the club, the remaining members held the groove until the pledge returned, preceded by his minder, who gave the signal to maintain the beat mentally. That silent meter the recruit now had to match, synchronizing his dancing with the inaudible grid to demonstrate that he could keep time—could shelter it, like a flame.

Being black wasn't exactly a requirement, but for many reasons, almost no white dancers ever entered the Hoofers' Club. Hal LeRoy was one of the few. He had learned the basics from a black kid in his hometown of Cincinnati and had stolen the rest from hoofers who passed through the local theater. "Maybe I didn't do the exact step," he remembered, "but more or less." He practiced five, six hours a day. In 1931, his rubbery, rapid tapping and boy-next-door manner made him an overnight star on Broadway. It got him into many movies, mostly short ones. And it earned him the respect of many black dancers. John Bubbles noticed what LeRoy was doing with Bubbles's steps, and he encouraged the kid with a gift of metal taps. According to LeRoy's memory of visiting the Hoofers' Club around 1931, the assembled members asked him to dance outside on a platform six feet off the ground. Some hoofers called out steps and watched; others, underneath the stage, listened. LeRoy passed the test and was appointed an honorary member. The hoofers awarded him a pin.

It was one thing for a talented outsider to be invited—especially if, as in the case of LeRoy, the outsider's sponsor was Bill Robinson, the most celebrated black tap dancer of all. This in itself was complicated, considering the mixed feelings that Harlem dancers harbored toward Robinson and his cozy relations with whites. Whatever LeRoy's skills and personal appeal, his sudden fame and the unequal opportunities that his skin color afforded him could be cause for resentment. The taps that

Bubbles gave him, the test, the pin—these all could have been tinged with irony and still have been genuine tokens of esteem. But it was another thing altogether for total outsiders to steal steps, or an entire act, then present that pilfered material in front of an audience that wouldn't recognize the difference between original and copy, perhaps in a venue where the originator and his friends might not be welcome. That happened, too. In either case, and in the vast gray area between, the history of tap is a history of stolen steps.

2

ORIGINAL STEPS

Leonard Reed could give an account of tap that went back some ninety years. It was only his version, but he lived it and was eager to tell. Any attempt to trace tap's roots back much farther faces multiple obstacles. Drawings of dancers in action can capture a gesture, a pose, but can only imply motion. Written accounts are often imprecise, contradictory, and—particularly in the case of forms, such as tap, that develop largely below the notice of official recordkeepers—simply scarce. Historians of pre-twentieth-century dance (which is to say, pre-film) are forced to recycle a few descriptions, arrange them by date and location, surround them with speculation, and patch them together with mutable oral traditions wherever those traditions have been fixed by documentation. Tracking development requires much gap-leaping and guesswork.

Consider the following story told by one James W. Smith about an event he witnessed while a slave in Texas just before the Civil War. By way of explaining how good and kind his master was, Smith spoke of how there was dancing on the plantation most Saturday nights, how his master built a platform for "jigging" contests, and how the colored folk came from miles around to compete. He spoke of a fellow slave, Tom, as "the jigginest fellow dat ever was."

> Everyone round tried to get some body to best him. He could put de glass of water on his head and make his feet go like triphammers and sound like de snaredrum. He could whirl round and sich, all de movement from his hips down. Now it gits round that a fellow has been found to beat Tom and a contest am 'ranged for Saturday evenin'. There was a big crowd and money am bet, but master bets on Tom, of course.
>
> They starts jigging. Tom starts easy and a little faster and faster. The other fellow doin' de same. Dey gits faster and faster, and dat crowd am a-yelling. Gosh! There am 'citement. They just keep a gwine. It look like Tom done found his match, but there's one thing he ain't done— he ain't made a whirl. Now he does it. Everyone holds his breath, and the other fellow starts to make the whirl, but jus' a spoonful of water sloughs out his cup, so Tom am the winner.

If this isn't tap, it sure sounds like an ancestor, a clear antecedent for cutting contests at the Hoofers' Club. *Tap dancing* is a twentieth-century term, but the practice it labels is much older, at least as old as the United States. Like most of the testimony about slave dance given by slaves themselves, Smith's account entered the historical record in the form of an interview conducted by members of the Federal Writers' Project in the 1930s. In it, the seventy-seven-year-old Smith is remembering his very early childhood. He is talking to a representative of the government, most likely a white person, in the segregated South. The words on the page are that interviewer's transcription of Smith's dialect—what the interviewer thought he heard, and maybe what Smith thought the interviewer expected or wanted to hear.

Caveats aside, what is happening in Smith's story? This contest—was it the master's idea or the slaves'? The glass on the head, the hip-down action, the feet behaving like "triphammers" and sounding like a snare drum up on a platform—where did these practices come from? Smith calls it all *jigging*, a word that seems to point to Ireland even as the lineage of the slaves points to Africa.

Any attempt to answer these questions is made difficult not just by the scarcity and ambiguity of documentation, but by the concept of race. Classifying humans by a rough set of physical features assumed to indicate ancestry is a scientifically dubious practice, especially when the physical differences are taken to stand for innate differences of intellect, aptitude, morality, or human possibility, and are used to establish and justify immutable hierarchies. Neverthless, it must be acknowledged that the socially constructed idea of race has been enormously influential in shaping how people regard, and treat, one another. Because of race, the question of tap's origins is always on the verge of becoming a property dispute, a question of who owns what. Or, as Leonard Reed would say, a question of who gets credit. The denials, evasions, rationalizations, and resentments of four centuries taint every fragment of evidence, and since indirection and dissimulation were essential defenses for blacks, nothing is necessarily as it seems.

AFRICA, OR, AN ECHO OF THE DRUM

What can we know of the dance that Africans might have brought with them and thus contributed to tap? If the West and Central African tribes from which the slaves were taken described their dancing in written form, then Western scholars haven't discovered it; it seems that the dancing, along with music and stories, *was* the record. Just about the sole written voice is that of Olaudah Equiano, a slave who purchased his freedom and who, in his 1789 autobiography, claimed that in his Igbo childhood, dancing was part of every occasion, translating stories and events into varied movement. That's about all he wrote on the subject, and so we have to rely upon accounts by European travelers and traders, filtered through their prejudices and likely miscomprehension, or we must extrapolate backward from scholarship on twentieth-century African dance, always keeping in mind how much could have changed in the interim.

Nevertheless, it's possible to venture generalizations across the slave-trading region. All accounts stress how very much the Africans danced. As the British trader Richard Jobson put it in 1623, "There is, without doubt, no other people on earth more naturally affected to the sound of musicke." (This generalization was already long in the tooth. In his eleventh-century guide to buying slaves, Ibn Butlan said of African slaves that "dancing and beating time are engrained in their nature.") Africans danced to celebrate victories and to mark seasonal cycles. They danced at weddings and at funerals. In some tribes, dance was part of the instruction given to youth during initiations, part of the education considered essential for adulthood. European observers marveled at the dancing of children so young they could barely stand: "One would be apt to say that they are born dancing, to see the exactness of their movements," a visitor to Senegal wrote in 1753. Later scholars would add that the aged danced, too, and that when they danced, they appeared young.

The Europeans identified patterns: a call-and-response between performers and spectators, blurring the distinction; the arrangement of dancers in a ring, with individuals taking turns in the center and those on the circle's edge clapping their hands in time. "With crooked knees and bended body they foot it nimbly," Jobson wrote about Senegambian dancers in 1620, catching what could be called the default position of West African dance: knees bent, torso piked forward, butt out. The crooked knees help the body to bend, freeing the pelvis and making it easier for upper and lower halves to operate independently. Supple knees absorb shocks, steadying the gait of someone carrying a load on her head. The crouch emphasizes a connection with the earth that deepens with rising intensity: when the music heats up, the dancer gets down. A great dancer was said to have no bones. Bent knees produced and signified flexibility, a quality prized not only in dance.

"The Negroes do not dance a step, but every member of their body, every joint, and even the head itself expresseth a different motion, always keeping time, let it never be so quick." So wrote a French botanist about a Senegambian funeral dance in 1749, identifying a core feature of West African dance, "keeping time." What struck the botanist as distinctive would continue to amaze Europeans—a rhythmic exactness, which, to have attracted such consistent attention, must have been very pronounced. Africans danced percussively. They beat their feet on the ground, but they also tied bells to their ankles and loaded their arms with bracelets, adornments that were noisemakers, rendering a dancer's precision audible. Even body parts without ornaments—shoulder blades, necks—behaved as if they could be making sounds.

This exactness, noted the botanist, was synchronized with drums. Europeans who wrote about African dance rarely failed to mention drums. African dancers studied by twentieth-century researchers were in constant communication with drummers. In the words of one Bakebe tribesman, the dancer "creates within himself an echo of the drum. Once he is seeing the echo, he is dancing with pride." The drummer directed the dancer, yet the dancer could also signal the drummer with gestures and rhythms; they could converse. (And since in many West African languages words could be distinguished by pitch, drums could "talk," transmitting messages with pitch patterns.)

"Every member of their body expresseth a different motion"—this might have registered a distinguishing trait of music in the region, what musicologists call polyrhythm. From a European perspective, the music of West and Central Africa uses at least two different rhythmic systems at once. (To take the most basic example, one drum plays three beats in the time it takes another to play two.) Though the individual parts are often simple, they interlock into a complex pattern that to many European ears throughout history—perceiving no pattern or only the repetition of one—has sounded chaotic or monotonous. Perhaps polyrhythm is what the botanist was seeing: the feet following one drum, the hips another. Such segmentation would pervade twentieth-century West African dance: polyrhythm encouraged isolation of body parts, and skilled dancers could follow three or four rhythms simultaneously. The best dancers could add more.

Music of that character, and the dancing to it, required a particular approach to time. One musicologist called it a "metronome sense," the listener's ability to hear the regular pulse of a metrical pattern, to feel it bodily, whether or not it's expressed aurally. In relation to tap, what's most intriguing is that, in addition to handling polyrhythms, a person with a strong metronome sense can divide or multiply the pulse, so that rhythmic accents that might seem off or random are sensed instead as being *on* the beat—the beat if the song were played at two or three times the tempo. Call it fractal rhythm, an apprehension of patterns across scales of magnification. It allows a seeming suspension of the beat that is, at a deeper level, no suspension at all. It sounds like essential equipment for a tap dancer, a secret to keeping time.

If the Europeans, in their appreciation of the Africans' exact timing, picked up on this, they likely missed much else. Several early European visitors noticed that the songs that accompanied dancing worked to "praise or blame" certain people, inducing laughter. The failure of these Europeans to mention the satirical *dancing* described by twentieth-century researchers might be explained by the probability that the earlier visitors, unfamiliar with norms or exaggerations, would have had trouble identifying the joke—particularly since they tended to find serious African dancing laughable. Among their descendants, those who could recognize themselves as the object of danced satire remained a minority. (And when they did recognize themselves, they tended to respond as the colonial government of Zambia did, by banning the dances.)

Also hiding in the silences of the record could be more of what a Dutch man of science witnessed in 1673: the propensity of dancers to "stamp on the ground vigorously with their feet . . . with a fixed expression on their faces." Robert Farris Thompson found something similar among twentieth-century Yoruban dancers, who performed the wildest movements while balancing upon their heads terra-cotta sculptures and containers of fire. Balance was the idea; a controlled dance style expressed self-mastery. "To do difficult tasks with an air of ease and a silent disdain," as was admired among the Gola, sounds universal, yet "the aesthetic of the cool" that Thompson identified in multiple Central and West African languages was "a special kind of cool," a spiritual principle, a metaphor for right living.

This is the kind of meaning that early European observers, who generally found sub-Saharan dance immoral from a Christian perpective, were least likely to intuit. Arranging serial solos within a circle of dancers is, like call-and-response, a way of negotiating the relationship between individual and group, between innovation and tradition. The set parts provide a foundation against which the swerves of the soloist acquire significance. It's safe to assume that for sub-Saharan Africans in the time of the slave trade, dance functioned as a mnemonic. Just as danced imitation could be a form of mockery, it could also be emulation of the most radical kind, the embodiment of ancestors or gods. In Yoruban tradition, the appearance of a god in a dancer is recognized as much by a signature rhythm and motion as by costume and mask. Across the region, it was commonly believed that ancestors lived on in the bodies of dancers, who entered a state of possession by disrupting a rhythm. ("Breaking the beat or breaking the pattern," as Thompson explains it, "is something one does to break on into the world of the ancestors.") It was believed that executing the ancestors' steps brought them back to life, a principle that in some measure carried over into tap. "When you're dancing," said Buster Brown, "I'm dancing with you."

The ships that transported Africans to the New World starting in the 1500s were densely packed. Diagrams of the hulls resemble the inside of a pomegranate. The cargo was chattel, yet those crammed-in bodies carried culture. The same immateriality of dance that frustrates the search for hard historical evidence helped African dance survive the Middle Passage. Among historians, a debate long raged between those who argued that the displacing forces of slavery had destroyed a usable African past in America, and those who insisted upon continuities. Until the 1960s, many blacks had no interest in being associated with an African culture assumed by majority opinion to be inferior; they and some well-meaning whites feared that admitting to African retentions would be giving ammunition to racists or be part of an argument that slavery wasn't so bad. With his 1942 book *The Myth of the Negro Past*, Melville Herskovits gave the continuity school a leg up, cataloguing hundreds of American practices with African analogues; he believed that dance had carried over the most. Other historians indentified more retentions, but more important was a "grammar of culture," the theory that it was an African way of doing things that affected how transplanted slaves adapted to the cultures of their Euro-American masters and neighbors and forged new cultures. The African heritage was less *what* the slaves danced and sang than *how*. Or, as Trummy Young and Sy Oliver, African-American musicians of the 1940s, would put it, "'Tain't what you do, it's the way that you do it."

BRITAIN, IRELAND, OR THE MOVING THING

Africans weren't the only percussive dancers who came to America. They weren't even the only ones who came as slaves. One might expect the history of dance in Britain and Ireland to be more fully documented than that of Africa, yet while the court dances and theatrical dances that emerged there left a wealth of records, the probable British ancestors of tap were not so highborn. For the most part, the folk traditions in question were deemed unworthy of mention by the literate, who either weren't aware of them or took them for granted. Often, the only way folk dance left a trace was by being adopted and altered by the upper classes—refined, polished, and tamed by "dancing masters," professionals who codified rules to teach and publish in treatises. This continual circulation of dance practices among the social classes, a process of imitation that was often parodic, further confuses any search for origins or authenticity, as does the constant traffic between folk customs and theatrical representations, particularly considering that when the dances changed, the nomenclature often didn't. In the oral tradition itself, the words used to label movements varied regionally: the same name might refer to different steps, or the same step might go by different names.

Take the word *jig*. The etymologist who traced it back to the ancient Sanskrit *jagat*, or "the moving thing," was probably overshooting, but he was onto something, because in the Europe of the late Middle Ages, the various cognates (*gigue, giga, Geige, jigge, jegg*, etc.) came to be applied to the fiddle and to almost any lively dance or dance tune—to anything that moved. In Elizabethan English, *iygges, gygges*, and *jigs* labeled various kinds of dance. In *Much Ado About Nothing*, Shakespeare characterized the "Scotch Jigge" as "hot and hasty" in a metaphor for wooing. (However, the dance that William Kempe, the great clown of Shakespeare's day, did with bells on his ankles, was a morris dance. When Kempe said he spent his life in "mad jigges," he meant bawdy song-and-dance afterpieces.) By the seventeenth century, *jig* had emerged as one of the most popular, if generic, terms for the dance and music of informal social occasions. Consider the good time Samuel Pepys recorded in his diary of 1665, watching his wife's maid dance a jig, "which she does the best I ever did see, having the most natural way of it and keeps time the most perfectly." Rhythmic accuracy and naturalness—meaning ease, lack of inhibition—were virtues that a university-educated, upwardly mobile son of a tailor might recognize, with some wistfulness, in his servant.

In the eighteenth century, the jig was danced alongside—and frequently conflated with—a dance called the hornpipe. The first uses, likely named after the instrument, include a Baroque court dance with a rhythm adopted by Purcell and Handel as characteristically English. But a different hornpipe popped up on London playbills in the 1700s. This denoted a solo step dance, a percussive style, usually performed in the character of a rustic. The dancer Nancy Dawson found fame in the class satire of *The Beggar's Opera*, hornpiping to the tune that would become known as "Here We Go Round the Mulberry Bush." (Earlier, it was called "Piss on the Grass.") Increasingly, the stage hornpipe grew associated with the character of a sailor, incorporating pantomime of sailorly activities. Actual sailors may have also done the hornpipe, for exercise and to stave off boredom. In any case, something called the hornpipe became basic equipment for performers in British fairgrounds and saloons, a dance that lower-class audiences recognized as an elaborated version of their own pastimes.

Scattered reminiscences of the early nineteenth century portray "stepping" as a standard feature of feasts and wakes and Saturday nights at the alehouse. These dances were percussive, too: even without a fiddler playing along, listeners could recognize the tune in the steps. Yet the dances were also meant to be seen. Dancers elevated their footwork closer to eye level by dancing atop tables; ladies raised their skirts. The upper-class attitude toward such stepping comes through in the remarks of a well-heeled witness to a Grasmere harvest dance in 1827: "The country lads tripped it merrily and heavily. They called the amusement dancing, but I call it thumping; for he who could make the greatest noise seemed to be esteemed the greatest dancer."

The county of Lancashire, associated with hornpipes since the seventeenth century, became associated in the nineteenth century with a dance called the Lancashire clog or clog hornpipe—the old hornpipe, perhaps, in different shoes. *Clog* as a term for wooden shoes was more than a century old. Farmers wore clogs, and during the Industrial Revolution, mill workers adopted the footwear as cheap protection against damp workplaces and cold stone floors. According to oral history, the workers, inspired by the beat of machinery, rattled their feet to keep warm and were pleased by the sound. During breaks, they held competitions on the cobblestones, folding in jigs and morris dances. Factory lads took the dance into alehouses, huddling on the flagstones by the hearth. (Their "quick, well-timed clatter" caught the ear of Edwin Waugh, who in his 1855 *Sketches of Lancashire Life* writes about following the curious noise into a tavern.) Clogs were originally loose-fitting, necessitating a flat-footed style lest the shoes fall off. Sole guards made of iron only encouraged further abuse. Metal against stone strikes sparks.

Clogs were associated with labor. Miners wore clogs, as did canal boat workers, who could practice their dancing on the job. Establishments wishing to exclude the "unwashed" put up notices that "Persons in Clogs" would not be admitted. Clog dancing was something most everyone could do, yet some people were experts. "Twopenny hops" of the 1850s might feature a paid exhibition by a "first rate professor." Street cloggers worked inside and outside of public houses, collecting coins, but competitions were also formalized with judges, rules, prize belts, and wagers. Clogging was an athletic event, taught aside wrestling and boxing. (One of the earliest mentions of "clog-hornpipe" is as a skill ascribed to the Lancashire pugilist Jack Carter in Pierce Egan's *Boxiana* of 1824.) In the second half of the century, the dance of the pub moved into the music hall. Stage dancers adopted the tighter-fitting clogs of dandyish young men, shoes snug enough for a high style, up on the toes. Compared with the more down-to-earth and presumably older "heel and toe" tradition, the new style was urban and social-climbing. Clogging of all kinds was referred to as "noisy shoe" and "shoe music," the difference residing not just in the skill of the dancer but in the ear of the beholder.

Considering that a large portion of the workers in those Lancashire mills were Irish, refugees from the famines of the 1840s and '50s, it's possible that much in Lancashire clogging could have been Irish in origin, or Irish-inflected. But Irish step dancing, at least from the late eighteenth century on, was generally called jigging. Prior references to jigs in Ireland are missing, but references to any dance in early Gaelic texts are few and unspecific: circle dances, sword dances. The accounts of traveling Englishmen, as shaped as European descriptions of Africa by the prejudices of a conquering power, repeatedly stress the Irish fondness for dance, often contrasting Irish vivacity with staid Englishness. The Irish stressed this about themselves. "An Irishman may be said to love fighting well, whiskey better, and dancing best of all," wrote the Irish antiquarian Thomas Croker in 1829. William Carleton, an Irish writer invested in defining Irish national character, charged (in 1840 but referring back to "racy old times" before the already compromised present) that "of all the amusements peculiar to our population, dancing is by far the most important . . . it may be considered as a very just indication of the spirit and character of the people." Furthermore, he boasted, "no people dance as well as the Irish," citing as explanation and proof the well-known Irish susceptibility to music.

Croker and Carleton were principally referring to dance figures and steps likely imported from England, Scotland, and Europe in the mid-to-late eighteenth century. The population learned these from itinerant dancing masters, upwardly mobile Irishmen who larded their high-flown speech with French and took pride in their shabby-genteel attire of tall hats, fine stockings, ornamental canes, and light pumps. Dancing masters taught deportment along with various kinds of dances. In the earliest descriptions of any specificity (from the mid-1800s, alas), jigs were danced by couples and distinguished by a 6/8 time signature and steps whose names—drumming, battering—suggested noise. The dancing masters demonstrated steps of common currency alongside those of their own invention, which might then enter the general fund under their name. Exhibitions of mastery came in solo step dances, interchangeably labeled hornpipes and jigs, full of hops and rapid crossings of the feet suggested by the adjective *twinkling* and the expression "cover the buckle." These solos were often beaten out atop a door pulled off its hinges, a sounding board in a land of sod or clay floors. The door was also a stage. Confronted with this spatial limitation, dancers embraced it as a preference. According to twentieth-century folklorists, those dancers who stayed most in place shot up highest in esteem. (The ability to execute every step starting with either foot was also prized.) If someone said you could "dance on a plate," you were dancing well. Dancing "on a sixpence" was better. There were stories of competitions in which the door started on the floor and was raised in successive rounds like a high bar—up onto the table, up onto barrels on top of the table. In one story, the contest ends with the door on top of the chimney.

In Ireland, the idea of dance as a competition, often with a cake as a prize, goes back at least to the seventeenth century. For rivalrous dancing masters, challenge matches served as advertising and a way to vie for fame, pupils, and territory. Many challenge stories have the sound of endurance contests, the winner being the man who lasts longest. Or the victor is he who spools out the most steps, displaying the most knowledge or invention. Where there's a suggestion of improvisation, it's treated as exceptional. Routines were set, and some sequences, mated to a matching tune, are still performed today, the oldest supposedly dating from around 1750, preserved through an unbroken line of teachers and students. The aesthetic became highly controlled. It wasn't just that the dance stayed in place; the body was disciplined, an ideal manifest in tales of dancers performing with a pan of water on their heads and not spilling a drop. It was dancing masters who fixed the arms to the dancers' sides, banning as vulgar the rhythmic rise and fall of upper limbs and the snapping of fingers mentioned in early descriptions. Some teachers, it is said, weighed down their pupils' hands with stones. That's one solution to the problem of what to do with the arms while the feet are making a racket. It made for a severe, unchanging front, all the motion from the hips down, a chest-forward martial rigor appealing to Irish pride and lacking in any show of sensuality to which the Church might object.

It appears that the influence of the dancing masters was greatest in the south, where the dominant style placed the weight over the ball of the foot, with the heels not touching the ground except when heel drops were explicitly part of the step. The north was characterized by a rocking between heel and toe, while in the west, the approach was flat-footed and low-slung, with the arms and torso unrestrained. While closely tied to music, the western style was more free-form; improvisation was encouraged and individual style linked to personality. It is sometimes presumed that the western style of dancing is the oldest. (Such is the assumption behind the name given to it by twentieth-century revivalists: *sean-nós*, Gaelic for "old-style.") But it was the southern style, the dancing masters' style, that Irish cultural nationalists of the early twentieth century codified and enforced: the rules, rigidity, and uniforms that came to dominate the teaching of Irish dance, both in Ireland and in America. It's worth remembering, though, that many of the Irish who came to America before that time might have danced quite differently.

In America's early colonial period, one of the functions of the British colonies was to serve as a dumping ground for what authorities considered "the dangerous classes": vagabonds, debtors, criminals, rebels. The Irish were well represented in each category. In the 1620s, the British began deporting Irish prisoners of war, tens of thousands of them, to Barbados, Jamaica, and Montserrat, lesser numbers to Virginia. The distinction between indentured servitude and slavery was not as fixed as it would become, and race relations were more fluid. Servants and slaves, white and black, often worked together, played together. More rarely, they rebelled or ran away together. Antimiscegenation laws passed as early as 1661, and their violation, indicate racial mixing in Virginia and Maryland. Cultural mixing is harder to trace but impossible to discount.

In the early 1700s, great numbers of Scots-Irish—Presbyterian Scots whose families had been settled as colonists in northern Ireland—migrated across the Atlantic, putting down roots in New England and Pennsylvania before spreading along the frontier regions of the Appalachian Mountains, where they would long constitute the majority of settlers and the dominant cultural force. Smaller numbers of Catholic Irish also immigrated, largely as indentured servants, but the largest tide of Catholic Irish immigration started flowing around 1814, when a swell in population combined with an economic depression and crop failures, and it surged with the famine and forced evictions of the 1840s and early 1850s. This wave of people, which mostly came from rural southern and western Ireland, concentrated in the eastern cities of the United States, but also in the South, establishing an Irish America that was urban and

Catholic. The propensity for dancing remained a just indication of its spirit and character.

Many of these Catholic Irish occupied a position in American society nearly as low as that of blacks. In one sense, they were lower: black slaves were worth money. In New York, Philadelphia, and Boston, the Irish would occupy the same crowded slums as blacks. That was also the case in Mobile and Savannah and New Orleans. Ships returning to New Orleans from exporting cotton to Liverpool filled their hulls with famine-fleeing Irish, who would often work alongside blacks in the same servile or dangerous jobs. Some of the same adjectives were used to denigrate both groups: savage, simian, low-browed, bestial. Closeness gave rise to competition, hatred, and bloodshed, but also to friendship, love, and shared recreation among people to whom dance and music were vital. The jigging of Tom, that black slave in Texas, might have been Irish after all.

THE AMERICAN CUT-OUT JIG

If tap is a mix, where and when might the mixing have begun? Perhaps on the very ships that transported slaves to the New World. In 1694, a commander of a British slave ship noted a curious practice in his diary: "We often at sea in the evenings would let the slaves come up into the sun to air themselves, and make them jump and dance for an hour or two to our bag-pipes, harp, and fiddle, by which exercise to preserve them in health." For as long as the slave trade continued, and even after it was outlawed, witnesses attested to such onboard dancing. Most accounts echo the suggestion that the exercise was compulsory, commonly enforced by the lash. A brief escape from the airless hold must have brought relief, yet claims that the slaves took pleasure in these dances are tainted by their use in apologies for the slave trade, as part of the argument that such dancing was evidence of good treatment and slave contentment. Other accounts, such as testimony before Parliament by abolitionists, characterize the dancing as joyless, in key with the slaves' songs of lamentation. This tension surrounding the pleasure expressed in slave dancing—what it might have meant to the slaves versus what it was perceived to mean by those who enslaved them—would prove long-lasting.

A slave might beat on a drum or kettle while others clapped their hands and rattled their chains. More rarely, a stringed African instrument would be on hand, an ancestor to the banjo, and the British commander's account isn't the only one to speak of bagpipes, fiddles, and harps. The few mentions of crew members joining in the dancing sound more like rape than like cultural exchange, but the possibility remains that there on those cursed vessels, on those wooden decks, English and Irish ways of dancing met African ones. Considering the tradition connecting sailors and the hornpipe, and considering how many Irish were pressed into naval service, hornpipes and jigs might have come up against African rhythms. In any event, the ships transporting African slaves to British colonies guaranteed such collisions.

Outcomes varied with the configurations of slave-based societies. Compared with the colonies of the Caribbean, the colonies that would become the United States imported far fewer slaves, and these were generally scattered, especially early on, among a larger white population in ratios that encouraged cross-racial interaction. Where the deadly work of sugar production in the Caribbean and Brazil necessitated a continual resupplying of labor from Africa, in groupings large enough to sustain distinct tribal identities, up north differences in climate, crops, and policy produced a slave birthrate that was eventually self-sustaining. The replacement of the international slave trade with a domestic one, as the eighteenth century met the nineteenth and slavery expanded westward in the newly established United States, reinforced local developments, sowing American hybrids across the land like cottonseed. As a result, the cultural expressions of West and Central Africa weren't preserved in forms as obvious as they were farther south. Just as the descendants of slaves brought to Cuba are much more likely to know the tribe of their ancestors than the descendants of slaves brought to Virginia or New York are to know theirs, so it is much easier to identify what is Yoruban in Afro-Cuban dancing than what is Kongo or Wolof in any African-American variety.

Until the American Revolution, Virginia and South Carolina were part of the same British system as Jamaica and Barbados—as until the

Louisiana Purchase, New Orleans and a huge swath of land west of the
Mississippi were connected to the French- and Spanish-controlled islands. Since slaves were often acclimated in the West Indies before being
shipped north, Caribbean slave culture influenced American slave culture. In Caribbean accounts from the seventeenth and eighteenth centuries, much more plentiful and detailed than contemporaneous northern
ones, slaves defy fatigue and distance to circle up and dance together in
perfect time to drums, and Caribbean blacks, enslaved and free, imitate
Europeans in dance and dress. The Europeans generally considered the
imitation amusing, though some of what the Europeans considered
"affectation" might have easily been satire. Europeans also laughed at
the seriousness of the slaves' African dancing, the cool combination of
"strange indecent attitudes" and "solemnity of countenance." That laughter was an expression of perceived incongruity, and it was likely echoed
in reverse as Caribbean-born whites adopted African-based dances,
dances that made it to Europe. Europeans documented the influence in
warnings against contagion; then, as African elements were absorbed,
reminders of African origins dwindled. But tap did not originate in the
Caribbean or in Europe. It required different conditions to grow.

One Sunday in 1739, in Stono, South Carolina, a region of rice plantations where the black population outnumbered the white one, a group
of slaves burst into a warehouse, beheaded two whites, gathered rifles
and ammunition, and marched south toward freedom in Spanish Florida.
Along the way, they killed whites and burned houses, beat drums and
gathered recruits. According to more than one account, they stopped in
a field to dance. Whatever the reason for this delay—a premature celebration, an invocation of divine assistance—it helped the white militia
catch up. Most of the rebels were killed, and selected heads were mounted
on mileposts. Soon, the colonial government issued a new, much more
restrictive slave code. Among many other measures, it sought to limit
the meetings of Negroes on Saturday nights, Sundays, and holidays, and
to ban them from "using or keeping drums, horns or other loud instruments, which may call together or give sign or notice to one another

of their wicked designs and purposes." Drums were loud, dangerous. Whites understood them to have a military purpose, because that's mainly how whites used drums themselves, in militias. So the slaveholders attempted to keep drums from the slaves. British colonies in the Caribbean had passed similar laws, but the mainland colonies were more successful in enforcement. In the territories that became the United States, records of African drumming, so deeply connected with African dance, are much more rare.

Yet no matter how effective, suppression of drums was not the same as suppression of drum rhythms. Those rhythms could be transferred to other instruments, including the body, including the feet. One might even speculate that the suppression of the drum encouraged the development of new outlets—that it created a need for tap that didn't arise elsewhere in the African diaspora.

Although Africans were imported into Virginia as early as 1619, evidence of African dancing in the American colonies before the mid-eighteenth century comes mainly in the form of churchmen objecting, ineffectually, to how the Negroes were allowed to profane the Lord's Day with their idolatrous practices. This dearth of documentation leaves nearly blank a long period when the line between African slaves and white indentured servants (many of them Irish) was more permeable, a time when much might have been exchanged. When white observers began recounting black dancing in more detail, they recognized rhythmic precision—the exact time and cadence with which slaves in Virginia in 1784 matched their "astonishing agility" to the music of a banjo and a drum. Yet when an English traveler characterized the dancing to a banjo that he witnessed at a "Negro Ball" in Maryland one Sunday in 1774 as so "irregular and grotesque" that he was "not able to describe it," both the demurral and the adjectives suggested an encounter with a foreign aesthetic. His response, and language, would prove typical, as would his observation that the dancing slaves were "exceedingly happy"—"as if they had forgot or were not sensible of their miserable conditions."

Perhaps some of the aesthetic is captured in a watercolor known as *The Old Plantation*, probably made in South Carolina in the late 1700s. A slave man wields a stick as he balances on the balls of his feet, with crooked knees and bent body; two women stretch handkerchiefs in his direction, one man plays a gourd banjo; another plays a drum. The slaves' attire, apart from the scarves on their heads, is in the style of their masters. Separate scholars, in ascribing distinct tribal origins to the headscarves, the handkerchiefs, the banjo, the drum, or the stick, collectively imply a potluck. Though it is to some degree possible to calculate the shifting ratios between points of origin for slaves in South Carolina at that time, arguments for the dominance of any one African region or tribe tend to break down—the general pattern in North America. At the moment of *The Old Plantation* or earlier, Africans from different cultures were discovering and negotiating a common culture. They were recognizing themselves as African, as opposed to Wolof or Kongo. Considering the importance of dance in those cultures, especially its function in cultural preservation, learning to dance together was a serious business. So was teaching dance to children who would never know Africa directly, children for whom Africa would be imagined and inherited, children who were becoming American.

Writing in his diary about festivities on a South Carolina plantation in 1805, a New Englander observed the African-born slaves dancing apart, "distorting their frames into the most unnatural figures." What the locally born Negroes were doing was more familiar to him. They were dancing to fiddles. At the same time that the slaves were working out commonalities among their ancestral cultures, they were also adopting aspects of Anglo-American culture, the English language above all. Fiddles had African analogues. The instruments were familiar to the slaves, too, and the most prevalent traces of the musical mixing are the abundant advertisements in colonial newspapers offering rewards for the return of runaway slave fiddlers. Slave fiddlers commonly played for the dancing of both blacks and whites. Their masters often hired them out for that purpose, and many notices described fugitive fiddlers as "well known."

If black slaves had a "mania" for dancing, which was often observed to be their favorite amusement, so did their white masters. European visitors remarked on the habit regularly, whether in pious disapproval or surprised admiration. The same newspapers that ran notices about runaway slave fiddlers also advertised the services of dancing masters. On many occasions, those two kinds of ads crossed in notices about runaway slave fiddlers who played for dancing masters. (More crossing: some of the dancing masters themselves were servants, "impudent" Irishmen with runaway notices of their own.) It seems safe to assume that these fiddlers absorbed dance instruction—minuets but also jigs—and even that they passed on such instruction to other slaves. "A good dancer and proud of it" was how an owner chose to characterize the escaped slave Sambo in a 1775 edition of the *Georgia Gazette*, the praise suggesting that slaves were mastering dance their masters could recognize and appraise as good. "He values himself for his fine Dancing," the owner of Tom, an escaped slave in Virginia, wrote about him in 1774, and the threat that a slave who valued himself could pose to the social order might be inferred from Tom's having run away.

Scattered stories in which members of the planting class—such as Thomas Jefferson's younger brother, Randolph—fiddle and dance with the slaves half the night point to boundary crossings more common than documents certify, meetings too furtive to mention, or too ordinary. The children of slaveholders grew up among slaves, and mutual habits formed early could endure into the separations of adulthood. Although there's much evidence of poor whites drinking and gambling together with blacks in dramshops and tippling houses, dancing is rarely mentioned. Yet the mixing did happen, and one outcome might have been the practice that whites labeled the Virginia Jig. In accounts from the mid-to-late eighteenth century, it's also called the "cut-out jig," since one couple engaged in amorous chase until either the lady or the gentleman was "cut out" by another. These jigs, which European visitors found "bacchanalian," often came at the end of an evening and might last until the fiddler quit. That fiddler was usually a slave, and at least one observer categorized the music as "some Negro tune." (In a Glasgow songbook of 1782, the transcription of a song labeled "Negro Jig" is built on a structure of repetitive cells that suggest African influence.) There are later accounts of similar jigs in Ireland, but one English traveler in Virginia was informed that the practice was "originally borrowed" from the Negroes.

———

Despite the oft-expressed anxiety of Puritan clergymen about the liber-
ties to which dancing might lead, dancing masters found plenty of business in eighteenth-century New England. Quaker qualms didn't exclude
dance from the middle colonies, either. The elite of Boston, Newport,
New York, and Philadelphia attended dancing schools, where they
learned minuets and country dances. White citizens did cut-out jigs in
Rhode Island and Pennsylvania. More advanced pupils studied hornpipes, which, as one student of the Boston dancing master William Turner
recalled, were only for boys. That same student also remembered
Turner's fiddler, Black Harry. As in the South, eighteenth-century peri-
odicals in the northern colonies carried plentiful notices about slave fiddlers for hire, slave fiddlers who had run away. Dancing masters relied
on their services.

They weren't the only ones. In 1760, a young John Adams recorded
in his journal a visit to a dockside tavern where a "wild Rable of both
sexes" was dancing "as if they would kick the floor thro." Who was
inspiring this vigor? "Negroes with a fiddle." Among the white revelers
was one Zab Hayward, whose fifteen-year reputation as the best dancer
in the region was known to the future president. Adams allowed that no
one could equal Hayward "in the nimbleness of heels" but judged that
he had "no conception of the grace, the air nor the regularity of dancing,"
a deficiency connected with his "low and ignoble" face. Was nimbleness
the standard by which the taverngoers rated Hayward so high? Those
who knew did not usually commit their thoughts to writing. Though
contemptuous, the Harvard graduate's description of how jigging Hayward caught the tavern girls in his arms betrays envy. The rabble was
having more fun.

One distressed informant of *The Boston Evening Post* discovered a
comparable tavern scene in 1740, except that the black violinist was
playing for black dancers. This particular party was private, yet dancing,
all night long or even a few days running, was a conspicuous feature of
northern holidays for slaves and free blacks. Negro Election Day, for
instance, was an annual festival during which blacks elected their own
ruler, then celebrated with parades, feasting, and dance: more banjos,
fiddles, and drums. "Most fatiguing" is as detailed as any source gets about
the dancing; what captured attention was the flamboyance of the slaves'

attire, finery often borrowed with permission from the closets of their masters. This was seen, with a patronizing smile, as an imitation of white Election Day, though, again, there's always the possibility that what whites understood as childish or pompous was actually parodic.

The case is similar with Pinkster, the main slave holiday in New York and New Jersey, a Dutch observance of Pentecost that by the late eighteenth century had largely been taken over by slaves. The evidence is shaky, but in Albany, a King Charles from Guinea was said to have presided, decked out in the ankle-length scarlet coat and tricornered hat of a British brigadier. Descriptions of the dance he led by thumping on an eel pot resemble descriptions of dancing in Martinique and Senegambia. It seems there was some Africa in Albany at the center of a Dutch carnival that had grown increasingly popular with "a certain class of whites" and a black population in a state that had, as of 1799, entered a gradual process of manumission.

By the time James Fenimore Cooper described a Pinkster celebration on a Manhattan parade ground in his 1845 historical novel *Satanstoe*, it was lore, a discontinued custom distinguished from the usual frolic by what Cooper called its African features: how the slaves danced not just to banjos but to drums. Cooper's telling was fiction, set before the author's birth. The researches of his contemporary Colonel Thomas De Voe are historically more trustworthy. Born in 1811, De Voe grew up as a butcher's assistant and became an expert on the city's markets. In his *Market Book* of 1862, he recounted how, at the turn of the nineteenth century, slaves from New Jersey and Long Island would gather on Pinkster at Catharine Market on the lower Manhattan side of the East River. They brought items to sell—roots, berries, fish—and they were always ready, De Voe wrote, "by 'negro sayings and doings' to make a few shillings more." This they did by engaging "in a jig or break-down, as that was one of their pastimes at home on the barn-floor, or in a frolic." *Do what you love and get paid for it*, as Buster Brown would say.

Each group of dancers brought its own dancing surface, a board called a "shingle," about six feet long, "with its particular spring in it." While one of the dancers jigged up a storm, two others would stand on opposite sides of the board, holding it down while beating time by dropping their heels and slapping their legs. Spectators rewarded the dancers with money, collected in a hat, and "if money was not to be had," the slaves "would dance for a bunch of eels or fish." (Eels were cheap and plentiful then, a staple of the poor.) Rivalry for reputation and spoils produced, as De Voe phrased it with patronizing quotation marks, "some excellent 'dancers.'"

This was the account of a man writing in the 1860s about dancing he may or may not have witnessed. Though elements seem African, he did not describe them as such. To him, the dance was Negro, and it was a jig, a Negro jig about making rhythms with the feet against a wooden platform, about making money in the marketplace of Manhattan. Everything about it sounds like tap.

FREEDOM DANCING IN SLAVEHOLDING AMERICA

In 1841, Solomon Northup, a free black farmer from New York lured south with the offer of a job as fiddler in a circus, was kidnapped and sold into slavery in Louisiana. A dozen years later, after he escaped, he published an account of his ordeal (the one adapted into the Oscar-winning film *12 Years a Slave*). In his book, Northup described how his master, soused and in the mood for sport, would call upon him to play the fiddle. The master would dance and would require his slaves to join him, slashing with his whip if anyone dared rest. (The master's wife, disapproving, could not always suppress a laugh.) This scene was an exhibit of a master's cruelty, but it was with pride that Northup wrote of slaves dancing in the starlight of a Christmas night: "If you wish to look upon the celerity, if not the 'poetry of motion'—upon genuine happiness, rampant and unrestrained—go down to Louisiana." On such occasions, Northup wrote, the slaves were "different beings from what they are in the field."

Whether or not Northup's account—written with the help of a white writer and with the expressed intention of converting whites to abolition— is entirely credible, those scenes capture the competing meanings of slave dancing. On one side was the coerced and degrading entertainment for slave owners, the stories told by former slaves about white folks coming to watch their dancing, coming to laugh, or about whites forcing them to dance, sometimes at gunpoint. And on the other was the happiness, genuine even in bondage, even if such a triumph of spirit could appear, to some, as a justification for slavery.

In an 1846 journal entry, the Harvard historian Francis Parkman described two slaves, chained together and dancing as another slave beat on a banjo: "They seem never to have known a care. Nothing is on their faces but careless, thoughtless enjoyment. Is it not safe to conclude them to be an inferior race?" A Virginia doctor, in an 1838 article, reported his wonder at slaves swigging persimmon beer and dancing to a banjo, merrily, percussively, ludicrously. The doctor recommended the scene as a rebuke to Northern abolitionists, as verification that the slaves were "the happiest of the human race," and also as proof for his Southern readers "that God has placed us high in the scale of human beings." These were the lines of thought, so pervasive as to be unremarkable, that led some abolitionists to insist that blacks did not dance and that all reports of slave dancing were proslavery propaganda.

The opportunities for slaves to dance varied from region to region and master to master. Although slave owners feared that slaves in large gatherings might plot rebellion, they also regarded recreation as a reward for good behavior and a safety valve of the kind Frederick Douglass meant when he characterized holidays as among "the most effective means in the hands of slaveholders of keeping down the spirit of insurrection." Holidays at Christmas, Easter, or the Fourth of July were occasions of license, often of liquor, and they always included dancing. Corn shuckings, quiltings, logrollings, and rice threshings all culminated in a feast and a dance, which served as a goal to inspire effort. Many masters allowed weekly dances or would allow slaves to attend dances on other plantations. "On Saturday nights," recalled the former slave James Campbell, "we'd dance long as de can'les lasted."

In their owners' eyes, the slaves were labor, merchandise, collateral, capital that reproduced itself. That they might also be family was among slavery's most awful complications. Through dancing, the slaves could reclaim their bodies for themselves. That was worth the effort of walking great distances after a long day's labor, worth the risk of a whipping or worse for attending a dance without a pass. Some slaves would recall dance explicitly as a form of resistance, glorying in remembrance of when they danced without permission. "Might whip us de nex' day," said Charles Grandy of Virginia, "but we done had our dance. Stay as late as we want—don't care ef we is got to be in de field at sunrise. When de dance break up we go out, slam de do' ef we wants, an' shout back at de man what had de party."

The slammed door resounds, flaunting the defiance involved whenever the slaves redirected energy to their own ends. Some meetings were secret, and thus required a short-term escape, as implied by the slave term for them, "steal away." But even sanctioned dances were interludes of freedom. In a clean shirt, a spare dress, adorned with a treasured ribbon, these people were different beings from what they were in the field, individuals who valued themselves for their fine dancing and could be so valued by others. Saturday evenings and holidays were the slaves' own time, and dancing was how they chose to spend it. Setting a high value on the community-strengthening powers of rhythmic synchronization came with the slaves' African heritage; associating dance with freedom became part of their American one.

Take it as heroic metaphor or as rules of the game, the dances of the slaves were dances of endurance. Solomon Northup, playing his fiddle in Louisiana, saw a man with a "placid bosom" and "legs flying like drumsticks" get cut out by a man shuffling and twisting his body into every conceivable shape as a woman outlasted them both, thereby sustaining her reputation as "the fastest gal." This was couple dancing but also individual competition. Slaves around the counterposed couple kept up the rhythm with foot tapping and body clapping. The Virginia doctor's similar account of jigging adds the slaves' comments, their aesthetic encouragement and criticism: "Molly move like the handsaw, see how she shake herself." "Cut him out, Gabe." Both scenes sound syncretic.

So does the competitive dancing that followed corn shuckings, events that blended European and African harvest customs. The slaves, divided in teams, worked to a beat in call-and-response with a singer who improvised rhymed commentary, commonly at the master's expense. For the dancing that followed, the slaves were said to prefer a plank floor or even the bottom of a wagon bed, concerned as they were with audible rhythms. (This observation, credible enough, comes from the 1914 memoir of a slaveholder's son, a man who missed the "faithful, patient, submissive, and happy creatures" of antebellum days.) Sharing a plank, two dancers would face off, spurred by the clapping and encouragement of those ringed around them into ever more rapid and violent motion until one of the dancers gave up.

Some former slaves would recall this use of a platform for public events, a sounding board that was also a stage. Yet Isaac Williams (in his as-told-to autobiography) attested that the clay floor of his slave cabin was hard enough to transmit the perfect time of bare feet as his friends danced to the music of his homemade fiddle, Saturday night right through Sunday morning. "Setting the floor," other slaves would call this practice, a couple squaring off and slapping their feet down on dirt. (The phrase also crops up in Scottish Gaelic songs for and about dancing.) Williams also remembered how he and his fellow slaves did the same dances—or at least dances with the same names—for their master's guests and how the best dancer won twenty-five cents.

Touring the South in 1851, Frederick Olmsted met the son of a small-scale Mississippi planter who informed him about the dancing favored "among common kind o' people." More than cotillions and reels, the young man enjoyed dancing on a plank balanced across two barrels "so it'll kind o' spring." Two people faced each other and danced as fast as they could while everyone else clapped and stomped and hollered phrases such as "Old Virginny never tire!" and "Heel and toe, Ketch a-fire!" The plank heightened the sport and turned up the volume. Between those barrels, it was like a door. But if dancing on a plank echoes Irish lore, it—and the competitive play and the clapping encouragement—equally resembles the dancing of African-American slaves.

The rowdy style of a country frolic was common ground. A handful of reports attest to whites dancing with slaves at communal events. A Rhode Island man who taught school in Georgia in the 1840s (and went to prison for aiding in the escape of a slave) wrote of dancing to fiddle music after a logrolling, whites and slaves together, inebriated and joking. But what astonished the Rhode Islander was the slaves' ability, the usual list of rapidity, accurate time, physical power, humor. "The sound of a fiddle makes them crazy," he wrote, speculating that in the case of insurrection, someone would merely have to strike up a tune and the slaves would drop their rebellion to jig. Dancing to the fiddle, he wrote, they were "at home."

> The slaves, as they become excited, use the most extravagant gestures— the music increases in speed—and the Whites soon find it impossible to sustain their parts, and they retire. This is just what the slaves wish, and they send up a general shout, which is returned by the Whites, acknowledging the victory. Then they all sing out, "Now show de white man what we can do!"

The ground might have been common, but not quite even.

ERECT AND DIGNIFIED

"Us slaves watched white folks' parties," remembered one former slave, "where the guests danced a minuet and then paraded in a grand march . . . then we'd do it, too. But we used to mock 'em, every step. Sometimes the white folks noticed it, but they seemed to like it. I guess they thought we couldn't dance any better."

Those words were written down in 1960, when the black actor Leigh Whipper, eighty years old at the time, recalled what his "nurse" had spoken on an occasion in 1901, when she was more than seventy. The events she was recounting had taken place some sixty years before that, when she was a young "strut gal" enjoying privileges for being a good dancer, taken from one plantation to another for competitions upon which her master wagered. This statement, so far from direct, is almost the only documentation of slaves imitatively mocking their masters in dance, the quote itself supplying one reason why evidence might be scarce: white folks' misinterpretations. Yet there's plenty of evidence of slaves mocking their masters in *song*, transcribed words whose meanings, overt and coded, we can now read. And it makes sense that from an African perspective a minuet might have appeared comically rigid. It makes sense that slaves would have been eager to send up the pretensions and hypocrisies of the planter class.

Derision, however, can't fully account for why people of African descent, to whom dance meant so much, borrowed from or adopted European dance. Certainly among black domestics and artisans, dance functioned as a mark of status. In his 1856 book *Virginia, especially Richmond, in By-Gone Days*, Samuel Mordecai fondly remembered the "colored aristocracy" of the early nineteenth century. Though Mordecai considered their "aping" of genteel behavior to be ridiculous, his account of the "erect and dignified" slave fiddler Sy Gilliat seems believable. Imagine the appeal of holding your body erect and dignified when, as Solomon Northup put it, "the attitude and the language of the slave," the demeanor expected and enforced by whites, was one of downcast eyes and bowed heads, a bodily lexicon of servility. An upright carriage, by contrast, was a show of pride, a trait disturbing enough to slaveholders that it merited mention in runaway slave notices.

"Erect and dignified" describes the manner of the black wedding party in Christian Mayr's 1838 painting *Kitchen Ball at White Sulphur Springs, Virginia*. Up north, the formal balls held by free blacks provided ripe matter for nasty cartoons and newspaper articles, often prompted by court proceedings treating the events as disturbances of the peace. *The Pennsylvania Gazette* rated one Philadelphia occasion of 1828 as "a joke of no ordinary magnitude." The mockery concentrated on fancy attire and high modes of address, yet most of the information about the dancing of Northern blacks comes in this form, with reported fact nearly indistinguishable from jest. A few genuine-sounding black voices cut through, such as the woman in a court proceeding who asked simply, "If the big white folks dance, why should not people of color?" That's a fair question, yet how did the people of color do the big white folks' dances? The most suggestive clue is the judgment of a white observer that Frank Johnson, a renowned black Philadelphian composer and bandleader who played at black functions and white resorts, showed "a remarkable taste in distorting a sentimental, simple, and beautiful song into a reel, jig, or country-dance." The "distortion" sounds rhythmic, a remix bent toward the preferences of rhythm-oriented dancers.

Interviewed in 1883, Sylvia Dubois would recall the superior dancing of her youth in the first decades of the century, when she was a house slave in New Jersey; the superiority, in her telling, lay in the quick, nimble crossing of feet ("ninety-nine times in a minute"): a value that sounds Irish. In the mind of the former slave Hannah Crasson, the way her aunt could "tote herself" was part of what distinguished her as a "royal slave." Crasson's aunt "could dance all over the place wid a tumbler of water on her head, widout spilling it." Many slaves would recall similar dances of balanced water. Water on the head was part of Set the Floor and other competitive pastimes. The idea could be an Irish dancing master's, or a game that conforms to the African aesthetic of the cool: the bosom placid while the lower limbs fly like drumsticks, the dancing style of people accustomed to toting loads on their heads. Beyond the allure of status markers, the slaves (and free blacks, too) must have been attracted to aesthetic qualities of European dance—to, say, the "easy careless manner" stressed by the influential dancing master William Turner. As much as African-derived dancing could strike whites as alien or absurd, the aesthetic of the cool was not incompatible with a European-derived ideal of grace.

We might speculate that slaves took to dancing with water on their heads much as some of them, recalling, if only dimly, the water deities and cleansing rituals of Africa, took to baptism. Efforts to convert the slaves to Christianity found greatest purchase in early-nineteenth-century camp meetings, where modes of worship were musically and emotionally ecstatic, drawing slaves in with resemblances to African spirituality that the slaves' participation reinforced. Yet among the most successful sects were Methodists and Baptists, who taught that dancing was sinful, causing many a pious slave to swear off it altogether. For people of African descent, this was an epochal conversion. It meant that the black church, already becoming a powerful, community-binding institution, set itself against dance, a proscription that persists in certain black churches to this day.

At least doctrinally. An 1819 catalogue of Methodist errors and excesses detected in the camp-meeting singing of blacks a rhythmic "sinking" of the legs, "producing an audible sound of the feet at every step, as manifest as the steps of actual Negro dancing in Virginia." Visiting a Georgia plantation in 1845, Sir Charles Lyell noted that while the Methodist missionaries silenced violins, the slaves were permitted to move around in a ring, "as substitute for the dance." Such dances became known as *shouts*. Northerners who journeyed south during the Civil War registered a shuffling dance of hand-clapping, foot-drumming, knee-bending, body-rocking motion that accelerated to a fever pitch. The shocked teacher who wrote home that the shout seemed "the remains of some old idol worship" and "like a regular frolic" was more right than she knew. In African-American culture, the line between feeling the spirit on Saturday night and feeling it on Sunday morning would ever remain thin—or rather, in tension, the body-denying doctrine contradicting a mode of delivery that forced the body to respond. And the expressive urge that kept the dance in church is among the urges that forged tap.

A SHARED LANGUAGE

Separately derived traditions could share much, and it was at points of commonality that they were most likely to blend. In dance, however, the most plentiful evidence is the most tenuous: a shared vocabulary of casually applied terms. Words that might reveal genealogies might just as well disguise them.

Ponder, for instance, "the pigeon wing," a phrase that former slaves applied to their antebellum dancing. Fannie Berry glossed it as "flippin' yo' arms an' legs roun' an' holdin' yo' neck stiff like a bird do," a description that suggests animal mimicry. But according to other former slaves, these from Texas, it was all about cracking the heels together, in the air, as many times as you could before landing. That's what the pigeon-winging young men, all white, do in one 1841 story of a Mississippi frontier wedding. (They're expressing their impatience with a tardy Negro fiddler, "indispensable at every frolic.") Everyone seems to agree on the appropriate verb: *cut*. Yet in the early-nineteenth-century New York ballrooms immortalized by Washington Irving, "cutting the pigeon wing" designated a difficult dancing-school step. This pigeon wing, an airborne beating together of extended legs, was then associated with French dancers and pirouettes; it may have derived from France and ballet's *ailes de pigeon* (or *brisé volé*). But by the mid-nineteenth century in America, the phrase was more associated with slaves and rowdy frontiersmen.

The situation is similar for "double shuffle," which the former slave
Isaac Williams used to describe his own dancing, both the audible dances
of the slave cabin and the funny dances that amused the master's guests.
Yet the double shuffle could also be a flourish that a white Bostonian, in
1827, inserted into a cotillion while following the calls of a Negro fiddler. The double shuffle is what a Negro banjoist in the 1833 *Sketches and
Eccentricities of Col. David Crockett of West Tennessee* directs the white frontiersfolk to do, along with such rural steps as "weed korn" and "kiver
taters." Corn and potatoes also cropped up in the dance steps of New
Jersey farmers, as recorded in the 1813 satirical poem *The Lay of the Scottish Fiddle* (attributed to James Kirke Paulding), and as an assumed terpsichorean skill of a Long Island Negro in an 1807 Washington Irving
story. But in both cases, the term linked to the hoeing and digging is
"double trouble" (which might be a corruption of "double treble"). Irving
called it Dutch, but for his friend Paulding, it was "undoubtedly of African
origin," a shuffling that kept accurate time without lifting feet off the
floor.

"Double shuffle" also shows up suggestively in *Life in London*, Pierce
Egan's scandalously popular British novel of 1821. The sports Tom
and Jerry, sampling life high and low, visit All-Max, an East End tavern serving sailors, garbage collectors, prostitutes, Indians, and blacks,
all swigging gin and jigging to a fiddle. The mood is "happiness—
everybody free and easy, and freedom of expression allowed to the very
echo," a freedom that includes "footing the double shuffle against each
other." George Cruickshank's illustration centers on Dusty Bob, a white
though grimy coal whipper, footing it against African Sall. A "comic pas
de deux" for those two partners made it into several stage versions, which
were hits in London and New York. Though fiction, Egan's scene offers
a creditable glimpse of free and easy mixing among the lower classes;
he was a connoisseur of urban slang, and for him, the double shuffle was
a dance of a motley clientele, conceivably as much African Sall's as Dusty
Bob's. In Britain and Ireland, the double shuffle, originally associated
with hornpipes, would remain a basic step in jigs and clog dancing. In
America, it would get combined, and confused, with the floor-scraping
"shuffling" of blacks.

Jig was the word that Henry Ravenal chose, writing in 1876 of his

1820s youth, to label the dancing of the slaves on his family's South Carolina plantation. "The jig," he maintained, "was an African dance and a famous one in old times, before more refined notions began to prevail." This was a cut-out jig, with a shuffling of partners. The woman moved with a "slow shuffling gait . . . edging along by some unseen exertion of the feet . . . sometimes courtesying [sic] down and remaining in that posture." The man's feet "moved about in the most grotesque manner stamping, slamming, and banging the floor, not unlike the patterning of hail on the housetop. The conflict between brogans and the sanded floor was terrific." Aspects of the music point to African influence, as do the woman's bent-kneed curtsy and those unseen exertions of the feet. Perhaps it's significant that *brogans*, the word former slaves would choose to refer to the stiff footwear their masters provided them, derives from Gaelic. The word *jig* would make a similar jump, adding to its Old World affiliation with Irishness a New World usage as a name for blacks.

Some jigs were called *juba*. *Patting juba* or *juber* was a term for body percussion. *Patting juba* is what Solomon Northup said the slaves were doing in the Louisiana starlight; it's what the slaves at the Georgia log-rolling were up to when they outlasted the whites. When the revels of poor whites in Baltimore got them hauled before a court in 1839, and thus reported in the newspaper, the story of their drunken spree also involved "patting juba." When a writer the following year related the amusingly rustic habits of Florida frontiersfolk, their dancing—to a "sable Paganini," naturally—consisted of "double trouble" and "juba," steps the writer categorized as "peculiarly cracker." Fragments of juba songs that Virginia slaves were singing in 1838—"Juber dis, and Juber dat," "get over double trouble"—would regularly resurface in accounts of Southern life over the next century. What happened to the words likely happened to the dance, less traceably.

As for the word *juba*, Bessie Jones, a black folksinger born in 1902, learned from her grandfather that *juba* meant "giblets," leftovers from the kitchens of whites slopped into troughs for blacks. Count on folk etymology for a flavorful metaphor. Juba was also the name of the king of Numidia in the time of Caesar, and Americans named their slaves Juba as they named them Pompey and Scipio. The word means something different in Zulu, Swahili, and Ashanti. Scholars point to a Bantu word for beating time, a harvest ritual from the Giouba tribe, and dances in the Caribbean. Robert Farris Thompson traces *juba* to the Ki-kongo words *zuba* (dance) and *nzuba* (hitting or slapping). Nineteenth-century enthusiasts focused on rhythmic properties. A Virginian friend of Edgar Allan Poe wrote to him about the possibilities for verse in "capriciously irregular" departures from meter that nevertheless maintained the cadence. Sidney Lanier, in his 1880 *The Science of English Verse*, would use *patting Juba* to explain syncopation. (His notated example—though he doesn't identify it as such—is a cross-rhythmic pattern found across Africa and known in Afro-Cuban music as *clave*.)

One final phrase was "buck dancing." In the slave trade, *buck* was an animal-breeding term applied to black males in advertisements. Before that, *buck* referred to a white dandy. Certain theories trace the word to the West Indian term *po'bockorau*—buckaroo, buccaneer, rowdy jigging sailor—or to the Gaelic term for playboy, *boc*. Others posit Native American origins, a black and white imitation of Native American dances imitating buck deer. (The Ute had their own stomping Buck Dance. Native American men were also called *bucks*.) Etymology by homophone can get you almost anywhere. In the 1890s, when *buck* first came into print as a dance term, the black poet James Edwin Campbell glossed the Mobile Buck as the dance of Negro roustabouts on the Ohio and the Mississippi, who bucked against each other.

THE BREAKDOWN

One platform that slaves had to themselves was the auction block. After their teeth were inspected and their backs scrutinized for whip scars, slaves might be made to dance—to demonstrate that their bodies were in good working order and to provide entertainment for those buying and selling them. In a 1931 book of interviews with former slaves, a man identified solely as Jolly Old Uncle Buck remembered one such incident vividly. As Buck sat waiting with other children to be sold and possibly separated from their families, he watched a slave named Fred stand on the auction block as another slave started to play the banjo:

Fred 'gin ter shuffle roun' on his big feet, an' fine'ly he can't stand it no longer. He gotta dance. He slap his big feet on de banjo table, an' we all pat wid de banjo music. White man laugh an' clap dey han's. Make him dance some mo'. Wouldn't let de auctioneer start till Fred dance de buck-an'-wing. Yo-ho! It sho'ly was funny! De white man what bought Fred say he done paid hundert dollars mo' fo' dat nigger cause he could dance like dat!

Everybody's laughing here, a laughter that courses through similar stories. But is the joke on Fred? Is he dancing because he can't resist the banjo or because they make him? Because he's dancing, his value has risen. Fred doesn't get the money or his freedom, but he gets some satisfaction, some glory, set apart up on the platform. Good dancers could win privileges. A slave who danced well might get himself out of the fields for a while. Dancing feet attracted coin. One former house slave reported being taken as a child by his master to dance "the jig and buck" for pennies in Annapolis stores; afterward, his master bought the talented slave a new pair of shoes.

Jolly Old Uncle Buck told his story about Fred to a white journalist in the segregated South. It's suspect yet not easily dismissed. When a black person being interviewed by a white person because he or she was once a slave recalls dancing for guests (and for food and drink) at the Big House and says, "You know a nigger is jest a born show-offer," how should that statement be taken? (Especially when the person goes on to say, "Niggers was all right on the plantations"?) These stories might tell us what they seem to on the surface, something about extroversion in African-American culture, or they might themselves be more examples of the performance that blacks in America found necessary for survival. Blacks told these stories and these stories became a staple of white Southern fiction and memoir. In Julia Morgan's memoir of the war, *How It Was*, she recounts how her faithful servant Joe cleverly avoided working for the Confederate army by pretending to be crippled. The ruse failed when this "celebrated jig dancer" who "cut the pigeon wing to perfection" saw a platform in the street and couldn't resist.

Which brings us back to Tom—that jiggin'est slave in Texas, up on a platform, making his feet sound like a snare drum, faster and faster, all the movement from the hips down, beating the other fellow because he could twirl without spilling water from the glass on his head. Where did all that come from? Though we can hear the acceleration, we can't quite hear the rhythm. Neither do we know who set the rules. Likely it was a negotiation, as with much in master-slave relations. But sorting out the ethnic origins of the behavior described in that anecdote, deciding the winner of the origin contest—it can't be done. Why not just call it American?

That's what the newspaper editor Ed James did in the 1871 dance manual *Jig, Clog, and Breakdown Dancing Made Easy. Breakdown* was one more term for slave dancing. The word suggests the breaking of pattern that induces possession in African dances; it seems kin to the breaks and breakaways and break-it-downs of later African-American dance and music. Yet in the printed record, the earliest "Virginia 'break-down'" I can find is in the diary of a governor of Mississippi, where he records the phrase as piquant slang encountered during a youthful keelboat journey on the Ohio River in 1819; here, it means a frolic attended by rough river men. The next usages, appearing in the 1830s, also refer to the dancing of whites—the dancing of whites imitating blacks. Here, a breakdown is a Negro jig, the kind of jig that Ed James, forty years later, considered "a peculiarly American institution." James located its origin in another peculiar American institution, "among the slaves of the southern plantations": "No white man taught the original darkies the arts of Jig or Clog Dancing, and it is equally as indisputable that they did not pick either one of them up from reading books on the subject. It was original with them and has been copied by those who, in the early days of minstrelsy, made that a feature of their business, and by them brought down to a complete science."

The question of origins can't be so easily fixed. Distinguishing original from copy would be hard enough, but what makes it nearly impossible is precisely this business of minstrelsy, a theatrical form in which whites imitated blacks. That the imitators altered the dances can be presumed, but with what mix of mimicry and mockery, distortion and invention? The questions are important, because it was through minstrelsy that the dances called jigs, juba, shuffles, and breakdowns became theater. It was through minstrelsy that they became tap.

3

IMITATION DANCE

The dancer's nose is flat and wide, his hair tightly curled. His clothes are patched. His arms float above his head, as in worship. His thighs splay. One bare foot is lifted high, in the act of crossing behind the other, which clings to a disintegrating shoe. Beneath the feet is a platform, a shingle, a door with its hinges still attached. This is an image on sheet music, published in 1840, for "Jim Along Josey," a popular song with backwoods drive and a dance break. Underneath the dancer appears the phrase "As sung by John N. Smith," a white man who danced as a black.

Smith had plenty of competition. He and other "Delineators of Ethiopian Character" bounced between circuses and theaters. A dancer-singer teamed up with a fiddler or a banjo player, or maybe both, to act out topical songs called "extravaganzas." The dancers referred to themselves as "heelologists" and "science niggas," and their dancing was percussive—jigs and double shuffles and breakdowns often sounded out on a plank in the center of a circus ring. "De ambition that dis nigger feels," one verse of "Jim Along Josey" explained, "is showing de science of his heels." The heels of Negroes, supposedly elongated, were staples of racial mockery, and Negro Delineators made audiences laugh. But science was skill, as in the "sweet science" of boxing, and the ambition was no joke.

Like many blackface jig dancers of his time and after, John Diamond was not yet of age, perhaps sixteen in 1839, when he began appearing on playbills as Master Diamond. The title Master, designating someone younger than a Mister, carried the association of expertise only inadvertently, yet Diamond may very well have been "a genius in the dancing line." That was the assessment of P. T. Barnum, then starting out as a promoter and peddler of humbug, who promoted Diamond, in 1840, as "the little 'Wirginny Nigger,' only 12 years old," who could "outdance the nation." Soon the New York papers were hailing the "extraordinary," "irresistible" local kid as "the best negro dancer in the country" and "King of Darkies." In high-heeled boots, Diamond did a Sailor's Hornpipe, a Camptown Hornpipe, and a Smokehouse Dance, but breakdowns were his specialty: Old Virginny breakdowns, Long Island breakdowns. Journalists punned about how sharply Diamond cut pigeon wings. "Exhibitions of suppleness" was how his performances were characterized by the theatrical manager Noah Ludlow: "He could twist his feet and legs, while dancing, into more fantastic forms than I ever witnessed before or since." The New Orleans *Picayune* rhapsodized about the kaleidoscopic variety and quicksilver grace of the "little nigger Apollo."

James Thomas, who was born to a slave mother and a prominent judge in 1827, would recall near the end of his long life the visit of Master Diamond to Nashville as part of a circus in 1842: "He would walk around the board, then jump on it, and dance in a manner as though he would pick it up with his feet, jump-off, again walk around, and say something nigger like and dance again. The people thought it was the best part of the show." An 1841 playbill for a Diamond appearance in Mobile depicted the dancer balanced between the heel of one foot and the ball of the other, wrists drooping. Sampling some black talk—"Now de heels, if dares any music in you it's got to come out"—it challenged all comers to compete with Diamond in a trial of skill at Negro Dancing, in all its varieties, for a wager of up to a thousand dollars. The wager was bait. As Barnum surely sniffed out, there was money to be made in Negro impersonation.

As soon as there were stages in North America, white performers were on them, imitating blacks. There were noble, suffering blacks (think Othello) and ignorant-but-clever comic servants and slaves. The comic servants drew from the Italian commedia dell'arte and its cunning figures such as Harlequin, who sometimes wore a black mask and whom some traditions linked with Africans. Other influences included court masques, carnivalesque folk theatricals, sooty-faced mummers, black men with diabolic connotations, fertility rites—a wide array of representations of blackness that had crossed the Atlantic.

In 1767, when a Mr. Tea offered a "Negro Dance in Character" in New York, his advertising the performance as a "grotesque interlude in dancing" was less disparaging than it sounds and more descriptive. Harlequin figures in eighteenth-century English pantomime were comics— our term *slapstick* stems from Harlequin's favored prop—but they were also virtuoso dancers. Their athletic, acrobatic style would come to be known as "character" dancing: the gestures that defined the characters of servants, sailors, and other low types, as opposed to the decorous and stately motions that marked nobles, heroes, and heroines. From the sixteenth to the nineteenth century, this comic dancing went by the label *grotesque*. That *grotesque* was also a common term for the dancing of blacks, an adjective for the abandon of slaves on holiday, was no coincidence. According to the hierarchical categories of European theatrical dancing, the dancing of blacks was comic. Like the Irish Jiggs and Drunken Peasant dances sharing stages at that time, a Negro Dance in Character, be it ever so nimble, wasn't to be taken seriously.

But with all the blackface on American stages, it's surprising how little evidence there is of blackface dancing—that is, until around 1828. Then, so goes the story, in Cincinnati, or Louisville, or Pittsburgh, some frontier town on the Ohio, a young actor from New York arrives with a traveling theatrical troupe. Strolling around, he runs into a black man, a Negro stage driver who sings a song and does a little dance. In multiple versions of this tale, the stage driver is lame, his right shoulder drawn up high, his left leg stiff and crooked so he walks with a limp. The actor, Thomas Dartmouth Rice, takes the slave's song, his dance, his name, and forges a new character. When Rice blackens his face, dresses in rags, and tries out the act, the audience calls him back to the stage thirty or forty times. The character, the song, and the dance share a name identified in the song: "Wheel about, turn about / Do jus' so / An' ebery time I turn about / I jump Jim Crow."

In the mix-and-match quatrains of the earliest printed variants, Crow speaks of himself as a skilled fiddler, a flatboat traveler on the Mississippi, a carpenter, a snapping turtle. He kisses the gals, knocks down Jersey niggers, and threatens white dandies with a trip to the gutter. The earliest illustrations depict a figure in a patched suit, knees bent, lolling on the heel of one disintegrating shoe and the ball of the other. One hand rests on his protruding rear; the other waves loosely. As later images of John Smith and John Diamond show, this stance would stick.

By 1832, Rice was all the rage, packing theaters up and down the eastern seaboard. His songs expanded into "extravaganzas," and adapting English farces and ballad operas, he cobbled together plays in which sassy black tricksters outwit white bosses. Touring England, Scotland, and Ireland, Rice was a runaway success, his song even more so. Journalists described a mania, an epidemic that spread Jim Crow onto every street corner and into every parlor. Nobility attended Rice's shows, but his core audience, as his detractors emphasized, was made up of carpenters, dustmen, and chimney sweeps—working youth. This was true in America as well, where his popularity drew vicious attacks from snobbish scribes.

What was the dance like? The lyrics grant a few clues—wheeling, jumping, an allusion to "double trouble," that possibly African variant of "double shuffle." "Sich a Getting Up Stairs," another song in Rice's repertoire, specified how its main character frolicked to a fiddle on a raft by striking toe and heel, cutting de pigeon wing, scratching gravel, and slapping de foot. These are foundational moves, or at least foundational terms: a century later, "scratching gravel" would be one name for the first step of the Shim Sham. An ad for a Rice engagement in 1833 promised "A Virginia Breakdown," the earliest theatrical use I can find of that term.

Soon, more blackface characters joined Jim. Out of the South came the song "Zip Coon," which told of a "larned skolar" who jumps "double trouble." The word *coon* had lately referred to a white hick, much as Daniel Boone's coonskin cap served as an emblem of rural folk. Yet as portrayed by Rice and George Washington Dixon, Zip Coon switched colors. The illustrations depict a black dandy in tight pantaloons, a tail-coat, and a top hat. Dangling a lorgnette, the character would seem to be an "Ethiopian exquisite," "a gentleman of color," already a figure of fun in stories and drawings that responded to flamboyantly dressed blacks on the sidewalks of New York and Philadelphia. Compared with the unmistakable racial contempt in such cartoons, however, the target of the song is less certain. Is it blacks acting above their station? Preten-sion in general? One in the guise of the other? The music is a lively jig. It's catchy, and it lasted. It's the tune of "Turkey in the Straw."

Music like that—music for dancing—was what attracted blackface dancers such as John Diamond. He often teamed up with a fellow New Yorker, the banjo player William Whitlock. Whitlock also worked with a dancer named Richard Pelham. The two pitch-black faces on an 1842 playbill for a circus stop in Charleston might depict either pair: the ban-joist on a barrel; the dancer, hat cocked and hand on hip, extending a heel. But this was another team: the Baltimorean dancer Frank Brower with Daniel Emmett, a fiddler and banjoist out of Ohio. A year later, two of these duos formed a band in lower Manhattan called the Virginia Minstrels (without Diamond, though he would sometimes join them). In addition to dancing, Pelham thumped a tambourine and Brower rat-tled bones. Whitlock gave a lecture in malaprop-laden "Negro" dialect and imitated a locomotive. All four men sang, swapped puns, and recited riddles. As they hoofed their jigs and breakdowns and pivoted through their "grapevine twisting," they shouted out phrases such as "Dars musick in dem old heels" and "dat deaph to creepin insects." A poster bragged about "knockin' de breff out o' bards," inflicting violence on floorboards.

The Tyrolese Minstrels, a family of Alpine singers, were popular with middle-class audiences, so for a group of Negro-impersonating circus entertainers to name themselves the Virginia Minstrels could have been a roguish travesty or a sincere appeal to a more respectable, wealthier audience. But if the marketing that assured "refined," "chaste" concerts wasn't a lampoon of the language used to lure middle-class women, it wasn't truth in advertising, either. A staple of the Virginia Minstrels' repertoire was "De Boatmen Dance," celebrating rough Ohio river men who danced all night till broad daylight and went home with the gals in the morning.

The idea of a minstrel band caught on quick. Imitators proliferated, and so many troupes adopted similar names that appending the word *original* nearly became a necessity. Minstrelsy was obscenely popular. Its strongholds were the cities of the Northeast—Boston, Philadelphia, New York—where as many as ten theaters might be devoted to minstrel shows and a minstrel troupe could sustain a run of a decade or more. But minstrelsy also spread west, jumping to the Pacific with the Gold Rush and then following settlers and railroads as they closed up the gap. Tours through the South were common, right up to the Civil War and resuming as soon as the smoke cleared. Everywhere minstrels went, they inspired stagestruck youth to black up and put on a show. John "Jim Along Josey" Smith, an immediate success in Britain, was one of many minstrels who went to Australia and never came back. The Virginia Minstrels immediately toured the British Isles. Their tambourinist never returned home. The United States finally had a cultural export that sold.

"Burnt-cork artists" they were sometimes called, in reference to their stage makeup. They dipped cork in alcohol and lit it on fire. After the cork burned to ash, they mixed it into a paste and smeared it on their faces. They painted on thick red lips and wore kinked wigs known as "wool." The rest of the costume could be the checked shirts of the Southern plantation slave or the long-tailed blue suit of the Northern black dandy. In time, the musicians at each end would take on fixed roles as the comic rowdies Tambo and Bones, named after their instruments. These wildmen would carry on jokey banter with the Interlocutor, a dignified, well-spoken, finely dressed man who sat in the center futilely trying to keep things under control.

The dance finale was frequently labeled a festival dance, a plantation dance, or maybe a walk-around. A promenading solo in playbills of the forties, the walk-around swelled into an ensemble act during the following decade. In one illustration from 1859, the men face in different directions, waving their arms above their heads; their feet and knees twist, squiggly lines indicating oscillation; everything is bowed, everything bent. As the company clapped and patted knees and shouted encouragement, one dancer would advance downstage, walk in a circle, execute a fancy step or a funny one, and return to the group. Then another dancer would repeat the sequence, displaying his own step and style. At the end, everyone would circumnavigate the stage. "A Cornshucking" was the subtitle of the most famous walk-around of all, a song advising the listener to "hoe it down and scratch your grabble" in the land of cotton: Daniel Emmett's "Dixie." (Yes, *that* "Dixie.")

The Virginia Minstrels peddled not just "the oddities, peculiarities, eccentricities, and comicalities of the Sable Genus of Humanity" but, quite specifically, the activities of "the southern slaves at all their merry meetings such as the gathering in of the cotton and sugar crops, corn huskings, slave weddings, and junketings." When they toured England, the *Manchester Times* reported with anthropological detail on a Corn Husking Jig and a Slave Marriage Dance, which the most expert dancer on the plantation performed for other slaves, and a Slave Match Dance, performed for whites, "who urge the negroes to their utmost skill by making small presents to the negro who can stand the most fatigue or remain upon the board for the longest time." What the Virginia Minstrels offered, their ads claimed, was "a true copy," "both new and original."

Early Northern reviewers often praised minstrels for accuracy, for "mimicry superb and true to life," and some Southern reviewers concurred. One of Rice's employers wrote that his strongest talent consisted in his "great fidelity in imitating the broad and prominent peculiarities of other persons," a talent most evident in "close delineations of the cornfield negro, drawn from real life." *Peculiarities*: that was always the word. But also: "drawn from real life." A newspaper editor who knew Rice well attested to his study of "the negro character in all its varieties," recounting how Rice ate, drank, and slept with them, "went to their frolics, and made himself the best white black man in existence." Analogous authenticating stories would be told of other burnt-cork artists. An obituary of the Virginia Minstrels' banjoist explained how he would "steal off to some negro hut to hear the darkies sing and see them dance, taking a jug of whisky to make things merrier."

We should be skeptical of such stories, but any attempt at scrutiny runs into obstacles. The information about early minstrelsy, especially about dance, is patchy and imprecise and encrusted with the embellishments of later scribes. Yet the more vexing problem arises from the other side, the scarcity and vagueness of the information about African-American music and dance. The problem isn't merely that to compare minstrel representations with black practice is to compare two ill-defined subjects; the problem is that minstrelsy, through its popularity and massive cultural influence, shuffled the evidence. Arguments can turn as circular as a Ring Shout.

Look at Jim Crow. It's quite possible that when he sings "I neeld to de buzzard / An I bou'd to de Crow," the scavenging birds echo trickster figures out of African-turned-African-American folklore. It's possible that Jim is cousin to the buzzard called John Crow in the Caribbean. In the mid-twentieth century, a song called "Knock Jim Crow" was still being sung with similar lyrics and acted out with patting-juba rhythms in the Georgia Sea Islands, but there's no way to know if that practice borrowed from Rice's ubiquitous ditty, or responded to it, rather than the other way around. The idea of Rice drawing from widespread folk practice is simply a more credible origin story than the one about him stealing from a single stablehand. It accounts better for what his contemporaries found true to life, what early audiences thrilled to recognize. Evidence also points to Rice's borrowing from black street performers, who borrowed from him. A back-and-forth business, it seems to have been—up to the edges of the stages on which Rice found fame and fortune.

If songs were traded, how about steps? In 1841, the New Orleans *Picayune* reported a police raid of a Negro ball. Gleefully arch, the article mocked how Sam Jonsing and Pete Gumbo were "dressed 'to kill,'" quoted the etiquette of their conversation in black dialect, and enlisted dance verbs to narrate how the authorities put the slaves in their place. Before that, the Sambos and Dinahs waltzed, someone did a Virginia breakdown in a corner, and then this: "In the refreshment room, an elderly 'nig' was strumming a sickly banjo, to which a 'science nigga' was dancing 'Jim Along Josey.'" Master Diamond, the article suggests, "might have employed himself very usefully in 'taking items.'" The *Picayune* had already praised Diamond, who was in town that week performing

"Jim Along Josey," for his "fidelity." According to the New York *Whip*, he handed coins to blacks on the New Orleans levees in exchange for steps; this was the source of his "modern improvement," a style of dancing "particularly his own."

The setting of New Orleans is intriguing: the most dance-mad American city, the one most closely tied to the Caribbean, the one where the slaves' African heritage was most openly on display (most famously in Congo Square), but also a place of much mixing, a nexus for trade in slaves, goods, and culture. What, though, should we make of the shared lingo? Does it help confirm the black roots of minstrelsy? Or is it rather an exhibit of contamination, demonstrating how minstrelsy was already determining the form in which whites represented, and even perceived, the behavior of blacks? The questions extend to much of the evidence. When the *Picayune* reports, in 1845, on blacks dancing "regular Ethiopian breakdowns" in Congo Square and singing "Hey Jim Along," those phrases might have been shorthand for black song and dance—for blacks acting, you know, like they do in the minstrel show. And then again, maybe they *were* acting that way, having taught the minstrels, or borrowed from them, or some combination that can't be untangled by pulling on this one thread.

Pictorial representations aren't any more or less reliable. The illustrations of breakdowns on minstrel playbills and songsters from the 1840s on depict bowlegged figures, legs hitched up to stomp, their body angles implying an imminent crossing of feet. The postures match, quite closely, those in illustrations of slave dances published in magazines in the 1850s and '60s (and those of blacks dancing through the end of the century). Some illustrations are so similar that their value as corroborative evidence is suspect, one representation either copying another outright or following the same set of conventions.

All of the parallels, linguistic and visual, could deceive, but my guess is that they don't. I would bet that the double trouble of Jim Crow is kin to the double trouble of Virginia slaves dancing juba, and also to the double trouble characteristic of Florida crackers. Minstrel scholarship has long noted how the bluster of Jim and Zip samples phrases found in the tough talk of the frontiersman Davy Crockett and the boatman Mike Fink, historical figures who became mythic. When Jim Crow

compared himself with a snapping turtle, he was borrowing the tag of
Fink and boatmen like him—the kind who referred to their dancing
frolics as Virginia breakdowns. These were men who worked the nation's circulatory system: the Mississippi, the Ohio. These were men
who got around. They had that in common with T. D. Rice and Master
Diamond and the Virginia Minstrels, who plied their trade on the same
rivers.

The boatmen traveled on flatboats, rafts that carried goods and
passengers downriver, or on oared keelboats, which could be gruelingly
forced upstream. Some of the passengers *were* goods; the boats carried
slaves, and some of the slaves labored as boatmen. "Gumbo Chaff," a
song Rice sang, was about such a slave boatman, who celebrates his master's death by taking a trip to New Orleans before retiring in Ohio.
Boatmen took that trip over and over, the roughest class of white men in
continual contact with black slaves, a floating wooden platform always
underfoot. When an 1844 account of the death of Mike Fink tallied the
uncivilized habits of his kind, dancing "nigger breakdowns" came in the
middle of the list, no explanation required.

These were the "joyous and reckless crews of fiddling, song-singing,
whisky-drinking, break-down dancing rapscallions" that Mark Twain,
poet of the Mississippi, would eulogize. Colonel T. B. Thorpe, who
carved a smaller career out of backwoods tales, listed the "rough frolics"
of the keelboatmen as dancing, fiddling, and fistfights, and characterized
black deckhands as favorites for "keeping time" with "the light fantastic
heel-and-toe tap" while someone fiddled "a Virginia hoe-down." In
Thorpe's stories of Fink and his tribe enjoying themselves by shooting
off people's hats or the tip of a Negro's heel, the climax of the trip is the
landing at Natchez Under-the-Hill, where boatmen got paid and "grat-
ified their humors." Natchez was another of the country's main hubs for
the trade in slaves (and the dancing that came with it). A "rough jig dance"
called "Natchez Under the Hill" was a source for the tune of "Zip Coon,"
which Daniel Emmett played as "Turkey in the Straw."

The twang in that tune is a clue to where many of the songs and
dances of early minstrelsy may have survived in their least altered form:
Appalachia. In the scene from the 1833 Davy Crockett story in which

the white frontiersfolk do the double shuffle, the tune that the black banjoist plays is "Jump Jim Crow." The descendants of those dancers are Appalachian cloggers, who (as can be seen in Mike Seeger's 1987 documentary *Talking Feet*) speak of their rhythmic stepping to banjos and fiddles as "buck dancing" and "cutting the pigeon wing." They are improvisers, flat-footed and aurally focused, whites and blacks who prize individuality and describe what they're doing as "freedom dances"—the freedom to express oneself, the freedom from work. It may be instructive to compare Appalachian clogging with the Anglo-Celtic variety of Cape Breton, where there was little slavery. "One lifts, the other sinks," says the British-born scholar-dancer Tony Barrand, contrasting the way the center of weight bounces up, then falls back in British and Cape Breton dancers with how it drops, then recovers in American ones. In Seeger's film, that sinking is more pronounced among African-American cloggers, whose accents tend to be syncopated even though their rhythms are even.

If it's hard to imagine Appalachian clogging as having African roots, that's for the same reason that people don't think of the banjo as an African instrument. More and more scholarship connects the "frailing" or "clawhammer" banjo playing described in minstrel training manuals to African practices. But that's not what the banjo stands for in popular culture. Since at least the 1930s, it has signified redneck, ultrawhite. The sheet music illustrations of bowlegged minstrels dancing in the 1840s look that way, too. Hillbilly. But so do contemporaneous illustrations of bowlegged blacks doing the breakdown after corn shuckings. The testimony of a circus manager that Daniel Emmett learned to play banjo from "a very ignorant person, and nigger all over except in color" pointed to an intermingled frontier culture. In his book *Bluegrass Breakdown*, Robert Cantwell establishes how the hillbilly persona of Nashville's Grand Ole Opry stemmed directly from minstrelsy—how it *was* minstrelsy with a new mask. As he points out, it's tough to find a pioneer of country music without a childhood tale of learning from black musicians. When such country musicians play, Cantwell writes, "if you turn your face away, you can hear the Africanized manner." You can see it, too, if you know what to look for. And you can find some of the same African-hillbilly roots in tap.

In his 1885 memoir, Isaac Williams would attest that, compared with his recollection of the breakdown back when he was a slave, the many minstrel shows he had seen were "as a counterfeit bill to a genuine one." The analogy was common, and though many of the people who denied minstrel authenticity offered definitions of genuine negritude that were at least as troubling as any minstrel caricature, it's probably safe to take Willams's judgment at face value. It's likely that minstrel mimicry left out subtle watermarks. That would be true of many later imitations.

In any case, identifying the African-American roots of minstrelsy only underlines what's most unsettling about minstrelsy's origin stories. The veracity of those stories is highly doubtful, yet the myths resonate because they are parables of appropriation—tales of stolen steps. They articulate guilt, or at least unease, about what whites have taken from blacks.

For early commentators, the standard explanation of minstrelsy's popularity was that it was fun and cheap. Since the 1960s, writers have indulged in all manner of speculation into the psychology of the minstrels and their audience, much of it facile and reductive. For a cultural theorist, minstrelsy is a feast and a Rorschach test. At first glance, it can appear to be simple racial denigration, but the more you look, the less simple it seems.

In T. D. Rice's farces, which minstrels performed into the 1850s, wily blacks invariably outwit white authority figures. During the "nullification crisis" of 1832, a foretaste of secessionist impulses, it was Jim Crow who suggested that if fighting broke out, the blacks might rise, "For deir wish for freedom / Is shining in deir eyes." In Britain, he commended his hosts on their recent abolition of slavery. More coyly, back home he sang:

> Now my brodder niggers
> I do not tink it right
> Dat you should laff at dem
> Who happen to be white
>
> Kase it dere misfortune
> And dey'd spend ebery dollar

> If dey could only be
> Gentlemen ob color
>
> It almost break my heart
> To see dem envy me
> And from my soul I wish dem
> Full as brack as we

How much of this comedic inversion was seriously subversive, how much naughty provocation? Who is being envied, who laughed at? Who addressed, who included? Solid answers are inaccessible. Everything depends upon tone, attitude, body language. The evidence of how Rice's mostly underclass public responded is limited to reports that he was immensely popular, that people laughed. If coded language was designed to fool hostile critics, it seems to have worked. But to fixate on the dialect or the word *nigger* and rest the case on minstrelsy as racial insult is to risk being as obtuse as those who missed the mockery in slave songs and dance.

Upsetting elites was uncontestably on the agenda. Acting black was a sure method for the proles Tambo and Bones to stick it to the stuffy Interlocutor, for young men to thumb their noses at middle-class moralizing. In turn, the guardians of refined taste looked down their noses at what they classed as low, common, vulgar trash. Elites found minstrelsy offensive, and not out of concern for the dignity of blacks. The sublimated aggression of black humor—mocking 'em every step—might have served as a model for how to make fun of those who have power over you: wear a mask. But just how deep the identification went is part of what the mask hides from historical inquiry.

Most often, blacks were the vehicle, not the target. Much satire was directed against European culture. Minstrelsy of the forties and fifties offered as many parodies of particular European operas, plays, and performers as it did plantation scenes. Minstrels worked up Ethiopian pas de deux and polkas. An 1840 playbill announced that William Whitlock would "jump, dance, and knock his heels in a way dat Mademoiselle Fanny Elssler neber did, neber can and neber will do." The Viennese ballerina, then on tour in New York, adored by the upper crust and raking in huge sums, was irresistible prey for local boys. How better to bring down to size an embodiment of European high culture than for John Diamond to portray Elssler or Zoloe Zelica Taglioni-rina engaged in a Grand Trial Dance during "La Bayadere in Ole Kentuck"?

Class attitudes overlapped with nationalist sentiment. Americans were stung by European charges that the former colonies had developed no culture of their own. This anxiety courses through a century's worth of commentary embracing minstrelsy as the only distinctively American contribution to theater and music. Minstrels made that claim for themselves, jigging around their role as middlemen, translators, thieves. What seems indisputable now—the disproportionate and defining influence of African-Americans upon American culture—was then a truth that could be told only slant, by white men in blackface.

In "Africanizing" European music, minstrels were Americanizing it, giving it American rhythm, attitude, style. Blacking up could serve as a form of cultural naturalization. That's the alchemy it worked for the increasing numbers of minstrels who were first- or second-generation Irish-Americans. The stage was an arena where immigrant Irish could grapple for a higher place in America's racial hierarchy; they could become more American by acting Negro, more white by blacking up. (That's the rub of the pun, which appeared in *Yankee Doodle* in 1846, tagging "Pat Juba" as an "Irish-American" dance.) Many minstrels played it straight, if still under cork, sincerely aspiring to excellence on European terms, an aspiration bound up with social class. The tension between the respectable Interlocutor and the rowdy end men was more than comedy; on playbills, the paired portraits of minstrels in and out of blackface bespoke a desire to have it both ways. As early as 1854, the snooty *New York Musical Review* was gloating over the demise of Negro Minstrelsy through a "bleaching process," and though the obituary was premature, the metaphoric cause of death showed the entwinement of class and color.

In dance, the bleach seems to have suffused more slowly. Aspiration would influence style, but this was counterbalanced by the exigencies of competition, the skill and speed and endurance displayed in Grand Trial Matches and valued by the culture of sporting and wagers. Dancing stayed low, with funny steps and gestures, and the "India rubber elasticity" attributed to Matt Peel's Virginia breakdown. It may also be that there was an alternative channel in cross-dressing, which was plentiful in minstrelsy. As much as the wench dancers played for laughs, they were also praised for ease and grace. Perhaps the cross-dressing, misogynistic on its surface, was another licensing disguise, like blackface, an escape from the kinetic confines of laboring-class masculinity.

In short, blackface minstrelsy was and was not about black people. The humor was usually about something else: hypocrisy, pretension, infidelity, shrewish wives. It was irreverence, puns, slapstick, nonsense—the imperishable staples of comedy, especially the American variety. The costume and the darky dialect were sometimes integral to this, sometimes incidental. When minstrelsy did turn directly to the subject of slave life, slave characters tended to get the best of their masters through cunning shows of stupidity. A few songs implied sexual exploitation and brutality, but the minstrels' preferred picture was singing and dancing, holidays, an escape from work, the kind of fun worth corking up for.

It's possible to view this portrayal as a justification of slavery. Undoubtedly, some people did. And that possibility was heightened by a nostalgia that arose as the Civil War loomed, troupes of 1857 peddling the old-fashioned minstrelsy of 1842. In the songs that Stephen Foster wrote at mid-century, compositions that would spread wide and sink deep, the sentimentalism of parlor songs found expression in a slave's longing for the old folks on the old plantation, rhetoric that fixed plantation life in a timeless past. As minstrelsy persisted and performers modeled their imitations on earlier performers, the conventions hardened and the jokes went stale. The slippery sass and sarcasm of Rice's tricksters seem to have receded as the stakes turned bloodier.

This was the context for the development of one of tap's ancestral dances: the Essence of Old Virginia. Dan Bryant (born O'Brien) may have given it the name in 1856, though other minstrels immediately adopted it as theirs. (Credit tended to go to whoever first put a dance's name next to his own on a playbill.) It was a "characteristic dance"— "characteristic," according to *The New York Clipper*, of "a rude and untutored black of the old plantation." (Around the same time, the A. M. Bininger Company of New York advertised its whiskey with the catchphrase "Essence of Old Virginia" and an illustration of blacks dancing to the banjo. Same idea.) The music for "Essence of Old Virginia" published in banjo manuals of the late 1850s suggests a promenade, the melody ambling out unhurriedly and then skipping back. Contemporaneous press reports indicate that the dance was popular and funny. In Billy Newcomb's essence, "the oddest outré positions and far fetched steps are executed with such apparent ease." The *Charleston Mercury* described it as "the most natural delineation of the negro character we have ever seen," and the word *natural* vibrates there, expressing the ease that reviewers valued in minstrel dancing, the persuasiveness of the characterization, and perhaps the idea of the Negro character being, in essence, close to nature.

The minstrel instinct was to lampoon, which is what minstrels did to *Uncle Tom's Cabin*. Serialized in 1851, Harriet Beecher Stowe's novel was swiftly on its way to selling more copies than any other book that century besides the Bible. The story was even more popular onstage; productions were mounted almost continuously for the next eighty years. These shows always held a place for plantation jigs and breakdowns; they were another nursery for tap. Along with contested facts, the book harbored minstrel elements: the black boy addressed as "Jim Crow" and made to perform for a slave trader who buys him; the antics of that "funny specimen in the Jim Crow line," the incorrigible Topsy, whose African Breakdown enlivened most stage productions and sometimes earned top billing for the actress or actor playing her. Some minstrel versions were antislavery; others presented slavery as a blessing or replaced tragic events with good times on the plantation. Frank Brower, after his Virginia Minstrel days, lived on his "Happy Uncle Tom" sketch, which turned Stowe's martyr into a dull-witted end man compulsively dancing to the banjo.

In 1861, a Massachusetts soldier wrote home from Virginia about two blacks in the Union barracks who tried to outdance each other. The dancers might have been seeking food or favor or even celebrating their freedom—General Butler had declared slaves free once behind Union lines. But all the soldier wrote was that "you don't see any true darkies in the North" and that the laughable dancers looked "exactly like our minstrels."

Minstrels liked to make fun of the rubes who mistook them for actual black people. These stories are of a piece with tales of backwoods audiences rushing the stage to foil a villain. They're jokes about mis-comprehension, and they're funny the way it's funny when Tambo and Bones misuse words. You have to perceive the error to get the joke. Recognizing the accuracy of the imitation presupposed recognizing it *as* an imitation. Yet recognizing accuracy also presupposed some prior conception of the subject, a preconception that the imitation might re-inforce, even circumscribe. Stereotypes sprout from such generaliza-tions, and they can turn malignant. Around the time that minstrelsy exploded, a coarseness entered into the visual representation of blacks and blackface minstrels: bulging eyes, giant lips, reptilian faces. No actual people could ever have looked like that, and this distortion of "peculiarities" was unequivocally dehumanizing. It is these images—which made it onto thousands of postcards and bottle openers and toys—that now color our understanding of minstrelsy and everything that came out of it. It is these images that make discussion of minstrelsy's ambiguities seem beside the point.

For the question wasn't only how the representation of blacks affected the way they were perceived; it was how the representation of blacks affected the way they were treated. Already, in 1841, *The Dover Morning Star* was editorializing against the outrage of respectable colored passen-gers being forced into the "Jim Crow or Negro Car" on Massachusetts trains. The white mobs who broke up abolitionist meetings were some-times heard to sing "Jim Crow." In 1845, Ralph Waldo Emerson gave a lecture arguing that the only defense of slavery that truly worked in the North was the assumption of Negro inferiority, encapsulated in the word *nigger* cried by rowdy boys who "jump Jim Crow in the streets and the taverns." If these were not the associations that T. D. Rice in-tended, they were associations that persisted. If blacks were more the weapon than the target of minstrelsy, they could still take the hit.

There were almost no blacks on antebellum minstrel stages, almost no blacks on any antebellum stages at all. (There were some in the audiences—laughing, reportedly.) Yet a professional black entertainer, especially a dancer, would be a minstrel by default, the role already defined—almost exclusively—by those who were not black.

4

DANCING JUBA FOR EELS

That Massachusetts soldier didn't have to go to Virginia to catch blacks dancing. Recall Thomas De Voe's account of how, at the beginning of the nineteenth century, Long Island and New Jersey slaves regularly gathered at Manhattan's Catharine Market to do "a jig or break-down" on a shingle. According to De Voe, some of these slaves were locally famous. One was Jack, who was "smart and faithful" and owned by Frederick DeVoo. When New York's manumission act forced DeVoo to free Jack in 1827, the former master gave his former slave a new suit and told him, "If you go home with me, you shall never want; but if you leave me now, my home shall never more know you." Jack chose the city. De Voe says he became "a loafer" and died in the market. An 1841 *New York Tattler* article parenthetically refers to the "black boys who usually dance juba for eels on Sunday morning," and an 1842 piece in the sporting newspaper *Flash* mockingly describes a similar scene (the shingles, the challenge dancing, the eels) in a Philadelphia market. But to the *American Angler's Guide* sixteen years later, the dancing was a custom of "some years ago," a scene unjustly neglected by artists, a lost part of "New York as it was."

About the neglect, the guide was mistaken. A folk drawing, labeled "Dancing for Eels, 1820 Catharine Market" but otherwise of uncertain provenance, shows two black men patting juba for a third one who jigs. The three white men who watch them most closely are recognizable as "b'hoys," rough members of lower Manhattan's working class whose sobriquet was meant to convey their Irish accent. In a very similar illustration from 1848, the dancer is caught mid-jig, thighs turned out, one boot-clad leg crossed behind the other. One hand rests on a hip; the other waves in the air, a stance that Robert Farris Thompson has traced to the Congo, but that in America signified Irishness and the hornpipe. The most prominent white observer leans in casually, approvingly. He, too, is a b'hoy, but not just any b'hoy. He is Mose, the pugilistic Irish-American fireman and local hero, star of the play that the drawing is illustrating, the Chatham Theatre's 1848 production of *New York As It Is*.

New York As It Is was very popular, and what made it so popular was how it reflected working-class patrons back to themselves. They recognized Mose. In the play, a city fellow introduces his country cousin to the wonders of the metropolis, attractions that include a Sunday morning at Catharine Market, distinguished by a "niggar dance for eels." This, too, must have been part of the world recognized by working-class theatergoers. But one of the ways they experienced it was through minstrel representations. The character of "Jack, a Negro and Dancer for Eels" was likely played in blackface, and other characters in the many plays starring Mose were known to express their love of minstrel performers, favorites at the same theater.

The pose of the Catharine Market dancer on the *New York As It Is* poster matches that of John Smith on the 1840 sheet music for "Jim Along Josey." It's nearly identical to an illustration of John Diamond, master of the Long Island breakdown, whose playbills promised "those unheard of, outlandish and inimitable licks, what is death to all de Long Island Darkies." Minstrel songs of the 1830s and '40s referred to Long Island niggers doing the double shubble. The Virginia Minstrels alluded to dancing for eels at the market, as did Jim Crow, who sang of Long Island niggers as rivals: "Dey raise a mighty dust / and tink dey make a show / but I neber seen one of dem / what could jump Jim Crow." (This is from the same 1832 song sheet in which Crow calls on his brother niggers not to laugh at envious whites and expresses the intention of obtaining a patent for his act.)

The man who sang that, T. D. Rice, was a New York City boy. He grew up just a few blocks away from Catharine Market, in the Five Points district. This was the poorest part of town, the place where immigrants were forced together, Germans and Italians and Jews and especially Irish. It was also one of the few places where free blacks could find accommodation. After an outbreak of fever in 1820, doctors from the New York Board of Health catalogued the district's inhabitants in detail: blacks made up a third of the population, and the report noted case after case of white women living with black husbands and of white prostitutes who served black customers. Court reports testify to couple after interracial couple put in jail for the crime known as amalgamation. Any harmony was tenuous. In an 1834 race riot, black-owned property was destroyed and blacks were lynched.

In music and dance, the crucibles of convergence were the many "negro dancing cellars." One 1799 ad seeking a runaway slave named Peter described him as "a great dancer and a very quarrelsome fellow, and is noted as such in the negro dancing cellars." The cellars were where people like Peter went to party, places documented in court records of brawls and murders. But not only blacks patronized such underground establishments. The white sailor Horace Lane was taken to one by a shipmate in 1804. In his 1839 autobiography, Lane remembered a black violinist and eight dancers "jumping about, twisting and screwing their joints and ankles as if to scour the floor with their feet." Lane says he ran away disgusted, but other whites felt differently about twisting the night away. The spirit of fun comes through even in the most contemptuous accounts. In an 1835 book attributed to Davy Crockett, the backwoodsman expresses disbelief at the patrons ("worse than savages") of a cellar: "Such fiddling and dancing nobody ever saw before in this world . . . black and white, white and black, all hug-em-snug together." A police raid in 1840 found "a knot of little amalgamationists . . . applauding the exertions of a bit of a niggar [sic], who was jumping 'Jim Crow.'"

The Five Points inspired moral crusades, evangelical missions, and a literature of shock. Ned Buntline's *Mysteries and Miseries of New York*, a bestselling dime novel of 1848, features an illicit excursion to the saloon run by Pete Williams, one of the "upper ten of darky-dom." There, the white narrator finds two hundred Negroes "of every shade" working up a sweat to fiddle and tambourine. What draws the narrator's attention away from feminine charms and the dice game is the performance of a "juba dancer," a young mulatto "laying it down": hornpipe, reel, "double-shuffles, heel and toe tappers, in-and-out winders, pigeon wings, heel-crackers," and to finish, "the winding blade." Buntline's novel was nominally fiction, but Pete Williams and his dance hall were real: the venue infamous enough to be included in the 1850 city guide *New York By Gas-Light*, newspaper reports, and the reminiscences of men about town; the colored proprietor prosperous enough to make it into the city directory and to get a paragraph in the *Times* when he died, in 1852.

The most famous name associated with the establishment, however, was not his. The dance hall was also known as Dickens's Hole, because Charles Dickens, the most famous author in the English-speaking world, had described his visit there in his 1842 *American Notes*. Dickens's account of the Five Points is a catalogue of squalor, yet once he descends into Pete Williams's place, the spirit begins to lift. The landlord orders up a regular breakdown, and a fiddler and a tambourine player set couples in action. Dickens finds the scene dull until the lead dancer, "the wit of the assembly, the greatest dancer known," makes a move. Because of this young man, "who never leaves off making queer faces," the mood of the room shifts:

> Instantly the fiddler grins, and goes at it tooth and nail; there is new energy in the tambourine; new laughter in the dancers; new smiles in the landlady; new confidence in the landlord; new brightness in the very candles. Single shuffle, double shuffle, cut and crosscut: snapping his fingers, rolling his eyes, turning in his knees, presenting the backs of his legs in front, spinning about on his toes and heels like nothing but the man's fingers on the tambourine; dancing with two left legs,

two right legs, two wooden legs, two wire legs, two spring legs—all sorts
of legs and no legs—what is this to him?

And in what walk of life, or dance of life, does man ever get such
stimulating applause as thunders about him, when, having danced his
partner off her feet, and himself too, he finishes by leaping gloriously
on the bar-counter and calling for something to drink, with the chuckle
of a million of counterfeit Jim Crows, in one inimitable sound!

Dickens doesn't name the wit, but there's good reason to believe that he
was describing a black dancer known as Master Juba. The nineteenth-
century theatrical-agent-turned-historian Alston Brown asserted that Juba's given name was William Henry Lane. Master Juba was also most
likely the "little negro called 'Juba'" who, as *The New York Sporting Whip*
announced in January 1843, was scheduled to participate in a match for
large stakes against "the best negro dancer in the country," John Diamond. In July 1844, the *Herald* announced another match between "the
Original JOHN DIAMOND and the Colored Boy JUBA," a trial for
"Champion Dancer of the World."

> The time to decide that has come, and the friends of Juba have chal-
> lenged the world to produce his superior in this Art . . . That challenge
> has been accepted by the friends of John Diamond, and on Monday
> Evening they meet, and Dance Three Jigs, Two Reels, and the Camp-
> town Hornpipe. Five judges have been selected for their ability and
> knowledge of the Art, so that a fair decision will be made . . . the vic-
> tory will be decided by the best time and the greatest number of steps.

The *Herald* did not publish the result, but the language is interesting: Juba
had friends, or supporters, men willing to bet on him.

Diamond had left P. T. Barnum's employ, and Barnum, incensed,
had circulated a letter to theater managers accusing the dancer of over-
drawing his salary and spending it in brothels. Soon after, Diamond was
jailed in New Orleans for stabbing a man. When this was reported,
The Boston Post scoffed: John Diamond was appearing in Boston. That
dancer, however, was a different John Diamond, a kid named Frank
Lynch whom Barnum had hired to impersonate his wayward star. The

existence of Frank Lynch, who went by "Frank Diamond" after the fraud was revealed, accounts for why the *Herald* announced John Diamond as the "Original." Yet questions of original versus copy were always at play. Diamond had been advertised as delineating "the Ethiopian character superior to any other *white* person," the italicized adjective there as hedge or challenge.

Announcements of Grand Trial Dances ensured a full house in the working-class theaters of New York. As the *Sporting Whip* explained, "he who can cut, shuffle, and attitudinize with the greatest facility is reckoned the best fellow and pockets the most money." The ideal was a "a real scientific, out-and-out trial of skill," a term that, in the sporting world covered by that organ of the press, grouped trial dances with cockfighting, dogfighting, and boxing. Since money was involved, rules were required. Much as a man in a duel chose his own weapon, each dancer chose his own accompanist. Judges determined the winner, though their presence did not preclude arguments about how a decision should be reached or entirely dispel suspicion of a fix. Newspaper explanations that victory was gauged by the "best time" and the "greatest number of steps," paired with times around five minutes and step counts around thirty, point toward a quantitative standard but leave vague what was being measured: Speed? Endurance? Invention?

Another contest between Diamond and Juba was described in a clipping printed around 1875. This contest supposedly took place a little earlier than the others, perhaps in 1842, when Diamond was performing at Barnum's American Museum, but the venue was Pete Williams's place. In this account, Juba's supporters included Negroes who "had bet all their coppers on their champion." Going first, he danced for an hour and fifteen minutes. When Diamond took his turn, "it was not only a case of Barnum's Museum against Pete Williams's dancehouse, but it was a case of white against black," and at some point, one of the blacks yelled, "He's a white man sure . . . but he's got a nigger in his heel." Diamond won, outlasting Juba. Their rivalry was inevitably racial, no matter how they might have seen it.

When Diamond appeared with the Ethiopian Serenaders in 1845, he was still billed as "the greatest dancer in the world." That same year, when Juba received top billing with the Georgia Champion Minstrels, the ads referred to contests with Diamond as having established Juba as King of All Dancers. "No conception can be formed of the variety of beautiful and intricate steps exhibited by him with ease. You must see to believe." Touring the South, as Diamond did, was not a sensible option for a free black man, so Juba headed north, alighting at smaller, cheaper theaters from Providence to Portland. In Boston, he was featured like a star actor, appearing with a different local troupe each evening. The *Evening Transcript* wrote of overflow houses and hailed Juba as "unquestionably the greatest dancer of the age." By 1847, he was back in New York, appearing at a bargain theater in the Bowery and acting with Daniel Emmett, the credited author of "Dixie," in a skit about a rigged dance contest. In 1848, the *New York Herald* crowned him with that ambiguous title, King of the Negro Dancers. (John Diamond was away, possibly fighting in the Mexican-American War, or on the lam, having stabbed a superior officer.)

From 1848 to 1850, Juba's fame spread across the Atlantic, as he toured England and Scotland with Pell's Ethiopian Minstrels. The ads promoted "Boz's Juba," a reference to Dickens's early pseudonym, and the playbills quoted the passage from *American Notes*. In a playbill cameo, Juba looks handsome, distinguished, no blackface, no wool. Another illustration pictures him in performance, snappily attired, with a cravat peeking out of his vest. His boots are shiny, with a thick heel that must have come down hard. Bending at the waist, he leans toward an upraised knee. The downward force of his hands, tucked into the pockets of his thigh-length topcoat, tugs tight the lapels. This arrested image bears some resemblance to minstrel illustrations of a breakdown, but it's inflected by an individual style. Juba looks cool.

The British press reported on him in far greater detail than the American press had: more adjectives, but also a real attempt to describe. British reviewers were familiar with minstrelsy. Two years before, Pell's Minstrels had toured Britain without Juba for a full year, garnering much press attention and a command performance before Queen Victoria. Presumably the British were also well versed in jigs, hornpipes, and double shuffles, at least in their own versions. Yet confronted with Juba, they were awestruck. "The dancing of Juba," a reviewer for *The Observer* wrote, "exceeded anything ever witnessed in Europe. The style as well

as the execution is unlike anything ever seen in this country. The manner
in which he beats time with his feet, and the extraordinary command he
possesses over them can only be believed by those who have been present at his exhibition."

The British reviewers said he was slender, copper-colored, about five
feet three, and maybe eighteen years old. Many tried to convey his performance as Dickens had, breathlessly. One Manchester critic spun out
the following:

> Such mobility of muscle, such flexibility of joints, such boundings, such
> slidings, such gyrations, such toes and heelings, such backwardings and
> forwardings, such posturings, such firmness of foot, such elasticity
> of tendon, such mutation of movement, such vigor, such variety, such
> natural grace, such powers of endurance, such potency of pattern, were
> never combined in one nigger.

For modern readers, that last word is a wall, but before the paragraph
slams into it, phrase after phrase piles up as if in awed imitation of un-
ending variety. "All of these marvels are done in strict time and appropriate rhythm, each note has its corresponding step and action."

Critic after critic echoed the last observation. "The most interesting
part of the performance was the exact time, which, even in the most
complicated and difficult steps, the dancer kept to the music." *The Illustrated London News* noted that Juba was "a musician as well as a dancer."
This was praise of his tambourine playing—like many tap dancers who
came after, Juba sidelined as a drummer—but the observation must have
applied equally to his footwork. The Pell's Minstrels playbill stressed
this auditory dimension, asking the audience to be as quiet as possible to
"hear the exact time he keeps with his extraordinary steps." Even a negative review took notice of the sound, if only to dismiss it as "a terrible
clatter."

But it was not just feet: "toes and heels, ankles and calves, knees and
thighs, elbows and wrists, nay even his eyes and the lobes of his ears, and
the wool on his caput dance." A few reviewers ventured technical specificity, writing of shuffles, double shuffles, pirouettes, loans from the
Highland fling and the sailor's hornpipe. Yet most of Juba's technique,

being "unborrowed from schools," struck the critics as foreign. It was frenzied, then subdued; wild and heavy, then airy and delicate. The tone kept changing, and Juba navigated the extremes with the composure that Dickens had caught. *The Advertiser* wrote of "the ease and grace which at once stamps execution as natural."

Pell's Minstrels were a high-toned outfit. They wore tuxedos. Juba sat on one end, beating his tambourine and harmonizing. In his featured numbers, he sped through patter songs or acted out the suggestive minstrel standard "Lucy Long" in a pink dress, a bonnet, a green parasol, and red boots. A critic for the *Manchester Guardian* seized on the way breaks of furious motion were preceded by slow, circular promenading ("with an air of satisfaction"). It sounds like a walk-around, like Master Diamond walking around his board in the circus ring, like contemporaneous descriptions of Irish dancers "circumambulating" before a jig (and, for that matter, like a flamenco *bailaor* or a break dancer catching his breath as he builds up anticipation, then diving in again). For the finale, the star banjo player would accompany Juba in the "Festival Dance (Original)" and the "Plantation Dance (Original)."

All of Juba's dances taxed the reviewers' powers of description, but these last two threw down challenges that were more interpretive, even ontological. What was this black man doing in a minstrel show? If he was "illustrating the dances of his own simple people on festive occasions," as the *Guardian* put it, how was that different from ordinary minstrel practice? What did it mean that Juba possessed "the additional attraction of being a 'real nigger,' and not a 'sham'"? The newspapers labeled Juba "a genuine specimen of the nigger," "a real undiluted Nigger," "a genuine gen'leman of color," "a genuine Son of the Southern Clime," "a true son of Africa," and "a genuine grit negro, from the far-west." The *Theatrical Times* found Juba's performances "far above the common performances of the mountebanks who give imitations of American and negro character." *The Illustrated London News* declared national dances such as the supposedly Spanish *cachucha* to be theatrical, erstatz; "but the Nigger Dance is a reality. The 'Virginny Breakdown,' or the 'Alabama Kick-up,' the 'Tennessee Double-shuffle,' or the 'Louisiana Toe-and-Heel,' we know to exist. If they did not, how could Juba enter into their wonderful complications so naturally?" The logic is knotted,

but there it is: Juba's ease must mean that he's doing what comes naturally, that both he and what he dances are authentic.

Of course, British critics had said similar things about T. D. Rice's
Jim Crow dancing: "There cannot be a doubt of its extraordinary
reality . . . [it] could never have been invented by Mr. Rice." Yet Juba,
everyone insisted, was different. "To say that he dances as man or nigger
never danced before; that he shakes his leg with the spirit of ten Jim
Crows . . . is nothing," wrote a reviewer for the *Mirror*, who had visited
South Carolina and had therefore seen "niggers dance before." Those
plantation dances, he declared, were "but poor shufflings compared to
the pedal inspirations of Juba"; in fact, the great ballet dancers of recent
memory could not compare—this from the same pen that wrote "man
or nigger." Juba confused by who he was, and by what he did. "Such
energy of continued motion is highly ludicrous," wrote the *Weekly Dispatch*, and yet, wrote the Manchester *Era*, "as eccentric as his style is,
every moment is replete with grace." Another critic found "an ideality
in what he does that makes his efforts at once grotesque and poetical."
The *Literary Gazette* considered Juba "a genius, in the fullest sense."

After Juba's tour ended, he chose to stay abroad. He went solo. To
the *Sheffield Times*, Juba still had no equal, but the *Era* reported on Juba
"jumping very fast at the Coliseum" and then, the following week: "Juba
has jumped away—by the way of an earnest yet friendly caution, let us
hope that he will not throw himself away." There would be a few more
newspaper reports about Juba dancing in working-class music halls, then
nothing. The minstrel historian Thomas Alston Brown would claim, in
1876, that "success proved too much" for Juba—that he had married a
white woman, "lived a fast life, dissipated freely, and died miserably."
The three-sentence biographies of most of Juba's fast-stepping, fast-
living peers end the same: John Diamond died a penniless drunk in
1857. Juba's story is like theirs, with a difference. According to Brown,
Juba's skeleton was put on exhibition in 1852 at the Surrey Music Hall in
Sheffield, a genuine specimen even after death.

In a 1947 article, the dance historian Marian Hannah Winter would
call Juba "the most influential single performer of nineteenth century

American dance," asserting that "the repertoire of any current tap dancer contains elements which were established theatrically by him." Because of his "vast influence," she wrote, "the minstrel show dance retained more integrity as a Negro art form than any other theatrical derivative of Negro culture." Most writing about Juba since has taken Winter at her word, and it's easy to understand why. Juba answers the need for a black hero. But was his art Negro just because he was? The descriptions provide some material for an answer that isn't automatic. Juba's full-bodied jigging, his rhythmic accuracy, the juxtapositions of hot and cool, the elastic contortions that made whites laugh, the grotesque *and* poetical, the style as well as the execution—all these might count as African, connecting Juba the dancer to the dance called Juba. Or rather, they count as African-American, and since tap was a child of such merging, Juba can be considered a founding father.

There's no evidence, though, that Juba had any more direct knowledge of the plantation dances of Southern slaves than the Virginia Minstrels did. There's not even any evidence linking him with the Long Island Negroes or Catharine Market. The only festival dancing we can connect him with is what Dickens witnessed in the Five Points. Winter claimed that Juba learned to dance from a "Negro jig and reel dancer" named Uncle Jim Lowe—an assertion solely based, as is much of Winter's essay, on a single anonymous article in an 1895 issue of the *New York Herald*. That article, in turn, seems to be based largely on the recollections of two minstrel dancers: Dave Reed, who was old enough to have known Juba, and Richard Carroll, who took Juba's place (under the name Master Marks) at Charlie White's Melodeon after Juba left for England. The article seems credible enough, but if we're to believe what it says about Uncle Jim, then why not what it says about how "the best in the profession" danced at Pete Williams's saloon? The continuity the article suggests isn't between Juba's dancing and that of the Long Island Jubas; it's between minstrelsy and the Negro dancing saloons. Perhaps even more than the levees and plantations, these miscegenated watering holes were the spawning grounds of tap, black and white dancers all hug-em-snug together.

In the United States, Juba didn't perform a festival or plantation dance as his finale. What he did instead would have been lost on foreigners.

An 1845 playbill advertised that he would give "correct Imitation Dances of all the principal Ethiopian Dancers in the United States," a list of white men including John "Jim Along Josey" Smith, the hoofer half of the Virginia Minstrels, Frank Diamond (the John Diamond imitator), and John Diamond himself. According to the *Herald* article, Juba did a similar imitation dance at Pete Williams's place. The men on the list were the men against whom Juba was judged. They were probably the men against whom he judged himself. Each had a style that could be imitated, recognized, and then bettered. For Juba followed the imitations with his "own jig." The point—in the promotional language of the playbill—was to demonstrate "the vast difference between those that have heretofore attempted dancing and this WONDERFUL YOUNG MAN." It's possible that Juba's dance was a form of racial revenge or reappropriation. It's impossible to know how much of the imitation was mockery, how much emulation. We can't be certain how vast the difference really was and whether it was more of kind or degree. The whole thing sounds like the mixture of homage and cutting contest that would take place, nearly a century later, at another dancers' hangout: the Hoofers' Club.

But it's minstrelsy and its conundrums that make the label that the playbill used for Juba's own jig so uncanny. It's a phrase that manages to express the make-it-your-own, stealing steps tradition and, at the same time, Juba's confusing position as a black man in minstrelsy. According to the playbill, when Juba does his own jig, what he's doing is "an imitation of himself."

5

THE AMERICAN CLOG

THE GENUINE ARTICLE

After John Diamond left the management of P. T. Barnum in 1841, the confidence man had to find a replacement. Here's how Thomas Low Nichols, in his memoir of 1864, described what happened next:

> Barnum, with the enterprise that has distinguished his whole career, on exploring the dance-houses of the Five Points, found a boy who could dance a better break-down than Master Diamond. It was easy to hire him; but he was a genuine negro; and there was not an audience in America that would not have resented, in a very energetic fashion, the insult of being asked to look at the dancing of a real negro . . . Barnum was equal to the occasion . . . He greased the little "nigger's" face and rubbed it over with a new blacking of burnt cork, painted his thick lips with vermillion, put on a wooly wig over his tight curled hair, and brought him out as the champion nigger-dancer of the world. Had it been suspected that the seeming counterfeit was the genuine article, the New York Vauxhaul would have blazed with indignation.

Back in 1841, a letter to the sporting paper *Sunday Flash* had already re-vealed the switch. The dancer billed as Master Diamond was "no more or less than a veritable negro," who had been presented the season before under the name "Rattler." "The boy is fifteen or sixteen years of age; his name is 'Juba.'" The letter writer was indignant because the advertising was false, not because Juba was genuine: "To do him justice, he is a very fair dancer. He is of harmless and inoffensive disposition and is not, I sincerely believe, aware of the meanness and audacity of the swindler to which he is presently a party." Was this how Juba began his career, under cork, his imitation dance of John Diamond used to perpetrate a fraud? The possibility that the fake Negro delineator was a real black tran-scends irony.

Barnum was the man who had exhibited an elderly black woman, claiming that she was George Washington's 161-year-old nurse. He was also the man who spread rumors that the woman was a dummy made out of rubber. The master of humbug found it profitable to keep people guessing—and paying admission to see for themselves. Maybe he wrote the letter. Regardless, the imposture made some twisted sense. Black-ness was a theatrical role, and blackface was part of the costume. Freder-ick Douglass, after seeing an all-black minstrel troupe in 1849, wrote that "in exaggerating the peculiarities," the performers "had recourse to the burnt cork and lamp black, the better to express their characters, and to produce uniformity of complexion." Before the war, such all-black minstrel troupes were extremely rare and short-lived, but after the war, they took off. And instead of resenting the insult of being asked to look at the genuine article, postbellum audiences greeted the novelty with eager curiosity.

Taking to the stage was part of what blacks did with their freedom. But they did so in slaves' clothing. The all-black Georgia Minstrels of-fered what the Virginia Minstrels had offered, only they claimed to have lived the plantation life they sang about. Black troupes called themselves the Slave Troupe Minstrels or the Georgia Slave Brothers, flashing their previous bondage as credentials. Advertisements stressed that they were "real," "genuine." Such already loaded terms as "original" got another spin. In recounting the origin of the Georgia Minstrels, the Macon *Tele-graph and Messenger* explained how the members, prior to emancipation, had been manservants who attended minstrel shows. To white reviewers, the black programs differed little in content from white minstrel shows; the black minstrels just seemed more "natural," and thus funnier. Eventually only the end men, the clowns, would regularly wear black-face and red lips, but blackface or no, the conventions of minstrelsy had been long established. Black minstrels followed them.

There were dozens of troupes. Audiences were white and black and large. Everywhere the black minstrels went, they had the same effect on stagestruck youth as their white counterparts. Indeed, for a black child, the sight of well-turned-out black men from elsewhere, parading through town with a brass band, held a special appeal. Dance, unsurprisingly, was emphasized: walk-arounds, plantation jigs. Occasionally, a publication such as *The Memphis Appeal* might appraise Dick Little and Bob Height as the "most laughable burlesque jig dancers in the world" or write of Charles Anderson that his "artistic dancing cannot be equaled in grace and finish." But mostly, there's no reliable assessment of how the dancing compared with that of whites in blackface, only the equivocal fact that many white reviewers deemed it superior.

A bit more remains of Billy Kersands, the most popular of black minstrels. Two hundred pounds but light on his feet, he did the Essence so well that people said he invented it. Like the Essence that Dan Bryant was doing in Manhattan while Kersands was a kid in Baton Rouge, Kersands's Essence was funny. It made Queen Victoria laugh. The ragtime composer Arthur Marshall, born in 1881, provided the most vivid picture: "The performer moves forward without appearing to move his feet at all, by manipulating his toes and heels rapidly . . . as if he was being towed around on ice skates." But Kersands described his own Essence as a "combination of knee work and head buttoning to keep time with the music." His fellow minstrel Sam Lucas recalled how Kersands used to "lie flat on his stomach and beat first his head and then his toes against the stage to keep time with the orchestra. He would look at his feet to see how they were keeping time, and then, looking out at the audience, he would say, 'Ain't this nice? I get seventy-five dollars a week for doing this!'"

The double edge of that joke is harder to discern in the ads that emphasized Kersands's gaping mouth. He stuffed his maw with billiard balls, or even a cup and saucer. "His mouth is his fortune," declared *The Daily Nebraska Press*. Were Kersands and his colleagues legitimizing cartoons of black life—providing opportunities for whites to say, *See, Negroes really are like that?* Kersands told a young black entertainer, "If they hate me, I'm still whipping them, because I'm making them laugh." Among his own people, Kersands was so popular that white theater owners accustomed to confining blacks to the balcony would open up half of the theater to accommodate his darker-skinned fans.

In his 1878 book about African-American musicians, the black educator James Monroe Trotter apologized to his readers for including a chapter on the Georgia Minstrels yet argued that the music was so "elevated in character" that it almost compensated for the distressing burlesque. Black minstrels introduced more spirituals, more hymns to freedom, more indirect jibes at racial injustice. They drew more directly from the black vernacular in music and dance—drew, and disseminated. (Reviews as early as the 1880s mention "swinging rhythm.") But drawing from dancing cellars struck men such as Trotter as facing in the wrong direction.

Looking back from 1930, James Weldon Johnson—a leading black novelist, intellectual, and man of the stage—added his voice to the consensus that minstrelsy was the "only completely original contribution America has made to the theater." Yet it was, he qualified, "a caricature of Negro life . . . It fixed the tradition of the Negro as only an irresponsible, happy-go-lucky, wide grinning, loud-laughing, shuffling, banjo playing, singing, dancing sort of being." The crucial word is *only*. As much as authenticity was a market niche, it was also a trap. Lower-class blacks laughed at the truth and the distortion and paid little regard to white reactions. Blacks who aspired to middle-class status feared that minstrelsy would, in Trotter's words, "reflect against the whole."

For the black minstrels themselves, the enterprise had another meaning. As Johnson admitted, "the companies provided essential training and theatrical experience which, at the time, could not have been acquired from any other source." Tom Fletcher, who started a long theatrical career as a black minstrel in 1888, wrote that blacks went into minstrelsy to make money, to educate the young, and to "break down the ill-feeling that existed toward colored people." Show business, he averred, was "a big break" for blacks "because singing and dancing was the way in which they had amused themselves for years"—a factual comment that skirts close to legitimizing a stereotype. *Do what you love and get paid for it.* But there was a price.

TOPSY'S SISTERS

With blacks taking on black roles, the charge of imitation flipped. "There is nothing like the natural thing," wrote one critic. "A negro can play the negro's peculiarities much more satisfactorily than the white 'artist' who with burnt cork is at best a base imitator." Partly for this reason, postbellum white minstrelsy strayed from the plantation toward urban vaudeville. Other ethnic caricatures increasingly vied for space— drunken Irishmen, coarse Germans, swindling Jews. Often these new caricatures were performed in blackface; often the old minstrel jokes required no alteration. Female impersonation surged in popularity. Not to be outdone, the black minstrels soon incorporated their own Irish Negroes and prima donnas.

The place of women, onstage and in the audience, was in flux. The working-class theaters where minstrels performed had been primarily male preserves, where the presence of prostitutes in the upper gallery repelled ladies not of the evening. But as attracting respectable female audiences became an economic goal, variety theaters severed the connection with alcohol and sex and gradually earned family patronage. Tony Pastor, a minstrel Tambo and circus clown, converted a beer hall into Pastor's Opera House in 1865 and pointed the way toward the polite vaudeville of century's end. Variety troupes like his built off minstrelsy, combining blackface comics and song-and-dance men with acrobats and animal acts. Women were invited along, too, mostly as singers. A few went in for song and dance.

Female dancers were even more suspect than actresses. Ballet, as a high art from Europe, could be partially excused, but American ballet girls were generally assumed to be fallen women. Arriving from Britain in 1868, Lydia Thompson and her troupe of blondes burlesqued high culture, but they did so as fleshy ladies in figure-revealing tights, physicalizing their impertinence with breakdowns, walk-arounds, and Juba patting. Denounced as indecent, the troupes toured profitably for decades. Female companies that were more explicitly minstrel followed the same model, offering what other minstrel shows notably lacked: actual women revealing the contours of their lower limbs. The female minstrels merged with the burlesque troupes and retained the name of burlesque even as they deemphasized or dropped parodies to stretch the limits of ever-relaxing standards in the allowable exposure of the female form. Down this path, a half century or so ahead, lay the striptease.

Dance by women, it seemed, was inextricable from sexual display. Yet a few women competed as men did, more or less. In one possibly apocryphal match reported in the New York *Libertine* in 1842, the contestants were prostitutes who traded hornpipes and Virginia breakdowns on a Boston wharf as a Negro fiddler played minstrel tunes. Twenty years on, one Julia Morgan, champion jig dancer of Boston, put out an ad challenging any man or woman to match her in the jig, reel, or walkaround. Naomi Porter of New York took the bait, arguing that five evenings would be necessary to exhibit the variety of her steps; those terms were accepted, but the male judges awarded Morgan the silver cup. In the burlesque context, even a relatively chaste dance—Miss Clara Burton and Her Championship Jig, Dollie and Bessie Warren in their Champion Clog Medley—though praised for agility and ease, read as immodest, brazen. The 1873 manual *Jig, Clog, and Breakdown Dancing Made Easy* lists the names of some twenty-two ladies beating the boards.

Jennie Worrell was on the list. The three Worrell sisters, daughters of a blackface circus clown, had standing engagements in New York. The dances of Jennie, considered the most vivacious, were encored every night. She was once caught wearing "trick heels"—shoes with rattling bullets hidden inside—but her private affairs produced bigger scandals. After her second husband, Mike Murray, the richest gambler in New York, divorced her for infidelity, she chased him with a pistol. She died destitute, in 1899, when a fire scorched the meadow where she was sleeping. An 1877 *carte de visite* photo of Kitty O'Neil, also on the list, shows a tough-looking colleen in breeches. You can see how she might have acquired the nickname "Never Smile Kitty." After debuting at ten with Tony Pastor in 1862, she moved through variety into Harrigan and

Hart's musical comedies of Irish assimilation. She was renowned for her sand jig and her Lancashire clog, and at her death in 1893, *The New York Times* noted her former reputation as "the best female jig dancer in the world." Lotta Crabtree, a much bigger star, learned to jig from a California tavern keeper and to do breakdowns from a black dancer in a mining camp. One of her signature parts was Topsy, and her name, too, became a byword for innocent impudence: Lotta, the petite personality who might dress like a boy and smoke a cigarette but who lived with her mother. She wedged her jigs and breakdowns into most roles, but they wouldn't have been enough on their own to make her the public's darling.

The author of an 1876 *Times* article about the swift rise of variety shows dismissed female clog dancers as a fad he hoped would disappear along with the "disgusting" female minstrels. His argument for the unsuitability of female cloggers has the sound of a man justifying his prejudices; his fear that women would "annihilate the old-style performers" is the petulance of a patriarchy under threat. But he was right about women bringing feminizing changes. To a writer for *The Washington Post* in 1891, the slippered feet of the sand-jig dancer Emma Pollock would suggest sunbeams and darting swallows. Though her art "came from the negro" and "smacked of the cornfield," she twinkled rather than pounded, and ten years of training insured that her dancing was "as different from ordinary clog dancing as possible."

CLOG DANCING MADE EASY

The postbellum script for a minstrel sketch called "Challenge Dance" features a "Hibernian darky" named Ill-Count McGinnis who brags to a group of musicians about his dancing skills. He's an outsider, a cheat, and all talk. The musicians call his bluff by arranging a contest with Farmyard Sam, an "Ethiopian exquisite" who is the favorite. Sam puns hard about how his cruel master died in a "werry unaccountable manner." All laugh except McGinnis, who only makes things worse by laughing too late. When Sam cuts a pigeon wing, McGinnis copies him "in a grotesque manner," and the two square off with "toe-heel snaking" and sand dancing. McGinnis stumbles, tires, falls. Sam is the winner, and McGinnis runs off with the wager.

While McGinnis appears to be the target of a typical minstrel parody of pretension, it's his cheating that triumphs. Taking this cynical plot as a parable would be overreading, yet whoever wrote it recognized one thing: the steps of the charismatic and newly masterless black man weren't necessarily improved when the Irishman tried to copy them. After the war, toe-heel snaking carried on in the Essence, yet jigs ceded popularity to clog dancing. Since jigs and clogs shared many steps, the succession was in part a swap of label, in part a swap of footwear, but the changes were also aesthetic and cultural.

Barney Fagan, born in Boston in 1850, claimed that clog dancing was brought to America early in the century by English, Irish, and Scottish sailors who danced in dives and brothels. By 1830, the stage form of clog dancing had also arrived from Britain, and as early as 1845, a "Lancashire Clog Hornpipe" was advertised at the Boston Museum, still unusual amid jigs and breakdowns. When Bryant's Minstrels debuted "Dixie" in 1859, though, Dick Sands's Wooden Shoe Dance was the number immediately preceding it, and by the 1860s, clogging was ascendant. The Lancashire clog was being formalized in England, and competition extended across the Atlantic, with champions sailing the ocean in both directions to defend their titles. Many leading clog dancers in America came from the Old Country, born in Ireland but raised in Sheffield or Manchester. They hopped between circuses and minstrel shows and moved into variety, where they were specialists or song-and-dance men, often of a specifically Irish character.

Their shoes were lace-ups, with leather tops and wooden soles. In Lancashire, these shoes would have been known as dandy clogs, Sunday clogs, tighter-fitting than work clogs and decorated for maximum flash. The American versions were closer to a regular dress shoe, but the men who wore them were unquestionably dandies. Their cameo portraits are a gallery of fashions in whiskers and cravats. They were theatrical men who lived in boardinghouses and belonged to Elks Clubs. Their salaries went to fancy dress and drink, and they tended to come to early ends.

In an 1860 illustration, the frilly attire of Fred Wilson, one of several dancers credited with introducing clogging, already fits the picture, except for his boots, woolly wig, and blackface. The later the illustration, the less likely the clogger's face will be corked. The men strike a proud posture, hands on hips, legs crossed tightly. Their embroidered shirts billow, tucked at the waist into a sash or a belt as big as a cummerbund. Over white hose, their velvet knee breeches grip thighs, with spangled floral patterns that ramify up the leg and around the central bulge. Such displays of male anatomy may have had something to do with why a prosperous minstrel manager characterized clog dance as "for the ladies."

Clues about technique can be gleaned from instruction manuals sold to amateurs. *Jig and Clog Dancing Without a Master*, published in 1864, offered the following advice on body carriage: "Stand erect, but not too stiff; hold the head upright; avoid looking at the feet, which obliges you to stoop; allow arms to hang straight and easy at the sides, hands open; avoid, as much as possible, any gesticulating movements with the arms." It was the posture of a dancing master, vertical, controlled, up on the toes. Henry Tucker's *Clog Dancing Made Easy* specified, "One must never stand with the heels touching the floor, unless required by the step in use at that moment."

Vague and inconsistent, the manuals were meant for people already familiar with the conventions of the dance. Certain sequences, though not labeled as such, seem to match the steps that twentieth-century Lancashire cloggers would call single shuffles, double shuffles, and so on. Along with hops and stamps, the manuals teach striking the tip of the toe against the floor and clicking toes or heels against each other, techniques that would feed into tap.

Clog songs usually fell into patterns of eight measures, or bars, divided into three sequences of two bars each and capped off by a punctuating two-bar "break." The steps in the manuals frequently hew to the same formula: do it to the right, repeat it to the left, do it to the right, break. This pattern would become the most common metrical (and spatial) structure in tap. Other, less common ways of dividing the eight bars would also carry over, but all of them finished with a break. Interviewed in 1889, one Bowery professor of dance distinguished between the clog, which came from England, and the shuffle, which originated with the darkies. Jigs were shuffles, he instructed, but the Irish Jig was danced in 6/8, while the Nigger Jig was danced in 2/4. The clog, danced in 4/4 in wooden shoes, was about cramming in as many taps as possible.

When Charlie Queen toured Britain with Haverly's Minstrels in the 1880s, audiences were impressed enough to demand that he pass around his clogs. Concealing noisemakers was not unheard of, but the newest Yankee tricks weren't hidden. People clogged on skates or a bicycle or, most pervasively, on a pedestal. Wooden platforms and shingles were traded up for slabs of slate and marble, narrow pedestals that might raise the dancer as high as eight feet. Some pedestal clogging crossed into acrobatics, but aural precision was still valued. These were the years when clog contests began to station some of the judges *under* the stage.

The title of the 1871 manual *Complete Dancing Instructions for Light and Heavy, Genteel and Plantation Songs and Dances* indicates the poles of a stylistic split. For the heavy plantation style, the author recommended goofy outfits and shoes three inches too long. The celebrated dancer Bobby Newcomb categorized the two main styles as "the light and easy, and the broad and the grotesque." Whereas the broad style consisted of "big jumps and extravagant breaks," the light style was to be done in a "gliding manner, or rather with a graceful swing." In Newcomb's opinion, the light style was superior, harder to master, and in his preference you can hear a professional's annoyance that his practiced subtleties might attract less attention.

Double acts became the favorite format. The team of Delehanty and Hengler, formed in 1866, was so popular that when one minstrel troupe hired them away from another, shots were fired. They wore little hats, did a little jig to their "Pickanninny Nig," and were one of many teams associated with the song "Shoo Fly," which some other minstrels discovered in a Negro dance house in Norfolk and made the walk-around hit of 1869. A pair of men dancing in perfect unison offered a nice mirroring effect, though many of the duos were comedy teams, trading on contrast. In variety theaters, double acts were frequently Irish—Needham and Kelly, Kelly and Ryan, men in plug hats and side-whiskers who used walk-arounds and clogging to mortar together verses about honest labor.

Unison dancing effectively precluded improvisation, but it doubled the volume, which must have been a concern as minstrel bands muscled up with brass instruments and augmented their ranks. In 1878, Haverly's Mastodon Minstrels boasted "forty—count 'em—forty" minstrels; by the 1890s, the troupe had a hundred. The amplification device of metal taps was still in the future, but accounts of the 1850s mention a do-it-yourself screwing of pennies into boots, and at least as early as 1871, mail-order clogs came with jingles attached. One enduring solution, which might date from the 1860s, was "stop-time": the band cutting out and keeping up the beat with a jab or two per measure but leaving the rest silent for the dancer to fill.

The clog duo of George Primrose and William West, formed in 1871, became the core of many top minstrel troupes. West, the dashing one, was known as a solid dancer, but his shorter and slighter partner was the sensation. Born near Toronto in 1852 or 1853 to English-Irish parents, Primrose said that he learned to dance by imitating "market men" in their jigs and clogs, "Juba dance," and Essence. Working as a runner at the railroad station, he wore down staircases with his practicing. By the time he was fifteen, he was a minstrel attraction in Detroit, billed as "Master Georgie the Infant Clog Dancer." He and West established themselves in their Double Clog, their Champion Challenge Clog, but it was as king of the "soft shoe" that Primrose became most celebrated. As with *clog*, the name indicated footwear and more than footwear. It was, in the words of one dancer, "a refinement of the Essence." Primrose's soft shoe was "neat," well groomed, the dance of a dark dandy sometimes performed in the suit of an English swell. No source describes it exactly, but people called it "picture dancing," emphasizing the visual. The soft shoe that became traditional called for a looser stance than clogging, a suppler spine, more birch bough than cedar trunk. While the feet were tickling the floor with tiny motions, the arms might float along. A soft shoe was never fast, so style was all-important.

Primrose enjoyed a long and influential career, performing as the "greatest soft shoe dancer in the world" right up to his death in 1919, the burnt cork worn so deeply into the creases of his face that it couldn't be washed off. Harland Dixon, born in Toronto in 1885 to Scots-Irish parents, spent a year with Primrose's troupe in 1906. What he remembered nearly sixty years later were his mentor's lovely shoulders, his flat stomach, and the way he never perspired, not even while parading on a summer day. "Prim was the greatest stylist of them all," Dixon recalled. But he was "not necessarily the greatest in technique," whereas Primrose's sometime rival Barney Fagan danced steps that "were so intricate that the audience and even the other dancers couldn't follow him." Fagan wasn't above showmanship—striking sparks as he clogged on a metal plate—but his aspirations inclined in another direction. He called one of his troupes the Progressive Minstrels. (An essay on the art of dancing he wrote around 1930 is a digest of a lifetime's worth of disputation, and the people Fagan most wants to correct are all the dancers who "habitually ridicule the technical thought, claiming that step dancing was intended to be a pleasure and a diversion." He felt that a dancer should know the names of steps and the note values. He envied ballet and music for their "scientific discourse," and his plea for systematic development sounds like that of a man long familiar with being shrugged off.)

Primrose's dancing was easier to follow, but he was cagey. "He did his best dancing when the other dancers were in their dressing rooms," Dixon remembered. The young Dixon caught something anyhow, and late in life, cataloguing the dancers of his youth in terms of who had copied whom and who had something no one else could copy, he pleaded guilty to modeling himself after Primrose: "My style was original with Primrose and I tried to copy it and what developed was my own style." As far as Dixon was concerned, Primrose "had a style that when he died he took it with him."

RAGTIME

In the mid-1890s, the Primrose and West troupe carried "40 whites and 30 blacks." The stage was no more integrated than the country. An ad stressed how the troupe required two of everything: two distinct performances, two parades, two separate train cars. The blacks ostensibly represented "Minstrelsy As It Was," while the whites portrayed "Minstrelsy As It Is," with the "leaders of modern minstrelsy" attired in the new fashion of antique court dress. Another Primrose and West poster, this one specifying "all white performers," advertised "new ideas in the terpsichorean art," including the American Clog Dance—a line of

pink-faced men in red, white, and blue, flanking Uncle Sam. As Barney
Fagan remembered it, the difference between the American Clog and
the Lancashire version was that American style spread out, abandoning
dancing on a plate for a trip across the stage. Yet the most significant
changes are the ones there's no solid record of: the developments in
rhythm. In this sense, it's much more likely that the modern leaders with
Primrose and West were the black performers: the Buck Dancers with
the Little Coon Band that the posters designated "hot stuff." James
McIntyre, of the prosperous white duo McIntyre and Heath, would
claim that he was the first to perform a syncopated buck-and-wing in
New York, in 1876. Where did he get the idea? "By watching Negroes
in the South."

Negro dance halls still generally made it into print only as crime
scenes. One exception was Lafcadio Hearn's vividly detailed 1876 description of riverfront dance houses on the levees of Cincinatti. Hearn
noted the prostitution and morphine addiction in Bucktown, but also
the way that while banjos and fiddles played, black steamboatmen and
their stogie-smoking gals crossed their legs in double shuffles rapid
enough to blur. (A quarter of the women were white, and, to Hearn's
eye, less graceful.) One mulatto girl with a blue ribbon in her hair, just
out of jail for grand larceny, was esteemed for her breakdown; one
stumpy fellow could jig with a glass of water on his head. "Amid such
scenes," Hearn wrote, "does the roustabout find his heaven, and this
heaven is certainly not to be despised." But despised it was, the ongoing
developments in music and dance largely unappreciated by the white
world, save for foraging white minstrels. Blacks in blackface could be
found on the levee, too, making mixed-race audiences scream with laughter. Hearn's descriptions of the professional dancing—including a young
lady with a razor-scarred face doing a breakdown in boy's brogans—echo
his descriptions of the dance houses.

Occasionally, Hearn noted, fashionably dressed whites came to watch,
escorted by the police. Fifteen years later, such people wouldn't have to
make the trip. In the 1890s, traveling shows selling Southern nostalgia
brought along blacks for local color. Productions of *Uncle Tom's Cabin*
began to let blacks take major speaking roles. *In Old Kentucky* had few
speaking roles for blacks, but that didn't stop the stableboys from stealing

the show by playing craps, boxing, buck dancing, and coaxing "discordant tunes" out of brass. These boys were billed as "pickaninnies," a patronizing name for black children since before Kentucky was a state. (Etymological theories abound: "pick" from picking cotton, or from picayunes, the coins they picked up, or from *pequeño*, for small.) Black minstrels had adopted the term, and white producers were catching on.

South Before the War set the fashion for "plant" shows, sketches of plantation life, by introducing its all-black variety program of 1892 with a scene of a runaway returning to contented enslavement. The pseudo-historical scenario gave black performers an opening, as the concept of plantation pastimes was vague enough to encompass their most up-to-date skills. It and the other plant shows launched the careers of children who grew into well-known dancers. In a change from black minstrelsy, several of these were female. In his memoirs, the black minstrel Tom Fletcher would remember Katie Carter as Queen of the Buck and Wing Dancers, "the largest box-office attraction in the country." Mentions in the press don't substantiate that claim, though the *Los Angeles Times* did call her "the greatest buck and wing dancer in the country."

The apotheosis of the plant shows was *Black America*, an outdoor exhibition complete with a cotton field and a cast of five hundred. The ads and programs had an ethnographic quality, and the white press took the event as an accurate representation of the Negro of the South, still careless as in slavery days, exhibiting a naturalness that put white imitations to shame, with perfect time in dancing "not to be dreamed of by people born with no touch of African blood in their veins."

The dancing came in two categories. One was the buck and wing, a variant of "buck dance" and Mobile Buck, all terms that entered the printed record around this time. The program characterized it as "the dance of the stalwart young darkies of 1820," known as bucks, who danced in heelless, extra-heavy shoes and finished exhausted after "a contest for supremacy." In other sources, *buck* functioned as a catchall for dances done by black people. One article about *Black America* listed a whole menagerie of buck dance steps: Rabbit Hop, Broken Foot Charley, Break de Chicken's Neck, Scratch Ground, Wake Up Black Man, Go 'Way Sugar Yo' Done Los' de Tas. These were loose-jointed, twisty combinations that called for feet to drag and slide; a sprinkling of sand was often a preamble. A buck dancer interviewed at a Kentucky barn dance gave an entirely different catalogue of steps, most of them sardonically named after such prominent whites as President McKinley. "T'aint no use for no white trash to come here and try teach us niggers how to dance," the dancer added. "The niggers aroun' dis town know as many different steps as anybody, new steps all the time."

The other dance in *Black America* was the cakewalk, which the program glossed as a Real Old Virginia Promenade, a holiday contest with a cake as a prize. A few former slaves would recall cakewalking (another practice with Irish analogues), and Tom Fletcher would pass along stories from his grandparents of a "chalk line walk," done for the master and his guests and involving pails of water carried on the head. Other accounts, also secondhand, portrayed the Cakewalk as a parody of white manners, mocking 'em every step. The name emerged after emancipation in notices for black church fund-raisers, then as entertainment by colored waiters at white resorts. In 1870s competitions between black contestants before mostly white audiences, promenading couples were judged by grace and ease, and fashionable attire was as de rigueur as a regal gait. "The style which is considered the most 'tony,'" explained the *New Haven Register*, "is to keep the head back at an angle of just ten degrees from the perpendicular . . . with a most melancholy expression, as if mourning the death of a life-long companion, or as if dreaming of some far off country." Diaspora had turned the aesthetic of the cool into underclass hauteur. But the dancers' elasticity extended into grotesque attitudes as well as stylish poses. Both drew laughter.

By the time of *Black America*, the cakewalk had grown into a national fad. No "plant" or "Tom" show could do without one. Beginning in 1892, an annual cakewalk at Madison Square Garden drew a mixed and betting crowd in the thousands. Across the country, respectable colored folk protested. High stepping smacked of the low, and the black bourgeoisie found such public displays doubly degrading, first because whites laughed and then because white promoters profited. Of course, some of the "exaggerated decorum" that amused a reporter at *Black America* could have been satirical. Indeed, the joke of the decade was what the *Baltimore Afro-American* noted with puzzlement: "The white people are picking up what the better class of colored people are trying to get away from."

Vanderbilts flaunted aristocratic independence by hiring colored enter-tainers as cakewalk tutors. And where the gentry promenaded, others would follow, trickle down converging with bubble up.

Vanderbilts did not buck dance, but most cakewalk events included a buck dancing competition, and most of the "Tom" and "plant" shows held buck dance contests, too. The contests were good business, drawing audiences to cheer local contenders. The buck dance contest for *In Old Kentucky* was soon a greater attraction than the play, and when the hotel bootblack emerged victorious over the boys in the band, he might turn professional. It was after winning a wing contest at a St. Louis cakewalk that Katie Carter hit the road. Wing contests were often for women only, and buck contests for men, though there were plenty of female buck dance champions, and women—white women—seem to have dominated the buck dance contests sponsored by the *Police Gazette*, one of the many tournaments promoted in its pink-papered sports pages. A "fascinating combination of all dancing steps," reported the *Milwaukee Journal* on a trend that had spread to Midwestern businessmen, clog and jig steps plus "rattles," "slides," "nerve executions," and more. It was the breakdown evolving, new steps all the time.

To the *New York Tribune*'s representative at the first Madison Square Garden cakewalk, the buck performed by Little Old Folks and Miss Lizzie Blizzard was "simply clog dancing of a high order." The Midwest-ern writer Rupert Hughes reported on another name for the amalgam: "Negroes call their clog dancing 'ragging' and the dance a 'rag.'" The dance, he wrote, was "largely shuffling": scraping footwork matching banjo notes and patting hands. In black Kansas of the 1890s, a *rag* was a social function at which, lamented the black-run *Leavenworth Advocate*, young people indulged in "low antics" such as the Mobile Buck. The music for such dancing spread with its name. By the middle of the decade, syn-copation and cross-rhythms under the label of *ragtime* were becoming a craze to define an era.

One of the earliest of ragtime's many origin stories appeared in the 1896 song sheet for "Syncopated Sandy" by Ned Wayburn. "RAG-TIME," Wayburn explained, "originated with the negroes and is characteristic of their people. The negroe in playing the piano, strikes the keys with the same time and measure that he taps the floor with his heels and toes in dancing, thereby obtaining a peculiarly accented time effect which he terms 'Rag-Time.'" Jig piano, some people called it, referring to the way that jigs, or blacks, played Wayburn, one of several white piano players billed as "The Man Who Invented Ragtime," later added that he took the tune for "Sandy" from an old darky playing banjo on an Alabama levee, "the beats corresponding to the taps of a buck dancer." (Wayburn put paper between the strings of his piano to mimic the sound.) The same theory was espoused by the black promoter William Foster: that ragtime was born from the stop-time of the banjo and the tapping of the Mobile Buck, transferred to beat-up pianos in levee dance halls. Foster and Wayburn agreed about where ragtime came from, but only Foster complained about who profited.

Foster might have complained about more. "Syncopated Sandy" is a song about a cakewalking champ, "a coon that leads a really reckless life." Wayburn also penned a version in the voice of a "bold bad nigger" who gets lynched. *Coon* was like *nigger*, a word that carried a different charge depending on who was using it. The bulk of ragtime songs, written by blacks and whites, were "coon songs," syncopated tales of chicken-stealing, craps-playing, razor-wielding blacks. Coon songs could be mock-sentimental—*coon* rhymes with *june* and *moon*—but mostly they were antisentimental, illicit scenes of underworld life such as the Chicago saloon anthem in which a woman throwing one man over for another who spends more freely cries, "All Pimps Look Alike to Me." The black minstrel Ernest Hogan, cleaning up the lyrics, revised the phrase as "All Coons Look Alike to Me," and so fashioned for himself a signature tune and, inadvertently, a jingle for racists.

Such were the opportunities, such the risks. An 1890s performance of Black Patti's Troubadours commenced with the skit "At Jolly Coon-ey Island" and a cakewalk or a buck dance contest, but it culminated in an Operatic Kaleidoscope. Bob Cole, the college-educated buck dance champion who wrote "Coon-ey Island," played a tramp in that sketch, in whiteface, and he put that quiet revolution of a character into *A Trip to Coontown*, an 1898 black musical comedy that disguised its grievances in ragtime insouciance. Around the same time, Charles Johnson and the full-figured beauty Dora Dean cakewalked onto white variety bills in evening clothes as the King and Queen of Coon Swelldom; Johnson's soft shoe, performed in top hat and monocle, garnered comparisons with George Primrose's. The team of Bert Williams and George Walker also rode the cakewalk to fame, billing themselves, boldly, as Two Real Coons. Onstage and off, Walker was the dandy in tight pants and mock diamonds, atilt and asway, his smile flashing white and gold. Williams—light-skinned and bookish when not in character—was the blackface clown, shuffling grotesquely but always in time. To James Weldon Johnson, a younger member of this generation, the ambition was "to compel the public to recognize that they could do something more than grin and cut pigeon wings." The musical comedies of Bob Cole and Williams and Walker would make incremental progress toward that goal, playing on what whites craved from a black show to expand what they would accept from one.

To white dancers, the changes were all rhythmic. Fred Stone was getting his start then, as a buck-dancing Topsy. In the 1920s, by which time he had become a musical comedy star, he would trace jazz back to an Ernest Hogan song and "the great changes as the dancers began to fit their steps . . . into the new jiggity time." These white dancers practiced all night, and "it wasn't long before every kind of step that any one could think of had been invented and named. Everyone was dancing ragtime, and the motif was to be found in the original buck dancing." The style was close-to-the-floor, with the dancers working "to catch the ear as well as the eye." Stone remembered that his friend Bert Jordan, a champion of flatfoot buck, used to find a rhythmic pattern on a snare drum, figure out how to manage it with his feet, then substitute two or three sounds for every one, multiplying the step mathematically. By the turn of the century, when Harland Dixon was learning the Lancashire clog, he found it difficult to maintain the even rhythms. "It took a lot of concentration to keep it from swinging." Ragtime had caught his ear, and everyone else's.

In black America, life got worse before it got better. By 1877, the North and South had made their bargain, and as the federal troops that propped up Reconstruction pulled out, white Southerners rode roughshod over the rights of black citizens. By 1896, the Supreme Court's decision in

Plessy v. Ferguson made it all official, providing a legal basis for segregation and the lie of "separate but equal." The South was carved up and divided, everything labeled "colored" or "white" in a system of discrimination that took the name of that double-shuffling trickster, Jim Crow. But *discrimination* is a paltry word for how boundaries were policed. The most extreme methods, the lynchings by which thousands of blacks were mutilated and murdered, were often community events. Crowds posed in front of hanged men or charred bodies as if before a tourist attraction, as if at a show.

During these same years, well before W. C. Handy gained the title of "Father of the Blues" by writing down the music, he was the bandmaster of William Mahara's Minstrels. The stories in his autobiography have what he calls a "grim, backwoods humor." In Texas, the idea of fun was to shoot at the black minstrels' train car as it passed through town. At one stop, a member of the company came down with smallpox, and the town doctor suggested that if anyone else got sick, the entire troupe might be lynched as a health measure; the company escaped only by sneaking the other ill men out in women's clothing while the rest of the troupe put on a diversionary show that involved a 280-pound minstrel repeatedly jumping in the air and landing on his "mighty buttocks." In Missouri, a friend of Handy's, a trombone player with the Georgia Minstrels, talked back to a gang of whites after they threw snowballs at him and his girl. The musician's corpse was shipped to his mother, tongue removed.

Life as a black minstrel could be tough all around. Handy sometimes needed a pistol to protect himself from the members of his own band. More often, the person holding the gun was a white man who wanted to be entertained. The *Topeka Weekly Call*, a black-owned paper, carried a story about a black boy who was ordered to dance by a crowd of white toughs. When the boy refused, he was knocked down, danced upon, and shot in the hips. He did not survive. Fast feet attracted coin, dodged bullets. Parading in Prince Albert suits, Handy and his fellow black minstrels made themselves conspicuous targets even as they provided diversions; when in doubt, they played "Dixie." Life up north was generally safer, but during the New York race riots of 1900, a white mob fastened on familiar names: "Get Ernest Hogan and Williams and

Walker and Cole and Johnson!" (Or so James Weldon Johnson wrote; the *New York Journal* reported that Hogan and Walker were attacked, but that the cry was "Get the nigger!") Handy noted that many of his fellow minstrels left the United States for good: "Perhaps they found it hard to erase from their minds the nightmare of those minstrel days."

W. C. Handy was far from the only early jazz musician to get his start in minstrel shows. The list would include many of the principal players and most of the journeymen. And then there were the comedians and the dancers, doing the dances that went with the music. As Handy put it, "The best talent of that generation came down the same drain . . . the minstrel show got them all."

Buck dancing came down that drain. Tap was at the other end. When Ned Wayburn, "The Man Who Invented Ragtime," made his first professional appearance, in Chicago in 1892, it was as a white comedian in blackface who played piano, "ragging the classics." When he arrived in New York five years later, and discovered that his act had already been presented there by someone else, he reinvented himself as a director, a teacher, and a producer. Over the next decades, thousands of dancers would study in his school and he would stage dozens of shows—many of the most lucrative entertainments of the early twentieth century. He developed hundreds of acts, and one he put together in 1902 was a line of sixteen girls he honored with the name Ned Wayburn's Minstrel Misses. They made their entrance as if in a minstrel parade, then stood behind a table and corked up, tucking their hair beneath woolly wigs and bellhop caps, stripping off their overcoats to reveal tuxedos with striped pants. On their feet they wore split-sole clogs—resonant like clogs but not quite as rigid. To describe the blackface buck dancing the Minstrel Misses did in those shoes, Wayburn coined a new term—or so he would let be said of him in *Life* decades later—a term that wouldn't go into wide practice for twenty years: "tap and step dancing."

PART II

EVERYBODY'S DOING IT NOW

We have come in the last fifteen years to care for nothing but a "rag" . . . We got our taste somehow from Mississippi niggers "sanding down" the "Mobile Buck."

—"The Present Craze for Dancing," *Hampton's Broadway Magazine*, 1908

Some persons believe that the Southern Negro was the originator of tap, or buck, dancing. This is not so. The Negro has an inborn sense of rhythm and his feet merely responded to impulses he felt while he was under the intoxicating spell of the music. The Negro shuffled aimlessly. There was no logical manipulation of his feet in a thoughtfully developed routine.

—JIMMY ORMONDE, *Tap Dancing at a Glance*, 1931

Tap dancing! Everybody's doing it now! It has actually assumed the proportions of a cure-all. The slim take it up to put on weight. The stout adopt it to take off weight. Tap dancers to the left of us, tap dancers to the right of us—and if they were all placed end to end, the one in front wouldn't know who to copy!

—*Los Angeles Times*, 1930

T wo young black men in headscarves and boots hunker down and pat Juba as a third takes a turn in the middle. His steps are crude: rough shuffles, some swiveling heel and toe. His friend starts in with shuffles, then hops into a twist. Unwinding, he stumbles backward and hits the ground in a roll that looks like an accident but sets him back on his feet right on time. The timing is visible, a pulse intermittently perceptible in clapping hands and the bounce of bodies. But it's nearly impossible to grasp a phrase, to catch the beat. The tempo seems slowed way down and the rhythms distorted by that stretching. There's no sound at all.

It's a silent film, less than thirty seconds shot at the Edison studio in 1894 and distributed as *The Pickanniny Dance*. Catalogue copy characterizes it as a scene of "Southern plantation life before the war, a jig and breakdown by three colored boys," a description that suggests any three colored boys, doing what colored boys did. Yet the catalogue identifies these three men as backup for the white soubrette Lucy Daly in *The Passing Show* on Broadway. Playing pickanninies was their job. The catalogue also gives their names: Joe Rastus, Denny Tolliver, and Walter Wilkins—probably the first African-Americans to be recorded by the recent invention of the motion picture camera, almost certainly the first tap dancers to be filmed in action.

The "Dancing Darkey Boy" in the 1897 film of that title doesn't get a name. He really is a boy, a child on a platform in knickers and a sailor's cap, surrounded by a crowd of white men who clap in encouragement. The boy begins his thirty seconds of buck dance upright, contained. An ambling-in-place step resembles the start of the Shim Sham, and the film might in fact be one of the "old films of kids shuffling their feet" that Leonard Reed cited as a source for that later-to-be-ubiquitous dance. Even though the boy's feet keep vanishing into the darkness of the print,

Opposite page: Bill Robinson, 1928

a downbeat is clear in his regular sinking. Every so often, he plants his feet and rolls his little hips.

The technology of recording changes history. Reading descriptions of earlier dance, I long to experience the dance directly and judge for myself. These films and those that followed come much closer to satisfying that desire. And you don't have to take my word for it. You can watch them, too. As evidence of 1890s dance, be it breakdown or buck, the films are, in a sense, arbitrary samples—others from the same time have been lost—and yet they're archetypal. Not intended as documentary, they document something early filmmakers thought the public would want to spend a few minutes looking at: pickaninnies and dancing darky boys.

Half of the dance is missing, of course. The sound. Fin-de-siècle technology could also capture that portion, only separately. Listening to the 1901 wax cylinder of "Pretty as a Picture" is like listening through a kazoo, such is the distortion and hiss, but about a minute in, there comes a rattling between phrases of melody, as if a stenographer were typing up what had just been sung. When the band cuts out for a break, typing fills the gap in soft-shoe cadences, the triplet rhythms of picture dancing. This typing might just be tapping, as might similar noises in other recordings of this vintage. You can't tell for sure just by listening.

In 1901, experiments were under way to marry the two technologies, but it would be decades before tap dancing was recorded in full—decades in which tap became tap.

6

BIG TIME

I n Boston in those days, the boys didn't worry about what they were
going to do when they grew up: you were going to be either a dancer
or a fighter." Those days were the first years of the century, and the
speaker did not become a boxer. Jack Donahue and his pals swapped
steps on the street corner or, if a cop chased them off, on a flatcar at the
freight yards. At the Howard Athenæum, they climbed three flights of
stairs to sit on benches and gaze down in judgment on professional dancers,
raining disapproval on a missed tap or a stolen routine. Donahue's hero
was George Primrose, though in the boy's eyes the minstrel man's soft
shoe belonged to the old school, beautiful but out-of-date. Where Primrose took a graceful tour of the stage in leisurely 4/4, the new style was
stationary, packing more taps into a faster 2/4. For young Donahue, the
modern mode was Paddy Shea doing a speedy buck dance in a Boston
barroom with a glass of beer on his head and not spilling a drop.

On the corner, the boys called out the names of steps to try. There
was Falling Off a Log, which really does look as if the dancer were
struggling to maintain his balance atop a rolling surface of timber, crossing his legs as he tilts, twists, and topples onto alternating feet. Then

there was Shuffle Off to Buffalo, in which the weight also rocks from foot to foot but the crossed legs don't change position as elbows and knees pump like the pistons of a train that propels the dancer across the stage, often toward the exit (and the next gig, in proverbial Buffalo). Both steps entered the general repertory of stage dancers. A version of Falling Off the Log would show up, before long, in the final step of the Shim Sham.

A certain kind of step was useful for setting a tempo and synchronizing with musicians. Steps of this kind became known as time steps, and their most common shape could be found in decades-old clog manuals: three-and-a-break. Repetition established a pattern that the break punctuated, a winding up that the break released, and the whole simple structure offered the tension of asymmetry within a reassuringly squared-off form. A few time steps—each known as the Time Step—became standard. These were the building blocks of tap, the basics. By executing the elementary syncopations of such a step cleanly, any dancer could demonstrate his ability to keep time. Still today, to say of a tap dancer that he can't even do a time step is to dismiss him utterly, while to say that he can make even a time step look good is to grant mastery. Back when Donahue was a boy, every self-respecting hoofer had at least one of his own, recognizable both as *a* time step and as *his*.

Many step names were onomatopoetic. The fact that someone heard the four-count rhythm of one step as "croppy lie down"—words from an Irish song—suggested the ethnic background of those doing the listening. But the ethnic mix was in flux. Benny Rubin, who grew up in Boston at about the same time as Donahue, began as both a dancer and a fighter, entering amateur contests in both fields. "I didn't know it was dancing," he remembered. "To me it was just a noise they were making, and we kids loved making noise." As a dialect comedian who danced a bit, Rubin joined a wave of Jews about to dominate show business— Balines becoming Berlins, Joelsons becoming Jolsons.

Jack Donahue turned professional after buying wooden shoes with his winnings from a dice game. He relocated his step swapping to the lobby of the Rexford Hotel and angled to dance in a theater. The fare at the Howard was burlesque—displays of female flesh offset with knockabout comedians and champion buck-and-wing dancers, a variety show distinguished by lower prices and lower standards of propriety. Burlesque theaters were now organized into circuits, or wheels, and a performer could arrange a series of bookings into an itinerary, a route. But those weren't the wheels that Donahue wanted to be on.

"The variety show was an outcast," a writer for *Everybody's Magazine* explained in 1905; "vaudeville is an institution, respected and respectable." Vaudeville shared variety's structure—its variety—but vaudeville was clean. Fabled backstage signs outlawed "slob," "son-of-a-gun," and "Holy Gee," along with everything sacrilegious and suggestive. Wholesome entertainment was big business. By 1905, New York and Chicago sustained several palaces of vaudeville, opulent structures seating more than a thousand. From the mid-teens onward, the zenith was the Palace Theatre in New York. To have "played the Palace" was a pinnacle of vaudeville success. That was the "big time," where the most famous acts performed, but the same cities supported dozens of smaller theaters. You could find vaudeville in just about every city in America. As in other national industries, competition led to consolidation. Big-time theaters in Chicago and points west were gathered into the Orpheum circuit, while Keith-Albee dominated the East. Keith-Albee's subsidiary, the United Booking Office, arranged a performer's route, and to maximize efficiency and kickbacks, it treated each act independently, to be moved around easily or replaced.

As many as twenty-one acts might appear on one bill, though the average was seven to fifteen. The guiding principle was "something for everyone." Vaudeville was singers, comedy teams, escape artists, hypnotists, jugglers, contortionists, mind readers, acrobats, ventriloquists, magicians, monologuists, impressionists, dancers, regurgitators, sports figures, celebrities with no discernible talent, actors from the "legitimate" theater slumming for better pay, and every sort of animal act. If you didn't like one thing, something else was coming. And the pace was quick. Exceeding the allotted time could get an act fined or fired, and the interval between performers was minimized by having a self-sufficient act perform in front of the curtain while a more elaborate act was set up behind it. Tap dancers served this purpose well.

In small time, the show might repeat three to five times each day, whereas another phrase for big time was "two-a-day." The order and composition of a bill was an art in itself. There was no universal formula, but in the ideal, a show might open with a "dumb" act—a trained seal, a troupe of acrobats, a dancer, something that wouldn't be too spoiled by the hubbub of latecomers. Next came something to settle the audience in, then something to wake them up. Everything built toward the headliner, who took the penultimate slot, and the show finished with a "chaser." This was often another dumb act, since folks on their way out make as much noise as on the way in—either flashy to send them off abuzz or awful to clear them out faster. The running order was a hierarchy of salary and fame, and every ambitious vaudevillian aspired to the rank of next-to-closing in a big-time theater. The default position for a strictly dance act was the deuce spot, number two, six minutes and off.

Vaudevillians showed you what they could do, fast. "They have to establish an immediate contact, set a current in motion, and exploit it to the last possible degree in the shortest space of time," explained the critic Gilbert Seldes. There was no room for mistakes, no chance for recovery. But if the format pushed vaudevillians toward a kind of perfection, it also provided plenty of practice. The circuits were vast and varied enough to embrace the best and the worst, and the ladder from small time to big time could extend to great length. Most bookings lasted three to six days, and then the performer started over in a new theater with a new clientele. The system gave vaudevillians opportunities to hone their acts in response to an ever-changing public and also insured that once an act was perfected, they might never need another. It could take years for a performer to cycle around to the same venue, and by then people had forgotten, or were happy to be reminded. One newspaper columnist estimated the average life of an act to be two years, but some lasted decades.

An act was a livelihood. Some vaudevillians filed theirs with the National Vaudeville Association in sealed envelopes to be opened when one trouper accused another of theft. These were scripts and sheet music; the method didn't work as well for dance. But more important than the act was the persona. Even in the largest theaters, vaudeville put little distance between performer and audience. "Personality" was everything, for comics and singers especially, yet not even the animal acts were exempt. The audience was always right, and managers' reports kept track of the public's verdict.

The soft shoe was prevalent. Vaudevillians who didn't specialize in dancing could manage one; it bestowed a little class and helped turn a comic into an entertainer, a candidate for next-to-closing. "The dance appropriate to the vaudeville stage is the stunt dance," Seldes decreed in the early twenties. He was protesting the "aesthetic dancing" that had crept in through the teens, supplementing the dominant buck-and-wing, and what he meant by stunts was gimmickry, which vaudeville encouraged in dance as it promoted speed in comedy. Milt Wood did his clogging atop a chair. Louis Stone did his upside down on his hands. Al Leach buck-danced on stairs as if drunk. The female winners of the *Police Gazette* championship medal for "wooden shoe buck dancing," when they danced in vaudeville as opposed to at smokers and stag parties, tended to pair up with a man. Bertha Gleason, who won in 1902, traveled with her dancing brother, John. Since so many stages, laid over concrete, were acoustically dead, the Gleasons carried a mat of wooden slats glued to canvas as a portable shingle. To handle their tricky musical cues, they also brought along their own pianist, a young man whom Bertha soon married.

Family was an especially effective gimmick. Among the most popular of acts was Eddie Foy and the Seven Little Foys, a first-generation Irish comic with his singing-and-dancing brood, lined up by age and height. The Four Fords worked as siblings: Dora, Mabel, Ed, and Max. Their dancing father instructed the boys; the sisters spied and figured it out for themselves. Reviewers praised the quartet as without equal for their perfect time and novel steps. Handsome scenery and costumes softened their strenuous dancing, and their lobby photo was genteel, a boardwalk stroll in boaters and bonnets. In 1910, they were headliners, but the act split soon after, the sisters yearning to express themselves in Grecian dancing, à la Isadora Duncan. This venture into Art flopped, and Dora and Mabel reverted to buck dance and headlined for another decade. Max went into teaching, and a ubiquitous step in his name proved the most lasting legacy of his clan—a lunging, scissoring burst of sound known as the Maxie Ford. (If you've seen Gene Kelly dance, you've seen this step.)

Pat Rooney, Jr., was also born into the business, the son and name-sake of one of the foremost clog-dancing Irish comedians of the 1880s. Twenty at the turn of the century, the younger Rooney toured first with his wife, then with his wife and their son, Pat the Third. Though billed as the premier dancing team of vaudeville, they likely wouldn't have been headliners without their catchy songs and patter. Rooney was five feet three, a leprechaun with a bright grin. The waltz clog, a step introduced during his father's day, became so associated with him that people assumed it was his invention. With his hands in his pockets, hitching his trousers up, he hopped, lifting one bent leg high and tucking the other underneath to click heels in flight—fixing the pigeon wing, which he called a "bell," as Irish for the new century.

As for Jack Donahue, that Boston Irish boy, he spent the teens on the Keith and Orpheum circuits, singing and dancing and talking non-sense with a nice-looking girl named Alice. His kind of dancing was called eccentric. "Nature helped me," he later wrote, "by endowing me with a pair of long legs and arms." His face was long, too, and on his gaunt frame, the standard steps looked funny, so he exaggerated further and milked more laughs. He packed more eccentric steps into a routine, one Rhode Island critic attested, than three or four other dancers combined. Donahue understood what another aspiring dancer, hoping to make use of the flat-footed style he learned from "the little darkies" in St. Louis, told the Cleveland *Plain Dealer*: "There's little enough money in dancing . . . you must mix comedy to get by."

UNDER THE RAG AND OUT FROM UNDER IT

Down the same drain—or, depending on your perspective, up it. Dewey "Pigmeat" Markham, born in North Carolina in 1903, preferred the analogy of educational advancement. "Show business for a colored dancer," he explained,

> was like going through school. You started in a medicine show—that was
> kindergarten—where they could use a few steps if you could cut them,
> but almost anything would do. Then you went on up to the gilly show,

which was like grade school—they wanted dancers. If you had something on the ball, you graduated to a carnival—that was high school—and
you sure had to be able to dance. College level was a colored minstrel
show, and as they faded out, a vaudeville circuit or even a Broadway show.
Vaudeville and Broadway sometimes had the best, although a lot of the
great dancers never got out from under the rag, never left the tent shows.

That was the path that led Leonard Reed to the Shim Sham and beyond.
Reed was born in 1906, and when he was a child, it took exposure to only
one or two of the traveling shows that came through Oklahoma—"the
pretty girls and the comedians with the cork on their face, doing funny
jokes"—to get him hooked. Whenever carnivals came through—"the
tambourine shakers and the black comedians doing what they called their
jig"—he was there every night. By the time he was fifteen, his dancing
talents had earned him a summer job in a medicine show.

For whatever ailed you, a medicine show could offer a miraculous
elixir. Turpentine and sugar, Coca-Cola and salt. Such outfits might be
a few guys peddling a snake-oil cure-all or a hundred men traveling
together by railroad, carrying an entire catalogue of dubious treatments.
More commonly, the show consisted of a "doctor" and two or three
assistants, a team that wandered from town to town in a wagon, on the
lookout for suckers. The assistants' job was to lure customers, which is
where the dancing came in. The wagon had a small platform, upon
which the assistants did their breakdown. The dancing, Reed remembered, was in "a comic, exaggerated, almost grotesque style"—whatever
it took, said Markham, to "put the yokels in a buying mood." After the
doctor made his sales pitch, the assistants would roam the crowd, exchanging bottles for cash and pocketing a little for themselves. It wasn't
much of a start for a dancer, but you learned how to attract attention—
how to sell.

A gilly was a small carnival, still a small-town operation, but it offered
steadier work at better pay. Black performers had their own tent. (Reed
remembered it as a "jig top," the tent for people called jigs.) To entice
customers, they put on a preview called the ballyhoo. Up on a platform
they went, everyone clapping and singing, the dancers trying to outdo
one another as a barker fast-talked people into buying tickets. Inside,

events proceeded as in a minstrel show. The blackface comedian traded jokes with a straight man and flaunted funny steps. Then came a section of specialties, and the whole thing would finish with a plantation afterpiece. This might repeat fourteen or fifteen times a day; one Fourth of July, Reed claimed, the count was forty-eight.

Carnivals and circuses and even Wild West shows carried something called a sideshow annex that was essentially an all-black minstrel show. The brass band was a big draw. Magicians, human corkscrews, trick cyclists, and trapeze acts shared the tent with champion buck dancers. They came solo or double, sometimes husband-and-wife, and most of them sang. Pigmeat Markham and his partner did a sand dance, the band going quiet so people could hear the scraped rhythms. Audience members called out requests for imitations: do a racehorse, do a train. The star of these shows was the dancing comedian. Markham remembered a "very funny" one named Joe Doakes, who would "shake his head from side to side so hard and so fast that the makeup on his lips dotted his ears." The dancers Markham rated the best were the craziest. "Exaggerating the peculiarities" was still sometimes referred to as "grotesque," but as in vaudeville, the term of art became "eccentric."

The activities of black entertainers were covered by the *Indianapolis Freeman*, often in the form of self-aggrandizing letters from the entertainers themselves. There you could also read about all-black minstrel shows that toured the South independently, under canvas. Long-enduring organizations such as the Rabbit's Foot Company, the Florida Blossoms, and Silas Green from New Orleans, along with more fly-by-night affairs, maintained Tambo and Bones while keeping up as ragtime gave way to the blues and early jazz. In 1911, Bessie Smith was not just "a great coon shouter"; she was "the girl with educated feet." Markham remembered "dancers who were so good you wouldn't believe it," such as Jim Green, known as the Human Top because he spun on his seat. Before, it had been Master Juba, Master Diamond; now it was Kid Checkers, Kid Slick, prizefighter names acquired in adolescence and then never outgrown.

They did start young. Robert Everleigh, who displayed his "eight minutes of footology" with Rabbit's Foot in the mid-teens, was a "boy wonder." His career was short, yet some lasted as long as minstrelsy held out. Eddie "Peg" Lightfoot was the One-Legged Dancing Wonder in 1916, a laugh machine in blackface and a squashed stovepipe; in 1923, he was nearly beaten to death by a white mob, but he would still be dancing beneath a Rabbit's Foot tent in 1954. His early years were not exactly years of obscurity. Even the backcountry was a high-traffic zone where minstrel managers pasted posters on top of the posters of other troupes. These performers were seen by hundreds or thousands—by blacks and whites—every night. But they are the dancers who never got out from under the rag.

THE BLACK CIRCUIT

One hope of getting out was to get into a theater. This usually meant a road show. Multiple companies of *In Old Kentucky* were still making the rounds with pickaninny bands and buck dance contests. (The favorite tune for contestants, a Baltimore regular recalled, was "Turkey in the Straw.") Around the turn of the century, if you wanted the gold medal, you had to get around Harry Swinton, who had a minuscule role in the play but a large reputation among black dancers. Eubie Blake joined the pickaninny band as a teenager and later painted Swinton in memory: "He came out in roustabout clothes with a paper cone full of sand and he did more dancing just spreading the sand than other dancers could do with their whole act."

Black Patti's Troubadours rolled on as well, with their eponymous opera singer and their own buck dance contest. Ida Forsyne, a dark and tiny dancer out of Chicago, joined the Troubadours at fifteen, doing her buck and pushing a baby carriage as she sang, "You're Just a Little Nigger but You're Mine All Mine." In 1905, she went abroad, securing fame as a Topsy in England and outdoing the Russians at Russian squat-kicks in St. Petersburg. Muriel Ringgold, from Alabama, joined the Troubadours at twelve as the "greatest child buck dancer." (Sometimes she was the "Honolulu Pickaninny Buck Dancer," playing to the Hawaiian vogue that followed American annexation of the archipelago in 1898.) In the Ernest Hogan shows *Rufus Rastus* and *The Oyster Man*, Ringgold's roles remained Topsy-like. She grew into a comedienne in oversized shoes, frequently dressed as a man, and danced and clowned into her fifties. She could "dance like a man," Forsyne would recall approvingly.

A positive review of the Troubadours might look like this one from a Dallas paper in 1910: "Don't look disgusted, they're pretty good stuff, these coon shows." In fact, the review continued, "a nigger that is willing to come right out and be pure nigger, to avail himself of the delicious peculiarities of his race, can be quite the funniest thing going, and the one who pompously apes the mannerisms of his brother in white can be just a tiny bit funnier." The music was fantastic, sounds "approached by no human," and the dancing, well—"From pickaninny days the buck-wing has been his own private possession, and the Negro comedian is in his element when his feet are describing eccentric circles." Supremacy in the buck and wing was conceded to blacks. It was their element, like the Jim Crow car, the sideshow annex, the balcony from which colored people could watch the Troubadours. And to profit from this possession, this peculiarity, this heritage, was to "come right out and be pure nigger."

Starting back in the 1890s, the musical comedies of Cole and Johnson and Williams and Walker had broken into the "legitimate sphere" of theaters. They had shown white audiences, as the *Freeman* phrased it, that black entertainers could do something "besides shouting coon songs and buck and wing dancing." But the early deaths of Cole, Walker, and Ernest Hogan, in a demoralizing cluster around 1910, appeared to derail that train. At the same time came a boom in the construction of black theaters—venues, many owned by blacks, that presented black performers to black patrons and were first organized into a circuit in 1912. This meant performers could set up a string of engagements with a single contract and organize transportation more efficiently, a real concern considering that throughout much of the country Negroes were not welcome at the local restaurant or hotel and had to rely on boarding-houses and the kindness of black strangers. Performers at these new theaters didn't have to worry as much about what might offend or please whites. If Keith-Albee was the big time, this was "colored time."

It was in a black theater in Jacksonville that "Ginger" Jack Wiggins burst onto the scene. The year was 1910, and soon he was in Memphis, boasting in the *Freeman* of never having lost a contest. Initially, he traveled with his brother, Henry, but Jack was the true "tanglefoot artist." Their act "All Black Stars Shine at Night" was hailed not only as the "danciest" but also the "swellest dressed." Even in grainy newspaper photos, Ginger Jack looks sharp. He made four "shining" wardrobe changes in ten minutes (aided, it was said, by his little dog). Through the teens, he toured black theaters with stock companies, acquiring and shedding partners male and female. The *Freeman* praised him as "a good self-impersonator" but also for originality in "twisting and turning"; among dancers he would be remembered for his Bantam Twist and Tango Twist, tap steps that leaned and reversed. His "Pull It" ended elegantly, with his back arched and one leg curling behind, but it also involved yanking an invisible object toward his pelvis. Wiggins introduced the move by announcing, "I'm going to do it!" (One version of this step wound up in the Shim Sham under the name Tack Annie—the nickname of one of Wiggins's girlfriends, a big, tough bouncer.)

Over the same circuits, the Whitman Sisters ran their own show, the most successful around. They wrote the sketches, composed the music, secured the bookings. Whenever they spotted a promising kid, they would ask his or her parents for permission to take on the child as part of their extended family, and in this way, a great many tap dancers— including some of the best—were reared. One reason that parents trusted the Whitman Sisters was the group's reputation. Their father, the Reverend Albery Allson Whitman, was born a Kentucky slave around 1851, but after the war, he studied at Wilberforce University and eventually published seven volumes of epic poetry. His daughters—Mabel, Essie, and Alberta—were born in the 1880s. Reverend Whitman made sure they had music lessons, and he taught them the double shuffle, Essie remembered, "for exercise." Soon the girls were accompanying him as jubilee singers whose camp meetings included minstrel songs and humor. By 1899, they were the Whitman Sisters Comedy Company, bolstered by a band of buck-dancing kids. In a photo from that year, Mabel and Essie are Southern belles cradling banjos, the ruffles of their hoop skirts cascading like fountains of white lace. The skin that shows isn't much darker.

After the Reverend died, in 1901, Mabel took over. When the troupe played Birmingham in 1904, the *Freeman* noted two facts indicative of

Mabel's mettle: first that she was the only colored woman managing her own company, second that it was the first time in the history of Birmingham that colored people had been allowed seats in the dress circle and parquet. In 1911, the Sisters split, and it was under the name Bert Whitman that Alberta developed her strutting skills as a male impersonator. One of the kids with Mabel was a ten-year-old named Aaron Palmer, whom the press followed Mabel's lead in dubbing the next George Walker. One of Alberta's Three Sunbeams was the fourth Whitman Sister, a "rompish" adopted girl named Alice whom the *Freeman* rated the best girl buck dancer. By 1914, the Whitmans were reunited and about to begin two decades as perennial box-office favorites, two decades of notices in the black press judging theirs the greatest of companies. By 1919, Alice and Aaron had a child of their own. His name was Albert, though everyone called him Pops. He wasn't four years old before he was stopping the show.

BLACKS IN WHITE VAUDEVILLE

On a Friday afternoon in 1912, an audience of record-breaking size gathered in a Philadelphia theater to witness a contest between Ginger Jack Wiggins and King Rastus Brown. Brown was the favorite, monarch of the East. It was announced in the *Freeman* that he had canceled engagements in order to stop the crowing of this upstart from the South. He went first, wearing a triumphant smile for all six minutes. In the end, though, it was Wiggins's name the Philadelphia public screamed as the winner of the world championship and fifty bucks.

King Rastus did not relinquish his sovereign title, but then he and Wiggins moved mostly in different circles, geographically and otherwise. Though Brown was brown-skinned, he danced in white vaudeville, billed as the Chocolate Drop or the Lively Coon. "The white people all say he is a wonder," reported the *Freeman* in 1909. Yet it was among black dancers that Rastus would be remembered. Questioned in the 1960s, they described a thin man who wore a derby, smoked long cigars, and loved his liquor. His endurance was as legendary as his imaginative fecundity: he could keep up his buck dancing for hours without repeating a step. Willie Glenn, half of a blacks-in-blackface team that toured the Keith–Albee circuit, recalled: "He could imitate anything, whatever the audience called for: a train, a drunk, different nationalities— Irish, Dutch, Jewish, Scottish. Then he'd say 'Now I'll go for myself' and top them all."

Since the days of Juba, blacks in otherwise white productions had become much more common. "The stage is the only profession open to the negro in which he has equal opportunity with the whites," asserted the *Kansas City Star* in 1901. Vaudeville might just have been the most integrated profession in America, though it was usually assumed that one black act on any white bill was enough. The pay, while generally below the rates offered white acts, far surpassed the going wages in almost any other profession open to blacks; the highest-paid black acts pulled down figures that most white Americans could only dream of.

Probably the greatest number of blacks entered white vaudeville as children. A female singer, usually white, would surround herself with a few black kids, usually boys, who would sing and dance and unfailingly please the audience with their adorableness. In showbiz lingo, these were pickaninnies or "picks," and they were "insurance." They never flopped. Whether dressed as street urchins or done up in opera hats and tuxedo jackets, they were an advertised part of the show: Mayme Remington and Her Picks, Mattie Phillips and Her Jungle Kids, Naomi Thompson's Brazilian Nuts. The picks normally put together their own numbers, and they didn't earn much, but the job beat being an assistant in a medicine show.

Around 1908, ten-year-old Willie Covan, along with five other kids, hooked up with the singer Cosie Smith and headed for California, dreaming of orange groves. In Roundup, Montana, they performed for a theaterful of cowboys. "They had never seen coloreds before," Covan remembered. "The cowboys didn't care nothing about no prejudice. They loved the dancin'." Afterward, a young fan took them to a saloon outside of town. "We tap danced like crazy. And they started throwin' money. We danced and we danced, and we picked up that money and stuffed it into our pockets." Then, along with the coins, came bullets. "They shot into the ground, and laughed, so we laughed too and danced like they told us to." Outside later, the boys discovered that the coins were gold. Roundup was a mining town. In one evening, Willie and his friends had made eleven hundred dollars, probably more than their parents could make in a year.

Covan was born in Atlanta, but by the time he was six his family had moved to Chicago, joining the tens of thousands of blacks migrating north during these years, seeking opportunity and fleeing Jim Crow. A city boy, he would claim he had learned to dance by listening to the rhythm of streetcars. The only lessons he would admit to were informal tutorials by Ida Forsyne's son, who had only one good leg and was known as Friendless George. In 1915, Willie was seventeen and ready to be recognized. When *In Old Kentucky* came to Chicago, he signed up for the dance contest, which drew the best from as far as Cleveland and Detroit. As was now traditional, judges were stationed on the stage and underneath it; a banjo player plunked stop-time through each contestant's allotted minute. Covan got lucky, drawing number eight, which gave him an opportunity to survey the competition ahead of him. He realized two things: everyone started with a time step, and a time step wasted time. When his turn came, he jumped right in with his fanciest stuff. He won the hundred-dollar prize, and his friends carried him home on their shoulders. "Everybody knew I was the greatest dancer in Chicago!"

Among those fancy steps were wings, a class of moves that in their simplest form work like this: Perched on one leg, the dancer jumps up, but as he takes off, he scrapes the outer edge of his jumping shoe, sending that leg off to the side as his body continues upward; while still airborne, he pulls the leg in and strikes the ground one more time before landing. That's three sounds in total: scrape, tap, land. The whole thing usually lasts a second or less, and calibrating the force of the jump requires musical timing. Many other fancy steps were "flash" steps— rhythmic but not necessarily rhythm-producing. Flash steps, more acrobatic, were helpful for a big finish or for whenever the band drowned out taps. What's special about a wing is that it's a cross between a flash step and a tap step. It's a jump that makes noise. The initial scrape adds another sound to the tap dancer's palette, longer than a tap, raspy or whooshing. Wings can be done with both feet—synchronized as three sounds or separated into six—or in alternation, with the wing launching off one leg and landing on the other. The leg that isn't winging is free to swing or kick or strike the floor from multiple directions. Visually exciting variations emerged: the Pump, the Pendulum, the Saw, the Fly. And the winging leg itself could pack in more sounds between scrape and landing. Once there was a three-tap wing, four- and five-tap wings weren't far behind.

Covan developed other tricks. A highlight of his act with his brother Dewey was Willie's execution of the Double Around the World, a step he had probably adapted from Russian dancers then prevalent on vaudeville stages. To pull off an Around the World, a squatting dancer swings one leg in a circle parallel to the floor, periodically shifting his weight to his hands and raising his squatting leg to let the circling one pass underneath; if the dancer starts alternating legs, he's doing the Double. During a matinee in 1917, the floor was slick, and the band kept accelerating. After they got offstage, Dewey turned to his brother and said, "You were doing it with no hands." Willie did not believe him. Nevertheless, the next time they performed, Willie concentrated hard and did it again. And the next time that the brothers were on Thirty-first Street and State, the corner where black dancers in Chicago gathered to challenge one another, Dewey started bragging. Bets flew down. Willie was wearing a brand-new, sixty-five-dollar suit, and as he changed the impossible to the possible, he cut his pants at the knee. "It was worth it," he remembered, even though he won only twenty bucks.

Covan would never forget how, around this time, he was given a pair of wooden shoes by the dancer he considered the best, King Rastus Brown. King Rastus didn't cut his pants doing flash steps, and he wasn't much of a comedian, either. Through the twenties, when King Rastus and Jack Wiggins could be seen only on the black circuits, Covan rose on the white ones. Yet he felt restricted, too. As an old man, he would tell about how he and his partner had stopped the show at the Palace in the early twenties, and got fired for being too good, and then moved to the Hippodrome, only to have the same thing happen, because the only spot for an act as good as his was second-to-closing and that spot was never ceded to a colored act. The story is partially verifiable in newspaper records, but the reasoning is still a bit off. It *was* possible for a colored act to play next-to-closing. If Covan wanted a role model for how a black tap dancer could be a headliner on the white circuit, one was readily at hand.

THE DARK CLOUD OF JOY

Bill "Bojangles" Robinson was born in Richmond, Virginia, in 1878. By the time he was seven, both of his parents had died. He and his younger brother moved in with their grandmother, who told them stories from her life as a slave. Robinson brought in money by shining shoes, and he danced in the street for pennies, often in front of the theater where George Primrose's minstrel shows played. Robinson would later tell white reporters that Primrose had inspired him to become a dancer.

The dancing didn't go over well with Robinson's Baptist grandmother. She also disapproved of the boy's petty thievery. He learned fast that he could dance and charm his way out of punishment, and it is remarkable, even considering his poverty, how many early Robinson stories involve theft. One of many accounts of the origin of his nickname (which might also be a Southern word for troublemaker or for "happy-go-lucky") traces it to a child's mispronunciation of Mr. Boujasson, owner of a Richmond haberdashery from which the young Robinson stole a hat. As for his given name, Luther, Robinson resented how other kids ridiculed him about it, so he beat up his younger brother, Bill, and took that name for himself. He forced his brother to go by Percy. All the misbehavior may have been too much for their grandmother, since she went to court to have the boys taken out of her custody. For a while, they lived with the presiding judge, but Robinson had other ideas. He had met a white boy named Lemuel Toney, who, dreaming of minstrel glory, had worked up a blackface act and needed a pickaninny. The interracial pair hopped a freight train and lit out for the nation's capital.

Toney, discovered by George Primrose, took the stage name Eddie Leonard and was on his way to becoming one of the last stars of minstrelsy. He helped Robinson get work as a pick in *The South Before the War*. It was at this time, according to his fellow performer Tom Fletcher, that Robinson began to notice how each of the top dancers had a style.

He started to do impressions, and out of those impressions he began to forge his own dance. Robinson traveled with the show and similar ones for a long time, not taking any of it as seriously as his poolroom activities. In after years, he would show reporters knife and razor scars from the period. During the Spanish-American War, he said, he served as a drummer in a colored regiment and was shot in the knee in a dance hall in North Carolina. The gunman was his unit's second lieutenant. "I think he was cleaning his gun," Robinson later told *The New Yorker's* St. Clair McKelway. When Robinson showed McKelway the scar from the bullet and the lack of a corresponding exit wound, McKelway came to a simple conclusion: "The bullet must be somewhere inside."

Robinson became a regular in the New York sporting clubs where black entertainers congregated. He was known for his comical singing— that is, until *In Old Kentucky* came to town and he won the buck-and-wing contest. His big break came when he was offered a job with Cooper and Bailey, a black vaudevillian duo. Cooper considered Bailey an unreliable drunk, so he hired Robinson as a replacement. In a derby and a tutu, Robinson played the fool to Cooper's straight man, and he did not dance much at first. He imitated a mosquito by blowing air through his lips, and he and Cooper amused audiences with their comic arguments and dialect numbers such as "Oiy Oiy Yoi." Since Cooper and Bailey had been advertised, not Cooper and Robinson, Robinson didn't perform under his own name for the first six months. He was working, though, and in the big time.

That's where he stayed, for more than a decade, honing his skills in show after show, town after town. When he and Cooper rolled into Denver in 1912, the *Tribune* found them the best thing on the bill:

> The men, who are honest to goodness Ethiopians, not burnt cork "make-believers," have that provoking flavor of real down Southern "darky" about them, which with homemade maple syrup is fast becoming a thing of the past. Cheap imitations have spoiled both. Both Cooper and Robinson are the genuine article and their chuckling guffaws, pigeon wing steps and cachinnating songs are a real vaudeville entertainment.

That same year, the *Freeman* cited the Cooper-Robinson act as a model that all colored performers should follow: clean, clever, up-to-date. "The negro gets a fair deal in modern vaudeville," Cooper told the *Duluth News-Tribune*, citing vaudeville as the one business where blacks had an advantage: "My partner and I seem to be able to dance to ragtime and to sing ragtime in a way that few white dancers or singers can."

Onstage, Robinson was a consummate professional. Offstage, he would draw both his partner's pay and his own and use the money to gamble. One time, he took a pool cue to a policeman's head. That predicament he talked his way through, but Cooper had to bail him out of trouble too often. This may have been why the act split up, and reunited, and split up again, though one of Cooper's later partners cited another cause for the final breakup: Cooper's marriage to a white woman. During the following decade, Cooper played the black circuits exclusively.

Whatever the reason, Robinson was on his own. He found help in Marty Forkins, a brash Irish-American manager from Chicago. Forkins's wife, Rae Samuels, herself a successful vaudevillian, had seen something in Robinson: "Bo had that personality," she recalled. "He could take the toughest audience in the world and take them in his hand and put them in his hip pocket." Over the next years, Forkins and Robinson worked his solo act up the ladders of the Keith and Orpheum circuits. Before long, Bojangles was at the Palace in the number two spot. In lesser venues, he played next-to-closing, his act now an expansive eighteen minutes. Even when he wasn't the headliner, reviewers often treated him as if he were. In 1922, the *Los Angeles Daily Times* could write assuredly, "Everybody must know Bill Robinson by this time."

At the Grand in Chicago, he was billed as "The Black Daffydill: A Cloudy Spasm of Song, Dance and Fun." On most marquees, he was "The Dark Cloud of Joy." White critics habitually remarked on his flashing teeth and rolling eyes. They admired the "exceptional artistry" of his dancing, his perfect rhythm, but they also loved his imitation of a man on a pogo stick. The magazine *The Dance* described him as "the most efficient buck dancing machine on stage," yet also took care to emphasize "that rare spirit of care-free abandon and sky-larking zest for which his race is noted."

Louis Armstrong noted something else. In 1922, just after the young trumpeter moved from New Orleans to Chicago and just before he almost single-handedly transformed jazz into a soloist's art, Armstrong caught Robinson's act. What struck him first was how the dancer was dressed: "That man was so sharp he was bleeding." In his dressing room, Robinson kept his suits spaced one inch apart, with matching shoes underneath. His favorite indoor sport, his wife once reported, was brushing his clothes with a whisk broom. For each performance, he changed outfits, and he always kept a towel in the wings so the audience wouldn't see him sweat. During the appearance Armstrong attended, Robinson had to wait long minutes for the applause to die down after his entrance—applause for being Bill Robinson. Then the dancer looked up at the lighting booth and said, "Give me a light, *my* color," and all the lights went out. The audience exploded in laughter, the kid from New Orleans loudest of all: "I hadn't heard anything like that before." The young trumpeter shared the crowd's joy in Robinson's jokes and mosquito imitations. "Every move," Armstrong remembered, "was a beautiful picture." Robinson was as dark-skinned as he was, and that meant something. So did the phrase Armstrong later chose to express what he was thinking as he watched Robinson that day in 1922: "Wow, what an artist."

There was more to Robinson's act than carefree abandon. A key part of it originated back in 1918, when Robinson saw some friends in the audience at the Palace and danced down the stairs to greet them. Thus was his stair dance born, or so he said sometimes. Other times, he said it came to him while he was dreaming of a different palace, in England. In that dream, he stood at the bottom of a staircase, waiting to be knighted. "I didn't like the idea of just walking up," he recalled, "so I thought I'd dance up. I danced up the stairs to the throne, got my badge, and danced right down again." He said that his best steps always came to him in dreams. These stories are probably apocryphal, which isn't to say that they hold no truth. Professional black and white dancers had been clogging on stairs since at least the 1880s. King Rastus Brown claimed that Robinson stole the idea from him, though Brown almost certainly stole it from somebody else. Notwithstanding such antecedents, Robinson was viciously possessive. There's many a tale about what he did to those who dared use stairs: stop the act mid-performance, slap the offender, pull out a pistol. Once, when the dancer Eddie Rector replaced him in a show, Robinson sent him a cablegram warning him not to do the stair dance, on penalty of death. His effort to protect his claim was largely futile. When he attempted to secure a patent on the stair routine, the U.S. Patent Office denied the application.

In the early years, he danced up and down stage stairs. Soon, he had a portable staircase built. The stairs were central to his act, his vaudeville gimmick, but they must have been important to him for another reason. They magnified the essential strengths of his dancing. The staircase was symmetrical. It was two staircases joined back to back, a terraced pyramid, five steps up, five steps down. Each step was just large enough to accommodate Robinson's two feet, and the connected top steps served as a platform. The entire staircase rose to the height of Robinson's ribs, and a triangle of empty space underneath it made for a resonant drum. Upon these steps, Robinson could portion out his own. These were mostly time steps, three-and-a-break steps, and what the stairs did for Robinson was reveal how he played with the structure of the music through how he played with the structure of the staircase.

He would become known for bringing tap "up on the toes." In contrast to the flat-footed style of dancers such as King Rastus Brown, Robinson carried his weight over the balls of his feet and drew his carriage up from there in an erect line. It's as if he were trying to balance a glass of water on his head, as if he had been studying *Clog Dancing Made Easy*. His arms swung more freely than a clogger's, but for the most part, he kept his feet neatly underneath him, which is why his dancing fit so well on the stairs. The small space emphasized the extraordinary efficiency of his movements, his impeccable control. The height gave his floor-bound dance a vertical dimension, amplifying his rhythmic wit. The staircase was an extension of his instinct to dramatize. It used the eye to direct the ear. From the back of a theater, you could perceive that it was an instrument, each stair of which rang a slightly different note. The tonal distinctions were subtle, but then, Robinson was a subtle dancer.

The Aiston Shoe Company in Chicago made his clogs special order, twenty to thirty pairs a year. If one sole split, he discarded the pair—using shoes with different levels of wear would have compromised the perfect

balance of his sound. He liked to challenge people to go beneath the
stage and try to distinguish his right from his left—an easy task with
many dancers, impossible with him. Robinson wore out shoes by dancing often, not by dancing hard. Wood met wood, two equals. It was a
warm sound, precise but with a soft center. His taps were even, measured.
"Indescribably liquid," wrote the critic Robert Benchley, "like a brook
flowing over pebbles." The *Chicago Daily News* compared them not just
with "the steady beat of a racehorse's feet," but with quail's wings; not
with firecrackers, but with "firecrackers heard in the distance." Audiences leaned in to listen.

To imagine Robinson's stair dance, first hear a song such as "Old
Folks at Home," Swanee River played in ragtime. He starts on the
ground with a time step, marking accents with sharp nudges to the face
of the bottom stair. Adjusting the angle of his bowler, he hops up a
couple levels and back. Then he repeats the rhythm by swinging his
right leg up and skipping it down, turning the stairs into a tilted xylo-
phone. His leg's momentum spins him around, and he hits an upbeat
en route before finishing out the phrase facing his instrument. The next
measure he splits between tapping on the floor and patting the stairs with
his foot. His knuckles handle the repeat. Then he's up and down the stairs,
half a phrase on one step, the remainder on its neighbor. The complexity
of the rhythms builds, then subsides, and builds again; the brook flows
over more pebbles, or fewer, but it does not cease flowing. All along,
Robinson's arms swing loosely, now drooping for a droll show of relaxation, now pushing out small circles as if to say, *That's nothing.* Sometimes he concentrates on one stair and sneaks in a tap on the stair below
it, or he slips a tap between stairs as he ascends. He scales the stairs backward with just as much ease. For a while, he uses the top platform to
showcase quick rolls and drum-tight wings. He keeps packing in more
stairs per bar, subdividing the beat with stairs. By the end, he's running
up and down the stairs. That's all he's doing: running up and down the
stairs. But it's music and it's magic and he knows it as he struts off the
stage.

The dance thrills, but not with acrobatics or speed or even inspired
rhythms. For much of the number, Robinson's rhythms are metronomic.
He can be plain. But you can trust him. You can relax. The stairs are a

stunt that conceals its daring. As generations of imitators would learn to their grief, the properties of the staircase that magnified Robinson's mastery equally magnify the slightest imperfection. Robinson's timing, his metronome sense, was legendary. Dancers tell a story in which he had his musicians cut out for three and a half minutes while he continued dancing. After the allotted time, the musicians came back in, cued by a metronome that Robinson couldn't hear. He was exactly on beat.

It was another sense of Robinson's timing, though, that would prove most consequential. Unlike, say, King Rastus Brown's stair routine, Robinson's signature number was filmed, most fully and simply in the 1932 all-black short *Harlem Is Heaven*. (That's the source of my description.) Bill Robinson came in at the right time. Or perhaps it would be more accurate to say that when the right time came, he was still there, on beat and in step.

7

THE PRACTICAL ART OF
STAGE DANCING

Yankee Doodle Dandy danced the buck and wing. His father was a minstrel clogger who shed blackface for Irish-themed variety, a song-and-dance man who recruited his wife, daughter, and son into a family vaudeville act. They were the Four Cohans, and the son—George M.—was born on the Third of July. He was twelve in 1890, when buck-and-wing was red-hot, and he set out to master every step he could. Brassy, self-assured, he introduced his Lively Bootblack act as "his own conception" of buck dancing, stressing difficult steps of his own invention. But vaudeville audiences weren't so interested. So instead of clogging in place, Cohan snapped his head back and ran up a wall. Or he started out lazy and let the music send him into a frenzy. His secret was his enthusiasm, energy unbound. That and a few trick steps, he soon realized, triggered a larger ovation than any carefully rehearsed routine. One term for this kind of act was "endurance dancer." ("I danced and danced for applause until I got a hand.") As Cohan would explain to the readers of *The Saturday Evening Post*, in an article titled "The Practical Side of Dancing," "The only way to make a hit with the public was to do something eccentric, something outside of the true art of dancing."

In billing and salary, he understood, masters of the true art rarely got very far. Cohan's own father, to pick the most searing example, wrote plays but was forever pigeonholed as a "song-and-dance man." The variety axiom "Once a dancer, always a dancer" had two sides. When George wrote his first nonmusical play and audiences literally cried out "Give us a dance," it was as much a compliment to the appeal of his footwork as it was a criticism of his fledgling skills as a playwright. All the same, it was an enforcement of status boundaries. "The mere learning to dance on the stage is no detriment," Cohan wrote. "It's the making of a reputation as a dancer that retards a man's progress." He was determined to break free.

That he did, escaping into—and helping to create—American musical comedy. Cohan showed 'em, becoming a song-and-dance man who owned a theater on Broadway named after himself. The populist, flag-waving plots of his shows were fables of underdog triumph in the American vernacular. A few of his songs would prove immortal— "Give My Regards to Broadway," "Yankee Doodle Dandy"—but Cohan knocked out his compositions in bulk. Many were coon songs, their rhyming patter bouncing along on the ragtime rhythm of dance steps. Though he had made his reputation as more than a dancer, his cocksure walk and the way he wore his hat over one eye were as central to his persona as the slang he delivered through one side of his mouth. His was an Irish style, an urban American one, part George Primrose, part George Walker. His shows had drive, and they were driven by dance. Even when, as a director, he adapted someone else's work, the ingredient he invariably added was more dancing. The phrase one critic applied to Cohan's 1922 production of *Little Nelly Kelly* might stand for all his productions: "a general dancing rough-house."

It was partly due to Cohan that American musical comedy danced. But his was also a dance-mad age, as the animal dances of vice districts stampeded across the country and up and down the social scale. There was a craze for the Turkey Trot and the Grizzly Bear. Irving Berlin's "Alexander's Ragtime Band," a ballyhoo in black slang, was the hit of 1911. The title of another song Berlin wrote that year was self-fulfilling prophecy: "Everybody's Doing It Now." "Syncopation is the soul of every American," he told *Theatre Magazine*. This was a creed that, as a Jewish immigrant whose family had fled Russian pogroms, he had learned from a Negro ragtime pianist in New York's Chinatown at a dive called Nigger Mike's. (Mike was also a Russian Jew.) The syncopations of James Reese Europe's black dance band propelled the foxtrot of Vernon and Irene Castle, a clean-cut white couple who made ragtime dancing respectable. (For *Dancing Times*, Irene explained how she and her husband took "nigger dances" and toned them down for the drawing room.) Their casual chic gave the middle classes access to upper-class taste and permission to enjoy American music from below. The main channels through which dance songs were introduced to the general public were vaudeville and Broadway shows—for example, the Castles performing Berlin's "The Syncopated Walk" in the 1914 revue *Watch Your Step*. A new dance that audience members might try was practically a requirement for a successful production.

While a tap step or two might enter the repertoire of average folk, tap—at least in white culture—was more theatrical than social. It could, however, be done in a group. When a vaudevillian like Frank Young—who informed the newspapers that he had learned his first buck steps from the Negroes of Evansville, Indiana, and that he had thereafter acquired finesse from a European dancing master—needed some extra cash, he could get a job in one of the many schools that taught chorines, en masse.

CHORUS LINE

There were chorus girls in musical comedies and chorus girls in vaudeville, but nowhere were they more essential than in the revue. The revue began as a review, a collection of topical songs and sketches lightly parodying the preceding theatrical season. The French spelling came courtesy of the impresario and publicity mastermind Florenz Ziegfeld, who modeled his revues after the Folies Bergères of Paris. From 1907 through the 1930s, Ziegfeld's Follies set the standard for spare-no-expense in costumes and scenic effects. Money, properly applied, could also buy the most talented star performers (including the top black star, Bert Williams). But "Glorifying the American Girl" was Ziegfeld's aim before it became his motto, and beautiful young women, dangled as a not-quite-attainable ideal, were the Follies' main attraction. Ziegfeld chose the girls himself, and only after an aspirant's beauty was established did she present her singing and dancing talents for inspection. These were usually limited, and the dancing in the first editions, staged by the partially deaf Julian Mitchell, was more fashion show than choreography: fifty girls personifying taxicabs in headlamp brassieres.

The staging of musical comedies wasn't all that different. In an article of 1913, Ned Wayburn—that Inventor of Ragtime and creator of the Minstrel Misses—characterized musical comedy staging as a search for "effects": turning chorus girls into table lamps, raising the curtain just enough to reveal pretty ankles and dancing feet. Wayburn spoke from authority. He regularly arranged five or six shows at a time. He amassed an ever-expanding directory of thousands of chorus girls, complete with names, addresses, and measurements, divided into the going categories of statuesque showgirls, in-betweens, delicate types, and dancers. He wrote articles about how the ample chorus girls of yore had been replaced by thinner girls, more lithe and livelier—in the lingo of the era, they had to have "ginger." Son of a Pittsburgh machinery manufacturer, Wayburn carried himself like a Captain of Industry, portly, self-serious, never without his pince-nez. He directed with a dog whistle and a megaphone. Through the thirties, he ran the biggest chorus-girl factory in America.

In 1915, Wayburn took over the staging of the Follies and introduced the swivel-and-pause Ziegfeld Walk so that the showgirls could negotiate steep staircases in style. When the critic Edmund Wilson, writing about the Follies in 1923, lamented a resemblance to military drills and goose-stepping, he was talking about the Walk, but also about "precision dancing," a tradition that stemmed from England and the turn-of-the-century efforts of the Manchester textile manufacturer John Tiller. Finding chorus dancing too untidy, Tiller applied industrial discipline to the training of his own Tiller Girls. (Rescuing the girls from poverty and its temptations, he argued, was a noble side benefit.) Their routines were, in fact, drills. The girls practiced them endlessly to achieve a perfect unison. Linking their arms around one another's waists, they formed a unit, a line that kicked and kicked and revolved and kicked some more. During the twenties, multiple squads of Tiller Girls and their many imitators overran Europe, an invasion of Girls between the wars. European intellectuals analyzed them as symbols of mass production in the Machine Age, the body broken down into component parts, the individual subsumed into the collective. To Siegfried Kracauer, their speedy step dancing made the sound "business, business." In his eyes, the Girls were an American product, but the Follies and other American shows first imported them from England.

Even Edmund Wilson considered the choral maneuvers of the Tiller Girls to be characteristically American—"what the American male really regards as beautiful: the efficiency of mechanical movement." But characteristic American chorus dancing was actually a bit different. Ned Wayburn gave his account in a mid-twenties instruction manual titled *The Art of Stage Dancing.* Essentially a book-length ad for his school, the manual explained "the kind of dancing that one can commercialize." On top of a foundation of limbering stretches, Wayburn taught Musical Comedy, Acrobatic, Exhibition Ballroom, and Modern Americanized Ballet. (The last promised to collapse tedious years of training into a few months.) The fifth category was Tap and Step, which included buck dance, soft shoe, waltz clog, and "straight (or English) clog." The term *tap dancing,* sporadic through the teens, was catching on. Tap and Step, Wayburn wrote, was in the tradition of George Primrose. It was dancing that "expresses American syncopated rhythms." His book explains how to build a time step and a break, the basic time step that would rule Broadway from then on. (Eddie Russell's 1924 manual *The Art of Buck and Wing Dance Simplified* outlines the same version, suggesting that a dancer hum eight bars of "Turkey in the Straw.") Surprisingly, Wayburn also stressed the distinct sound produced by each way of striking the floor, an attention to tone that was likely to be lost in the thunder of massed chorines.

For shoes, Wayburn recommended ankle-strap Mary Janes or laced Oxfords. Only very advanced pupils needed to consider clogs or split soles. Most professionals, Wayburn added, preferred the "Haney metal plates," which appear to have been a recent development. Dancers in search of a louder, brighter sound had been hammering nails into their soles since way back, but the mid-twenties was when the concept spawned a mass-marketed product. One story puts the plates on the shoes used in *No, No, Nanette* in 1925, but if so, the metal passed beneath the notice of reviewers. The earliest patent seems to be the one issued to William John Haney of Indiana in 1927, quickly followed by James Selva and Salvatore Capezio, men whose main business had been making ballet shoes. (Later ads for Selva taps pointed back to 1925 as the beginning of the line.)

Wayburn described tap numbers as "bread and butter dances, something you can sell most easily in the present show market." Yet the core of his teaching was Musical Comedy dancing, the most eclectic category of all, "a cross between the ballet and the Ned Wayburn type of tap and step." This mix might include handstands, cartwheels, splits, or high kicks, but Wayburn drew a firm distinction between straight acrobatics and acrobatic dancing. Doing one trick after another was for the circus; dancing spiced with tricks was the more lucrative stuff of musical comedies and revues. Largely interchangeable, the routines Wayburn taught were constructed to fit any thirty-two-bar song, the standard template on Tin Pan Alley. One step brought the dancers onstage, another took them off, and those in between were built to goad applause.

To a writer in *The New York Times* in 1925, a chorus with some ballet training was the mark of the new. Technical standards were rising, and chorus girls were working harder than ever. As the decade progressed, dance directors piled on references to modernity in crankshaft dances and skyscraper routines. They arranged people like pistons and made metal strike metal. Fad dances came and went. Tap persisted.

Simply executing the routines wasn't quite enough. "You must throw your personality into it," Wayburn advised. More important than the step was the manner in which the step was sold. It could be a smile, an attitude, or something more intangible such as "atmosphere." Personality, idiosyncrasy heightened into style—this made the difference between a dancer in the line and a soloist, between a chorus girl and a star. (Wayburn's instruction was directed almost exclusively toward young women; the book's references to "boys" are few and perfunctory; his school offered males only private lessons.) Wayburn and Ziegfeld always said that they were on the lookout for a girl who, often unconsciously, phrased or accentuated in some slightly different and pleasing fashion. As much as the story of the chorus girl who becomes the leading lady was a fantasy, it did actually happen. The dancing stars of the Follies had that extra something. Ann Pennington made the most of her four-foot-ten-inch frame and dimpled knees. Her every move was devil-may-care: tossing her curls, shaking her hips. In Wayburn's book, he brags about his former student as one of the "leading exponents of 'Tap and Step Dancing,'" but the tap Pennington does in films of the late twenties is minimal and messy, a side effect of her pep.

Marilyn Miller, another Wayburn pupil, was Ziegfeld's biggest success. She was four when she joined her stepfather's vaudeville act, and her performing never lost a childlike exuberance. Framed by blond ringlets, her darling smile and sunshiny eyes captured the hearts of a generation of theatergoers. In 1918, when she joined the Follies, she was twenty. Two years later, she shot to fame in the Ziegfeld-produced Jerome Kern musical *Sally*. It was a Cinderella story, the era's favorite plot, tracking the rise of an orphan who makes it into—where else?—the Follies. By the time of Miller's next show, *Sunny*, she was the highest-paid performer on Broadway, the ingenue queen of musical comedy in the twenties.

At the end of that decade, when sound films came in, Hollywood hired Miller to reproduce those landmark performances, and so, acknowledging the time lag and the change of medium, we can still catch a glimpse of what the fuss was about. Miller's joy shines through, though not quite with movie-star projection. "Come on, let's have some fun," she says before her tap number in *Sunny* (1930). Flat-footed, in pants, she starts at an easy tempo, knocking out stop-and-start rhythms before building to turns and leg-crossing ballet jumps. In "All I Want to Do, Do, Do Is Dance," a tap number added to the film of *Sally* (1929), Miller wears a skirt, but there's still a disjuncture between the feminine styling of her upper body and the drags, swivels, and heavy breaks of her lower half. The fun she's having is that of a girl playing at boys' games with no intention of being mistaken for a man. Her technique may be beginner-intermediate and sometimes wobbly, yet her smile never dims. When Miller tied on her ballet shoes, critics of her own time found her "poetical," but her sloppy, superficial ballet technique holds up less well on film. A musical theater star of the twenties could count on the trick of turning on her tiptoes to make an audience swoon. Sally's debut with the Follies, the culmination of the Cinderella plot, came in the form of a Butterfly Ballet. It had to. Ballet signified aristocratic refinement and fairy-tale endings. Tap was for horsing around.

ECCENTRICS

Horsing around is what the era's male musical comedy stars did. Leon Errol, a Follies regular and Marilyn Miller's co-star in the stage version of *Sally*, was a physical comedian, but his drunk act was a dance. He specialized in "rubberlegs," a term that explains itself, as does the similar label "legomania," both in the general category of "eccentric." The cartwheels, splits, and walkovers favored by women constituted a female parallel—Evelyn Law hopping across the stage with one foot nuzzling her ear. But "eccentric" was principally reserved for men, for funnymen. Most tapped.

A child of the prairie, Fred Stone grew up as a blackface breakdown dancer. With David Montgomery, he broke into musical comedy playing a buck-and-winging Moses and Aaron. In 1903, the pair found greater fame as the Tin Man and the Scarecrow in the original *Wizard of Oz*, where, in straw-stuffed clothing, Stone fashioned the archetypal eccentric dance character, ever on the verge of collapse. One critic noted the "perfect rhythm with which he does the anatomically impossible." Montgomery died in 1917, but Stone lasted as a Broadway draw through the twenties. When he made it into movies, it was as a nondancing character actor. (He's the bulb-nosed father of Katharine Hepburn in *Alice Adams*.) It was Stone who said that ragtime changed stage dancing, and it was his eccentric type that he meant. Ragtime syncopations expressed through African-derived isolations: that could make white America laugh.

Lauded as Stone's successor, Harland Dixon was a superior dancer. This was the same Harland Dixon who had tried to copy George Primrose's style and it came out funny. In the beginning, he was a wing dancer, stringing together eight different wing steps in sixty-four bars of music. One day, he put in what he considered a "rest step," slowly drawing in a leg. The step got a laugh and also a bigger hand than any of his exhausting wings. "From then on," Dixon later said, "I never did wings except in hotel lobbies when other dancers were around." Around 1912, Dixon gave up blackface, and he and his partner, Jimmy Doyle, moved from burlesque into vaudeville. They did challenge dances, imitation dances: Italian, Chinese, Russian, Negro. Dixon's Irish jig was a display of confrontational temperament, a style he admitted to having stolen from Jimmy Monahan, who jigged with a glass of beer on his head at Coney Island. Dixon was less concerned with coining steps than with using them to convey character; when he played a man in a dentist's office, he tapped out his trepidation all over the chair. This helped him and Doyle fit into musicals, and after the pair split in 1921, Dixon continued to move between vaudeville and Broadway. Critics adored him, but it wasn't until well after Dixon retired that he appeared in a movie, *Something to Sing About*, a 1937 film starring and produced by his buddy James Cagney; in a sailor number, he shows his knack for turning an ordinary tap routine into farce.

James Barton may have been an even greater comedy dancer. Born into an Irish-American theatrical family in 1890, he performed from age four, but he didn't make it onto Broadway until he was nearly thirty. In 1923, he carried *Dew Drop Inn* with some fourteen different routines, including burlesques of a dying swan and of a waltz danced earlier in the show. For the critic Alexander Woollcott, Barton could be compared only with Nijinsky and Chaplin. Heywood Broun hailed him as a genius, citing his ability to be "sublime and grotesque at the same time." Reviewers described Barton, like Master Juba, as dancing with his toes, his legs, his ribs. His role in *Dew Drop Inn* had been created for Bert Williams just before Williams died, and the reviewer's comment that Barton was "as negroid as Bert Williams used to be" was likely prompted not just by his blackface but by his pelvic freedom. Tap dancers—black and white— recognized Barton as a great in their field, and he called himself a drummer who danced best with a good jazz band. Nevertheless, as one tap master phrased it, Barton was "more fun to watch than to listen to." In 1933, he began a five-year run as a sharecropper in the play *Tobacco Road*. He played Hickey in *The Iceman Cometh* and memorable cowboys. When cast in a musical, he would break out his soft shoe, but few thought of him as a dancer anymore. Only the 1929 short *After Seben* preserves his early style. There, his wit is evident—anarchic, self-mocking—but it's hard now to see him as more than a white guy in blackface, shown up by the film's black dancers.

Jack Donahue—the Boston lad who became a dancer, not a fighter— was in the Barton-Dixon line. He and Dixon were good friends, and their third musketeer was Johnny Boyle. Modestly, Donahue wrote of Boyle as the "best all-round tap dancer," and Dixon agreed that Boyle was a great tap dancer—with zero personality. Boyle went into teaching. In a 1929 ad for the school he ran with Donahue, his photo looks like the mug shot of a man who could work for Capone. (He also appears in that 1937 Cagney film with Dixon, where he somehow manages to leave almost no impression while doing flips.) Donahue was different. Playing an orderly, he used a whisk broom to turn his sand dance into comedy. In *Sunny* and *Rosalie*, he played opposite Marilyn Miller, a pairing that indicated his rising professional stature. He was lauded for his "almost endless variety of steps" and for such tasty tapping that "the very orchestra stops to listen," yet by the time of *Rosalie*, in 1927, he was, in the words of Brooks Atkinson, "more clown than hoofer." He died in 1930 and made no films.

George White's early life followed a similar trajectory, except that he started out on New York's Lower East Side, as Isadore Weitz. After his bankrupt family decamped to Toronto, young Weitz discovered he could earn more by hoofing than by hawking newspapers. (He would recall "the sharp sting as the nickels and pennies hit your legs.") He ran away to New York and worked for such underworld characters as Steve Brodie. His first dance partner was a black boy. With a white boy, Benny Ryan, he broke into musicals and traded steps with Dixon and Donahue on Forty-second Street at midnight. In the Follies, he paired up with Ann Pennington, of the dimpled knees. Instead of becoming a comedian, however, White became a producer, at age twenty-six. His "Scandals," starting in 1918 and running annually through 1926, then more sporadically into the late thirties, gave the Follies its strongest competition in the revue business. White still danced—the *Times* called him "an adept stepper and a facile imitator of the steps of others;" he does a competent soft shoe in *George White's 1935 Scandals*, one of two films he directed. But mostly he hired dancers: Pennington and Dixon and Tom Patricola, a knock-kneed zany who tapped heavily while strumming a ukulele. Almost no white eccentrics of the twenties made it into the thirties as dancers. It was one of their own who changed the mold.

"He is one of those extraordinary persons whose sense of rhythm and humor have been all mixed up," wrote Alexander Woollcott in 1919 about one more eccentric: Fred Astaire. This one performed with his older sister, Adele, the obviously gifted child in the family. Born in Omaha, of Austrian and Alsatian parentage, they began as a child act on the vaudeville circuits of the teens, stepping up and down a wedding cake as bride and groom in one number and dancing as a lobster and a glass of champagne in another. For his solo, the boy managed buck-and-wing on toe-tip. They studied at New York dancing schools, including Ned Wayburn's factory, and Wayburn designed an act for them. (A 1907 profile of Wayburn mentions the Astaires as "wonderful little clog dancers from Omaha.") Later, a vaudevillian named Aurelio Coccia taught them "smart" dances in the mode of Vernon and Irene Castle. They passed their awkward years touring small-time theaters in the opening slot, trudging their way up the billing and into the big time. Fred labored ceaselessly to improve, scrutinizing other acts and beginning to choreograph. Adele couldn't be bothered. She got all the good notices.

Adele had a gamine charm, a refined outrageousness, ready-made for the twenties. After she and Fred appeared in their first Broadway revue, *Over the Top*, in 1917, she continued to receive most of the attention, from critics and college boys alike. But the critics also began to notice her gangly, big-eared, already balding brother, who was nimble and "ease-limbed." The siblings became known for a jokey bit called the Runaround, during which, shoulder to shoulder, deadpan, they accelerated in a circle to an oompah beat. Their dancing was brightening, bubbly—all the more so since it looked, in the words of a *Times* reviewer, "apparently impromptu." And they could handle the comedy part of musical comedy and take on speaking roles.

In London, critics greeted their dancing as a new American art. "Grotesque and eccentric dancing is familiar, but humor combined with vivacity and art and nimble daintiness is a novelty." Royalty and the smart set invited the Astaires into their social circle, putting a permanent crease in Fred's mid-Atlantic sense of style. Back in New York, the siblings were cast in *Lady, Be Good!*, with the first full score by Fred's buddy from vaudeville, George Gershwin. The tricky pattern of "Fascinating Rhythm," a song actually addressed to a maddeningly catchy cadence, required a rhythmically adept singer. Offstage, Astaire and Gershwin played stride piano together and traded tap steps. Woollcott was soon writing about the affinity between Gershwin's rhythms and Fred's feet. Others would soon note how Astaire's dancing visualized music and how audiences held their applause in order to listen. A year into the run of *Lady, Be Good!*, Fred got bored with his solo and inserted tap. It stopped the show, so he added more. Virtuosic tap was something Adele did not do.

While *Lady, Be Good!* was knocking 'em dead in London, Astaire made an audio recording. The time is April 1926. The number is " 'Half of It Dearie' Blues." The composer is at the keys. When Astaire goes into his dance, his rhythms are clear and thumpy. There's a little Shim Sham *avant la lettre* and sections that sound like a heavy-footed Bojangles, but Astaire is much less tidy than Robinson, much more apparently impromptu in sound. "How's that, George?" he asks, and Gershwin answers: "That's great, Freddie. Do it again." Now Astaire goes to town. When he almost misses an offbeat, he screams like a motorist swerving to avoid a collision, and when he pulls out the quick stuff he chortles. Gershwin's right. It's pretty great. And in 1926, especially in Britain, it must have sounded new.

8

IT'S GETTING DARK ON
OLD BROADWAY

Ziegfeld's weren't the only Follies. In 1913, a Follies opened in Harlem. As a result of overdevelopment, the area had recently been made available to black tenants, who could be charged higher rents. The long migration of New York's Darktown up Manhattan from the Five Points stopped and pooled, converging with a rising tide of blacks from the South and the Caribbean. The growing numbers of black tenants caused white tenants to flee, and so Harlem became Harlem, the great black metropolis. Neighborhood theaters—the Lincoln, then the Lafayette—acknowledged the demographic shift by opening their doors to black patrons and by booking productions those patrons might appreciate. J. Leubrie Hill's Darktown Follies fit that qualification perfectly. His shows toured the same black theater circuit as those of the Whitman Sisters. Increasingly, Harlem was a hub for colored time.

The first Darktown Follies show at the Lafayette was *My Friend from Kentucky*, a broad and conventional comedy of social climbing. What made it distinctive was the dancing: the Texas Tommy, the tango. For the finale, the entire cast formed a hands-to-hips chain that circled backstage and on again. Ethel Williams, the girl on the end, did her own thing entirely. For Carl Van Vechten in the *New York Press*, this approached that undiscoverable grail, "the negro as he really is—and not as he wants to be on stage." Van Vechten enjoyed how the performers enjoyed themselves. He enjoyed how the spectators enjoyed themselves, rocking and screaming like worshippers at a camp meeting. Writing again six years later, after he had established himself as the white authority on happenings uptown, Van Vechten could still remember the spontaneity and joy of "the real nigger stuff" in the Darktown Follies and how the rhythm had "dominated" him for days.

Florenz Ziegfeld paid the show a different kind of compliment. He bought the finale for his own Follies. He did not buy the cast, though he hired Ethel Williams and other Darktown players as tutors. It's unlikely that the copy matched the original. (Van Vechten didn't think so. The girls were pretty, he wrote, but "the Congo had disappeared.") The Ziegfeld Follies program made no mention of J. Leubrie Hill or Ethel Williams or the Darktown Follies at all. Appropriation was an old story, but Ziegfeld's purchase was a tentative indicator of a new surge of power in black theater. The Darktown Follies moved downtown onto Hammerstein's Roof Garden and into the Bijou, a "theatre for colored people." Neither of these incursions lasted more than a year, yet they softened up defenses. Rebuffed, the Darktown Follies rallied on colored time. In 1914, the troupe helped inaugurate the Standard Theatre in Philadelphia, one more stop on an expanding black belt.

By 1914, the show also had an added attraction in Toots Davis. Sylvester Russell, the severe dean of black critics, judged Davis "the greatest buck dancer on the American stage, a whirlwind of science." The First World War was on, and trench warfare in Europe suggested names for two tap steps credited to Toots. The first was called Over the Top. In this maneuver, the dancer leans forward and bounces off the tip of one toe as the opposite leg vaults over the top of it and lands with a heavy crash. Performed on alternating legs, the step makes a figure-eight pattern, and each crash looks perilous, as though the dancer might land on his face. When Davis played the Palace, the *New York Tribune* praised him for "a variety of new and surprising ways to be just on the point of falling on his ear."

Similar praise would have served for the companion step, Through the Trenches. Bent over again, with all his weight on one leg, the dancer slides that leg backward along the outside edge of the foot, falls forward onto the opposite leg, slides backward, and so on. The arm across from the falling foot reaches for it, the other arm for the sky, and both arms swing as the legs alternate, the whole package going nowhere in style. Executed correctly, the step is beautiful in cross-body oppositions and a fluid sluicing of weight through the slide. A swoosh shunts into a bass note each time the weight shifts. Though trenches have been described as running in place, the best dancers make the step look more like speed skating. If you've seen a Broadway show or a Hollywood movie with tap in it, you've seen trenches, though likely in inferior form. Trenches are the most consistently faked step in the history of tap. The essential and hardest part—the slide—gets left out, transforming something smooth and free into something jerky and hectoring, the sound clomping along as outstretched arms beg for the applause that the step undeservedly receives. A proper trench is "pulled."

DIXIE TO BROADWAY

Trenches and Over the Tops quickly became standard, and their combination a default finish. The new steps seem not to have made it to Broadway until black dancers did, and that wasn't until 1921 and the advent of *Shuffle Along*. The story is a classic showbiz tale of perseverence: an ordeal of one-night tryouts in the boondocks, a booking in a broken-down New York lecture hall at the upper edge of the theater district, encouraging reviews, and slow ticket sales gradually ramping up through word of mouth into a society fad and some five hundred performances, a record surpassed that season only by Marilyn Miller's *Sally*. All of this was particularly remarkable considering the obstacles a black show faced, such as the white backers who saw it in tryouts, laughed their heads off, then confidently insisted that white audiences wouldn't enjoy it. On tour before and after the Broadway run, the production had to start over in each city and persuade the skeptical. But persuade it did. *Shuffle Along* proved again that black musicals could play white theaters and make money.

It was the brainchild of two vaudeville teams. The Dixie plot about a mayoral election came from the burnt-cork comedy pair of Flournoy Miller and Aubrey Lyles. The songs, slangy but clean, came from the duo of singer-lyricist Noble Sissle and composer-pianist Eubie Blake. Before the New York opening, the creators were most worried about an operetta-style song that broke taboos by treating romance between two black characters seriously, but white audiences ignored it in favor of "The Baltimore Buzz," the dance-craze number with lyrics advertising raggy-draggy sliding and gliding. Critics mostly disparaged the plot to rhapsodize over the music—"a breeze of super-jazz blown up from Dixie!"—and especially the infectious vitality of the dancing: struts, strolls, slow drags, one-steps, two-steps, and more.

Not much of that dancing was strictly tap. The already vintage "Fisti-cuffs" routine—during which Miller, who was tall, held the head of Lyles, who was not, as the shorter man kept swinging and missing—used buck-and-wing to give jazz timing to the slapstick. The precision-kicking chorus did some syncopated stenography for the mayor. There was Tommy Woods, a young veteran of the Whitman Sisters troupe, who launched out of a time step into flips on the beat as the porter Old Black Joe, and Charlie Davis, who did Over the Tops and trenches while playing a traffic cop named Uncle Tom. Few reviews mentioned either man. The stars who emerged were Florence Mills, a replacement soubrette, and Josephine Baker, a replacement chorine whose cross-eyed clowning at the end of the chorus line would propel her to France, where she was embraced as an icon of glamorous negritude. Mills and Baker were not tap dancers per se, though tap was an ingredient in their music-makes-me-crazy style.

Shuffle Along inaugurated a fashion for black shows, and it became the standard against which those shows were judged. "The first reporto-rial responsibility of any reviewer who goes to a Negro musical comedy," explained Heywood Broun, "is to say whether or not it is as good as *Shuffle Along.*" Over the next few years, *Strut Miss Lizzie, The Chocolate Dandies, Lucky Sambo,* and many others—some of them musicals with a plot, some revues—snuck into out-of-the-way or seasonally vacant theaters. The 1922 edition of the Ziegfeld Follies, staged by Ned Way-burn, acknowledged the trend with a number for the naughty Gilda

Gray. "We used to brag about the Broadway White Lights," she sang, announcing that those lights were now growing dim. "Real darktown entertainers" had taken over, "pretty chocolate babies" and the "dancing coon." It was, the lyrics explained, like an eclipse. Suddenly, the Great White Way was white no more, and, as the lights went out and the dancers cavorted in phosphorescent costumes, Gray sang the refrain: "It's Getting Very Dark on Old Broadway."

Can you hear the nervous laughter? The black shows couldn't approach the opulence of the Follies, but it became an instant critical platitude that black chorus lines surpassed every white equivalent. Writing about *Liza*'s chorus, for instance, *The New York Sun* judged that "clog dancing, such as Ned Wayburn sponsors, seems very tame in comparison." In 1923, the all-black *Runnin' Wild*, for which George White as producer hired away Miller and Lyles, popularized the dance that defined the decade. The origin stories of the Charleston are as murky as you might expect: Geechees doing it on Charleston levees, Kongo parallels. The dance got into *Runnin' Wild*, Miller once explained, because he caught some kids—two black boys (one from Charleston) and an Italian kid who went by "Champ"—doing it with garbage can lids outside the Lincoln Theater. He had Willie Covan elaborate it into a routine with a song by the stride-piano king James P. Johnson. A group of Dancing Redcaps clapped their hands and stomped their feet, up on a platform in their porter uniforms. The Charleston had been danced in black neighborhoods for years and in black musicals the year before *Runnin' Wild*, but it was this version that set off a vogue.

The cultural brushfire of the Charleston spread farther and faster than even the cakewalk had. It embodied the spirit of the twenties: Throw away your cares, fling off the old restraints. The dance enacted abandon in kicks and swivels. Its turned-in knees were eccentric but not necessarily comic; the action could be sexy, depending on the knees. What was crucial was the rhythm; that's what made a Charleston a Charleston across an abundance of variations. Doing it, a broad swath of America might learn to hit the beat just before the beat, to feel that little rush. The Charleston was the self-expression of youth and the characteristic dance of the flapper, whose fringed fashions it threw into bold motion, but soon it was also the businessman's indulgence. Prohibitions against it were about as effective as Prohibition. And in this latest phase of the commerce between black dance halls and white, Broadway was the bridge. For a talented few, the Charleston served as a gateway into the theatrical profession. Many a tap dancer learned his first steps to a Charleston beat and first walked the boards during a Charleston contest. Strong traces of it would endure in their style.

But there was tap on Black Broadway, too. To read the reviews is to watch the terms *clog* and *buck-and-wing* get replaced by *tap*, with a consensus coalescing around mid-decade. Audiences at *Put and Take*, in 1921, woke up at the late appearance of Maxie McCree and his "dizzy hoofing." A husband of Alberta Whitman, he had broken off from the Whitman Sisters troupe. Black dancers would remember him as a pioneer in combining tap with the trend toward ever-more-daring acrobatics. Suddenly, he would sink to the floor on an accent, landing on his knees; just as suddenly, he would pop back up. Freakish in the wrong hands, the move could seem superhuman if done with the right aplomb. (Ankles and calves helped break the fall, but the patella still got a beating. It was a young man's step.) At the time of *Put and Take*, McCree was crossing over, integrating white vaudeville circuits and Reisenweber's, New York's most fashionable cabaret. George White hired McCree and his partner, George Brown, for the Scandals of 1922, and "Maxie and Georgie" got good reviews in Boston. When the production made it to New York, though, McCree wasn't in it. A drowning accident was the official story, though there were rumors that connected McCree's death, at age twenty-three, with his interest in one of the Scandals showgirls.

Some of the tap in *Dixie to Broadway* (1924) was handled by McCree's cousin Willie Covan, that accidental inventor of the Double Around the World with No Hands. In addition to his strutting impersonation of a "Georgia Cohan," Covan tapped in front of a curtain graced with the picture of a pickaninny chomping on a watermelon. His partner for that number was Ulysses "Slow Kid" Thompson, an eccentric dancer who had worked his way out from under the rag with his wife, Florence Mills. She was the star of *Dixie to Broadway*. A few years before, the producer Lew Leslie had hired her to sing and dance, at 12:30 and 2:00, in his Plantation Club on Broadway. Leslie exported the revue to London, and a silent snippet of that production shows Covan and Thompson in striped convict oufits, trading rubbery steps and huge cross-body wings. When the company returned to America, a different trio wore convict outfits and tapped while chained together. ("Lincoln freed the slaves for America and for Lew Leslie" was the going quip in the black theatrical community.) One of the production's showstoppers was a burlesque of "The Parade of the Wooden Soldiers" from the Russian revue *La Chauve-Souris*. Where the original had employed snare drums, the *Dixie* version beat its tattoo with an ensemble of precisely tapping feet. That's how America answered Europe. The military routine had been a specialty of the Darktown Follies tap dancer Eddie Rector, but Leslie had Rector teach it to a chorus led by Florence Mills, who was an adequate tap dancer, an enchanting personality, and the most celebrated black entertainer of the day. That's how Darktown adapted to Broadway.

Of all the tap specialists in the black shows of the early twenties, Johnny Nit attracted the most press. It's fairly clear why. U. S. Thompson identified Nit's foremost assets as "a broad smile and ivory teeth." Rarely did a critic fail to mention that smile. According to Charlie Davis, Nit was "a good buck-and-wing dancer and a better showman." He would do the same steps as everyone else, "and when he added that grin of his, the audience went crazy." It wasn't that Nit was a faker. He was known to train like a boxer so he could keep up high speeds for long stretches and pump out wings by the dozen. But it was his showmanship that sold. When Nit performed in Britain, a critic called him perfect, and he returned the compliment by staying for the rest of his life. (He married an Englishwoman and had children.) In 1932, British Pathé filmed his act. He dances to a quick 2/4, up on his toes and really pounding. The grin is there and the wings, too. Midway through, he pulls out a chair, sits down, and continues tapping as a show of nonchalance. Yet his next move is to lay the chair sideways and lie down beside it, tapping feebly on the seat—showmanship tipped over into mere novelty.

While the Black Broadway shows brought renewed attention to black dance, the greatest black hoofers of the time—the ones most respected by later black hoofers—didn't play much of a role. They danced elsewhere. In 1921, the same year as *Shuffle Along*, the Theater Owners

Booking Association was organized, binding theatrical houses in the East, South, and Midwest. On this circuit, blacks performed for blacks, and black producers had a shot at surviving. Toby Time was a theatrical ghetto, a home and a prison, and the acronym TOBA was said, with some affection, to stand for Tough on Black Asses. Material conditions were inferior to those of white showbiz, but opportunities for black artists were far more abundant. The fare inclined toward road shows: traveling revues with comedians, blues singers, dancers, a line of girls, and a jazz band. These seem not to have differed much from the black revues on Broadway—many of those played TOBA on tour—except in being a little looser, a little faster (the ads all boasted about speed), and perhaps a little racier. The sets and costumes were less costly and the comic situations not always ones that whites would immediately recognize, yet the crucial difference was to be found out in the audience: a crowd that was harder to please and more enthusiastic when won over.

Irvin C. Miller (brother of *Shuffle Along*'s Flournoy and producer of *Put and Take* and *Liza* on Broadway) might have three or four shows touring TOBA at any one time. One of them was certain to be the latest edition of his Brownskin Models, through which he sought to glorify the Brownskin Girl. The Whitman Sisters were the queens of TOBA, packing houses to overflowing fifty-two weeks a year. Their accelerated revues—titled *Rompin' Thru* or *High Speed*—carried blackface comedians such as Rastus Airship, Daybreak Nelson, and Willie Too Sweet, or the ribald henpecked-husband-and-nagging-wife team of Butterbeans and Susie. Little Pops Whitman always stopped the show, tapping and flipping like his uncle Maxie. His mother, Alice, was "Queen of Taps," the "China Doll of Syncopation." Chappy Gardner of the Philadelphia *Courier* once crowed that "Broadway has no superior girl dancer." Her hair was bobbed, her costumes abbreviated. One dress had a large bow on the back. "If I ever lost that bow," she would recall, "I'd sure catch cold." "I don't know what you call it," she might say of her dancing, in a baby voice with a squeak, "but it sure feels good."

Alice danced solo or with Bert, her male-impersonator sister. In photos, they look like a gangster and his moll. Alice might also team up with a fresh recruit, such as the teenaged Willie Bryant, whom the sisters discovered selling candy at the Grand Theatre in Chicago. By his own estimation, Bryant was an excellent tap dancer. "There was no step I saw I couldn't do," he later boasted. But his pride and joy was his nerve-control step, a protracted spasm. "Kids called it the Tommy Gun." No more Rattlesnake jig or galloping horses: this was the twenties. When Bryant wasn't outgunning Dillinger with his feet, the six-foot adolescent was partnering the three-foot Princess Wee Wee, the World's Smallest Perfect Woman.

"A colored audience is our favorite," Mabel Whitman told the *Baltimore Afro-American* in 1931. "For there we get full appreciation without grudge, and there is no such thing as a nasty little feeling that we are breaking in where we are not really wanted." TOBA was where you could find Ginger Jack Wiggins, still challenging everyone as the World's Greatest Buck Dancer. In the twenties at Atlanta's 81 Theatre, the future comedian Nipsey Russell was stunned by Wiggins, "the first black man I ever saw in a good suit with great dignity and speaking good English." TOBA was where you could find King Rastus Brown. The British-born vaudevillian Leslie Hope caught Brown's act in Cleveland, the King pointing his cane as if it were a gun and shooting off nerve taps. (Hope built an act out of steps he learned from Brown, well before he switched to comedy, swapped the cane for a golf club, changed his first name to Bob, and conquered Middle America.) When Prince Spencer, a Toledo kid whose career as a tapper was just beginning, came upon Brown a few years later, the cane seemed the crutch of an old man. When someone in the audience complained about not being able to see Brown's feet, the King made a remark that permanently altered Spencer's conception of tap: "You don't have to see my feet to enjoy my dancing. My dancing tells a story." It was a story you could see or hear only on TOBA.

Of the strong hoofers who did make it into Broadway revues, most found little success outside of them. Others, revered within the tribe, such as Willie Covan, never got much press attention and never starred. Or if they were given top billing, like Eddie Rector, it was in shows that flopped. The headliners were comedians and singers, not mute tap dancers. Only one black tap dancer achieved the status of a star, and he didn't debut on Broadway until 1928.

THE NEW LOW DOWN

That one exception was Bill Robinson. The vehicle was *Blackbirds of 1928*, another Lew Leslie revue. Late in the second act came a number called "Doin' the New Low Down," Robinson's sole appearance. People who had seen his vaudeville act wouldn't have noticed much that was new, yet the critical response was nearly unanimous: Robinson was the high spot. And the reviews he received were of a different order from the usual enthusiasm for fast and furious black dancers. His dancing was "extraordinarily beautiful." His feet were instruments that conveyed "true esthetic emotion." Reviewers saw the comedy in his pantomiming, but they also heard the wit in his rhythms. Fifty years old, he was no unknown, yet the outpouring of praise brought him an unprecedented level of prestige. It also may have saved the show, which ran for 518 performances, much longer than any of the other black musicals after *Shuffle Along*.

In 1930, Robinson starred in *Brown Buddies*, a musical comedy about blacks serving in the First World War. Again he did his stair dance, now flanked by chorus girls; again the reviewers asserted that he alone redeemed the show's weak material, making the audience hold its breath with his "lullaby hoofing." Critics remarked on how he watched his feet and chuckled at them, "as if he were talking to them gently and coaxing them to do the impossible." His gaze guided the spectators'. His delight stoked theirs. His pantomime traded on an eccentric dancer's sense of self-surprise, though Robinson could hardly have been startled by anything his feet said—the same steps, often on the same set of stairs. Much of his appeal came from a kind of standing still. Tap dancing was accelerating, growing more complex and athletic, whereas Robinson, wrote Brooks Atkinson, "reduced his act to its essentials." Where other hoofers looked as if they were risking cardiac arrest, Bojangles never lost the crease in his pants. "Robinson was absolute tops in control," recalled Pete Nugent, a hoofer who debuted around this time. "The toughest thing about imitating him is to get that perfect balance which seems so natural. He would never impress a novice." And yet he did impress. "It's really very simple," Robert Benchley wrote in *The New Yorker*. "All you have to have is God-given genius and take your time."

"There are hundreds of tap dancers," explained a *Times* review of a program at the Palace, "but there is only one Bill Robinson." Robinson's dancing put him in a different class in other ways, too. By the middle of the thirties, he would be making $3,500 a week. In Harlem, he owned seven rooms in the prestigious Dunbar Apartments. His chauffeur drove a Duesenberg limousine. In 1934, a group of New York's prominent white citizens elected him the unofficial "Mayor of Harlem," but on his home turf, the title was superfluous. All of Harlem knew Uncle Bo. They knew that he didn't smoke or drink but ate ice cream at every meal. They knew that he burned those calories by dancing and by running backward, a skill for which he held the Guinness World Record (8.2 seconds for 75 yards—a record that stood until 1977). They knew him as someone they could count on to buy a week's groceries, to cover funeral costs or bail, to settle the doctor's bill for a sick child or the back rent for an evicted family. They knew that he appeared in benefit performances almost as frequently as the paying kind—as many as four hundred a year, as many as six in one day.

His 1934 *New Yorker* profile noted that, along with a "gold-inlaid, pearl-handled, thirty-two-caliber revolver" given to him by the police of his Harlem precinct, Robinson carried a diamond-studded case in his upper right vest pocket containing a gold badge designating him Special Deputy Sheriff of New York County (an honorary position); that under the lapel of his coat, he wore another badge identifying him as Special Inspector of Motor Vehicles (another honorary position); and that in his left hip pocket, he carried a pistol permit and his credentials as Admiral in the Great Navy of the State of Nebraska. He also carried documents establishing his friendship with the police chiefs of most major American cities, and he always made a point of performing at benefits for police widows and orphans. When he arrived in a new town, the first place he would visit would be the local police department.

During a Pittsburgh tryout of *Brown Buddies*, Robinson heard a scream and saw two black kids mugging an elderly white woman. He yelled, took up the chase, pulled out his revolver, and fired in the air. A white policeman, coming on the scene to find a black man discharging a gun, shot Robinson in the shoulder and let the muggers escape. Collapsed on the ground, Robinson showed the cop a letter of friendship from

Pittsburgh's chief of police, who later confirmed the relationship by visiting Robinson in the hospital. The victim of the mugging brought
flowers. Robinson was famous enough that the incident made headlines
across the country, and according to *The Chicago Defender*, the policeman
offered the excuse that "all black men look alike to me." At the New
York opening of *Brown Buddies* two days later, Robinson was tapping
again, his arm in a satin sling, his grin bright. The bullet must have been
somewhere inside.

ANOTHER IMITATION DANCE

The most frequent charge lodged against the black shows of the twenties
was the charge of imitation. Over and over, white critics rang variations
on the same complaint: "another childlike imitation of dull white
extravaganzas," "aping the more ambitious and generally less endurable
features of the Broadway extravaganza." Look past the condescending
adjective and the simian verb and note the nature of the disappointment.
Of Lew Leslie's *Plantation Revue*, the *Times* said, "There are places when,
if you love the things these natural entertainers can do best, you wish
they would not slavishly imitate the usual Broadway stuff." The Chicago
critic Ashton Stevens, a great admirer of *Shuffle Along*, described Sissle
and Blake's follow-up as seeming to "suffer from too much white man."
That meant "too much politeness . . . and not enough of the racy and
razor-edged, too much 'art' and not enough Africa."

Along with their new success, black artists such as Sissle and Blake
found themselves in an old bind. After *Shuffle Along*, they felt they could
write any show they wanted. "We were wrong," Blake remembered.
"People who went to a colored show—most people, not *all* people—
expected only fast dancing and Negroid humor, and when they got
something else they put it down." Blacks were chided for stepping out of
character. Reviewing *Put and Take* in 1921, *Variety*'s critic put it frankly:
"Colored folks seemed to have set out to show the Whites that they are
just as white as anybody. They may be as good but they're different—and,
in their entertainment at any rate, they should remain different—distinct—

indigenous." (Which part of *Put and Take* did that critic like? "The reg-ular darkie business" of Maxie McCree's tapping.)

The sharpest journalistic response came in the *Chicago Defender* col-umn of the black actor and producer Salem Tutt Whitney. Sixty-four years old, with a career stretching back into the preceding century, Whitney had seen enough of the imitation charge. *Deep Harlem*, his Broadway show of 1929, had attempted to chronicle the progress of the Negro from African kingdoms through slavery to Harlem; most white critics called it pretentious with some good dancing, an attempt to "play the white man's game" redeemed only when the performers "became themselves." Tutt sneeringly explained that it was difficult for black per-formers "to be ourselves" when the average white person found the title characters of the popular radio show *Amos 'n' Andy*—the minstrel-like creations of white actors—to be more authentically black than black people. Even more galling was the way that white performers would fre-quent black dance halls, pick up a few moves, then introduce them to white audiences as original creations—with the result that black perform-ers later doing those same moves before white audiences became de facto imitators, people doing imitations of themselves. Whitney was complain-ing about stolen steps.

This was the other side of "It's Getting Dark on Old Broadway." Gilda Gray, who introduced that song about shimmying chocolate babies, was herself best known for her shoulder-shaking shimmy, which she claimed to have invented. Negroes had nothing to do with it, she insisted in 1927, even though the Shimmy and the Shake were ubiqui-tous in black juke joints and tent shows before she was born. Similar claims of white origination were made for the Charleston and for the Black Bottom, a slow, hip-swiveling dance with off-beat stamps that Ann Pen-nington brought into fashion in George White's *Scandals of 1926*. According to the black songwriter Perry Bradford—whose "Black Bottom Dance," referring both to a body part and the black section of Southern towns, came out in 1919—White bought the dance from Irving C. Miller after seeing it uptown in Miller's show *Dinah*. A 1926 *Times* article credited White with the sole creation of that dance and the Charleston, too.

It's hard to say whether Gilda Gray was lying or ignorant or just telling a very narrow truth. It's also hard to imagine who believed her. The song she sang in the Follies teased with an open secret. The source of the "new" steps and rhythms was no more of a mystery than it had been in minstrel days. Indeed, the origin, barely disguised, provided much of the attraction. One 1930 magazine advertisement for Old Gold cigarettes equated its product with Marilyn Miller: just as Nature had blessed the musical comedy star with "a charm all her own," so Nature was responsible for the better tobacco that made Old Golds popular. The illustration showed Miller in her childhood basement, getting her feet educated by "Grandmother's kinky-haired old furnaceman." Elsewhere, Miller told the press that her first teacher had been a colored boy who brought coal to her home. Either way, Nature had help.

For many, many white dancers, help came in the form of one particular colored boy: Clarence Edward Bradley. He was a kid from Harrisburg whose parents had died by the time he was fourteen. Looking for work, he ended up in a Harlem rooming house whose residents just happened to include a few dancers. As a boy, he had learned the time step from an uncle, but he couldn't figure out how to do it on the left side and gave up. Now he progressed quickly, spurred by the other young hoofers who practiced with him and by the prospect of a job in a Harlem nightclub. He got one of those jobs, and then another in Lew Leslie's *Dixie to Broadway*. In 1925, now going by the name Buddy Bradley, he met Billy Pierce, an enterprising black businessman who owned a one-room dance studio near Times Square. Pierce asked Bradley to put together a routine for Irene Delroy, a white client who was appearing in the *Greenwich Village Follies*. The number stopped the show, and the next morning at the Pierce studio there was a line of girls from the *Follies* looking for what Delroy had found. Pierce expanded his establishment, taking over a whole floor and hiring five assistants. Bradley worked twelve-hour days, shuttling back and forth between rooms. It was a rare week that the teenager pulled down less than a grand.

The Pierce studio merely made a formal business out of the kinds of transactions that were happening all the time: the black dancer Freddie Taylor teaches the Black Bottom to Ann Pennington and she buys him a car. The number that Bradley devised for Delroy was a Charleston with some strut and tap trimming. He had realized he would have to tailor to the ingenue's limited abilities. This became his specialty: he cut down the tap to what his client could handle and padded with what he and his Harlem friends called "jive" dancing, stuff they considered corny because everybody they knew could do it. The Sugar Foot Strut, the Jungle Stomp, Harlem Hips, the Virginia Essence—Bradley didn't invent the steps any more than W. C. Handy invented the blues, but they were novel enough to Broadway, not part of Ned Wayburn's syllabus. (They were "marvelous, new, dirty steps" in the words of one of Bradley's more successful pupils, Adele Astaire.) Bradley decided that girls doing tap looked awkward and required cute styling. Bill Robinson's steps were simple, Bradley once explained, "but he made them *look* great." That's what counted.

Over the next four years, according to Bradley, there wasn't a Broadway production that didn't have one or more of his routines in it. Any attempt to substantiate that claim is complicated by the fact that Bradley's name never appeared on programs. A publication such as *The Dance* might print photos of Bradley demonstrating low-down steps, but white dance directors got the credit for Bradley's contributions to the stage, or there was some fiction about the number being of the star's "own devising."

In 1930, Charles B. Cochran, the British Ziegfeld, began hiring Bradley to choreograph his London revues. Bradley's name went in the program, and Cochran paired him with the ballet choreographers George Balanchine, Antony Tudor, and Frederick Ashton. Bradley taught the British stars Jack Buchanan and Jessie Matthews, and he served as choreographer for Matthews's films, such as the 1934 *Evergreen*, in which one can catch six seconds of the man himself Charlestoning with kids on the street. *Evergreen* also shows how good he could make a hardworking charmer like Matthews look. In show after show and film after film, as well as through his large and prosperous Soho school, Bradley exercised an influence on British theatrical dancing that was significant and prolonged. He stayed abroad for thirty-eight years before returning to the country that wouldn't give him credit. In 1972, not long after his repatriation, he died little known.

———

The increasingly ornate black productions competing with the Scandals and the Follies struck white critics as pretentious. Many of the sketches in the black revues were burlesques of white shows and performers, so the question rises again of how much imitation was mockery. But by the end of the decade, the imitation charge was as likely a complaint about stale blackface comedy, "a bad imitation of what was not a very good imitation in the first place." One motif in the charge sounds reasonable—something like "play to your strengths." To the extent that black performers adopted white performance practices, they became more ordinary. The white critics didn't want blacks to conform to worn-out white conventions; they wanted blacks to do what blacks, in the opinion of the white critics, did best. Black critics, such as the young Caribbean-born intellectual Eric Walrond, could agree that the black revues, in following white models, did so "at the expense of a genuine negro spirit," though that didn't necessarily mean that Walrond agreed about what genuine Negro spirit was.

Pretty much everyone agreed about one thing: blacks could dance. A reviewer might disparage every other aspect of a show, but dancing was dependable. "Negro performers are dancers first of all," generalized Brooks Atkinson in a review of *Brown Buddies*. Writing about the same production in *The Washington Post*, Robert Littell generalized further that dance was the one thing white folks would never succeed in imitating. Covering *Dixie to Broadway*, Heywood Broun had quipped, "When I see a Negro child two or three years old come out and dance a little better than anybody at the New Amsterdam or the Winter Garden"—where the Ziegfeld Follies and *Earl Carroll's Vanities* played—"I grow fearful that there must be certain reservations in the theory of white supremacy." But everyone conceded black superiority in this realm. "Regular darkie business" was "rhythm that's born, not made."

That last phrase, applied by a reviewer of *Blackbirds of 1930*, was what prompted Salem Tutt Whitney's article. He protested the natural-born idea, recounting how none of the blacks he grew up among could dance and some of the whites could. In the 1903 book *The Souls of Black Folk*, W.E.B. Du Bois had coined the now-famous term "double-consciousness" to capture the Negro's "sense of always looking at one's self through the eyes of others," the eyes of the white world. African-

Americans, from Du Bois's point of view, had a surfeit of self-consciousness. Yet what white critics, and probably the majority of white audiences, saw in black entertainers was a lack of self-consciousness—an effect that must have been in some measure genuine and in some measure cultivated. Lew Leslie understood one reason that the black performers he hired were more eager: "They learn to dance faster and smoother and easier and to sing more heartily," he once explained to the press, "knowing they've got to be far better than white entertainers to overcome their handicap and get across to a white audience." But then the same man could say that "they don't know what sadness is" and that "they'd rather perform for nothing than work for money," making merry "in their natural, never-serious way." He also complained that Negroes wore out their shoes faster.

One of the most intriguing editorials on the imitation question came from John Martin, the first full-time dance critic hired by an American newspaper. "Negro dancing itself," he claimed in a *New York Times* article in 1928, was "not benefiting from the experience." For Martin, the problem had gone beyond imitation. "The Negro's attempt to give white audiences what they choose to consider negro dancing" was, he wrote, "as far removed from the real thing as Tambo and Bones of the old minstrel tradition." The real thing, Martin asserted, was based in relaxation, "not just physical but mental and even moral as well." What was once "simple" and "naïve" had become "brazen, sophisticated and vulgar." According to the Kentucky-born critic, "Dixie heritage" resided in the "laziness of the Southern negro," and this was to be admired as "the ability to employ the minimum of muscular exertion in the performance of a physical action," an ability that "dancers of the white race generally attain only by diligent effort, and in the vast majority of cases never attain at all."

> The negro has not yet proved for himself any claim to be regarded as a serious artist in his dancing. He seems not to care a whit for beauty of line or movement for its own sake. But in his grasp of relaxation and control lies a contribution to the art that is quite sufficient in itself, even if we omit the subject of rhythm of which he is obviously and admittedly a master.

How easily an insult could be converted into praise. How thin the line between illuminating generalization and damning stereotype. Martin was calling for blacks to behave as they used to. It was a plea for aesthetic conservatism that could sound socially reactionary. His diagnosis was not entirely negative. I'll bet you can guess which dancer he singled out as an exception.

Two years earlier in *The Nation*, Mary Austin, known for her novels and essays about Native American life, had written that Bill Robinson restored for his audience "the primal freshness of their own lost rhythmic powers." Though Robinson himself was apparently unaware, the buck and wing, Austin explained, was a dance for the increase of spiritual power, "the mysterious *wokonda*." This "earth-medicine" is what Robinson was offering to his audience—"the gift of the Negro," "the great desideratum of modern art, a clean, short cut to areas of enjoyment long closed to us by the accumulated rubbish of the cultural route."

There was an idea in the air: blacks could save white America from itself, set it free. Black rhythms, black tap dancing. To Alain Locke, however, it was the black performer who was "in vaudeville chains" and needed to be unshackled. Locke was a Harvard graduate, the first black Rhodes scholar (in 1907), a professor with a PhD in philosophy. In his writings, he argued for the importance and influence of Negro music, particularly the "instinctive mastery of rhythm" stemming from a culture in which dancing was a natural and spontaneous activity. But Locke was even more worried than John Martin about commercial pressures, and he dreamed of black symphonies and ballets, not jazz and not tap, which he considered "a terrible hybrid." "A Bojangles performance is excellent vaudeville," he wrote in 1936, "but listen with closed eyes, and it becomes an almost symphonic composition of sounds. What the eye sees is the tawdry American convention; what the ear hears is the priceless African heritage."

What *was* the heritage of black Americans? The gift, the contribution to modern art? What part of it was African? What part American? These questions lay at the heart of *The New Negro*—the anthology, edited by Locke and published in 1925, that announced a new phase in African-American culture. One name for this phase is the Harlem Renaissance. To Locke and many others, culture seemed to be the realm in which blacks could lay aside "the status of a beneficiary and ward for that of a collaborator and participant in American civilization."

The writers of the Harlem Renaissance, and the many books about them, would not have much to say about tap. But Bill Robinson, just about the only tap dancer who does rate mention by those writers, sounded a similar note in describing *Blackbirds* to *The Chicago Defender*. "A safe and sane advertisement for a better understanding of my people" was how he labeled a show that, like all of the *Blackbirds* revues, moved in historical progression from scenes set in Jungle Land and Dixie to scenes set in a Harlem gin mill; a show that had blackface comics cowering in graveyards and cheating at poker; a show bursting with jazz; a show that made a star of Bill Robinson. "To give our hearts and souls to the spirited impulses of joy that are our national heritage, that is our pride," Robinson said. If separating priceless heritage from tawdry convention was the goal, black tap dancers would find themselves in an especially difficult position. Making people listen with closed eyes was not really an option.

INTERLUDE: THE COLOR LINE

Leonard Reed joined the Whitman Sisters in 1927. Moving up from carnivals, he had learned his trade on the TOBA circuit. His headstrong personality collided with Mabel Whitman's, and he lasted only a few months with the sisters, but during that time, he met Willie Bryant and assembled the Shim Sham, the two young men thinking little of it as they moved on to what they saw as bigger things.

Their eyes were not on the TOBA circuit. Reed was born in a teepee in Lightning Creek, Oklahoma. His mother was Choctaw Cherokee, and her great-grandfather was black. As for his father, Reed said, he was "white and Irish or something. He was a huckster. He sold blankets and whiskey to the Indians. He had an affair with my mother and her sister. They run him out of Oklahoma." When Reed was two, his mother died. Later, he was adopted by a mixed-race high school principal. Willie Bryant's mother was a French-Canadian showgirl, and his father was part black, part Native American, also from Oklahoma. Both Reed and Bryant were light enough to pass.

The dance that gained Reed his first carnival job was the Charleston. He learned it on the playground of his white school. All the local theaters

in Kansas City held Charleston contests, and after Reed entered his first
and won, he began entering as many as he could. He would enter
one, perform, run to the next theater, perform, run back to the first, get
the prize, run back to the second, get the prize, and so on, through an
exhausting and lucrative evening. Eventually, a black usher snitched
on him.

> I was standin' there after the contest. I saw the manager and could tell
> that something was up. So I grabbed the prize money and ran. The
> manager started yelling, "Catch that nigger! Catch that nigger!" When
> somebody said, "Where?" I didn't even think about it, I was so nervous.
> So I chimed in with, "Catch that nigger!" The theater was letting out,
> and everybody was coming out the side entrance. I just ran through
> that shuttle, right through the alleyway. And when I was running, yell-
> ing, "Catch that nigger," they all started runnin' along with me tryin'
> to help.

Another time, when Reed was performing the Charleston with black
dancers, someone pulled him off the stage and told him not to be up
there with those niggers. Reed was forced to blacken his face, though
even that wasn't sufficient. His sweat made the cork run. Reed's foster
parent, a graduate of Cornell University, arranged for him to attend the
college, but Reed had been there only a few weeks when a white minstrel troupe arrived and put on a promotional Charleston contest. Reed
couldn't resist entering, and after he won, he was asked to join the outfit.
Again he blacked up, this time to share the stage with whites. The cork,
he said, made his face sore.

Ever the chameleon, Reed worked in both black and white theaters.
"Every time you looked up, you'd see me. But I always had a different
act: Pen and Ink, Cutout and Leonard, Leonard and Crackaloo . . . Nobody knew what I was or wasn't." His vaudeville act with Willie Bryant
was a carefully paced, eight-minute package. The men looked dashing—
checked blazers and straw hats for the afternoon show, tuxedos for the
dinner program, top hat and tails in the evening—and every rhythmic
accent was carefully matched by an accent in their arrangement. Their
slogan was "Brains as well as Feet," which meant that in addition

to dancing, they told jokes. Performers who talked were usually paid better.

Traveling with Reed and Bryant was their valet, a much darker-skinned child named Frankie, who excelled at a sitting-in-a-chair dance. Bryant would introduce Frankie as the team's valet and egg him on, saying, "Come on, boy! Show 'em how you can dance!" Offstage, Bryant would call the boy a little black son of a bitch. ("Well, we had to be white, and he had to be black," Reed explained, years later.) By the time they reached Birmingham, Frankie's hometown, the boy was fed up. "If you call me any more names," Frankie said, "I'm gonna tell 'em you're a nigger." Frankie was also sick of being presented as the pair's valet. That evening, Bryant introduced him as "a gentleman with us who can really dance."

During their layoffs from the white theaters, Reed and Bryant would work in black ones. But again, they were told on. "They found out that we were colored who could go white and be around the girls. They didn't like that," Reed remembered. "After that I never did work white again." It was 1933. Reed became a successful dance director of black revues. Bryant took over a big band and taught his musicians to do the Shim Sham. Later, he became a popular emcee, a radio host, and an honorary mayor of Harlem. When his band toured the South, a sheriff made him stand on a platform, because it was against the law for whites and blacks to share a stage. "You may be colored like you say," the sheriff said, "but the audience doesn't know it."

If Reed and Bryant had been seeking advice about these matters, they could have asked the Whitman Sisters. Decades before, the sisters had also performed in white theaters. They, too, were light enough to pass. But they turned away from white showbiz. As Mabel Whitman explained, "You never have a real light colored star on the white stage. When we get too light, as we are, they won't really welcome you." Women like the Whitman Sisters and men like Reed and Bryant made certain people nervous, afraid that someone might make a mistake.

Essie Whitman told a story about how, in the late 1890s, the theater owner Oscar Hammerstein had hired her and her sisters, but had required them to wear blackface and woolly wigs. That in itself wasn't unusual—a convention that might have also served as a disguise. For the finale, however, Hammerstein asked them to set free their chestnut hair and take off their makeup. It was like Ned Wayburn's Minstrel Misses, but in reverse. "The audience was always puzzled," Essie remembered, "and someone was sure to ask, 'What are those white women doing up there?' Then they would recognize us as the performers and laugh in amazement."

Was the audience initially fooled into thinking that the makeup was the sisters' actual skin? If so, when spectators recognized the sisters as "the performers," were they recognizing them as white women masquerading? Were they laughing at the effectiveness of the blackface deception or suddenly seeing the sisters as colored and laughing at how silly it had been to think of them as white? Did anyone recognize the deeper joke, the mockery made of racial categories? It would be nice to think so. So few stories about playing across the color line end in laughter.

PART III

AMERICA'S NATURAL WAY OF DANCING

Tap dancers are very popular in the U.S.A.—silent Negroes, as mechanical as a sewing machine, inexhaustible, holding your interest by beating out a rhythmic poem on the stage with the soles of their shoes . . . The popularity of tap dancing shows that the old rhythmic instinct of the virgin African forest has learned the lesson of the machine and that in America the rigor of exactitude is a pleasure.

—LE CORBUSIER, *When the Cathedrals Were White*, 1936

When you come to the evolution of the dance, its history and philosophy . . . I don't know how it all started, and I don't want to know.

—FRED ASTAIRE, *Steps in Time*, 1956

9

RHYTHM FOR SALE

C layton Bates, born in 1907, learned to dance among the sharecrop-
pers of Fountain Inn, South Carolina. "The white man owned the
land," he would remember. "You didn't work from nine to five. You
worked from can to can't. The white man gave you a portion, and you
had to take his word for it. I think I would have murdered to get away
from farming."

"I lived in a completely black neighborhood," he recalled. "For relaxation, the black people used to dance, play guitar, and drink corn liquor. There were other neighbor dancers and we would challenge one
another. We didn't know too much about the names of steps. I was tap
dancing and didn't know I was." Whatever you called it, Bates could
do it. He liked the attention—especially, as he grew older, the attention
from girls. His dancing, however, had to be fit in on the sly, because his
Baptist mother disapproved. Sometimes Bates would go into the white
part of town, where he would dance in front of the barbershop in a little
red jacket, and the white folks would clap along and throw pennies.

Opposite page: Fred Astaire in *Blue Skies*, 1946

When his mother found out, she walked to the barbershop and grabbed her son to take him home for a whipping. "Make a monkey out of your own kid," she told the gathered crowd.

When Bates was twelve, he wanted to buy a suit, so he got a job at the local mill. He had been working there only three days when, late one evening, a light went out. Investigating the problem, he fell onto a conveyer belt and soon felt metal drilling into his flesh. Another employee—a man who had already lost an arm to the mill—heard the kid's screams and stopped the machine. The one-armed man took the injured boy home, where, on his mother's kitchen table, a doctor amputated his mangled leg below the knee. At first, Bates didn't understand why his mother was so distraught. "I thought it was like a toenail, it would grow back."

At school, he watched as the girls turned their attentions to another boy. On crutches, he challenged his rival to a race and fell trying to keep up. When he explained the scrapes to his mother, she gave him another whipping, saying he had no business challenging a boy with two legs. "Momma, you can whip me all you want," he told her, "but one of these days, I'm gonna beat that boy." His uncle fashioned him a peg leg, and so equipped, the young amputee tried horseback riding, bicycling, baseball. Mostly, he danced. "If I saw a two-legged dancer doing a step, I would copy that step. But I would do it with one leg, which made it look like an entirely different step." Not only would the step look different, assymetrical, but Bates's wooden peg—eventually tipped half with leather for sound, half with rubber for grip—produced a powerful thump that no two-legged dancer could quite match. At dancing, he could beat that boy.

When his family moved to Greenville, a nearby town large enough to have a theater, Bates discovered something else the peg gave him: a gimmick. He started winning amateur contests, and after he had won eleven times in a row, the manager of the theater hired him as a featured attraction. As an escape from sharecropping, this was much better than working in the mill. The dancing that Bates eventually developed transcended gimmickry, but the peg was a fabulous gimmick nevertheless. People began calling him Peg Leg Bates.

From the pit band, Bates learned how many measures were in a song and when to stop. A minstrel show hired him, and in Texas, after he kicked a sheriff's son for peeking into the girls' tent, Bates escaped a lynching by hiding in the baggage car. It wasn't long before the company ran out of money and he had to cable his mother for return train fare. He hadn't told her about the job. Another whipping. Closer to home, he started playing the state fair, working in blackface. ("All comedians had cork on their faces," he would recall. "I wanted to be funny too.") Someone told his mother, and when she came to see him this time, her response was a washing of hands. "That ain't my son," she said, and meant it. When another carnival came through town, Bates ran away again, got stranded again, and could no longer count on his mother for rescue. He put out a hat and danced on the street corner for change until he convinced the management of a road show called Eddie Lemons' Dashin' Dinah to take him along. ("What do you dance, kid?" they asked Peg Leg. "The soft shoe," he answered.) Within two weeks, his was the featured act. Awed spectators threw so much money onstage that he used it to pay room and board for the entire troupe. Lemons was sure that Bates could be a star if he could make it to New York.

HARLEM

When Bates arrived in Harlem, it was 1927 and he couldn't believe his eyes. "Not seventh heaven, *first* heaven." It's a sentiment often echoed in reminiscences of artistic youth drawn to Harlem in the 1920s. Whereas in 1890 barely 1 percent of the population of Manhattan was black, in 1930 more than 10 percent was. To Bates, the sheer numbers were dazzling. "I'd never seen so many black people." But not just the numbers. "Everybody was well dressed. Black people had everything. They had style."

Harlem could seem a fairy-tale land. On Bates's second day there, he was standing in front of the Lafayette Theatre when someone tapped him on the shoulder. "You Peg Leg Bates?" the man asked. "Leonard Harper is looking for you." One of Harlem's leading dance directors, a Birmingham-born out-from-under-the-rag Ned Wayburn, Harper was the best-dressed black man Bates had ever seen, and he was putting together a show to go into the Lafayette, the uptown equivalent of the Palace. Bates found himself in a number about soldiers in the Great War celebrating in Paris. His brief appearance earned him an offer to stay on for the next show at triple the salary. The producer Lew Leslie had a scout in the audience, and before Bates knew it, he was tapping on Broadway in *Blackbirds of 1928*. In the show's challenge-dance number, "Four Bad Men from Harlem," Bates was slotted in last, so that the audience would wonder what the one-legged guy was going to do. He stopped the show. (This irritated Bill Robinson, who countered by joining Bates onstage and publicly co-opting him as a protégé.) Then *Blackbirds* took Bates to Paris, the real Paris, a place he'd never imagined he would see.

Things didn't progress so vertiginously for all tap dancers. Not all tap dancers were Peg Leg Bates. Still, the Tree of Hope planted outside the Lafayette Theatre was no site of blind superstition. Entertainers rubbed the elm's bark because they believed in its magical powers to grant wishes for employment, but they also gathered on the sidewalk around the tree because producers really did come by. Miracles weren't necessary. The Lafayette was part of a black theater circuit informally known as 'Round the World, which included select theaters in Philadelphia, Baltimore, Chicago, and Washington, D.C. This was the top of black showbiz, which would still thrive while smaller TOBA venues suffered the brunt of the Depression. Tap dancers were an assumed part of the entertainment package.

On the same block as the Lafayette, still just steps away from the Tree of Hope, was the entrance to the swanky nightclub Connie's Inn. When Bates returned from Europe, that's where he took his act. This, too, was a place he might never have seen had he not been a dancer. With few exceptions, blacks were admitted only as entertainers or as staff (though that hadn't always been true). The segregation also applied at the even swankier Cotton Club a few blocks away. The existence, in the middle of Harlem, of whites-only clubs, owned by bootleggers and gangsters and specializing in black entertainers, was the convergence of two trends. First, Prohibition had spawned a profusion of nightclubs and cabarets uptown. One block of 133rd Street alone had more than a dozen. That this block was known as "Jungle Alley" pointed to the other trend. *Shuffle Along* had attracted attention to black entertainment (when Connie's Inn first opened, in 1921, it was called the Shuffle Inn), and Harlem had acquired a reputation not just as somewhere you could get a drink, but as a place where repressed whites could strip off their inhibitions temporarily. "One by one, our cherished biases are taken off like arctic overcoats," explained a white journalist. "It becomes natural to laugh and shout in the consciousness of an emotional holiday. Then, when the last ambiguously worded song is done, one puts on again one's hat, coat, and niceties, and once again is staid, proper, and a community pillar."

Jazz was part of the attraction, but also the scantily clad chorus line, young ladies who gyrated much more suggestively than the girls downtown but whose complexions might not be much darker. ("High yellows" were desired; "tall, tan, and terrific" became the motto.) Harlem had its own eccentric dancers, too—crazies like Jigsaw Jackson, who kept his chin planted on the floor as his feet chattered. Where Jazzlips Richardson flapped his mouth to the music, Dynamite Hooker worked in blithe disregard of it, flailing until a gong told him to stop. Earl "Snakehips" Tucker was both sexy and eccentric. Waves rolled out from his pelvis, swelling undulations that fractured his body into zigzags and might propel him sideways, with one foot pivoting and the other dragging seductively behind. With astonishing elasticity, he sank and rose, each move connected to every other by a finger-snapping pulse. If this was sex, it was also operatic emotion and spiritual possession. The shake that made his satiny shirt shimmer could break into trembling sobs as he hid his face in his hands. Before Tucker, snakehips and shake dancing had been associated with women, yet no one would have dared question his masculinity. The black press chronicled his arrests for stabbings, assault, and rape, and his dancing had a coiled menace. When he took his gyrations downtown for *Blackbirds of 1928*, his "New Low Down" was on the same program as Bill Robinson's upright version, but up until his death by a "mysterious illness" in 1937, his act—best preserved in the 1930 short *Crazy House*, made when Tucker was twenty-three—was the kind you generally had to go to Harlem to see.

Zora Neale Hurston was probably thinking of Tucker when she wrote, "Negro dancing is dynamic suggestion. No matter how violent it may appear to the beholder, every posture gives the impression that the dancer will do much more." Tucker's act matched the Cotton Club's forbidden allure better than any tap dancer's (though male tap dancers were known to be popular, after work, with white women patrons). There were, however, other faces to the cabaret aesthetic. Despite its promise of leading into some fantasy of darkest Africa or the antebellum

South, the door to the Cotton Club opened onto the height of urban elegance. There were plantation columns and palm trees, yes, but the scene
at the venue Lady Mountbatten dubbed "the Aristocrat of Harlem" was as
much about Putting On the Ritz as about Taking It All Off. Duke Ellington, whose band was hired by the club in 1927, composed and played what
was labeled "jungle music" while attiring and carrying himself like nobility. That's why they called him Duke. (Perhaps the savage context helped
make his blinding sophistication more palatable to white egos.) Among
tap dancers, immaculate Bill Robinson set the standard of dress. Peg Leg
Bates soon had a peg to match the color of each of his suits. Posing in
his promotional photos, he cut a figure to be envied, not pitied. "The way
you looked," he remembered, "was how you was judged."

EDDIE RECTOR AND THE CLASS ACT

Just as Ellington's suaveness went beyond fashion, tap dancers' wardrobe
choices were outward symbols of a deeper refinement under development, most explicitly in a tradition that came to be called the class act. It
derived from the soft shoe, from the Picture Dancing of George Primrose. Sartorially, the class acts drew upon the fin-de-siècle cakewalker
Charles Johnson and also Rufus Greenlee and Thaddeus Drayton, a
tuxedo-and-monocle duo who filled the breaks of their soft shoe with
repartee in seven languages. Ginger Jack Wiggins swung the tradition a
little harder, as did Willie Covan, billed as "poetry of motion" with U. S.
Thompson or Leonard Ruffin. "Effortless steppers who mix some light
trick stuff in with pure soft-shoe rhythmatics" was how *Variety* described
Covan and Thompson in 1923.

Eddie Rector took it from there. His first stage costume was a dress, the
outfit of a pickaninny in a white singer's act. In the Darktown Follies, he
danced a military tattoo in a porter's uniform. With Toots Davis, Leonard
Ruffin, and later with his second wife, Grace, Rector toured TOBA
and the Keith circuit. By the time it was getting dark on Broadway, he
had exchanged his bandanna and blackface for a top hat, tails, and a cape,
all in pearl gray. The cornerstone of his "Bambalina" routine was a time
step, but Rector didn't stay in one place; he spread his taps around, float-

ing from one side of the stage to the other, tilted like a man blown by the wind. He danced with his arms, with his hands. In one *Dixie to Broadway* sketch, his character came upon ladies drinking tea. He asked each woman to dance, and one by one, they refused. Undefeated, he did the Bambalina by himself, his arms shaped around an imaginary partner. Pete Nugent, who modeled himself on Rector, remembered the routine as one that could make you laugh and cry at the same time.

Photos show a light-skinned man, elegant to his fingertips. In one shot, Rector cups a hand next to an ear, anticipating applause or reminding the audience to listen. His innovations weren't exclusively visual. He appropriated the Waltz Clog, a step and meter associated with Irish performers in the line of Pat Rooney and his progeny. What most impressed Nugent was how the older dancer "dovetailed" his steps together—his transitions, his rhythmic grammar. The only document of Rector's dancing is in audio form. At the Cotton Club one night in 1931, the German broadcaster Hellmut H. Hellmut set out to give his radio listeners a short emotional holiday. Rector's taps flow like Robinson's, grouped into three-and-a-break. But the brook over pebbles has hit the rapids. The accents are sharper—triplets tumbling irregularly over the beat, rhythms doubling back in little whirlpools. Deep thumps open up greater contrasts between bass and treble and a less predictable conversation between the two registers. To hear this music, one has to listen through some minstrel-show voice that asks, "How many legs you got?" and orders a barking dog not to bite. Hellmut confuses Rector's name with that of Eddie Cantor, the Jewish blackface comedian. Cantor could tap, but not like this.

Through the twenties, Rector had appeared in several black Broadway revues, mistaken for Johnny Nit in *Liza*, overshadowed by Florence Mills in *Dixie to Broadway*, outshone by Robinson in *Blackbirds of 1928*. When *Blackbirds* migrated to Paris and Robinson left for higher-paying vaudeville, Rector crossed the Atlantic in Bojangles's place. (That's when he received the telegram from Robinson threatening murder if he attempted a stair dance. Rector called Robinson's bluff, but Parisian critics largely ignored him.) He was a regular at Connie's Inn and the Cotton Club. On Broadway, in Lew Leslie's *Rhapsody in Black* (1930) and in the quick-sinking *Hot Rhythm* (1930) and *Yeah-Man* (1932), he earned praise from the *Times* as a "footloose aristocrat." The veteran critic

Burns Mantle suggested that Rector did things that Robinson wouldn't try, and in the black press, where Rector's name had long been attached to superlatives, Theophilus Lewis proposed that Rector's stair dance might be superior. But Rector didn't have Robinson's showmanship. Or maybe there just wasn't room for more than one.

He migrated to Los Angeles, where he danced, played trumpet, and directed revues for the Cotton Club there but appeared in no films. When he returned to the Lafayette in 1934, resplendent in beige satin, he was greeted as a prodigal son. The homecoming was not only a return from California. He had also spent time in a mental institution. All along, alcohol had been a problem. Before Buddy Bradley embarked on his career as the Invisible Man of Broadway choreography, he worked as a Connie's Inn chorus boy when Rector was in the show. Sometimes Rector would be too drunk to stand, so Bradley and the other chorus boys would hold him up while he dressed, push him onstage, then watch in wonder as he executed a six-minute routine perfectly. Bradley considered Rector the most inventive of tap dancers, the most beautiful and ahead of his time.

A week after his comeback at the Lafayette, Rector requested a conference with the theater's manager, Frank Schiffman, and showed up for the meeting with a loaded .38-caliber Colt revolver. Alerted by his staff, Schiffman summoned the police. According to Rector's dance partner Ralph Cooper, Rector was upset that Schiffman was paying him less than promised, a common complaint about this manager. Bill Robinson came along with the cops, presumably to intercede, but considering the bad blood between him and Rector, who knows? Rector, unlike Robinson, had no gun permit. After pleading guilty to a weapon possession charge, he was declared insane and committed to an asylum in Long Island. After a year or so, he was released, but he spent the remainder of the thirties convalescing as his imitators spread his influence.

FLASH

Dan Healy, the producer of Cotton Club shows during Rector's day, had been a vaudeville tapper himself, a principal in the Follies. The guy was a Damon Runyon character, cozy with mobsters and entirely convincing as a sleazy dancer in the 1929 Ziegfeld-produced film *Glorifying the American Girl*, where he manages some ancient moves his character speaks of as "new steps." Interviewed in the 1960s, he would remember the end of the twenties as the time when black dancers "became as good as anybody." Their main contributions, he thought, were "wings, personality, and a lot of enthusiasm."

Healy wasn't thinking of Eddie Rector. He was thinking of "hot" dancing to go with "hot" music. He was thinking of flash. For years, tap dancers had been incorporating stunts picked up from foreign acrobatic troupes on vaudeville circuits. Now they went wild. Splits proliferated, not eased into gently but thrown down like exclamation points. These splits went splat, which looked not just difficult but painful. Competition between acts—and within them via the ubiquitous challenge-dance format—insured that the ante was continually upped: not just a flip or a split, but a flip into a split; not just a flip into a split, but a run up the wall into a backward flip into a split-and-recover. Flash acts piled it on and kept up the pace, but what most distinguished flash act acrobatics from the European or Asian variety was rhythm, jazz rhythm. The stunts were danced. A spin was a windup; stopping made the sound. Jumps and flips made flash dancers masters of the air, but the emphasis was less on going up than on coming back down. When flash dancers hit the floor, they hit an accent, one simultaneously visual, aural, and kinesthetic—felt in the spectator's own joints.

If Eddie Rector could make you cry, flash acts were more likely to make you gasp. You couldn't necessarily tell a flash act from a class act by costume, though. The flash acts dressed classy, too. What almost all black dance acts had in common was rhythmic execution, which almost always included some tap. Even the acts that specialized in acrobatics tapped a bit. Snakehips Tucker tapped. At the same time, however, the technique of tap specialists was developing at an unprecedented clip. And if you wanted to gauge the state of the art, you didn't have to walk far from the Tree of Hope.

The Hoofers' Club was on the same block. It seems to have started, in late 1924, as the Colored Vaudeville Comedy Club, an elaborately furnished clubhouse, frequently raided for violations of the Volstead Act, where off-duty entertainers held professional meetings, performed for hundreds, and fought with one another. In late 1925, it reopened under the name of the Hoofers' Club, was raided, and reopened again. An article in *The Pittsburgh Courier* about this "place of recreation for the tired actor" announced officers, committees, and a board of directors (Bill Robinson, chairman); it mentioned a dancing studio with classes by Leonard Harper and a membership of five hundred. Since the president was Rudolph Brown, a notorious black gangster, it's likely that the club was a front for gambling and liquor. That's how Leonard Reed would remember it. Founding a club was a common strategy for getting around Prohibition. By 1930, after closing and reopening several more times, the place had changed its name to the Symphony Club, run by Lonnie Hicks, a black businessman with close ties to the Democratic Party machine. Hicks was the owner of the Hoofers' Club who would be remembered by dancers who arrived in New York after 1930, the guy who let them beat the floor in the back room of his gambling den.

Front or annex, this was where hoofers danced for other hoofers, without regard to theatrical conventions or time restrictions. The room served as rehearsal hall, academy, and prizefighting ring. The names of the greats were scratched on the walls. When Peg Leg Bates arrived in New York, it wasn't long before he visited the Hoofers' Club, for that was where a new kid in town had to go to prove himself to his peers. One day in 1927, it was Peg Leg Bates from Fountain Inn. A few years earlier, it had been John Bubbles, a singer from Louisville who was laughed out of the place on his first visit. When he visited a second time, nobody would laugh but him.

BUBBLES CUTS THE TEMPO, MULTIPLIES THE RHYTHM

The first time John Sublett went to a theater, he was seven years old. Convinced that he could outsing anybody in the show, he went backstage and said so, thereby gaining himself a job. From that point forward, although he worked many other jobs (stableboy, bat boy, dishwasher, seller of coal that he hauled with his pet goat), Sublett was a professional entertainer. He wasn't dancing yet. "You don't dance with the voice I had." His self-confidence brought him work but also trouble: when white kids threw rocks, young Sublett threw rocks back; when whites attacked, he pulled out his knife. Setting up pins in a Louisville bowling alley, he met Ford Lee Washington, an even younger boy, who played piano. Sublett's nickname was Bubber, Washington's was Buck, and as Buck and Bubbles the pair began performing in bars and carnivals. Eventually, the manager of the theater where they ushered asked them to replace a weak act. This was, Bubbles later insisted, the first time blacks had played that theater, and the duo wore burnt cork "to fool the public." A traveling show offered to take them to New York, and so, in 1920, the seventeen-year-old Bubbles and the thirteen-year-old Buck hit the road.

Roller-skating to the office of a New York music publisher, the boys met an acrobat named Nat Nazarro, who agreed to tack them onto his act. As Nazarro's sons balanced on his body, Buck and Bubbles would run on from the audience, ask where colored boys were allowed to sit, then dart through Nazarro's legs and launch into their own songs. A few days after the meeting, while waiting to go on at the Columbia Theatre, Bubbles overheard the house manager telling Nazarro he didn't want any niggers on his stage. That was before Buck and Bubbles performed. Afterward, the manager was asking, "Where are those two colored boys?" and locking them in their dressing room so they wouldn't get away. Reviewers started reporting on the amazing pickaninnies who were taking over Nazarro's act, and how Nazarro didn't seem to mind.

Around this time, Bubbles's voice cracked on a high note, and he decided that he ought to acquire another skill, just in case. Soon he visited the Hoofers' Club, where, after he took a turn, he heard the regulars tell him he was hurting the floor. Driven by humiliation, he worked on his dancing nonstop. One step in particular, a Double Over the Top, finally came to him during an all-night breakthrough practice session (the one in which he took off his shoes in deference to the downstairs neighbors). When he debuted his new variation at the Hoofers' Club, the sniggering ceased. Bubbles's contribution to tap would far exceed a single step. Many of his innovations were by-products of theft protection. "I didn't want 'em to copy *me*," he once explained, "so when I did a show I never did the same step the same way. If I got four shows, I'd do it four different ways . . . I'd do new steps and I'd do old steps and turn them into something else." For the same reason, he also blended his steps together into longer phrases that enjambed over bar lines, grouping them into rhythmic units less contained than Bill Robinson's.

Initially, like everybody else, Bubbles concentrated on dancing fast. Then, to set himself apart, and "thinking about when I got older," he cut his tempo in half, trading a brisk march for four-to-the-bar swing. Historically, this was a swing of the pendulum, reversing turn-of-the-century acceleration, except that while Bubbles cut the tempo of his accompaniment, he didn't always cut the tempo of his tapping. Instead, he used his metronome sense and gave himself options. He could coast at a soft-shoe pace, or he could shift gears, subdivide the beat, and fire off a burst of double or triple time. The slower base tempo gave him rhythmic room. Also, Bubbles explained, audiences appreciated the more leisurely pulse. Where flash dancers could seem frantic, Bubbles conveyed nonchalance, though his ease was less lulling than Robinson's. The eruptions of speed suggested reasons for the audience not to relax entirely.

Among dancers, Bubbles became known for "dropping the heels." Bubbles himself would later declare, "That's what I added to dancing: the heel." This is curious, considering that heels had been part of tap from at least as far back as the minstrel "heelologists." Even the cloggers and up-on-his-toes Bill Robinson used the back end of their feet, if sparingly. Bubbles's innovation, then, was not that he dropped his heels, but where he dropped them—where in the music. He used the thump to emphasize offbeat accents and to ground his more complex syncopations. The cramp roll, which involved an even dropping of toes and heels to sound like a short drumroll, had been around for decades before Bubbles compressed it into a crunch. He stuck a kick on the front and a stomp on the end, squeezing and shaping a drum-major step into something much more swinging. His drawn-out phrases and eased-up tempos had similar effects, and his looser, more weighted physicality sank into the rhythms. Small wonder Bubbles's style of tap acquired the label "rhythm dancing."

These signal developments transpired sometime between, say, 1922 and 1931. First interviewed around 1960, the dancers who had been there to note the changes and mark them as transformational weren't very solid about dates. Reviews from the time offer detail on the order of "clever on his feet." The earliest extant recording of Bubbles, in the

1929 short *In and Out*, looks like a haphazard Bill Robinson imitation, with an up-on-his-toes Bubbles dancing up and down packing crates rather than stairs. Most of the rhythms are Robinsonian, too, until the end, when his legs do figure eights, his heels strike, and the tap firecrackers pop in longer strings. Could this be Bubbles becoming Bubbles?

The larger dearth of documentation—very few recordings of tap at all until sound film took off in 1928—frustrates any systematic attempt to trace tap's rhythmic evolution, as well as any empirical examination of the idea, proposed by later tap dancers, that Bubbles actually anticipated and guided the rhythmic evolution of jazz musicians, rather than vice versa. The mid-twenties were the years when Fletcher Henderson and Ellington, among others, were developing big-band swing, trading a two-beat orientation for a smoother four-to-the-bar—changes it is partially possible to follow on recordings, changes that were accelerated by recordings. Reattributing any of those developments exclusively to one dancer would require a conspiracy theory, but it's worth remembering that the musicians were accompanying floor shows featuring tap dancers. Eddie Rector was at the Roseland Ballroom with Henderson when Louis Armstrong raised the bar for New York. He was in Chicago at the Sunset Café with Armstrong and Earl Hines at the time of their Hot Five recordings. So were Buck and Bubbles. If tap dancers, more free to concentrate on rhythmic innovation than time-keeping drummers or players of melodic instruments, were working out new approaches, innovative musicians were right there to hear them.

In the absence of better evidence, it seems safe to say that Bubbles was whipping up a novel blend. Though he often insisted that he had been influenced by no one, the truth was that he stole from everybody. His vaudeville touring exposed him to Harland Dixon's Lancashire clog, from which he admitted to pilfering toe-to-toe and toe-to-heel clicks. From dancers in the George Walker tradition, he took the strut. The intricate footwork of the former met the diagonal bodylines of the latter to produce, among other steps, off-kilter turns that did not cease shooting out rhythms just because the dancer happened to be revolving, and spins that rolled smoothly across heels and toes and doubled back on themselves without stopping for breath. Bubbles also copped to taking slides from white dancers—slipping and scooting steps from the white-black eccentric tradition. These he fashioned into a thing of beauty, later captured on film. Moving in a single direction like a man on a conveyer belt, Bubbles kicks and twists backward and forward and backward again. He tilts as if he were being dragged, but it's obvious who's in command. Though Bubbles crossed his legs as quickly as any legomaniac, someone so suave could hardly have been called eccentric. "I took the white boys' steps and the colored boys' steps," he liked to say, "and mixed 'em all together so you couldn't tell 'em, white or colored. I made it *me*." (Or, phrased differently, "I was everybody when you saw me for the different things I did, but I didn't have their style. I had my style.")

As much as other dancers revered Bubbles, he was best known as half of a colored comedy team. It was Buck and Bubbles, like Williams and Walker or Miller and Lyles before, like Stump and Stumpy, Moke and Poke, Red and Struggy, Slap and Happy, and countless other teams that followed. Bubbles was justly proud of his singing voice, a light, husky tenor that never lost the honey of a onetime boy soprano. Buck was an accomplished pianist, good enough to accompany Bessie Smith and Louis Armstrong on recordings. "He played a lotta piano," reported Mary Lou Williams, who played a lotta piano herself. "Especially while jamming," she specified. "Everything he did was unusual." As part of the act, Buck simultaneously played "Twelfth Street Rag" with his right hand and "Yes, We Have No Bananas" with his left.

Their comedy seems, from a historical distance, less distinctive. Buck, much shorter than Bubbles and bandy-legged, wore clothes that were too small, often a Little Lord Fauntleroy number. Along with manning the piano, chiming in with his serviceable baritone, and bickering with his partner, Buck pretended to challenge Bubbles as a dancer. The biggest applause, Buck later told *Dance Magazine*, came when he stubbed his toe. While Bubbles tossed off his rhythmic surprises, Buck fell off his piano stool, as if drowsy, and reached up to plunk notes from the floor. Between Buck's exaggerated indolence and Bubbles's nonchalance, the pair could have seemed the embodiment of John Martin's theory about the laziness of the Southern Negro. Neither wore blackface, but their jokes and patter sound pretty stale, or shrouded. Bubbles would wipe his face with a handkerchief, and Buck would ask him why he was taking off his makeup. "I'm not taking it off," Bubbles would reply, "I'm rubbing it in." To many white reviewers, all of this convention was the height of naturalness—compared with minstrel conventions, it might have seemed so. It was as if, one critic wrote in 1921, Nat Nazarro had grabbed two crap-playing kids at random off State Street. In 1927, after Buck and Bubbles had been touring continually for nearly a decade, another critic could watch them play musically talented stableboys in *Weather Clear, Track Fast* and proclaim them "utterly unconscious of the audience." It was meant as a compliment, and they *had* been stableboys once.

Buck and Bubbles were vaudevillians, highly successful ones. Nazarro, who had sensed through his thick glasses an easier way to make money than playing Atlas to his children, managed the team—the first in what would become a stable of Nazarro-managed black acts. Bubbles and Nazarro endlessly feuded and made up, leaving a trail of court battles three decades long in which Bubbles vainly tried to extricate himself and his partner from a series of exploitative contracts. (Where most agents took a 10 percent cut, Nazarro took 30 or 40.) But Bubbles always returned to Nazarro, resenting the tug of a loyalty he described in filial terms. (Maybe he felt as Louis Armstrong did about his own exploitative manager: always keep a white man behind you that'll put his hand on you and say, "This is *my* nigger.") Nazarro kept Buck and Bubbles on the white circuits. By 1922, the team was playing the Palace, where, according to *Variety*, they "tied the show in a knot." The audience wouldn't let them leave the stage. This was the pattern: Buck and Bubbles show up at a theater where few or no black acts have played before; the skeptical management demands that they cut precious minutes from their act; Buck and Bubbles perform, and the audience keeps them performing well beyond their originally allotted time. While most black acts worked in the number two slot, Buck and Bubbles played next-to-closing.

Their greatest triumph along this line came in 1931, when the pair joined the Ziegfeld Follies, the first black performers to do so since Bert Williams died in 1922. During the out-of-town tryouts in Pittsburgh, it was the same story: Buck and Bubbles, the colored specialty act, stopping the show. None of the white stars would follow them. The only place they could fit was right before the finale. And on opening night on Broadway, that was their spot, in a number titled "Harlem." It says so in the program, where, unlike the stars, Buck and Bubbles get no bios. White reviewers mentioned them barely or not at all, while the black press feted them as heroes. The previous year, the team's featured billing in *Blackbirds of 1930* hadn't garnered them much more attention from Broadway critics. "Bubbles got rhythm" was as far as it went. His innovations were apparently difficult to discern in his role as Aunt Jemima's husband, Cream of Wheat.

During the Follies run, the pair also played a week up in Harlem at the Lafayette, repeating the same act in two places each night. This practice was called "doubling," and this particular instance of it was, Bubbles recalled, like "going from the ridiculous to the sublime." Backstage downtown, "you could hear a pin fall." Backstage uptown, "you couldn't hear anything there was so much noise and so little respect." The audiences out front were equally contrastive. "At the Ziegfeld, it was a challenge between the acts; uptown, it was a challenge between the entertainer and the audience." Bubbles altered his dancing accordingly: "not different steps but with a different feeling." It's clear that the Harlem audiences demanded more, and it's also clear that Bubbles resented their participatory clamor. Throughout his career, the majority of the audiences he appeared before were white. Thinking back on that 1931 week of doubling, he would recall the thrill of making "this extreme transition" between the two venues, the two worlds. But it wasn't just that week. Bubbles was making the transition, culturally, all the time.

He had one protégé. As Bubbles and Buck matured enough not to look like boys anymore, Nazarro got the idea of bolstering them with a kiddie act. Around 1932, the manager found what he wanted in Shorty and Slim, a prepubescent pair out of Georgia. Christopher Samuel Columbus Green was the slim one, tall and gentle to James Walker's squat and cocky. Nazarro dubbed them Chuck and Chuckles and had the boys study their elders until they had memorized the act. (Sixty years later, Green could still recount all forty minutes of it.) During a Buck and Bubbles performance, Chuck and Chuckles would repeat portions in miniature. Before long, the junior team branched off, and their mix of comedy, song, and dance made for a popular act into the forties. Originally, it was Chuckles Walker, the better tap dancer back in Georgia, who was supposed to shadow Bubbles, but Chuck Green showed more interest. He moved into the Bubbles residence, where the master permitted him to steal steps and even taught him a few. From time to time, instructor and student would take a field trip to the Hoofers' Club.

DIME A DOZEN: ACTS OF THE THIRTIES

John Bubbles did not spend much time in the Hoofers' Club. He liked to say that the place had been "full of good dancers—good out-of-work dancers" while he was making big money on the Orpheum circuit. Nevertheless, a song he recorded in 1933 (and may have written) would have made an apt choice as the club's anthem. It set to music the leading business model for black jazz musicians. It was called "Rhythm for Sale." In a rhythm-mad world, the lyrics declared, "Colored folks are mighty glad / 'Cause they've got rhythm for sale." Another stanza recounted how Africans used to beat their tom-toms for free and how things were different in Harlem.

Having rhythm for sale became particularly important as the Depression settled in. An expanding tier of Hoofers' Club habitués was made up of young men who lived with their parents and had few prospects of ordinary employment. "We had lots and lots of time to practice," one of them remembered. And with all the nightclubs and revues in a rhythm-mad nation, demand for tap dancers seemed to be high and rising. In Harlem and other black urban zones, young dancers met, and after a while, a few of them would decide to put together an act, a team. The team might not last long. The Midnight Steppers, a trio out of Chicago, made a splash at Connie's Inn in 1929, but an argument over gambling debts split them up within months. Other teams persisted for years and years, perhaps holding on to a name as members shuffled in and out. Groups came in twos and fours and especially threes, and they kept coming—a flood of tap acts that wouldn't abate for two decades. Some sold flash and some sold class, but they all sold rhythm. Some were recognized by the white world, some not.

———

Maceo Anderson, whose family had come up from Charleston on a cotton boat in 1916, organized his own Hoofers' Club in the basement of his Harlem apartment building. The neighborhood kids would challenge one another half the night, fueled by a big pot of beans and rice. Having outgrown a job as a pick, Anderson joined up with Al Williams and William "Red" Gordon, both also in their late teens and from families recently arrived from the South. The three of them kept sneaking into the Cotton Club through the back door, pleading with Duke Ellington until he let them go on during intermission. As the Three Ebony Steppers, the boys were a hit, and Ellington composed numbers for them. They added a fourth member, Sherman Robinson, and lasted at the Cotton Club for four years as the Four Step Brothers. The name was more than a pun. In their signature challenge dance, each man was allotted four four-bar steps. The arrangement formalized street practice, with the boys clapping the beat for one another. The serial structure gave each dancer time to shine but also to rest, which meant that during his turn, he could shoot the works.

Though black acts were barely represented in Hollywood musicals of the early sound era, the Vitaphone Corporation, a subsidiary of Warner Brothers, experimented with all-black shorts, filmed in New York. In *Barbershop Blues*, from 1933, when a barbershop proprietor picks a lucky number, he uses his winnings to spruce up his place of business, hiring a band to play and the Four Step Brothers to shine shoes in rhythm. These dancers may do a Bill Robinson step or two, but Bojangles would have cracked his soles if he struck the ground so hard. The Step Brothers don't just tap out a rhythm; they hammer it into the floor, punching holes with the tips of their toes and occasionally loading their full weight onto those precarious perches. No glass of water would have a chance on their heads. During the challenge dance, the last guy does two-legged wings from a deep crouch, opening and closing his limbs like scissors, five sounds to a snip. For the finish, the men form an indomitable front line of trenches and Over the Tops. That's how the Four Step Brothers faced hard times, head-on. Al Williams would remember, "We were never aware of the Depression because we were working all the time." With a shifting lineup, the group would last nearly until the end of the century.

The parents of the Nicholas Brothers played in TOBA pit bands and were, by all accounts, excellent musicians: she a stride-piano adept, he a "show drummer" who juggled his sticks. The children of such parents couldn't escape jazz, whether rocking in a bassinet in the orchestra pit or loitering in the wings each day after school. Starting in Mobile, the family trekked from theater to theater, Chicago to Winston-Salem. In Baltimore, young Fayard saw Ginger Jack Wiggins do a split and tried it himself, sliding all the way down and squeezing back up without using his hands. His muscles were young and elastic, and it came easy. The time step, however, Fayard initially found difficult. Enlisting his sister and brother, he formed an act. Leonard Reed, who came through Baltimore in 1926, remembered that the Nicholas Kids stopped the show there, especially when Harold, the youngest, toddled out. The family settled in Philadelphia, where the parents ran the pit band of the Standard Theatre, calling themselves the Nicholas Collegians and dressing in preppy white sweaters. Fayard observed and absorbed: Eddie Rector, Buck and Bubbles, the Whitman Sisters. "Fayard was in everybody's way in the wings, watching everybody," Reed recalled. "He could do anybody he wanted to do."

Fayard practiced in his living room, practiced on the fire escape, practiced in his dreams. "If I thought of something," he once recalled, "to keep from losing it, I'd start performing it." Another tactic was to teach his brother. (His bookish sister bowed out early.) Seven years younger than Fayard, Harold was a preternatural mimic who entertained the family with his Louis Armstrong imitiation. At first, Harold also struggled with the time step, but the logic clicked one day while he was washing the dishes. Keeping up with his big brother was no sweat. They made their debut over the airwaves, on the popular radio program the *Horn and Hardart Children's Hour*. It would be their last amateur show. The boys' father insisted on professional engagements, and from then on, it was the typical early-life-of-a-tap-star story, accelerated. Everywhere, they stopped the show; everywhere, they earned the next-to-closing spot. One night near the end of 1931, Frank Schiffman, the manager of the Lafayette, knocked on their dressing-room door. The whole family packed for Harlem.

Not just anywhere in Harlem. The Nicholases moved to Sugar Hill, Harlem's most exclusive residential district. And after the boys triumphed at the Lafayette, their father did not consider just any job. The managers of Connie's Inn and the Cotton Club both bid for the act, but the Cotton Club offered more cash, and the club's front man, Herman Stark, took the boys under his personal management. Six nights a week, two or three shows per night, the brothers did their bit, now decked out in tiny tailcoats. At home, the boys had a private tutor, and a chauffeur drove them to the club, where they also enjoyed privileges. Playing downtown at the Paramount Theatre with the Ellington band, they were pulled out of the show by truancy officers. Uptown, under the protection of the mob, child labor laws did not apply. Unlike the other Cotton Club performers, the Nicholas kids were allowed to mingle with the patrons, to sip orange juice at the table of Tallulah Bankhead. Recalling these actions for interviewers, Fayard would stress their importance: "because we could show them that black people had class."

The brothers' Lafayette debut led to their being cast in the Vitaphone short *Pie, Pie Blackbird* (1932). According to their biographer Constance Valis Hill, Fayard is eighteen in the film; Harold, eleven. They could pass for much younger. (Fayard told Marshall Stearns that he and his brother were fourteen and seven, which at least looks more accurate.) Harold comes up to Fayard's lower ribs. The brothers play pickaninnies to Nina Mae McKinney's mammy figure as she sings to them about a blackbird pie she's making for the master. In close-up, the pie peels back to reveal Eubie Blake's band, cooking up some jazz in pastry-chef uniforms, and soon the Nicholas Brothers skip on for a challenge dance to set before a king. Fayard opens with Over the Tops, bent way over, his limbs crossing and slashing far more than the step requires. He finishes on toe-tip. "Yeah!" screams his little brother, hopping to the beat on his toes and screaming "Yeah!" for himself. When Fayard tries to break in, Harold brushes him off—he's not done yet—and punches out Over the Tops piked even closer to horizontal than his brother managed. Fayard's next turn, building intensity by repeating a step, crests with no-hands splits. "I can take that!" Harold yells, executing Over the Tops and trenches with such reckless force that he's either going to lose a tooth or levitate. Gravity seems to operate differently on his insubstantial mass. The band accelerates, and the brothers' time steps are obscured by smoke. When the smoke clears, two dancing skeletons remain, a disturbing joke about "hot" jazz.

The routine is a summation of twenties tap in two and a half minutes, everything that Fayard assimilated at the Standard Theatre. The phrases are Robinson-tidy—eight-bar segments divided into three-and-a-break or tiled with one step—but these brothers hit the ground just as hard as the Four Step fraternity, and they put even more planes into motion. Stories of their stopping every show need no more proof than this clip. Yet the special charm of the number lies in their attitude toward each other, which really does feel fraternal—loving, with a strong undercurrent of rivalry. Fayard's dancing is more complicated, physically and rhythmically, shifting in and out of double time, but his artistry is trumped by Harold's charisma. The elder brother, the gentle one who has choreographed the dance, gets upstaged by his impish pupil. Teacher looks pleased.

In two later shorts, *All-Colored Vaudeville* (1935) and *The Black Network* (1936), you can watch the Nicholas Brothers develop, their technique broadening to include wings, their theatricality expanding in cute gestures. They smooth their hair. They tighten their ties. Fayard places a finger on top of Harold's head and Harold revolves. In *The Black Network*'s "Lucky Number," they're a real team, tapping out a tricky routine mostly in unison. Both brothers sing, but Harold's the singer, flaunting the adult vocal skills with which he imitated Cab Calloway at the Cotton Club. Fayard, for his part, has achieved a new level of grace. Early on, his father the show drummer encouraged him to pay attention to his hands, not just to his drumming feet. Fayard rented a room with mirrors in a Philadelphia rehearsal hall and worked on those upper extremities. To the end of his life, his hands would rank, next to his brother, as his greatest point of pride.

The Nicholas Brothers weren't relegated exclusively to all-black shorts. After catching their act at the Cotton Club, Sam Goldwyn hired them for the 1934 Eddie Cantor comedy *Kid Millions*. In one number, Harold dons white tails and a top hat to sing "I Want to Be a Minstrel Man," and though the lyrics speak of a longing for "those minstrel days," Harold's aspirations are better explained by the line of white minstrel-loving Goldwyn Girls who surround him. (Harold played the same precocious game with the chorus girls at the Cotton Club and with a sepia chorus in the 1933 film of *Emperor Jones*.) Later in *Kid Millions*, Harold and Fayard do a challenge dance with Cantor, the Jewish black-face comedian. The brothers don't let the film's star take a turn, and when they finally wave him in, he scoots away in surrender. The idea of Cantor challenging the Nicholas Brothers is treated as farce, no contest. The tone matches that of an earlier scene in which Cantor, working hard to apply his blackface, looks at his dark-skinned servant and says, in all sincerity, "You know, you're lucky."

The next two years found Harold and Fayard in the more obscure *Jealousy*, *Coronado*, *Don't Gamble with Love*, and *My American Wife*. Even when they weren't alloted much screen time—thirty seconds in the middle of a finale—they were always presented as exceptional. For the *Big Broadcast of 1936*, an all-star extravaganza, the brothers were even allowed small speaking roles. Harold, in coat, tie, and shorts, gives tap lessons over the radio. (Not a screenwriter's fancy, this: people actually did it.) In the middle of one number, the film cuts to another pair of tapping feet, these belonging to Bill Robinson, who taps down the sidewalk like a Pied Hoofer gathering a crowd in his wake. Figuratively, it was the Nicholas Brothers who were right behind him.

The "most important colored discovery of the season" was what *Billboard* called the duo of Pops and Louie after their 1933 debut at the Paramount Theatre. That year they appeared regularly on NBC radio and made a Warner Brothers short (*The Big Benefit*) with Bill Robinson. The following year, their "acrobatic fireworks," along with their "magic feet and ingratiating personalities," earned encore after encore at Loew's State, and after they played the Cotton Club, *The Chicago Defender* rated them "the only rivals" to the Nicholas Brothers. At the Earle in Philadelphia, Eddie Cantor affectionately spoke of them as sons, but the black press knew Pops as the scion of the Whitman Sisters. Louis Williams was a dark, sunny New Orleans boy whose parents had signed him over into Mabel Whitman's care. As teenagers, he and Pops developed what Williams described as an "ad lib song-and-dance act, singing duets together and doing whatever we felt like." Often, what Pops felt like doing was some of the most impossible-seeming acrobatic tapping ever—including the out-of-nowhere flips that inspired Buster Brown. Pops and Louie regularly appeared in white venues and headlined in black ones, but there would be no follow-up to that one film—which may or may not still exist— until 1943. Management by Mabel, as opposed to by better-connected and less scrupulous white agents, may have held them back.

Most duos were comedy teams. Tap acts did come in foursomes—in addition to the Four Step Brothers, there were the Four Flash Devils, the Four Bobs—but trios were definitely in: the Three Speed Kings, the Three Speed Demons, the Three Princes of Rhythm, the Three Sparks of Rhythm, the Three Bits of Rhythm, the Three Rhythm Steppers, and the Three Pepper Pots. The Three Browns—not to be confused with the Three Brown Jacks, the Three Brown Spots, the Three Brown Buddies, or the Three Brown Brothers—had combined tap with knee drops and splits in the mid-twenties. The Three Eddies were known as the fastest team of that time. This trio of Tiny Ray, Chick Horsey, and Charles Woody took its name and its look—oversized white-framed glasses, bowler hats, and blackface—from Eddie Cantor. As filmed by British Pathé in 1930, they sang spirituals in barbershop harmony before Horsey unleashed an onslaught of frenzied wings, his torso stiff, his feet spinning like a cartoon character's off a cliff. Their challenge dance was absurdly accelerated, with struts, slides, Chaplinesque waddles, Bojangles steps, and backward steps all thrown at a breakneck tempo, taps falling where they may. Around the same time, another trio, the Three Little Words, was popularizing the Shim Sham in Harlem.

The team of Teddy Frazier, Sammy Green, and Raymond Winfield debuted in 1929 as the Three Rhythm Kings, an accurate-enough billing. But there were too many groups with similar names, so Frazier and his pals, experts in tip-of-the-toe tapping, adopted the moniker Tip, Tap, and Toe. (This was a nonnumerical way to title a trio, as in Pot, Pan, and Skillet.) In the 1935 Vitaphone short *By Request*, up on a knee-high platform just large enough to fit them, the three men put down rhythms in bellboy caps. While the man in the middle stays put, the outside guys make a shell game of themselves, occasionally holding down one phrase while the middleman holds down another. When it's time for solos, rhythm-making cedes to flash. One guy stabs a toe tip into the ground and wings the other foot, with one of his arms churning as though he were cranking himself. Bearing his full weight, the toes curl over, which looks impressive but also unpleasant.

Only the man in the middle, Raymond Winfield, truly stands out. He indulges in the most obvious flash—both legs winging, both arms windmilling—but much more characteristic is the way his torso lingers before snapping around in a turn, or his cool ascent from splits, with one hand raised high as though he were hoisting himself by an invisible hook. There's just a taste in *By Request*, but Winfield would become master of the slide, shedding the clownishness of slipping to bring into staccato tap a species of legato. Not that Winfield was too cool for fun. In one of his signature steps, he slid his legs open and closed, open and closed, snapping an offbeat accent with the out stroke as he reflected the lower-body action with his hands, his languid fingers dragging behind his wrists as he batted his eyelashes. It's as if he were operating his legs through the telekinesis of a flirtatious carnival magician. Tip, Tap, and Toe held their own in advanced technique, but Winfield set the act apart.

CLASSIFICATION

"Our trio had class," said Jimmy Mordecai of Wells, Mordecai, and Taylor, a.k.a. the Three Klassy Kids. His evidence? "We had six changes of costume." At the Cotton Club in 1929, the trio, billed as "Hot Feet Boys," was known for a routine called "Hittin' the Bottle," which gave a winking Prohibition title to an old Southern game of dancing as close as possible to bottles without knocking them over. In the 1929 short *St. Louis Blues*, Mordecai looks brutally suave while giving Bessie Smith something to sing the blues about, and it's a show of his pimp-worthy arrogance when, after grandly entering a nightclub where waiters spin trays, he pulls out slashing wings and Over the Tops that are wardrobe-testing enough for any flash team. His team didn't last long. Dickie Wells opened a club, Ernest Taylor died in 1934, and Mordecai strutted on as a man about Harlem. Their trio would be remembered as a class act.

Precision was involved in that distinction, multiple men tapping as one. In the late twenties, Eddie Rector and Ralph Cooper finished their act shoulder to shoulder, unifying their rhythms so that, as Cooper described it, "you could close your eyes and think one person was dancing." Rutledge and Taylor were credited with establishing the One Man Dance, stacking themselves one behind the other. The Five Blazers, also known as the Five Hot Shots, multiplied the effect (as can be seen, further multiplied by a glassy floor, in the arty 1929 Ellington short *Black and Tan*). Attire carried enormous significance. "Correct Dress More Than Steps Make Pete, Duke" read a 1935 headline in the *Defender*. Explaining that the trio of Pete, Peaches, and Duke attributed their success to their appearance, the article catalogued the team's 26 suits each and 26 pairs of shoes, plus a collective total of 190 shirts, 30 sets of cufflinks, 300 handkerchiefs, and more than 300 ties. As Gary "Pete" Nugent would recall it, their act was built on acceleration: after a unison soft shoe or military drill in yachting uniforms, Irving "Peaches" Berman started his solo nice and easy; Nugent cranked the tempo up a notch, and Duquesne "Duke" Miller finished at a gallop. The structure was a little more sophisticated than the standard challenge form, more interwoven, in that the entire trio reconvened briefly in the middle of each solo. They exited as one.

Restraint was also a distinguishing characteristic. "With the accompaniment fortissimo," Nugent explained, "it's a terrible temptation to let go with some flash steps." Class acts resisted that temptation. (Onstage, at least; in offstage cutting contests, Nugent said, "we'd never let anybody shoot us down.") The Lucky Seven Trio, according to one of its members, was a class novelty act. That meant that although they danced on dice, they eschewed knee falls and splits. They, too, had six changes of costume.

At some level, though, the class–act distinction was about social class—about class and color. Pete Nugent stemmed from the light-skinned Negro aristocracy of Washington, D.C. His pale mother was descended from a Scottish Loyalist; his slightly darker father was an elevator man in the Capitol. Passing for white in New York, his mother boarded her more Negro-looking sons apart from her in Harlem. Pete's older brother, Richard Bruce, became a leading writer of the Harlem Renaissance (the period during which, as Richard archly explained in a late-thirties essay, "Northern dilettantes discovered that Negroes possessed cultural as well as tap-dancing ability"). Pete began dancing on the black circuit at sixteen, and all his life he swore like a sailor in defiance of his proper upbringing. Pete, Peaches, and Duke, "Society's Sepia Sons," were all light-skinned, with thin noses and lips. Nugent once said that during the first ten minutes of their act, the taps were drowned out by the sound of people asking one another, Are they white or colored?

"I'm a tap dancer, of course," Nugent declared, "but if you have to make a choice, I prefer all body motion and no tap to all tap and no body motion. Any hoofer can execute all the steps, but the way a man handles his body and travels is what gives it class." That aesthetic preference carried connotations beyond aesthetics. The class acts sought to replace demeaning stereotypes with a dignified image—to show whites, in Fayard Nicholas's phrase, that black people had class. Yet "class" also remained a way of distinguishing *between* black people. "Class" and "flash" could be fighting words. Flash acts faulted class acts for lacking punch; class acts disdained flash acts as vulgar. "Class act" tended to be a self-definition, "flash act" a label imposed from without. Who, in the 1930s, didn't want to be classy?

Duke Miller died of influenza in 1937, at age twenty-seven. Peaches formed an unsuccessful Negro Ballet, while Pete earned fresh acclaim as a single, noted for advancing the elegant style of Eddie Rector, billed as Public Tapper #1 or the Sepia Fred Astaire. The team never made any films, but one group that copied them did. In a 1933 Vitaphone short, the Three Dukes (Leslie "Bubba" Gaines, Arthur "Pye" Russell, and James "Hutch" Hudson) crash a party in police uniforms. Their model's structure of solos interlaced with unison is there, but only roughly: it looks as though one guy didn't learn the routine. There isn't much routine to know, and each solo is basically a different wing repeated. There's little hint of the sophisticated dancer Gaines would become, and curiously, the team's specialty doesn't appear. "The Aristocrats of Dancing," as the Three Dukes subtitled themselves, were amateur boxers, skilled at jumping rope. For their 1933 debut at the Alhambra, they dipped their ropes, gloves, and shoes in radium paint, and asked for a blackout with an ultraviolet spotlight. The intended haunted-house effect of ropes, gloves, and shoes dancing by themselves combined with an unintended one of flaking paint scattering like sparks. The outcome was what they hoped for: a contract with Buck and Bubbles's agent, Nat Nazarro. Into the Cotton Club they went.

The jump-roping, tap-dancing redcap in the 1932 Vitaphone short *Smash Your Baggage* could be Hutch, but even if it's Danny Alexander (also known for his rope specialty), the film documents the general idea. The guy jumps rope while doing time steps, while squatting, while bouncing off his knees. But tapping while jumping rope isn't only a stunt. As the rope ticks steadily against the floor, its circling manifests the inexorability of the beat, the way it's always coming around again. The rope compounds the physical consequences of a tapper's timing. And the jump-roping tapper in *Smash Your Baggage* clarifies something else about the style of tap dominant in the film and popular in its period. The other dancers look like they're jumping rope even when there's no rope in sight. Quick tempos make them frantic, comic, "crazy." This is the style of tap that John Bubbles eased away from.

ONE-MAN DANCE

Single black tap acts were always rarer, perhaps because minstrelsy and vaudeville had trained audiences to expect black dancers in units no smaller than two. Peg Leg Bates was a kind of novelty, set apart first by his peg and then by his talent. The "flashy monopede" worked alone and continually through the thirties, traveling by limousine between vaudeville theaters, nightclubs, and revues, bowling over audiences black and white but mostly white. "I don't want no sympathy," he sang, and his flamboyant display of not needing any made people stand up in gratitude. As a single, he was second in fame to the perennial exception, Bill Robinson.

Bill Bailey, born in Virginia, spent his adolescence in Philadelphia. In New York, he was discovered by Lew Leslie, who promptly threw the eighteen-year-old into *Blackbirds of 1930*. Soon, he teamed up with Derby Wilson, a habitué of the Hoofers' Club five years his senior and already a veteran of black revues. Together, they challenged each other at the Cotton Club and toured with Ellington's band on its triumphant visit to Europe in 1933. (An ecstatic reviewer for Britain's *Melody Maker* regretted the inclusion of tap dancers; though brilliant, they interfered with his listening.) Within two years, the men had each gone solo with a Robinson imitation, talking and tapping. It was a strategy that proved successful for both but especially for Bailey, who sometimes replaced Robinson in nightclubs when the star was filming in Hollywood. The black press kept making false predictions that Bailey would follow Robinson into film stardom.

Soloists who only tapped were especially scarce. In his late teens, Roland Holder taught with (and learned from) Buddy Bradley before earning esteem in the 1929 *Hot Chocolates* at Connie's Inn. The 1931 film *The Exile*, by the black filmmaker Oscar Micheaux, preserves his act. A small man under a top hat, he works up on his toes like Bojangles, his phrasing similarly symmetrical, but he puts that formal regularity in tension with a slanting body, lackadaisical revolutions, and meandering stage patterns. Diffident yet distinctive, he knocks off wonderful steps that show up nowhere else on film. Holder was a regular feature in black revues until mid-decade; by decade's end, his press mentions would turn to burglary charges. (Dope did him in, according to Bailey.)

When Charles "Honi" Coles went solo, it was not exactly by choice. He began as one of the Three Millers. (George and Danny Miller were brothers. Their sibling Duke performed with Pete and Peaches.) Coles had been given the nickname Honey by his older sister, and it was sewn onto the jacket he wore as a member of the boys' club the Jolly Buccaneers until continual razzing induced him to alter the spelling. He and the Millers were all sons of Philadelphia, a town so teeming with tap dancers that the street corners were categorized by skill level—this one for beginners, that one for intermediates, the rankings determined in challenges under the spotlight of a streetlamp. "That was our only form of entertainment," Coles remembered, which wasn't entirely true, since he also recalled attending shows at the Earle and Standard theaters and stopping in every doorway on his way home, trying to remember the steps. The coins that Coles and his friends earned dancing on the street bought them tickets to see their betters on stage before they broke into showbiz themselves.

The Miller Brothers practiced an act on pedestals six feet high and about a foot wide. Up onto these platforms they transferred trenches and barrel rolls, sensationalizing their superior balance. A booking with the 1931 revue *Dixie on Parade* carried the young dancers to New York, where their careers floundered without an agent. Back in Philly a year later, Coles learned to his surprise that the Millers were performing—without him. Fueled by visions of revenge, he holed himself up in a small room from which he removed all the furniture and practiced all day, every day, for at least a year. When he emerged, he was by his own estimation the fastest dancer in show business. He looked to Robinson for clarity, to Bubbles for rhythms. Where almost everybody else danced in eight-bar patterns, Coles stretched his phrases to double that length. He also crammed more in, doubling and tripling the beat. "I felt I couldn't leave any space open," he recalled of this phase so typical of youth. In pursuit of both speed and elegance, he began dancing in thin-soled shoes rather than his street companions' heavy footwear, their equipment for toe stands. His long legs extended the elegance, but his speed was unusual for a dancer so tall, made possible only by extreme efficiency. The man barely lifted his feet.

Returning to New York, Coles became king of the Hoofers' Club for a while. When he practiced at Joe Price's acrobatics studio downtown, white dancers came around to challenge him and walked away confused. He worked up three routines, but when he showed them to agents, the agents asked where the routines were. The patterns were too intricate or went by too fast. He danced a few solo gigs uptown, but ahead of his time for now, he mainly supported himself in the pool hall. He replaced a member of the Lucky Seven Trio, rivals to the Millers who changed their name to the Three Giants of Rhythm after Coles joined. In 1938, he teamed up with a comedian, then went single again, and was occasionally mentioned, in the black press, as a candidate for the position the black press was always trying to fill: the next Bill Robinson.

SISTER ACTS

What about the female royalty of rhythm? They were the rarest of them all. There were black women who broke out of the chorus, but almost all of their careers were shorter and less recognized than those of their male peers. Nat Nazarro, agent to so many male teams, also handled the Three Rhythm Queens. They commanded the stage of the Cotton Club in 1935 and disbanded the year after. The Edwards Sisters, Louise and Ruth, fared better, playing most of the same venues as the top brother acts into the forties. They came out of Columbus—trained, choreographed, and managed by their hoofer father, Jay, who ensured that the black press tracked his girls' bookings coast-to-coast. In photographs, they're cute kids, but these Twin Torpedoes of Rhythm left few traces beyond their impressive itineraries. There were black female singles, too. Early in the thirties, Elma Turner tapped at the Cotton Club as a soloist. As her career continued in Chicago clubs, she was one of several lady tappers promoted in photos that emphasized shapely legs and one of several praised in black newspapers as the best female dancer. But she was never very famous and was soon forgotten.

Women were accepted as singers, and tapping women often sang. On Broadway in the late twenties, a pudgy, owl-faced comedian named Mae Barnes did the buck and wing. Billed as the "Bronzed Ann Pennington," she cultivated a sleepy, deadpan style that *The New York Times* described as "bored, faintly annoyed." After a car accident thwarted her dancing, she had no difficulty sustaining a long career as a cabaret singer. In surviving fragments of the 1929 Micheaux film *Darktown Scandals*, Maud Mills, known as the sister of gone-too-soon Florence but also as Hardfoot Maud, caps off a growling blues number with a double-time chorus of time steps. Like many blues queens, she hoofed the way she sang. The 1933 short *That's the Spirit* shows Cora LaRedd as unusually dark-skinned for a gal who worked the Cotton Club, her chipmunk cheeks shining, her mighty thighs revealed in shorts. She goes all googly-eyed belting out "Jig Time," then keeps her smile bright as she pounds quick time steps with downward-driving intensity. LaRedd briefly led a band called the Red Peppers. She starred in several late-twenties black musicals downtown and even a short-lived white one. She cruised Harlem in a lavender Packard, and her career rode the Harlem vogue, up and down. By the early forties, she would be driving a taxi for a living.

Alice Whitman remained active as a main attraction of the Whitman Sisters. The black press regularly hailed her as the female Bojangles. In photos, she poses like a swimsuit model, and her "fabulous figure" was what Pete Nugent would remember about her, her pristine tapping almost an afterthought. The only time the white press took notice was in 1935, when she appeared as a soloist downtown. Louis Sobol, the syndicated Broadway columnist, selected her for special mention, "a blond, pretty, fast-stepping gal." He expressed disbelief that anyone so youthful-looking could be the mother of Pops, but youthfulness wasn't the aspect of her appearance that caused trouble. Soon, she was out of the show, and her sister Mabel claimed that she had been released from her contract on account of her light skin and blue eyes, the wrong look for a show called *Hot Chocolates*. After a brief spell in Chicago nightclubs, she returned to the Whitman fold. She was never filmed.

Louise Madison didn't make any films either, though fellow female dancers insisted that she outdanced everyone. "She danced like a man" was how male dancers put it, intending the supreme compliment. "She wasn't just a woman dancer because she surpassed all tap dancers," remembered Honi Coles, who grew up with Madison in Philadelphia and admitted, when pressed, to having learned from her. Bill Bailey made a similar confession and called Madison "the greatest of them all." The superlatives resound in a near vacuum of biographical data. She had a featured number in the unsuccessful *Blackbirds of 1933*, and in a group photo taken during that show's European tour and printed in *The Chicago Defender*, her dark face looks out happily. But thereafter even the black press seems to have mostly ignored her. LaVaughn Robinson, a slightly later Philadelphia hoofer, remembered seeing her at the Cotton Club in Lawnside, New Jersey, in the mid-forties, gleaming in white tails, wearing low-heeled shoes, and "doing so much dancing it was unbelievable." She was, he recalled, "tougher than any man." There were rumors about dope and the wrong crowd and her sexual orientation; the effects of her appearance or behavior on her career are unknowable.

Of all the black female soloists, the one who brushed closest to mainstream stardom was Jeni LeGon. Born on the South Side of Chicago in 1916, she grew up trading taps with the boys on her corner. On Saturdays, she spent all day at the theater, catching every step: "I would take it and tear it to pieces and make it my own." She did the same with the steps shown to her by girls who could afford dance classes. When LeGon auditioned for her first chorus line, she couldn't fill out the dress ("no bubs and no hips"), so she wore pants instead, a wardrobe choice that became a trademark. When the Four Step Brothers came through Chicago, they were so impressed—she had memorized their routine and improved upon one of the steps—that they recommended her to the Whitman Sisters. After six months with the Whitmans, LeGon broke off with her foster sister, forming a boy-girl duo in which LeGon played the boy. The young woman's flash style, replete with toe stands and other tricks, was considered unusual for a girl. Yet there was nothing butch about her cute, coquettish manner. A job offer at the Los Angeles Cotton Club fell through, but the prospect drew her to Hollywood, and it was through a misspelling in the influential gossip column of Louella Parsons that Jennie Ligon became Jeni LeGon.

For her film debut in RKO's 1935 *Hooray for Love*, she was cast opposite none other than Bill Robinson. In their routine, LeGon is evicted but the Mayor of Harlem cheers her up, singing that as long as she has "a snap in her fingers" and "a rhythm in her walk," she's "living in a great big way." While dancing, LeGon has all that, plus a jazz-baby bobble in her head and shoulders. Side by side with Bojangles, she puts enough pixie charm into their Shim Sham variations to complement her illustrious partner. There are bumps in her turtleneck now, but no hint of sex in the pairing. LeGon seems less a character than an expression of racial happiness, like the adorable black kids who peek out from under a blanket and the furniture mover who plays piano and sings like Fats Waller. It *is* Fats Waller, but this is a Bill Robinson number, climaxing in one of his bubbliest solos.

Even before the film was released, LeGon was already living in a great big way. Black newspapers made much of her, their movie star, the "Sepia Cinderella Girl." Her manager was Earl Dancer, the big-talking black manager-producer who had helped steer the great singer Ethel Waters onto white circuits. He crowed to the *Defender* that LeGon was "a child without race" who would "reign in moviedom without being typed" and "bridge the gap between the distinctly white and the distinctly black in films." MGM signed LeGon to a five-year contract. Promotional photos for her upcoming *Broadway Melody of 1935* showed her in a glamorous gown. In New York, someone, possibly John Bubbles, brought her to the Hoofers' Club: a woman into the temple, the one girl allowed in the treehouse. Yet *Hooray for Love* would turn out to be the premature peak of a film career heavy on parts for nondancing maids.

White female tap dancers didn't run into the same problems in Hollywood, but the problems weren't just about race, and they weren't restricted to Hollywood. The people who booked talent into nightclubs and theaters generally thought of black female dancers as chorus girls or shake dancers, as sex objects. If a tap dancer was required, a man was asked. One of those men, Cholly Atkins, remembered occasions when a club owner would solicit his advice about a replacement; if Atkins suggested a woman, the owner would say, "I want a man doing this thing." (Atkins recounted this only after his ghostwriter, Jacqui Malone, pressured him to address the woman question.) A tap-dancing woman was a hard sell, and few female tap dancers had agents to represent them. Representing themselves, they were shut out of backroom deals. They were also shut out of places like the Hoofers' Club, which served as an informal employment center, somewhere one could put together partnerships and learn which jobs were available. Most retired after they became mothers, a role difficult though not impossible to balance with life on the road. But the strongest cause-and-effect loop was probably the assumption of male supremacy. Black male hoofers tended to disregard women as inventors or thieves of steps made by men, for men's bodies; women who did pose a threat were more actively ignored. In tap's culture of competition, there was a feeling that virtuosity wasn't feminine. Quantitatively, chorus girls might have laid down the most taps, but they did so in a man's world.

THE APOLLO AND THE BIG BANDS

In Harlem, the repeal of Prohibition in 1933 was followed, a few years later, by a race riot, an enticement replaced by a deterrent. The Harlem vogue tapered off. The Cotton Club and Connie's Inn relocated downtown, where white customers felt safer, and the center of New York jazz drifted to clubs clustered on and around Fifty-second Street, dark and smoky places stuffed into the ground floors of brownstones where the bandstands were tiny and the music was for listening. In 1934, when Seventh Avenue was widened, the Tree of Hope was chopped down. A crowd of hundreds sighed when it fell. Shards and slivers were sold as souvenirs and talismans, and the stump, salvaged by Bill Robinson, was lacquered and bolted beside a new tree that Robinson persuaded the park commissioner, Robert Moses, to plant. That same year, the Hurtig and Seamon's burlesque theater on 125th Street reopened as the Apollo, and when the management of the Lafayette took over the venue in 1935, it replaced the Lafayette as Harlem's foremost live entertainment venue. A piece of the Tree of Hope ended up on the Apollo stage, a remnant of the True Cross to be touched by believers and aspirants.

Every week at the Apollo saw a different revue, six or seven acts, four shows a day with an extra midnight showing on Wednesdays and Saturdays. The Three Rhythm Kings were on the first bill, and tappers followed them on every bill thereafter. All the top black entertainers—and always a handful of white ones—played the venue, at prices that regular Harlem folk could afford. The house chorus line, long led by Ristina Banks, was the finest around. Week after week, as different acts passed through, the chorus girls stayed put, learning a new show's worth of routines, often choreographing numbers themselves. Chosen as much for their youth and beauty as for their dancing ability, many of the ladies were nevertheless perfectly capable of stealing any step they saw, though very few left the line to start dancing acts of their own. At the Apollo, there were seats for seventeen hundred, but four or five hundred more might squeeze in. These people, especially the tough customers in the second balcony, did not keep their feelings to themselves. Shows were routinely dialogues between performer and crowd, and the hecklers were often funnier than the comics. Apollo audiences showed no tolerance for the second-rate or the lazy, but they rewarded excellence with effusive love. In the thirties and forties, those audiences were frequently a third or more white—for the Saturday midnight show or the famous Amateur Night, whites sometimes formed the majority—but success at the Apollo meant something particular, a stamp of approval from Harlem. Black entertainers came to think of the place as home.

Tap dancers loved the Apollo's maple stage. For them, the toughest part of the tough crowd consisted of other tap dancers. Howard "Sandman" Sims, who was booed during his first Amateur Night appearance, described the scene when a tap act was on the bill: "Up in the balcony, dancers, and the first six rows, you saw nothing but tap dancers, wanta-be tap dancers, gonna-be tap dancers, tried-to-be tap dancers. That's the reason a guy would want to dance at the Apollo. But he would be scared to death; he'd do most of his dancing backstage, trembling." Dancers in the audience regularly challenged the dancers onstage. The Apollo was a proving ground, a high-visibility site for a cutting contest. Still, for everyone who wasn't a tap dancer, tap acts were seldom a major draw, and tappers were normally the lowest paid. One of the treasured stories of Amateur Night concerns a young lady who signed up intending to tap, but grew too intimidated watching the Edwards Sisters on the regular bill and decided to sing instead and use her rhythm that way. Her name was Ella Fitzgerald, and she made the right choice.

For all the ways in which the Apollo was special, its format was typical. Vaudeville had been dying for years. Records and then radio, nationalized in the mid-twenties, gave audiences more and more reasons to stay home. Films, initially absorbed into vaudeville bills as chasers, gradually took over their host. Hundreds of vaudeville theaters converted to cinemas, some preserving the stage show as a first course. During the twenties, the trend was toward "presentation houses," mammoth movie palaces that combined films with live entertainment. Like the vaudeville theaters they replaced, presentation houses were organized into national circuits. Variety acts were packaged into touring "units," most of which included tap dancers—soloists, small ensembles, or at the very least a chorus line.

In 1932, even the Palace was forced to abandon its two-a-day format for four-a-day with films. That same year, Radio City Music Hall opened as a cavernous Art Deco update of the all-variety theater. Within weeks, the venue capitulated to the presentation format. And although S. L. Rothafel, more popularly known as Roxy, had originally intended Radio City to feature an array of dance ranging upward to ballet and the highbrow modernism of Martha Graham, the face of the institution turned out to be its precision girl troupe. The troupe's creator, Russell Markert, had envisioned an American version of the Tiller Girls—taller girls, with more leg to flaunt, girls who could really tap. When he transplanted his Missouri Rockets, formed in St. Louis in 1926, to New York

and the Roxy Theater, he renamed them the Roxyettes, and after they
moved to Radio City, he split the difference. Selected for uniformity,
the thirty-six Rockettes made a wholesome machine, a sweet team
effort. Their trademark was the eye-high kickline, their most enduring routine a Parade of Wooden Soldiers who collapse onto one another in slow domino motion. But tap was the group's foundation—time
steps in rearranging formations, never too advanced but always exact.
The troupe set the standard for the satisfying lift of synchronized tap,
and through that satisfaction it endured. For a good portion of the
many, many people who applauded the Rockettes week after week,
tens of thousands each day, those pretty faces, long legs, and dancing
feet represented Radio City. They represented *New York* City, stood
for the U.S.A. and Christmas. In years to come, when tap would grow
scarce elsewhere, the Rockettes would abide, dependably tapping away.

There would be no black Rockettes until 1988. In the thirties, the
Apollo sometimes advertised its chorus line as the Apollo Rockettes, but
this was less emulation than opportunistic marketing. The main current
of imitation flowed in the opposite direction. At the Apollo, the show
was built around the band. The music was jazz acquiring the name *swing*,
a verb transformed into a noun to indicate a rhythmic approach. It was
dance music, unmistakably. Underneath the syncopated strikes of massed
horns or the swerves of a soloist were four steady beats to the bar, a horizontal bounce. In ballrooms and dance halls, more steps sprouted from
the line of the Texas Tommy and the Charleston. Folks were Truckin',
swiveling their feet and wiggling an index finger high. They were doing
the Suzie Q, scootching sideways on a grinding heel. They were Peckin'
like chickens and doing the Shim Sham, too—steps traveling from stage
to dance floor and back.

Many of the steps aggregated around the Lindy Hop, which put a
pair of dancers in mutual orbit, low and smooth, as centrifugal force
periodically spun them apart into "breakaways" or "swing-outs," opportunities for independent improvisation. For Lindy Hoppers, a swinging big band offered a superior ride, with plenty of horsepower and
deluxe suspension. The bands and the dancers challenged each other,
especially at Harlem's Savoy Ballroom, which became a kind of a Hoof-

ers' Club for Lindy Hoppers. Dance contests led to professional Lindy Hoppers, and the Lindy grew more theatrical; from its horizontal base, it went airborne and acrobatic, as the men flung the women around with apparent recklessness. The upended bodies, flailing legs, and exposed drawers conveyed an innocent exuberance despite the inevitable charges of indecency once whites took it up. "Those Lindy Hoppers made it tough for everybody," reported Pete Nugent, speaking from the tap dancer's perspective. "They made all the other dancers look like they were standing still."

"Rhythm is our business / Rhythm is what we sell." When the Jimmie Lunceford band sang those words in 1935, business was "swell," since big bands were becoming big draws, promoted through radio broadcasts and recordings and put in high demand by teenagers who wanted to dance. That year Benny Goodman, fronting a white band but using black arrangers, discovered a whole generation of middle-class whites responsive to swing moderated with pop. Swing became the nation's music, the label for an era. Goodman, the son of poor immigrants, Russian Jews, had learned jazz from black and white musicians who migrated from New Orleans to his hometown of Chicago, and his celebrity, predicated as much on his color as on his exceptional musicianship, was the latest chapter in the story that starts with minstrelsy. Daringly, he used his commercial clout to hire black musicians, but the rhythm business was still segregated, and business opportunities were better for whites.

Black bands reigned at theaters such as the Apollo. Before an appearance there, Earl Hines and his band threatened to walk out unless they were allowed to remain onstage the whole show. "I'm not going in the pit," Hines insisted. Other bands and bandleaders also refused to descend. The band became the headliner, and a unit was assembled to tour with it: a small chorus line, a comic, a singer, a dance act or two. Tap dancers were a standard component, especially with the top black bands. When Lunceford, Ellington, Cab Calloway, or Count Basie went on the road, tap acts went with them, often more than one at a time. Buck and Bubbles started their own band just to stay current.

It was now necessary for a tap act to provide musical arrangements.

Since few dancers were musically literate, this usually meant singing their ideas to an arranger, who translated the scatted rhythms into musical notation. In this way, the fit between dancers and their accompaniment grew tighter, more worked out in advance. Each flip could be reinforced not just with the cymbal crash of an alert drummer but with a blast from the entire brass section. An arrangement expertly tailored to a routine left less room for improvisation, but there wasn't all that much improvising in the unison work of the duos, trios, and quartets anyway. "The only time we'd improvise is *after* our act," Fayard Nicholas would explain. "People would want more and more, so we'd go back on, and my brother and I would improvise for the ladies . . . But that's not our act, improvising." The trick, for dancers and arrangers alike, was to maintain an impromptu spirit while coordinating many moving parts. Challenge dances, usually but not always choreographed, helped sustain the illusion.

Outside of the presentation theaters, tap dancers played nightclubs and cabarets. In Philadelphia and Boston, St. Louis and Kansas City, there were hundreds of lesser-known clubs, many here today and gone tomorrow, and these clubs were home to hundreds of lesser-known tap acts. Top spots such as Small's Paradise in Harlem, the Club DeLisa in Chicago, the Club Plantation in Detroit, and the Club Harlem in Atlantic City presented the bigger names in luxurious intimacy. The clubs were situated in black districts and sometimes had black owners, but the mob still ran the show. Los Angeles had a Cotton Club. So did Cincinnati and Cleveland, Spokane and Lawnside, New Jersey. The New York original maintained its prestige in its new location on Broadway and Seventh Avenue. Throughout the late thirties, Bill Robinson was the default headliner there. Leonard Reed often staged the programs. In addition to the chorus girls, a male chorus called the Cotton Club Boys executed precision numbers, and the other dance acts included ballroom teams and Lindy Hoppers. The tap acts were top-notch: Bill Bailey, Peg Leg Bates. It was common for these acts to double, during the day, at downtown presentation theaters such as the Paramount. Or they might take the very same act up to the Apollo. The "extreme transition" Buck and Bubbles had known a few years earlier had grown a little less extreme.

Competition was as hot as ever. In the fall of 1938, the Nicholas Brothers shared the Cotton Club headliner spot with Cab Calloway. As a kind of dare, Herman Starks, who both ran the Cotton Club and managed the Nicholas Brothers, scheduled the Berry Brothers to close the show. Born in New Orleans, Ananias and James Berry had made their New York debut, aged thirteen and eleven, at the Club Alabam in 1927. Then came the uptown Cotton Club, a tour of *Blackbirds* that took them to Paris, and a Broadway run in *Rhapsody in Black*. During the tour of the last show, Ananias, now eighteen, had eloped with a glamorous older woman—Valaida Snow, who sang, danced, conducted the band, and blew trumpet—and when Ananias broke off to tour with his wife, James recruited the youngest Berry, Warren, as a replacement. Which meant that in 1936, when Ananias, having divorced Snow, rejoined his brothers, they were now a trio. The siblings fashioned an act so perfect and unfailingly popular, they didn't dare change it.

It's fitting that Ananias's screen debut was as a cakewalker (a few seconds in the 1936 *San Francisco*), since the Berrys were masters of the strut. Ananias was the greatest strut dancer ever put on film. When he did a high kick, his leg swung first back, then out and up, up, his pointed toe ascending effortlessly over his head and nearly tugging the other leg off the ground. Ananias discharged one kick like that after another, as if it were just the way he preferred to take a stroll. His spins were blurs. Unlike a ballet dancer, he didn't "spot," or reset his focus after each revolution. Someone pulled a string and around he whirled. James offered lesser versions of all this—lesser only in comparison to his brother—but he concentrated on selling what Ananias did with singing and mugging. Sometimes, James's facial features seemed to stretch double, his gap-toothed smile yawning wide enough to accommodate a large object. In dancing skill, Warren was somewhere between his brothers; in the act, he was often between their legs, sliding through. Onto slides, struts, and spins, the Berrys stacked flips into splits, framing one another beautifully and building to an explosive finish. They called what they did "acrobatic soft shoe dancing," and their tapping was basic, keeping up the rhythmic momentum between strikes of lightning.

At the Cotton Club in 1938, forced to come up with something to top everything, the Berrys changed the end of their act. Behind the band stood a platform, twelve feet high, where the chorus girls would sometimes pose. For their new denouement, Ananias and James, leaving Warren onstage, ran up to that platform and jumped—out over the heads of the musicians to land in splits on either side of their brother, who flipped backward into his own simultaneous split before all three brothers popped up in unison, flipped, touched down in splits, bounced, and bowed. Without the aid of ropes and harnesses, it's hard to imagine a flash finale going farther.

LESS DARK ON BROADWAY

"Let them kill themselves," Fayard remembered thinking. He and his brother were headliners. They had been in Hollywood movies and big-ticket Broadway shows. The Berry Brothers had performed on Broadway themselves, in *Blackbirds of 1930*, but that debut came at the beginning of the end for black Broadway revues. In 1930, a reviewer for the *Brooklyn Eagle* could watch the Berry Brothers and see that "no one, black or white" could dance like Ananias, while the erudite critic George Jean Nathan looked at the same show and saw darkies, who "like most darkies, simply go on repeating the one or two little tricks they have, and get pretty tiresome after you've been looking at them for a number of years." Cleansed of its racist overapplication, the claim might have had some merit. The Berrys, like most vaudevillians, clung to their act. They gave the public what it wanted, until it didn't want that anymore. As professional theatergoers, critics hit their satiation point earlier than most. In his review of *Rhapsody in Black*, in 1931, Robert Benchley, joking that he was "probably uttering a great American heresy," praised the show for *not* including much tap: "Up until three or four years ago . . . it didn't seem as if I could get enough tap-dancing. But I did. More than enough. With every revue and musical comedy offering a complicated routine every seven minutes throughout its program, and each dancer vying with the rest to upset the easy rhythm of the original dance form, tap-dancing lost its tang."

Like Nathan, Benchley was tired of tap dancers, but for almost the opposite cause. "They are all good," he wrote, "and are getting better each year, so there is no excitement in seeing a good one any more." (Benchley made an exception, needless to say, for Bill Robinson.) Between Nathan's implied dictum that an artist must do more than repeat and Benchley's displeasure in losing the original easy rhythm lay a dilemma for dancers. And pleasing the public was treacherous enough. The critic Heywoud Broun, lamenting how audiences applauded acrobatic stunts while ignoring the "sweet sound of the shoes," suggested the need for a book called "How to Listen to Tap Dancing."

But Benchley's ultimate point was to praise Lew Leslie, *Rhapsody*'s producer, for breaking with the conventions of Negro revues on Broadway—for injecting "a little dignity," cutting back on minstrel sketches, substituting a choir for chorus girls, and, along the same line of reasoning, limiting the tap acts to two (the Berry Brothers and Eddie Rector, both excellent in Bentley's view). Leslie must have sensed that the formula had been overdone. Yet the concert model of *Rhapsody in Black* didn't catch on, either. The appetite for black shows of any kind on Broadway appeared to be sated. A sequel to *Shuffle Along* barely passed the starting gate in 1932, and black shows with lesser marquee value closed after a performance or two. Even with Bill Robinson as a guest star, Leslie's *Blackbirds of 1933*, a return to the old pie recipe, lasted only a month.

The unabating Depression didn't help, though low production costs had initially worked in favor of black shows. White Broadway was also hurting, reeling from the double blow of economic collapse and competition from the movie musical. But for a black act to make it into a white revue remained a coup. George White's *Scandals of 1936* featured the trio of "Sam, Ted, and Ray"—otherwise known as Tip, Tap, and Toe. Raised on a dais, Sam and Ted appeared as Ethiopian soldiers in shorts. Ray was in between, robed in the white tunic, black cape, and pith helmet of Haile Selassie: Emperor's clothing for the King of Slides. *Time* magazine, in the same issue in which it bestowed Man of the Year status on Haile Selassie for resisting Mussolini, rated Sam, Ted, and Ray as the high point of that year's Scandals. *The Chicago Defender* objected, assuming that to show an emperor tapping was to make him a minstrel clown, but the attention helped get Tip, Tap, and Toe into their first Hollywood film. It was called *You Can't Have Everything*.

When the Nicholas Brothers appeared in the Follies of 1936, they had already made the jump to Hollywood, but the revue was their Broadway debut, and despite Ziegfeld's death in 1932, the Follies retained cachet. The boys were not the only blacks in the show. This Follies marked the American return of Josephine Baker, that St. Louis–born star of the Folies Bergère in Paris. The Nicholas Brothers played pages to the chanteuse. Harold imitated her, in French, and both brothers, buttoned up as bellhops, did a challenge dance of their own devising (with no help, as usual, from the credited choreographer, Robert Alton). Brooks Atkinson commented that while Baker had "refined her art until there is nothing left in it," the Nicholas Brothers "restore your faith in dusky revelry." The double-edged compliment did not die with the black revue. (Nor had the black revue died overseas; the Nicholas Brothers were a great success in London's *Blackbirds of 1936*.)

The Nicholas Brothers were next cast in Rodgers and Hart's 1937 musical *Babes in Arms*. The choreographer was George Balanchine. Trained at Russia's Imperial School of Ballet and Theatre, Balanchine had served as ballet master for Diaghilev's Ballets Russes, the company that revitalized ballet in Europe and transformed it into a twentieth-century art. Now he was struggling to establish a ballet company in America and working on Broadway to pay the bills. Admiring black dancers for their suppleness and sense of time, he had originally planned his American ballet company to be mixed-race, but that didn't prove feasible. Preparing *Babes in Arms*, he watched the Nicholas Brothers do their regular act and fixed on the moment when Fayard jumped over Harold and Harold slid through Fayard's legs. Balanchine added chorus girls, directing Fayard to jump over two of them, then three, until there were eight girls, pressed together, bent over with their legs spread. Harold slid through the arches. That was the kind of effect the brothers suggested to a great theatrical imagination.

Harold and Fayard were often asked if they had been trained in ballet. Balanchine asked them this. "Maybe it comes natural," Fayard answered, "from watching you." Fayard watched rehearsals of *Babes in*

Arms the same way he watched everything else. If Balanchine had an influence on him and his brother, it was a reinforcement. Long lines, a lift in the torso, bravura attack—these were already in Fayard's idea of elegant showmanship. From the other direction, elements of the Nicholas Brothers style—angularities, syncopations, speed—were among the elements Balanchine absorbed from black dance and would use to modernize ballet and make it American. Strong talents take what they need, intuitively; that's what a phrase like "comes natural" means. Such mutual influence produced better results, aesthetically speaking, than more conscious attempts to hybridize ballet and tap—whether the bag-of-tricks jumbles of the twenties or the anxious, oil-and-water mixtures of high and low that were now beginning to proliferate.

The question of what comes natural, as it happens, was raised by the number the Nicholas Brothers were given to sing in *Babes in Arms*. In a score stuffed with songs destined to last (including the grammatically punctilious "I Wish I Were in Love Again"), this one didn't. "Pale-faced babies don't dance in the street / All dark people is light on their feet." Offended more by the dialect than by the stereotype, Mother Nicholas instructed her sons to replace "is" with "are." The dark people she raised spoke Standard English. After the stage manager yelled at the brothers to deliver the lyric as written, they obeyed, except when they forgot. At one point in the plot, a wealthy Southerner agrees to bankroll the kids' show only if the blacks are excluded; the other kids refuse, of course, taking the stance of good Northern liberals on segregated Broadway. *The Wall Street Journal* reported it "good to see a little real old time Harlem dancing again," welcoming the return of a style distorted by misguided directors "until it was only a noisy imitation of itself." The Nicholas Brothers were already finding much more success in Hollywood movies than almost all of the pale-faced babies in the cast, but with even less integration into those plots than into this one. So it was going to go. Bankrolling producers feared offending white Southerners. Black tap acts might be included in the show but not in the story.

Porgy and Bess, which premiered on Broadway in 1935, was a black story, but its white creative team had to work even harder to teach its black cast to speak in dialect. Most of the leads that George Gershwin hired for his "folk opera" were classically trained. The starkest exception was the man playing the drug-dealing gambler Sportin' Life. John Bubbles didn't read music. Todd Duncan, the college-educated baritone who played Porgy, remembered that Gershwin had to teach Bubbles his part by patting out the rhythms—by translating the score into tap. "After he learned to dance it, he never made a mistake." Duncan found Bubbles's performances "electric," but resented how "he caused problems in the rehearsals because he wanted to use his own rhythms." This interpretive freedom upset the conductor, Alexander Smallens, and caused other cast members to miss their cues. (Duncan also told on Bubbles for giving "performances in his dressing room" in the company of various ladies; Anne Brown, the college-educated soprano who played the bad girl Bess, was shocked by how Bubbles smoked marijuana with the chorus girls.) When Bubbles showed up late to rehearsals, Smallens assumed this was just Sportin' Life behavior, but in an interview in 1975, Bubbles explained that he had been arriving late on purpose, in an effort to appear more important in front of a cast that looked down on him.

When Smallens, exasperated, suggested that Bubbles be replaced, Gershwin protested—crying out (in Oscar Levant's account), "Why he's—he's the black Toscanini!" Even if those aren't Gershwin's exact words, it makes sense that Gershwin would rush to defend Bubbles. The composer cited Sportin' Life as an example of the opera's mix of light and serious, calling the character "a humorous, dancing villain, who is likeable and believable and at the same time evil," and he stood by Bubbles as the perfect man for the part. Perhaps Gershwin felt a kinship with Bubbles and his mix of white boys' and colored boys' steps. It's not clear how much tapping Bubbles did—the *Times*'s music critic mentioned "clogging"—but in photographs and silent amateur-movie snippets of the show, his cane-twirling strut commands attention. Bubbles was proud of the role for the rest of his life, especially after the show was consecrated an American classic. But he accepted the part only on the condition that Buck also be hired. Bubbles never took a job without his partner. Whatever the gig, it was going to end. What sense did it make to break up the act?

PALE-FACED RHYTHM BOYS

The year before *Babes in Arms*, George Balanchine had worked on another Rodgers and Hart musical, *On Your Toes*. The plot was a classic example of 1930s nervous populism. The hero is the son of vaudevillians who have pushed him to become a professor of music though he really wants to be a hoofer; he helps out a Russian ballet troupe and is seduced by the ballerina but returns in the end to his nice American girl. It's a tale that provided its makers with the opportunity to spoof foreign art while showing off witty high-culture allusions and indulging some high-art aspirations of their own. One ballet satirized the orientalisms of *Scheherazade*, with the hero in blackface, and for the show's climactic number, its modern meeting of European classical tradition and vernacular American themes, Rodgers composed a "jazz ballet" called "Slaughter on Tenth Avenue." It's an eleven-minute battle for the affections of a stripper, and as the show-within-a-show is performed, two gangsters hover over the action with orders to shoot the hero on the loud final chord. The hero learns this, so he keeps the orchestra playing the last bars over and over as he dances and dances, comically exhausting himself in avoidance of death, until the police arrive. Since this bit of narrative suspense was generated through dance, "Slaughter on Tenth Avenue" has been looked back upon as inaugurating a new direction in musicals: the integration of dance into the plot. This development, barely there in *On Your Toes*, would turn out to have negative consequences for tap dancers, but such an outcome would have been hard to foretell in 1936. For one thing, the "Slaughter on Tenth Avenue" ballet was part tap. The hero, dancing for his life, hoofed. In tap shoes. (Balanchine's assistant for the tap choreography, listed in the program, was Herbert Harper, a black hoofer who learned tap by watching the white students in Buddy Bradley's classes.) And the performer who played the hoofing hero was an outstanding tap dancer: Ray Bolger.

As a boy, he had idolized Fred Stone, whom he would come to eclipse in the role Stone originated, the Scarecrow in *The Wizard of Oz*. Bolger's early career conformed to the eccentric dancer model. A stringbean with a toucan nose, he was as elongated as Jack Donahue, whose successor he was promptly named. Bolger grew up in Irish Catholic Boston, about a decade later than Donahue, learning his first steps on the sidewalk from a retired vaudevillian. "My ears could hear the rhythms and I could do them," Bolger remembered, "but I didn't want to do what the others did. I felt it in a different way." When he danced, the other kids laughed. Unlike the eccentrics who preceded him, Bolger studied ballet. One difference between coming of age in the aughts and maturing a few years later was the presence of Soviet-fleeing Russians such as Senia Russakoff, who taught ballet in the same building where Bolger was learning to buck-dance. Yet when Bolger performed in the ballet school recital, the pattern held: his serious dancing was taken as comedy, so he started taking his comedy seriously.

Vaudeville, bit parts, a spot at the Palace, then roles in George White's Scandals and other revues—the path was still there, and now it extended into Radio City Music Hall. Bolger continued the eccentric tradition of satire. In the Scandals, he sent up precision tap trios, and the *Times* patted him on the back for stamping out "the rhythm boys' madness," those "teams of three dark, smiling and separately indistinguishable young men." The success of *On Your Toes* earned Bolger a contract with MGM, an option not available to his eccentric predecessors at similar points in their careers. Bolger's first film appearance was in the 1936 biopic *The Great Ziegfeld*. Under an absurdly large hat, Bolger's weak chin keeps rising, as if to put more distance between itself and the dangers below. When he repeats a step to fill out an eight-bar phrase, the step gets away from him, and the perfectly timed syncopations of his recovery look like stumbles. When he shakes a nerve tap, the convulsions nearly knock him off his feet. Doing splits, he gets stuck. Twice, he pulls himself up halfway only to sink back to bottom, and when he finally pulls erect, it's a little man's victory. His pretty soft shoe gets interrupted when the band comes back in, blasting a bugle call as bands always did and startling Bolger into the requisite double-time finish. The number is a devastating parody of an early-thirties tap act.

In the opinion of Frank Condos, "the best dancers were colored." But the top rhythm boys weren't all dark, or dark in the same way. Emigrating from Greece, the Condos family tried St. Louis and Pittsburgh before opening a restaurant across from Philadelphia's Standard Theatre. As a high school student in the early 1920s, Frank carried meals to hungry performers. The Standard was a black-owned establishment that booked both white and black performers, but it was the black dancing acts that most fascinated young Condos. With his buddy Mateo Olvera, he formed a duo called King and King that became known for dancing while chained to each other at the ankle. They used slatted tap mats to heighten the scrape of their specialty wings, and their act fit the standard pattern—soft shoe, medium tempo, high-speed challenge—except that the one-upmanship was unusually strenuous. "We nearly killed ourselves trying to out-dance each other," Condos recalled. Back and forth they went, wing after wing, accelerating with each trade. "Other guys would be fresh after sixteen bars," Condos said. "We were exhausted."

"From the waist up," Condos admitted, "we didn't have any personality." Nevertheless, their wings won them jobs in rowdier Broadway revues such as *Artists and Models*, the kind with the crude comics and the naked girls. In 1929, the pair split into two bona fide brother acts. Olvera enlisted two of his siblings into an expanded King, King, and King, thereby stoking the vogue for trios with names picked from a pinochle deck, the rhythm boys that Bolger would parody in Scandals. (Condos: "It got so that when the stage hands would come out and put a mat down on the floor, the audience would say, 'Oh no, not again!' because some of these trios were pretty bad.") Condos formed a duo with his brother Nick, ten years his junior. It was as the Condos Brothers that Frank and Nick developed their five-tap wing—five sounds emanating from a single winging foot. Few dancers could match the manuever, and at first only Nick could do it on either side.

Such skill gained the team respect from the colored dancers they admired. It earned them a near-the-finale spot in *Earl Carroll's Vanities* of 1930 and inspired *Variety*'s rhetorical question, "Are there any faster steppers than they?" Trying to keep up with the growing sophistication of the tap around them—with "the colored dancers," Frank specified— they doled out their most arduous steps more sparsely. Nonetheless, when the brothers stopped the show in the number two slot at the Palace, one reviewer, noting the boys' "Turkish bath sweat," predicted that their nine-minute act would continue to stop all shows, but only if they could sustain the pace "without breaking down." It wasn't unusual for critics to fear for the Condos brothers' health. They went abroad, wowing London and baffling Paris. Around 1936, Frank left the duo, tried a little solo work and dance direction, and retired to a less strenuous career as a welder. The youngest Condos brother, Steve, quit school and took Frank's place. It was Nick and Steve who would make it into the movies as the Condos Brothers.

In the *Ziegfeld Follies of 1931*, the last one before Ziegfeld's death, the dancer whom the press was already naming as successor to the eccentric Jack Donahue was an eighteen-year-old named Hal LeRoy. With a lanky frame and an overbite, LeRoy was shaped like an eccentric, but his dominant quality was youthfulness. *A High School Hoofer* (1931) was the first in a series of short films he starred in, and that's how people saw him, an affable boy wonder. LeRoy looked a bit like a holdover from the twenties: his ever-swiveling legs, dangling loosely from his hips, were pure Charleston, legomania with taps. His rhythms, however, were more up-to-date.

LeRoy grew up in Cincinnati, where he sold papers and learned his first steps from a fellow newsboy, who was black. You can surmise the rest: the stealing from vaudevillians who came through town, the making it his own through hours of daily practice. (It was he who said, "Maybe I didn't get the exact step, but more or less.") He moved from Cincinnati grill rooms into a Boston revue, became an overnight sensation in *The Gang's All Here* on Broadway, and was immediately snatched up by the Follies. This wasn't your average chorus boy. He couldn't remember the routines, for one. Not that it mattered. When the Follies' dance director berated the kid, Ziegfeld supposedly yelled, "I didn't hire him to learn your routines. I hired him to dance." LeRoy was, in his own words, an "ad-lib dancer." He improvised, and the reviewers, responding to his spontaneity, called him a natural. LeRoy had his surefire steps, his applause-getters, but every night went a little differently, and every night he took in a little more of the other hoofer in the Follies of 1931, John Bubbles.

The older black dancer encouraged the younger white one; the Father of Rhythm gave the boy a set of taps. Bill Robinson also befriended the kid. LeRoy considered Robinson his best friend at the time. It was Robinson who escorted LeRoy to the Hoofers' Club, where, in LeRoy's telling, the dancers tested him in various styles and gave him an honorary member's pin after he passed. What the other dancers thought about Robinson bringing the white kid uptown and what exactly they meant by the pin aren't recorded. (Nick Condos, according to his brother Steve, also earned entrance. Maceo Anderson of the Four Step Brothers said Nick "licked them colored guys, they run back and hide.") Still, in some important sense, LeRoy was the rare white hoofer deemed worthy of being inducted into the club.

It's surprising, nevertheless, to read in *Life*'s review of the 1931 Follies that Hal LeRoy was "the most stylish and accomplished tap dancer the white race has to offer at the moment." The racial qualifier is intriguing, especially since the magazine explained it by citing Eddie Rector and Bill Robinson but not John Bubbles, who was in the same damn show. The superlative is remarkable because there was a more obvious candidate, an established star who was about to become, if he wasn't already, the foremost model for tap dancers of the white race. Many decades later, Bubbles would tell inquiring journalists a story about charging that dancer four hundred dollars for one hour-long lesson in 1930. This guy was a slow learner, but his female friend picked up faster, so Bubbles taught her instead. That way, the fellow would get more value for his money. The woman was Ziegfeld's aging ingenue, Marilyn Miller. The guy was her co-star in Ziegfeld's *Smiles,* Fred Astaire.

Astaire never told that story. He did, however, tell stories about what a slow study he was, and in his autobiography, he talked about Bill Robinson—about how he and Bojangles were both on the same vaudeville bill in Iowa in the early teens, how Robinson gave him a lesson in being a pool shark, how they compared steps, how Robinson told him, "Boy, you can dance." In retirement, Astaire would sometimes mention in private conversations (with people who later snitched) how, as a child performer, he used to watch the black dancers on the bill or in the alley

by the theater and ask for a step. Sometimes he would mention how he
studied with Bill Robinson. Diana Vreeland recalled witnessing one of
those lessons, during an excursion to Harlem with Astaire in the twenties. The lyricist Howard Dietz remembered another Harlem trip, circa
1931, when Dietz took Astaire to a nightclub to see a dancer who had
some steps "he might want to look at." The nameless Harlem hoofer
demonstrated a tricky maneuver, Astaire copied it right off, and the
hoofer asked Astaire if he wanted a job. Dietz offered the anecdote as
authentication of Astaire's talent but also as an ironic joke—he didn't
need to say that Astaire had better employment opportunities.

To a biographer in the 1980s, Astaire stated that he admired Robinson but didn't do what Robinson did: buck dancing, wooden-shoe stuff
on stairs. "John Bubbles was different," he continued. "I don't know
whether he used tap shoes or not, but he was stylish. I used to meet him
occasionally and we would try steps together." There's no mention of
Bubbles in Astaire's self-effacing autobiography of 1959. (Soon after it
was published, Marshall Stearns wrote Astaire a letter asking about the
omission, and Astaire wrote back saying the material about Bubbles must
have fallen out in the editing, adding cryptically, "Bubbles and I have
had some interesting meetings in dance.") Once, on TV in the sixties,
Astaire explained how dancers borrow steps—"like a library book: if it's
good you forget to bring it back"—and recounted how Bubbles once
gave him a step: "He gave it to me for one of mine."

These stories, these pieces of stories, are pieces of a larger and even
more elusive tale: the intersection of tap's segregated worlds. The story
fragments can be set next to others in which white dancers make research
expeditions to the Lafayette and the Apollo, more trips uptown to have
a look at some steps. They can be joined with more allusions to black
dancers on otherwise white bills trading steps with white dancers in the
wings or in the alley out back. And they can be combined with a third
type of meeting in dance, mentioned casually in tap dancers' reminiscences
but otherwise undocumented, the cross-racial tap challenge: Barton and
Donahue and Bojangles, Barton and Bojangles and Rector, Bolger
and Bojangles and Astaire. It was customary, apparently, for white dancers to catch the Sunday night show at the Cotton Club and have Dan
Healy call them up for a challenge session against the house champions.

Like the interracial battles of a generation earlier during the *In Old Kentucky* amateur contest, these contests seem to have occurred mostly on white turf, or in venues where whites were in charge. These fragments raise the perennial questions of imitation and theft. They stir up suspicion that Astaire wasn't entirely forthright about the sources of his art, implying omissions and evasions that are commonplace yet matter because he does. There was, of course, much more to Astaire's style than stolen steps, much, much more than what he might have picked up in a cram session with Bubbles or a dozen trips to Harlem or from whatever his sister bought at Buddy Bradley's. As with Gershwin and Balanchine, the question of what he took is worth notice because of what he made of it.

Talking to that biographer in the eighties, Astaire was careful to specify that tap had been "strictly a sideline." "When I'm called 'a tap dancer,' it makes me laugh. Because I *am* in a way, but that is *one* of the kinds of dancing I do." True enough. "I had a little different treatment of how to apply it. I didn't just set out and hop into the 'buck.' I'd move around and do things." Also true, and true of Cohan and Rector and Bubbles. Early reviewers didn't have much better success at isolating what was different about Astaire, just that he *was* different. "Fred Astaire can dance as probably no one else ever did or will, when it comes to dancing rhythm," wrote *Variety*. This was in 1930, when Astaire was dancing in *Smiles*—the period during which John Bubbles was playing Cream of Wheat in *Blackbirds of 1930* and possibly giving Astaire that one formal lesson.

That same year, Astaire tapped on recordings of "Puttin' on the Ritz" and "Crazy Feet." The style advances the unpredictability of his 1926 recording. It is not a graceful sound. Shapes can be discerned in the phrasing but they're irregular, interrupted. The beat is stomped around and kicked down the stairs thumping. Astaire's stamped rhythms have the logic of tantrums, impatient, sputtering. If not quite crazy, the feet aren't entirely under control, either, so that a few of the offbeats sound unintentionally off—missed. The sound conjures an image of someone moving around a lot and getting off the floor. It's a wilder sound than most people would come to associate with Astaire, but it's recognizably his.

"The greatest tap dancer in the world." Robert Benchley tucked this assessment of Astaire into a qualifying clause in his review of *Smiles*, expecting no objection. A year later, when uttering his heresy about tap having lost its tang, Benchley exempted two dancers. Bill Robinson was one. Here and elsewhere, Astaire was the white exception, built like an eccentric but graceful as a leading man, his rhythm-boy feet guided by theatrical ideas. *Life*'s review of *The Band Wagon* in 1931 called Astaire "our most accomplished dancing actor," conceding that "there may be a number of young men along Broadway who are better hoofers than Fred from a technical standpoint." Just a week later, in fact, the magazine would be designating Hal LeRoy the most accomplished white tapper. "But that is just the difference. You never think of Fred as a hoofer."

In the "High Hat" number of *Funny Face*, Astaire tapped tuxedoed in front of a male chorus of twenty-four. "Say, Young Man of Manhattan" in *Smiles* embellished the concept in the manner of King Rastus Brown, Astaire aiming his cane at the line of gents and gunning them down as his feet fired away. After *The Band Wagon*, Adele Astaire married into the British aristocracy and retired from the stage, breaking up the family act. Fred's first show without her was titled *Gay Divorce*. No longer paired with his sister, he was free to seduce his partner, the glamorous and sexy Claire Luce. He did it by dancing. Their ballroom-style adagio to Cole Porter's "Night and Day" revealed a new Fred Astaire, not just humor and rhythm but also romance. More than ever, Astaire was not someone you thought of as a hoofer.

In years to come, hoofers would be quick to echo that assessment. Some meant it as a compliment. In the forties, the Condos Brothers would repeatedly gush to reporters that Astaire was the greatest dancer who ever lived, while they were mere hoofers. Other hoofers agreed, but in a different tone. Astaire might be the world's greatest dancer, they'd say, but his tapping wasn't so great. Honi Coles, a dancer who prided himself on the way he moved around a stage and disparaged other black hoofers for offering nothing above the waist, would disqualify Astaire because he didn't drum in one spot. This was protesting too much. Fred Astaire was a great tap dancer and his greatness arose, as he suggested, from the application of what he called his "outlaw style." It was Broadway and Britain and Harlem, white boys' steps and colored boys' steps mixed together. Astaire didn't like being called a tap dancer for some of the same reasons that Duke Ellington didn't care to be called a jazz musician. What Astaire termed "outlaw style," Ellington spoke of as "beyond category."

Opinions like Coles's reacted against the opportunities afforded by Astaire's skin color and, even more, at the enormous cultural space Astaire occupied through his films. If Bill Robinson came in at the right time, so did Astaire, but Astaire was white. Yet neither race nor timing entirely explains what happened. *Gay Divorce* was Astaire's last stage show. In 1933, he got the attention of RKO pictures and a ticket to Hollywood. His success there was far from sure. In retrospect, Astaire's nonchalance seems made for the camera's close gaze; his "apparently impromptu" air, the product of a perfectionist work ethic, best suited to a system of multiple takes. But Astaire's dancing wasn't ideal for film as he found it. It was ideal for film as he made it.

10

HOW TO HOOF IN HOLLYWOOD

Before the widespread adoption of synchronized sound, filmed tap dancing didn't make complete sense. It couldn't. But American film-makers could hardly ignore it. A Dancing Darkey Boy was as necessary an American subject as *Uncle Tom's Cabin*, which, in the first of many filmings, in 1903, occasioned a cakewalk sequence, a spastic breakdown from a blackface Topsy, and some incoherent buck dancing by black kids at the slave auction. *Fights of Nations*, from 1907, provided a more extended visual record. During the section titled "Sunny Africa, Eighth Avenue, New York," before the patrons of a black Tenderloin bar pull out razors, one of them gets up to show off. The dance is eccentric, studded with twists, drags, and a twining and untwining of legs spaced out with shuffles. The dancer signals the end by knocking one foot out with the other, a finish that would become traditional. At such moments, it's possible to imagine what the dance sounded like, but on the whole these early films reveal silent tap to be an art diminished by more than half.

Tap in the pictures demanded sound. From Edison on, filmmakers experimented with combining sound and image, but amplification and

synchronization posed difficult technical problems, and silent film established its own powerful aesthetic and infrastructure. It wasn't until the late
twenties that the rise of radio spurred the film industry to undertake the
expensive conversion. The bits of talking and songs spliced into *The Jazz
Singer* in 1927—Al Jolson blackening his rendition of "Toot, Toot, Tootsie"
with some snakehips—were enough of a hit to inspire a deluge of movie
musicals. Most were imported from Broadway, and tap came along as
Broadway's bread-and-butter dance.

Initial conditions were far from ideal. The microphone was fixed and
kept picking up the wrong sounds. The camera couldn't move much,
either, enclosed in a booth to muffle the noise of its motor. During
the filming of *The Broadway Melody* in 1928, a new technique was tried
out. A musical number would first be recorded, as audio; then, during
filming, the performers would key their movements to the prerecorded
track, lip-synching. This method, soon standard industry practice, saved
the expense of keeping an orchestra on set for every take, made it easier
to balance the sound, and freed up the camera. But it didn't eliminate the
problem of synchronization. Matching sight and sound became part of a
performer's job, and, especially, an editor's. In terms of dance, that job
was made easier if the relationship between music and motion was either
simple or loose; the amateurish dancing of the early sound films was usually both. Cutting to a reaction shot was a cheap way around any trouble.

Tap dancing, however, compounded the difficulty. Exact synchronization is crucial to the reproduction of any dance, but with tap, it's
everything. One of the trials facing a tap dancer who wishes to study
the recorded history of the art is the torture of imprecisely matched
footage. You have to remember the sound or the image, whichever lags
behind, and try to reconnect the two in your mind. Sound was recorded
continuously, but film is a series of still pictures flashed past the eye quickly
enough to trick the brain into seeing motion. Trying to reconstruct
routines, tap dancers slow the film down, going frame by frame if they
can, and sometimes they hear a tap but can't find it with their eyes. It fell
between exposures.

However rare, such disjunctures are reminders of the process behind
the document. At the outset of the movie musical, the sound of taps was

sometimes recorded during filming, and sometimes beforehand, which required the dancers to foot-synch. Later—by 1936, but perhaps earlier—it became customary to record music before filming and dub in taps after filming. The separation of sound and image introduced some complications for dancers but increased the control available to filmmakers. It enabled more illusion—the sound of taps during the number but not during the walking on either side of it, the sound of taps hitting surfaces more solid than the hollow plywood of sets, the relatively clean sound of a small group of tapping people matched to the image of many more, the sound of someone tapping masked by the dancing image of someone else.

Imperfectly or deceitfully, in cutting tap dance apart and sewing it back together, sound films preserved it and reproduced it, vastly expanding its dominion. *The Broadway Melody* inaugurated the movie musical. It was a Broadway story, a backstager. Even when Broadway didn't provide the plot for musicals, it usually provided the dance directors. It's impossible to know how much to take as an accurate reflection of contemporary Broadway practice or how much to ascribe to the technological adjustments and the rush to pump out product, but the level of both artistry and execution was low.

Although George Cunningham was credited as dance director on *Broadway Melody*, the dances were probably staged by Sammy Lee, whose stage work had included the landmark productions *Lady, Be Good!*, *No, No, Nanette*, and *Showboat*. The film's title number would prove typical. A man in top hat sings the song, backed by a line of bare-legged chorus girls who kick high and muddle a few time steps before hopping off unsteadily, each gripping a hoisted leg. There's also a female soloist, who taps in kitten ears and toe shoes. This freak hybrid, toe tap, was not uncommon. For a moment, the film cuts to a close-up of the poor girl's misused feet, an innovation in filmed dance that in this case only magnifies viewer discomfort. For another example of early movie musical style, look at the finale of *Gold Diggers of Broadway* (1929), a film that set a long-standing record for gross profits. It's a Broadway finale enlarged. Masses of dancers parade on and off, weaving through routines of some sort that include time steps. Two of the anonymous specialists are impressive wing experts, but they're just part of the frenzy, one crazy thing after another. "For the screen, it isn't the step that counts," explained the dance director Maurice Kusell in 1930. "It is the formation." Many in Hollywood evidently felt the same, which meant plenty of work for chorus girls. All you needed, said Larry Ceballos, dance director for *Gold Diggers*, was good health, good looks, and a sense of rhythm. Prior training wasn't necessary. "If you can walk in time, you can dance."

That seems to have been the norm for dancers, Hollywood stars included. Every studio showcased its stable of talent in revue films, and just as some stars of the silent screen surprised audiences with their voices, others broke out time steps. MGM's never-released (but subsequently rediscovered) revue *The March of Time* allotted a minute or so to the eighty-year-old Barney Fagan, the rival of George Primrose in minstrel days. This was around the same time that Fagan wrote his jeremiad against low expectations in tap. The tap he encountered in Hollywood must have driven him batty. It looks like something everyone could do and everyone was doing. "Everybody Tap" was, in fact, a song in *Chasing Rainbows*, a MGM backstager that also included the song "Happy Days Are Here Again." They weren't, not in 1930. But they might seem so while people were tapping. "Everybody Tap" was an invitation that the movies extended to the world. In 1930, the Dancing Masters of America announced that demand for tap shoes had increased 150 percent since 1928: "America has gone tap-crazy."

On with the Show, filmed in 1929, follows the same formulas as the other early movie musicals, with a few significant differences. One is Ethel Waters, who is segregated from the plot but treated as the great artist she obviously is. Another is that the show that must go on is set on a Southern plantation, and during the big chorus dances (once again by Ceballos), two black couples come out and take care of the real work. In a levee number, they hoedown in straw hats and striped overalls; during a party, they dance while carrying trays with champagne bottles attached. Props don't impede their hoofing. It's fast, vibrant, up-on-the-toes but weighted, thick with wings and one-leg-over-the-other jumps. The taps don't all register aurally, but you can sense that's not the fault of these dancers, manifestly in-the-pocket, especially compared with whatever it is the white chorus is doing behind them. (Calisthenics? Patty-cake?) Who was this scene-saving quartet? The credits don't give names, but when *On with the Show* was shown at Philadelphia's Standard Theatre, moviegoers such as Fayard Nicholas recognized the Four Covans.

Child dodger of cowboy bullets, Chicago master of the Double Around the World, Willie Covan had formed a family act, around 1927, with his brother Dewey and their wives, Florence and Carita. As Willie described it, their eight-minute act included a tap waltz, a military drill, and a challenge dance, in addition to up-tempo precision work. In *On with the Show*, Willie's dancing stands out, in time with the others but on a larger scale. You watch him to learn how the step *should* look. As a personality, though, Willie is a blank. The Four Covans tapped in a few more films the same year, but Willie's career in front of the cameras ended just about as it began. By 1934, he had officially retired. He opened a dance studio and made himself a kind of Buddy Bradley for the West Coast, a private coach to the stars. MGM put him on the payroll.

In its initial borrowings from Broadway, the studios mostly ignored the blacks that Broadway had borrowed from. The Four Covans did dance in *Hearts of Dixie*, one of two tales of the black South released in 1929. The other film, *Hallelujah!*, a distinguished romanticization, used some buck-dancing black kids to evoke rural simplicity and some low-down steps to signal urban seduction. The only major career to emerge from either film was that of Stepin Fetchit, with his canny hyperbolizing of laziness. (Avoiding work in *Hearts of Dixie*, he puts his energy into a sand dance.) It would be a long while before the big studios made any more all-black musicals, but black two-reelers were a briefly plentiful experiment. By the middle of 1930, Buck and Bubbles had starred in six all-black shorts based on the Uncle Remus–like stories of Hugh Wiley. *In and Out*, from 1929, has the earliest footage of Bubbles's dancing, the number in which he seems to be imitating Bill Robinson and saving his John Bubbles steps until the end.

Robinson's film debut in *Dixiana*, an antebellum spectacle of 1930, comes near the end of the movie. Out of nowhere he appears, alone, in rags, holding a feather duster. As he dusts, his feet carry him, inevitably, down a flight of stairs. The number is not his finest work, yet for two minutes or so, a master tap dancer fills the screen. Then the plot finishes up without him. Robinson would have to wait five years for another chance in a mainstream film. Until then, he starred in "race movies," all-colored films produced on tiny budgets and distributed to black theaters. Two were the backstagers *Harlem Is Heaven* (1932) and *King for a Day* (1934). These films make *Broadway Melody* look sophisticated. Robinson plays himself, or nearly: Bill, the world's greatest tap dancer and compulsive gambler. *King for a Day* features a minstrel-show number during which he and some blacks in blackface commit terrible puns about color. Bill doesn't wear cork, though. He dresses nattily, and his dance, nearly four minutes of wooden-shoe brilliance, confirms just about everything Broadway critics had praised in him. *Harlem Is Heaven* contains Robinson's stair dance—one for the ages.

COME AND MEET THOSE DANCING FEET

As soon as Hollywood learned how to make musicals, it made too many of them. The public recoiled, and the studios pulled way back, but the retrenchment didn't last long, because, in 1933, Warner Brothers released *42nd Street*. It was another backstager, but a tough-talking one in which putting on the show was given the desperate urgency of jobs on the line. An ingenuous chorus girl steps in for the injured lead at the last minute, and the director gives her a pep talk climaxing in the immortal phrase "You're going out a youngster, but you've got to come back a star!" For tap, the more telling line is the director's exasperated rant at the chorus line he's drilling in time steps: "Faster! Faster!" It gives you an idea of the dance values that California imported from New York. But at least most of these musical numbers were designed for the camera. And the raw kid out of the chorus, the character you're meant to root for, is a tap dancer. The actress playing her was so suited to the role that she seemed not to be acting at all. Yet by the time she made this, her first film, the twenty-three-year-old Ruby Keeler was a Broadway veteran.

Ruby was born Ethel, in Nova Scotia, one of six children in a poor Irish Catholic family. She grew up in New York, and she learned her first jigs at her parochial school. Informed that Ruby was talented, her parents transferred her to the Professional Children's School and into the Jack Blue School of Rhythm and Taps. Mr. Blue had worked with George M. Cohan, and he taught in the Cohan mode. It was in a Cohan show, *The Rise of Rosie O'Grady*, that Keeler joined her first chorus, at age thirteen. Winning a dance contest earned her jobs at nightclubs and speakeasies, El Fey and the Silver Slipper, working for the mob under the protective wing of the notorious mistress of ceremonies Texas Guinan. Keeler's boyfriend was a mobster, Johnny "Irish" Costello, until an infatuated Al Jolson, more than twice her age, convinced her to become his third wife. Keeler was a specialty act, a Champion Charleston and Buck Dancer. When she moved into featured spots in Broadway musicals, the *Times* commented that although tap dancers were plentiful, this one had personality.

That personality was peculiar. Early silent films and photographs preserve the look. Pretty in a flapper's bob, she goes through the motions of over-the-shoulder seduction, but those big, beautiful eyes—they're dewy to the point of dopey, innocent to the point of oblivious. In *42nd Street* and films that followed, Keeler isn't like the other girls. They're golddiggers: jaded, wisecracking, mercenary. She's naïve, guileless, hard-working. Even when she's wised up, she stays nice, with only a hint of demure rebellion that says, as her character in *Dames* does, "I'm free, white, and twenty-one. I love to dance, and I'm gonna dance." But a Ruby Keeler character doesn't live fast and she doesn't dance fast, either. She taps clearly and hard. "I dance like a man," she once said, "because all my teachers were men." (She studied with Buddy Bradley, and possibly with Bill Robinson.) In the title number of *42nd Street*, Keeler peels off her skirt to unveil her gams in shorts, but though she holds up her arms, she's much less concerned with posing than with pounding out clog steps in her wooden shoes. The rhythms are simple, mainly swung eighth notes with a heavy backbeat, but they're solid. Keeler is solid. She was right to call herself a hoofer.

Keeler claimed to have choreographed her own solos. It's entirely plausible. The hoofing she does in *42nd Street* is all her. When the camera tilts to reveal that she's dancing on top of a taxicab and the scene opens

up to a fantasia of New York that discloses a crime of passion and finishes with the chorus girls creating a skyline with their bodies—that's
all Busby Berkeley, who directed the number. Berkeley also came from
Broadway. In the late twenties, he had made a reputation for himself as
an up-and-coming dance director. That he brought to the position no
training in dance or music raised no eyebrows back then. What did was
his approach to rhythm. In the *Times*, John Martin praised him for delv-
ing "into the actual rhythmic structures of jazz," pointing out how
Berkeley had his chorus girls execute a five-against-four rhythm with
one part of their bodies and a three-against-four with another. It sounds
positively African. When Martin interviewed Berkeley about it, the dance
director couldn't explain what he had done. He got the girls together,
watched what they did, and experimented. The things he tried in Hollywood, however, wouldn't have much to do with rhythm.

He made the camera dance: that's the standard line on Berkeley's
contribution to film. It's partly true. His camera eye swooped high
above the scene and it moved into the action, gliding between the parted
legs of chorus girls as if it were Harold Nicholas. Berkeley had holes put
in the studio ceiling so the camera could gain further altitude, and he
had a monorail built so the camera could travel faster. But he was even
more interested in what he arranged in front of the camera: enormous,
metamorphic sets and lots and lots of girls. Berkeley had a multiplying
imagination: if he saw four pianos, he imagined sixteen; if he saw one
girl with a violin, he imagined dozens, with violins in neon. His sense
of scale was extreme. The young women were pretty faces in close-up or
they were pieces in a kaleidoscope. They were sex *and* the machine. As a
field artillery lieutenant in the First World War, Berkeley had organized
parade drills, and that sense of pattern found full expression in his Hollywood work, where what had been latently militaristic in Ziegfeld precision routines often became explicitly so. His musical sequences took
Ziegfeld-style spectacle and magnified it to dimensions that could never
exist onstage, though the fiction that the numbers *were* happening onstage was often maintained, at beginnings and endings, almost in jest.

The other joke was that Berkeley was a dance director who wasn't
really interested in dance. He selected his girls for looks. ("I never cared
whether a girl knew her right foot from her left, so long as she was

beautiful," he said. "I'd get her to move, or dance, or something.") When
he let a tap dancer do her thing, it was usually in a stagebound introduction to the cinematic fantasy, as in Keeler's taxi dance in *42nd Street* or
the soft shoe she performs (not so softly) before the teasing, voyeuristic
spectacle of "Petting in the Park" in *Gold Diggers of 1933*. Alternatively,
tap soloists served as pockets of individualism dwarfed by the collective
vision: Lee Dixon on a giant rocking chair about to be blown to bits in
the mammoth battle of the sexes of *Gold Diggers of 1937*. In the finale
of *Footlight Parade* (1933), James Cagney is an American sailor searching
for Shanghai Lil: Ruby Keeler in slanted eyeliner. They celebrate their
reunion by hopping on a bartop to trade snare-drum cadences with
their feet, then get swamped by a parade of marching sailors who merge
like puzzle pieces into an American flag and the face of Franklin Delano
Roosevelt.

Cagney had started out as a song-and-dance man in Broadway revues and vaudeville, and he remained one while a movie gangster. An
electric presence on-screen, he was more graceful when not dancing. He
and Keeler grew up in the same heavily Irish neighborhood, but where
she was winsomely ungainly, Cagney tended to force his stiff-legged
tapping in pseudo-balletic directions. He came from the school of Irish
posturing in which an arch high in the back suggests something stuck in
lower down. Make a quip like that and he'd slug you. It was an odd
style, but it worked for *Yankee Doodle Dandy* (1942), in which Cagney,
playing George M. Cohan, out-Cohaned the original, careening around
a stage in a complete triumph of personality over technique. (His dancing coach on that film was Johnny Boyle, the personality-bereft associate of Jack Donahue.)

There's one major exception to Berkeley's general disregard of dance:
the "Lullaby of Broadway" sequence in *Gold Diggers of 1935*. The dancing
doesn't begin until a good six minutes into the number, after a montage
contrasting the nocturnal revels of a Broadway baby with the daily grind
of working folk. In what might be a dream, the film's leads, Dick Powell
and Winifred Shaw, find themselves the sole guests in a cavernous nightclub. An army of tap dancers marches in, fifty women with bare stomachs
interpenetrated by fifty men doing something like a Nazi salute. When
the orchestra cuts out for twenty-four measures, all you hear are distinct

rhythms, the women holding up their skirts to take a turn, the men answering. Later, a trio of rhythm boys raises the difficulty level with wings, Berkeley filming them from above and also below, through a glass floor. Yet it's the surrounding ensemble tapping that's most striking. Normally, a multiplication of bodies decreases the intensity of tap, perhaps because ensemble tapping overwhelms the perception of *this* foot producing *that* sound. The editing helps subvert the craving for that synchronicity, delaying the cuts from group to group so that we hear the beginning of each phrase before we see it, and the predictable patterns of time steps bind together images of pretty faces and bared flesh filmed from oblique angles. The choreography hardly deserves the name, but the cold setting chills the tapping—relentless in its thundering, at once martial and erotic—and when the mob sings "Come and dance!" at Shaw, the friendly invitation takes on menace as the Broadway baby is crowded onto a balcony and off it to her death. The lullaby transforms into moral fable, and for once, massed tap dancing signifies something other than shared mirth.

Dozens of musical sequences mimicked Berkeley's effects. Few matched his audacity. "Too Marvelous for Words" from *Ready, Willing, and Able* (1937) ends with Ruby Keeler and Lee Dixon tapping on an enormous typewriter with chorus-girl legs for hammers. The conceit is Berkeley Lite, but the dancing is more technically challenging and cleverly choreographed than anything Berkeley filmed. The duo circulates their steps all over the keyboard's four tiers of round platforms, each the size of a tom-tom. They toss in wings and switch direction for the hell of it, as if trying to touch as many keys as possible while playing a variety of musically apt rhythms. The number was staged and directed by another Broadway transplant, Bobby Connolly, who appears in the film, stubby in stature and New York in accent. But the technique might be ascribed to Dixon, a talent out of Brooklyn, blond, twenty-two, and free. An inoffensive presence with a floppy style common among white hoofers of his generation, he had one big year in films.

Keeping up with Dixon, Keeler rises to the challenge. She wasn't given many such opportunities in her movies, four with Berkeley followed by five choreographed by Connolly. After *Ready*, she made one more film, divorced Al Jolson, remarried, and retired into motherhood.

PERFECTION

By the time of *Gold Diggers of 1935*, there was already an alternative to Berkeley. For his debut film, Fred Astaire, loaned out to MGM for a lavish imitation of *42nd Street* called *Dancing Lady* (1933), wasn't allowed to do much. (Joan Crawford, who rose to stardom as a Charlestoning flapper, handled the tap, her style even more ungainly than Keeler's while also more glamorous.) Astaire's solo in his second film, *Flying Down to Rio* (1933), is chopped into many gratuitous cuts, interrupted by reaction shots, crowded by other stuff in the frame, and cheapened by a close-up of the dancer's feet. As soon as his success afforded him control over how he was filmed (quite soon, since *Flying Down to Rio* was a hit), Astaire minimized all of these elements, insisting that he and his partners be filmed in full figure. "Either the camera will dance or I will," he declared. Actually, the camera often danced with him, tracking his movements on what studio technicians came to call an "Astaire dolly." But the goal was to make viewers forget the camera and attend to dancing that warranted complete attention.

Apart from how it was filmed, there's much in that first solo that Astaire did not discard. The song is "Music Makes Me," and the premise is that Astaire, trying to teach some chorus girls a routine, can't help but dance to the rhythms of the band rehearsing nearby. He resists, then gives in—the band leaves a break open and he just has to fill it. In the brief tap dance that the music makes him do, he has the quality of a man not entirely in command of his own body. It's like an eccentric routine, in other words, though Astaire plays it cool, and finishes by going right back to what he was doing before. The number exemplifies, at the most basic level, Astaire's manner of dramatizing a tap dance. It looks as though he doesn't have a choice in the matter.

The reality was almost exactly the opposite. In advance of filming, Astaire would rehearse each number for weeks upon agonizing weeks, not pausing for Sundays or holidays, perpetually unsatisfied. During filming, he was commonly the first on the set and the last to leave. On the set of *Rio*, he met two members of what became his creative team, the rehearsal pianist Hal Borne and the dance assistant Hermes Pan. When Astaire was working out a new number, Borne would play, im-

provising an arrangement of the song in question, and Pan and Astaire
would ad-lib along. Days might pass until one of them came upon an
idea that Astaire thought he could use. Slowly, meticulously, he would
build that idea into a dance—"like writing music," Astaire explained.
But that was only half of the job, for once the dance was set, he would
rehearse it until he could do it without thinking, as if he were just ad-
libbing in the rehearsal studio. The potential for such paradoxical illusions
as rehearsed spontaneity was part of what attracted the masochistically
self-critical Astaire to the film medium: "You give your best performance
all the time."

Yet there was more to the appearance of spontaneity than grueling
rehearsal. It was inherent in Astaire's style. "A Needle in a Haystack," his
character-defining solo in the first film he starred in, *The Gay Divorcee*
(1934), shows him getting dressed to go out and search for the girl of his
dreams. He's surprised to find one of his feet tapping, and though the
rest of his body catches the beat, that's not enough for Astaire. He dances
with the whole room. In a single shot, he drums on the mantelpiece,
smoothly swivels out of a turn into the jacket held by his valet, vaults the
sofa in the midst of pinning his boutonniere, hops onto a chair in time
to catch a tossed bowler and umbrella, and twirls the umbrella under his
arm for a slow-churning, tip-of-the-hat exit. The dance is exploratory
but never tentative. Each eruption is cushioned by a casual recovery.
Astaire makes it look easy.

Already, that's what he was known for. Less acknowledged is how
he doesn't make it look *too* easy. His percussive bursts are a bit rough, his
spins a bit wild. The number builds to a trio of cabrioles—pigeon-wing
jumps during which the legs beat together in the air. These typify
Astaire's borrowings from ballet: the time off the ground is but a breath
in the rhythm before a barrage of noisy turns. In those turns, he lifts his
torso and arms as a ballet dancer would, but he doesn't set them. Ever so
slightly, they flail, conveying naturalness. In "I Won't Dance," his solo
for his third film, *Roberta* (1935), the arms flail even more as he turns
twister. Coiling and uncoiling, he gets as tangled as Ray Bolger, but
Astaire lyricizes the self-entwining. He imparts it with feeling. His im-
perfections are what allow you to believe him as a man making it
up, someone you can root for. Debonair as he might be, this bony fellow,

betraying his anxiety as he strains for the high notes, wasn't going to win the girl without dancing exceptionally well.

"A Needle in a Haystack" is also notable as the only film routine in which Astaire used a wing. He didn't do Over the Tops. He didn't go for flips or splits. He didn't even find need for much articulation of the feet. Astaire's toe has a tip, and his heel may drop, but he loved nothing better than to stamp a flat foot. Even at high speeds, his tap steps are, to a surprising extent, just that—steps, the foot lifted off the ground and set back down audibly. He was, in the words of Hermes Pan, a "master of the broken rhythm." A common feel for rhythm was what drew the two men together; rhythmically, they could finish each other's sentences. (They also looked alike.) Pan had paid his dues as a Broadway chorus dancer, but he had acquired his underlying sense of rhythm much earlier, in an equally traditional fashion: from Sam Clark, a black kid who worked as a houseboy and driver for his family in Tennessee and was the son of Pan's mammy. Born Panagiotopoulos, Pan was half-Greek, half-Irish, yet, as he explained to an interviewer in 1989, his rhythms "became strictly black." Rather than the up-on-the-toes mechanical tap he found on Broadway, he preferred the flat-footed black style of his youth or that he found during trips to the Cotton Club, a style he found again in Astaire. "Fred and I used to call it gutbucket." The first time Astaire asked him for help in finishing a sequence, Pan pulled out a break Sam Clark had taught him. It was just what Astaire was looking for.

Astaire's dancing, of course, was not exclusively solo. In *Flying Down to Rio*, he had been thrown together with Ginger Rogers. At twenty-two, she was a champion Charleston dancer and a Broadway star–turned–Hollywood starlet. Astaire, because of his sister, was exceedingly wary of getting trapped in another team, but the movie public knew better and asked for more. During the next six years, Astaire and Rogers made eight more films together, films probably best remembered for their romantic ballroom duets of resistance and surrender. It was in these duets, in the words of Arlene Croce (whose *The Fred Astaire & Ginger Rogers Book* is the best book on the subject), that "dancing was transformed into a vehicle of serious emotion between a man and woman." Yet their more playful duets, interlacing ballroom and tap, were also vehicles of emotion. And for tap, this initiated a new mode.

Take "I'll Be Hard to Handle," from *Roberta* (1935), which finds the childhood sweethearts played by Astaire and Rogers reunited in Paris. As Ginger rehearses with Fred's band, they banter about the old days. Fred punctuates his wisecracks with tap, his own cymbal crashes. When Ginger moves to swat him, he catches her wrists, and just like that, they're dancing together. The illusion of spontaneity could hardly be more convincing. Getting reacquainted, Astaire pilots Rogers around the stage, and as they tap out the breaks together, the tap and ballroom elements gradually mingle, the tap growing more expansive, the ballroom more rhythmic. A bugle call announces the band's exit for thirty-two measures of a cappella hoofing: it's a tap conversation, a challenge-dance-turned-courtship-ritual with all flirtatious repartee relocated to body language and foot sounds. Mock offended, Ginger slaps Fred in the face, smack on the afterbeat. Then she stamps on his foot. When the band kicks in again, the dancers take to each other's arms, touring the floor, and by the end of the dance, it's clear that theirs is a romance rekindled and that tap has provided the sparks. The erotic charge of this kind of Astaire–Rogers number is generated by rhythmic badinage. Their sublimated sex does not live by ballroom alone.

Some of the number's immediacy might be ascribed to how the sound was recorded: directly, the band playing on the side as the stars tapped on a maple floor. Some of Astaire's early solos were recorded this way, but for production numbers, dubbing and postsynchronization became the norm. The Bakelite floors shining in those scenes scarred easily and would've made for a lousy sound. As one might expect, Astaire dubbed his own taps. "I used to do it," he remembered, "because I—I don't know, I wanted to kill myself, I guess, or something." He worked carefully with the musical arrangers, specifying tempos, showing where the dance followed the music and where it worked in opposition, and he watched over sound editors. (One editor told a story about Astaire calling him in on a Sunday to fix the synchronization. There are four sprocket holes alongside each of the twenty-four frames of film that go by per second. Astaire's correction was an adjustment by one sprocket hole.) In the recording studio, Astaire and Pan experimented with different kinds of wood, once laying the boards over a pool of water to dull the tone. Early on, they rarely wore taps. Later, when Astaire started wearing them more often, he hammered them onto the shoes himself and filed the aluminum thin.

Ginger Rogers did not dub her own taps. Instead, in most of the Astaire-Rogers routines, what the eye sees is Ginger Rogers and what the ear hears is Hermes Pan. The voice you hear is Rogers's own, and it would be disappointing to learn otherwise. But only in a history of tap might it count as shocking that someone else dubbed her feet. It goes to show how little a recognizable, personal sound mattered in Hollywood tap. Rogers wasn't a great tap dancer. The feminist quip about how she did everything that Astaire did, only backward and in high heels, just ain't so. Rogers faked things. But she had technique to suffice, and qualities that would prove rarer. Her vulgarity was in just the right proportion to ruffle Astaire's aw-shucks detachment. She knew how to let the play of toughness and vulnerability in her acting permeate a dance. Through her elegant frame and facial expressions, Rogers conveyed a casualness that made her flaws winning. (As Croce observed, "She sometimes threw away stuff she never had.") Her reactions taught moviegoers the appropriate response to Astaire's magic: bedazzlement. Her one tap solo in the Astaire-Rogers series (it's in *Follow the Fleet*) sounds like elementary Astaire. The Ginger is all in the shoulders, hips, and eyes. (That's true as well of the sexy tap dance on a fire escape that Pan would make for her in the 1942 *Roxy Hart*.) No one would have said of her, "She dances like a man."

Astaire and Pan created most of the routines without Rogers, who was always busy making other films, but she contributed ideas. One was the segue into dancing during "Isn't It a Lovely Day" in *Top Hat* (1935). Taking advantage of a storm that has trapped the two of them in a gazebo, Astaire, who's been chasing Rogers to little avail, sings to her back. He sets off on a circular stroll, whistling, and she mimics his masculine stride, signaling her willingness to play. This is a challenge dance that pretends not to be one. When Astaire ventures a tap turn, Rogers tops it, then keeps walking. The tension is delicious. Finding themselves face-to-face, they stop just short of touching, and the sequential imitation, previously mocking, turns collaborative. A tap break answering a thunderclap jolts the number into a faster tempo and the lovers into each other's arms, spinning. Tap has done it again.

It is tap dancing, earlier in *Top Hat*, that has caused Astaire and Rogers to meet. In a London hotel room, Astaire proclaims himself romantically unattached and confirms his fancy-free-dom by tapping around the room, assimilating the decor into his dance. For once, the camera moves away with a good reason, craning down to the room below and the fearsome raised eyebrow of Rogers, who's trying to sleep. When she goes up to deal with the matter in person, she catches Astaire in the act. "Every once and a while, I suddenly find myself . . . dancing," he explains. "I suppose it's some kind of an affliction," she retorts, to which he can only answer yes, and that he shouldn't be left alone. Rogers walks off in a huff, the pleased smirk on her face telling the camera all. But that's not the end of the scene. Astaire sprinkles sand and with the soft white noise of his caressing feet soothes the lady below to sleep. Only Astaire made tap so seductive.

Top Hat's title number demonstrates what he could do with a male chorus. He wears what he sings about: top hat, white tie, tails. But as much as the penguin suit, the rhythms out of which Irving Berlin crafted the song are quintessentially Astaire, especially in the anticipated accents of the bridge ("I'm stepping *out* my dear *to* breathe an *at*mosphere *that* simply *reeks* with *class*."). The male chorus frames him at first and trades a tap phrase or two. In the middle, they leave altogether, and Astaire expertly incorporates his cane into his rhythm-making like a third foot—"I couldn't get enough satisfaction with just the feet noises," he once explained—and does a bit of misterioso twisting in response to an unseen threat. When the men return in a menacing line, Astaire treats them as a shooting gallery, taking out a clump with a tommy-gun foot-rattle and dispatching a pesky survivor with mimed bow and arrow. Astaire took the concept from his 1930 Broadway show *Smiles*, repeating it because he liked it. He also liked repeating what James Cagney once told him: "You've got a little of the hoodlum in you." He liked to think of himself as a gangster, and a violent streak runs through his outlaw style, an urge to startle underneath the formal attire and good manners. In *Top Hat*, it's a plot point and a character trait, this impulse to disturb the peace as an American in stuffy London. But across Astaire's career, whenever he's tapping, the violence is there, the suspense of it and the satisfaction.

In *Follow the Fleet* (1936), in which Astaire plays a dancer-turned-sailor,

his gum-chewing swagger is forced. A running tap joke about his Pav-
lovian need to answer a bugle call with his feet runs aground. But the
tapping in his solo-with-chorus, "I'd Rather Lead a Band," amazes in
how it plays with the music. For anyone who doubts Astaire's purely
musical abilities as a tap dancer, this is the number to listen to. If you
shut your eyes, though, you miss much of the music—the way he swabs
the ship's deck with rhythms; the way he sets hard, quick sounds next to
slow, viscous turns. During the song, he conducts with a baton, but for
the dance, he leads the band more subtly, adjusting tempo with his feet.
When he taps triplets against the band's 4/4, he makes a miniature skit
out of the cycling rhythmic relationship, lumbering as if he were tipsy,
and when the male chorus stands at attention, Astaire taps drill sergeant
commands. Just as the gag starts to get old (just *after*, actually), it's company march again, and over that steady clomping, Astaire taps out a
tune. There's a principle here: whenever Astaire the choreographer brings
on more bodies, they aren't just more bodies. They're opportunities: for
comedy, for musical drama. It's characteristic of Astaire to set himself
against them.

Swing Time (1936) is the zenith of the Astaire-Rogers series. No
dance musical is finer, and in it, tap and ballroom are most thoroughly
blended. In "Pick Yourself Up," the get-on-Ginger's-good-side duet,
Astaire, who has pretended he's a klutz to get a dance lesson with Rogers,
unleashes his true skills to save her job. (Watch Rogers's dance-acting
here: confused and rigid at first, she loosens up as the duet proceeds, her
joyful realization spreading to self-mockery in her chin and hands.) The
dance contrasts elegance and effrontery, but tap is involved on both sides,
the tapping giving the closed-position turns the texture of swing and
the turns allowing the tapping couple conjoined flight, right over the
dance-floor railings and out of the room. Whether they will dance together again is the guiding question of the film's story, and the dance
they finally get to do is "Waltz in Swing Time," which is like other
waltzes except that it's impossibly intricate and fast, with foot sounds
that are absolutely essential to Jerome Kern's music, whispering sweet
nothings as the enraptured lovers trace circles in circles. Only in "Never
Gonna Dance," the duet that reprises all of Swing Time in disintegrating
snatches of remembered songs and steps, the dance in which Fred loses

Ginger (later to win her back only through plot machinations), does tap play no part. The lovers are too out of synch. The taps speak by their absence.

If Astaire wasn't convincing as a sailor, he was still less convincing as a ballet dancer, even as an American one posing as a Russian—the premise of *Shall We Dance* (1937). He's a ballet dancer who falls in love with Astaire-Rogers dancing and with an Astaire-Rogers dancer, played by Ginger. The high-low subject was likely inspired by the ballet-themed Broadway hit of the previous year, *On Your Toes*, which Rodgers and Hart had originally conceived for Astaire. At the film's start, Astaire blathers about combining "the technique of ballet with the warmth and passion of this other mood," a concept he demonstrates by tacking taps onto a "grand leap." The moment is more absurd than it intends to be. Ballet in the film is represented by hack choreography and Harriet Hoctor, a Follies contortionist in pointe shoes. The ideal mixed form that the actual Astaire had already created appears in "They All Laughed," Ginger and Fred's only duet excepting a novelty number on roller skates. When they get together, she turns and turns like a ballerina under his finger while his feet take care of the sound.

Throughout his *Shall We Dance* solo, "Slap That Bass," whenever Astaire finds himself falling into a ballet position, he shakes it off with disgust. Astaire, not just his character, had a reflexive aversion to anything "arty," but more is going on in the number than an allergy to pretension. It takes place in the pristine Art Deco boiler room of a New York–bound ocean liner, where members of the black crew—to complete the fantasy—have gathered for a jam session. Astaire watches in admiration, like Mose at Catharine Market, then jumps in with a sly smile. The Gershwin song he sings has one of those lyrics presenting jazz as a panacea: "the happiest men / All got rhythm." Slumming below-decks, Astaire's character wants to impress the blacks, show them he's got rhythm, too. He performs for them, though they soon fall out of the frame so he can perform for us, imitating machines. (According to Hermes Pan, the idea was inspired by a cement mixer on the studio lot; like many tap dancers, Astaire heard rhythms where others heard noise.) Astaire's imitation of machinery is the number's novel gimmick; Astaire's imitation of the crew is taken for granted. In some unacknowledged way, it's part of his character's re-Americanizing, a mid-Atlantic trip to Harlem.

The scene reminds me of a story about George Gershwin in Charleston doing research for *Porgy and Bess*—studying, like T. D. Rice, to be the best white black man in existence. He attends a black church and jumps into the Ring Shout, uninvited, clapping away. An old man puts his arms around him and says, "You sure could beat out those rhythms, boy . . . You could be my own son." Gershwin's sense of entitlement is troubling, even as his openness endears; the old man's response could have easily been sincere.

Astaire was not known to fraternize with blacks. When the Nicholas Brothers visited him on the set of *Top Hat*, he traded steps with them, but these interactions stopped at the studio gates, and the only filming was done by Mother Nicholas and her home-movie camera. The place of blacks in the Astaire-Rogers movies—absent or in the background— was by no means unusual. The omission of Vernon and Irene Castle's black collaborators from the Astaire-Rogers *Story of Vernon and Irene Castle* (1939) was Hollywood convention. Still, Astaire's appearance in *Swing Time*'s "Bojangles of Harlem" number (1936) demands some explaining. Two giant legs extend to the back of the stage, with a collar and bow tie, a pair of lips, and a bowler stuck on their giant black soles as if to make a minstrel Mr. Potato Head. When the chorus girls part the legs, there's Astaire in the crotch, smiling in blackface. The girls immediately haul away the appendages, vestiges of a much more stereotyped scenario, with staircases, that Astaire wisely scrapped. He leaves to the chorus girls most of Jerome Kern's insufficiently syncopated song and takes for himself a "jig piano" vamp by Hal Bourne.

He wears a bowler, but his polka-dot jacket and minstrel-clown collar are much louder than anything Bill Robinson would've worn. Cocky and crouched, he makes no attempt to dance in the Robinson manner. The number is not parody, and if it's homage, what Astaire offers in tribute is his own brilliance. Rather than just dance in front of the chorus girls, he partners them en masse, a brilliant bit of choreography. In his first use of trick photography, he dances with three giant shadows of himself, brilliant shapes in silhouette. (The joke is that they can't keep up.) The whole number is rhythmically brilliant, even by Astaire standards. The final section, when the music slows to half-time, is the most Bojangles-like in the metronomical way that Astaire subdivides the beat—though he keeps things visually interesting by cycling the steady ticking through his hands and feet, playing Hacky Sack with eighth notes as the rest of him rotates.

Bojangles occasionally patted juba, but it was Astaire who was commended for a fuller use of the body. He was, in the words of a 1941 profile in *Life* magazine, "the first American tap dancer consciously to employ the full resources of his arms, hands and torso." The historical validity of that claim hinges on the meaning of *consciously* and *full*, but in the article it's a link in a pernicious chain of logic: "As Astaire technique evolved, the American Dance washed off its black pigmentation and put on white tie and tails." That sounds like a supplanting, or a forgetting. Did Astaire know that the limp wrist with which he finishes "Bojangles of Harlem" was a gesture of Jim Crow?

But Astaire technique truly was an advance. Later in his career, he tried more trick photography, but no special effects ever equaled Astaire effects. When he played piano, he actually played piano; when he played drums, he played drums. Canes, umbrellas, and other props were extensions of himself. His golfing solo in *Carefree* (1938), in which he drives a teed-up line of golf balls, perfectly, in perfect rhythm, tapping in between swings—that's Astaire taking advantage of the film medium, using multiple takes to capture one real-time moment of perfection. "Every dance ought to spring somehow out of the character or the situation," he once said. "Otherwise, it is simply a vaudeville act." Before starting a new film, he watched his previous ones to remind himself which options were off the table. His act was never to repeat himself.

Astaire technique: John Martin put a finger on the spine of it. "Tap dancing can be a desperate bore to watch," he explained, because of its emphasis on the ear. Astaire was different, not by a "mere superimposition of visual movements upon a base of foot-tapping," but by expressing "one central dance impulse in terms of as many mediums as the body can muster." With many tap dancers, the body follows the feet, functionally, or upper and lower halves seem barely on speaking terms, but with Astaire, the impulse could flow in all directions. His appeal to the eye wasn't separate from his appeal to the ear. And although Astaire was inimitable, his example could serve as a standard for how much could be done with tap. He inspired millions to imagine that they might dance like, or with, Fred Astaire—a fool's dream, some kind of affliction.

SANDBAGGED BALLERINA

Astaire never found a partner to equal Rogers, but he did work with one woman who came closer to matching him as a tap technician: Eleanor Powell. They made a single film together, *Broadway Melody of 1940*, in which, Astaire explained, they "rather specialized in tap dancing." In Astaire's estimation, Powell was a woman who "put 'em down like a man," but during her girlhood in Springfield, Massachusetts, she was pitifully shy. It was in an effort to overcome her bashfulness that Powell's mother delivered her at age eleven to the local dance school, where she studied basic ballet, "esthetic dancing," and acrobatics. Showing off these skills on the beach in Atlantic City got her a summer job in a dinner show. Her family was poor, and seeing her divorced mother work in menial jobs, she later said, gave her determination to succeed. In Atlantic City, she looked down her thirteen-year-old nose at the tap dancers on the bill, but soon, when she ventured into New York, she found that the only question producers asked was, Do you tap?

So she enrolled for ten classes at the school of Jack Donahue, that Boston-bred eccentric. After the first session, Powell wanted to quit. She couldn't get the routine. The next time, Donahue held Powell's ankles in his hands as she drilled the steps. The time after that, he cinched an army belt around her waist and attached a sandbag to each side. The ballet-trained dancer sank into the ground like a hoofer. All Donahue had her do was shift her augmented weight from leg to leg, a tap dancer's most fundamental skill. After about seven lessons with the belt on, something clicked. It was, Powell remembered, "like an algebra lesson which baffles you until the light suddenly shines."

Those first ten classes were Powell's last formal tap lessons. (So she said, though one can find counterassertions that she studied with Buddy Bradley, Frank Condos, and others.) The routine she learned from

Donahue served as her specialty number in her first Broadway shows, in 1929, as a tapping tennis-player type with a boyish figure and a Louise Brooks bob. It wasn't long, though, before she started devising her own dances and was being called "possibly the best lady tap-dancer in the business" by *Time*. On Broadway she worked for George White and Ziegfeld. She tapped at Carnegie Hall with Paul Whiteman's band. When she wasn't onstage, she was practicing, some sixteen hours a day. Nothing else interested her. Donahue had suggested that she cross her ballet and tap skills, so she tried that. By her own report, it took her three years to teach herself how to turn while tapping. (Chuck Green, the protégé of John Bubbles, claimed to have taught her how to incorporate taps into her turns one day at Billy Pierce's studio.) Her favorite practice records were by Fats Waller.

"There must be some colored blood in me somewhere," she told an interviewer in 1971 (probably not a comment she would have offered to a fan magazine in the thirties). "I often used to kid my mother, 'Did you have a colored milkman or something?' Because it's a black sound." During the same interview, Powell told an uncanny and not altogether believable story about her first major movie appearance, in *George White's 1935 Scandals*. Thinking she was an extra in a different film, the Fox makeup department darkened her skin to play an Egyptian. White, too drunk to notice, filmed her like that. "Because I'm doing this low-to-the-ground tap number, they think I'm a Negress." Someone told her that Louis B. Mayer, scanning Fox footage for talent to grab for Metro-Goldwyn-Mayer, saw the take and said he could use a girl like that if she weren't colored.

In the take that made it into the movie, Powell's character is introduced as "the greatest female tap dancer," the title that would remain attached to her throughout her career and after. She doesn't look colored, or even Egyptian, but she does sink rather than lift. Her spotless rhythms are largely even, tacked together by gunshot upbeats, and she brings her hips into the dance, samba-style. Like many performers of her time, Powell habitually affected a pose of ecstatic pleasure, head back and mouth open. In some close-ups, she looks ready to eat the camera. Her faux-sophisticated mannerisms don't date well, unless you emphathize with a good girl's struggle to be glamorous. The *Scandals* number is a nightclub routine, made up of steps repeated to get a hand. Powell's ballet-tap turns come by the dozen, with one tapping foot out in front counting. Perhaps her self-schooling accounts for the bizarre way she always held her arms in a spin—elbows pulled to her chest, hands drooping, as if in imitation of a *Tyrannosaurus rex*.

Someone must have alerted Mayer to his misunderstanding, because MGM tried to sign up Powell to do a dance in *Broadway Melody of 1936*. Put off by the sinful ways of Hollywood, she insisted on a speaking role and an astronomical salary, expecting MGM to balk. Instead, MGM called her bluff and gave her the lead. After the film succeeded, the studio offered her a seven-year contract. Studio staff capped her teeth, plucked her eyebrows, and feminized her hairstyle, yet Powell wasn't your average starlet. For one thing, she did her own choreography. Like Astaire, she educated herself about the camera and learned to sit in the editing room when her numbers were being cut. She also dubbed her own taps. (Marjorie Lane dubbed much of her singing.) To ensure the right tempos, Powell first did her routine while the orchestra was recording, muffling her taps on a mattress. During filming, she danced to that recording and only later did she lay down the shoe music, watching her filmed image and synchronizing with the score through headphones as she tapped on a maple board in shoes more practical than those she wore onscreen.

In the Astaire-Rogers films, the plots don't rise to the level of the dancing, but the movies are still watchable. Powell's films aren't, really. The great Cole Porter songs introduced in them deserved better launchings. Powell was a specialty act with no experience in carrying a story, and flimsy backstage plots didn't help. She is courteous, bland, wholesome. She usually has a love interest, but he is usually a nondancer: Robert Taylor, Jimmy Stewart. He doesn't win her through dancing; he's in love with dancing's display of her. Powell is a soloist, and her most common dance partner is a male chorus that expresses its affection by tossing her around.

Her numbers tend to be exhibitions, gymnastic floor routines with tap. On top of the endless turns, Powell layers high kicks, deep lunges, and pliant backbends. One Powell number might impress, but watch a few and you can track the recycling of a small vocabulary—steps such as the rolling one she liked to repeat for measures on end with a finger pressed coyly against her cheek. The essential sameness of the dances is partially disguised by varying costumes—a sequined majorette's uniform, a sequined tuxedo, a Hawaiian grass skirt—and by the production elements, on which MGM spent lavishly. For the finale of *Born to Dance* (1936), the studio built her a white battleship. For the finale of *Rosalie* (1937), Powell danced up and down sixteen drums, arranged in ascending order of height from ten inches to fifteen feet, and spun her way through a sixty-acre set into a crowd of five hundred extras. It was a lot to look at, though nothing Powell played on those drums was much to listen to.

She was a soloist even if there were other tappers in her films. Ray Bolger was in *Rosalie*, but almost all of his dancing was edited out. Buddy Ebsen, lanky of limb and thick of eyebrow, was an appealing eccentric. He and his sister, Velma, had been a successful comedy team in vaudeville and nightclubs. In "Sing Before Breakfast," their rooftop romp with Powell in *Broadway Melody of 1936*, they're more lovable than she is, more believably relaxed. True to the eccentric pattern, Ebsen ended up as a character actor specializing in hayseeds, most famously as Jed Clampett on *The Beverly Hillbillies*. George Murphy, Powell's opposite in *Broadway Melody of 1938*, was a Yale athlete–turned–dancer: leading-man material. He, too, was likable, but his song-and-dance style was standard-issue white-Broadway-and-nightclubs of the twenties: competent, stiff. He ended up as a Republican senator.

In *Broadway Melody of 1938*, Murphy and Powell get caught in the rain, in a gazebo. But even their splashing in puddles doesn't slosh up any fun. As Murphy would have readily admitted, Powell's other co-star in *Broadway Melody of 1940* was of a different order. Working on duets with Astaire was difficult, Powell reported, since they were both accustomed to choreographing their own numbers. She danced mostly on the beat, he mostly off. Rehearsals were halting, gummed up by a coagulation of courtesy and perfectionism, until Mr. Astaire and Miss Powell were improvising in different corners of the room and happened upon the same rhythm. This musical convergence didn't translate into much on-screen chemistry—the most romantically credible moment in the film is Astaire's solo, during which he dances with a picture of Powell—but it did produce some shared rhythmic sophistication.

Their first duet, supposedly impromptu, is nearly all unison and side by side. It starts with a groove, no song, and in that groove it spirals, accelerating halfway through and going out on flag-waving riffs. The bits of rhythmic repartee are so subtle that you might miss them, a few comment-and-answers slipped in on the fly. Because there's no flirtation, there are no sparks when the dancers touch, as chastely as siblings, but they do manage a beautiful, unusual turn together in ballroom position. According to the positioning, he's leading, but she provides both propulsion and sound as he holds a one-legged pose, displaying his superior line and squeezing in a few offbeat stamps of his own. The climactic ten-minute "Begin the Beguine" takes place in two parts. The first section, floating on the rumba-like rhythm, is a circling soft shoe with Spanish lace, dreamy but also dry in the sommelier's sense. Powell's stiffness never looked so lovely. The second section swings into a zenith of deluxe Hollywood tap. It's a challenge dance, politely playful up top, serious and witty down in the feet. In a tacet segment, Astaire and Powell set up a basic time step. Onto the front of the step they serially append one, two, then three and four forward-creeping chugs. They do this addition separately, Astaire ahead of Powell, so that they're in canon. Aurally, the effect is echo upon echo; visually, it's like ripples on the set's reflecting pool of a floor. Thrillingly, the tapping accelerates into a series of turning Maxie Fords that build as they repeat, first with the dancers side by side, then orbiting each other, then firing missiles with their arms. For once, Powell's turning ability has been taken advantage of for a purpose more choreographically significant than "repeat ad infinitum."

Without Astaire, Powell never reached the same heights, but it shouldn't be surprising that one of her most effective numbers was directed by Busby Berkeley. In "Fascinating Rhythm" in *Lady, Be Good* (1941), Berkeley's camera stays fixed on her as pianos and their boogie-woogie players rotate past. Powell delivers some of her pithiest tapping, finessed with slides and swivels, and she takes a slightly different rhythmic approach to each pianist. At the end, Berkeley's swooping camera heightens the impact of her usual moves. Elsewhere, formulas made for missed opportunities, such as in *Ship Ahoy* (1942), where her interactions with the Tommy Dorsey Orchestra's drum virtuoso, Buddy Rich, remain limited to a few drumstick swaps. What with Powell's tapping on tables and across a diving board and her bounding in and out of the arms of anonymous men, she has little time for Rich. Even a woman who "put 'em down like a man" was expected to do more than challenge-dance.

Though Powell was respected by black tap dancers—Fayard Nicholas, Bill Bailey—rhythm wasn't her core business. "I would try to think up something that is still tapping but with something else," Powell remembered. "After all, you can't just come out and tap." In *Honolulu* (1939), she jumped rope; in *I Dood It* (1943), she twirled a lariat. Whatever the skill, she trained with experts and practiced as if for a new profession, hard work that shows. The routine she taught a terrier to do with her in *Lady, Be Good* is most excellent vaudeville. But her turn as a human pinball and her duet with a horse, both in *Sensations of 1945*, are no more than gimmicks. In the films that followed *Broadway Melody of 1940*, Powell still received top billing but not always a leading role in the plot, and the stuff around her degenerated from bad to worse. In 1944, she married the on-the-rise actor Glenn Ford and, a year later, gave birth to a son and pretty much retired. Her final film appearance came in 1950 with *Duchess of Idaho*, as a specialty act in an Esther Williams movie.

UNCLE BILLY AND SHIRLEY

In *Honolulu*, Powell had put her own Bill Robinson homage on film, wearing blackface at a costume ball while doing a close copy of the stair dance of her favorite entertainer. Except for a contrivance—the stairs pop up from the floor as needed—it's simple impersonation of the kind that puts into relief the original's inimitable virtues. When Powell first arrived in Hollywood, the papers quoted Robinson's boast that she had been his pupil for five years. Powell said she had learned just one routine from him. Near the end of her life, she also recalled the time she had played on the same vaudeville bill as John Bubbles in 1928. Between shows, they would trade steps in the basement, and during Bubbles's performances, she would lie on her stomach in the wings and watch as he angled his dance in her direction, challenging her. Powell knew Willie Covan, too. It was she who suggested that MGM hire him as a tap teacher. She insisted on black piano players for "Fascinating Rhythm," and that number—with an opening featuring the Berry Brothers and gigantic shadows—is another open-secret tease, telegraphing a source of her "black sound." Cholly Atkins, who arrived in Hollywood in the mid-thirties as a young hoofer from Buffalo, recalls in his autobiography that Powell hired a stable of black tap dancers, including himself, to come to her studio and supply her with ideas and steps. She would take what she thought she could use. "If she thought certain steps were too masculine," Atkins remembers, "we'd leave them out."

Of all of the black dancers who influenced her, though, Powell was closest in friendship to Robinson. Sometimes, they would perform together at benefits or private parties. Once, because Robinson was not allowed in the front elevator, Powell traveled with him in the back one. Another time, she remembered, they were both given glasses of water. After finishing his, Robinson broke the glass, then paid for it, informing Powell that their white hosts wouldn't drink from it after he had. There was no way that Powell and Robinson would be allowed to dance together on film.

In 1934, Bill Robinson, aged fifty-six, signed a contract to appear in *The Little Colonel*, starring Shirley Temple. Six years old, Temple was already a movie star; during the next three years, she would be the top box-office draw in the country. She had learned to tap at the Los Angeles dancing school of Ethel Meglin, and whatever effort Meglin had invested in the child reaped dividends, because every time one of Temple's movies was released, enrollment in tap classes soared countrywide. Similar surges followed the release of each Astaire-Rogers or Powell movie, but the most requests by far came in for Shirley Temple routines. Kids wanted to have as much fun as she seemed to be having; mothers of the Depression had visions of meal tickets. It's probable that Shirley Temple lured more people into tap class than anyone else, ever.

Her films were commonly titled after her character, a girl often nick-named after one of her physical attributes: *Bright Eyes, Curly Top, Dimples*.

In *The Little Colonel*, she played the willful granddaughter of a curmud-geonly former Confederate. Bill Robinson was cast as the colonel's loyal servant. The mansion had a staircase; ergo, Robinson would dance on it. Before filming started, someone suggested that Temple join him on the stairs, and so Robinson taught a simplified version of his precious rou-tine to the child. "Let's get your feet attached to your ears," he told her, and they practiced until she had the steps in her muscle memory. In the film, his character is trying to get hers to go up to bed. He goes first, showing her "the brand-new way" to climb stairs, *his* way, accompany-ing himself with kazoo-like lip buzzing. Temple responds as the child in anyone would. "I want to do that, too," she says. And then she does, holding Robinson's hand, matching him step for step.

She was an angel of love. Her characters softened hard hearts. And say what you will about the treacle of her films and their corny resolu-tions, the little lady was a pro. In her shrewd autobiography, *Child Star*, published in 1988, she recalls how Robinson taught her how much work it takes to appear relaxed. She also tells a story about dubbing her own taps perfectly, take after take, while one of her adult partners kept mak-ing mistakes. The number in question, the military finale of *Poor Little Rich Girl* (1936), was complicated, requiring from the eight-year-old the independence of some elementary counterpoint and canon. She applied Robinson's lessons of clarity to her routines without him, palling around with Buddy Ebsen and George Murphy. In *Child Star*, Temple writes that the smile on her face in her scenes with the man she called Uncle Billy wasn't acting. Of all the actors she worked with, Robinson treated her most as an equal. Robinson's smile is harder to read. In his homes and dressing rooms, Temple's portrait was prominently displayed, and he was always buying the child presents: dancing shoes, a miniature car, a gold-plated police badge with a diamond set in the middle.

The Littlest Rebel (1935) begins in the South before the Civil War. Robinson's character is the faithful slave. When Temple asks him to dance for her juvenile guests, he obliges with a nice little solo to that enduring minstrel ditty "Turkey in the Straw." This idyll is interrupted when the Yankees invade the plantation. At one point, as a disguise, Temple blacks her face with shoe polish. She and Robinson dance together twice: first they do the Shim Sham as a diversion so that Temple's Confederate father can escape, then they busk for train fare to find Dad in a prisoner-of-war camp. Throughout, Robinson's character is capable, cool-headed. He makes a point of distinguishing himself from the slaves who take advantage of the fog of war to run away. Uncle Billy takes care of Shirley.

This was, as the film historian Donald Bogle has pointed out, the first instance in motion picture history in which a black character was responsible for a white one. Bogle has also called the pair "the perfect interracial love match"—perfect because sexless. In *Child Star*, Temple writes proudly of herself and Robinson as "the first interracial dancing couple in movie history" and reports that shots of them holding hands had to be excised for Southern distributors. Is it really possible that people were threatened by a snowy-haired black caretaker? Robinson didn't appear in the film in which Temple, unavoidably, played Little Eva. (This was *Dimples*, which he choreographed, uncredited—and in which Temple did a minstrel routine, clean-faced with everyone around her corked up.) But the Uncle Billy character was nevertheless related to Uncle Tom. Robinson's persona in the films, for all of his displays of illiteracy, stands in contrast to the slow-witted, easily spooked Negro played by Willie Best and the outrageously lazy one played by Stepin Fetchit. Robinson's loyal slave or servant was a comforting white fantasy, yet there's an undeniable dignity in how he treats the child, even when they're just fooling around.

Much in Robinson's long-established style was ready-made to amuse a minor: the lip-buzzing cuteness, the nursery-rhyme rhythms. And he didn't have to alter his dancing, that Essence of Old Virginia, to suit a story of the South. (One of his favorite foot-crossing steps—hands on hips, head tilted—can be seen in the dancer illustrated on the sheet music for "Ole Virginny Break Down" in 1841.) In time, these facts and associations would come to haunt him. During the Depression, though, millions of people were cheered by the old black man and the little white girl tapping their troubles away together. Reflecting back on the Robinson-Temple films in the late 1970s, Honi Coles, who knew Robinson well, insisted that the older dancer had been proud of them: "He was the happiest man in the world doing things like that with Shirley

Temple. Part of it was the generosity that black entertainers showed to whites. We were so happy somebody wanted what we did, we were ready to just give it away."

Robinson's other films didn't offer him much more scope. Wash, the sensible servant character of *In Old Kentucky* (1935), is described by his employer, played by Will Rogers, as a "boy" who's "absolutely the best in the world"—the best dancer. Yet most of Robinson's dancing is confined to domestic duties, embellishments while he's setting the table. Wash entertains at the white folks' party and the roles reverse, partially, when he patiently teaches Rogers a step. This step Rogers subsequently uses, while blackened up, to impersonate Wash and break out of jail. Such blackening-up episodes played on an absurd dramatic irony. What audience member wasn't going to recognize Will Rogers under cork? He was a beloved figure, second only to Temple as a box-office draw. As a friend to both stars, on-screen and off, Robinson grew more beloved himself. For his specialty spot in *Hooray for Love* (1935), he got to play Bill Robinson, the Mayor of Harlem, and was cast with a female partner slightly closer to his age, that black teenager Jeni LeGon. Rather than a love duet, the number is a we've-got-plenty-of-nothing trio with the magnificent Fats Waller, whose flamboyant irony telegraphs, as Robinson's clowning does not, that he's in on the joke.

In *One Mile from Heaven* (1936), a social-issue movie about a black woman who adopts a Shirley Temple lookalike, Robinson was given a straight role, or almost straight. His good-hearted policeman first appears while summoning the neighborhood children with the sound of his feet. In *Café Metropole* (1937), an Americans-in-Europe feature, Robinson was given a more glamorous specialty spot. After prancing down the steps of a Paris cabaret in top hat and tails, "Bill Robinson of Harlem" delivers an exquisite soft shoe, softly accompanied by a string orchestra. (Such high-toned backing was not unheard of for his stage appearances.) Lasting three minutes, the number is his longest-sustained dance in a major motion picture. It's beautiful, with a low percentage of the steps recycled through his other film appearances. Robinson mugs, but it's nevertheless an unprecedented image of an adult black dancer as a sophisticate.

It was his other appearance in the film, however, that sparked controversy. The problem was not that the number was an Apache Dance, the
Parisian pantomime form in which a pimp roughs up a prostitute. The
problem was his partner: Geneva Sawyer, a twenty-three-year-old
white girl in dark makeup. (She had already appeared in blackface as
one of Temple's dolls in *Poor Little Rich Girl*.) The rumor that Robinson
had pushed Sawyer forward for the role raised hackles in the black
press, objections that came barbed with comments about how popular
Bojangles was among whites and reminders of the expensive presents he
was always giving that little white millionaire. Robinson's response—
that the role was too small to justify importing a black girl from New
York—seemed to evade the issue. Sawyer's performance, evincing little
discernible talent, doesn't clear up the mystery, either. Why did the studio
allow a white woman to perform a sexually themed dance with a black
man? Ultimately, it didn't. Both numbers, superfluous to an overlong
plot, were cut.

For the most part, it was back to Shirley Temple vehicles. In *Rebecca
of Sunnybrook Farm* (1938), Robinson is a farmhand who joins Shirley
for a toy-soldier number on a staircase. In *Just Around the Corner*, later that
year, he's the doorman in her building, running down stairs, and during
the benefit she stages to help out Uncle Sam, he and Temple pretend to
pick cotton. Temple's tapping continued to improve. She moves like an
adult in *Young People* (1940), but that's the trouble. On the cusp of adolescence, she's just about lost her fascination. In any case, a black man was no
longer an acceptable partner for the young lady. In 1938, Robinson's contract with Fox was canceled. He was relegated to tiny roles in B movies: a
pit mechanic in *Road Demon*, a cheery convict in *Up the River*. He tapped
up and down the auto shop stairs, and down and around the circular jail-
house stairs, cleaning as he went. For *Up the River*'s inmate talent show, he
got to wear top hat and tails again, introduced as "that dark cloud of joy."

Robinson had to wait until 1943 to play a leading man in a movie,
the all-black musical *Stormy Weather*. Here, in what would be his final
film, he is lover to the much younger Lena Horne. As his character (Bill
Robinson–like but also based on Noble Sissle and his service in the First
World War) rises to fame, he does a little sand dance on a riverboat—he's

dead tired but he just can't resist the music. Later, in an exotic African number, he steals focus, bare-chested, tapping on various-sized drums. There's not much to these numbers or to his tuxedoed routines with Horne. Before the film was released, the *Amsterdam News* reported that it was going to be redone, so unbelievable was Robinson's performance as a lover. Though the rumor proved false, the article treated it as a sign that Hollywood was finally beginning to care what black audiences thought. High-profile negotiations between the NAACP and the Hollywood studios in 1942 had led to an agreement to broaden the film representation of blacks beyond comic and menial figures. In this light, the very mediocrity of *Stormy Weather*—an all-black equivalent of countless white morale-boosting entertainments—could be taken as progress.

THE TAP-DANCING JANITOR

Stormy Weather might have seemed to herald an era of all-black films, especially because it wasn't the only one released in 1943. The other one, the far superior *Cabin in the Sky*, also provided a role for a tap great: John Bubbles. In the film, Bubbles plays Domino Johnson, a sharpie like his Sportin' Life in *Porgy and Bess*. His acting suffices, the blankness of it conferring menace, and the cane-twirling strut he does to "Shine," backed by the Ellington band, is first-class. It isn't a tap dance, though. The only hoofing in the film is done by Bill Bailey, the erstwhile Bill Robinson impersonator. While Ethel Waters, the film's devout heroine, sings a heartfelt "Takin' a Chance on Love," Bailey puts on a fixed grin to execute a series of rhythmically precise but physically unkempt wings, throwing in a trademark sliding step that would become known, decades later, as the Moonwalk. In the folk morality play that *Cabin in the Sky* is, Bailey's dance represents domestic bliss against the temptations of the nightclub where Bubbles thrives. And while Bailey's gestures are clearly of the happy darky variety, Bubbles's coquettish eye rolls are more ambiguous. His dancing has what the film critic Pauline Kael remembered from seeing him onstage around the same time: a "slinky sexy" quality. "I thought he was evil," Kael wrote, "but I loved it."

Bubbles had already exhibited his tap skills in the 1937 film *Varsity Show*. That story takes place at a college, where Buck and Bubbles are janitors named Buck and Bubbles. Taking a break from shoveling coal in the basement, Bubbles shows the students some steps: sand-dance scrapings, heel-heavy rhythms, masterly dancing done in a goofball manner. At the end of the film, when the Varsity Show moves to Broadway, Buck and Bubbles are asked to contribute their amateur talents. In a Prince Albert suit, Bubbles slides down an enormous curving ramp—an entrance from the mind of the director, Busby Berkeley. After alighting, Bubbles taps sitting next to Buck on the piano bench, then taps on top of the instrument, his legs but not his rhythms blurring as he falls off the log double-time and crunches into whip-around turns with the greatest of ease. The number is exciting but it's mere prelude to a Berkeley collegiate extravaganza.

The Buck and Bubbles number in the 1938 Mentone short *Beauty Shoppe* closely resembles descriptions of the duo's nightclub act. As bellmen pushing a piano, the two insult each other, playing the dozens, before Buck dazzles on the piano and Bubbles goes into his song and dance. Much of that dance is deceptively simple, tucking its rhythmic complexities into strolling motion and more talking. Only a break near the end drop-kicks the beat around with unmistakable force. In *Atlantic City*, Buck and Bubbles do a routine to a song like "Rhythm for Sale," enlivening an excisable Harlem sequence that they share with Louis Armstrong in the otherwise worthless 1944 film. Just as Bubbles starts heating up rhythmically, the number ends. The comment of a *Life* reviewer about their act at the Zanzibar in 1943 applies: it would be better if Bubbles clowned less and danced more. For the duo's next and final Hollywood appearance, in the 1948 Danny Kaye musical *A Song Is Born*, they were cast again as musically gifted janitors and didn't dance at all. They weren't even billed—a sorry ending to a film career that never took off.

In the case of Bill Robinson, despite the limits placed on his career, something approaching a full representation of his artistry as a dancer seems to have been captured on film. The footage accords with the descriptions laid down by those who saw him perform live, and it's

possible to perceive now what his contemporaries did then. With Bubbles, the situation is more equivocal. The stories—say, those about no one
being able to steal from him because he didn't repeat—match the films
only in fits. Insufficient footage is partly at fault. And the conditions of
Hollywood filmmaking, over which Bubbles had little control, were far
from ideal for capturing a great improviser. Yet his might also be a case
of an innovator whose innovations were so thoroughly absorbed by
everyone else—and built upon—that it's difficult to appreciate the originality in the original. During an interview Bubbles gave in 1979, a few
years before his death, when he was asked about some of the films, such
as *Atlantic City*, the titles meant nothing to him. Though he could recall
countless details from his long career (the interview lasted ten hours), he
did not remember making those films. In that case, the interviewer asked,
did the films mean nothing to him? "The films had more meaning,"
Bubbles retorted. "Because I was entertaining more people. The film was
going more places than I could be." Places that included posterity.

THE FLYING BROTHERS

Bill Robinson is not the only tap dancer in *Stormy Weather*. The film is
stolen out from under him by a pair of younger hoofers who appear only
in the finale. The Nicholas Brothers were in their twenties in 1943,
and their routine is a stair dance like nothing Robinson ever dreamed
of. Cab Calloway is jiving and scatting with his band in a nightclub
when the Nicholas Brothers suddenly hop onto the stage from a table in
the audience. Dancing, the brothers jump up onto narrow, waist-high
platforms and leap from perch to perch. Then they pounce on the piano,
beat out some punch-in-the-gut rhythms up there, soar to the ground,
land in splits, and bounce back upright. For most acts, this would constitute a spectacular finish. The Nicholas Brothers simply amble to another
part of the set, where a giant staircase awaits them. The staircase is a semicircle, made of two curving flights of six stairs apiece, each stair as high
as the dancers' knees. Harold and Fayard ascend one side in gulps and
descend the other as only they would, one brother leaping over the other

into splits, stair by punishing stair. And still that's not the end. Each taking a side, Harold and Fayard mount the stairs one more time in a suspense-producing stutter rhythm, then slide back down—once again in splits—on ramps that run along the inside curves of the staircase. Finally, they stop, stand, and open their arms in a conclusive gesture of munificence, a signal that the ovation may at last commence.

Of all the tap numbers ever filmed, this is the most universally fail-safe: show it and people go nuts. Much of the effect derives from the elastic, safety-be-damned acrobatics, but the number would not have the same impact without its binding to the music. Every movement the brothers make is matched by an accent in the arrangement. When they climb the stairs, the music climbs a scale; when they do their leapfrog descent, the music climbs again, as if counting the rising tally of feats. The rhythms are simple and swinging, and Harold and Fayard make them visible. In Robinson's stair dance, the staircase is a musical instrument; with the Nicholas Brothers, the instrument is their bodies, and the staircase mostly a means of elevation.

The Nicholas Brothers were not new to films, yet their style had developed since their juvenile appearances. Much of the change stemmed from a partnership with Nick Castle, a white choreographer for Fox, the studio that had awarded the Nicholases a five-year contract in 1940. Born Nicola Casaccio, Castle was an ex-vaudevillian from Brooklyn. He was short and he stuttered, but, as he said in a 1965 interview, "colored people called me the white boy with Negro rhythm." He claimed to have visited the Hoofers' Club, and he idolized Eddie Rector, Bubbles, and Bill Robinson. In 1935, Castle came upon an article written by the Fox star Dixie Dunbar, titled "How to Hoof in Hollywood." He wrote her a letter, offering his services as a teacher, and after she responded, he talked his way into the job of assistant to dance directors who didn't dance. Soon he was choreographing a dozen or more mostly undistinguished films a year. *Stormy Weather* was his fourth with the Nicholas Brothers.

For the Nicholas Brothers' number in *Orchestra Wives* (1942), Castle remembered a stunt by the Mosconi Brothers, an acrobat troupe, in which they would run up a wall and flip. His idea was to have Harold run up a column, flip backward off it, and land in a split—an extension of Nicholas Brothers technique that Harold might not have hazarded on his own. ("Let me see *you* do that," Harold initially told Castle.) Castle harnessed him with ropes and pulleys to practice, and in the filmed number, the new stunt is worked into a challenge dance. Fayard runs up one slick marble column and bounces off into a split. Harold trumps him by adding the backflip. It's breathtaking.

Most of their routines had a challenge dance at the core. Harold and Fayard's number in *Down Argentine Way* (1941), their first film for Fox, essentially documented the stage act that Fayard had choreographed for the Cotton Club in the late thirties. It was a challenge dance to beat all challenge dances, jammed with spins and kamikaze flips delivered with panache: at one point, Fayard grips two ends of his handkerchief and hops it as if it were an undersized jump rope (Castle's idea), landing each time in splits; reversing the slide to rise to his feet, he suavely returns the handkerchief to a lapel pocket, only to have Harold pop through his parted legs in more sliding splits. The dynamic between the brothers endured: Fayard more solicitous, always making an effort to frame and complement his brother; Harold the show-off, spoiling for his turn. Harold's looks had caught up to his precocious voice. Fayard also sang, but usually in embellishment or comment on Harold's song. As dancers they were equals, though Harold was a little less conscious of his arms and hands than his choreographer brother. Fayard could be too conscious, swirling the air around him like a magician. Astaire "used his hands like I do," he once said. "I just did more of it." Precisely.

"Classical tap" was Fayard's preferred term for their style—he loathed being labeled a "flash act"—and by "classical," he meant graceful, elegant, classy, "the whole body from our heads down to our toes." Their extended lines still prompted people to ask them if they had ballet training, but the Nicholas Brothers were no more ballet dancers than Astaire was. In both cases, the aspects of their style that reminded people of ballet derived more from adagio ballroom teams than from academic technique: the lifted torso, the rounded arms, the twist-tie tautness of one leg wrapped behind the other. How much one style drew from the other is an open question. Publicly, Astaire and the Nicholases expressed great mutual admiration. When asked directly, Fayard disavowed any influence: "We were like inventors on different continents coming up with an invention at the same time." Astaire, it seems, was never asked, but Fayard did recall that Astaire once said to him, "I have always wanted to dance like you." That's a phrase it's easy to imagine the well-mannered Astaire speaking.

Tap was the base. When they were on their feet, the Nicholas Brothers pounded out rhythms that swung. They rarely wore metal on their soles (even during dubbing, which they handled themselves), and their tone was generally low and heavy, though they could be light when they wanted. In their number for *Down Argentine Way*, Fayard spools out a strand of wings that are stork-sized yet delicate; they mate perfectly with high, harplike arpeggios in the score. Certain surface similarities obscure the variety across their routines. In *The Great American Broadcast* (1941), they don railway-porter outfits to tap on suitcases and leap through a train window, and in *Tin Pan Alley* (1940), they go topless in turbans and briefs to portray eunuchs in a harem, but most often they dress in tailcoats. And in all of their numbers, they leap into splits so frequently that the exclamatory move becomes as common as a period or a comma.

Apart from that habit, however, few steps recur, as a vocabulary of spins, stamps, and wings is crafted into fresh statements. In their "Chattanooga Choo Choo" routine for *Sun Valley Serenade* (1941), the brothers split a rhythmic phrase between them, sliding a foot to evoke a train leaving the station; later, they repeat the alternating idea without the train motions, abstracting it. In *Orchestra Wives*, their split-and-recovers go into slow motion during a spotlit adagio section like one of Astaire's misterioso passages. It's short, but it's an advance into a broader range of mood, never revisited. By Astaire's structural standards, the brothers' routines could be a tad rickety; tethered to their arrangements, they could be musically single-leveled. But Fayard's choreographic invention went far beyond the attention-grabbing stunts thought up for him by Nick Castle. How much Castle and the other nominal choreographers contributed is another mystery of Hollywood collaboration. Castle recalled spending hours with the brothers as they mimicked him in front of a mirror. According to Fayard, "Castle would say, 'How about doing this step, fellows?' and we'd say, 'Yes, great, how about adding this to it?'" Hermes Pan, the choreographer on *Sun Valley Serenade*, remembered that he "mostly just let them go."

One place Harold and Fayard weren't allowed to go was into the film's story. *Great American Broadcast* momentarily floats the pretense that they're train porters. ("Those boys are terrific," remarks Jack Oakie. "They ought to be onstage.") In *Orchestra Wives* and *Sun Valley Serenade*, Glenn Miller and his band speak dialogue and serve a small function in the story, while the Nicholas Brothers do not. Performing with a white band was a kind of integration for the black dancers, but they remained entirely segregated from the plot. Their appearance in *Sun Valley Serenade* is the most incongruous. The film, a vehicle for the Norwegian figure skater Sonja Henie, is set in a ski lodge in Idaho; as the band is rehearsing a soon-to-be-number-one tune about a train ride down South, Harold and Fayard and the fetching Dorothy Dandridge appear out of nowhere for the third trip through the song. Once their number's finished, they vanish. That was their role, you might say—tap dancers and singers, not actors. But Sonja Henie was no actor, and the brothers provide the best three minutes in the film. Someone might have given them the chance to spread out.

The Nicholas Brothers' contract with Twentieth Century–Fox elapsed in 1945, and according to Fayard, it was he and his brother who chose not to renew it. They felt underutilized. In her biography of the Nicholases, Constance Valis Hill suggests that Fox didn't know what to do with a pair of sexually potent young black men, too old to be pickaninnies, too young for Uncle Tom. Applied to Fayard, the argument holds less water: it's difficult to conceive of his cherubic manner and elvish voice as sexually threatening, though for some viewers his color may have been sufficient. Harold is a different story. He was inarguably sexy. You can imagine him as a romantic lead. But the number with Dandridge—a twenty-year-old beauty who would soon become Harold's wife—is chummy rather than amorous. Harold and Fayard were already bound as a unit of two.

No buddy films were in the works, but an opportunity opened up in 1943, when Fayard was drafted into the army. (He entertained other soldiers in the Special Services.) Harold was also drafted, but he fell short of the minimum height requirement. Without his brother, he appeared in two B-movie musicals and proved he could carry a number on his own. His dance in *Reckless Age* is just him, his talent, and a Carmen Miranda song, plus some tables and a ladder to treat like the columns in *Orchestra Wives*. In *Carolina Blues*, he holds together an elaborate production number built around him as "Mr. Beebe," a local Harlem celebrity too classy to wear a zoot suit; going from solos to duets, threading his dance over heads and through legs, Harold is, quite convincingly, "the man who knows." But he's still a man confined to a specialty turn. It would be at least a decade before Hollywood was at all ready for a sexy black leading man, and that guy would be a calypso singer: Harry Belafonte.

THE HARLEM NUMBER

In the mid-thirties, the young Nicholas Brothers and Bill Robinson had been just about the only black tap dancers in Hollywood films. Once the swing craze went national, in 1936, white movie characters began to wander more frequently into black areas. In *New Faces of 1937*, the Peckin' dance spreads from chickens through the Three Chocolateers and into the white cast like a merry form of avian flu. Something was catching, all right, but the black dancers stayed quarantined in specialty numbers. Most often, the setting was a mythical Harlem. Now that whites weren't venturing into the real place much, Hollywood was all over it.

That's what Harold Nicholas's "Mr. Beebe" number in *Carolina Blues* is, a Harlem number. He shares it with the Four Step Brothers, that Cotton Club team from *Barbershop Blues*. The men saunter on to tap in sharp precision before getting down to splits and flips and one member launching himself over the others. Most film appearances by the Four Step Brothers are like this, with the fellas turning up when white characters enter a nightclub or go to the theater. In *It Ain't Hay*, they materialize as unusually agile furniture movers, blithely tossing and tapping upon boxes labeled "Fragile." Their numbers in the wartime flicks *Hi, Buddy* and *When Johnny Comes Marching Home* are as segregated as the armed forces still were, but the grinning men appear in army fatigues for some of their routines, in top hats and tails for others. Accessorized by rifles or

canes, these outfits were symbolic achievements, signifiers of professional dignity. Sometimes their challenge dancing invited a variation in
which the film's star comic joined in, making a fool of himself against
their skill. Or the star, hiding from pursuers, might try to blend in with
the boys, the joke residing in the obvious inadequacy of such camouflage.
The gag derived from vaudeville MCs and would survive in nightclubs
and television shows. In the movies, it facilitated for the Step Brothers a
kind of integration with the plot, the most they were going to get.

One measure of the anonymity of black tap acts is the fact that the Four
Step Brothers who appear in *Carolina Blues* (1944) are not the same
Four Step Brothers who appear in *When Johnny Comes Marching Home*
(1942) or in *Greenwich Village* (1944). From 1942 to 1946, the Four Step
Brothers did their thing in at least nine films, but the membership kept
shifting. At the beginning of that period, the roster had already turned
over by half from the original Cotton Club incarnation, with the veterans
Al Williams and Maceo Anderson joined by Sylvester "Happy" Johnson
and Freddie James, who was famous among his peers as a multitalented,
endlessly inventive cutting-contest champion but who looks neutered
and bored in the films. When Anderson was drafted in 1941 (after filming *When Johnny* . . .), he was replaced by Ernest "Sunshine Sammy"
Morrison, whose career had languished since his days as cinema's first
black child star in the "Our Gang" films of the twenties. When Morrison
was himself drafted, suave Prince Spencer joined the group (in time for
Carolina Blues). Right after the war, Happy died, and Anderson returned,
only to see Freddie James die (of a drug overdose) and Flash MacDonald
take his place. The Four Step Brothers lived on.

In the 1937 Fox backstager *You Can't Have Everything*, Tip, Tap, and
Toe do the Ethiopian emperor number that had been acclaimed by
Broadway reviewers. Movie critics ignored them, as did the studios,
until Universal put them into *Pardon My Sarong*, an Abbott and Costello
flick of 1942. Some white characters are listening to the Ink Spots sing
"Shout, Brother, Shout," a spiritual in which rhythm subtitutes for religion, when three black waiters—Tip, Tap, and Toe—shout "Hallelujah!"
and take turns getting happy atop a table. Slipping around, Raymond
Winfield's feet are like ice riding on its own melting, as Robert Frost said

a poem should do. He's so kingly about his seeming defiance of natural laws that the chef's hat on his head might as well be a crown. In *Honeymoon Lodge* (1943), the trio gets its railway-porter number, up on suitcases, and in *All by Myself* (1943), they do their thing in cowboy garb. Whatever the costume, Winfield's art remained cheerfully regal, though he looks particularly magnificent in evening dress and a full beard in *Hi, Good Lookin'* (1944), sitting at a grand piano, then tapping across its surface and almost off its edges.

Winfield is marvelous, yet taken together, his group's film routines betray enough repetition to suggest that we aren't missing much in not having more of them. The Apollo Theater manager Jack Schiffman remembered that in the late forties, Winfield had to be pushed onstage and that after he performed his magic, he would stand in the wings, nodding in a private world. By 1952, he would be out of the act, deep into drugs and serving a prison sentence for burglary. Fifteen years later, he was dead. The films preserve his blissful art. The same might also be said of Pops Whitman. The Harlem number in *Hit Parade of 1943* isn't much, but the ad-lib brilliance that Pops and Louie were known for wasn't likely to be netted in a production number. What is captured are a few signature moves for the inadvertent library of American dance: a can't-believe-your-eyes corkscrew spin into a knee drop; the unannounced flip that made Buster Brown want to become a dancer. In 1950, when Pops was thirty-one, he would die in Greece, after what the *Defender* described as a "short illness."

The Berry Brothers were better served by the studios. According to Warren, the youngest Berry, what he and his siblings do in MGM's *Lady, Be Good* (1940) is essentially their nightclub act, lavishly filmed. In *Panama Hattie* (1942), Warren, Ananias, and James top off a cane-twirling exhibition of unrivaled coordination and cool by re-creating the legendary feat of their Cotton Club tenure—leaping over the band into splits, bouncing into more flips, and walking off as if it were nothing. That makes one fewer story we have to take on faith. Hollywood used the Berrys once more, but Warren would've been happy if the act had been put to rest after *Lady, Be Good*. "I hated it," he admitted decades later. "It *never* changed." The people who hired them didn't want it to change. His older brothers didn't want to change it. The act *was* the Berry

Brothers, and it stopped only after Ananias died, in 1950. Warren mourned that death, but he felt no regret, soon after, when one of his hips gave out. At long last, he was free.

ALL-BLACK

The Berry Brothers had also appeared in a different sort of movie. *Boarding House Blues* (1948) was an independently produced, all-black film with a tiny budget, the kind of movie shown only in black theaters. James and Warren's appearance in it is a poor copy of their number in *Lady, Be Good*, minus the keystone of Ananias and badly filmed. Among the other acts, Stump and Stumpy, a big-man-small-man comedy team whose tapping was up-to-date, had already appeared in the 1942 Eleanor Powell movie *Ship Ahoy*, and to far better effect. Still, such fledgling productions did provide opportunities for black performers (such as the racy comic Moms Mabley) whom Hollywood ignored. *Killer Diller* (1948) features the Clark Brothers, your average virtuosic tap duo, and Patterson and Jackson, equally virtuosic despite their combined weight of more than five hundred pounds.

In the thirties, films by the pioneer black director Oscar Micheaux used a few hoofers Hollywood overlooked. The esteemed Roland Holder appears in Micheaux's *The Exile* (1930) and nowhere else. In the forties, Ralph Cooper, Eddie Rector's former dance partner, found a place for tap in his all-black independent films *Duke Is Tops* (1938) and *Gang War* (1940)—tap in the form of Willie Covan, much more debonair than he had been in *On with the Show* ten years before but not much more charismatic. Also in the forties, black tap dancers could be seen in bars and diners in the coin-operated jukeboxes that projected musical short films known as "soundies." Pop in a nickel and the Three Chefs might appear, tapping out "Breakfast in Rhythm." Pop in another and you might see a young Buster Brown.

The black independent gangster flicks *Double Deal* (1939) and *Hi-De-Ho* (1947) gave Jeni LeGon her only starring roles. After she shared the screen with Bill Robinson in 1935, Hollywood had offered her just a few specialty appearances. In *Ali Baba Goes to Town*, after Eddie Cantor, playing an American Jew visiting the sultan of Baghdad, finds he can communicate with African musicians in Cab Calloway jive, LeGon comes out in a grass skirt and a bikini top to do a bright tap solo of finger-wagging Harlem steps and perky toe stands. Otherwise, she was mostly cast as a nondancing maid. Her two attempts at Broadway success—the lead in *Black Rhythm* in 1936 and a smaller role in Fats Waller's mixed-race *Early to Bed* in 1943—were both in shows that flopped. By the early fifties, she had largely retired to teaching.

What happened to this career upon which the black press had pinned its hopes? Back at the beginning, ten months after LeGon signed her MGM contract, the studio dropped her. According to LeGon, someone from MGM called her manager to explain that they had discovered another female tap dancer and didn't have room for two. The other dancer was Eleanor Powell. This happened, LeGon claimed, directly after she had overshadowed Powell in a stage appearance. LeGon also claimed that in the films she did make, other white leading ladies had her dance numbers cut. It's all possible, though the argument that LeGon was un-justly denied stardom as an actress isn't bolstered by her performances in the black independents, where she's even more stilted than the scripts. Her acting wasn't much worse than Powell's, however, and the system was certainly rigged against her. The arrival at MGM of the white hoofer with "the black sound" may have provided a convenient excuse. For a long time, there was no room for even one of LeGon's kind. (In Holly-wood, that is: after MGM dropped her, LeGon was a hit in a London revue, doing the "Got a Bran' New Suit" number that Powell had just done on Broadway. She subsequently appeared in a few British films, but unlike the revue's choreographer, Buddy Bradley, she didn't stay abroad.)

There were other things for black tap dancers to do in Hollywood besides perform on camera. The Caribbean number that the Berry Brothers perform in *Panama Hattie* is "The Spring," a song written and staged by an uncredited Jeni LeGon. When Cholly Atkins wasn't suggest-ing steps to Eleanor Powell, he organized a crew of his fellow black danc-ers to dub taps for such films as *Big Broadcast of 1938* and *Broadway Melody of 1938*. The films show a chorus line of raggedly tapping white men; the soundtrack plays the tight rhythms of Atkins and his friends. When the black dancers didn't get dubbing jobs, they found work as extras, impersonating slaves, jungle natives, Indians, Mongolians. At night, they performed in the thriving black nightclubs around Central Avenue—Club Alabam, the Plantation—where they were often watched by the white Hollywood elite. On the set, Atkins used his access and his lunch breaks to study films in rehearsal, his curious mind sponging free lessons in choreography. Occasionally, he would look with resentment at someone like Johnny Downs, a white "Our Gang" kid who grew into a singing-and-dancing college-boy star of B movies, at least once in blackface. Downs wasn't half the dancer Atkins was. Why Downs got the breaks and he didn't—that was one lesson Atkins didn't need to learn.

COEDS AND CONDOS BROTHERS

That is not to say that Hollywood lacked capable white tap dancers. Indeed, there were more of them, populating musicals and not just musicals. Some might have roles in the stories, though many were confined to specialty spots, even as their dancing outshone the stars and stories around them. Hal LeRoy, honorary member of the Hoofers' Club, was King of the Tap Shorts. His only lead in a full-length film would be as the title character in *Harold Teen* (1934), Warner Brothers' failed attempt to launch a franchise off a popular comic strip. But by the time he was cast in that role, the rubber-legged hickory stick had already starred in two-reelers and was established enough in films that when Astaire came to Hollywood, a movie magazine suggested that the new hoofer might be the next Hal LeRoy. LeRoy wasn't any better-looking than Astaire, and his acting was pretty much aw-gee. But he was personable. He almost always played a character named Hal.

In *High School Hoofer* (1931), Hal's the guy with the "inferiority complex" who wins the heart of the popular girl by tapping well. In *Use Your Imagination* (1933), he's the daydreamer who can't hold a job because he taps too much. In more than one film, he works as an elevator operator, a position with the irresistible temptation of a personal practice floor. Tap is his outlet for good-natured rebellion, but his busy footwork does sometimes prove useful. In *Private Lessons* (1934), he sells more slip-on taps by offering instruction all the girls crave. In *The Knight Is Young* (1938), his sign painting doesn't benefit from his scaffold hoofing, but the dance does attract the attention of a damsel in distress. The film is about a courtship, as are most of LeRoy's films, ten to twenty minutes long. He always wins the girl but tends to prefer dancing to romancing. Whatever tender feelings he has, he expresses with his feet.

That's where the girls train their admiring eyes, and so does the camera, routinely in close-up. They swivel like windshield wipers on high, those feet, and the impulse to oscillate occasionally travels up to his knees. His arms wave at the elbow, as if throwing Frisbees. His dances look improvised, like a scrambling of favorite steps with nifty new ones. His rhythms were swinging before swing was a fad to be advertised in titles such as his *Swing for Sale* (1937). In *The Prisoner of Swing* (1938), he's the commoner who impersonates the king in order to overturn a royal ban on swing music. In *Public Jitterbug #1* (1939), he dances with the swing-crazy criminal when he's supposed to be nabbing her. These movies were on the side of teenagers. While some of LeRoy's co-stars—June Allyson, Betty Hutton—grew into leading roles in features, the closest he came was a few cameos in the collegiate musicals *Start Cheering* (1938) and *Too Many Girls* (1940).

Rhythmitis (1936) diagnosed his restlessness of foot as a condition affecting the young. In *Picture Palace* (1934), his character explained his involuntary response to syncopated music by singing "I was just born that way." The actual Hal LeRoy, you may remember, learned his first steps from a black boy in Cincinnati. LeRoy's cameo in the 1934 Al Jolson film *Wonder Bar* comes in "Goin' to Heaven on a Mule," an over-the-top afterlife of minstrel clichés as only Busby Berkeley could imagine. Chorus girls pull apart slices of a giant watermelon to reveal LeRoy, wearing angel's wings, a top hat, and a terribly short white robe. The image is even more ridiculous than that of Astaire in "Bojangles of Harlem" the following year. LeRoy's face is blackened, and so are his hairy legs.

Nick Condos was the first of the tapping brothers from his Philadelphia family—the relentless wingmasters about whose health reviewers expressed concern—to make it into the movies. In *To Beat the Band* (1936), he dances all over an empty bandstand, spreading taps across a drum kit, the seats of chairs, and the lid of a piano at an astonishing rate. The one-man band conceit is Astaire-like and some of the tanglefoot steps recall Hal LeRoy, but this is a dogged tour de force, devoid of charisma and executed in a spirit of just getting through. In *Wake Up and Live* (1937), Nick and his brother Steve perform in white tails at a swanky nightclub, but again, the sophistication is almost entirely technical. They wheel and slide, letting loose a near-constant stream of complex taps, yet the effect is curiously flat until Nick starts in on his wings. He looks like a rocket ship, thrusters firing. He sounds like the Superchief, scraping and thumping at full speed. This is a step that demands applause. It's thrilling that a human being can do such a thing.

What splits were to the Nicholas Brothers, wings were to the brothers Condos. At another point in *Wake Up and Live*, Nick and Steve do their wings while seated. It sounds like the sharpening of a drawerful of knives. Decent-looking young men, the brothers smile and feint a gag, but, really, all of the important action happens from the waist down. This was also true when they danced standing up. In the Sonja Henie vehicle *Happy Landing* (1938), they do their number atop platforms, tricked out in feathered headdresses and war paint. The music, forward-thinking jazz by the Raymond Scott Quintette, is called "War Dance for Wooden Indians," and "wooden" is apt. Though the dancers do not just stand in place and hoof, their wandering turns and arms like a baby splashing in a bath are graceless enough that you might wish them to keep still. The Condos Brothers are statues come only half to life.

It's this perfunctory upper-body work that makes Condos Brothers numbers appear interchangeable, despite the changing costumes: sailor suits for *In the Navy* (1941), hayseed overalls for *Pin Up Girl* (1944). In *The Time, the Place, and the Girl* (1946), they wear no cork for a blackface sequence; their bowl-cut wigs for the Seminole number in *Moon over Miami* (1941) are more embarrassing. From number to number, however, more varies than attire. In *Song of the Open Road* (1944), they tap up on a piano and a pair of drums, but that kind of spectacle isn't what a Condos dance is about. By the yardsticks of speed, intricacy, and technical difficulty, their footwork equals or surpasses anything else that made it into a Hollywood film. Choreographed by Steve, the rhythms are fresh and inventive, a running chatter in which you can hear melodies, though only if you listen very closely.

Nick was a bon vivant at home in showbiz, but Steve preferred the company of jazzmen and thought of himself as a frustrated musician. Outside films, the Condos Brothers performed with Benny Goodman, the Dorsey brothers, Count Basie, and Ellington. When Steve started improvising his solos on movie sets, it annoyed his brother and made cameramen nervous. The real test came in the dubbing studio, weeks after filming, when he had to reproduce whatever he had made up. The synching, at least, is exact—partly because, like Astaire, Steve learned to make friends with the sound editor. He is, to my knowledge, the only person to have improvised his tap dancing on camera in a Hollywood film. You can't really tell, or I can't, but it made a difference to him and his self-respect as a jazz musician. In a 1949 short subject with Buddy Rich's band, he dances in front of a park bench, but the only story is in his rhythms. Unlike in Rich's cameo with Eleanor Powell, when Rich and Condos trade tap phrases, it's unmistakable that two master drummers are at work.

"Turkey in the Straw just ain't the thing / Hollywood's gone tap-swing." So sang the chorus girls in *Three Cheers for Love* in 1936. The swing craze prompted Hollywood to hire many young white tap dancers. *Three Cheers for Love* saw the debut of Louis DaPron in a number called "Swing Tap." He had been born to a touring family of dancers, outside Chicago, in 1913. A Buck and Bubbles performance turned the boy's ear, and he gleaned some Broadway technique at Ned Wayburn's in New York. By the time Paramount signed him up, he had developed a shoulder-shrugging, hangdog style. "I don't have it from the waist up," he once confessed to a colleague, though it would have been truer to say that what he lacked was full coordination between waist-up and waist-down. In "Swing Tap," he has ideas of what to do with his body, but he can't quite execute them and also keep his balance. His manner seems to apologize for this, agreeably. Like many white male tappers of his era, his looseness had a lope to it, a bit of hayseed. In "Swing Tap," he looks more at home playing a hick than when he puts on dinner clothes. Still, the boast implied in DaPron's confession—that he *did* have it from the waist down—was justified. "Swing Tap" isn't *Swing Time*, but it's a fine number—a male-female duet with fancy steps, cute styling, and rhythmic dialogue that generates its lift by tap means. DaPron never pretended to be able to act, so it was a good thing that at one of his initial meetings with Universal in 1941, his agent said, "Louis choreographs, too." ("That was the first I ever heard of it," DaPron remembered.) Over the next ten years, he choreographed some thirty films.

Just as black specialty tap acts were mostly male, white ones were mostly female. Many ladies went in for tricks: time steps while twirling lassos, strings of walkovers as if to impersonate a pinwheel. In *Strike Me Pink* (1936), after Ethel Merman sings "Shake It Off with Rhythm," Sunnie O'Dea taps a routine, imaginatively choreographed by Robert Alton, in which the tapping reflection of herself in the floor gets away from her. Her crisp footwork and Charleston body-flinging look less interesting in later, less interesting numbers. Lorraine Krueger, one of the new faces in *New Faces of 1937*, could move with much of the under-stated charm of Ginger Rogers—she could have been Rogers's body double—and she had tap technique to equal or surpass any of the reign-ing stars, but that didn't earn her a film career.

Eleanore Whitney, DaPron's partner in "Swing Tap," may have done propeller turns atop pianos in previous numbers, but she could really swing, too. She was a five-foot Kewpie doll, a Charleston champion of Cleveland (and also the niece of Adolph Zukor, head of Paramount Pictures). It was often reported that Bill Robinson had given her back-stage lessons and that she had moved to New York to study with him daily. In "Swing Tap," her solo is an assortment of Robinson steps, rhyth-mically perfect but with a less disciplined physicality and more feminine shoulders. Although she had a period mannerism of letting steps knock her chin back, as if she were downing a pill, her tapping was much less swamped in syrupy affectation than that of Eleanor Powell, whom she matched in ability. Though the press pushed her as a rival to Powell and took to calling her the world's fastest tap dancer, her dancing didn't emphasize speed any more than Robinson's did. Sometimes starring, sometimes not, she made a dozen unremarkable, mostly unremembered films. (In *College Holiday*, she and Johnny Downs do a cute tap number on a train, and appear in a blackface minstrel routine). In 1938, she married and retired from films, aged twenty-one.

Over at Fox, there was Dixie Dunbar, just under five feet tall. A Charleston champion of Atlanta, she was sixteen when George White caught her nightclub act—she danced in diapers and a biblike brassiere—and took her to Hollywood for his Scandals films. In *King of Burlesque* (1936), she taps in a tuxedo top and leg-baring shorts. A male chorus provides protection as she moves into a Harlem nightclub where the great Fats Waller is at the keys. While Dunbar taps, inflecting her steps with wiggles, Waller works his eyebrows in asides: "Looka dere, looka dere, what a pair, what a pair!" Tap in the movies didn't get more suggestive. (Imagine the reaction of the people who wanted to excise scenes of Shirley Temple and Bill Robinson holding hands.) Dunbar had something special, but, like Whitney, she got mired in college musicals. The minor roles she was offered dissatisfied her, so she left Hollywood at twenty.

The Jivin' Jacks and Jills were a gang of talented teens. They were studio kids who took their schooling on the set, and from 1942 to 1944, they made fourteen films for Universal, in a hurry before the boys got drafted. With titles in the vein of *Get Hep to Love*, these were jitterbugging teen movies, spiced with the conventionalized slang of black musicians to mystify the square adults in the plot and the parents they stood for. The kids did their tapping in ensemble but also in pairs, six couples partnered up for the Lindy. Then each Jack, each Jill, would show off a lively specialty: flips, turns. The films' open-secret moment can be found in *Mister Big* as the Jacks and Jills put their hearts into a swing-spiritual while black kids sing in the balcony. In the interest of sonic clarity, the taps would be dubbed by only three or four members, and often just one joined by their choreographer, Louis DaPron.

Among the Jills, Peggy Ryan was the cut-up. When she was eleven, her accurate dance impression of Eleanor Powell had earned her a place in *Top of the Town* (1937). She claimed that Bill Robinson had once complimented her by asking, "You sure you haven't got any black blood in you? You dance like *us*." But while her rhythms were firm, her body was unruly, like a chicken with its head sewn back on. In the Jacks and Jills, this blinking teenager was paired with the only guy as tall as she was, a klutz named Donald O'Connor. Their wisecracking carried them from the back of the line into larger and larger roles in the films. Under DaPron's tutelage, O'Connor's dancing improved swiftly, but just as his duets with Ryan were evolving from pratfalls into a rougher Fred and Ginger, the army nabbed him. After the war, his career would scale new heights, but Ryan's had peaked, as had the careers of most of the other Jacks and Jills.

For *That's the Spirit* and *On Stage Everybody*, in 1945, Ryan was paired with Johnny Coy, a Canadian tapper whose medical discharge from the Canadian army made him attractive to studios losing men to the draft. His matinee-idol face didn't hurt, either, and the ballet positions he used to frame his rapid tapping weren't faked: he finished his shapes. But though his dirt-devil spins were impressive enough for *The Baltimore Sun* to imagine he might be "one of the great ones," those skills couldn't break him out of small spots in B movies for Universal, almost all of them released in 1945.

That year, for a soldier's homecoming number in *Duffy's Tavern*, Coy was cast opposite a pretty Broadway tapper named Miriam Franklin. Coy pantomimes war stories and Franklin uses her wiles to get him into the chapel. The number was a big break for Franklin, a contract player who usually played a hatcheck girl, only rarely using her accomplished if nondescript tap technique. But instead of becoming a star, she dubbed the stars' taps. She was the sound of Betty Hutton, Ginger Rogers, Bing Crosby, and Bob Hope. In the footage she was supposed to dub, often the movements of the performer wouldn't be in time with the score, so she asked the technicians which she should follow. Match the music, they told her; the ear is faster than the eye. It worked: the dancer appeared to be in time.

PINUPS AND BABES IN ARMS

The musical stars that Franklin envied, the ones with dialogue—most of them tapped, too. In between her debut in a tight sweater and her prime as a femme fatale, Lana Turner was a tap-dancing coed. (A mediocre one, but that hardly mattered.) It was expected that a figure such as Alice Faye, the nice-but-tough star of some thirty musicals from the mid-thirties to the early forties, would hoof a little. The all-out tap numbers in her films were handled by specialty performers—the Condos Brothers, the Nicholas Brothers—but the rags-to-riches entertainers that Faye portrayed needed to muster a soft shoe. In *Poor Little Rich Girl* (1936), she holds her own with Shirley Temple. In *Tin Pan Alley* (1940), she and Betty Grable tap in a Hawaiian routine.

Grable was the future, despite her having been around since the first wave of movie musicals. She was thirteen for her film debut in the 1930 *Let's Go Places*, and by 1940, she had appeared in some fifty films, including bits in two Astaire-Rogers movies. "Buried on the campus" (her words) along with Eleanore Whitney and Dixie Dunbar, she had made a well-timed detour to Broadway, thereby convincing Darryl Zanuck she could handle adult roles. Her comeback appearance, starring in *Down Argentine Way*, made a much bigger splash than that of the Nicholas Brothers in the same film. Suddenly, everyone noticed the blue-eyed blonde, the one in the white swimsuit in the photograph of 1942, smiling over her shoulder and the rest of her curves, half of the image dominated by legs famous enough to be insured (as they were) for a million bucks. She was the ultimate forties pinup, attractive yet approachable. For millions of American soldiers she served as an idealized version of the girl back home, and the girls back home saw her as one of them. Not coincidentally, she was the top box-office draw in 1943; near the top through 1951, she was one of Hollywood's highest-paid stars and one of its least pretentious. "People like to hear me sing, see me dance, and watch my legs," she once said. "I'm just average, maybe a little below."

The Technicolor movies Grable made for Twentieth Century–Fox, set in exotic resorts or costume-rich periods, were full of all-purpose song-and-dance numbers, mostly undistinguished as song or dance. Her leading men weren't tap dancers, not until 1948, when she was teamed with Dan Dailey. Before that, she was sometimes partnered by her usual choreographer, Hermes Pan. Astaire's right-hand man had a beautifully relaxed quality on film, as if still in the rehearsal studio, and this helped him recede into a supporting function. His numbers without Astaire are shards of their shared style, underdeveloped varieties from the same stock of ideas. He didn't give Grable anything she couldn't do or fake, but in *Moon over Miami*, she joins the Condos Brothers, and though somewhat simplified—no five-tap wings for Grable's million-dollar legs—it's a real tap routine, and Grable, always a hard worker beneath her "just average" manner, appears to keep up. Since she moves in unison and was almost certainly dubbed by someone else, it's difficult to gauge how accurate she is, but the answer probably isn't all that important. Nobody watched Betty Grable's feet.

When Mickey Rooney and Judy Garland get the kids together to put on a show in *Babes in Arms* (1939), *Strike Up the Band* (1940), and *Babes on Broadway* (1941), of course they tap. Tap was an assumed tool in the skill set of professional children. Rooney's tapping as a twelve-year-old in 1933's *Broadway to Hollywood* was timeless: the boy had no time. His rhythm improved with age, at least in his drumming—a good outlet for the puppy energy that made him the biggest box-office draw from 1939 through 1941. In the Mickey-and-Judy films, tap is treated as old-fashioned and folksy, like the blackface routines. In *Babes in Arms*, Judy and Mickey apply all of their amphetamine zeal to the full gamut of minstrel style. (Judy vamps in sepia skin tone, as, in *Coney Island* (1943), Betty Grable flirts in café au lait makeup.) Unlike the stage version, the movie includes no Nicholas Brothers; there are no black entertainers in the series at all. But, as the Interlocutor announces in the minstrel show finale of *Babes on Broadway*, you expect to see dancing in a minstrel show, and so a corked-up Ray McDonald does a George Primrose soft shoe, introduced as "Mr. Rufus Rastus Jefferson Davis Brown." These minstrel sequences are meant as innocent fun, and so is the tapping, often faked. The films' big musical numbers, all directed by Busby Berkeley, are textbook examples of faked tap, marching that marks time instead of making music. In *Girl Crazy* (1943), Mickey and Judy tap out a few flaccid trades in the middle of a western-themed extravaganza to "I Got Rhythm." Footwise, they don't have much. But with her voice and her febrile presence, Garland had all that she needed.

TOO DARN HOT

A star did not have to be an accomplished tap dancer, yet it was still possible for an accomplished tap dancer to be a star. As a child in Houston, Johnnie Lucille Ann Collier showed signs of rickets and was enrolled in ballet classes as physical therapy. She loathed ballet. She wanted to dance to drums. By age eleven, she was supporting both her divorced mother and herself with her dancing. She called herself Ann Miller and her style "machine-gun." In the early forties, Ripley's *Believe It or Not* would officially designate her "the world's fastest tap dancer," clocking her at 598 taps per minute in a contest with a typist. While her feet were firing away, her hands ran up and down her body, hinting at burlesque. The sounds she made with her feet were self-accompaniment, drums she could shake to. Where Eleanor Powell held her mouth open, Miller bit the air, ardently, with a hard-sell seduction that many people found sexy.

At thirteen, she was in *New Faces of 1937*, and in her early films, the influence of Powell is apparent, down to the broken wrists in endless turns. During a successful sojourn on Broadway in *George White's Scandals of 1939*, a more distinctive persona emerged, and in *Too Many Girls* (1940), it was captured on-screen: Miller in a sombrero and a split skirt, tapping in a manner to match Desi Arnaz beating bongos. For Columbia she made a dozen films in half as many years, cheap B movies that almost always turned a profit. They were war-effort films, and Miller's numbers were morale-boosting. In *Reveille with Beverly* (1943), she taps a V for Victory, her path outlined in flames. In *Jam Session* (1944), she rivets the floor, backed by a chorus of Rosie the Riveters. Like Grable, Miller was a serviceman's dream, just not the kind the men wrote home to Mom about. Her solo in the otherwise army-based movie *Hey, Rookie* (1944) is an ersatz belly dance with taps.

In 1948, after Powell had retired, Miller moved to MGM, taking to the big-budget glamour as to her natural habitat. In *Easter Parade* (1948), she gets to dance with Astaire, though Judy Garland is his love interest. (There are worse fates than second billing: Miller's maid in the movie is played by Jeni LeGon.) In her libidinous number in *On the Town* (1949), she actually says, "I really love tom-toms," and in another tom-tom-loving number in *Small Town Girl* (1953), eighty-six musicians hide under the stage, with their arms and instruments poking up through it. Miller dances around this obstacle course, a late flourish by Busby Berkeley, and her long chain of tap turns outdoes Powell. Yet the quintessential Miller routine is "Too Darn Hot" in *Kiss Me, Kate* (1953). In pink heels, elbow-length pink gloves, and a pink bustier with a bit of fringe for a skirt, she taps all over the furniture while musicians scream, "Go, girl, go!" Stripping, spinning, shimmying, she beats out the same rhythm as the bongo player, then pumps out sixteenth notes as she fans herself. The steaminess is pleasurably absurd, yet the full impact can be appreciated only, as intended, with 3-D glasses.

As a movie star, Miller always made an impression. As a tap dancer, she stepped within a narrow territory. She worked with many choreographers, sometimes more than one at a time. For *Easter Parade*, Robert Alton choreographed her movements, but he didn't tap, so Nick Castle helped her with the steps. For "Too Darn Hot," Hermes Pan could offer her both steps and styling, but Busby Berkeley was a different kind of director. The surreal mise-en-scène was his concern, but for tap steps, Miller had to look to her uncredited coach, Willie Covan. The inventor of the Double Around the World with No Hands was one of many craftsmen and experts who worked behind the scenes, or under the floor, of the studio system. Movies like Miller's required that system, and it wasn't as stable as it looked.

ASTAIRE EFFECTS

In the meantime, tap in the movies thrived. How could it not when Astaire was still at work? The age gap between him and his partners kept widening. Rita Hayworth was the most stunning, a schooled dancer who looked at ease in the ballroom numbers and whose youth allowed Astaire to keep current with the bobby-soxers, building a tap-and-swing duet around the Savoy step Shorty George. Vera-Ellen, on the bland side of pretty, had the technique of a true all-rounder. In her films without Astaire, her pert tapping gravitated to arrhythmic tricks and tap on pointe, but her skills inspired one of Astaire's most intricate and beautiful mixes of tap and ballroom in one of his least popular films, *The Belle of New York* (1952). Astaire's other partners couldn't tap much. Cyd Charisse, with her ballet training and never-ending legs, didn't even pretend.

The tap concentrated in Astaire's solos. In *You'll Never Get Rich* (1941), his enlisted-man character is sentenced to a guardhouse where his fellow inmates improbably include a band of black musicians. Smitten with Hayworth, Astaire can't help but beat out rhythms, and his dance manages to appear sportively and improvised even though it's constructed with the theme-and-variations logic of a composer. In his solo for *Holiday Inn* (1942), a dance for the Fourth of July, he walks on jauntily, a cigarette between his lips and his hands in his pockets. The pockets are stuffed with firecrackers, which he detonates in between taps. New gag, old effect: Astaire's tapping was always setting off strings of explosions. "Sometimes," he later wrote about the solo, "you want to bang your feet down so hard in a tap dance that you get shin-bucked or stone-bruised. In this one I had a completely satisfactory outlet with those dynamite noises."

And in *The Sky's the Limit* (1943), an underrated film about the home front, his tap explosions serve as an outlet for frustration and anger. Rejected and misunderstood by his beloved and soured by the war, Astaire's character sings "One for My Baby (and One More for the Road)" in bar after bar until he's alone and thoroughly drunk. Astaire's previous drunk dances had been comic. Here, launching himself onto a bar top, he taps away furiously, smashing three stacks of glasses and shattering a mirror with a barstool. In truth, his tapping and his marvelous gliding along the bar's surface seem more an expression of what-the-hell than of rage, yet the outright destruction must have been startling at the time, exposing the violence in Astaire's style.

Astaire didn't go there again. In his tap solos, he played with tricks of process photography and mechanical illusion-making—dancing with a chorus of Astaires (*Blue Skies*, 1946), dancing in slow motion (*Easter Parade*, 1948), dancing with shoes that come to life before he shoots them (*The Barkleys of Broadway*, 1949). Most famously, he danced up walls and across the ceiling (*Royal Wedding*, 1951). But it remained true that no special effects were as good as what he could do on his own. *Blue Skies* has its own slow-motion section and *Royal Wedding* has a hat rack that comes to life, but in both of those cases, it's Astaire who effects the magic, just by dancing.

Even in terrible films, Astaire managed great solos—such as the screwball routine all over two pianos in *Let's Dance* (1950), with its sublime sailing exit, Astaire riding a series of chairs to the ground with all the finesse he applied to dipping Ginger. Through the fifties, he kept minting numbers good and great as the culture shifted under his feet. From the mid-forties on, the scores for his films tended to borrow from the twenties and thirties. Irving Berlin wrote "Puttin' on the Ritz" in 1929, and in 1946, when Astaire used the song for *Blue Skies*, its staggering syncopations remained his comfort zone, recalling the days when Broadway stars took trips uptown. Ensconced in Hollywood now, Astaire got his inspiration from records, at home, drumming and dancing along.

THE TAP-DANCING TRUCK DRIVER

"Puttin' on the Ritz" was advertised as Astaire's last solo, since he planned to retire. But two years later, Astaire agreed to star in *Easter Parade* in order to replace Gene Kelly, who had injured an ankle playing volleyball. It was a gracious move, or a cunning one, since Kelly was already assumed to be Astaire's chief rival, if not his replacement, as Hollywood's premiere song-and-dance man. Comparisons between Astaire and Kelly were and are inevitable. Astaire: slim, elegant, understated in his evening clothes. Kelly: brawny, athletic, forceful in his tight-fitting T-shirt. This is the contrast that Kelly promoted. "Fred," Kelly liked to say, "represented the aristocrat when he danced. I represented the proletariat." That's a tendentious way to put it, unless we're talking about an aristocracy of talent, but it's true that costume signified as much for Kelly as it did for the black class acts. He shunned the associations of formal attire as eagerly as the Nicholas Brothers sought them. That was one of many ways he altered the image of a tap dancer.

Kelly was indeed a product of working-class Pittsburgh, the third of five children in a tight-knit, upward-striving Irish Catholic family. His mother insisted that he and his siblings attend dancing school, and for a while they performed together in a vaudeville act called the Five Kellys.

In Pittsburgh, this made Gene and his brothers a target. The neighborhood boys would attack the dancing sissies, and the Kelly boys would fight back. For the rest of his life, Gene was sensitive to the suggestion that dancing wasn't manly. Initially, he didn't want to be a dancer at all. In high school, he earned varsity letters in football and gymnastics and played with a semipro hockey team. Fred, the baby of the Kelly boys, was the most precocious entertainer, the one his mother expected to become a star. Gene started to change his mind about dance when he realized the effect it had on the girls at school: "Some of them thought I was bloody marvelous and pretty soon I began to believe them." The Kelly family took over ownership of a dancing studio, and since Gene was the main teacher, they named it after him.

Before long, the Five Kellys had shrunk to the Kelly Brothers, Gene and Fred. The younger taught the older, and the fraternal pair became experts at stealing steps, pooling their plunder by spying on tap acts together and comparing notes. Gene would remember being particularly impressed by George M. Cohan, whose cocky swagger is obvious in the style Kelly would fashion for himself, and by Clarence "Dancing" Dotson, whose eccentric pantomiming isn't. Dotson wasn't the only black influence. Gene and Fred admired Bill Robinson and took classes from a black New Yorker named Frank Harrington. Once, when the Cab Calloway Orchestra was appearing nearby and needed an act to replace the Hollywood-bound Nicholas Brothers, the Kelly Brothers filled in. As Fred told the story, Calloway was shocked to discover that the Kelly Brothers weren't black (the agent hadn't indicated skin color), but impressed enough to put their names next to his on the marquee.

During the early years of the Depression, when their father was out of work, Gene and Fred supplemented their teaching income by doing their act in the lowest of dives. When customers threw coins, Gene was offended, barely restraining himself from punching somebody; when people yelled "Fag!" he swung. Being ignored was even worse. Wanting out of that world, Gene worked his way through college—a signal difference from vaudevillians like Astaire, not to mention black hoofers— and on summer visits to Chicago, he took classes in ballet and modern dance and traded steps with blacks in a seedy South Side rehearsal hall called the Snake Pit. In the Chicago public library, he read all the books on dance he could find, struck by the insistence of the Russian choreographer Michel Fokine that movement and gesture arise from character. Back at the Gene Kelly Studio of Dance, enrollment swelled, a tide of children floating in on fantasies of Hollywood glory, but Gene Kelly himself hesitated in his hometown, teaching and choreographing local productions. It wasn't until 1937, when Kelly was twenty-five, that he chanced New York.

As a chorus boy in musicals, Kelly stood out immediately: talent, drive, a killer smile. But it was in a straight play that he revealed true distinctiveness. In William Saroyan's *The Time of Your Life*, a boozily sentimental story about the regulars in a bar, the character of Harry the Hoofer is an unemployed vaudevillian. Playing him was a chance to create a character through dance, to find a dance style appropriate to the role. A Pittsburgh truck driver, Kelly would say, couldn't come out and do a classical pose. (That was the example he always used, for the rest of his life.) But such a character could tap. Kelly was also trying to forge a specifically American style. It was an aim he shared with many ballet and modern-dance choreographers of the day, but unlike them, Kelly wanted to dance to the popular songs he had grown up with. Besides, as he later remembered, "At the time, the quickest way to establish yourself as an American was to throw a little bit of tap into your dance—even when it wasn't called for."

Kelly's performance garnered him a greater opportunity along the same lines, the title role in the musical *Pal Joey*. Based on stories by the hard-boiled writer John O'Hara, *Pal Joey* had as its central character a small-time nightclub performer, a hustler, a heel. A potentially unsympathetic protagonist was unorthodox territory for American musical comedy, and Kelly was largely responsible for making it work. "After some scenes," he remembered, "I could feel the waves of hate coming from the audience. Then I'd smile at them and dance and it would relax them." The audience hated Joey, but it loved Gene. Even in the silent fragments of a bootleg film, the effect registers. He dances and he flashes that crinkly-eyed grin, and you forgive the cocky bastard, at least for a moment.

Kelly's performance was exceptional in another way, and John Martin devoted one of his *New York Times* dance columns to explaining it. "A tap dancer who can characterize his routines and turn them into an integral element of an imaginative theatrical whole would seem to be pretty close, indeed, to being unique." *Integral* was the operative term, as opposed to the usual removable specialty. It was the watchword of the theatrical era and would remain a guiding principle for Kelly. The show's choreographer, Robert Alton, let Kelly craft his own routines to display different sides of Joey: a little pseudo-Spanish tap here, a little ballet there. Martin noted this influence of ballet in the oppositions and balances of Kelly's body, an answer to the tap dancer's problem of what to do with his torso and arms. Compared with the more natural-seeming solutions of Astaire or Bill Robinson, Kelly's approach struck Martin as a bit too academic, but the dancer was young, attractive, the most promising talent since Astaire. Hollywood would be calling for sure.

In his first film role, opposite Judy Garland in *For Me and My Gal* (1942), and in many to follow, Kelly plays an egotistical, maddeningly charming cad, much like Joey except that he mends his ways at the end to win the gal. In a character arc like that, Kelly is always a little more convincing at the beginning. His dance duets with Garland are period pieces and pleasing as such. Kelly's solo in *Du Barry Was a Lady* (1943) is also pedestrian, thickened only by his pantherine grace; in white tie and tails, he's a swollen Astaire. A solo added to the wartime romance *Thousands Cheer* (1943) gave him more room. It's a prop dance à la Astaire, the kind in which the dancer partners the room, but Kelly is a GI in T-shirt, jeans, and loafers. A mop and broom are his cane and partner. The number is thin on ideas and rhythm-poor, yet Kelly carries it with magnetism and muscle, boosting morale with a run of airplane turns, propeller arms whirring.

Like Astaire and Powell, Kelly soon gained control of his musical numbers. For his solo in *Cover Girl* (1944), he attempted a duet with his own conscience, played by himself in double exposure. The ambition was threefold: the idea was distinctly cinematic; it grew out of the story, expressing his character's internal conflict; and everyone said it couldn't be done. Bucking studio policy, Kelly took on the direction of the number himself, aided by Stanley Donen, a twenty-year-old chorus boy who

had followed him from New York and who would be his chief collaborator for the next decade. A Jewish kid from South Carolina, Donen got
hooked on dancing after seeing Astaire in *Flying Down to Rio*. For *Cover
Girl*, the fact that he was a hoofer proved crucial, as he could play Kelly's
double in rehearsals and call out timings during shooting.

In the finished product, Kelly's conscience emerges from his reflection in a window and asserts its tug in traded tap phrases. Kelly resists by
fleeing, and as his conscience takes up the chase, the dance *moves*—up stairs
and down poles and all over the street, climaxing in the kind of leaping
turns that serve as strong evidence that Kelly, with more thorough training, could have made it as a ballet dancer. The conscience ends up in the
window again, and Kelly smashes the glass, an echo of Astaire's drunken
rampage in *The Sky's the Limit* (released just before *Cover Girl* was filmed).
Despite that precedent, the alter-ego sequence was a breakthrough number. It was also a road not taken. Throughout the rest of his career, there
would be a brooding Kelly and a tapping Kelly, an ambition and a talent,
but seldom would they meet.

Emboldened, Kelly and Donen tried more. In *Anchors Aweigh* (1945),
they paired Kelly with Jerry the cartoon mouse. According to the fairy-
tale premise of the dream sequence, Jerry is a king who has outlawed
singing and dancing because he believes that he cannot sing or dance
himself. Kelly teaches him otherwise: all you need is a big, warm,
happy heart. This is what tap means in *Anchors Aweigh*. The two tap out
a nursery rhyme with their feet. The live dancer and the animated one
interact ingeniously (the frame-by-frame preparation was grueling),
and the whole thing ends with Kelly in a squat, attacking the camera as
it tracks backward. That kind of movement of dancer and camera
accorded with Kelly's theories for generating three-dimensional force
in a two-dimensional image. Astaire's style, Kelly often explained, required one kind of filming; his more robust style, another. That sounds
sensible—it worked for Kelly—but his innovations weren't always
improvements.

The technical difficulty of synchronizing with a double image or a
cartoon put some limitations on what Kelly could do as a dancer. Working with Astaire posed different problems, the collision of two sharply
defined styles. In *Ziegfeld Follies* (1946), their only appearance together,

they treat each other respectfully, crack nervous jokes about their rivalry, and end up with an unhappy medium that draws heavily on the weakest aspect of Astaire's humor—lots of one guy kicking the other in the butt— while suffering from Kelly's greatest deficiency: a poverty of rhythm. The routine's musical humor remains confined to the ancient "SHAVE-and-a-HAIRcut, TWO BITS!" which is pretty much the outer border of rhythmic wit in any Kelly number.

In tap, this might be the most significant difference between the two men. Kelly had the lower center of gravity, the muscular torque in form-revealing costumes, the manly sex appeal, and the strength to do Douglas Fairbanks stunts, but, as a tap dancer, he was the lightweight. His hockey-player crouch gave him the appearance of digging in, yet his feet didn't hit hard. This contrast between Kelly's bulk and his feline lightness of step was part of his appeal, the reverse of Astaire's airy racket-making. But there were no firecrackers in Kelly's sound, no surprises. His rhythms were utterly predictable, with an Irish lilt and a triplet feel. In the age of swing, he seldom swung.

Both men tapped on albums, where their differing approaches to rhythm are all the more striking. Tapping to the Astaire-associated "Let Yourself Go" in a 1948 recording, Kelly is plodding: you can hear him falling into the same stock phrases. ("The Daughter of Rosie O'Grady" and "Yankee Doodle Dandy" are much more up his alley.) It's difficult to conceive of Kelly recording what Astaire did in 1940, a single with the Benny Goodman band in which the taps sound like one instrument among others, and it's impossible to conceive of Kelly recording what Astaire did in 1952, a greatest-hits double album backed by Oscar Peterson and a combo of other top-flight jazz musicians. Kelly didn't have the catalogue, the swath of the American Songbook that had been written for Astaire. But beyond that, Kelly wasn't a jazz artist and Astaire was—in the Gershwin sense, a category unto himself that overlapped with jazz. Astaire's vocal time was loose and unmeasured, Peterson recalled, but "dancing, his time was so strict that he could make an accompaniment sound early or late." On the album, Astaire apologizes that his tap isn't very effective on records because he gets "off the floor a great deal and there may be a lot of empty spaces." Yet he chooses to "ad-lib with the boys" on a few tracks anyway, and you can hear the real thing happening, music made in the moment.

In films, Astaire had danced with black musicians, but only Kelly put himself side by side with black hoofers. An outspoken liberal, Kelly insisted that the Nicholas Brothers be hired to join him for a number in *The Pirate* (1948). There, they aren't servants or bellhops, but neither do they have lines. Nor do they tap: the common denominator of Kelly and the Nicholas Brothers is gymnastics. Was Kelly making a political statement? Was he fulfilling a fantasy? Whatever the motivation, "Be a Clown" represented progress in the racial integration of the film musical. Kelly is clearly the star, but he tumbles with the brothers, touches them. Almost nothing comparable was again attempted for nearly two decades. (Fayard later expressed pleasure that many audiences hadn't realized that he and his brother were in *The Pirate*. "They thought they were looking at somebody else," he said. That integration might result in a kind of invisibility was a possibility the Nicholas Brothers did not get to explore. "Be a Clown" was their last number together in a Hollywood movie.)

Kelly and Donen charged forward, pressing against studio conventions as co-directors. They filmed a sliver of *On the Town* (1949) on the town, opening the story of three sailors on twenty-four-hour leave in New York City with actual footage of the sailors in New York City. Pride of place is given to a dream ballet near the end, a recapitulation of the story in a higher key. Dream ballets were a vogue imported from Broadway. The stage version of *On the Town*, much more charged with wartime carpe diem, had itself grown out of a ballet, Jerome Robbins's *Fancy Free*. Yet Kelly's predilection for dream ballets went beyond fashion. His dream ballets were ballets not because of academic technique, which he barely used, but because of their attempts at a poetic abstraction of the story's emotions, a shift out of a naturalistic frame more extreme than the usual heightening of song and dance. There were things that Kelly desired to express that tap, he believed, could not.

From this perspective, *Summer Stock* (1950) was regressive, a Mickey-and-Judy flick without Mickey. Kelly agreed to do it only to aid Garland, burnt-out and drug-addled, and he puts in his best tap dancing on film. One number is a pep talk in the form of a mock Holy Roller service. Kelly testifies with his feet, and for once his rhythms have drive. His solo in the empty barn is even better. He discovers a squeaky board and a sheet of newspaper and out of these he builds a seemingly improvisational, carefully constructed dance worthy of comparison with Astaire. Just before, his character has kissed Garland's for the first time, so it's a number about love, but, uncharacteristically for Kelly, it's also a number about sound. (The newspaper idea came from the choreographer Nick Castle.) As he plays the board's squeak and the paper's swish and rip, the predictable rhythms build in waves. The ending is just right—the way he halves and quarters the newspaper with his feet, gets interested in a headline, walks off absorbed in his reading, and happens upon the errant board for one final creak.

By contrast, Kelly's grand achievements in film aren't grand achievements in tap. In *An American in Paris* (1951), when he gives English lessons to French children, the *"danse américaine"* he teaches them, amid imitations of cowboys, choo-choos, and Chaplin, is Le Time Step and Le Shim Sham. It's adorable, more tap as kid's stuff, but Kelly also taps a lot in the adult portion of the movie, off the cuff. Like Astaire's American in London, Kelly's American in Paris has to tap. (Unlike the self-described "hard-headed Irishman" Kelly played in *Cover Girl* or his Eddie O'Brien in *Take Me Out to the Ball Game*, his postwar Jerry Mulligan is only incidentally Irish.) There's even a little tap, of the Cohan variety, in the big dream ballet. This ballet was of a length, scale, and cost unprecedented in a Hollywood film, and its ideas—befitting the painterly director, Vincente Minnelli—are concentrated in the production values, the French paintings come to life. It shows Kelly the choreographer straining to inflate *la danse américaine*, but something hems him in, the character perhaps, his dance vocabulary for sure.

Singin' in the Rain (1952) is set in the early, awkward days of sound musicals and built around songs from that era. The period setting allows Kelly to indulge in that to which he fondly condescends. A flashback to the vaudeville roots of Kelly's matinee-idol character, played for irony against his professions of dignity, is a delightful hoard of corn, a culling of what Kelly picked up in Pittsburgh. This was home territory. To attend to Kelly's numbers in bulk is to notice not just the same few steps and rhythms over and over, but the same shadings, the same emphases. One can say of Kelly, as one can't of Astaire, that he has *a* step: a series of Maxie Fords, assertively lunging from side to side, that appears, along with the shave-and-a-haircut rhythm, in nearly all his routines. Both show up in *Singin' in the Rain*'s "Moses Supposes" duet, a fine example of how much fun Kelly could spark with his restricted lexicon. Because Donald O'Connor is trying so hard to follow Kelly's example in their revolt against an elocution lesson, he gets close enough to put his model into relief: almost getting the easy-swimming arms, the coquettish twisting of manly shoulders, the self-satisfied uptilt of chin. When the routine starts really moving, O'Connor loses his grip on the upper-body styling. Kelly doesn't. He lays on the personality, and your eye goes to him.

The seventh child in a family of vaudevillians, O'Connor had amassed an overloaded suitcase of vaudeville clichés himself. His "Make 'Em Laugh" solo is a career's worth of schtick encapsulated. It was working with Kelly, O'Connor later said, that started him dancing "from the waist up." His tapping from the waist down had already excelled Kelly's in lower-profile films choreographed by the waist-down expert Louis DaPron. See O'Connor tear around a set in *Yes Sir, That's My Baby* (1949) or trade phrases with his choreographer in *Are You With It?* (1948). (O'Connor dubbed some routines, DaPron others. "You can tell, at least I can," O'Connor would later say.) One of the film musical's most likable performers, O'Connor grew into the age's most underrated dancer. Check out the physical wit of his drunk routine with balloons in *Call Me Madam* (1953). In *Walking My Baby Back Home* (1953), he puts down thirty beautiful seconds of tap that any great hoofer might want to steal. Consider, also, the grace of his post-*Rain* duets with Debbie Reynolds, Vera-Ellen, and Mitzi Gaynor. He wins the girl with charm, but he could do it just by dancing.

The most extravagant number in *Singin' in the Rain* is "Broadway Melody/Broadway Rhythm," which scores some satirical points in its tracking of a hoofer's rise by presenting the same song in costumes that get fancier as the movement grows more restrained. But the number as a whole follows Gene Kelly's idea of progress in dance, building to a kitchsy wind-machine ballet (lots of flimsy material blown about by Hollywood-sized gusts of air) before retreating to a vision of Broadway rhythm as hollow razzmatazz. Contrast that with the imperishable title number. The old soft-shoe steps, exactly as needed; the euphoric climax of mere splashing in a puddle; that wet face, stretching into rain as if to bask in sun; that smile—this is what Kelly could do best.

There is, however, an asterisk. The taps and splashes in this, Kelly's most famous routine, were dubbed by his talented dance assistants Carol Haney, Jeanne Coyne, and Gwen Verdon. This was standard practice but ironic in context, since the film's plot hinges on Debbie Reynolds's character dubbing the voice of Jean Hagen's character. For the film itself, Reynolds's voice was dubbed—at one point, by Jean Hagen. Donen dubbed taps for Reynolds and Kelly, and Kelly was concerned enough about Reynolds, who could barely dance when cast, to dub some of her taps himself. *Singin' in the Rain* takes as its chief object of satire everything that went wrong in Hollywood's early coupling of sound and image, but it's consistent with the film's self-congratulation that it dodges the compromises that became conventional in Hollywood. The filming of tap isn't central to those compromises, but the compromises are central to the filming of tap. The movie most often cited as the best musical that Hollywood produced contains a half-hidden reminder about Hollywood musicals: what the ear hears isn't always what the eye sees.

FADE OUT

Gene Kelly didn't advance the art of tap on film so much as preside over its eclipse. *It's Always Fair Weather* (1955), Kelly and Donen's last film together, is a kind of companion piece to *On the Town*, its three soldiers vowing to reunite ten years after the war and discovering, when they do, that they have nothing in common. If such a premise counted as new candor, the dance numbers mainly addressed the new challenge of a widescreen format. Kelly and his co-stars, Dan Dailey and Michael Kidd, run and leap all over the soundstage, sweating to span the broader frame, expressing their prewar drunken camaraderie by inanely flogging the shave-and-a-haircut rhythm and slamming down the Gene Kelly step with one foot attached to a trash-can lid. The film's best number is its most traditional: a tap-dance solo on roller skates in which Kelly takes the slide to rapturous new lengths.

The state of the art could be seen in the spread of Kelly's buddies. Dailey was old-school—big, tall, Irish, a decent-seeming guy who could play a vaudevillian, do a natural-looking soft shoe, and win Betty Grable's heart. (No matter that he showed up to the *Fair Weather* press screening drunk and in drag.) Kidd barely came up to Dailey's shoulders but could almost close the difference when they both jumped. A Brooklyn boy, a.k.a. Milton Greenwald, he had studied at Balanchine's School of American Ballet and danced with Ballet Caravan and Ballet Theatre, two of America's first ballet companies. Kidd was also a choreographer, with a string of Broadway and Hollywood credits. For *The Band Wagon* (1953), he put Astaire through the "Girl Hunt Ballet," a weak parody of Mickey Spillane novels that looked like a weak parody of Gene Kelly ballets but suggested, in muzzle flashes, how Astaire's style might be muted when tap went out of fashion.

And tap *was* going out of fashion, even as new tap dancers emerged. At the turn of the fifties, Gene Nelson played leading roles in Technicolor musicals for Warner Brothers. Another kid who enrolled in dance lessons on the way home from seeing Astaire in *Flying Down to Rio*, he was a six-footer descended from Swedes, blond and broadly built. Before arriving in Hollywood, he had studied ballet and toured with a Sonja Henie ice show, and these other modes marked his acrobatic, rhythmically dull tapping. Nelson's shoe-salesman amiability made him a tonal match for his frequent co-star Doris Day—that sparkly scrubbed icon of the fifties, who could handle the basic tap still expected of an all-rounder. Nelson saw himself in the Astaire-Kelly line, fighting to integrate his dances into the story despite studio resistance. The role for which he would be best remembered was in *Oklahoma!* (1955), the film version of the Broadway musical that hoofers were already blaming for displacing tap on Broadway.

Established hoofers could still blossom. Ray Bolger's greatest tapping on film came late. In the course of embodying his Bostonian predecessor Jack Donahue in the lame Marilyn Miller biopic *Look for the Silver Lining* (1949), Bolger pulled off a spontaneous-seeming, use-all-the-props routine, beginning with a soft shoe that's both traditional and sui generis and finishing by converting a dance with a sandbag into a sand dance. In the 1952 film *Where's Charley?*, based on a show that had been a triumph for Bolger on Broadway, his performance of "Once in Love with Amy" is the ultimate Bolger dance: a staggering soft shoe that stretches like Silly Putty into outrageous slides, all to express the bumbling hero's expansive heart. That same year, he starred opposite Doris Day in the harmless *April in Paris*. It was the last major vehicle a studio offered him.

Tap teams grew much scarcer. In *Call Me Mister* (1951), the ever-capable Betty Grable taps in navy togs, playing at being just one of the rhythm boys. The boys around her are the Dunhills, a dopey but skilled white trio that would survive into the sixties with a rusting formula of precision unison and challenge-dance acrobatics, assembling steps from Eddie Rector, the Four Step Brothers, and Tip, Tap, and Toe. (Some of these steps might have been paid for; Pete Nugent claimed to have coached the team.) The challenge dance that the Four Step Brothers do in *Here Come the Girls* (1953) is there so that Bob Hope can unsuccessfully hide from a killer by joining in with the colored boys. Someone still thought that gag was funny, but the demand for any tap teams in Hollywood seems to have run out—which meant, effectively, no more work for black hoofers.

"The trend," Hermes Pan had informed *Dance Magazine* in 1947, was "to modern or what might be called American ballet." In *White Christmas*, the biggest hit of 1954 and a landmark for its minstrel number done without blackface, the modern dance of Martha Graham was fodder for satire. Danny Kaye, a jester in serious black, sang about the zeitgeist—"Chaps who did taps aren't tapping anymore / They're doing choreography"—but the number was another rigged tournament in which the populist contender (Vera-Ellen, tapping perkily) could not lose. Tap had more to fear from former friends like Pan, who was inclining toward "jazz dance," choreography that flashed the accents of jazz arrangements without contributing many foot rhythms of its own.

Pan had an eye for trends. The most exciting dance in *Kiss Me, Kate* (1953) is the sixty seconds he let Bob Fosse handle. Limbs splay to tally with the screams of horns and women; bodies slump, angled inward at the joints, to mark time insinuatingly. This cool was cutting-edge for the movies. Fosse, a boy-at-the-soda-fountain type in his first year at MGM, talented enough to trigger fantasies of another Astaire, snuck a little tap in between backflips and knee slides (see his Nicholas Brothers–like challenge dance with the ballet-trained Tommy Rall in 1955's *My Sister Eileen*). Fosse had grown up as a hoofer but was far too ambitious to anchor himself to an idiom on the wane. Part of the plot of *Give a Girl a Break* (1953) turned on the question of what a choreographer should do now that tap was going out. In the film, Fosse represented one answer, while Gower and Marge Champion embodied another. They were an attractive team whose clever ballroom routines told stories and engaged the set. Seldom did they make sounds with their shoes.

Behind all of them—Champion, Fosse, Pan, Kidd—was Jack Cole, who had trained a company of dancers at Columbia Pictures in the forties. A student of the modern-dance pioneers Ruth St. Denis and Ted Shawn, Cole had defected into nightclub work to make a living. He took from East Asian, Caribbean, Harlem swing, everything but tap. In Hollywood, he became best known for choreographing Rita Hayworth's stripteases and for showing Marilyn Monroe how to make her sexpot image move to music, but his tense style of body-part isolations and bent knees was so heavily borrowed from as to become ubiquitous, the dominant mode in theater dance. In 1957, Cole choreographed *Les Girls*, Gene Kelly's final film at MGM. The principal reason that Cole was choreographing Kelly was that Kelly's previous film had been a big flop. It was *Invitation to the Dance*, Kelly's most ambitious and pretentious project: an all-dance film, no dialogue. Kelly aimed to popularize ballet, but ballet needed a better choreographer, and it didn't need him as an advocate.

It was tap that needed saving. Likewise, the movie musical. Chief suspects to blame for its decline surfaced in anxious parodies within the musicals themselves: television in *It's Always Fair Weather*, rock and roll in *Silk Stockings*. Television depleted the audience; rock and roll split it generationally. One series of court cases forced the studios to divest themselves of the movie theater chains they owned; another undermined their long-term contracts. And so the studio system, with its standing armies of specialists, gave way to independent production. The contract system had produced *Swing Time* and *Singin' in the Rain*, not to mention swarms of Bs. It was the factory for that kind of product. Going forward, musicals would still be filmed, but far more sporadically. A few were hugely successful, yet these were specials, no longer staples.

Tap dance, so long a Hollywood staple itself, disappeared almost entirely from the big screen. The leading star of musical films from the late fifties through the sixties was Elvis Presley, and not only did Elvis not tap, nobody tapped to Elvis's music. Almost everything else was imported from Broadway, and tap had gone out of fashion there first. I wonder if what Robert Benchley felt, in 1931, about tap in Broadway shows—that he had seen more than enough of it—was felt by the whole moviegoing public as the sixties loomed. With all of the great, good, and mostly mediocre tap churned out over the preceding three decades, perhaps people were just tired of it. The film industry certainly acted as if that were so.

What's remarkable in retrospect is how *much* tap was preserved—so much more than of any other kind of dance. Most musical films of the thirties, forties, and fifties did not disappear, and for each succeeding generation, they could live anew. Yet because production dwindled, those films would also fix tap, in the cultural memory of Americans and of Hollywood's worldwide audience, as a period artifact. The movies would make tap a thing of the past.

11

BEFORE THE FALL

Tap dancing is what we think of as a natural way of dancing in this country." Edwin Denby, the most perceptive dance critic of his day, wrote that in 1943. It was not his main point. He was writing about dance on film and why Astaire's intimate, understated movement, his "exquisite salon style," had been more effective on film than ballet, a form designed to be seen from a distance. With Astaire, the dynamic range was "narrow but sharply differentiated." The dance didn't need much room, and a complete dance phrase could be photographed without a cut or change of angle breaking the continuity. These advantages were the concern of Denby's article and his insight into why tap looked good on film. The idea that Americans thought of tap as a natural way of dancing was what he could assume. Americans had thought of tap that way before tap went by the name. Movies, once they got wired for sound, had reinforced the idea. Tap was Shirley Temple and chorus girls doing time steps. It was Astaire, who, in 1943, still had more than a decade of films ahead of him. It was Bill Robinson, who had another six years to live. And while these images of tap were being spread by

Hollywood, the dance was developing in ways that the movies mostly missed.

TAP-DANCING HAMLET

In 1941, the dance critic Walter Terry had made a comment similar to Denby's: "Tap is the style of dance which Americans find most natural to do and most entertaining to watch." Here, too, the idea was assumed. Terry, however, introduced it to contrast it against the low opinion of tap held by "serious dance lovers." This was a time when modern-dance fans believed ballet to be frivolous and passé, corrupt and ill-suited to a democracy, while ballet fans judged modern dance clumsy, faddish, and probably Bolshevik, yet both camps could band together in their contempt for the most popular form. Allowing for the standard exceptions (Astaire and Robinson), Terry catalogued the perceived deficiencies of tap, availing himself of the word *limited* six times in three paragraphs. Tap dancing was limited in music: "the popular and ephemeral tunes of the day." It was limited in range of expression: "About the only human quality it can project is good spirits." It was limited in technique: "There is a limited number of things that can be said with the feet." Terry also complained about the typical tap posture—"that of an anthropoid ape." Nevertheless, he did find hope that "America's only indigenous dance form" could become a "valid facet of the American dance art," and thus "no longer be limited to the field of pure entertainment." The cause of this hope was one particular tap dancer: Paul Draper.

Point by point, Draper was a direct answer to Terry's litany of limitations. He danced to Bach and Handel. He presented characters in his dances and told stories. As John Martin explained, "He does not think up a series of tricks and merely join them together by means of time-steps; he composes in terms of rhythm." Draper carried himself like a ballet dancer and borrowed from ballet its complementary arms and extended lines. There was nothing simian about him.

Terry was echoing the critical consensus. In 1942, *The Saturday Evening Post* cited, as common opinion, Draper's ranking as the best tap dancer in the world. And even that superlative was comparatively faint praise.

For most, Draper had transcended the category. Nelson B. Bell, a theater critic for *The Washington Post*, wrote of Draper that "to denominate him a 'tap dancer' is a desecration." Stark Young, a drama critic for *The New Republic*, called him "one of the major achievements to come out of our American theatre," evincing "an elusive and beautiful quality of mind." This kind of talk had started as early as 1934, when John Martin had characterized Draper as "unique among tap dancers in that he considers his work as an art," but Draper's greater distinction was his ability to make reviewers and audiences consider his work that way, as what *The Christian Science Monitor* called "art—solacing and stirring and elevating." Critics imagined Draper moving tap up, "into the realm of serious art," as Cecil Smith wrote of Draper's 1938 appearances at Chicago's Chez Paree. "He proves himself to be as near to genius as any one the American dance has brought to light."

If Draper elevated tap, it was a matter of lifting from above. He didn't break his way into high culture; he was born into it, and looked the part, patrician to his nose. He wasn't from Pittsburgh or Irish Boston, and he certainly wasn't from Harlem. He came into the world in 1909, in Florence, Italy, where his father, a tenor from a socially prominent American family, was studying bel canto. Soon afterward, the Drapers moved to London, where Paul's mother, Muriel, established a salon frequented by Arthur Rubinstein, Pablo Casals, Henry James, Gertrude Stein, and John Singer Sargent, among other luminaries in the arts. In the Draper home, there was Music at Midnight—the title of Muriel's memoir—and the sound of Rubinstein's piano and Casals's cello seeped under the door of young Draper's nursery. Muriel was the draw, flamboyant, formidable, grand, a conversationalist capable of producing, in the words of her fellow *saloneuse* Mabel Dodge, "a downpour of language." In retrospect, her son would suggest that the stutter he developed in childhood was a reaction against his mother's volubility, an unconscious strategy for grabbing attention. Muriel had other theories. In any case, she was the great force in his world.

By the time Paul was six or seven, his mother had moved back to New York and divorced her husband (who would die in 1925). Paul was sent off to his mother's parents, then to an uncle, and finally to a series of boarding schools, where he excelled academically and misbehaved.

Expelled from two institutions, he ran away from a third. He dug ditches, enrolled in a civil engineering college, dropped out, found a job as a music critic, was fired, tried teaching ballroom dance for Arthur Murray, and was fired again. It was at this point that he took a few tap lessons from one Tom Nip, who told him not to bother taking any more. "I thought it would be a soft way to make money and a good way to show off," Draper later explained with characteristic dry candor. "I wanted to do something you didn't have to study and I thought dancing was something you didn't have to study." Tap, it seemed, was "the natural way to express myself."

Unable to find work in New York, Draper sailed to London carrying letters of introduction and talked his way into a touring show. At first, he elevated his art the traditional way, by tapping high on a marble-topped pedestal. Stranded in France, he finagled passage money home from his family by promising that he would give up his tap foolishness and join his uncle on Wall Street. Upon returning, he immediately took his pedestal on the vaudeville circuit, with minimal success until an anonymous donor (possibly his mother) paid for his salary at the Sutton Club. That engagement led to more at the Casino de Paris and Radio City. Poised in high-waisted trousers and a double-breasted jacket, his salmon-tinted hair slicked, Draper was a class act automatically. He was a Draper—it wasn't your average hoofer who was profiled in society magazines such as *Town and Country*. E. E. Cummings, one of his mother's lovers, wrote a poem about him.

Some kind of atavistic pride kicked in. Draper began to practice, diligently, four to seven hours a day. He devised the most difficult steps he could imagine. Like Honi Coles in his furnitureless bedroom a few years earlier, he strove to dance faster than anyone else. The exercise, he later said, worked all the tricks out of his system. He admired Jack Donahue, Bill Robinson, Bubbles. (He had made trips to Harlem with his mother and Carl Van Vechten.) He tried to imitate them and failed. Sensing a dead end in the direction of speed and difficulty, he changed course. He picked up his pedestal and, dramatically, smashed it. Now he began to try to tell a story with each routine—"style instead of speed" was how he phrased it. He set about experimenting with pieces in the classical tradition, the music he had grown up with. The arpeggiated

gaiety of the Gigue in Bach's B-flat major Partita seemed to him to beg
for tap. And, as he would later point out, using classical music, a tap dancer
rarely had to compete with a drummer.

He wanted to expand—make use of his legs and arms—and ballet
seemed "the most available way of expanding." Every time he ventured
to make a step more "meaningful," it would come out looking like ballet. And so while he was headlining at the Persian Room at the Plaza
and the Empire Room at the Waldorf, he attended classes at the School
of American Ballet, newly founded by George Balanchine. (Lincoln
Kirstein, the school's other founder, had been a devoted habitué of
Muriel Draper's New York salon. In 1941, on tour in Rio, Paul would
marry Heidi Vosseler, who had been one of Balanchine's ballerinas and
who would later brag about having been the balletmaster's first American conquest.) Passing into his mid-twenties, Draper was a late starter,
but he took what he needed, including the discovery that "some kind
of organized learning is necessary to any freedom." Draper adopted
ballet placement, positions, and steps—adding, for example, the high-
swinging leg of a *grand battement* to his wings. But more than ballet
technique, he coveted ballet's rigor, its systematic methods for broadening
expressive powers. He practiced just as long and doggedly as before, but
now more intelligently, breaking down steps into component parts, isolating the muscles involved, working toward the efficiency of movement
that creates the illusion of effortlessness. His principle was control: moving as he chose to, not as gravity or habit demanded, getting the rhythm
and the motion he desired without distorting either.

Yet for all of his ambition, Draper bristled when people suggested
that he might graduate to a higher form. He liked tap, he said. "It's not
a case of being badly brought up." His use of ballet was not, he stressed,
a branching off into another form; it was an enlarging of tap. "Perhaps
I'm limited," he conceded, "but who isn't? A ballet dancer is limited in
not knowing tap."

That last statement never had more professional significance than in
the mid-thirties, when Hollywood's appetite for tap dancers seemed in-
satiable. Though Draper stuttered in his screen test for Warner Brothers,
he was cast in the 1936 Ruby Keeler film *Colleen*. The routine Draper
choreographed for himself and Keeler tells the story of a courtship,

engagement, wedding, and honeymoon. There's a tapped tiff, a tapped exchange of "I do"s, a tapped train leaving the station. Clear as panto-mime and sort of clever, the number gives a glimpse of the nascent Draper style: up on the toes, light, crisp, brittle. Even allowing for the restrictions imposed by his partner, the dancing feels timid, the use of arms suggesting an aim for delicacy that reads as half-finished. What-ever Draper was, he was not a musical comedy dancer. Warner Brothers told him as much and didn't hire him again.

Colleen was not, however, his last encounter with Hollywood. In 1945, perhaps in response to all the acclaim, Paramount cast him opposite Bing Crosby in *Blue Skies*—only to replace him, a few weeks into shoot-ing, with Fred Astaire. Three years later, he took a role in James Cagney's film version of *The Time of Your Life*, the bit role of Harry the Hoofer, Gene Kelly's part in the Broadway show. As casting, this was either total ineptitude or genius. Harry is supposed to be a comedian who isn't funny, a small-time dancer with a big heart. ("Is that good?" an average Joe asks about Harry's tapping. "I don't know," answers another, "but it's honest.") Draper's performance is so unfunny that it's almost funny, and his dancing is so odd that the character's repeated insistence that he's "a natural-born dancer" is almost poignant. At one point, Harry acts out a political speech with taps, something that Draper did in his nightclub act, a dance that the tough-witted *New Yorker* satirist Wolcott Gibbs would later claim was a more hilarious criticism than anything done with words. In the film, it's so embarrassing, so earnestly right for a pathetic charac-ter, that it could be self-parody. Or is this what a Draper performance always looked like?

The question nags, for these awkward Hollywood appearances are the only film records of Draper in his prime. It's those films against the critics' effusive praise. The films preserve little of the musicality that critics lauded, the sensitive touch and dynamic shading. Edwin Denby had faulted Draper for merely embroidering the rhythms of his chosen compositions rather than contributing independent lines of his own. Denby also found Draper's academic arm work stiff in the shoulders and neck, and he acknowledged the conflicts involved in the ballet-tap mixture, the way the bent knees and loose ankles required for sound production blunted ballet's taut extensions. Still, Denby found Draper charming—refined, innocent in a touching way. And he noted that audiences loved the dancer unfailingly.

This wasn't a case, in other words, of critics pushing some rarefied taste. Draper was popular. In the Broadway production *Priorities of 1942*, a vaudeville-style throwback, he stopped the show every night, tapping to Bach. He had the same effect in presentation houses, where bobby-soxers who came to scream at Perry Como cheered Draper's "Flight of the Bumblebee," and in nightclubs, where his repertory ran to Gershwin. He took requests. He invited the audience to sing along. His stage manner was enthusiastically informal. ("Let's have a great big hand for Mr. Bach.") Draper gave people a little culture with their entertainment, and they adored him for it. In 1939, when he wasn't yet thirty, a lengthy *New Yorker* profile of him—titled after Muriel Draper's description of her son, "Dancing Hamlet"—estimated his annual earnings at $75,000 and climbing.

He teamed up with Larry Adler, a virtuoso of the harmonica who also tackled a classical repertoire not intended for his instrument and garnered notices expressing astonishment at how much music he drew from that limited medium of expression. Together, the short, wisecracking Jew and the tall, stuttering Wasp embarked on a concert tour: Adler did his thing, Draper did his, and then the two improvised in tandem to selections shouted out by the audience. (Another unusual feature: one of their regular accompanists, J. Calvin Jackson, was black.) An initial tour of twelve auditoriums mushroomed to sixty a year. They sold out Carnegie Hall in New York, Symphony Hall in Boston, Orchestra Hall in Chicago, and so on across the nation. An annual Christmas–to–New Year's engagement at New York's new City Center became a holiday tradition. Draper bought a townhouse and a Mercedes and hired five servants. And then, in December 1948, someone called the cops.

Earlier that year, Draper and Adler had performed in Birmingham, Alabama. Later the same day, they had addressed a rally for Henry Wallace. Newspaper headlines conflated the events, and Hester McCullough, a society lady in Greenwich, Connecticut, and wife of a senior editor at *Time*, wrote a letter to her local paper announcing that she was canceling her tickets to the Greenwich appearance of Draper and Adler, because the artists were "pro-Communist in sympathy." To purchase a ticket to their concerts, she wrote, was to "indirectly make cash contributions to Moscow." This was not a light charge in 1948. Adler and Draper were advised to sue for libel, which they did. The two men swore under oath that they were not Communists or Communist sympathizers. They were, however, left-leaning. Along with many entertainers (such as Gene Kelly), they had protested the investigations of the House Un-American Activities Committee. Draper had performed at benefits for Loyalist refugees of the Spanish Civil War and the National Council for American-Soviet Friendship. His mother belonged to organizations that probably were Communist fronts.

Before the trial began, Draper and Adler were viciously attacked in the Hearst newspapers. Igor Cassini devoted no fewer than fifty of his syndicated columns to condemning the pair, equating the importance of their trial to that of Alger Hiss, and once challenging them to a brawl. Another columnist suggested that readers happening upon the "mincing," "dainty" Draper and Adler should "beat them bowlegged." Walter Winchell invited Adler to come on his enormously influential radio show and denounce Draper and Henry Wallace as Communists, and when Adler refused, Winchell mentioned in his column a mouth-organ-playing leftie who "spouts the party-line." *The New York Times*, among other newspapers, covered the trial on a nearly daily basis. It ended, in May 1950, in a hung jury.

The damage had been done. Bookings were canceled. New ones did not materialize. Adler and Draper were on the blacklist. Adler decamped to England, established a successful career in Europe, and never moved back. Draper also fled to England, then to Switzerland, but he returned home in 1954. He could find work, but then the American Legion would protest and the work would disappear. With his aunt Ruth, a famous monologuist, he put on a well-received show at a Broadway theater, but touring proved impractical. Year after year, the 92nd Street Y in New York presented him in solo programs. He introduced new material, including a seventeen-minute a cappella "Sonata for Tap Dancer" in which he developed themes and suggested melodies, fascinating critics with shifting textures of sound. John Martin congratulated Draper for finally achieving an integration between his feet and the rest of his body and granted his approval, long half-withheld, for the improbable task of making a work of fine art out of tap. In 1959, Draper went on tour again—driving himself, a pianist, and a student between high school auditoriums in Rockland, Maine, and Lead, North Dakota.

He went into teaching: small classes on his own, then at Juilliard and the American Dance Festival. Each class began like a ballet lesson, with exercises at the barre, before Draper demonstrated one of his concert pieces, using precise musical terms but breaking down very little. ("His classes were not well-attended," remembers Bob Audy, a student who became a teacher. "Nobody could do it.") From 1967 to 1984, he taught movement to actors at Carnegie Mellon.

Draper's example exerted more influence than his teaching. Georgie Tapps also danced to the classics. His given name was Mortimer Alphonse Becker, and he acquired his necessary stage name at age sixteen, working in one of the same speakeasies as Ruby Keeler and studying at Ned Wayburn's factory. In his nightclub number in the film *Vogues of 1938*, his ballet looks rigid and his halting rhythms make little sense, but nightclub reviewers and audiences appreciated the classy packaging. In his nightclub program, he satirized a vaudeville hoofer, distancing himself from vulgar roots before tapping to Bach, Chopin, and de Falla's "Fire Dance." In 1953, he formed a troupe of dancers, which was to survive another decade, and in *Dance Magazine*, he lashed out at those who said that tap jobs were drying up: the people who said that, he wrote, were the ones who didn't study ballet. "There has never been a time," he whistled in the dark, "when there were better opportunities or a greater audience for the art of the tap dancing."

Back in 1935, Draper had spoken of making a tap ballet, with himself acting as the soloist does in a concerto amid an orchestra of tap dancers. In the late forties, Morton Gould, a classical and Broadway composer, had approached Draper with a similar idea, but Draper's troubles got in the way. In 1951, Gould was inspired to try again by a younger dancer, Danny Daniels, a Broadway hoofer with ballet training. The Tap Dance Concerto that Gould composed for him came with the tap dancer's rhythms written into the score. "The important point," Gould told the

Herald-Tribune, "is that this isn't hoofing." Daniels posed during the rests. He pretended to read the music. He borrowed ballet steps, and danced in shoes "as much like a ballet slipper as I could get while still holding the tap." John Martin found the debut ingenious and enjoyable, remarking on how, for the first time, dance was indispensable to a musical work. Daniels performed the concerto for pops concerts in Boston, Los Angeles, New York, London, and Berlin. Columbia Records issued a recording. (The score, in a Bernsteinesque mode, is competent but undistinguished.) Though not quite a living, this was a prestigious kind of fun. Gould wrote one more piece for Daniels, but other composers failed to take up the idea. The hope that Daniels expressed to *Dance*—that tap would become a concert art—seemed unlikely, so he went into choreography, mostly for television. Following the times, he used little tap.

Paul Draper also wrote about tap for *Dance*. In the first of a near-monthly series of articles from 1954 to 1963, he gave what he considered to be basic advice about equipment and technique. Letters he received from readers expressed bafflement. The standard teaching of tap was based on routines: provincial teachers stocked up in New York or at conventions or by mail. Ads for mail-order routines abutted Draper's assertions that routines did not qualify as dancing. "Not every student can learn to dance," he wrote, "whereas almost anybody can learn a routine, if it is simple enough. Very few students learn how to dance no matter how you teach them." Draper recommended exercises for developing muscle control, the strength necessary for lightness. He insisted that the study of ballet and music precede the study of tap, and he spoke in terms of thousands of hours of training, over ten to fifteen years.

This "Serious Approach to Tap Dancing" must have been bracing. Draper was advocating his own aesthetic, sometimes tendentiously. ("A heavy-footed tap dancer is a contradiction in terms, since 'tap' means to strike lightly.") He fought against the "traditional belief that there is something essentially flat-footed about tap dancing," and he tried to convince readers "to stop being in love with the feeling that all tap dancing must be done in a loose and easy fashion." The goal, he wrote, should be not the making of sound but "communicating something special we have discovered about the world we live in." Drawing on his own experience, he noticed a bashfulness bordering on shame that hindered tap dancers from approaching their art as an art. Buck up, Draper told his readers—treat tap "as an expression of the very best and most valuable part of you."

Fine words, useful words. Draper's attack on tap routines could only do tap good. He drew attention to true deficiencies and tore down some of the false limitations imposed by arbitrary hierarchies. Others, he reinforced. John Martin had exalted Draper for using tap dancing "as a medium for art rather than hoofing," and Draper, in a later interview, would echo the dichotomy, even as he cited Bill Robinson as the best tap dancer he ever saw. "He could do slaps"—the simplest of steps— "and make you cry. It was in that hoofer genre, but it was that genre developed. He never lifted a leg, but it was lovely. You wouldn't have wanted him to . . . Somehow or other he expressed everyone's idea, rhythmic joy . . . It was never that complex. It just made you feel good." Draper considered Astaire "an exceedingly fine artist," and praised his "well-bred quality" and inimitable style. That, however, was also the fault Draper found in Astaire and Robinson: they were inimitable. Their kind of dancing, he wrote, had little value in itself: the value was in the performer. Of Robinson's heirs, Draper could only say, "It is entertainment. It hasn't really got much to do with dancing, but it's undeniably fun. I don't mean to knock it. It isn't going to go any place. It hasn't a design, a structure." This is a respectable view of art—it sounds a lot like the mid-century polemics of Lincoln Kirstein—but one that is deaf and blind to a great deal of value.

As for what the hoofers thought of Draper, even Pete Nugent, the Harlem class act who preferred all body motion and no tap to all tap and no body motion, said that Draper didn't have a rhythmic bone in his body: "He learned all the algebraic mathematical business about dancing and worked hard." Hal LeRoy, the ad-lib dancer with the crazy legs, thought Draper had "a very odd style. You could see that everything was worked out." Buddy Bradley credited Draper with "no more sense of rhythm than a flea." Avon Long, who played Sportin' Life in the 1942 revival of *Porgy and Bess*, didn't think much of Draper's dancing at first, either. It took him a while to realize that Draper was "saying things with his feet that most dancers don't say or even understand. I've heard him say, 'Hello.'" Few black hoofers listened to what Draper was saying, whether with his feet or with his pen. Their ears were tuned to something else.

TAPPING BIRD

Edwin Denby caught it in in 1942, at a "coffee concert" at the Museum of Modern Art: "a man who did a tap dance as purely acoustic as a drum solo." It was interesting, Denby noted, how the man "ignored the 'elegant' style in shoulders and hips, sacrificing this Broadway convention to the sound he made." The man was called Baby, and he wasn't accustomed to giving concerts at museums. But the sound he made was modern art, modern jazz.

Born in Baltimore in 1921, Laurence Donald Jackson was on the road with Don Redman's band by age eleven, as a singer. His parents died soon after, in a fire, and instead of living with an aunt, he ran away to New York. Dickie Wells, who had parlayed his membership in the early class act Wells, Mordecai, and Taylor into ownership of a Harlem nightclub, unofficially adopted the young singer and gave him his stage name, Baby Laurence. The kid sang with the Four Buds, who joined with the Three Gobs to become the Six Merry Scotchmen or the Harlem Highlanders, an act that wore kilts to voice Jimmie Lunceford arrangements in six-part harmony. At the same time, Laurence was hanging out at the Hoofers' Club, learning to dance. Robinson and Bubbles weren't much help, but Eddie Rector was, along with young guys such as Raymond Winfield and Honi Coles, and an otherwise unknown member of the Three Playboys named Harold Mablin. When Laurence executed a step differently from how Mablin had demonstrated it, Mablin would get mad. All Laurence could say was, "I just don't feel it that way." At the Hoofers' Club, that was all he *had* to say.

One reason Laurence felt steps differently was that he was listening to different music. In the mid-thirties, he sang at the Onyx Club on Fifty-second Street, where Art Tatum made his New York debut. Tatum was the piano player other piano players called God. His technique was orchestral, bewilderingly rapid and dexterous at the service of a bewilderingly quick and inventive mind and ear. His music ran in cascades and cataracts, in and out of tempo, in flights and adventures of harmony and time. When Laurence heard Tatum play, he felt the urge to move his feet in emulation of Tatum's fingers. A boy could dream. Around 1940, with the assistance of Leonard Reed, Laurence put together a solo tap act, and soon he was slotted into touring revues with the bands of Count Basie and Duke Ellington. The Basie band had the most solid and swinging rhythm section in jazz, support so trustworthy it inspired bold departures. The band's drummer, Jo Jones, was a selfless accompanist, gently assenting and escorting. At one time a tap dancer himself on the carnival circuit, he understood what a tap dancer needed, how to stay out of a hoofer's way and "catch" him with complementary fills and cymbal crashes. (Decades later, he would release a pedagogical album with sample rhythms by Bill Robinson, Eddie Rector, Pete Nugent— and Baby Laurence.) In the tenor saxophonist Lester Young, the band had an example of rule-changing rhythmic originality, an improviser who floated across bar lines on phrases that rose and fell like a breeze and teased the beat with dancing accents. During the same years, the Ellington band, less accommodating to a dancer but inspiring nevertheless, was at one of its greatest peaks. And for a few numbers per set, it was backing up Baby Laurence.

Already known as "the show folks' dancer," the hoofer who most impressed other professionals, Laurence began listening to a saxophonist his own age, one who had also been listening to Tatum and Young but who, in his mind's ear, had heard further developments. Several aspects of the playing of Charlie Parker were novel, but perhaps the most fundamental revisions—certainly the most important for Laurence— were rhythmic. Parker's asymmetrical phrases stopped and started unexpectedly, even as they maintained logic and balance. The accents inside the phrases were themselves irregular, struck on and off and in between the beats in unpredictable and subtle patterns. Whether playing ballad-slow or at a furious clip, Parker subdivided the beat very finely. Laurence could hear all of that, and it thrilled him. And so, like countless other awestruck musicians, the tap dancer memorized Parker's solos and tried to play them on his own instrument. The effort required him to break his steps into fragments or run them together. It required him, to a great extent, to forgo steps altogether, in favor of notes.

"I called him Bravery," recalled Chuck Green, "because he feared no sounds." Even John Bubbles had to admit that Laurence was the toughest hoofer he had ever faced. To Cholly Atkins, an expert dancer slightly older than Laurence, Laurence's new style was familiar and yet not: "When you watched him you could see in his combinations the basic techniques that everybody else came up with, but there was a way it was put together that made the difference." Musicians said similar things about Parker. By 1944, Laurence was performing with Parker informally, showing up with his tap shoes in a trumpet case. By 1945, he was on the bill for Parker's gig at the Three Deuces on Fifty-second Street, sharing a stage the size of a pool table with the other musicians and a drum kit. Miles Davis, who was then starting out as Parker's trumpet player, remembered Laurence trading fours and eights, like any other member of the band. In his autobiography, Davis—a great artist and talent spotter—honored Laurence with his highest term of praise, calling him "a motherfucker . . . the greatest tap dancer that I have ever seen, or heard, because his tap dancing sounded just like jazz drumming." Dexter Gordon, who was playing saxophone with Parker and Laurence at the Spotlite in 1947, recalled that Laurence "was the show but he was really part of the band . . . just like a drummer."

To sound just like a drummer didn't mean quite what it used to. In the music that was coming to be known, onomatopoetically, as bebop, the drummer's role shifted from that of a timekeeper who soloed infrequently to a more up-front participant in the musical conversation. Where the bass drum had once broadcast a steady pulse, now the ride cymbal offered a lighter, more flexible beat, a shimmer. The drummer became freer to contribute polyrhythms and textural subtleties, and the bass drum was made available for accents—kicks in the band's ass to which musicians gave the wartime label "dropping bombs." Tap dancers and jazz drummers had always been kin, and the back-and-forth between them continued, along with the sibling rivalry. (According to Buster Brown, "musicians with the big bands didn't like us dancers, because we could get the girls.") Max Roach, one of the pioneer bebop drummers, remembered playing with Laurence, call-and-response-style, each imitating and learning from the other. Laurence, in turn, remembered playing with Roach and speculated that it might have been from drummers that he learned the most.

For older tap dancers, however, the new drum style could seem like crowding, a usurping of the dancer's rhythmic role. In 1944, Pete Nugent, the Sepia Fred Astaire, was hired to dance with Billy Eckstine's orchestra, a band that included bebop's central innovators, Charlie Parker and Dizzy Gillespie, as well as the up-and-coming drummer Art Blakey. One of Nugent's numbers was a pretty soft shoe arranged for delicate clarinets and chiming piano; into the middle of this garden party Blakey dropped his bombs. Whether that was an act of bored rebellion or a misplaced attempt to help, for a dancer expecting to be "caught," it was unsettling to be blitzed. "This guy had absolutely no respect for dancers," Cholly Atkins recalled of Blakey. After Eckstine told the young drummer to ease off or the dancers might quit, Blakey responded, "We don't need them."

Blakey was right. Over the next forty-five years, his thunder would goad and catapult the astonishing list of major musicians who came through his Jazz Messengers band. Tap dancers were the ones who needed to adjust. And it wasn't only Laurence's generation who could. In *Jivin' in Bebop*, a black variety film from 1946, Ralph Brown dances with Gillespie's orchestra, and though Brown learned his trade at the Hoofers' Club in the early thirties, he handles the bebop song "Ornithology" with aplomb. In lieu of taking on the song's rhythms, he rides over them, unspooling almost an unbroken string of swung eighth notes interlaced with stomped accents, his own little bombs. Periodically, he inserts some Bill Robinson patterns, but in general, discrete steps have been relinquished in favor of continuous chatter. Tap dancers didn't have to deal with the closely spaced hurdles of bebop harmonic changes, and the rhythmic challenges should have been up their alley. (The right hand of the bop pianist Bud Powell produced, to my ear, some of the era's greatest tapping.) It shouldn't have been so hard for them to adapt.

But it wasn't just aging hoofers who were thrown off. In 1945, Gillespie took his newly constituted band on a tour of the South. The Nicholas Brothers, then at the crest of their Hollywood fame, were the headliners of the stage show that preceded a public dance. Harold and Fayard, as band member Max Roach recalled, did "what they were known for doing," and Southern audiences, white and black, adored them. Audiences loved the heavyset hoofers Patterson and Jackson. They loved the shake dancer Lovey Lane. Gillespie's music they found bewildering—too fast, too hard to follow. Instead of dancing, they stood around with blank faces. (Though, as the Lindy hoppers in *Jivin' in Bebop* prove, the music was wonderfully danceable once the ear rehabituated.) During one show, someone yelled out, "Can't you nigguhs play no blues?!"

In that disconnect was a sign of things to come: most broadly, the failure of bebop to attract a mass audience. Many older jazz critics attacked it as nonsense or heresy; the mainstream press treated it as a silly cult or a dangerous subversion. White rebels and militant blacks adopted it as an expression of nonconformity. Even for sympathetic whites, the demeanor of black bebop performers could be discomforting. Gillespie was an ironic clown, but the others—most influentially Parker and Miles Davis—rejected the traditional manner of the entertainer, attempting to cut loose from the embarrassments of minstrelsy and the subservient associations of playing for Massa. Into their public performances they brought some of the insular attitude of jam sessions, of musicians playing for other musicians—as if to say, *Listen if you like, we're not putting on a show.* They insisted that they were artists, not entertainers, and the distinction mattered to them even more than it did to Paul Draper.

For young musicians, the embodiment of the old, compromised manner was Louis Armstrong. For young tap dancers, their Uncle Tom was Bill Robinson. And for them, rejecting the role of entertainer was even more complicated. *What the eye sees is the tawdry American convention; what the ear hears is the priceless African heritage.* "Jazz tap," Baby Laurence decreed, was percussive, "mostly from the waist down and the emphasis on sound." He resented the influence of Hollywood and the promoters who urged him to smile and use his hands; being conscious of poise, he opined, inevitably took away from what a dancer said with his feet. Sound was pure, and the visual aspects of tap were tainted. They should be sacrificed.

Perhaps Laurence wouldn't have been displeased, then, that there are no films extant of him in his prime. In photos from that era, he's hand-

Sheet music cover for "Jim Along Josey,"
1840 (George Endicott lithograph, Picture
Collection, New York Public Library)

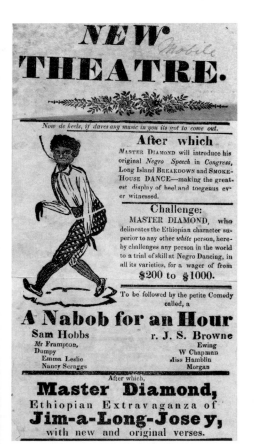

John Diamond performs in Mobile, 1841
(Harvard Theatre Collection)

T. D. Rice as Jim Crow, 1832 (Harvard
Theatre Collection)

Sheet music cover illustration for "Ole Virginy Break Down," 1847
(Rubenstein Library, Duke University)

"The Sabbath Among Slaves," from *Narrative of the Life and Adventures of Henry Bibb,
an American Slave*, 1849 (Library of Congress)

Master Juba in *The Illustrated London News*, 1848
(Photographs and Prints Division, Schomburg
Center for Research in Black Culture,
New York Public Library)

Dance manual, Henry Tucker's *Clog Dancing Made Easy*, 1874 (Library of Congress)

George Primrose, "the greatest soft-shoe dancer in the world" (Jerome Robbins Dance Division, New York Public Library for the Performing Arts)

Ned Wayburn's
Minstrel Misses in 1903
(Sheet Music Collection,
Brown University Library)

Ned Wayburn teaches musical comedy dancing at the Ned Wayburn Studios of
Stage Dancing in New York City (Collection of Bill and Sally Sommer)

Ginger Jack Wiggins in
The Freeman, 1915

Alberta and Alice Whitman,
queens of the 1920s black circuit
(Institute of Jazz Studies, Rutgers
University)

Peg Leg Bates: "The way you
looked was how you was
judged." (James J. Kriegsmann,
Photographs and Print Division,
Schomburg Center for Research
in Black Culture, New York
Public Library)

John Bubbles as Sportin' Life in *Porgy and Bess*, 1935
(Photograph by Vandamm Studio, copyright © Billy Rose Theatre
Division, New York Public Library for the Performing Arts)

Eddie Rector, defining a class act
circa 1924 (Photographs and Print
Division, Schomburg Center for
Research in Black Culture, New
York Public Library)

The Miller Brothers, with Honi Coles in the middle
(Institute of Jazz Studies, Rutgers University)

Harold and Fayard
Nicholas, circa 1938
(Photograph by
James J. Kriegsmann)

Ginger Rogers and
Fred Astaire in *Swing
Time*, 1936 (Photofest)

Bill Robinson and Shirley Temple in *The Little Colonel*, 1935 (Photofest)

Eleanor Powell in *Born to Dance*, 1936 (Photofest)

The Nicholas Brothers in *Stormy Weather*, 1943 (Photofest)

Gene Kelly in *Thousands Cheer*, 1943 (Photofest)

Paul Draper,
ascendant in 1942
(Photograph by
Barrett Gallagher)

Ray Bolger,
parodying Paul Draper
(Jerome Robbins Dance
Division, New York
Public Library)

Lon Chaney and Baby
Laurence at the Purple
Manor, 1963 (Jack Bradley)

Baby Laurence, Pete Nugent, Honi Coles, Cholly Atkins, and Bunny Briggs at the
1962 Newport Jazz Festival (Joe Alper Photo Collection LLC)

The Hoofers, 1969 (Leticia Jay, second from left; Chuck Green, center, clapping; Sandman Sims, far right) (Jack Bradley)

The Copasetics in *Steps in Time*, 1979 (Honi Coles, Phace Roberts, Cookie Cook, Bubba Gaines, Buster Brown) (Johan Elbers)

Brenda Bufalino and Honi Coles, 1978 (Photograph by Shelley Farkas Davis)

Jane Goldberg and Cookie Cook, 1977 (Photograph by Bob Crimi)

The Jazz Tap Ensemble (Camden Richman, Paul Arslanian, Tom Dannenberg, Keith Terry, Lynn Dally, Fred Strickler), 1980 (Jazz Tap Ensemble archives)

Dianne Walker, C. B. Hetherington,
Pam Raff, and Leon Colllins in 1982
(Copyright © L. Barry Hetherington)

Gregory Hines, tap star of the 1980s
(Photograph by Kenn Duncan, copyright ©
Billy Rose Theatre Division, New York
Public Library for the Performing Arts)

Honi Coles, Steve Condos, Jimmy Slyde, Eddie Brown, and Gregory Hines
preside at the 1986 Colorado Dance Festival (Bill Warren)

Savion Glover in his 2005 show *Classical Savion*, backed by a photo of the recently departed Gregory Hines (Copyright © Jack Vartoogian / Front Row Photos)

Jimmy Slyde, sixty-seven and still sliding in 1994 (Copyright © 1994 Karen Zebulon)

Michelle Dorrance, Dormeshia Sumbry-Edwards, and Chloé Arnold perform "Charlie's Angels" at the 2007 New York City Tap Festival (Copyright © Julieta Cervantes)

Roxane Butterfly in front of the Jimmy Slyde Institute, Barcelona, 2014 (Fred Fogherty)

some, dark-skinned, and dapper, armed with a ladykiller grin. Unless one of the television appearances he made in the late forties surfaces, the earliest documentation of his art will remain the album he recorded in 1959 and 1960. Even at that late date, the concept was unprecedented: an album with the tap dancer as the lead instrument. Laurence does not sing. He astonishes. The first thing that strikes the ear is extraordinary speed, the sheer number of distinct taps. But this isn't Ann Miller rattling away for a world record. The sound is fine-grained, molded, more like the work of fingers than of feet. Thumping bass notes anchor it to a deep bottom. As with Charlie Parker, what's most remarkable isn't the rapidity but the imagination persistently meeting impossible demands of tempo. The album is an exhibition of range. Laurence does a sand dance, a military number, a "modern" version of a Bill Robinson stair routine, using the hollow boom to drop bombs on himself. He does an unaccompanied "conglomeration of rhythms" he calls "Concerto in Taps." That's a tour de force, but the other numbers aren't routines plus backup; they're conversations among musicians, and the rhythmic ideas are developed with such sly wit, such pedal prestidigitation, that you don't miss the visual element. You can imagine it in the sound, which is recorded so that the ear-tickling scrapes and scuffs are distinctly audible, as is Laurence's path from microphone to microphone. You can also look at the photographs on the album cover: Laurence at his most eye-catchingly dynamic, corkscrewed in a turn, even airborne in a balletic leap. His art wasn't exclusively aural.

SIDEWALK MUSIC

Such efforts of imagination are less required for Laurence's foremost rival, Teddy Hale. Hollywood didn't find Hale, but television did— Mr. Television himself, Milton Berle, who introduced the hoofer as his discovery on his variety program in 1949. Into Teddy Hale's three minutes of national fame, which turned out to be his testament to posterity, the twentysomething appears to squeeze everything he knows. There's not a hint of strain. After about thirty seconds, the band cuts out. Hale unwinds skeins of variegated taps as his legs trace figure eights; he makes

a gift of really wrapped three-a-break steps; he tosses off a crunchy, astonishing self-lassoing tap turn; and he does a bit seated in a chair, his
arms folded cheekily across his chest—all in a minute and a half. His
rhythms are lucid, unostentatiously swinging. When not loosely swaying, his arms counterbalance the tight crossing of his legs or their abrupt
splaying, lightly complementing the footwork, as if hands and feet were
connected by a slack string. The coordination of sound and motion is
superb. When the band overpowers his taps, he pulls out a fortissimo
assortment of swivels, slides, ice-skater spins, and flips into jive splits.
His near-constant smile is neither servile nor cocky. Hale's gifts are obvious, and he takes pleasure in sharing them.

Born to a Cleveland chorus girl, Theodore Hailey followed her onstage as soon as he could walk. Before long, he was sidekick to the popular white clarinetist and nutty bandleader Ted Lewis; when Lewis sang
"Me and My Shadow," the shadow was little Teddy, in synch with the
star, his miniature top hat raised high. By age ten, he was a nightclub
single in New York, singing, telling jokes, and shaking his head in impressions of Jimmy Durante. He worked at the Apollo and the downtown Connie's Inn and Cotton Club, hounded by the watchdogs of
child labor. He once told a reporter he had three ages: a low one for the
railroad, a high one for the Children's Society, and a real one he didn't
remember. After Hale had outgrown such troubles, on the other side of
the Second World War, fellow hoofers noticed a change in his dancing.
(The Chicago hoofer Leon Collins later claimed he had been teaching
Hale while they were both in prison.) Pete Nugent caught Hale at the
Paramount, doing the seated bit and the flash assortment finale, and was
flabbergasted—by the bravura but also by the "transitional steps that
only another dancer could appreciate." Nugent dragged his colleague
Derby Wilson to see the next show. Wilson's response: "Sweet Jesus."

Stories gathered about Hale like those about Bubbles—tales of no
two performances being the same, reports of Hale tapping for an hour
and not repeating a step. Old-guard theatrical reviewers provided some
corroboration with their complaint "on too long." The black press had
already, back in 1935, mentioned Hale as a contender to fill Bill Robinson's shoes; now the suggestion was serious, imminent. Among tap dancers, Hale's high reputation derived from his offstage battles with Baby

Laurence, repeatedly fought to a draw. "They was music themselves," recalled Chuck Green. "When they finished, you could hardly hear your ears." In an art based in improvisation, it's a statistical probability that much of the best music was never recorded, and awareness of all that missing music lies behind the obsessive collection of bootleg recordings. Tap might have been thought of the same way, but if anyone cared enough to tape Baby Laurence challenging Teddy Hale, those recordings are lost or hidden. Other recordings of Hale do exist: audio from a few TV broadcasts, collected by jazz enthusiasts interested in the band. One is with Charlie Parker; Hale is barely audible. Others, from *The Eddie Condon Floor Show*, are more distinct, though the visual footage of Hale and Laurence challenge-dancing on that program appears to be irretrievable.

You can find recordings of some of the jam sessions inside Minton's Playhouse, the small Harlem club that would be eulogized as a laboratory of bebop experimentation. But there aren't recordings of the duels that took place outside Minton's, on the sidewalk. These, Miles Davis recalls in his autobiography, were often between Baby Laurence and a hoofer called Groundhog, two musicians who were battling not just for preeminence. "Baby and Groundhog were junkies," reports Davis, who was a junkie himself at the time, "and so they used to dance a lot in front of Minton's for their drugs, because the dealers liked to watch them. They gave them shit for free if they got down."

This was the other way that musicians emulated Charlie Parker—some convinced, despite Parker's denials, that the heroin he injected was the source of his inspiration. Young tap dancers were part of the same crowd, and many of them picked up the same habits. They jigged for new masters now, the dealers. (Baby Laurence later boasted that it was he who had introduced Parker to heroin in the first place.) Laurence and Hale spent the fifties in and out of jail, convicted of drug possession or of stealing more than steps. The trumpeter Chet Baker, a fellow addict and convict, remembered coming upon Laurence in 1959, tap-dancing up the walls of a prison yard. Whenever the dancers were out of the pen, they headlined at the Apollo and sundry nightclubs. Hale made it to London, where he was again arrested for possession, and to France, from where he was deported on similar charges. Leslie Uggams, a child performer back then, remembers once watching Hale's act from the wings as she stood next to the cops who were waiting to bust him. Hale tapped down the stage stairs, up the auditorium aisle, and out into a taxi. "That was the last we saw of Teddy."

In 1955, Hale was on the bill at the Moulin Rouge, the first integrated casino in Las Vegas, a black-and-tan on the dark side of town where all the city's entertainers gravitated after hours. During the run, he was arrested as a suspect in the death of the sharp-witted saxophonist Wardell Gray, whose corpse had been found in the desert with a broken neck. While strapped to a lie detector, Hale said that the thirty-four-year-old Gray had overdosed while he and Hale were shooting up heroin, and that Hale, panicking, dumped the body. No autopsy was ever performed, and that lapse, combined with the setting of a mob-run, racially segregated town, fertilized several noirish theories. The tap dancer was sentenced to ninety days for illegally moving a corpse. That same year, Charlie Parker died, at age thirty-four, so weakened by years of drug and alcohol abuse that a doctor who examined the body estimated the age of the deceased to be fifty. Two years later in Harlem, Hale, just released from another prison term on another narcotics possession charge, was shot in the leg by a stray policeman's bullet. No chief of police visited him in the hospital, and the $2.5 million lawsuit he filed against the city, claiming career-ending paralysis in his right foot, seems to have gone nowhere. Only a few months passed before he was arrested again. In May 1959, he died of a brain hemorrhage, likely drug-related. He was just shy of thirty-three.

"If you weren't in the 'in' crowd," wrote Miles Davis, "you didn't know nothing about the dancing in front of Minton's. Those tap dancers used to talk about Fred Astaire and all of them other white dancers like they were nothing, and they weren't nothing compared to how these guys could dance. But they were black and couldn't ever hope to get no break dancing for real money and fame." Being black certainly had much to do with it, though not everything. (Davis's next sentence begins: "By this time I was getting really famous.") Once during the fifties, when Baby Laurence was released from jail, Jack Schiffman, who had taken over as manager of the Apollo from his father, offered the ex-con a job. According to Schiffman, Laurence's dancing was better than ever, but halfway through the engagement, he disappeared. Months later, Laurence returned and Schiffman hired him again; again, Laurence failed to last a week. This sequence repeated a half-dozen times before Schiffman gave up.

As for Groundhog, Pete Nugent called him "a short, dumpy guy with no style who couldn't sell but could really dance." Leonard Reed told me that Groundhog was "the best street dancer" he had ever seen, but "put him on stage and he died. No personality." Even to Laurence, Groundhog was a wonderful drummer who knew all the flash steps but who was also "short and slovenly and unreliable." His given name was probably Clarence Taylor, though in one interview he gave while drunk he said (perhaps in jest) it was Earl Basie, and that he hated the name Groundhog, which derived from his stature and persisted because of his hygiene. He was born in Birmingham to the TOBA comedian Showboy Holland and a chorus girl, taken on the road by the Whitman Sisters when he was five, and kept on as Pops's partner for eight years. Alice Whitman remembered him as "a boy who was always disappearing." Then came sporadic appearances in the Midwest and touring in Europe. Many dancers would report on his fearsomeness in cutting contests— some on the sidewalk at five in the morning, after the nightclubs had closed. Max Roach claimed to have learned a lot from Groundhog, and Miles Davis rated him as a motherfucker. But a dancer's dancer, particularly a homely one with a drug habit, was not a likely candidate for big money and fame.

Another factor is suggested by Davis's anecdote. The dancers are battling *outside* Minton's, during the daytime. Laurence performed inside Minton's at least once, but in general, the small combos and tiny clubs in which bebop musicians found their niche weren't very hospitable to tap. Jazz was becoming a listening music: not something you danced to, not a show you watched. One cause was a federal entertainment tax instituted as a wartime revenue-producing measure in 1944. Starting at 30 percent and reduced under protest to 20, the tax applied to floor shows and public dancing, but not to instrumental music. In order to avoid the tax, thousands of nightclubs—and these were the days when there *were* thousands of nightclubs—either eliminated floor shows and dancing or closed up entirely. Larger clubs survived by raising prices, but the strongest effects were felt after the war, when the economy contracted and the tax was not repealed. Then it combined with other trends—the exodus to the suburbs, the rise of television—that sharply reduced nightclub attendance. As musicians and stagehands unionized, the cost of putting on shows ballooned, eventually causing most of even the larger clubs to close. Subject to the same forces, the presentation theaters also began to drop their stage programs. There were fewer and fewer places for a tap dancer to dance.

BROADWAY RHYTHM

Broadway wasn't one of them. Not anymore.

Jerome Kern and Oscar Hammerstein's *Showboat* had led the way in 1927, with a grander story than the usual formulas, a saga shaded by tragedy, but, unlike the operettas imported from Europe, one told about Americans in an American vernacular. *Showboat* crossed the two problems of integration in American musical theater: it put together dialogue, song, and dance in a plot that turned on miscegenation and racial passing. (The cast was nearly a third black.) Yet *Showboat*, however serious, was stuffed with tap and its relatives. The entertainer characters did cakewalks and "nigger shuffles" in the 1890s section, eccentric tap numbers and the Charleston to represent the now. But in 1927, the leading dance directors were already talking a different game. "No longer are routines a matter of speed and noise," Seymour Felix told the press. A dance needed some connection to the story, an idea. "The cycle of acrobatics, 'hot' dancing, and stomping is over," Felix said, which didn't bode well for a dance form considered exclusively hot, stomping, and mindless. Still, throughout the thirties, the sporadic incursion of ballet into Broadway productions such as Rodgers and Hart's *On Your Toes* didn't do much to threaten tap's dominance. As late as 1940, it was still taken for granted that even a more sophisticated musical, such as Rodgers and Hart's *Pal Joey*, could be based in musical comedy dance, in tap.

Then, in 1943, Richard Rodgers teamed up with Oscar Hammerstein and made *Oklahoma!*. To a greater degree than in previous musical comedies, the songs in *Oklahoma!* advanced character and plot. So did the dances. The choreographer was Agnes de Mille, a well-bred young

woman from an intellectual-theatrical family and an artist of high ambition who had grown up near Hollywood, where her uncle Cecil was
one of the biggest directors in town. After years of struggle, her first
great success came in 1942, when she created the ballet *Rodeo* for the
Ballet Russe de Monte Carlo, one of the two similarly named troupes of
Europeans that brought ballet, foreign and glamorous, to the American
heartland. Set to a genre-defining score by Aaron Copland, *Rodeo*—
with its cowboys on imaginary bucking broncos and its funny, clumsy,
lovestruck cowgirl heroine—made good on a decade of attempts at
American-themed ballet. It was a story ballet with a square dance in the
middle, and even a little tap. The Champion Roper won the heroine's
heart by making noise with his feet.

There was tap, too, in de Mille's choreography for *Oklahoma!*. When
the character Will Parker reported on his trip to Kansas City, he showed
off some fancy steps acquired there. Parker was played by Lee Dixon,
who had tapped on a typewriter with Ruby Keeler in the movies. What
got all the attention, however, was the dream ballet that ended the
first act. A dream ballet was in itself no innovation, but this one was
more psychological, more Freudian; it let audiences in on the core emotional conflict of the heroine, expressing desires and fears that she might
not admit to herself. Perhaps more important, the Western setting and
idiom of *Oklahoma!*—cowboys, a hoedown—made ballet familiar, do-
mesticated it. During the Second World War, de Mille's dances touched
national chords of feeling.

Oklahoma! was enormously successful, both critically and commercially. Rodgers and Hammerstein began their reign as the monarchs of
Broadway, and their kind of "musical play" became the American musical's high standard. Immediately, others tried to duplicate their success,
and in the process, ballet went from being an exotic spice or the butt of
a joke to a nearly essential ingredient. During the year after *Oklahoma!*
opened, nearly half of the musicals produced included ballet; over the
next three years, more than half did, dream ballets abounding. De Mille
was the most sought-after choreographer in town, her name printed in
the advertisements along with those of the composers and the stars.

Choreographers like her, from ballet or modern dance, were suddenly prized. Balanchine, the trailblazer, was still active, and now others

joined: Anna Sokolow, Hanya Holm, Michael Kidd. Jerome Robbins, the twenty-five-year-old choreographer of the sailor ballet *Fancy Free* (1944), expanded that inspired work into the musical *On the Town*, in which dance played an even greater role in the storytelling than it did in *Oklahoma!*. Like de Mille, Robbins was fashioning a new kind of ballet, rooted in classical technique but dressed in costumes and gestures that made it seem less foreign to American audiences. Seeking to control their theater work as a ballet choreographer controls his ballets, de Mille and especially Robbins created for themselves a new role, the director-choreographer, organizing an entire Broadway production almost as if it were one long dance.

As a result of all of this, dance on Broadway became more central and prestigious. Dance, but not tap. The choreographers were not tap dancers. Most of them knew much less about the form than had the breed of dance directors they replaced. And with the new choreographers came a new kind of dancer. In one of her tartly eloquent autobiographies, de Mille described the changeover: "The chorus girl and the chorus boy of the past, corrupt, sly, ruthless and professionally inept, gradually disappeared. And in their place came singers and dancers, trained and self-respecting." The days when any fresh and eager kid could walk off the street into a Broadway chorus were over, but self-trained, self-respecting tap dancers didn't fit into the system either. And as the condescencion in de Mille's tone hints, there may have been an element of revenge at work. Ballet dancers had always lost jobs to tap dancers; tap had always been more popular than ballet. Here was a chance to turn the tables.

In one sense, tap—America's natural way of dancing—should have been easier than ballet to integrate into the native plots of American musical plays. Yet as the musical's subject matter broadened, tap's associations remained constricted. Other forms seemed better suited for Rodgers's soaring melodies, and perhaps the special shoes were viewed as impeding fluid transitions from scene to song. (The most distinguished precedent—Astaire's numbers for film—had largely sidestepped such technical problems.) In any case, Broadway choreographers of the forties had no interest in tap dancers, didn't know what to do with them. (The only choreographer who was interested, in his conflicted way, left for Hollywood: Gene Kelly.) "Bravura display for its own sake or for the glory of the performer," de Mille decreed to the *Times* in 1943, "belongs to an outmoded style." Tap dancers had trained themselves to stop shows, not to further the plot. (Black dancers knew they had no role in the plot anyway.) Showstopping numbers did not vanish from Broadway, but the tap dancer's art—self-contained—lost value in the marketplace.

The tapping of a star comic was still viable, for a while. *By Jupiter* in 1942—the last full-length Rodgers and Hart show before Rodgers joined Hammerstein—was a hit for Ray Bolger. Reviewing Bolger's previous show, Brooks Atkinson had rated him the "best hoofer in the business," and now Milton Bracker explained that Bolger "strives to convince his audience that he is feeling something, not just hoofing." John Martin presented Bolger in one paragraph as a reason to consider tap dancing an art and insisted in the next that the comedian could not be confined to the category: "He uses taps, as he uses everything else that can serve him, merely in passing to create a unified, altogether individual style," an older form of integration. (The dancer himself explained to *Dance* that "to be good you've got to be a person doing a dance, not a series of steps.") Bolger's stage career peaked in 1948 with *Where's Charley?*, in which, Martin observed, everything Bolger did was dancing.

For an old-fashioned musical comedy, a just-hoofing tap act still might be brought in for a little color and verve. That happened with *Kiss Me, Kate*, in 1949, when Fred and Sledge, a young black duo out of Texas, were hired to provide some rhythmic heat for Cole Porter's "Too Darn Hot." That same year, the recently formed pair of Honi Coles, the ex–Miller Brother whose speed baffled agents, and Cholly Atkins, late of dubbing in Hollywood, was hired for a spot in *Gentlemen Prefer Blondes*. De Mille, the show's choreographer, had nothing to do with the Coles and Atkins number. With the help of an outside arranger, Coles and Atkins adapted one of the routines from their nightclub act. That de Mille received the credit was standard practice, though it was irritating, a little while later, for Coles and Atkins to have to ask her permission to perform their own routine on television.

Coles and Atkins didn't think of themselves as choreographers. "Putting an act together" was the phrase they favored, and they did it with care. Their mode was tap-centered variety, everything in twelve and a half minutes: a song, a couple of jokes, some twizzly jazz dancing, a soft shoe. The duo balanced sound and sight. In his solo, Coles dazzled with intricate footwork, what his friend Pete Nugent dubbed "centipede steps"; Atkins countered with wings and Lindy steps and what he called "balletic flash stuff." Theirs was a class act, so attire and demeanor were paramount. Both men were tall and debonair, suave in thin mustaches, though their sophistication didn't preclude audience-pleasing antics: Coles playing the showboat, Atkins stealing Coles's bows.

In film from the early fifties, Coles and Atkins dance and sing well and acquit themselves in mildly wry comedy sketches. The glory of their act, however, wasn't documented until 1965, when the duo performed their soft shoe for educational television. It was the slowest around, with an eternity yawning between the first note and the second. Such a tempo demanded extraordinary control, especially in continuous unison. All that silence was exposing. In the dance, Coles and Atkins play with the soft-shoe form without rupturing it, applying pressure to its easy ambling with a brief suspension of the beat in a jump or an intensification of it in a burst of double-time. They indulge in the drama of a spread-eagled slide but immediately rein it in with mincing heel drops. The dancers carefully place each pearlescent click and bridge the chasms between notes with grace. Smiling, Coles and Atkins take on the tawdry American convention as their own.

The duo had come together in Cab Calloway's band after the war. They had traveled with Billy Eckstine and Count Basie, played the Apollo, and toured Europe. But those bands broke up, and it was in search of new opportunities that Coles and Atkins auditioned for *Gentlemen Prefer Blondes*. It was their first audition: before, an agent had always booked their act, or a friend had hired them. They auditioned as a team.

There would have been few or no individual roles for them anyhow. The Great White Way, bent on integration of form, was still almost entirely racially segregated. A pared-down revival of *Porgy and Bess* in 1942 was a bigger hit than the original, and *Cabin in the Sky* (1940), another folkloric all-black show by a mostly white creative team, had found enough favor to inspire MGM to film it. (That's the movie in which John Bubbles struts.) In 1946, the mildly successful *St. Louis Woman* starred Harold Nicholas as a short-statured, big-talking jockey of the 1890s. There were also black-cast adaptations of white shows: Gilbert and Sullivan operettas played in swing, *Carmen* set in the South as *Carmen Jones* with Buck and Bubbles. Duke Ellington's *Beggar's Holiday*, an integrated adaptation of *The Beggar's Opera*, had a brief run in 1946, but his *Jump for Joy*, a hit in Los Angeles in 1941, never made it to Broadway. *Jump for Joy* was a revue, like *Blackbirds*. (Pete Nugent contributed his tap act; Nick Castle, the choreographer, struggled to get him to tell a story.) But tonally, the show was ahead of its time. Its satire of Uncle Tom theatrical conventions and Jim Crow injustice drew death threats from the local KKK. An immediately sinking Broadway revival of *Shuffle Along* in 1952 indicated that bringing back the old black shows wasn't going to work, either, despite an entirely new story and a lovely old sand dance by Eddie Rector.

Gentlemen Prefer Blondes ran for two years. After the tour ended, Coles and Atkins started taking jobs in Scranton and Wilkes-Barre. In New York, Coles knew the manager of the Fourteenth Street Academy of Music, so sometimes the pair could work there two weeks in a row, billed first as Coles and Atkins and then as Jenkins and Foster or some other invented pairing. They added more comedy into the act, filling spaces in the soft shoe with repartee. Promoters advised them to stick to dancing and stay out of the headliner's turf. Their manager, Joe Glaser, told them they were too good, too classy, "doing a white boys' act," and that club owners feared that they might appeal to white girls. Atkins thought the problem was that he and his partner were too smart to be taken advantage of and that agents knew it. Coles and Atkins could get by, but one of the best acts in the business began to look into other ways of making a living.

THE WAR AND AFTER

During the war, Atkins had been stationed near New York and free to perform on weekends. Luckier enlisted tap dancers worked in the Special Services and spent the whole war performing. A special unit was formed for Irving Berlin's morale-boosting show *This Is the Army*, the only racially integrated unit in the armed forces. Pete Nugent choreographed the black routine; Fred Kelly choreographed the blackface one. (In the *Times*, John Martin commented that the "Negro cast makes it unmistakeably clear that Negro rhythm is an inborn gift and that white men might as well give up trying to acquire it.") Meanwhile, civilian tappers worked for the USO. Fred Astaire hoofed on the hoods of jeeps all over Europe. Peg Leg Bates visited the wounded in hospitals, suggesting that a loss of limb was not the end of the world. Gene Kelly performed in hospitals, too, assiduously, before he was called up in late 1944, went through boot camp, and started making films for the navy. When war was declared, Jimmy Smith, a young hoofer out of Chicago, worried about the wartime rationing of metal. He tapped on a self-made vibraphone, playing melodies across thirty-two aluminum bars. As it happened, the war was good for business, and Smith, having worked out a supply line, flourished. The postwar obstacles for hoofers proved more difficult to surmount.

At first, it seemed only a matter of succession. Starting around 1940, black newspapers began speculating more often about who might replace Bill Robinson. The candidate most frequently cited was Bill Bailey. His derby-topped, tap-and-patter act was such a close copy of Robinson's that the comparison made itself. Aside from his rough, chipper performance in the 1943 film of *Cabin in the Sky*, the earliest extant footage comes from the fifties. The dancer chats as he demonstrates some Robinson steps, replicating the master's rhythmic precision without the economy of movement. Everything is heavier: rhythmic sighs coarsened to grunts, erect effortlessness replaced by clenched strain. Another clip is more modern-looking, alive with spasms and snapping motions as if to shake more sound onto the floor. *Cabin in the Sky* didn't lead to more film work for Bailey, but he remained in demand and highly paid in nightclubs and theaters.

In 1946, he sensed the change. "The nightclubs and theaters were closing and the places left were just joints." He couldn't stand the noise, couldn't concentrate. He was smoking a lot of dope. While performing at Café Zanzibar one evening, he heard a buzzing in his ears, a voice that whispered, "The wages of sin is death." Night after night, the voice returned, until one time it added, "The gift of God is eternal life." Bailey walked off the stage and quit showbiz. Like his father before him, he became a Pentecostal minister. On the sidewalks outside his former places of employment and in a small church behind the Apollo, he preached to sinners like the one he had been, show people, addicts. The Apollo donated seats, and stagehands built the altar, but running a church was expensive, and in 1951, Bailey returned to dancing—"Suddenly God gave me the OK"—using his talents to finance God's work. By this time, however, it was his sister, Pearl, who was the star, and Bill became an added attraction to her act. Pearl could tap, but it was as a singer with hit records that she made her name.

"When I leave this world, I choose this boy to take my place." Bill Robinson said that about Harold Nicholas and Honi Coles and also about Bunny Briggs, who found a path through the postwar shrinkage. Born in Harlem in 1922, Briggs loved watching stage shows because they took him into a more glamorous world. To him, Robinson was "the greatest thing onstage. Black dancers were expected to *get hot*. I detest that word. But Bill came up all calm. He was dainty." Briggs noticed that while other black dancers wore bellhop uniforms, Robinson was in a suit, "dressed like a gentleman that's walking down Fifth Avenue." After the five-year-old danced for his idol, Robinson asked Briggs to join him on the road, but Briggs's mother, who had heard of Robinson's gambling habit, wouldn't let him go. Doing the Charleston for coins in front of a record shop, he was hired by Luckey Roberts and his Society Entertainers, a black band that played exclusively for the Vanderbilt set. This was another world indeed. Society people sat on the floor around him, and he danced softly so they could relax. In the 1932 short *Slowpoke*, you can see him, doe-eyed, waifish, shimmying his little shoulders. After apprenticing with the Whitman Sisters, he danced as a teenager at the Ubangi Club, where he met and was dazed by Baby Laurence. In the early forties, Louise Crane, an heiress who dabbled in management, chose Briggs as a replacement for Laurence, who had left her. She put Briggs into Kelly's Stables on Fifty-second Street, with Coleman Hawkins. Sometimes billed as the Prince Charming of Tap, he went onto the circuit, with the Basie band and the band of Earl Hines when Dizzy Gillespie and Charlie Parker were in it. He had a step that sounded like the rhythm Gillespie put into "Salt Peanuts." Briggs adapted to bebop, practicing all day in the basement of Detroit's Club 666 until it came to him, a way of connecting steps that he called "continuation."

This had something to do with the paddle and roll, a combination of dropped heels and a controlled flopping from the ankle (the "paddle") that could produce a shuttling sound like a train. Older East Coast dancers considered the paddle and roll a Midwestern kind of cheating. (It came to their attention, they said, in 1937, with the New York arrival of the now otherwise forgotten Chicago dancer Walter Green.) Carnell Lyons, who grew up in Kansas City with Charlie Parker, claimed to have created the paddle and roll while trying and failing to copy Baby Laurence in Chicago in the early forties. Later the step, easily variable and extendable, entered Laurence's vocabulary, and just about everyone else's.

Briggs's version can be found in a 1950 Universal musical short with the Benny Carter Orchestra. Giving the ground a close shave, his feet churn out a roll so quick and constant that it's nearly impossible to isolate the source of each tap. His torso is fairly still (he told me he derived this from Irish dancing; he told someone else he took it from a lady in the movies), but he sits in his heels. When he breaks his continuation, it's with a high contrast two-footed stomp or with big triplets in half-time, fording against the flow of the beat. Otherwise, the sound is so light and dappled that it takes microscopic earwork to absorb its full complexity. It's like Baby Laurence with the damper pedal glued down. Briggs wore his taps loose to get that click, as crisp and soft as raindrops hitting gravel. He lets the tiny motions propel him, a sewing machine stitching figures into the floor. Sometimes the figures are from skating as he slides on his metal taps, pantomiming the cold and falling snow. He dramatizes—suddenly shifting direction or level, swiveling like a marionette. The easy-to-follow patterns of traditional tap are gone, but in their place is another kind of show.

Decades later, Briggs would say that Laurence "couldn't sell himself. The public has to understand and like what you're doing, not other dancers." Robinson was Briggs's lodestar, and he handled an audience delicately. Briggs had bebop cool but also a babyface, which he sometimes powdered in skin-whitening makeup. With the mixed-race band of the white saxophonist Charlie Barnet, he toured theaters both black and white. Barnet thought that Briggs had what it took to be a big star but that his mother held him back: Mrs. Briggs once told the bandleader that she would rather see her son running an elevator than performing, or performing with Barnet's band. The visual side of Briggs's dancing proved an asset as amplification came in, drowning out taps. In the years to come, he would often be described as an exception, the one who stayed clean, the one who kept working.

WOMEN OF THE FORTIES

Female tap acts remained the greater rarity and were destined to fall into greater obscurity. The Edwards Sisters, those Twin Torpedoes of Rhythm, finally made a film appearance in 1949, a brief spot in the Duke Ellington short *Symphony in Swing.* In double-breasted Eton jackets and high-waisted pants, they look like twins. Poor sound makes their rhythms hard to follow, and the frequent crosscutting to Ellington shreds the routine's continuity, yet it's nevertheless possible to discern a boogie-woogie bounce and a tidal motion similar to the style of their male contemporaries. And while the brevity frustrates qualitative comparison, it accurately reproduces the role that the Edwards Sisters would have played in an Ellington show: an appetizer. Within a few years, they had quit performing to become wives and mothers.

Trading steps with the boys, recalled Jewel "Pepper" Welch, made girls dance just like them. She grew up hoofing on the same Philadelphia corners as Honi Coles before starting an act with Mildred "Candi" Thorpe, who hung around the Lincoln Theater asking guys like Honi Coles for steps. Perhaps to look like the boys, or not to look like shake dancers, Welch and her second partner, Edwina "Salt" Evelyn, costumed themselves in male attire, with six suits to choose from and "nurse shoes" to match. In the late forties and early fifties, Salt and Pepper toured with big bands, played nightclubs, and were rated by the *Amsterdam News* as the "greatest among the femme dancing teams." Edith "Baby" Edwards, another daughter of Philadelphia, was the kind of female hoofer men were always advising to dance softer. Decades later, when LaVaughn Robinson was a respected tap elder and Edwards was nearly unknown, Robinson would suggest that she could have been the greatest tap dancer had she not quit to take care of her sick mother. According to her female contemporaries, Edwards carried her act with Willie Joseph, billed as Spic and Span, holding back so as not to show up the male partner who gave her necessary protection on the road. Juanita Pitts danced with her well-regarded husband, Leroy, but when he took ill, she went on without him. That's how she appears in *It Happened in Harlem*, a black short of 1945. Slim in a suit and flats, she taps in the low-slung style of the day, swinging with low-key savoir faire. Except for her gender, her act doesn't seem that distinctive, but that one distinction seems to have been a handicap in a career that lasted through the mid-fifties in smaller clubs.

In 1939, when the Miller Brothers were in the market for a new member, it took a lot of convincing from Cholly Atkins before they gave an audition to one of his friends, a chorus girl named Lois Bright. Danny Miller doubted a woman could cut it. After Bright proved him wrong, he married her. The act that the Miller Brothers and Lois developed was a peak of platform tapping—captured, after years of polishing, in the 1947 black short *Hi-De-Ho*. The first section is prime class-act precision. The two men, in tailcoats and top hats, swivel around Lois, who wears the same getup except for a skirt and Cuban heels. She does what the boys do and throws in high kicks or walkovers as garnish. Then, across the buttes and valleys of five narrow platforms a few feet high that spell out M-I-L-L-E-R, Lois and one of the guys range sideways and backward, spreading a brisk and daring routine that would be impressive enough on the ground. The final section introduces loftier platforms, one a board almost tall enough to reach Lois's shoulders, and the tempo races even faster. The brothers break out their craziest wings, but the climax comes with Lois, elevated like a woman walking the plank, doing trenches and rotating like a stunt biplane. The act dissolved sometime in the early fifties, and the marriage between Danny and Lois didn't last much longer. She went into teaching.

LAST STEPS

In the final decade of his life, Bill Robinson was largely insulated from tap's shifting styles and fortunes. *He* didn't change. In 1939, at the age of sixty-one, he tapped in gold pants and gold shoes in the title role of *The*

Hot Mikado. During the same period, he headlined at the downtown Cotton Club. After his 7:30 show there, he raced to the *Mikado* theater in time for his second-act entrance at 8:40, then raced back for the midnight and 2:00 a.m. shows at the club. The storied venue closed for good the next year, but the Mayor of Harlem kept on, starring in an otherwise all-white Broadway revue called *All in Fun*, and in *Memphis Bound*, another all-black Gilbert and Sullivan in swing. He did his stair dance, and the praise from the *Times* could have served as an epitaph: "His dancing is the same as always."

Plans for a swing version of *Uncle Tom's Cabin* starring Robinson and Shirley Temple fell through, which was just as well for Robinson's reputation among young blacks. In the forties, coverage of Robinson's performances in the black press included reports of hecklers. "We don't want to hear that old Uncle Tom stuff," yelled a disgruntled youth in Cleveland. "We came here to see you dance." Buster Brown recalled Robinson's ingratiation more indulgently: "We call it Tom, but white folks call it diplomacy." If a Harlem kid got in trouble with the law, Robinson might talk to the judge and do a dance and walk the kid out of jail. Stories like that jostle with stories of Robinson's temper: the story of Robinson taking out a gun to convince the manager of a Midwest diner to serve him and the Ellington band, newspaper accounts of Robinson pistol-whipping a white football player who had insulted him. "He proved he was no Uncle Tom," reasoned the dancer U. S. Thompson, "because Uncle Tom didn't fight."

On November 25, 1949, Bill Robinson died of heart failure. "His death takes from us not only a great performer who entertained us but a great human being who made our lives richer and happier," wrote the *Times*, honoring Robinson, as did other papers, for his generosity in spreading joy. The line of people filing past his body as it lay in state at the 369th Regiment Armory extended long into the night. On the day of his funeral, the schools in Harlem closed at noon, as did many theaters, and three thousand mourners packed the Abyssinian Baptist Church. Thousands, perhaps tens of thousands, listened outside. A motorcade of nearly a hundred cars made its way from Harlem, past the Palace Theatre and the crowds lining the streets, five and six rows deep, to the Evergreens Cemetery in Brooklyn and Queens, where hundreds more mourners had been waiting in near-freezing temperatures for hours. All told, the police department estimated that at least half a million people turned out to mourn Bojangles.

He had many friends. The roll of honorary pallbearers—there were a hundred and fifty—was heavily studded with show business royalty: Bob Hope, Bing Crosby, Jack Warner, Louis B. Mayer, Lee Shubert, Rodgers and Hammerstein, and more. Joe DiMaggio was on the list, as were Jackie Robinson, Joe Louis, Duke Ellington, and Louis Armstrong. New York's Edward Mulrooney was far from the only police commissioner represented. There were judges and senators, Governor Thomas Dewey and J. Edgar Hoover. Mayor William O'Dwyer delivered the eulogy, praising Robinson's good manners and decency, and Ed Sullivan, in charge of the service, said, "No performer and very few Americans ever touched the heart of this city, and this nation, with greater impact." The Reverend Adam Clayton Powell, Jr., pastor of the church and New York's first black congressman, called Robinson "a legend because he was ageless and raceless. Bill wasn't a credit to his race, meaning the Negro race. He was a credit to the human race. He was not a great Negro dancer, he was the world's greatest dancer."

Eulogies are supposed to eulogize. Robinson had always looked younger than his years, but he could never be raceless in America. He wasn't the world's greatest dancer or even the world's greatest tap dancer. Yet he was a great one, an artist and an entertainer, a legend, the face of his art, out front and smiling.

In hindsight, tap dancers would come to view Robinson's death as the turning point. "After that," said Buster Brown, "everything just fell. Bang. No more jobs." The question of who would succeed Robinson was supplanted by the question of whether tap would survive at all. By 1955, a writer for *The Chicago Defender* would be asking, "What happened to the great tap dancers?" and similar articles would appear periodically over the next decade, written by black journalists who remembered. Some of the hoofers would go abroad. Some would try teaching. Most took up regular jobs, hanging on as hotel clerks, elevator operators, cabdrivers, night watchmen. They would dance at night, dance when nobody was watching. The days when every show had a tap dancer, when tap was taken for granted—those days were coming to an end.

PART IV

OUT OF STEP

There is no danger that the art of tap dancing will dissolve into any state that is not rhythmically, dancingly and agelessly alive.
—ELSIE A. LITTLE, *The Dance Encyclopedia*, 1949

It is a sign of these strange times that an Art Form as interesting and original and as natural to the shows of yesteryear could now be called a novelty.
—HONI COLES, *New York Amsterdam News*, 1964

12

THE BREAK

A SMALLER SCREEN

Television should have been good for tap. Better than radio, at least, which had brought the sounds of Astaire, Eleanor Powell, Buck and Bubbles, and dozens of amateur kiddies into the homes of millions. Tapping on radio wasn't like juggling on radio; it was only a joke if you didn't think of tap as music. Bill Robinson, in his many radio appearances of the thirties, combined his tap with corny stories, one-liners ("I haven't been this proud since I was colored"), and catchphrases ("Shoot me while I'm happy!"). When the airwaves were awash in the ventriloquism of white actors pretending to be black—most prominently in the number one show, *Amos 'n' Andy*—Robinson was one of the only black actors on radio, the perfect order of his rhythms suggesting an immaculateness listeners could not see. Tap on the radio left out a lot. Tap dancers were present for some of the earliest television experiments. Buck and Bubbles appeared on the debut program of the British Broadcasting

Opposite page: Sammy Davis, Jr., with Sammy Davis, Sr., and Will Mastin, 1955

Corporation's television service, in 1936, and on what was reported to be the first televised cabaret in America, in 1939. When commercial television caught on in the United States, in the late forties and early fifties, the new audiovisual medium provided abundant opportunities, above all by giving a second life to vaudeville.

Officially number one as soon as the Nielsen Company began compiling ratings, in 1950, *Texaco Star Theater* and its zany host, Milton Berle, were credited with a huge spike in the sale of TV sets. (In 1948, less than one percent of American households had TV; by 1952, one-third did; by 1957, two-thirds.) *Texaco Star Theater* was a variety show. At its premiere in 1948, an ad, in *Variety*, crowed, "Vaudeville is back!" And with vaudeville came comedians, singers, magicians, acrobats, trained animals, and tap dancers. Bill Robinson danced on the second episode of *Texaco Star Theater*. (In his second appearance, two months before his death, when he still looked twenty years younger than he was, he grabbed a cane and gave his impression of himself forty years hence—"and believe me, I'm going to be here.") Within the program's first two seasons, it also featured Buck and Bubbles, the Berry Brothers, the Clark Brothers, Peg Leg Bates, and Teddy Hale, among other hoofers. Hal LeRoy—the onetime Harold Teen, his rubberlegs now middle-aged—had made his last film in 1940, and his nightclub career was coasting, but in the first four years of *Texaco Star Theater*, LeRoy tapped on the show at least five times. It was almost a comeback.

The situation was similar on the rival series *Toast of the Town*, which premiered in 1948 and grew into a national Sunday night ritual by 1955, when it took on the name of its mortician-stiff host, Ed Sullivan. Bunny Briggs was invited on the show once a year, Peg Leg Bates and Hal LeRoy and the Four Step Brothers more frequently than that. Those tap acts and others popped up on *The Morey Amsterdam Show*, *The Ken Murray Show*, *The Jack Carter Show*, *The Bob Hope Show*, *The Frank Sinatra Show*, *The Kate Smith Evening Hour*, *Cavalcade of Stars*, *Cavalcade of Bands*, *The Four Star Revue*, *The Colgate Comedy Hour*, and more. (Coles and Atkins were on the short-lived all-black variety show *Sugar Hill Times*, hosted by Willie Bryant.) Variety shows were all over early TV, and not even the movies had offered such instant and vast exposure. By the time *Toast of the Town* started airing, Peg Leg Bates was already well-known among the thousands who had seen him perform live in theaters and nightclubs. Yet as soon as the dancer appeared on Sullivan's TV show, he was immediately confronted with a radically different level of recognition. People came up to him on the street, saying, "I saw you on TV."

For vaudevillians, this exposure was a blessing and a curse. Instead of the old system of creating an act, then touring it around the country for months or years, now a single performance reached a potential audience of millions, all at once. Do a single gig, and it was time for a new song, outfit, steps, or at least a new arrangement of the old ones. Movie appearances had similar consequences, but television programs, airing weekly, had a much more ravenous appetite for material. Even so, the time allotted for a tap act was only a few minutes, and the acts booked most frequently weren't hired more than once a month, an interval presumably long enough for the creation of a few more minutes of tap.

Peg Leg Bates claimed that he performed on the Ed Sullivan Show nineteen (or sometimes twenty-two) times between 1951 and 1960—an impressive total but still less than twice a year. His act looked terrific on the small screen: the dapper man with one leg, tapping out rhythms as swinging as any man with two; the supposedly disabled man with the quiet confidence, turning his own rhythmic clapping into a prompt for applause; the man with a peg leg finishing big with his version of trenches—diving forward and leaping onto his good leg, his peg, his good leg, his peg, hopping backward on his peg with the good leg pointing the way. No wonder Sullivan kept asking him back to do essentially the same thing.

Early television differed from film in another key sense: the variety shows were broadcast live. No retakes, no spliced-together numbers, no dubbing. Good, then, to hire an improviser like Hal LeRoy, who could just get in front of the camera and go. And if Ed Sullivan wanted him to dance with Peg Leg Bates, as happened several times on *Toast of the Town* in the mid-fifties, the two hoofers could, without rehearsal, face off in a challenge and finish with the Shim Sham, and that lazy formula could produce something as wonderful as LeRoy tauntingly quoting one of Bates's steps, only to have Bates vanquish him with a flying stunt that no two-legged man could replicate. Early TV transmitted some of the risks and rewards of live theater, and it was almost as ephemeral—sound and image sent out over airwaves or along cables to die with the signal. Before videotape was introduced in 1956, the only way to preserve a live broadcast was in the form of a kinescope, a film made by pointing a camera at a television monitor. The primary reason that television stations made kinescopes of their broadcasts was in order to broadcast them later in a different time zone. Most were then discarded. Yet it is in the form of kinescopes (since converted to videotape or digitized) that the performances of many tap dancers survive. Since Bates didn't make any movies, the kinescopes of him are our only record of the great dancer in his prime.

From the beginning, there were technical problems. Fred Kelly, brother of Gene, remembered directing *The Steve Allen Show* around 1951: "I used more tap dancers in six months' time than have played in the entire history of the Palace." But then, he recalled, the soundmen insisted on hiring an extra guy to mike the taps, and the sound engineer said he would need an extra man to balance the tap mikes, and the executives put a stop to this by issuing a directive banning tap dancers on CBS. Tap dancers did appear on CBS again, but the anecdote reveals how tap could cause hassles. The most common snag was sound. Louis DaPron, the former movie choreographer, found work on TV and would remember having prerecorded all the taps, often himself. On television, too, the eye saw Donald O'Connor while the ear heard Louis DaPron.

Still, in the early days, you might tune in to O'Connor's former Jivin' Jill partner Peggy Ryan and her squeaky clean husband, Ray McDonald; they were on *Texaco Star Theater* every six months or so. Or the Dunhills, the dopey white trio in the black mode; they were on *Texaco* a couple of times a year. On *Toast of the Town* in the mid-fifties, you might meet Joan Holloway, button-nose adorable, introduced by Ed Sullivan as "little Joan" though she was over twenty. In extant footage, she taps quickly, cleanly, her poise interrupted by appealingly odd spasms of over-excitement. Bubbles-style toe clicks, heel drops, and rhythm turns in pumps abut high kicks, backbends, and whirls in the mode of Eleanor Powell. Her five-minute act starts at an amble, eases into a lullaby, and finishes allegro, with an impressive a cappella cadenza and pirouettes with one extended leg raising her skirt.

Holloway's charm was idiosyncratic, but the form of her act was common: the trite music arranged into a progression of tempi, the tricks cut and pasted from ballet. It was the style shared by Betty Bruce, a dancer with some ballet training who had won high praise as a Broadway tapper in the early forties and was enough of a celebrity to have a brand of taps named after her. By the fifties, tap was in short supply on Broadway, but Bruce appeared regularly on TV variety shows, tapping like a bushy-tailed bunny, and her sort of act hadn't yet disappeared from nightclubs. A 1955 article in *The Chicago Defender* went so far as to suggest that "Ofay Femmes"—white women—were taking over tap. One ofay femme, Billie Mahoney, would remember instead that "tap dance in the fifties was a white man's game," dominated by Paul Draper and other exponents of ballet-tap. ("The 'colored' tap acts looked all the same," she wrote in 1995.) Mahoney, who had studied ballet and modern dance, soon dropped her baton-twirling tap and converted to the new style they were calling "modern jazz." As for Holloway, there's little evidence of a career outside the circuit of TV variety shows. She tapped for *Toast of the Town* and its massive audience because Ed was fond of little Joan.

Dean Martin and Jerry Lewis, frequent hosts of *The Colgate Comedy Hour*, were partial to Ray Malone, a gawky kid in a bow tie who sometimes joked around with Dean and Jerry in a challenge dance. More often, Malone's high-energy dancing was engulfed in productions with backup dancers, flimsy scts, and flimsier scenarios. His unkempt style was more spin than sound, though appearances can deceive. As part of the regular cast of the daily late-night variety show *Broadway Open House* (1950–51), Malone tapped, sang, played the bongos, and squealed in skits. One night, Charlie Parker was on, and in the audio that remains, Parker and Malone trade fours and—surprise—the nebbishy hoofer holds up his end. In 1956, Malone tapped on a record with Moondog, a blind musician who performed on New York streets in a Viking helmet and would influence the minimalist composers Steve Reich and Philip Glass. On the track, which you might confuse with a field recording of African drumming, you could mistake the tapper for Baby Laurence.

Malone hadn't made much of an impression in his two movie cameos in the early forties. TV gave him a second chance. For others, an appearance on *Toast of the Town* or *Texaco Star Theater* was the fifties equivalent of playing the Palace. It stamped a performer with prestige. But where an appearance at the Palace had almost guaranteed more bookings, television was luring audiences away from the places where tap dancers made a living. Though chorus girls could earn more money per week on a TV program than they did in a Broadway show, Cholly Atkins remembered that the top fee for an act like Coles and Atkins was $150 an episode—which, after the agent's cut, bought some groceries. Fifty was more common. At best, TV could serve as a temporary refuge, and only for a few.

Paul Draper was not one of them. The footage of him on *Toast of the Town* suggests that television wasn't his ideal medium any more than movie musicals were. Buttoned up in a three-piece suit, Draper flits about with his pseudo-ballet to the jazz played by his black accompanist. As he invites the audience to sing along with "Pop Goes the Weasel" and "Turkey in the Straw," he sounds as if he were about to cry. I'm with Ed Sullivan in preferring Joan Holloway to this patrician populism, but the differences between Holloway and Draper weren't just aesthetic. Draper appeared on *Toast of the Town* in January 1950, in the midst of his defamation trial and public redbaiting. CBS and the show's sponsor, Ford Motor Company, were barraged with letters and telegrams protesting the broadcast of a Communist sympathizer. Under front-page headlines, Hearst papers demanded that Ford drop Sullivan. Draper wasn't booked on any more TV shows. *Toast of the Town* was his only paying performance that year.

TV tap was seldom so controversial. Not even around race. Milton Berle, in his autobiography, recalls when his sponsor objected to the Four Step Brothers. "If they don't go on, I don't go on," Berle replied in the early flush of his popularity, and the Four Step Brothers went on. Likewise, Ed Sullivan regularly scheduled black artists, and when Lincoln-Mercury dealers in Southern cities objected, he convinced Lincoln-Mercury not to worry. These actions took courage, yet despite persistent fears about the Southern market, a few black entertainers did not make for an especially threatening image. On *Toast of the Town*, black boxers tapped. Sugar Ray Robinson, the recently retired welterweight and middleweight champion, hoofed well and sang poorly, promoting his second career as a nightclub entertainer. Joe Louis, the former heavy-weight champion, a national hero, lumbered gently through the Joe Louis Shuffle, a variation on the Shim Sham that was part of his comedy act with Leonard Reed. A tap-dancing black boxer looked as dangerous as a tap-dancing bear.

Tap on TV was what the sixteen ladies known as the June Taylor Dancers did, in between the kick lines and the Berkeleyesque overhead shots, in the numbers that opened and closed every episode of *The Jackie Gleason Show*. Tap was how the female legs protruding from the bottom of human-sized packs of Old Gold cigarettes advertised product. Tap was what most TV hosts could do, Gleason topping off his heavy-man's soft shoe with a pratfall, Berle taking a jocular turn in a Four Step Brothers challenge. Tap was a skill demonstrated on *The Mickey Mouse Club* by talented teenaged girls.

And tap was what an otherwise forgotten duo named Conn and Mann did on the night in 1956 that sixty million people tuned in to *The Ed Sullivan Show* for the first appearance of Elvis Presley. Conn and Mann's act wasn't quite the corny vaudeville bit that would make for a simple symbol of what rock and roll shoved aside. Though Conn and Mann did dance to that twenties chestnut "Tea for Two," they did it as a half-realized satire of how a British team might handle the song. Their soigné nightclub routine with modern tap earned polite applause and chuckles. Elvis was sheepish and incited hysterical screams. The Southern white boy with undeniable sex appeal, goofing around with juke-joint music and snakehips—this was a new wave of minstrelsy. But where in the 1840s minstrels could signal rebellion with the Vir-ginny breakdown, in 1956, tap dancing wasn't going to upset anyone's parents.

A generational gap was spreading, but you couldn't necessarily see the fault line on television. For decades, rock acts shared variety programs with vaudevillians. Through the late fifties and into the sixties, Ed Sullivan continued to hire hoofers. He was especially keen on Conrad Buckner, a black dancer from Kansas City who was younger than Chuck

Berry and went by the name of Little Buck. More skilled than smooth, Buckner tapped to studio-orchestra jazz, and he wasn't averse to rumpling his tuxedo with a mess of acrobatics. Critics remarked upon his "indestructible constitution" and "terrifying vitality." (Bunny Briggs recalled that it was after Briggs had asked Sullivan not to say "Get hot" while he was dancing that he stopped appearing on the show and Little Buck started.) When Sullivan took a troupe of performers to the Soviet Union in 1959, he brought along Little Buck as a representative of American freedom.

Five years later, the Beatles debuted on Sullivan's program, changing everything. Two months after that, Little Buck was back, challenge-dancing with Peg Leg Bates. When the Rolling Stones first appeared, that same year, the bad boys of the British Invasion were surrounded by acrobats, Itzhak Perlman, Phyllis Diller, and Peg Leg Bates. All through the sixties, John Bubbles, who hadn't performed much since the death of Buck in 1955, reemerged as an old-timer. On *American Musical Theater* in 1961, he did imitations of Harland Dixon, Pat Rooney, and Bill Robinson, and then he showed his own style. He tapped and sang on the shows of Perry Como, Jack Paar, Steve Allen, Jerry Lewis, Dean Martin, and Bob Hope. Sometimes he came with his partner of those years, the twenty-something Italian singer Anna Maria Alberghetti. Evidently, producers found nothing controversial in an aging black man and a nubile white woman stepping in tandem to "Me and My Shadow." Bob Hope brought Bubbles along on USO tours to Vietnam, and during a 1964 Christmas show before an integrated audience of servicemen, Bubbles, the only black on the program, asked Hope if he was in favor of integration. Hope answered in the affirmative, so Bubbles said, "Kiss me."

Bubbles and Alberghetti also tapped on *Hollywood Palace*, a popular variety series that ran from 1964 to 1970. It was on *Hollywood Palace* in July 1964 that the Nicholas Brothers reunited after a seven-year separation during which Harold had lived in Paris. In Europe, he had been received as a singer, an actor, a multilingual ambassador of America like Josephine Baker, with whom he performed. On *Hollywood Palace*, the brothers mounted and descended a huge staircase, leapfrogging each other into splits. Their subsequent television appearances were in this mode— re-creations of their famous routines, refurbished in polyester suits and wider lapels. Bob Hope took them on a USO tour of Asia, milking whatever comedy was left in the contrast between their speedy turns and his slow, foolish soft shoe. All veterans of the *Ziegfeld Follies of 1936*, the three men did the Shim Sham together in Guam.

And then there was *The Lawrence Welk Show*. Loyal, aging fans of the North Dakotan accordion player's "champagne music" kept the program on the air for nearly thirty years. Among the show's regulars were Jack Imel, who could tap while playing the marimba, and Bobby Burgess, a tapping former Mouseketeer. Starting in 1964, the "musical family" also included one dark face. Arthur Duncan was a thirty-year-old song-and-dance man from Pasadena who had studied with Willie Covan and Nick Castle. He considered Castle's influence to be greater, summed up in the advice, "Do something that people can understand." His tapping, always adept, rarely inspired, generally followed a standard recipe of solid rhythm and big finishes, yet the variety of steps was impressive; stealing from many sources, he rarely repeated himself. He was not a relaxed dancer. His forearms tended to swing stiffly from the elbow, like parallel drawbridges going up and down, and on a show sponsored by Geritol, his demeanor was old-time, calculated to please old-timers. Though a hint of sarcasm might occasionally escape, the look on his face was strained, wavering between smarmy and scared, the smile of a man concerned about the pistol sticking into his back.

"I didn't take chances," Duncan told me. So that the band wouldn't drown him out, he prerecorded his taps—a technique that solved the sound-balance problem at the price of spontaneity. "It locked me in a situation where I couldn't experiment," he said. But the situation Duncan was locked in wasn't just the dubbing process. It was *The Lawrence Welk Show*. And it was being the only black guy on *The Lawrence Welk Show*. When Welk introduced Duncan as "the young man who is keeping tap dancing alive," the epithet was based in fact. For nearly twenty years, the decades in which the art was dormant, Arthur Duncan tapped on television once a week, giving the art its most regular exposure in that era. Yet because he did so on *The Lawrence Welk Show*, he kept tap alive at the cost of associating it with the nearly dead.

———

Movie studios were at first dismissive of television, then wary, barring their employees from the rival medium just as vaudeville managers had barred theirs from the movies. The strategy was no less futile. Ray Bolger moved over in 1953, starring in his own TV show. Donald O'Connor danced often as one of the rotating hosts of *The Colgate Comedy Hour.* Soon, the practice of a movie star plugging a new film on TV became a common form of free publicity, and it was in that guise that Fred Astaire first sang and danced on *Toast of the Town.*

In 1958, he tried something more ambitious: an hour-long special called *An Evening with Fred Astaire.* It was a typical Astaire product, meticulously rehearsed. Videotaped in color (a technical breakthrough), it won nine Emmy awards and critical raves. (Jack Gould, in the *Times,* wrote that Astaire had "done more for the cause of dancing on television than anyone else in the first decade of TV.") It captured the fifty-nine-year-old star in good shape, but his young and competent partner, Barrie Chase, was not a tap dancer, the chorus dancers did not tap, and Astaire barely tapped himself. The dance numbers were choreographed by Hermes Pan in a modern-jazz style that would not date well, and the cleverest routine was retrospective, a mimed compendium of Astaire's prop-dance solos. The follow-ups *Another Evening with Fred Astaire* (1959) and *Astaire Time* (1960) did not advance the cause of tap on television, either, even though the last one had Count Basie. The swingingest band around inspired only some pantomime from the aging master of broken rhythm. Mid-sixties appearances on *Hollywood Palace*—Astaire cutely stumbling through "Top Hat" with go-go dancers, trying to explain the definition of "camp," silently applying old steps to Jimmy Smith's soul-jazz organ—told the same message: his tapping days were behind him.

Gene Kelly made TV specials, too. His most ambitious was a 1958 episode of the educational program *Omnibus* called "Dancing: A Man's Game." An elaborate defense against Kelly's childhood fear of being seen as a sissy, the program was packed with smug reminders that the male is dominant and that even though a man is stronger and capable of more intricate steps, women can do a few things better, such as bear children and sing soprano. Another target: men who "confuse beauty of movement with effeminacy of movement" and thus provide "the prime reason that men don't go into dance." As obnoxious as the message was, the means were brilliant. Kelly took America's most beloved sports stars and their motions—Johnny Unitas hiking a football, Mickey Mantle sliding into base—and forged them into a routine. He taught a macho version of dance history, did buck-and-wing with Sugar Ray Robinson, and danced a history of tap.

Tap, Kelly explained, is "like America itself," "a real melting pot of the folk dances of several countries." He talked about the Irish and their sporting-event dance contests, and though he didn't mention Africa, he did discuss the American Negro in the South dancing to blues. When Kelly described how clog dancers adapted their steps to Negro music and learned to relax, he demonstrated the process, acting out a strikingly persuasive account of the stages by which a clog step could become the Shim Sham. Yet the most important development, Kelly insisted, was the emergence of musical comedy: "Now the dancer must play a dramatic role, not be a specialty act." How, for example, would a truck driver from Pittsburgh dance? The answer was implicit. Gene Kelly's history of tap culminated in Gene Kelly.

Tap-dancing movie stars appeared on TV in one more form: in their old movies. In TV's early years, only minor film studios such as Republic, maker of all of those Ann Miller Bs, would license their back catalogues. By the mid-fifties, however, the big studios had decided to sell or rent to TV, realizing that such deals were almost pure profit. Programs like *Million Dollar Movie* (sixteen telecasts per week of the same film), *The Early Show*, *The Late Show*, and *The Late, Late Show* began to proliferate. On them, many of the musicals of the thirties and forties could be seen—chopped to fit schedules, interrupted by commercials, and often censored, but seen, over and over, in the homes of millions: a continual reminder, among other things, of what tap had once been.

SUNNIER CLIMES AND IN-BETWEEN PLACES

Eleanor Powell had her own early-fifties television show. It was called *Faith of Our Children*, and it was electronic Sunday school. She had not given up dancing. On a 1952 episode of *All Star Revue*, she tapped, as a woman of forty, almost exactly as she had tapped as a twentysomething—more cleanly, in fact, without the acrobatics. Seven years later, she got a divorce, went on a diet, lost thirty-five pounds practicing six hours a day, and made a comeback as a nightclub act. In footage from *Perry Como's Kraft Music Hall* in 1962, she's still at the top of her game, her style adamant against the passage of time. (When she appeared on *The Tonight Show* the following year, John Bubbles popped out of the studio audience and engaged her in a friendly challenge dance.) For sixty-five of her stage act's hundred minutes, Powell tapped, sometimes dancing along with scenes from her movies to demonstrate dubbing. She brought along a staircase to honor Bill Robinson and also her own maple floor. An adequate surface was something a tap dancer could no longer take for granted.

Powell jumped back in and right back out, retiring for good in 1964. But before that, she played some of the prime remaining spots: the Latin Quarter in New York, the Diplomat in Miami. For her debut, she chose the place where the idea for a comeback had suggested itself, the place where it seemed possible, the new capital of nightclub entertainment: Las Vegas. The resort destination in the Nevada desert had been growing fast, dominated by the mafia. Legal gambling was at once a perfect front and an economic motor. The entertainment on offer was a lure, not a profit center, so admission could stay cheap. The casinos could afford to bring in the big names and advertise them in enormous letters on the enormous, bright signs attracting customers to the gambling tables and slot machines. Occasionally, the name would be that of a tap dancer, Ray Bolger or Donald O'Connor or even the Nicholas Brothers, former movie stars who did more than hoof. In the Nicholas Brothers' act, Fayard would do dance impressions of Astaire, Bolger, Powell, Robinson, and Kelly, and then go into a split and say, "Who's that? That's me."

But the names of tap dancers were more likely to appear at the bottom of those signs and in smaller letters. Most often, the small letters spelled out the Four Step Brothers. That band of hoofers had a reputation as the World's Best Opening Act. One time, in 1952, at the Lido in Paris, they were headliners; in America, they were the headliners' choice. Jerry Lewis and Dean Martin, Tony Bennett, Sinatra—all the top acts wanted the brothers in their show. Watch any of their many appearances on *The Colgate Comedy Hour* in the early fifties, and you can see what good sports "the boys" were, doing their solos, then cheering on Dino as he imitated a few of their moves (surprisingly well) and Jerry as he made a mockery of them. On *The Dean Martin Show* in the mid-sixties, the guys did the same thing in color: the same solos, even as their eldest member, Maceo Anderson, lost power and leaned more on his face-filling grin. The four men could be counted on to get an audience excited, but not to be too funny or sing too well.

And so, as tap became a hobby for many of their colleagues, the team kept working, forty weeks a year. "It didn't bother us not to be headliners," Prince Spencer told me. "We tried once and thirty-five people came." Though the Step Brothers had been in the movies and though they appeared on TV more frequently than any other tap act, they weren't the kind of celebrities who could draw an audience by themselves. Truth be told, they probably couldn't sustain an entire show on their own. Yet the pigmentation of their skin was not irrelevant. "They said colored people had a place," Spencer explained. "We accepted what it was. We'd go onstage and set it on fire."

As an opening act, the Step Brothers opened doors. In the forties and fifties, Vegas might have reminded Anderson of the Cotton Club, and not just because of the mobsters. Blacks were welcome onstage but not in the audience. Black entertainers could not stay in the hotel, gamble in the casino, or eat in the restaurants. After doing their act, they were expected to withdraw to the black side of town, where the janitors and maids lived, to sleep in rooming houses that charged three times as much as the white hotels. In the early forties, Lena Horne and Pearl Bailey had sometimes been allowed to stay where they were performing (though, the story goes, their bedsheets were burned after they left). The tighter restrictions came in with postwar prosperity and an anxiety about upsetting high rollers from the South. For the four months it was open in 1955, the interracial Moulin Rouge casino, where Sinatra and Hollywood celebrities jammed with jazz greats after hours and Teddy Hale was implicated in Wardell Gray's death, represented an opening. When policies began to change on the Strip, it was usually because a white headliner, Jerry Lewis or Sinatra, was shocked to find his opening

act, the Four Step Brothers, eating in their dressing room, and threatened to cancel the show unless his guys were invited into the restaurant.
These kinds of gestures had to be made repeatedly. It wasn't until 1960
that the NAACP and the threat of sit-ins convinced publicity-conscious
casino managers to allow blacks as customers. The Four Step Brothers
led the way. Or perhaps more accurately, they were pushed in front.

Vegas may have been called the Mississippi of the West by some, but
Miami was actually in the South. As Vegas was on the rise, Miami was
still the most popular winter resort destination in the country, and its
hotels and nightclubs all provided live entertainment, which still sometimes included tap. Around 1950, when Dean Martin and Jerry Lewis
were the highest-paid nightclub act in the country, they played Copa
City, Miami's top cabaret, and insisted on bringing the Four Step
Brothers with them, even though blacks had never been allowed to perform in the venue before. Prince Spencer remembered a sign in Miami
that read "No Jews, No Niggers, No Dogs." He recalled riding on the
floor of Lewis's limo because of the curfews that banned blacks from
Miami Beach at night. Black entertainers carried IDs indicating permission from the police department, and they slept in the black section of
town and did late shows in the area's black clubs. In the sixties, sit-ins
and political action would force the gradual integration of Miami, too,
but for a long time, the Four Step Brothers and other black entertainers
inhabited an in-between place, both privileged and exposed.

The situation was similar on the Borscht Belt, the thriving colony of
Jewish resorts in New York's Catskill Mountains. In the forties, Peg Leg
Bates and Buck and Bubbles had been among the well-known acts to
perform at the large hotels. Honi Coles and Bunny Briggs learned a
lot of Yiddish. But blacks in general were not welcome to stay. Jewish
Americans, excluded from gentile establishments, had built establishments of their own, excluding whom they wished. In 1951, Bates followed their example, in part, converting a Catskills turkey farm into the
Peg Leg Bates Country Club. From a four-room house, it grew into a
150-room complex with swimming pools and tennis courts. Unlike the
Jewish resorts it was modeled on, Bates's club was an integrated institution from the start. Whites frequented the nightclub to watch performances by the owner's famous friends, though almost none of them chose

to stay overnight. Blacks came by the busload, until they were welcome elsewhere and the club became one of many unintended casualties of integration.

THE KID IN THE MIDDLE

Again, there was an exception. A black tap dancer who was a headliner, a hoofer who was a star. On the signs in front of Vegas casinos, his name beckoned in the largest letters available: Sammy Davis, Jr. Born in 1925 to a Harlem chorus girl, he grew up on the road, touring TOBA theaters and small-time vaudeville with his father, Sammy Davis. With them was Will Mastin, a strut dancer of Bill Robinson's generation who held together his own road show, a tough operator whom little Sammy learned to call Uncle. Mother left the picture very early. The younger Sammy was a preternatural mimic, an extraordinary stealer of steps and voices. Often, his face was corked in homage to Al Jolson and in hope of fooling child protection societies. You can see that Sammy Davis, Jr., in the 1932 all-black short *Rufus Jones for President*. He plays the title character, a boy who dreams that he gets elected president of the United States—a nation that, in this case, is a coon-song republic where voters are offered two pork chops for each vote and senators are required to check their razors at the door. The seven-year-old Davis transcends all that, putting most adults to shame as he slides all over his rendition of "I'll Be Glad When You're Dead, You Rascal You," knocks out time steps with Robinsonian flair, and sticks tiptoe stands like the Nicholas Brothers.

Little Sammy didn't make it to Hollywood, though, or even to the Cotton Club. He stayed in vaudeville as vaudeville died. The Will Mastin Gang shrunk to the Will Mastin Trio, a flash act with Sammy as the kid in the middle. Gaining in power as the men flanking him aged and tired, he radiated so much energy that it could seem that he was siphoning it from his elders. The impression that he was carrying them was nearly the physical truth. From Mastin, the boy learned a performer's code: Leave your troubles in the wings, always come on smiling. Constantly pestering other performers to show him a step, he sopped up everything, Bojangles to Bubbles and beyond. But it wasn't until 1941, when the Trio filled in for Tip, Tap, and Toe as the opening act for Tommy Dorsey, that Davis met the man he most wanted to emulate: the vocalist with the band, the one the girls were swooning over. In Frank Sinatra, Davis found a buddy, a brother, a booster, and a role model for life.

Growing up in the sheltering culture of show people, Davis seems to have had little exposure to the contempt his skin color could inspire. That shelter did not accompany him into the army. His performances in the camp variety shows attracted attention both admiring and resentful. As Davis describes his basic training in his bestselling 1965 autobiography *Yes, I Can!*, it was one long fistfight. (The Davis biographer Gary Fishgall isn't alone in questioning the likelihood of such constant racial violence in a still-segregated army.) One story he tells has archetypal force. A gang of white trainees, unappreciative of Davis's friendliness toward a white member of the Women's Army Corps, lures him into a latrine, where they paint the words *Nigger* and *Coon* on his chest and forehead. Then they force him to dance, driving his tempo with punches to the gut, shoving him metaphorically back up onto the plantation platform, making him shuffle on the auction block. And yet the lesson that Davis took away from his army experience and the reaction to his performing was that talent could give him "a pass" from prejudice, or should.

"I've got to have them *pulling* for me," Davis would say in a 1966 *Playboy* interview. "I wanted them feeling, 'Oh, God, if he doesn't make it, he might run off and cut his wrists.'" That desperation jumps out from the 1947 musical short *Sweet and Low*. The older two-thirds of the Will Mastin Trio are dapper and dull; even while executing their specialty flash steps, they seem to recede into the background. Twenty-two-year-old Sammy is a dynamo, crossing his legs in corkscrewing squat-kicks and crossing his eyes, too. Davis was now incorporating impressions of celebrities that made his partners nervous—not just Nat King Cole and Louis Armstrong, but Cagney, Bogart, Cary Grant, white celebrities whose idiosyncrasies he exaggerated with mocking accuracy. To Mastin's surprise, white audiences loved it. Davis would do a whole song of impressions, rotating through his repertory of voices on successive choruses, and then he would say, "This is me," and finish the song in his "own" voice, sounding like an imitation of himself. He spoke with careful diction that could seem strained, periodically dropping into the black vernacular for comic effect. The way that he twisted his jaw to get at the sounds for his impressions eventually hardened into an affectation that made for an easy impersonation of Sammy Davis, Jr.

Bookings for the Will Mastin Trio, Featuring Sammy Davis, Jr., improved: opening spots for Mickey Rooney and Sinatra, both of whom encouraged Sammy to sing more and do more impressions. He started making records (as a singer, though on the 1949 Capitol recording "Smile, Darn You, Smile" he taps out a modern-style chorus). The turning point came in 1951, when the trio opened for the B-movie actress Janis Paige at Ciro's, the toniest nightclub in Los Angeles. By the second night, Janis Paige was opening for the trio. Davis hadn't only broken out of the opening act slot; he had broken into a citadel of white privilege. In Miami, he still had to sleep on the dark side of town, but when he returned to Vegas, the Last Frontier put him in the best suite and gave him the run of the resort. He had a pass.

The asking price of the Will Mastin Trio, Starring Sammy Davis, Jr., doubled and quadrupled. The act was invited onto *Toast of the Town* and *The Colgate Comedy Hour* with Eddie Cantor, whose hospitable dabbing of Davis's brow inspired hate mail. (Cantor responded by booking the trio for three additional episodes.) But it meant more to Davis when the trio headlined at New York's Copacabana, probably the foremost nightclub in the country. He had always wanted to get in. A Broadway musical carried similar significance for him, and though *Mr. Wonderful*, written for Davis, was little more than a package for his nightclub routine, it was a Broadway show, and Davis made it a hit by sheer effort. He had hit records, too. He was all over television, in sitcoms and dramas and westerns. He made it into all-black movies: as a streetwise sailor in *Anna Lucasta* (1958) and as Sportin' Life in *Porgy and Bess* (1959), slinky and sinister in John Bubbles's role. *Ocean's Eleven*, released the next year, did not have an all-black cast. Davis was now a member of the Rat Pack, a public pal of Sinatra and Dean Martin, a quintessential Vegas hipster: hard-drinking, cigarette-smoking, philandering, adult. Everyone, it seemed in those days, wanted to be Frank or at least to be with him, and there was

Sammy at his side, doubling over in laughter at the race jokes ("Smile, Sammy, so the folks can see you") and trying his best not to upstage the Chairman of the Board. The pass had a price.

In the mid-sixties, Sammy Davis, Jr., was arguably the most famous black man in America, up there with Martin Luther King, Jr., and Muhammad Ali. He was certainly one of the two or three highest-paid. The whole country knew about the car crash in which he lost an eye, about his conversion to Judaism, about his marriage to the Swedish actress and blond goddess May Britt. Transitively, he was the most famous black tap dancer in America. Hoofing had become a small part of his act—what with the singing, the wisecracking, the drum playing, the gun twirling—but his tap shoes were always under the piano, to be worn when the mood struck him. He inserted a little tap in his next Broadway show, *Golden Boy* (1964), though few noticed it amid the controversy about an interracial kiss. His Astaire-inspired, bust-up-the-bar number in the Rat Pack gangster flick *Robin and the Seven Hoods* (1964) was more gunplay than footwork, but when Count Basie appeared on the single-season *Sammy Davis Jr. Show*, in 1966, Davis asked for some "buck dance music," hopped on the piano, and took two minutes to remind America how tap could be jazz.

And in 1967, on one of the many episodes of *Hollywood Palace* that Davis hosted, in addition to singing and dancing with the Supremes, after making an awkward joke about the white drummer not being born with rhythm, he humbly brought on "the greatest tap dancer in the world," Baby Laurence—"to prove," in Davis's words, "that tap dancing is not a lost art." In the footage, the earliest extant of the Babe, Laurence proves that *he* hasn't lost it. In his mid-forties, with gray in his hair, he's effortlessly cool in coat and tie, which isn't to say that he's without ardor or bite; speed that would impress anyone conceals subtleties to astound a connoisseur. His benefactor in the Nehru jacket is not effortless, and though Davis holds up his end of a challenge dance for a while, Laurence keeps turning up the heat until Davis has to avert a rout with a comic surrender. Davis's tapping was like his singing: expert, dazzling in flourishes, but never quite achieving the singular authority of a great artist. He wasn't Baby Laurence the way he wasn't Sinatra.

From the seventies on, one of Davis's signature songs was "Mr.

Bojangles," a tale of a down-and-out hoofer that had nothing to do with Bill Robinson and everything to do with Davis's fears of where he could always end up. Back in the first bloom of his crossover success, when an interviewer called him "the most exciting Negro performer to come along since Bill Robinson," the young man objected. The comparison was all wrong, he said. He danced in a different style and did all kinds of things that Robinson did not. But the objection went deeper. Davis wasn't content to be considered the greatest Negro performer. In his naïve, driven, self-serving, and courageous way, he lived his life as if skin color didn't matter, naked in his desire to be accepted by the white world, bold in his rejection of the idea that colored people had a place. There were some who called him the World's Greatest Entertainer, yet to many blacks, he was a sellout who wanted to be white, and despite his philanthropy and his marching at Selma, they booed him for many of the same reasons that Bojangles had been heckled. (Marrying a white woman was one thing, but hugging Richard Nixon—who courted where the Kennedys had snubbed—was an unforgivable sin.) To a younger generation, across racial lines, he became a joke, an embodiment of the worst of showbiz unctuousness, weighed down by too much jewelry, trying much too hard to stay hip—out of synch with the present, like the hoofer's art he was born into.

THROUGH THE GRAPEVINE

Even at the Apollo, the place that so many tap dancers had considered home, they were pushed aside. In the fifties, as the popularity of rhythm and blues and rock and roll exploded, Bobby Schiffman, who was inheriting the theater from his father, realized that "people weren't coming to see the tap dancer and other acts. They were coming to see the vocal act that had the hit record that was being played on the radio." So instead of the variety shows that the Apollo had always presented, young Schiffman began packaging "R&B revues," as many as a dozen R&B groups on a single bill, one after the other. Leonard Reed, then the theater's production manager, didn't approve, but he couldn't argue with full houses. When Reed tried to slip Foster Johnson, a distinguished tap dancer, into one of the revues, Johnson got booed off the stage. By the mid-fifties, the R&B revue was the dominant mode at the Apollo, and tap dancers were few and far between.

One of the rare ones was Bobby Ephram, a young hoofer out of Chicago who idolized Teddy Hale. When Ephram first appeared at the Apollo in 1951, the management (which kept track of its opinions on index cards) considered him "a good opening act," and in 1953, "a very good opening act." In 1956, he was a "better than usual single tap dancer," and in 1960, he was still "worth playing." 1963: "Hasn't changed anything. Still does nice job." 1964: "Usual good job. Nothing new." That same year, the thirty-year-old Ephram assured the *Amsterdam News* that "tap may be a vanishing art but it will not die. I will not let it die." He complained that agents who could get a cut of a singer's $5,000 per week weren't interested in booking a tap dancer for $500. Doing his usual good job, he eked a career in Miami and Atlantic City.

While on tour in Australia, Ephram recorded an album, but his tapping got no airplay back home. Disc jockeys, the career-makers of the day, paid no attention to tap. But many tap dancers themselves refused to keep up. Accustomed to Count Basie or Charlie Parker, they found the currently popular music simplistic, lacking rhythms they could imagine playing their rhythms against. And except for Frankie Lymon, the pubescent lead singer of "Why Do Fools Fall in Love," who studied with Pete Nugent, almost none of the kids with hit records were interested in learning to hoof.

Even if tap dancers had wanted to join in with the Drifters, and even if they had been welcome, a perplexing technical obstacle stood in their way. Instruments went electric, singers crooned into microphones, but no one seemed to understand how to amplify the sound of a tap dancer effectively. For sound balance, an engineer needs to isolate the signals of individual sound-making devices, and the tap dancer's instruments— transient soles and the stage floor—were relatively difficult to isolate. With tap out of fashion, there was little incentive to work out a solution, and so the problem became yet another reason not to hire a hoofer.

Nevertheless, in the R&B revues, tap could, in a sense, still be seen. In 1960, Honi Coles and Cholly Atkins retired as a duo, putting on their tap shoes only a few times a year for special appearances with old friends

like Billy Eckstine. Coles succeeded Leonard Reed as the Apollo's production manager. The teenagers in the R&B revues appalled him. Flush
with cash and suddenly famous, the kids were entirely ignorant of the
theatrical traditions Coles held dear. Worse, they didn't care. He would
offer to teach them a few basics, like how to bow, and they would ask
him what his hit record was. He began spending more time at the bar
down the block. Meanwhile, Cholly Atkins had built a reputation as a
choreographer, someone the managers of the new vocal groups could
hire to give the kids some polish and make their re-creations of their
records worth watching. Atkins would meet with the Moonglows, the
Cleftones, the Bowties—then the Crystals, the Chantels, the Shirelles—
and give them some easy moves to go with their singing, sometimes elementary tap steps in regular shoes.

In this way, Gladys Knight and the Pips became a kind of class act
without taps, smoothly gliding through routines descended from the
Coles and Atkins soft shoe. Their synchronized finesse attracted attention, and in 1965, Atkins was hired by Motown Records as the resident
choreographer for its Artist Development program, an essential tool in
the Detroit music factory's astonishingly successful strategy for crossing
over into the white market. Smokey Robinson and the Miracles, Martha
and the Vandellas, Marvin Gaye—they all came under Atkins's tutelage. When grooming the Supremes or the Temptations for the Copacabana, Atkins might teach them something nostalgic, like a hat-and-cane
number to "Rock-a-Bye Your Baby with a Dixie Melody." But it was
what Atkins called "vocal choreography," his dances for singers, that had
the greatest influence. At concerts or through *American Bandstand*, millions of teenagers fixed upon the minimal steps—copied them, made
their own variations, kept them in circulation. Jazz dancing continued,
in R&B clothing. Tap remained muffled.

13

CONTINUATION

A HOOFERS' CLUB

In 1949, on their way home from filing past Bill Robinson's body, a few tap dancers gathered in the apartment of Luther and Lucille Preston, the husband-and-wife tap act known as Slim and Sweets. The comedy team of Leroy Myers and James "Chuckles" Walker was present, as was Charles "Cookie" Cook. Since the men enjoyed each other's company, Lucille suggested they form a club. For a name, a bartender called Youngblood suggested one of Bill Robinson's pet words, a word he claimed to have coined, though others insisted it was a common expression in the South. When someone would ask Robinson how he felt, he would say, "Everything is copasetic," meaning fine and dandy. In his honor, the Hoofers' Club was reborn as a formal association, a fraternity called the Copasetics.

The group took on more members, soon expanding to twenty-one. Cook's partner joined, the four-foot-ten-inch Ernest "Brownie" Brown, along with Peg Leg Bates and Cholly Atkins and the filthy-mouthed class act Pete Nugent. Honi Coles was elected president. The club wasn't

for dancers only; select musician friends were invited to join: Billy Eckstine, Dizzy Gillespie. Billy Strayhorn, Duke Ellington's right-hand
man, succeeded Coles as chief executive, holding the position until
1967, when he died and the office was retired. Every Sunday the members met, rotating from apartment to apartment. They followed orga-
nizational protocol, establishing subcommittees, taking minutes, and
drafting a charter, which read:

> The Copasetics is a social, friendly benevolent club. Its members pledge
> themselves to do all in their power to promote fellowship and to strengthen
> character within their ranks. With these thoughts ever foremost in our
> minds, it should be our every desire to create only impressions that will
> establish us in all walks of life as a group of decent, respectable men.
> Bearing in mind that these achievements can only become reality by
> first seeking the aid of God.

It was an Elks Lodge where the meetings might end in a cutting contest.
"We communicated with our bodies," Honi Coles told the Strayhorn
biographer David Hajdu. "If we were celebrating, if we were debating,
if we were fighting, we did it in dance." Instead of collecting dues, the
treasurer passed around a hat to cover expenses; excess funds went to
whoever needed help with the rent or with a doctor's bill, be that a fellow member or just a friend. The club was in the tradition of African-
American mutual aid societies, and it was also a group of drinking
buddies. "We had great times," recalled Buster Brown. "That's what we
did mostly, laugh."

On a Monday each September, the Copasetics put on a show for
charity. Strayhorn composed the music. Milton Larkin, another musician Copasetic, led a big band. Cholly Atkins and Pete Nugent handled
the choreography, which usually included at least one Robinson routine.
Each show had a theme and roped in a guest star: the comedians Redd
Foxx and Dick Gregory, the Nicholas Brothers, Sammy Davis, Jr. The
performances were lighthearted, though the 1963 show, "Down Dere,"
acknowledged the civil rights movement, expressing solidarity in a cel-
ebratory tone. Most years, the show took place at a big banquet hall such
as the Riverside Plaza Terrace, and the Copasetics had no trouble filling

a thousand seats. A Copasetics show was a social occasion for the black elite, who paid to print their congratulations in bound souvenir booklets. To the white press, the events were invisible.

NEWPORT, THE GATE, AND BERLIN

Writing in *The New Yorker* in 1962, the magazine's jazz critic, Whitney Balliett, reported on a concert "of the kind that becomes legendary the next day and that is described with firsthand relish years later to children and grandchildren by people who were not even there." It took place at the Newport Jazz Festival, an annual summer event in the Rhode Island resort town. Founded in 1954 by a Newport couple and the young nightclub owner George Wein, the festival was groundbreaking in its approach to presenting jazz. "The idea," Wein once explained, "was to make live jazz appealing again to a generation that didn't go to nightclubs anymore . . . You could have a picnic. The kids could play." The concept was ecumenical: all styles were welcome, and at one time or another, just about every great jazz musician alive played the festival, to crowds in the tens of thousands. A standout appearance could jump-start a stalled or idling career, as happened for Miles Davis in 1955 and the Duke Ellington Orchestra in 1956.

The concert that Balliett was writing about wasn't exactly a concert. The festival had pedagogical aims. A panel discussion the first year had grappled with "The Place of Jazz in American Culture," and one on that soon-to-be-legendary day in 1962 addressed "The Economics of the Jazz Community." A frequent organizer of these panels was Marshall Stearns, an English professor whose enthusiasm for jazz dated back to his undergraduate years at Harvard. In 1952, he had established an Institute for Jazz Studies, which grew out of his own sizable collection and which was located at first in his apartment. His book *The Story of Jazz*, published by Oxford University Press in 1956, was one of the first histories of the music. In the late fifties, he began to tackle a related and even more neglected topic: the history of jazz dance. The legendary concert that Balliett described was a Stearns lecture-demonstration on a Saturday afternoon: "A History of the Tap Dance and Its Relation to Jazz." The living examples were Pete Nugent, Coles and Atkins, Bunny Briggs, and Baby Laurence.

In his horn-rimmed glasses and wispy mustache, Stearns looked the part of a 1950s professor hip to jazz. In anecdotal style, he explained tap's origins in a fusion of Irish jigs, clogs, and Negro shuffles, while the dancers did the Shim Sham and displayed time steps, wings, and trenches on temporary maple flooring. They demonstrated the styles of Rector, Bubbles, Wiggins, and Robinson, and then each did his own. Together, they satirized the Twist and showed what they thought of rock and roll. The veteran drummer Jo Jones helped to underline the Relation to Jazz part, and jazz critics slapped their heads at the connection. During the more heavily attended evening concert that same day, Duke Ellington introduced Laurence and Briggs as "The King and Maharajah of Terpsichore." Several witnesses deemed Briggs, with his more visually eccentric style, to be the victor. (His strategy: "If you get in there with a champion, bang him in the mouth as soon as you walk in the ring.") Before Laurence walked off the stage, he leaned into a microphone and addressed his new fans: "This is a great American art. Don't let it die."

At his afternoon program at Newport the following year—called "A Night at the Hoofers' Club"—Stearns explained stealing and challenge dancing. On a Voice of America audio recording of the event, the dancers chime in to clarify, or, more often, to josh each other and the professor. Stearns: "The colored dancer Jack Wiggins . . ." Coles: "We don't say that anymore, Marshall. You remember Malcolm X, now." Stearns: "Where's Charlie Mingus?" According to Briggs and the *Boston Sunday Herald*, during the previous year's program, the jazz bassist Charles Mingus, enraged by Stearns's use of the word "pickaninny," had stormed onstage and had to be restrained by policemen.

Illustrating the style of Bubbles in 1963 was the master's own protégé, Chuck Green, who demonstrated how a dancer might tap to any style of accompaniment: waltz, march, tango, bebop. Even more than for the other dancers, his appearance was a comeback. Chuck and Chuckles had broken up in the late forties, when Chuckles decided to get married and move to Europe. Green, who couldn't conceive of going solo, brought in other dancers to play Chuckles's role. Then he checked into a psychiatric hospital and stayed, for at least a decade, hibernating through tap's

winter. He never gave up tapping. "It was a daily prayer," he would remember, "self-preservation," a way to "keep company with memory."
Soon after he was released, Bubbles invited him onstage at the Apollo
and gave him the signal to carry on.

Green was dancing well, yet now and ever after he would seem not
all there, smiling from some other, happier place. "Chuck was having
some problems with his mind," recalled Buster Brown, "but the minute
they said, 'Ladies and Gentlemen, Chuck Green,' he was normal." Or
closer to normal. Often his pupils would roll toward a high corner, giving his face the coquettish, crazed expression of someone enjoying a
private joke. In film footage from the late sixties, Green's demeanor and
his big, bump-toed shoes suggest a clown. There is something square
about his tall, large frame—like a man wearing a sandwich board—and
as he heaves it into Bubbles-style turns and quick-changing footwork, he
appears on the verge of toppling. The play of such lumbering awkwardness against the absolute rhythmic control of his tapping has curious,
even subversive effect, telling the eye and the ear conflicting stories. In
the Voice of America recording, his tapping pours out steadily, with what
Balliett accurately characterized as an "infallible pendulum rhythm"
and the kind of rhythmic wit that makes the audience giggle and the
kind of musical logic through which small surprises are instantly converted into inevitabilities.

The audiotape stands as the earliest record of Green's dancing. It's the
only record of Pete Nugent's. After serving as tour manager for the Temptations, Public Tapper #1 would die in 1973. On the 1963 tape, he demonstrates the style of his idol, Eddie Rector, and notes the recent passing of
that forgotten luminary, a janitor at the end. The men onstage, Stearns
repeats, are a dying breed.

Marshall Stearns was writing a book about jazz dance, and this was good
news for tap dancers. It made them feel valued, important. Most immediately, the professor got them work. Baby Laurence, in and out of jail, had
come under the mothering wing of Mary Lou Williams—an outstanding
pianist, a mentor to beboppers, and a Catholic convert who ran a charity

devoted to addict musicians. She accompanied the dancer on street corners, aiming to save the souls of passersby. In 1960, Stearns helped Laurence secure a nightclub gig with Charles Mingus. A gargantuan force, firmly rooted in the Ellingtonian tradition and the blues yet able to harness the convention-breaching energy of free jazz, Mingus was running an experimental workshop, hiring and firing at whim. His drummer, Dannie Richmond, would remember trading phrases with Laurence, copying him and learning much. The gig, alas, lasted only a few weeks. It didn't reconnect tap with jazz, but Whitney Balliett did show up, likely tipped off by Stearns. A connoisseur of drummers, Balliett was surprised to discover a great one in a dancer. The short *New Yorker* article in which he said so was the most extended press attention Laurence ever received.

The same year, in protest against low pay, Mingus and Max Roach organized an alternative Newport festival and invited Laurence. There, according to the singer Babs Gonzales, Laurence stole the keys and wallet of the saxophonist Eric Dolphy, made a drug run for New York in Dolphy's car, and wrecked it outside of Providence. Soon after, Laurence was back in jail, hitting up Stearns for money in grandiloquently polite letters that sampled the dancer's formal, self-pitying verse. A few months later, Stearns hired Laurence as a guest lecturer for his jazz history course at the New School, then got him and some of his colleagues into the official Newport festival two years in a row.

In 1964, Stearns arranged to squeeze a two-night tap exhibition in between the regular acts at the Village Gate in Greenwich Village. The lineup included John Chivers, formerly of the Two Zephyrs, whom everyone called Rhythm Red. He was big and bald, aptly described by Stearns as "a kindly Mr. Clean." His style was dainty, on his toes with his butt out and up. Isaiah Chaneyfield was unknown then but would become less so, under the cinematic sobriquet of Lon Chaney. A prizefighter and drummer from South Carolina, he had fallen in love with tap in 1951 upon encountering Baby Laurence. Chaney was working in a grocery store then, and he traded Laurence milk and bread for steps. Barrel-chested and thick-necked, though not as heavyset as he would soon grow, Chaney danced to type, grunting and sweating and dropping his weight with precision into the paddle and roll he sometimes claimed to have invented.

The event was a mess. Everyone went on too long. The man of the hour was Groundhog, the ever-disappearing junkie cutting-contest king, who had been lured out of his hole in Cincinnati by the chance to challenge Chuck Green. "I've been waiting to battle Chuck Green for twenty years," Groundhog told Stearns. "Hoofing is like the gangster world. Every dancer is my enemy." The battle between them was both furious and curious. Groundhog, flashing a gap-toothed grin, threw down physical challenges and verbal taunts that Green answered in calm wordlessness. "It was not exactly a battle between a dancer with one great style and another with an endless bag of tricks," Stearns wrote; Groundhog, the foxier one, was fusing new combinations, and each combination "had a style of its own." In some photographs he looks as poised as a matador. Bouncing off his knees, he laughed, hugged Green, and declared himself the winner.

"Dancing jumped about twenty years ahead of itself," Groundhog explained to Stearns. "People don't understand it." He said that dancing and drumming were the same, and also that he admired Paul Draper. Drunk at a bar not long afterward, he showed Stearns the calluses on his hands from manual labor and said that "dancers have been persecuted as bad as the Jews." He promised to give Stearns "the inside story of tap." Then he disappeared again.

Stearns wasn't the only one finding work for hoofers. Duke Ellington had been hiring Bunny Briggs, and he wrote him into *My People*, a pageant for the Century of Negro Progress Exhibition in 1963. (The program also included the company of the modern dancer Alvin Ailey, a sign of expanding options for black dancers.) Ellington took his modern spiritual "Come Sunday," doubled the tempo, and retitled it "David Danced Before the Lord" in reference to King David's dance of joy as he brought the Ark of the Covenant into Jerusalem. When Ellington gave a "Concert of Sacred Music" in San Francisco's Grace Cathedral two years later, he used "David Danced" as the finale. Briggs's heel-propelled, train-leaving-the-station step could've been part of a Ring Shout, yet Briggs, a Catholic who always wore a cross around his neck, was nervous about dancing in church. Ellington introduced him as "the most super-Leviathonic rhythmaturgically syncopated tapster-magician-ism-ist," and Briggs danced as he always did. The Sacred Concert was released on record, and a film made for educational television is the highest-quality document of Briggs's art.

There was also George Wein, who was not just producer of the Newport Jazz Festival but now also an international impresario. In 1965, he organized a drum-battle tour of Japan, and along with the hoofers-turned-drummers Buddy Rich and Philly Joe Jones, he sent Baby Laurence. In 1966, he sent Laurence, Chuck Green, Buster Brown, and Jimmy Slyde—a younger dancer—to the Berlin Jazz Festival with an all-star Swing-era band. The effusive appreciation of audiences in Paris and Switzerland and Sweden raised the dancers' hopes for respect and steady work. But after the tour was over, Wein didn't hire tap dancers again for nearly ten years, and only infrequently after that. Jimmy Slyde, feeling betrayed, figured that the dancers must have been too hard to follow, that they had upstaged the musicians. He blamed "the American mentality" and never forgave Wein. Decades later, when I asked Wein about his hiring decisions, he gave as explanation a specimen of a mentality often called American: "Tap," he said, "is not a big ticket-selling situation."

Some fragmented footage exists of the Berlin Jazz Festival, filmed by German television. There are a few seconds of all four men together, as a voice explains how tap is the only authentic form of jazz dancing and how the black tap dancers taught Fred Astaire and Gene Kelly. The single complete number is the solo of the most camera-friendly dancer, Jimmy Slyde. That footage, along with an appearance of Slyde on the Los Angeles TV show *Club Checkerboard* in 1959 and Baby Laurence's cameo on *The Hollywood Palace* in 1966, is for my money the best tap caught on film during the dark years.

Slyde: the name advertises the specialty, the spelling signals the manner, as laid-back as a lowercase *y*. Out of what could be a gimmick, he fashions an entire expressive idiom. His slides go in all directions, now as if pushed, now as if pulled. They come in all sizes, too, all parts of speech, from connective scoots to long, stage-traversing slalom runs. Feet flat on the floor, he pulls up from the hip to get moving, regulating momentum by bending his knee. His reedy frame tilts in opposition, twisting for balance and achieving beauty. Visually thrilling in their elongation and slant, Slyde's slides are equally musical. He uses them to tease the beat, to suspend it, to fall behind and to catch up. The slides are silences, dancing rests, but those same silences, stretched in a slide, also imply sustained notes, just as Slyde's physical dynamics, speeding and slowing, imply crescendos and diminuendos. He would stress that slides couldn't be metered out exactly; there was an aleatory element that kept both him and his public alert. He often described the function of slides in aural terms—as a breath, a hush—and their variety could be detected in the sounds they elicited: giggles, gasps, sighs of wonder, wild applause.

Confronted with potential conflict between sight and sound, Slyde answered with a balance to rival Astaire's. Actually, he was smoother. His vocabulary included whirling-top spins and shifts of direction that pressed into the floor at one point and spurted out at another. Exiting a spin, he might freeze in a pose, tip his head down, and point one finger loosely, as if to say, *Did you catch* that? His movements solicited musical comparisons by being fully integrated into his phrasing, which was plenty percussive, lyricism with a kick. Arriving at adulthood in the late forties, he matured in the bebop era, and his approach to rhythm revealed that idiom as a way of swinging harder. His sound was light, crisp, carefully modulated. Compared to a Baby Laurence bombardment or a Bunny Briggs burble, his tapping was sparser, pithier. It had wit. He used his shoulders the way other people use their eyebrows. He considered *improvisation* too exalted a word for what he did: deploying his signature steps in response to the musical moment, branching off into fresh creations only when inspiration struck. "Ad-lib dancing," he called it, or "accidental dancing" or "fumbling and stumbling." His best steps, he would acknowledge, were sometimes mistakes.

Born James Titus Godbolt in 1927, he was fourteen years younger than Buster Brown, six younger than Baby Laurence. Besides that age gap and its effect on where his career fell in tap's decline, he differed from his Berlin colleagues in one crucial respect. Their motto was "Never took a lesson in my life"; he learned his craft in a dancing school. Located in Boston across the street from the New England Conservatory of Music, where young Jimmy took violin, Stanley Brown's studio was a Boston hub of black entertainment. Brown had been a dancer himself—one of Naomi Thomas's Brazilian Nuts, then a single with the Savoyagers—before he opened a school, around 1938. Robinson and Bubbles, friends of his, came by to observe, teach, and inspire. Their kind of tap stayed alive in such places, the schools of ex-dancers such as Sammy Dyer and Jimmy Payne and Tommy Sutton in Chicago and Henry LeTang in New York. At Brown's academy, the students were required to take tap *and* ballet. The recitals were like professional shows, with talent scouts and agents in the audience. Most of the students were white, most of the instructors black. One of the regular teachers, "Schoolboy" Eddie Ford, was a specialist in slides, and he put together an act for Jimmy Godbolt and another student, Jimmy Mitchell. As the Slyde Brothers, the two teenagers did flips and splits as expected of a young black duo. Slides set them apart.

The act was short-lived, breaking up when Mitchell got drafted. But Slyde faced a larger problem. The world that he had been trained to enter was fast vanishing. As a single, he got on a burlesque circuit and tried Chicago and San Francisco. In the late fifties, he moved to Los Angeles with the aim of breaking into the movies, only to discover that Hollywood no longer wanted tap dancers, especially not those of his color. He practiced in Willie Covan's studio and found a job here, a job there, dancing for his supper. With the TV nebbish Ray Malone and sometimes another skilled white dancer named Jack Ackerman, Slyde put together an act optimistically called "Just in Time." But he and his partners were now even later in tap's ebb and still a little too early for an interracial team (though one of their jokes referenced *I Spy*, the hit TV show with the interracial buddies, played by Bill Cosby and Robert Culp, who avoided the subject of race.) Then came Berlin and the ecstatic crowds. "I just knew we were going to be working on the festivals," Slyde remembered. "And everything was going to be all right."

JAZZ DANCE

Marshall Stearns's *The Story of Jazz* had been a synthesis. Much had been written about the music, and Stearns drew upon that literature to produce a sensible, entertaining consensus history. Stearns's *Jazz Dance* was much more pioneering. As Clive Barnes pointed out in his glowing review in the *Times*, the book was "not merely the best in its field," but "also the first." Where almost all of the endnotes in *The Story of Jazz* point to books and articles and recordings, the most common citation in *Jazz Dance* is the phrase "from interviews." The primary source was the memory of dancers, hundreds of them whom Stearns and his wife, Jean, had hunted down over a period of seven years. It was to their many stories that Stearns applied his skill.

The book had a subtitle, *The Story of American Vernacular Dance*, which the introduction defines somewhat circularly as "American dancing that is performed to and with the rhythms of jazz." This story, Stearns notes, is parallel to that of jazz, a matter of European and African traditions blending in America—a variant of the story Stearns had already told. The prologue sets up the tale in its largest dimension, the inexorable spread of African-American styles and rhythms, and casts a bemused look at contemporary rock-and-roll dances, "unrealized revivals," pieces of the Charleston and the Eagle Rock returning as the Mashed Potato and the Fish. The story *Jazz Dance* wants to tell is one of continuity. It opens with a 1950s meeting between dancers from Sierra Leone, Trinidad, and Harlem discovering the similarities in their traditions, which are really "one great tradition." (That these similarities had to be rediscovered was also, of course, a measure of discontinuity and diaspora.) This tradition had not only survived, it had secretly triumphed. The culture of an oppressed minority had influenced and eventually dominated that of the majority.

Yet imbedded within this story was another one, the story of professional dancers, tap individualists, and in the sixties, this was not a story of triumph. "The most highly developed dancing of the past—tap dance—is the most completely lost," Stearns argues, "partly because it is so difficult, but also because a revolution in mass culture apparently needs to begin all over again with something new and relatively simple."

The final section of the book, the part that covers Baby Laurence and Bunny Briggs, is titled "Requiem."

Simply as a vessel of oral history, *Jazz Dance* was and is invaluable. A book such as the one you're reading would be immeasurably diminished without it. But *Jazz Dance* is more than interviews; it attempts to categorize and make sense of often-contradictory testimony, and as the only book on the subject for decades, its influence would be high. In later years, dancers quoted in it would repeat its ideas, not clarifying whether Stearns had learned from them or vice versa. The book's structure implies that class acts were the most advanced, and interview transcripts suggest that Stearns was most influenced by Pete Nugent and Coles and Atkins, class acts he considered friends. (They said the same of him.) The Nicholas Brothers must not have been too pleased to be paired with their old rivals, the Berrys, as flash acts. Except for a chapter on Astaire, tap in Hollywood is ignored. The Whitman Sisters get a chapter, but women in general are scarce. Eleanor Powell is rated the best woman in a single throwaway sentence. Part of Stearns's argument on behalf of his neglected subject is that "the question of whether or not dancers were sissies *never arose in the native tradition of vernacular dance.*" (The italics are his.) Stearns and his subjects stress how masculine Astaire was, how Robinson was "no faggot." The only way that Gene Kelly makes it into *Jazz Dance* is through his assertion that dancing is a man's business that women have taken over and that has become dominated by homosexuals. At a time when anxiety about men dancing was a frequent subject in magazines and newspapers, the notion that dancing *wasn't* a man's game did need combating, but the underlying problem wasn't the misperception of dancing as sissy; it was the fear of sissiness.

Jazz Dance's occasional knocks on ballet and modern dance are its least informed bits, seeming to rely on no experience more direct than television watching. But there were reasons to feel embattled. Ballet and modern dance tended to treat vernacular dance as frivolous or as shorthand for naughtiness or, at best, as raw material to refine. Funding decisions reflected such attitudes. In 1963, the Ford Foundation allotted an unprecedented $7 million to dance, most of it to George Balanchine's New York City Ballet and its affiliated School of American Ballet, the rest to regional ballet troupes. Private foundations and corporations

followed the precedent, as did the federal government, after the formation of the National Foundation on the Arts and the Humanities in 1965.
The National Endowment for the Arts granted money directly to dance
companies, money that kept those companies solvent. None of this money
went to tap.

In the ensuing "dance boom," tap was left out, while modern dance
and ballet attracted larger audiences than ever before. Most recipients of
funds were deserving—Balanchine was a national treasure, among the
greatest artists of the twentieth century in any medium. Moreover, they
were supported by institutions—companies, schools—in which it was
responsible to invest. All tap had was dancers in need of jobs, and the
idea of subsidizing what had always been commercial entertainment
may have seemed bizarre. When Stearns, in his program for the Newport festival, blamed the decline of tap on the rise of ballet and complained about how "like artistic colonials, we threw away the wonderful
swinging rhythms of tap for a lot of agonized swooping, sliding, posing, and gliding," his dismissal of concert dance was itself provincial.
(Though one can recognize certain qualities of modern dance in his
description.) Modern dance was also American; so was ballet as Balanchine had reconceived it for American dancers. Still, Stearns's fundamental charge was sound: Americans, especially those Americans who
doled out money, undervalued tap.

As Whitney Balliett encapsulated it in 1969, tap had gone from being
"taken for granted as just another example of those picturesque gifts
Negroes are born to" to becoming "an art whose proponents were celebrated by being offered jobs as bellhops and elevator men." In *Jazz
Dance*, Stearns recorded tap's traditions and clarified what he called its
"usable past." Except for TV appearances with the jazz dancers Leon
James and Al Minns and once with Coles and Atkins, his plans to film
the dancers didn't come to fruition, but his work on the book came
just in time. Throughout *Jazz Dance*, there are glimpses of the book's
creation—scenes of senior citizens getting up to demonstrate the dances
of their youth, occasions when the Stearnses reunite friends long out of
touch, a continual bridging of white and black worlds. Penciled in at
the top of the interview transcripts are more than a few notes like: "Interviewed Feb. 1960; Died, Nov. 1960." On December 18, 1966, Marshall

Stearns died of a heart attack, having just turned in his manuscript. *Jazz Dance* was published two years later.

MONDAY NIGHT HOOFERS AND THE VEILED LADY

By the time Stearns died, his flame had already set other candles alight. Out of a Ned Wayburn home-study course, six hours of lessons with the modern-dance pioneer Ruth St. Denis, and years in various dancing schools, Leticia Jay of Jaytown, Texas, had made herself into an "ethnic" dancer who combined notionally East Asian techniques with back-bends and multiple veils. In the forties, this style counted as exotic in burlesque. (Duke Ellington and Billy Strayhorn composed "Strange Feeling" for her burlesque act at the Hurricane in 1943.) In the fifties, Jay transferred it to concert dancing, performing with her East-West Dance Group at serious-minded venues such as the 92nd Street Y. In 1963, she caught Stearns's lecture-demonstration at Newport and tap gained another convert.

Inspired, Jay wrote a report for *Dance*, pages and pages, of which the magazine printed one. In it, she asked why tap, "one of our two really indigenous forms (jazz is the other)" was so seldom seen, and she argued that the form was worthy of concert staging. (Six months before, in the same publication, Paul Draper had calmly dismissed the tap dancing of Bunny Briggs as not dancing at all. Two years later, Ann Barzel would write in the magazine that "trying to show that tap dancing is an art is like trying to make a silk purse out of a sow's ear.") Jay envisioned tap as ethnic dance, "our character dance," and she continued the argument in a rambling, quixotic, and ultimately prescient proposal that she sent to leading figures in the dance world, calling for a "United States of America National Ethnic Dance Company," a folkloric troupe along the lines of Russia's Moiseyev. She described tap as "one of the highest forms of abstract art in our American culture." (Abstract art carried great prestige in 1963.) She recognized that "the problem of transferring an entertainment medium into an art form" was largely a problem of perception: for tap to be received as Art, it had to be presented as Art. Her proposal suggested how tap might explore storytelling and a wider emotional range.

She imagined tap "orchestras" sounding off in counterpoint and the eventual maturation of an "American Classical Dance."

Jay wasn't the first to make such proposals. But for her, promoting tap became all-consuming. She began looking after Chuck Green—dancers referred to her as "Chuck's ladyfriend"—and she traveled with him to Berlin and elsewhere. On occasion, she performed alongside him, prompting reviews that unfavorably contrasted Green's ease with her self-indulgent straining. In combining the roles of caretaker, promoter, and performer, Jay was setting a precedent, as well as providing a test case for the perils involved therein.

As a champion of tap, her most important achievement was selfless. It came about through a confluence of uptown and off-Broadway. Around 1963, Lon Chaney, the heavyweight of Harlem, had the idea that he might save tap by gathering dancers together. His mentor, Baby Laurence, advised him that it would never work, because hoofers were too competitive. Chaney's solution was to organize a Battle of the Taps, "like a big prize fight," after midnight at a small lounge on 125th Street called the Purple Manor. With Laurence and Chuck Green among the contenders, other dancers couldn't resist. Someone, probably Marshall Stearns, wrote an unsigned report about it for *Downbeat*. It's not clear how many Mondays the hoofers competed, but by 1967, Honi Coles—who, when he attended a Battle of the Taps, was inclined to sit at the bar with his Copasetics buddies, looking unimpressed—used his position at the Apollo to transfer the arena from a small club to a big theater, still on Mondays.

Downtown, people were tapping again for different reasons. *Dames at Sea*, which premiered in 1966 at a Greenwich Village coffeehouse and grew into a long-running hit, was a pastische of Busby Berkeley movies, a Berkeley extravaganza with a cast of six. Here was a newly popular way of appreciating the past: camp nostalgia. "The real lovers of the 30's," Clive Barnes wrote in a review of surprised praise, "are the people who have absorbed them through the new time machine called the late-nite movie on television." The producer Robert Dahdah repeated the formula in 1967 with *Curley McDimple*, an affectionate spoof of Shirley Temple movies. Playing the Bill Robinson role was the Harlem veteran George Hillman, and as the run continued into 1969 and Hillman went on vacation, he called his old friend Chuck Green to replace him. Leticia Jay saw an opening. Buttonholing Dahdah, she informed him of the great talent languishing up in Harlem and persuaded him to let her put on a tap show on *Curley McDimple*'s night off. Hoofers were accustomed to dancing on Mondays.

She called the show *Tap Happening, a Reminisce with Chuck Green* and she dedicated it to the late Marshall Stearns. Derby Wilson, the one-time Bill Robinson imitator, crippled in a car accident three years prior, emceed with jokes from well before Robinson's death. In the first half, Chuck Green, now fifty, reminisced in between introducing other performers. After intermission came a Battle of the Taps, with the men taking solo turns before going into what Lon Chaney called the Track, everyone doing a paddle and roll like a group metronome while Chaney chanted like a chain-gang leader and each man stepped out again in succession. The lineup varied. Jay invited everybody she knew and sent out a flyer calling in the missing. (There were no women on the list, though Jay did perform. In one photo, she wears a black Afro wig like a minstrel Black Panther.) Neither Steve Condos, who was semiretired in Florida, nor Baby Laurence, who was alternating between construction work and gigs in a Maryland mall, appears to have made it to New York. Honi Coles had been announced as emcee, but he and his Copasetics buddies seemed to have chosen not to participate. John Bubbles wasn't available. His sixties comeback as an old-time song-and-dance man had culminated in 1967, when he was warmly received at the revived Palace Theatre as a guest of Judy Garland and the *Times* praised him as "a veteran trouper from the uncomplicated, naïve, pre-Stokely Carmichael era." With the rise of Black Power, the man who had once embodied Bad Negroes seemed quaint. After one of the Palace performances, he suffered a stroke and never danced again.

At *Tap Happening*, the regulars were Chaney and Rhythm Red and Jimmy Slyde. Howard "Sandman" Sims poured sand into a box before stepping in himself and swiveling his toes. On top of this time-keeping, he added longer swirls, like a train picking up speed and letting off steam. At his best, he was like a drummer working brushes, churning all that scraping into speech or song. Exiting the box, he'd sweep his feet backward, finishing his business as dogs do. Born in 1918, Sims was known to inform interviewers that he had invented the sand dance. More plausibly, he claimed to have discovered it for himself in the mid-thirties, messing around in a rosin box as an aspiring pugilist in Los Angeles. He said he was inspired by Hal LeRoy, then by Bill Robinson, who, thinking of his own stair dance, advised the young man to hold on to his gimmick. After Sims moved to New York in 1946, the sand got him work, but his steadiest job came in the mid-fifties, when he served as "executioner" for the Apollo's Amateur Night, responsible for removing dud acts entertainingly. For that role, Sims was a natural. A cantankerous showboat, he was forever drawing focus, cheering on other dancers when he wasn't mocking them. His chest, exposed in open-necked shirts, jutted as he roostered around. His dancing was rough-edged, ropy, drawing from a seemingly limitless catalogue of steps pulled out in no particular order, like a man emptying his pockets. Never did he surrender a stage gladly. He whipped off flashy combinations with downcast eyes, then demanded applause. "That step was for you," he liked to tell an audience, "and this one is for me."

Like a negative of *The Lawrence Welk Show*, *Tap Happening* took in one white face. As a Jewish boy in Queens, Jerry Abrams had idolized Astaire. He had studied in the Broadway dancing school of Jack Stanly, had taken classes from Paul Draper, and, under the name Jerry Ames, had worked on Broadway, cruise ships, and television before settling into teaching. From that biography, his style might be fairly imagined. Finding Jay's flyer, Ames treated its open invitation as genuine, and Green took a liking to him. To interviewers Ames gamely joked about "token integration."

And there *were* interviewers, because *Tap Happening* was a sleeper hit. The show moved from the Hotel Dixie to the Mercury Theatre for eight shows a week under the name *The Hoofers*. (The new incarnation included "Gotta Go Tap Dancing Tonight," a theme song by Rhythm Red that Buster Brown would be singing at Swing 46 at century's end.) "You may not think tap dancing would be interesting enough to look at for a whole evening," wrote Marcia Siegel in *New York*, "but each of these performers has his own distinctive approach." Along with expressing surprise at the variety, other critics joined Siegel in marveling at what she called the "ingenuous, unrehearsed quality," "an innocence, an almost mystical honesty," and at how the dancers "remain themselves."

In his column, Walter Kerr appreciated the camaraderie, noting how the dancers seemed to want each other to be impossible to follow, while Clive Barnes, in the *Times*, sensed cutthroat competition beneath the smiles. Confirming the rumor that *Tap Happening* was the best dance event in town, "some of the most gorgeous dancing you are ever going to see in your life," Barnes was the only critic to address race directly. (Siegel did notice the absence of young blacks in the audience.) "What makes American dance American is its blackness," wrote the British-born Barnes. "The white liberal is forced to note the marked over-all superiority of the black over white, and it is enough to turn the more sensitive into racists." Astaire and Kelly he deemed "more personalities than dancers," though he insisted on Paul Draper as a "great artist" even if "black tap dancers do not really dig" him. (When Draper attended *Tap Happening*, the band played "Once in Love with Amy," Ray Bolger's theme.)

There was, across the reviews, a sense of revelation. This was not the tap of Astaire or Kelly—nor of Ann Miller, who was concurrently reminding Broadway audiences about her brand as a replacement for the lead in *Mame*. This tap was about sound. "To see the show is to realize it IS an art," declared Alvin Klein on WNYC. "It is the real thing." Long disregarded, these dancers and their art could now be discovered.

Leticia Jay had one evening of *Tap Happening* filmed. The reels that remain are partial: solos of Green and Sims, the Battle of the Taps. In the battle, Jerry Ames, with his rhythmless pirouettes, seems out of place. (Barnes, justly, called Ames "too uptight," but Richard Watts of the *New York Post*, judging by different criteria, found him "the most skillful dancer of the lot.") During his earlier solo, Ames recalled, the red recording light shut off, and when he asked Jay about it, she replied, "We have enough footage of Fred Astaire and Gene Kelly."

The success of *Tap Happening* made Jay jubilant. Her program note for *The Hoofers*, a discourse on "Man's Role in the Rhythmic Pattern of the Universe," built up to a declaration of victory: "This year, 1969, is the Time of Truth for our American tap dancing. It is making a comeback." Yet *The Hoofers* didn't last three months. There are several stories of what happened, most of them involving money. Jay, who had invested her own savings in the show, lost it all.

Various assemblages of the Hoofers continued to perform sporadically. One 1972 performance was filmed for the TV show *Camera Three*: vintage Green, Slyde, Ralph Brown, Buster Brown, and, as token integration, Fred Kelly. Jay continued what she called the First Tap Company— largely jam sessions in church basements, which, as Jay bitterly indicated in her homemade flyers, were not sponsored by "the open sesame of grants" she assumed would follow *Tap Happening*. The Hoofers' style of tap was still underground.

PART V

PUTTING THE SHOES BACK ON

No, the emotional range of tap dancing is not unlimited: it cannot express tragedy or pain or fear or guilt; all it can express is gaiety and every shade of emotion pertaining to the joy of living. (Yes, it is my favorite form of the dance.)

—AYN RAND, 1971

Tap will forever be a nostalgia thing. It's an art that couldn't go anywhere.

—PATRICK O'CONNOR, dance critic, 1977

If the only form of tradition, of handing down, consisted in following the ways of the immediate generation before us in a blind or timid adherence to its successes, "tradition" should be positively discouraged . . . It cannot be inherited, and if you want it you must obtain it by great labour.

—T. S. ELIOT, "Tradition and the Individual Talent," 1919

14

REVIVAL

If theater audiences were primed for the entertainment that Ruby Keeler and Busby Berkeley had once provided, why not bring back Ruby herself? Last seen onstage in 1929, retired since 1941, Keeler returned, at age sixty-two, for a 1971 revival of *No, No, Nanette*. Just as *Dames at Sea* had billed itself as "the new 1930s musical," so this production called itself "the new 1925 musical." Berkeley signed on as a consultant, lending his name and little else. Keeler offered her ever-likable self. Her first dance number, "I Want to Be Happy," toyed with the question of whether she could still dance. Backed by boys in sweaters, she handed off her ukulele and eased into a soft shoe. Then, in the up-tempo second chorus, she let loose in time steps, shuffled off to Buffalo, and pumped her arms in fake trenches like the Ruby Keeler in the old movies. On opening night, an elderly woman in the audience cried out, "Thattagirl, Ruby!"

The revival of *No, No, Nanette* racked up more than twice as many performances as the original production had. It won four Tony Awards,

Opposite page: Savion Glover and Gregory Hines in *Jelly's Last Jam*, 1992 including one for choreography by the Astaire-inspired, ballet-trained Donald Saddler, who came of age around the time Keeler retired. "I wanted to show that all my early tap dancing lessons weren't in vain," he later said, professing his rekindled love for tap. "It says what we are as much as, say, corn bread." Walter Kerr wrote about a "lost pleasure," a playfulness "like a puppy without a purpose." Clive Barnes confided that he had forgotten that tap could be so much fun. Since *No, No, Nanette* was the hit of the year, its formula—exhume an old show with an old star—was copied, less successfully, by *Irene* with Debbie Reynolds and *Good News* with Alice Faye. But the fun that Barnes meant wasn't the personalities of yesteryear. He meant the tapping chorus line, the unison time steps, the whole pre-*Oklahoma!* style. If, after the upheavals of the late sixties, people just wanted to be happy again, wasn't it time for the happy dance?

In the words of Ron Field, the choreographer of *Cabaret* (1966) and *Applause* (1970), "If you do a musical or a number with the feeling of the twenties, thirties, or forties, you put the taps on because that was the definitive dance form." Yet precisely because the associations were so fixed, tap could also be used ironically, and among the artistically adventurous Broadway choreographers of the seventies, irony was irresistible. For *Company* (1970), a musical without a linear plot, centered around a commitment-shy bachelor and his not-so-happily-married friends, the twenty-seven-year-old choreographer Michael Bennett staged the climax of the number "Side by Side by Side" by having the husband-and-wife teams each share a call-and-answer tap break. Down the line they went until the bachelor took his turn, answered by no one. This was an affecting application of a tap tradition. More typically, the use of hats and canes, a sartorial style so distant from the mod present, suggested playacting, false cheer, and social lies, while the acidic lyrics told the grim truth for laughs.

(We've also reached a new chapter of our story in another sense. The original production of *Company* was preserved, in the freeze-dried form of videotape, as Broadway productions were with increasing regularity through the seventies. I don't have to take the word of contemporary witnesses about Broadway shows, and you don't have to take mine.)

In *Follies* (1971), showbiz was both story and metaphor, nostalgia and resentment clashing in form and content. The plot concerned the reunion of Follies showgirls and their husbands, thirty years on, questioning the choices they'd made, and the structure borrowed from revues. The casting put to good use many former Broadway and Hollywood stars, including Gene Nelson, the gymnast tapper, and though his unfaithful traveling salesman did frustrated spins rather than tap, at one point some of the ladies tried stumbling through a distantly remembered routine and its big tap finish. The number that Bennett devised for this was pastiche; his twist was to have younger versions of the women join in mid-routine, a brutal contrast between past and present. This was brilliant stagecraft, the whole show in a single image. But the stage was raked and slippery, so the tapping ghosts wore rubber soles and the phantom sounds of tapping came from chorus members offstage. As the Broadway authority Ethan Mordden has pointed out, the ghosts were supposed to materialize magically; taps on their shoes would have given them away. The choice to dub is an example of Bennett's mastery of detail. It's also an example of how the compromises of film could migrate to the stage.

The scores for these shows, with music and lyrics by Stephen Sondheim, were more than just parody or evocation; they were an extension of Broadway's traditions by its most intelligent and talented young artist. The tapping, by contrast, was routine, stock, there to make a point. The most obvious point-making came in *Mack and Mabel* (1974). Placed late in the plot's timeline, at the dawn of movie musicals, the song "Tap Your Troubles Away" was an echo of a hundred similar songs of pluck, a hymn to one of the traditional musical's articles of faith. As the chorus tapped, the heroine snorted cocaine, watched her husband cheat on her, and murdered him with a pistol. The show's director-choreographer, Gower Champion, had turned to Broadway after MGM stopped making his kind of musical. His choreography deemphasized steps in favor of group patterns, one thing gliding into the next, but he had nevertheless made use of some non-ironic soft shoe in his hit shows *Bye Bye Birdie* (1960) and *Hello, Dolly!* (1964). By 1974, he was getting in on the musical of disillusionment. "Tap dancing on the stage is boring," he told reporters. "You've seen *No, No, Nanette*."

Two years earlier, Champion had tried, or had allowed for, an alternative. *Sugar* was a musical adaptation of *Some Like It Hot*. During out-of-town tryouts, the part of the mob don Spats Palazzo was changed into a dancing role and given to Steve Condos, now in his fifties. (This was at the suggestion of assistant choreographer Bert Michaels, who had been a student of Condos.) His Palazzo gave orders in taps, and in the chase number "Tear This Town Apart," he did his town-tearing with tommy-gun hoofing. Champion let Condos ad-lib, making the hoofer, as he had been in Hollywood, an improviser in a no-improvisation zone. But Condos's use of tap—as comic storytelling, as jazz improvisation— must have seemed a one-off. It didn't go on the cast album. No other Broadway roles followed for the dancer, so he went back to Florida and the occasional cruise-ship gig.

Champion had already been eclipsed as a director-choreographer by one of his co-stars from the MGM days. Growing up in Chicago in the forties, Bob Fosse had been half of the Riff Brothers, a teenaged tap duo that did precision unison in tails, stealing from the black brother acts and looking up to Draper and Astaire while performing in strip clubs. As a contract player in Hollywood, a kid with dreams of succeeding Gene Kelly, Fosse had shown himself a charming dancer, but his mature style didn't retain much tap. Often, the feet were nailed to the floor, the better to isolate a flexed hand or a jutting pelvis. It was a slinky, sleazy style, comic or cynical or both. In the seventies, though Fosse still fetishized hats and canes, the closest he usually came to tap was a scrunched soft shoe, used ironically. In *Pippin* (1972), he placed a nifty soft shoe in front of a pantomime of war, the dancers coolly indifferent to the carnage behind them. In his *Chicago* (1975), vaudeville served as a symbol for life's essential phoniness. The twenties setting allowed for tap, as did the distancing style—numbers explicitly framed as vaudeville turns— borrowed from Brecht, but here tap was a method by which the murderess heroine could hoodwink her husband or a mercenary lawyer could razzle-dazzle a jury. Here it was a trick a disillusioned choreographer could use to throw sequins in the eyes of his audience.

In the audition around which the plot of Michael Bennett's *A Chorus Line* (1975) was built, the dancer-characters were required to learn a tap routine, a boilerplate traveling soft shoe that was presented as another chore and a mindless background against which a dancer could express her individuality. Early in the show, one of the men told the stereotypical story of following his sister into dance class; his show-off solo, "I Can Do That," was a compilation of tap clichés, and the other kinds of dancing that formed the bulk of the show were equally undistinguished. The routines were supposed to be routine; that was part of the show's honesty about the life of a chorus dancer. Bennett had started out tap dancing, but his true gift was for fluid staging, seamless and as if spontaneous. *A Chorus Line*'s emotional impact came from the group-therapy confessions and the assertion that "we're all special," however much that message was undercut by the hackneyed, endlessly repeating, anonymous, and unfailingly applause-generating kick line. *A Chorus Line* quickly moved from Off-Broadway to On, where it stayed for fifteen years and was seen by millions. Millions more saw it via various tours, amateur productions, and the unfaithful 1985 film. This quintessential dance musical of the seventies was extraordinarily influential, and one of its incidental effects was to perpetuate impoverished notions of tap.

There was one black character in *A Chorus Line*, a minor one, and Ben Vereen, a black actor in *Pippin*, was a major Fosse dancer. *The Wiz* (1975) was all-black, a disco *Wizard of Oz*, like the swing Gilbert and Sullivans of the forties. The choreographer was even black himself, the first black choreographer to win a Tony. But George Faison came from the modern-dance company of Alvin Ailey, and though his tap for the Tin Man gestured at Bojangles, it was no *Tap Happening*.

Gower Champion returned to the tried and true. His final show, in 1980, didn't bring back Ruby Keeler again, but it brought back her debut film. In the old days, shows had traveled from Broadway to Hollywood, but Broadway wasn't what it used to be. Still, *42nd Street* was at least *about* what Broadway used to be, when tap reigned. Champion, however, was not a tap dancer. Choreographing the show, he clapped out rhythms and his assistants filled in steps. The curtain rose slowly, lingering to isolate a long line of tapping feet: an audition, in the pre–*Chorus Line*, pre-*Oklahoma!* sense, with chorus hopefuls hammering away at a time step, knees flying up to their chests. *42nd Street* was an expert resuscitation of showbiz conventions, a tale of Broadway hoofers who have everything they need to cheer themselves up. When Champion died hours before opening night, his passing was plausibly seen as the end of an era. The

production's eight-and-a-half-year run convinced many that the future
of the Broadway musical was to be found in the past.

The idea to put *42nd Street* on Broadway may have had its seed in *That's
Entertainment*, the musical anthology that MGM released in movie theaters in 1974. The advertising slogan, in that year of Watergate and Vietnam, was "Boy, do we need it now!" *That's Entertainment* presented a past
neither lost nor forgotten but, in those days before videotapes, not readily
accessible—and not in this form, with the numbers snipped out of the
plots, a culled genre history. It was an MGM anthology, so, in terms of tap
dancers, it had Eleanor Powell, Ann Miller, Kelly, Astaire, even Joan Crawford, but no Bill Robinson or black acts at all, save the Nicholas Brothers,
who made it in only as backup for Kelly. The film and its two sequels
were, shall we say, selective. But they brought to a mass market the interest in the films of Berkeley and other thirties musicals that had burgeoned
in art-house cinemas and on college campuses in the sixties. Arlene
Croce's *The Fred Astaire & Ginger Rogers Book*, the smartest possible advertisement for the Astaire-Rogers films, had been published in 1972.

It was now that "Tap Is Back" stories began to sprout in newspapers
and magazines—as they would periodically for decades to come. This
round wasn't so much about tap returning to Broadway as about Americans returning to tap. The dancewear supplier Capezio reported that
sales of tap shoes had tripled or quadrupled. The teaching of tap to children had never ceased, but housewives and suburban fathers and cabdrivers learning—that was news. Those interviewed explained how tap
was exercise and what a snap it was to learn. As one tap instructor said,
"The worse the economy gets, the better my business gets."

In 1977, Jerry Ames, the self-described token representative of integration in *Tap Happening*, put out *The Book of Tap*, which, despite its
quasi-biblical title, was a modest thumbnail history. Venturing to account
for tap's new popularity, Ames and his co-author, Jim Siegelman, argued
that Americans were "trying to salvage something of value from our no-
longer-innocent heritage." Tap dancing came from better times; it could
put people "in touch with an older vision of America." Most fundamentally, they wrote, "it makes you happy."

The Book of Tap also found room for voices of caution and dissent. The longtime teacher Jack Stanly argued that because tap had been disregarded for so many years, the sudden exposure might be harmful to the art. Current standards weren't high enough, and having gained people's attention, tap might quickly lose it again. And then there was this from Paul Draper:

> Why did tap die out? I suspect largely because the other forms of dance which began to emerge in other shows were so much more imaginative, so much more musical, and so much more meaningful that nothing as ordinarily idly based as tap dancing had been could conceivably survive in the face of it . . . With all the other things that dancing was, I don't see how tap survived even as long as it did . . .
>
> I don't think there is a tap revival. I've only seen one sign in a national magazine . . . It said there was a revival in tap dancing and that the reason for the revival was because it was so easy to learn—you could learn to tap dance in about twenty minutes. I've been trying to learn tap dance for about thirty-five years and I haven't learned how yet. I don't know what all these people are doing, but it is not tap dancing.

"The final challenge," wrote Ames and Siegelman, "is for tap to move out of the shadow of its nostalgic associations. It must go someplace other than where it has been in the past." Some interviewees vested their hopes in a choreographer, someone to do with tap what Agnes de Mille had done with ballet. Others suggested a company, something along the lines of modern dance. (Ames had founded such a company, all-white and super-square, in 1975.) George Church, who had danced in *On Your Toes*, believed that all tap needed was a charismatic star, an Astaire, a Kelly, a "tap messiah." Jimmy Slyde prophesized that the next great tap dancer would come from Europe: "We had our chance and we blew it."

After a stint in the Maryland House of Correction—where, according to a friend, he converted to Islam—Baby Laurence found work with Leticia Jay. For a while, in the early seventies, he hosted a Sunday jam session at New York's Jazz Museum, a novel kind of institution funded by the New York State Council on the Arts. (One week, he invited Jerry Ames. "When my solo came," Ames remembered, "Baby took the mic and said, 'Tap dancing is a percussive art. You don't spin like a top or leap like a duck.'" Later, in *The Book of Tap*, Ames represented Laurence with a photo of him in flight, his leaping limbs more artfully arranged than Paul Draper's.) In 1973, Laurence was invited back to Newport, along with Buster Brown and Chuck Green, for a concert with Charles Mingus, a children's matinee. In Monterey, they served as between-the-acts filler. In Berlin, Laurence danced with the Ellington band. Back home, he appeared on *The Mike Douglas Show* and *The Flip Wilson Show*, a popular TV variety program with a black host. Things were looking up. A few months later, in April 1974, he died.

The cause was cancer. He was fifty-three. At his funeral, Copasetics and Hoofers danced in his memory. "Each one of us spoke to God in tap dancing," remembered Chuck Green. "Joyful noises, see." A short documentary about Laurence had recently been shot, catching the master expending his subtleties on a riser at a street fair, a film that wouldn't be released until 1981. Though Laurence taught a bit and planned to start a school, he left no disciples. Even amid the Tap Is Back fever of 1974, the aging black men at his funeral could feel that something—the most important thing—was still in danger of being lost. The Copasetics and the Hoofers weren't getting any younger. Who would be interested in furthering *their* tradition? The answer was going to surprise them.

15

RENAISSANCE

In 1973, the Copasetics played Carnegie Hall. They were guests of Cab Calloway, who joked about having to dig up his Cotton Club band, as if he were exhuming the dead. By way of introducing the Copasetics, he made the offhand assertion that "tap dancing is a thing more or less of the past."

After the show, Honi Coles was greeted by a former student, one of the few he'd ever had. Her name was Brenda Bufalino, and she had brought along her own students, plus some ideas about tap. Brenda Bufalino was bursting with ideas. She wanted to make a documentary about the Copasetics. She wanted to transform tap into a concert form. And she wanted Coles to join her. His retort was swift. Nobody is interested in that stuff, he told her. And nobody wants to see a broken-down buck dancer.

Bufalino was not so easily discouraged. She had been born into the business. Her Italian father was a contractor, but her mother, a Yankee with some Native American blood, was a soprano and elocutionist who worked with Bufalino's pianist aunt in an act called the Strickland Sisters. As they traveled from their home in Swampscott, Massachusetts, to Rotary clubs and Masonic lodges throughout New England in the forties, performing Dutch and Hawaiian medleys and reciting Long-fellow, hyperactive little Brenda tagged along and shared with the folks what she had learned at dancing school. She did tap in a hula skirt, tap on roller skates, tap while jumping rope. At age fourteen, she decided she wanted to add a "primitive" dance. In leopard-skin tights and a hat spouting ostrich feathers, she danced to *Bolero* atop a drum. Her mother's agent understood what she was after. He sent her to Stanley Brown.

Bufalino walked into Brown's Boston studio just a few years after Jimmy Slyde had walked out. Only she walked in wearing a pink dress, white pumps, a white hat, and white gloves. The person inside that out-fit heard the drums and felt immediately at home. "You don't belong here," she would remember Brown telling her. "There is no place for you in this world." For someone of Bufalino's temperament, no more inviting words could have been spoken. At Brown's, she studied Afro-Caribbean dance, what they called "modern primitive," along with jazz-based tap. "I was built for it. It was like I knew it. I could just do it."

Brown taught the old-fashioned way, demonstrating a phrase and then leaving the room as his pupil worked it out for herself. Even through this hands-off method, Bufalino learned to think of her tapping less as a stringing together of steps than as musical phrasing. From the arrangers Brown employed she gleaned that it wasn't the tune that mattered; it was how you played the tune. Other lessons were less happy. At sixteen, Bu-falino joined a troupe based at the school, an interracial troupe that per-formed in seedy clubs around Boston. Every night there was a fight. If her black colleagues escorted her to her bus, white thugs rewarded them with a beating. Rocks broke the windows of her home. She was ac-cused of hiding a black baby she didn't have. As soon as she graduated from high school, she moved to New York.

It was then that she met Honi Coles. At Dance Craft, a studio set above Jimmy Ryan's jazz club on Fifty-second Street, Bufalino was awed by Coles's subtle phrasing and understated delivery. As a teacher, he had no truck with terminology; he demonstrated the rhythm or scatted it with syllables. He and his business partner, Pete Nugent, didn't have many students in 1955. "They used to stand at the window waiting for people to come in," she would recall. On Monday nights, they would invite their out-of-work buddies for a bring-your-own-booze jam. Bufalino had been improvising her whole life; remembering routines was hard for her, so she made things up. Yet she was disturbed by how a cutting contest made her feel: not as a nice girl should.

She kept performing, studying with members of Katherine Dunham's company and getting more work as an Afro-Cuban and calypso dancer than as a tapper. She dyed her hair dark and sometimes passed as black or Latin. (You can see her, topless in Capri pants, on the cover of *Bohemia After Dark*, the 1955 jazz album that introduced the Adderley brothers.) Four shows a night, seven days a week, expected to "mix" with the customers, forever hearing some guy yell, "Take it off!": this was her life as an artist. A burnt-out twenty-year-old in 1957—the year Coles gave up teaching and took his job at the Apollo—she quit dancing, got married, bought a farm upstate, and proceeded to raise two children.

Around 1966, Ed Summerlin, a jazz saxophonist she had known in Boston, started including her in the contemporary liturgics he put together for the National Council of Churches. These were very 1960s productions. Bufalino tied up her audience, flashed lights in their eyes, recited *Sex and the Single Girl* into a bullhorn. The jazz was avant-garde, free. "You have to give up rhythm," Summerlin told her. "Rhythm is dead." Bufalino often brought her tap shoes along as another crazy prop, and at an avant-garde festival in 1973, when the electrical system overloaded, she laced up her acoustic instruments. The arty crowd seemed to miss rhythm, she felt, and so did she. Was she an entertainer or an artist? The question would persist.

After parting ways with Summerlin, and with her husband, too, Bufalino opened a dance studio in New Paltz and began incorporating tap into her teaching. In a space of her own, she practiced hard, with a clear intention, much as Coles had in his furnitureless room forty years before. Yet she also approached her practicing analytically, taking the technique she had acquired intuitively and pulling it apart so she could teach it to others. In 1974, she brought in the Copasetics to do lecture-demonstrations. (When she approached faculty in the local college's black studies department for help promoting the events, they formally boycotted them.) Then she took advantage of a tool that she had discovered in the avant-garde: the grant application. The National Endowment for the Arts awarded her funds to make a documentary about the Copasetics. She titled it *Great Feats of Feet*.

Here was something that Marshall Stearns hadn't quite accomplished. Recorded in black-and-white video in 1977, *Great Feats of Feet* is a decidedly amateur product, yet it succeeds in capturing the men in action. As they teach, perform, swap stories, and wander though New Paltz in their suits and hats, the people of the town fall for them. Who could resist? Honi Coles: so dry and distingué even while teaching the Shim Sham to beginners. Cookie Cook: sardonic and softhearted, a curmudgeon who complains about how people don't love each other like they used to. His undersized partner, Brownie Brown: so elastic of body and spirit that he bounces back, chest out, every time Cook grabs him by the face and thrusts him to the ground. Albert "Gip" Gibson: doubled in diameter since his days with the Chocolateers, his cane now a necessary support after all those knee drops from the balcony, hobbling through routines with undiminished gusto, so excited he squeaks. Buster Brown: slim and groovy, the hippest one in his applejack hat, swiveling into snakehips, dropping into splits, reheating his schtick. Bubba Gaines: more circumspect, capable of the most feathery time steps but also of whipping an audience into a frenzy with the jump-rope tap from his tenure with the Three Dukes before flashing a dazzling smile and wheezing, "If you keep encouraging me like that, I will completely destroy myself."

Even discounting the years off, the men had accumulated decades of stage experience. As retirees, they had nothing to prove, and though they appeared not to take themselves very seriously, their technical mastery was unmistakable. They behaved like old friends, because that's what they were, a social club formed a quarter century before. Yet adoration after such sustained neglect aroused in them an eagerness to share. The men didn't need to be half as good as they were. Anything they managed now looked miraculous. They could execute the traditional routine profanely known as the B.S. Chorus while sitting in chairs and get a bigger hand than when they did it standing up. They could disinter their antique jokes and it didn't matter whether the gags were still funny.

If the men were behind the times, that only made them more adorable, and their dancing redeemed all.

The showbiz adage about not performing with animals or kids needed an update: never share a stage with old black hoofers. Especially not these old black hoofers. And yet that's just what Bufalino did. As demand for the Copasetics grew, she occasionally joined them as a guest. For an opener, they used a routine that Coles had put together for nondancers on *The Perry Como Show*. The Copasetics called it the Walkaround, though after Cookie Cook started teaching it at New Paltz, Coles changed the name to the Coles Stroll. Like its minstrel-show ancestor, it was a circle dance. The Copasetics entered in a line, just ambling around to the music, each man introducing himself to the audience by his gait. Still circling, every eight bars they added a beat to the repeating pattern: a brush, a hop, a toe hit, until they had built up, right before your eyes, a nice skipping phrase. When the Copasetics did the routine, it was a casual demonstration of their favorite saying, "If you can walk, you can tap." When Bufalino joined them, she always entered last and always got a laugh.

However incongruous she appeared, Bufalino was the next in line. Including Coles in her own 1978 concert *Singing, Swinging, and Winging* was at once opportunistic, collegial, and courageous. He did his Bill Robinson tribute—a patter song followed by a collection of Bojangles steps, leaner even than the original—then went into his own style, gradually increasing the intricacy to a refined height of solo hoofing. Between the two parts, he told the audience, Juba-like, "That was Uncle Bo. This is me." Later, Bufalino joined him for a rechoreographed, lesser version of the Coles and Atkins soft shoe: same song, same glacial tempo, mostly new steps. The obvious physical differences between the partners—black, white; male, female; tall, short—played against a less obvious similarity in how they held their bodies and moved, giving the partnership a distinct charge. They played their arguments for comedy. At a few points in Bufalino's choreography for herself and her two students, each dancer set up a phrase of her own, and when all three phrases locked together, the gears meshed, and the combined rhythm took off like a Wright Brothers test flight. Bufalino, who considered unison tap a waste of multiple dancers, was putting her toe into the polyrhythmic water. The evening ended with some of Coles's Copasetic buddies joining the cast in the Shim Sham.

Coles, the variety veteran, had been skeptical about a whole evening of tap. "The audience won't sit through it," he assured her. He was equally skeptical about polyrhythm: "The audience won't understand it." When she suggested that he dance at greater length, Coles told her to try it herself. Bufalino constructed *Tapestry*, a forty-five-minute duet for herself and a student, a progressively complex composition performed a cappella, with a few sections drifting in free time. At its 1981 premiere, she would recall in her autobiography, she could feel the small audience growing restless as the dance's duration spilled over the five-minute mark. Then she felt them relaxing, adjusting. At the finish, they stood up.

Bufalino, changing the man's game, had one more vision for Coles to judge impossible: a tap-dance orchestra. It was to be big—twenty, forty dancers—so that she could divide the company into sections, each section holding its own rhythm, all of the rhythms interlocking. Done right, she imagined, it could blast the roof off a building.

STEARNS, JR.

Tagging along through *Great Feats of Feet* is a young woman with frizzy curls, a fondness for thrift-store dresses, and a chronic giggle. Meet Jane Goldberg, soon to be known as the Tap Goddess of the Lower East Side, the form's greatest evangelist since Leticia Jay. In 1972, Goldberg was a New Left graduate of Boston University with aspirations of becoming a muckraking journalist. "If you can't liberate the world," Professor Howard Zinn had told her, "you must liberate the ground under your feet." That was an inspiring goal, but reading a *Newsweek* review of Arlene Croce's Astaire-Rogers book and then seeing *Carefree*, Goldberg fell in love with the romance of it all and started fantasizing about dancing with Astaire. As a child, she had tapped in Mary Janes with bows. Thinking to begin again, she looked up "tap" in the Boston yellow pages and found one studio listed: Stanley Brown's.

The place that had changed Brenda Bufalino's life did not have the same effect on Goldberg. She enjoyed the steps, but she was equally interested in modern and postmodern dance. She had started publishing dance criticism, and it was a critic mentor, Deborah Jowitt, who handed her a flyer for "Mama J's JazzJoint or Tap Happen." In a church basement in New York, Goldberg discovered a group of old black men cracking jokes and dancing on linoleum, along with a gyrating lady with a Southern accent. It was John T. McPhee, Raymond Kaalund, Rhythm Red, Chuck Green, and Leticia Jay, about to shatter Goldberg's notions of what tap could be. That church basement was the site of her conversion.

"Somebody," she wrote in her report of the event for *The Patriot Ledger*, "should grab them fast and learn their special brand of tap-dance." Why not her? As Goldberg watched Chuck Green do what few tap dancers in history could equal, the thought that came into her head was, I can do that. She asked Green for lessons, and she recorded her first instructional session: a loop of Green demonstrating a step, Goldberg trying it, and Green grunting in disapproval. But Goldberg also asked Green about himself and he began telling his story—how he danced on Georgia sidewalks with bottletops stuck with tar to the bottom of his feet, how he tricked John Bubbles into teaching him. Goldberg was as fascinated by the stories as by the steps. She would collect both.

Back in Boston, after she described her problems learning from Green to Stanley Brown, Brown said simply, "Oh no, they cannot pass it on." And there it was: a challenge, a cause, a story to uncover, an injustice to right. After moving to New York, she called Honi Coles for six months before convincing him to teach her and some curious modern dancers she gathered together in a SoHo loft. After she trekked to Pittsburgh to consult the oracle of Paul Draper, he told her that what the hoofers did wasn't dancing; she took a course with him, but his ballet-tap felt artificial to her, so she quit halfway through. Dropping Coles's name earned her entrance into the 1976 Copasetics ball, where the only other white people were Brenda Bufalino and one of Bufalino's students. One by one, doing the Coles Stroll, the rest of the Copasetics entered her life. Portly Gip Gibson gave her the number of Sandman Sims, and in her basement apartment on Bleecker Street, Goldberg and Sims yelled at each other for half a year as he broke down the paddle and roll. While at first he suggested that she might play Shirley Temple to his Bill Robinson, Goldberg knew she was getting somewhere when he told her, "You're dancing like a little black boy."

When Goldberg's father took a trip to Las Vegas, she went along and looked up Cholly Atkins and Maceo Anderson of the Four Step Brothers. Through Goldberg's tape recorder, Atkins sent a message to his former partner Honi Coles, with whom he had been out of touch. The connections were accumulating, and the tapes, too, the physical evidence of an obsession. Tapes of Goldberg talking to tap dancers and jazz musicians piled up next to tapes of Goldberg talking to herself, later to be joined by tapes of Goldberg talking to her therapist, all about tap. There were tapes of Goldberg tapping with others, tapes of her tapping alone. Beside them crowded articles and photos and videos and shoes and the five hundred remaining copies of Baby Laurence's album, rescued by purchase just before they were to be scrapped. Goldberg was on a scavenger hunt, and Marshall Stearns's *Jazz Dance* provided the list. The title page of her copy of the book was soon dense with signatures of the living. Cookie Cook started calling her "Stearns, Jr."

Cook had taken over Coles's class. He had never been known as a tap dancer; he was a comedy dancer, back in the days when everyone tapped. One of the early effects of the new attention, however, was his blossoming as a hoofer. He enjoyed teaching. He discovered that it could be a mode of choreography; students remembered his improvisations. Goldberg loved his classes. In other dance forms, she would later explain, she had often felt fat. Cookie taught with his back to the class, listening. He didn't give a damn what she looked like. His kind of tap also seemed to mesh with her politics and free-spirit impulses. "That's what the time steps were all about: everybody had his own. It was a democratic form." All the hoofers urged her to find her own style.

What Goldberg loved best about Cook, though, was his sense of humor. She yearned to do comedy with him, to be funny *and* tap. And where could one do that? Vaudeville was dead. Independently, Goldberg and Cook were selected for the Comprehensive Employment Act Training Program, a WPA-type initiative, and they began working together in nursing homes and libraries. Mounting a siege on the NEA, Goldberg discovered that Rhoda Grauer, the head of the organization's dance program, was a closet hoofer, symphathetic enough to offer Goldberg a $1,800 choreography fellowship. The initial plan was a lecture-demonstration, but Cook, drunk one evening, insisted on bringing along Gip Gibson, who brought along Jazzlips Richardson. Then Goldberg invited another of Cook's students, Andrea Levine, and Levine's drummer boyfriend and a piano player and a saxophonist and suddenly she had a show. The choreographer Elaine Summers offered Goldberg her fifth-floor SoHo loft for a weekend run in late February 1978. Goldberg picked a punning and pointed title: *It's About Time.*

The evening began with Goldberg dancing to a voice-over recording of Stanley Brown, who had recently died, telling her about how the hoofers could not pass it on. The rest of the program proved him wrong. Goldberg improvised with the saxophonist; Levine traded eights with the drummer. The old guys doing their old numbers earned the warmest response, but the heart of the show was Cook and Goldberg dancing side by side, doing material from Cook's old act and new dances Cook had just created. One was called "Let's Be Buddies," and that's what the pair looked like—he in a pink suit; she in top hat, tails, and knickers. At the end of the show, tappers in the audience, veterans and beginners, streamed onstage for the Shim Sham.

"Break down the doors if you have to," wrote Jennifer Dunning in *The New York Times.* Other reviewers were equally ardent, even grateful. All at once, Jane Goldberg, not yet thirty, was hot. She and her gang played the Village Vanguard and were invited to perform at prestigious summer venues such as the American Dance Festival, where tap hadn't been welcome since Draper was there in 1963, and Jacob's Pillow, where the preceding tap act had been the company of George Tapps in 1948. She enlisted more hoofers. Ralph Brown, that genial gentleman of the Cotton Club and *Jivin' in Bebop*, offered his "heelology," balancing on the heels of his pink shoes to suture the stage with tiny steps, clicking his toes together and holding up his hands to silence applause until he was finished. Bubba Gaines taught Goldberg a Three Dukes number on miniature suitcases. Marion Coles, the wife of Honi, adapted Apollo chorus line routines.

Goldberg's next show, *Shoot Me While I'm Happy*, opened in the dark,

with the sound of someone doing the paddle and roll. This was a reminder to listen, warming up the ears by depriving the eyes. It was also,
though perhaps not intentionally, a version of the blindfold tests once
organized by jazz magazines like *Downbeat*, in which prominent musicians were supposed to listen to records without being told who was
playing and offer opinions about quality and sometimes about the race of
the players. In *Shoot Me While I'm Happy*, the person doing the paddle
and roll was Goldberg, but the sound could have been Cook's. With
the lights on, she had the appealingly eager awkwardness of early Joan
Crawford and an unpretentious manner that one critic likened to "a favorite aunt serving up treats." Later, she did a "Hebrew" soft shoe. She
also tapped to a poem about a neighbor driven crazy by her practicing, a
poem recited by that neighbor to the rhythms of Poe's "The Raven."
She took one of the best-known songs from *No, No, Nanette* and war-
bled it thusly:

> I want to be happy,
> But I don't feel happy,
> Friends say I sing crappy, too.

> I thought I found the answer.
> Became a tap dancer.
> But still I feel crappy, too.

When the show played New York, it was accompanied by a screening of
tap numbers from the film collection of Ernie Smith, an advertising executive and swing dancer who had volunteered for Stearns and the Institute of Jazz Studies in the sixties. Scouring vintage copies of *Variety* and
Billboard, Smith had compiled a thorough appendix of tap in film for *Jazz
Dance* and had, through purchase and trade, amassed a stockpile of jazz in
film. He had Bill Robinson's stair dance, some Buck and Bubbles, the
Coles and Atkins soft shoe. Smith's reels were, in a sense, film companions to *Jazz Dance*, compilations of tap left out by *That's Entertainment*.

   This kind of tap had a history, and it had a future—Goldberg stressed
both in the articles that were written about her wherever she went. A
journalist herself, she knew how to attract coverage. (Philadelphia's *Jew-*

ish Community Voice gave its profile of Goldberg the headline "She Saved Tap Dancing from Death.") She insisted that her project had nothing to do with nostalgia, and she continued the argument in the articles she wrote herself, including an interview with John Bubbles. (He called her Jane Allison—"Goldberg is not a stage name"—and told her from his wheelchair, "You've got to surpass me, darling. Not just do me but surpass me.") Goldberg didn't use the word *revival*, so suggestive of restaging and return; she preferred the word *renaissance*—the birth of something new, informed by the past.

She formed a nonprofit corporation, and she and another tap aficionado, Jackie Raven, shared visions of an updated Hoofers' Club. Their initial idea involved a twenty-week program of classes by tap masters and eight performances. The budget estimate came to $43,000. The NEA granted $16,000, and the whole thing got condensed into a single week of classes. Still, it was a tap festival, the first. By Word of Foot, as it was called, attracted 150 students, a motley gathering crammed into the makeshift classroom of the Village Gate nightclub in 1980. Each afternoon, Bubbles held court, expressing his pleased amazement that so many people were "interested in this idea." Leticia Jay remarked that if she had attempted such a festival in 1969, there would have been no young dancers eager to learn, "not one."

RECAPITULATION

Writing about By Word of Foot, both Noël Carroll in *Dance* and Sally Sommer in *The Village Voice* were disturbed by how many students failed to absorb, instantly and on the spot, all of the stylistic and rhythmic nuances of the masters. Carroll noted the incongruity of these men, who had learned their art on street corners, teaching in a classroom setting. Sommer remarked on how the majority of the students were uncomfortable with improvisation while the ad-libbing masters frequently could not remember the sequence they had just demonstrated. Neither writer overlooked the most obvious contrast: almost all the teachers were old black men; almost all the students were young white women. Sommer wasn't surprised—tap classes, she pointed out, had been rites of passage for the white middle class when these women were children—yet she was troubled. "This has got to change," she wrote, "if this unique black dance art is going to survive with vigor and integrity. If it isn't passed on to large numbers of young blacks, the tradition—as it now exists—will simply erode."

Sommer was a young white woman herself, though old enough to have witnessed *Tap Happening* in 1969. She was new to New York then, trained in modern dance, with multiple degrees in theater, and the Hoofers, she would later write, "rearranged" all her "ideas about art in dance." When Goldberg and others started importing tap into modern-dance venues, Sommer was an eloquent advocate. She was even a participant in By Word of Foot—she gave a lecture on tap as black culture—and in her article about the festival she wrote, "It's not that I want the young white women to fade away." She thought they deserved "gratitude, admiration, and respect" for fund-raising and organizing. Yet they were, in her view, not appropriate heirs because of "unavoidable cultural distinctions." Style, she asserted, "is as profoundly imprinted as the way we walk and talk," and since the tap style of Honi Coles was "thoroughly embedded in Afro-American culture," white women had no access to "black rhythms." By citing a counterexample of a black Savoy Ballroom dancer who was passing her tradition on to a son, Sommer implied that the only legitimate transfer was genetic. In an earlier review of a Goldberg show, Sommer had gone further still. "The greatest tap dancers are (and were) black," she wrote, and the reason most people didn't know that was racism. She called the young white women's efforts a "recapitulation" of "the great white ripoff."

Marcia Siegel, in her *New York* review of *Shoot Me While I'm Happy*, noted that while Dance Theatre of Harlem, whose classical ballet performances she was also reviewing, was trying to prove that black dancers could do white dance, Goldberg and her ilk were attempting the opposite. That's the kind of comparison that arises through the serendipity of scheduling, but consider this: if Siegel or Sommer had suggested that Dance Theatre of Harlem (founded in 1969 by Arthur Mitchell, a one-time tap dancer who had become the first black soloist in the New York City Ballet in 1955) could not do ballet because of unavoidable cultural distinctions (as had been argued, routinely and openly, about blacks into the seventies), their publications would have been inundated by protest mail.

As it happened, the *Voice* did publish a letter of dissent. It was from Jan Leder, a white female jazz flutist who spit the racist label back at Sommer. In one sense, the young white female tappers had it easier than white female jazz musicians. The tradition they were adopting may have provided few female role models, but the business and culture of the modern-dance world into which they were transplanting that tradition had largely been created by women and was much less sexist than the boys' club of jazz. In another sense, they had it tougher. All talk of "black rhythm" aside, music doesn't have a color or a gender; bodies do. And while a musician can, to some extent, hide behind an instrument, a dancer's body *is* her instrument. The eye is more discriminating than the ear.

While Sommer was suggesting that the young white women couldn't accurately emulate their mentors, Arlene Croce was arguing that they shouldn't. The reason women had seldom ventured into virtuoso hoofer territory, Croce wrote in *The New Yorker*, was that the technique was physically unflattering: "Those who study with aging hoofers have to beware of absorbing their heaviness." Absorbing heaviness from Honi Coles would seem paradoxical, but Croce was advocating different expectations for female dancers, particularly a cultivated body line. "I'm aware that these sexual distinctions probably don't interest the new breed of female tap-dancers, but who could be interested in the low-primate stuff they're turning out now?" Croce's dismissal, it seems to me, unnecessarily conflated beginner's awkwardness with an African-derived dance posture well suited to tap. That the women would absorb heaviness was less of a peril than that they would fail to absorb the aesthetic of the cool. The danger wasn't that they would look like apes; the danger was that they would look like they were aping.

All of this commentary signaled another twist in the spiraling history of the imitation dance. Sommer's talk about filtering and dilution, her phrase "a pale copy"—here was the same language of bleaching and refinement that surrounded minstrelsy, the same imitation charge leveled at the black musicals of the twenties. Here was the latest stage in the treacherous and futile and irresistible pursuit of the Real Thing, or what

Sommer called the "true tradition." Was it possible to acknowlege the worth of African American culture without treating race as some essential category? If racial lines had been kept pure, there would be no African-American culture and certainly no tap. Sommer's understandable anxiety seemed to miss the point the old black masters were always stressing: make it your own. The central idea in her articles was the interconnectedness of tap and the cultural context in which it grew. But the context had changed. As Goldberg wrote in defense of By Word of Foot, "That tap dancers no longer jam on street corners was the whole point of organizing such a festival."

Still, it was good to be wary of what might be lost, and the paucity of interested young black people was certainly sad. Reverberations of racism past could make things awkward all around. When Cookie Cook accused his student-turned-partner of paying herself more than she paid him, he had some cause for suspicion. For decades, he had been ripped off by white managers. (A producer named Jack Goldberg, no relation to Jane, had been one of the most notorious exploiters of black talent.) But Cook's accusation was false. Even though Goldberg was arranging the gigs, she split the fees evenly. Cook also told Goldberg that the Copasetics were giving him hell for teaching their material to her. Honi Coles told Brenda Bufalino that he was getting the same message: Why are you giving our stuff to the white girl? According to Bufalino, Coles's response was simple: "Because no blacks want it and she does, and because nobody else can do it and she can."

There's a telling moment in a 1981 interview between Bufalino and Coles. For almost the entire four hours of videotape, made for a public television oral history project, the two dancers are the closest of colleagues, frequently touching hands as they joke and chat and recall steps. At one point, though, Bufalino mentions the difference between their kind of tap and the tap on Broadway, and in an instant, everything turns tense. "You've put me in a funny spot," says Coles. The question of ethnicity has been raised, "and there is a great difference." The Condos Brothers, Coles allows, could swing like blacks, having learned from them, and Bufalino, he says, swings as well as anyone he knows, though she "swings Italian." When Bufalino suggests that if it weren't for the mixing of cultures, tap wouldn't have existed at all, Coles responds coldly: "I don't know how you mean that." His supple body language stiffens. He brings up an article he once read about how Mozart stole from Africans. He talks about how you don't need shoes to dance out rhythms. Sensing a segue, both he and Bufalino grab for it, pulling themselves out of the pit of race by way of a technical discussion of the kinds of taps he prefers. But the pit did gape, as it could anytime, even between them.

TEACHERS AND STUDENTS

Honi Coles, heading into his seventies, was more famous than ever. Age became him. It put a dignified patina on his elegance and gave his courtly geniality some sharp and bitter edges. He took to the role of elder statesman, and the newly listening audiences encouraged him to concentrate on musical subtleties, shadings, moods. During the filming of *Great Feats of Feet*, he was absent for the performances because he was touring in the Broadway revue *Bubbling Brown Sugar*, a black response, featuring all black composers, to Broadway revivals like *No, No, Nanette*. That same year, Coles was invited by none other than Agnes de Mille, the Woman Who Killed Tap, to personify his art in her lecture-demonstration about dance for the Joffrey Ballet. The witty and cultivated talk-show host Dick Cavett, guest-hosting *The Tonight Show*, invited Coles on and fawned over him as an exemplar of urbanity, the same way he fawned over Astaire. Cavett also studied tap with Coles, sometimes in the company of his friend Woody Allen. On his own PBS program, Cavett broadcast the Copasetics' entire act and modestly stumbled through the routines himself.

The Copasetics, too, were more famous than ever, and more active. They still held their annual benefit, but their schedule now included the college circuit: Duke University, Yale. *New York* magazine ran an adulatory profile illustrated with a photo of the men, spread across two pages, glowing in white tails, top hats, and smiles. No longer were they an uptown secret. The Hoofers were also on the go. From 1979 through the early eighties, Jimmy Slyde, Lon Chaney, and their gang of fifty- and sixty-year-olds formed the dancing half of the internationally touring revue *1000 Years of Jazz*, contributing their ages to the sum in the name. The Hoofers and the Copasetics were rival tribes. Chuck Green would point out that not all of the Copasetics were dancers, insinuating that they were showmen in a shallow sense. Honi Coles would imply that the Hoofers were ragged, lacking in polish. Sandman Sims, a Hoofer, was rebuffed by the Copasetics, so he made a habit of waiting outside their meetings to heckle. It was a measure of Buster Brown's amiability that he could hop from one group to the other, the only dancer to do so.

Nevertheless, Green and Sims joined the Copasetics for a signal event at the Brooklyn Academy of Music in the final days of 1979. It was called *Steps in Time*. A nearly four-hour program, it was the prototype for what would prove a durable model: the tap show overstuffed by justification of historical redress. The finale was a screening of Nicholas Brothers movie routines, after which the Nicholas Brothers broke through the screen to appear in the flesh. Harold, his facial hair now styled like Fu Manchu's, announced that they didn't do splits anymore, then threw one in anyway. Fayard, older and arthritic, conducted Harold's trip to the floor and back with his magician hands. These brothers were different from the other hoofers: slicker, grander. Time in Vegas, as much as time in general, had shrunken and hardened their schtick, though they could still make it shine. And they were shadowed by their younger selves, unaging on film. It became a standard joke of theirs to announce that they didn't dance like they used to—that *nobody* danced like they used to. The movies made the Nicholas Brothers larger than their tap colleagues, but the movies also diminished them. You weren't free to imagine, as you were with the others, that they were dancing better than they ever had.

Steps in Time was, in the words of Arlene Croce, "biographies, inescapably, of black men," the lives you could sense behind the performances. The concert inspired another round of articles about tap's hidden history, "the real tap dancing," and in answer to the nagging question about the paucity of young blacks onstage and in the audience, Honi Coles mused, "Maybe they're not ready to remember." *Steps in Time* wasn't just about aged black men, though. Cookie Cook had Jane Goldberg and Marion Coles join him. Leon Collins, a guest elder, insisted on performing with five of his students: four of them young women, all but

one white. These women weren't invited back for the repeat performances a few months later, but they were already part of the story.

The tap renaissance wasn't happening only in New York. There was, for
example, a Boston chapter. Leon Collins was a hoofer, Chicago-born.
In the forties, he toured with the Jimmy Lunceford Orchestra, shared
bills with the Four Step Brothers, played the Apollo. His epithet was
"Gangs of Dancing." His models were Baby Laurence and Groundhog.
Dizzy Gillespie would remember him dancing Charlie Parker solos,
note for note. He traded steps with Teddy Hale, who, he would later
claim, set him up for a drug bust that left him beaten by the police so
badly he was imprisoned for eleven months to hide the evidence. Through
the fifties, he worked the Catskills, and when the jobs disappeared, he
settled in Boston and devoted himself to polishing and reupholstering
cars. For fourteen years, he did not dance. His new friends did not know
he ever had. Then, in 1976, Tina Pratt, a friend from the old days, put
together a little evening called "The Artistry of Jazz Tap" at a Boston jazz
club and convinced Collins to participate. He began teaching tap in
Stanley Brown's school, and in 1982, helped by his devoted students, he
opened a school of his own in a former bowling alley. It was named after
him but known as Tapper's Paradise.

   He was tall and thin, with basset-hound eyes, a grizzled beard, and,
for a while, a godawful toupee. His style was fastidious, each sound placed
just so. Among his peers, he was a fierce competitor, equipped with a
deep enough "trick of bags," as he called it, to answer most challenges.
Yet with his pupils, the mostly young women he called his "dumplings,"
Collins was all generosity. "It makes me disgusted," he would say, "when
I make up a step and there's no one there to give it to." Because then he
might forget it; because then it would disappear. "It doesn't belong to
us," he said about his tradition. "It's like the air we breathe. It's for everybody." With his few male students, Collins was notably less generous,
and for his own solos he hoarded wonders that none of his students had
seen before. To aid his apprentices, he developed a graduated series of
étude-like routines, and he pushed his best students by performing with
them. He liked to "throw you to the wolves," as one of those students

recalled—waiting until the last minute to select the routine or abruptly leaving his charges alone in the middle of a number. When offered a gig, he insisted on bringing his dumplings along, especially his three protégées: a neuropsychophysiological technician named Clara "CB" Heatherington, a college dropout and sometime astrologer named Pamela Raff, and Dianne Walker, a clinical psychologist and mother of two. They were three women in their twenties—Walker was the only black one—who had taken tap as children and had rediscovered it through Collins. None had considered tap as a career, and now all of them would have careers in tap.

The most apparent impact on Collins's late style, however, came from a woman much closer to his own age. When he met Joan Hill, she was newly divorced after twenty-eight years of marriage, a white classical pianist who was following her bliss into jazz. They fell in love immediately, moved in together, and as she worked on her jazz skills, he grew fascinated with her classical repertoire. Together, they began performing von Suppé's "Poet and Peasant Overture" and de Falla's "Ritual Fire Dance." Her arrangement segueing from "Flight of the Bumblebee" into "Begin the Beguine" became his signature piece, marked by a you-weren't-expecting-*this* drollery that was part situational, part rhythmic, and part physical. His renditions of Bach's Prelude and Fugue in C Minor were less comic. He treated the notes as he would a Charlie Parker solo, matter-of-factly adapting bebop steps to baroque rhythms. This final stage of Collins's life didn't last long. He died in 1985, of cancer. His students kept his influence alive.

California had its own sets of neglected masters and hungry acolytes. But the masters tended to be more obscure, and the acolytes, oddly, were mostly modern dancers from the Midwest. Among the least known and most influential elders was Eddie Brown. He was born in Omaha, as one of nine children. The street corners of the prairie city's black section reverberated with foot rhythms back then—the late twenties, the early thirties—and Brown, who learned the basics from an itinerant teacher uncle, practiced with his buddies after school, or instead of school, until it got dark or even after they couldn't see anymore. Brown also had a higher-tech method of stealing steps. He studied Bill Robinson's 78 of "Doin' the New Low Down," slowing the Grafonola to catch all the beats, then matched them with steps he had seen Robinson do in movie and stage appearances. When Bojangles hosted a dance contest in Omaha, Brown performed the routine for its originator, who was impressed enough to invite him to New York. Brown's parents wouldn't give him permission to go, but the sixteen-year-old took off on his own a week later, train-hopping with two friends. In New York, he danced up-tempo and acrobatically, and though he was at first confused by the more easeful style that John Bubbles had introduced, he set himself to mastering it. He used it touring with big bands, though his own renown never grew large. Washed up in San Francisco, he spent much of tap's Dark Ages drunk.

Around 1975, he got a job dancing in a production of *Evolution of the Blues*, a historical revue by the jazz singer Jon Hendricks. Brown was short, slight, low-riding. His body draped as loosely as the large double-breasted suit jackets he favored. He let his arms swing, and the soft folding of his elbows reflected the folding of his knees as they lifted his feet, rarely more than a few inches high. His body language physicalized the attitude behind his favorite expression, "Can you dig it?" He called his style Scientific Rhythm, the adjective apparently intended (as in minstrel days) to emphasize the tight logic of his impromptu constructions. His dancing generally contrasted strolling-in-place phrases with spurts of double time, his punctuating pauses as important as the ricocheting stamps before them, accents popping off in unusual places like mini-shocks of static electricity. Brown was such a thorough improviser that you could watch his appearance in *Evolution of the Blues* night after night and never hear the same thing twice. That was the experience of a twenty-six-year-old modern dancer named Camden Richman, and it changed her life.

Richman convinced Brown to teach her. This meant visiting the home of the aging bachelor, rousing him out of bed, giving him his medicine, sobering him up, then trying to absorb as much as possible as he danced on an old piece of wood in the basement. Usually, Brown couldn't remember the step he had just done, but if Richman could catch it, it was hers, he said. This was the philosophy he imparted to the many students who followed. Unlike many of his black contemporaries, he was eager to be videotaped; after a taping, he would eagerly ask, "Is it in the box?" "It was more than just picking up steps as fast as you can," Richman would recall. "It's the way he moves and the way he approaches them. You find it in yourself how to do that." Brown encouraged individual expression, which he pronounced "express-see-ohn." Asked to explain improvisation, he once said, "I like to get up and let myself go down strange paths. I don't know where I'm going . . . There's a little man in there telling me what to do."

When Honi Coles came to San Francisco with *Bubbling Brown Sugar*, Richman went backstage and introduced herself as a "tap percussionist." She asked for lessons from him, too, and Coles granted them. "And, like, I didn't have to see what he did," she would recall. "I wasn't watching so much as I was listening." Richman was fascinated by tap's past, reverent toward it, but she also had ideas about the future. She formed a jazz trio to try them out.

Something was coming together. Richman took classes with Lynn Dally, another modern dancer, a little older, who had been raised as a tap dancer. Dally's father, Jimmy Rawlins, was a retired vaudevillian who ran a rigorous dancing school in Columbus, Ohio. When Dally enrolled at Ohio State in 1959, she brought her tap shoes with her, but at the audition for the university dance ensemble, she noticed that everyone else was barefoot. University dance departments had been created by modern dancers, a clan that didn't consider tap worthy of academic study. Into a locker went Dally's shoes, there to remain, at least metaphorically, for more than a decade. She got a master's degree in dance, taught, and eventually formed her own dance company in California, while teaching at UCLA. Fred Strickler, who had grown up as a scholarship student at the Rawlins studio, also studied dance at Ohio State. Drawn by the same cultural wind, he moved west to join a modern-dance company (Bella Lewitsky's) and teach. He followed this path independently, but reconnected in Los Angeles with Dally, who introduced him to Richman, who told him about Honi Coles and Eddie Brown.

But when Strickler and Dally went to see the L.A. production of

Evolution of the Blues, it featured the tapping of Foster Johnson. "He had a white Afro," Strickler would remember. "This was the Angela Davis era. A beautiful man. Danced like quicksilver, like sand pouring from a bottle. I was awestruck." Born in Virginia around 1917, Johnson had worked on TOBA with the Whitman Sisters and danced (sometimes in a duo with Bobby Johnson) with the best big bands at the Cotton Club, at the Apollo, and in Vegas. After the war, he ran the Finale Club, a hip jazz joint in Los Angeles. By the fifties, the press was referring to him as "the former tap dancer," an emcee who taught. He drove a forklift, edited a magazine, and made it back onstage as a ballroom dancer, which informed his gliding style once he laced up his tap shoes again in the seventies. Handsome, articulate, and ultra-urbane, he might have made as fine an elder statesman for tap as Honi Coles. But he would die, of an aortic aneurism, in 1981.

The night that Dally saw him, Johnson recognized her from when he had taught at her father's studio. "You're Lynny," he said, grabbing her cheeks. Lessons were arranged.

Dally and Strickler also began practicing tap together, smoking dope and remembering things they didn't know they knew and revaluing their early training. Hooking up with Richman, they started choreographing tap pieces. People wanted more, so a company was formed: three dancers and three musicians. They called themselves the Jazz Tap Percussion Ensemble, the name serving to emphasize historical roots and a collective ideal—a collaborative of musicians, not dancers plus accompaniment.

Their concerts experimented with configurations: Richman and Dally with the bassist, Strickler with the drummer, the dancers without the musicians or vice versa. The music was a mix of originals and jazz standards, picking up where jazz and tap had gotten estranged to assimilate now-classic bebop compositions. The dances went in and out of time, testing out sonic possibilities, including silence. Dally's choreography showed the most obvious modern-dance influence, incorporating torso movements that were neither functional nor strictly decorative, semi-narrative concepts, and clipped endings. Strickler's background and intelligence came through in the exploratory shape of his dances, best exemplified by "Tacet Understanding," a brooding, introspective solo of cumulative and degenerative patterns. Body percussion pieces by the drummer, Keith Terry, were clever and amusing. Richman's work was the closest to the approach of her teachers, even when she was in flirty conversation with her boyfriend's New Wave playing of the electric bass.

Because Dally sometimes wore her hair short and Rod Stewart–spiky, reviewers called her "funky," but there seemed to be a permanent tilt to her head. Trying for thoughtfulness or bluesy soul, her body went slack and floppy. Strickler, with a patrician nose, was the most balletic in carriage, casual but also rigid. The entertainer in him snuck out in smirks during show-off solos titled "Cadenza" or "Tone Poem." Richman had more charisma. A gamine brunette, fragile-tough in leg warmers and a ponytail, she had absorbed Honi Coles's speed and floor-skimming lightness. She could be ungainly, too, landing in a deep squat like an impudent kid; it was easy to imagine her playing Peter Pan. That sense of play, combined with her beauty, made her stand out, yet the ensemble was remarkably balanced, very much a six-way conversation, which kept things interesting through a full concert.

Compared with the style of Coles, much less to Broadway or Hollywood modes, the group sensibility was, as Arlene Croce wrote, "a little overstarched." When the dancers put their hands in their pockets, the gesture seemed more a reference to casualness than casualness itself. The company could also exude a soft-edged quality that was stereotypically Californian. But in interviews and lecture demonstrations, their mentors were all they talked about. For the ensemble's New York debut in December 1979, it opened with a piece made by Foster Johnson and closed with one dedicated to Coles. While on the East Coast, the dancers met Brenda Bufalino, Jane Goldberg, and the rest of the community to which they now realized they belonged. They participated, as students, in Goldberg's By Word of Foot festival, and when their group performed at the Smithsonian in 1982—by then the name had been shortened to the Jazz Tap Ensemble—it started a tradition by bringing along a venerable guest artist: Honi Coles.

Tapdancin', a documentary directed by Christian Blackwood in 1979, is a survey of tap in the late seventies. It opens with the Hoofers grunting through the Track and includes footage of a Copasetics show, the Nicholas Brothers in Vegas, and Jerry Ames doing Morton Gould's Tap Dance Concerto in a tight white jumpsuit and a paisley shirt with a butterfly collar. No dance is shown in full, and as the film cuts quickly, the juxtapositions serve to make the Jazz Tap Ensemble look precious, the Nicholas Brothers shallow, and Ames ludicrous. All the same, *Tapdancin'* captures Maceo Anderson happily marveling at the difference between the old Four Step Brothers days, when he would fight if someone stole his steps, and a present in which he gives them away. John Bubbles seethes at the opportunities denied him—"To get on the stage you had to be everything else but what you were . . . world's greatest dancer . . . janitor," he says, and the way he spits out the last word is frightening—while Honi Coles's take on historical injustice turns enervating: "I think I'd have had the opportunity of an Astaire or Kelly if I'd been white. But if I'd been white maybe I wouldn't have been a dancer."

George T. Nierenberg's *No Maps on My Taps*, released the same year, is a narrower, deeper film. It concentrates on three dancers, all pushing sixty as they prepare for a public challenge backed by Lionel Hampton's band at Small's Paradise in Harlem. The men are vivid: Sandman Sims the wiry extrovert, Bunny Briggs the sad-eyed gentleman, Chuck Green a sort of autistic savant. A fragment of song Green makes up gives the film its title: a metaphor for improvisational, individualistic freedom. But Nierenberg's camera also takes in the flip side—the extent to which Green is lost, the hurt child in Briggs's faded-matinee-idol glamour, the bluster in Sims's bravado and his tender heart. The performance at Small's was an anachronism arranged by the filmmaker, though Hampton was one of the only bandleaders to hire tap dancers in the seventies. A phone call in the film between Green and John Bubbles is almost absurdly contrived, and the sidewalk arguments look fake, yet this tension between the film's documentary aspects and its apparent artifice makes it more poignant, drawing out the extent to which these men were always performing. As Green once explained, "You're supposed to be someone, a make-belief—for the public in general, not only in the theater. You have to play the part all the time."

The film took five years to make. Nierenberg, who was twenty-seven when it was released, was another member of his generation fascinated by tap history and shocked by his ignorance. He also recorded oral histories with Bubbles and Green, ten to thirteen hours each, that document the difficulty of interviewing these men. Bubbles is self-aggrandizing and irascible, berating Nierenberg for not understanding whenever Nierenberg asks a question. Green speaks figuratively, chuckling. Before the interview, Dee Bradley, the British widow of Buddy Bradley and girlfriend of Baby Laurence, advised Nierenberg that feeding Green walnuts would make him more lucid. Nierenberg followed that advice, but long tracts of the tape drift back and forth teasingly across the edge of sense. "I like to talk about into these degrees," Green says, "because someday, the world is going to want to take baths in these things." Here he is at the end of the interview, stuffed with walnuts, explaining why he never quit dancing:

> Well, there's what you call registration. Without registration, there's no force. There is no censorships to oppress you. If you could understand the physics of, uh, showboat. Which is something we are indebted to for all this new technologies that's going on today. The showboat is like a scratch rock is to the ancients [the Injuns?]. Understand? We must always have a family head. If you're gonna be an author, you must have a library. And we must never give out of describing the immensities of compassion, which is some sort of power that God has distributed to, see, our great greats. Like: the higher you go, the closer you see. Shed God's graces in the places to be.

No Maps on My Taps was partially funded by the NEA. It was broadcast on PBS and later on the BBC. Nierenberg packaged showings of the film with a live performance by its three stars (sometimes with Buster Brown and Jimmy Slyde as additions or substitutions), a touring double bill that made real the kind of gig the film had to fake. Traveling with Green posed challenges, such as when Green had to pass through metal detectors and would pull item after item from his many layers of clothing, a collection of junk emerging like clowns from a clown car. The show was presented at the Smithsonian, where tap had a new friend in the institution's dance consultant, Sali Ann Kriegsman. She had caught the tap bug at a Jane Goldberg show, and she told audiences that it was shameful that a dance historian such as herself had been unaware of Baby Laurence when he was performing nearby. Penitent, she hired Slyde and Steve Condos.

Condos was also featured in *About Tap*, a half-hour documentary Nierenberg released in 1985. Where *No Maps* is dramatic and biographical, *About Tap* is a film essay in tap aesthetics. Chuck Green says, "You can't always do what you want to do. You have to do what's needed." Condos lays out his method of building beats into rolls, explaining how shifting the accents ("sculpting" the rhythm, he calls it) keeps those otherwise mechanical patterns alive. "I leave my body alone," he says. "Whatever it does after my feet talk, that's unconscious." And that's how it looks, like a linebacker doing one of those keep-the-feet-moving drills. Of all the hoofers to come out of retirement, Condos was probably the most freed up. The new context gave him permission to be the pure musician he had always wanted to be. "I get in a trance," he once explained, "and the only thing that wakes me up is if somebody applauds." Condos still sang songs and cracked one-liners, but his late style was visually plain—save for his face, which brimmed with joy. It's possible that no one ever loved tap more than Steve Condos. In *About Tap*, Nierenberg films him dancing against a simulation of a star-pricked sky. When Condos accelerates into a roll, his face lights up and you could believe he's about to blast off.

The presence of Condos, the improvising white elder with Philadelphia street cred and a Hollywood résumé, complicated the race issue. In *No Maps on My Taps*, Sandman Sims makes a point, echoed by Bubbles in *Tapdancin'*, about how blacks dance from the soul and whites from counts. At one level, this was a difference in pedagogy. Dancing-school teachers counted out rhythms; hoofers scatted. Counts are less efficient and less expressive than scatting, and since they break down after a few levels of rhythmic subdivision, they're of limited use. (Even Paul Draper complained about this; it's why he wanted tappers to learn to read music.) But that wasn't what Sims and Bubbles were driving at. They were making a heart-versus-head argument, a division that supposedly broke down along racial lines. In an interview with a black researcher, Sims said that his art was not America's heritage but Africa's. "They mixed it in with *our* dancing. That's where you got 'tap dancing.' But hoofing is like . . . they say beauty's skin deep but ugly is all the way to the bone."

Sims was right that there had been mixing. Back in 1876, a writer for the *Times* had judged dancing according to values similar to his, praising an impromptu quality of "genuine American invention" that can't be learned over the arithmetical calculations of ballet. That writer was praising blackface minstrels. In *No Maps on My Taps*, Sims says, "For us this will probably be the last hooray," but he also says, "There will be others." He could have been more accurate: in 1979, there already were.

16

LINEAGE

PRODIGAL SON

Gregory Hines is standing in the alley behind the Apollo, reminiscing about the many hours he spent in that spot as a child performer three decades prior. In this scene from the 1985 documentary *About Tap*, he recalls the attention paid to him by Sandman Sims, an adult who took the time to trade steps with a kid—who took the kid seriously, pushing him to work on his weak left side. Watching Sims, Hines says, he could see himself "as a man." He singles out the moment when, after trying to steal steps from Teddy Hale by watching his act multiple times, he realized that Hale had no routine, that Hale was improvising. He remembers what older hoofers had to say when Hines, then nine, declared that he wanted to *be* Teddy Hale. "'That's great,' they said, 'but you can't hope to be a great artist, like he is, by copying him. No, you have to take all these steps that you're stealing from him and that we're feeding you and assimilate it. And have it come out in your own way, in your own style.'" Each of his heroes had that: a style. Hines says he can recognize each one with his eyes closed. He says he owes them every-thing: "I found myself through them."

First there was his brother, Maurice, two years older. At four or five, Maurice was already enrolled in a neighborhood tap class. Gregory was supposedly too young, but he could copy his brother's steps. Their mother sought out the best teacher around, and in the late forties that was Henry LeTang. As a Harlem kid in the twenties, LeTang had himself started out at the Peter Pan Kiddies School before graduating to Buddy Bradley's. He also studied at the Hoofers' Club and backstage with Bubbles. The Cotton Club said he was too short, but he toured with Sophie Tucker's son, billed as "Bert Tucker and Friend." By 1937, he had opened a Times Square studio of his own, following in Bradley's foot-steps, grooming white stars and choreographing Broadway shows and nightclub acts for which he sometimes got credit. Like Bradley, LeTang could cater to people with minimal dancing talent. He likened his job to that of a tailor and frankly labeled it "commercial." Most of his students were white. Profiled by *Ebony* in 1948, he gave his take on racial differ-ence. The average Negro hoofer, in his experience, had no more "natural rhythm" than the average white dancer. But the average Negro tended to learn faster and work harder—perhaps, LeTang suggested, because the field for Negro dancers was so much smaller.

LeTang didn't normally teach children, but he saw something in the Hines kids. He gave the boys private lessons, standing between them and holding their hands as they mimicked his steps. He made them take ballet and he brought them to the Apollo, both to perform and to study. The theater was their day care center. Alma Hines regularly dropped off her sons to watch three or four shows while she was at work. In the audience and in the wings and in the alley out back, the boys soaked up a tradition on the wane. Once in the mid-fifties, they watched as Bubbles performed on a bill that was otherwise rock and roll. Maurice and Gregory figured the audience would reject the old man, but the veteran sang "Shine" and the crowd loved him. "So we went to his dressing room afterward," Maurice would remember. "And we asked him how he did it. And he said, 'Always tell the truth to the audience. Don't pretend to be some-thing you aren't. They'll know. And they'll get you.'" Apollo audiences loved the Hines Kids, too. In 1954, they were cast as a newsboy and a shoeshiner in the Broadway show *The Girl in Pink Tights*. People were saying they might be the next Nicholas Brothers, a prediction that Maurice and Gregory believed until they saw the Nicholas Brothers.

Kinescopes of early Hines Kids TV appearances make comparison possible. Maurice and Gregory aren't quite Fayard and Harold, not quite as bursting with talent and life. There's something similar, though, about the sibling dynamic. Maurice, the brother with the French name, is more polished, more balletic, leaning effeminate where Fayard was pixieish. Gregory is offhand, digging in to his solo steps but otherwise not quite bothering with the arms. "Even back then," Maurice told me, "I was like Fayard and Greg was like Harold. Even in temperament." Maurice was the conscientious brother, Gregory the mischievous one who hated to rehearse. TV footage separated by years shows the brothers growing physically, but the act changing little. The routines, tightly bound to the arrangements, operate on the LeTang Principle of Repetition. As Gregory later explained it, "Henry would insist there were four or five steps in the routine that we would repeat six times. Because by the fourth time, the audience would understand the step, and start to applaud."

As the fifties passed into the sixties, the Hines Kids played the contracting circuit. In Las Vegas, they replaced Teddy Hale at the Moulin Rouge after Wardell Gray's death. Just as Tallulah Bankhead had once bought little Harold Nicholas a bicycle, Gregory got a drum kit from Marlene Dietrich. In Miami, the Hines brothers discovered segregated water fountains, a confusing revelation for the boys, who were growing up in the predominately white populations of professional children's schools in New York. As an opening act, they performed in the Catskills and toured with Count Basie and the Will Mastin Trio Starring Sammy Davis, Jr. Like Davis, whom Gregory idolized, they gradually mixed in more singing and comedy, relegating their tapping to a number or two. In the early sixties, they added their father, Maurice, Sr., on drums, and it was this act—Hines, Hines, and Dad—that you could see on *The Tonight Show* and *Hollywood Palace* and that is captured on the 1968 live album *Pandemonium*. Amid jazzy renditions of show-tune medleys, tap enters as sibling-rivalry schtick. In this joke, Greg has the upper hand, but as the clown, he generally comes in for abuse. During the bows, Dad introduces his younger son as "our lovable idiot."

By 1973, the lovable idiot was ready to quit. "I wanted to be real," he would recall. "My family would tell me to smile. I never wanted to smile." He thought smiling was phony. He was twenty-seven. Five years before, he had married a waitress he met in the Catskills, and their child was now three. All of that—marriage, parenthood, his brother, his father, showbiz, tap—he left behind for the beaches of Venice, California. This was his missed adolescence, his version of dropping out. He worked as a busboy, taught karate, and did nothing if he felt like doing nothing. He got his ears pierced, let his hair grow, dabbled in free love and acid, and did not own a pair of tap shoes. He didn't stop performing; he played rhythm guitar and sang in an otherwise all-white rock band, aptly called Severance. (Their sole album sounds like a child of Steely Dan and the Eagles.) He fell in love and learned how to take care of himself, yet he missed his daughter. His desire to be a responsible divorced father, rein-forced by the two men's-sensitivity groups he had joined and the wake-up call of a buddy from childhood being murdered in a drug deal, prompted him to move back to New York in 1978.

He had no money, no job. But his brother told him about an audition for a musical, and he got the part. *The Last Minstrel Show* concerned a black minstrel company shut down by reformers. It closed in Philadel-phia, shut down by insufficient audience enthusiasm, but Hines's next show made it to Broadway. *Eubie!*, a revue based around the songs of Eubie Blake, the still-living composer of *Shuffle Along*, ran for a year and earned Gregory a Tony nomination. Maurice, who was cast in the show first, and Henry LeTang, who was choreographing it, had to lobby hard to get Gregory hired; he wasn't an ingratiating auditioner. Once perfor-mances started, however, it was Maurice, the brother who had stayed in New York and in the business, who was upstaged. What had been true of the brothers as teenagers was even truer now; as Maurice admitted to me, "I was afraid of the audience. Greg wasn't. I tried to grab it. And Greg let them come to him."

Gregory's next project, *Comin' Uptown*, an all-black musical of *A Christmas Carol*, was a flop, yet his portrayal of a slumlord Scrooge earned him his second Tony nomination. For the three-week run of the histor-ical revue *Black Broadway*, which featured John Bubbles, Hines credibly replaced an ailing Honi Coles, and did so for free. Then, in 1981, came

Sophisticated Ladies. It was another revue, this time of Ellington songs, but it was lavishly produced, with a band stocked with actual Ellingtonians. "It's no secret that Mr. Hines may be the best tap dancer of our day," wrote Frank Rich in his rave for the *Times*, "but he's more than a dancer; he's the frisky Ellington spirit incarnate." Hines could sing— wring the feeling out of a ballad, hold his own in scatted trades with a trombonist. And he was attractive, with hooded, droopy eyes set in a long and leonine face. He could be romantic, funny, sexy. Tap had a star.

In *Sophisticated Ladies*, Hines's dancing contrasted with that of two other male dancers, both about ten years his junior. Gregg Burge had grown up as a Long Island talent-show champion who brought his shoes to a performance of *The Hoofers* and briefly became the boy wonder of Leticia Jay's First Tap Company. By the time of *Sophisticated Ladies*, that exposure was hard to trace, covered over by formal training in ballet at Juilliard. Though his tapping was clean, it was wanting in subtlety and grit, and his perpetual display of flexibility had a preening quality. Hinton Battle's background was almost entirely balletic. He had studied at the School of American Ballet before playing the Scarecrow in *The Wiz* (Burge replaced him, *42nd Street*–style, after Battle sprained an ankle) and had performed with Dance Theatre of Harlem before starring in Bob Fosse's *Dancin'*. When he was cast in *Sophisticated Ladies*, he knew almost no tap, and a crash course with LeTang could get him only so far.

What Burge and Battle proved was that you didn't have to be white to tap white. The two men could have served as exhibits for what the author of *Jazz Dance* and his trusted sources had been worried was going to happen, as poster boys for an abandonment of the American vernacular in favor of the most superficial features of European dance: pulled-up spines, pointed toes, pirouettes, and compulsive ear-high kicks. Dancing next to Burge and Battle in video footage, Hines is different. In his big solo, that's even more true, since he's improvising. He toys with one idea, moves on to another. This isn't esoteric: he's talking to the people with his feet, pleasing himself and letting the audience share in his pleasure. As the number segues into a stair dance on multiple staircases, Hines plays with the levels in the same spirit. His ascents and descents aren't as symmetrical as Robinson's, no more than his get-down vigor reproduces Robinson's erect daintiness. But critics listened to Hines the way they listened to Bojangles. For the first time in a long time, a tap virtuoso, a hoofer in the jazz tradition, was starring on Broadway.

As his brother took over his role in New York, Hines headed up the Los Angeles production, hoping to expand his career into the movies. He already had completed two films: as a wily dancing slave in Mel Brooks's *History of the World, Part I*, and as a nondancing medical examiner in the horror flick *Wolfen*. Such roles, followed by a co-starring turn in the comedy *Deal of the Century*, were important for Hines's acting career, but when he learned that Francis Ford Coppola was working on a film about the Cotton Club, he knew that such a film needed Gregory Hines. He showed up at the producer's home in period costume and tapped on the man's coffee table.

The making of *The Cotton Club* (1984) was a notorious fiasco: an exploding budget, thirty drafts of a script, multiple lawsuits. Along the way, Hines's role became Sandman Williams, half of a brother act. Maurice was cast and the plot grew to incorporate elements of the Hines Brothers' own split and reconciliation. This storyline ran in parallel with that of another pair of brothers, played by Nicholas Cage and Richard Gere, who was the white star needed to finance the picture. On top of this were piled love stories for Hines and Gere, plus a complicated gangster war between ethnic mobs. Pared down to fit with all these other stories, the Williams Brothers' story lost whatever emotional impact it might have had. More important, the music and dance that might have been at the heart of a movie about the Cotton Club ended up relegated to background color.

Henry LeTang (credited for "tap choreography" while Michael Smuin was credited as "principal choreographer") re-created numbers for many of the Cotton Club's greatest acts, none of which made it into the film. The nightclub numbers that weren't cut survive in the release print only in scraps, and the two fragments of the Williams Brothers' act are incoherent excerpts from Hines Brothers' routines. A scene set in the Hoofers' Club gives more while falling farther from its potential. For the first time in a major motion picture, Honi Coles dances. And Buster Brown. And Jimmy Slyde. The frenetic editing allots each dancer a few seconds while the framing butchers their bodies. Their camaraderie injects a surge of warmth into a film that otherwise lacks it, but the movie doesn't treat the hoofers with much respect.

Editing serves a more expressive purpose at the movie's climax, when an impassioned tap solo by Hines is intercut with a series of mob hits, as the Italians take over the black numbers game. It's like the crosscutting of mob war and baptism in Coppola's *The Godfather*, but with a murkier moral point. In an earlier scene, Hines's character, frustrated by racial injustice but realizing that retaliatory violence is a game he'll lose, has vowed to kill with his tap shoes. Is the juxtaposition meant to reveal a balance between the cultural power of blacks and their weak position in a racist society? An imbalance? Or is it just about the sonic similarity between Hines's hoofing and the chatter of tommy guns? Hines's anachronistic performance looks like nothing anyone would have seen at the Cotton Club, yet it was important for Hines to dance in his own style in a mainstream movie, just as it was important for him to take off his shirt in a sex scene. Both gestures telegraphed that this was not Uncle Billy and Shirley. The dancing was new and Hines had come up with a neologism for its protean mix of worked-out steps and impromptu adaptations, a word that debuted in the film's credits: "tap improvography by Gregory Hines."

Eubie!, *Sophisticated Ladies*, and *The Cotton Club* had established Hines as a modern representative of tap's past. His next film brought tap into the eighties. The implausible Cold War plot of *White Nights* (1985) cast Hines as Raymond Greenwood, a tap dancer of his own generation, a onetime child star who, after growing disillusioned with America while serving in Vietnam, has defected to the Soviet Union. His first appearance finds him relegated to a tiny theater in Siberia, performing with a Russian company of *Porgy and Bess*. He is Sportin' Life—Bubbles's role, Sammy's role. He sings the hell out of "There's a Boat Dat's Leavin' Soon," and though he twirls a hooked cane as Bubbles did, the virile aggressiveness is his own. At the end of the number, his wife appears, played by Isabella Rossellini. This casting was not Uncle Billy and Shirley, yet reviews didn't make much of the interracial romance, nor of the offscreen fact that Hines's second wife was a blond Jewish divorcee. Much had changed since Davis's sixties.

In a later scene, drunk on vodka, Greenwood narrates the story of how he went from being a "cute little colored kid, a real novelty" to being a hired murderer and rapist in the army. When Hines's volume goes up, his believability goes down, but the emotion he's able to express through his hoofing—the bitterness, the frustration—is striking and novel. Much of the monologue, apparently, came from Hines himself. In interviews, he said that the speech had helped him get a lot of things off his chest, like his resentment that "the rich don't patronize tap" and the monologue's assertion—at once prideful and self-denigrating—that "most black people in America can tap," an idea close to one that Hines grew up hearing: that all black people have rhythm. "Sure, he was putting the guy on," Hines told *The Washington Post*; "but there was also a lot of anger behind it." This was a complex anger, the anger of a black tap dancer who loved his tradition but struggled to come to terms with it. By dancing that anger—a black anger, long after it had become commonplace in music and other arts—Hines was altering the image of tap at least as much as Gene Kelly had by dancing in a T-shirt.

The guy Raymond is putting on is the film's other main character, Nikolai Rodchenko, a Soviet ballet star and defector to the West who gets trapped in the Soviet Union and—this is just part of the film's implausibility—put under the supervision of Hines's character by the KGB. In playing Rodchenko, Mikhail Baryshnikov, the Russian ballet star who had defected about a decade before, was also drawing on his own biography. One of the film's high points is Baryshnikov and Hines dancing together. What they do is a hybrid, choreographed by the hybrid choreographer Twyla Tharp: a little of Hines's karate, some slackened ballet. It's not a great dance, but it's good enough to show both men as great dancers. It's difficult to choose which one to watch, which shade of cool to savor. For Hines to hold his own against the man justly considered the greatest dancer in the world—that said something about Hines. For a tap dancer, and a black one, to be framed as an equal to ballet's prince— that said something about tap, and where Hines might take it.

The Hines-Baryshnikov duet has no tap in it, though. The news about where Hines was taking tap comes in his solo. He's in the studio, improvising to a tape that Rodchenko has brought from the decadent West. Charging forward, grapevining sideways, swooping backward, Hines covers ground. There's something of Sandman Sims in the way he bounces on the balls of his feet, yet he groups his rhythms like someone who once played in a jazz-rock band. Hines improvised the scene without music. Only afterward did the songwriter David Foster compose a track, drenched in synthesizers and heavy on backbeat, that, with the addition of vocals, could have played on FM radio in 1985. Hines looked contemporary and he sounded contemporary, too.

He didn't dance in the buddy-cop movie *Running Scared*, and though the film was successful, his movie career sputtered. A guest duet on a Luther Vandross album turned into a hit single, but Hines's subsequent solo recording, credibly executed in a satiny Vandross style, didn't sell many copies. Just because Hines could do it all didn't mean he could sustain multiple careers across genres. He spent much time touring as a soloist in nightclubs and small theaters, singing standards and R&B and always tapping. As a quality control measure, he brought along his own stage, a costly shingle outfitted with microphones. The platform raised the volume, righting the balance with amplified instruments. It satisfied the eleven-year-old boy in Hines who had once thrilled to the vibrations of Chuck Berry turned all the way up. But the custom stage didn't just allow him to dance loudly; it allowed him to dance quietly, subtly, with the confidence that those quiet subtleties would be heard.

It was also a platform he was willing to share. Regularly, he would ask if there were tap dancers in the house. Then he would invite them up. Hines may have been a movie star, but anyone with a pair of tap shoes was a member of his tribe.

EXTENDED FAMILY

In 1986, when the Jazz Tap Ensemble appeared at New York's Joyce Theater, the guest artist was Gregory Hines. His performance, captured on video, is beyond nightclub casual. In a T-shirt, Kelly-tight and bodybuilder-sleeveless, he chats with the crowd, stops to sip from a water bottle or to pull up his socks, laughs at himself. He makes a sound like African drums with his heels, then mocks it by mouthing jungle noises. As he feels out the floor, you can see him listening to himself, see him thinking. If he repeats a step four times, he does so mindful of the LeTang Principle of Repetition, but also because he enjoys it. Hines brought his own stage to the Joyce and danced on it alone, apart. That the troupe invited him as the guest artist, a position it had previously offered only to tap elders, was a gesture indicative of his unique position. He had marquee value, and yet as someone who had grown up in the tradition, with the right skin color, he also could bestow legitimacy. His participation connected his mass entertainment success with the subculture that had been developing at the same time.

But he wasn't the only standout. Of the original members of the Jazz Tap Ensemble, only Lynn Dally remained: the one who never improved as a performer but also the one who kept the company going and brought in superior dancers. Among the new recruits was a thirty-six-year-old virtuoso named Sam Weber. The core of Weber's childhood training had taken place in the San Francisco studio of Stan Kahn, a vaudevillian who, in addition to staging nightclub shows and the Ice Follies, had systematically broken down the mechanics of tap, developed a series of graduated exercises, and invented and copyrighted a pictographic notation system. (Rodney Strong, a student of Paul Draper's who later founded a successful vineyard, also taught at Kahn's studio.) Kahn made his students study ballet, and though his ace pupil resisted at first, in the late sixties a career in ballet seemed much more possible than Weber's true dream of becoming a concert tap dancer. Weber spent the seventies in the employ of ballet troupes, and in the early eighties, he brushed up his tap to perform the Tap Dance Concerto with symphony orchestras. The first time he saw the Jazz Tap Ensemble, he thought, They're doing what I always wanted to do. When Fred Strickler left the company, Weber leaped at the opening.

On the tape of the 1986 performance, he taps to Cole Porter and to Bach. With his lifted torso aligned over the balls of his feet and his ankles loose, he hovers, skims, floats, flutters. When he uses ballet port de bras, it's with a fullness and fluidity far beyond Paul Draper's; in speed, intricacy, and diversity of steps, he surpasses Hines. Weber's rhythms are flawlessly accurate, his sound a dense nest of tones. Instead of awkwardly grafting ballet onto a narrow base of tap, as Draper did, Weber assimilates steps from Coles and Slyde and Condos into his own balletic system; the way he threads steps together and swirls them around the stage retains a ballet dancer's measured sense of *enchaînement*. In a manner that would only intensify over the coming years, he takes efficiency—the greatest number of sounds activated by the fewest and smallest movements—to such a seemingly effortless extreme that some of his extraordinary flurries fail to register, and his filigree sometimes obscures the pulse. Compare that to Hines, who always keeps the beat handy and for whom grimacing effort is an expression of naturalness. There are other differences, of course: race the most obvious, charisma the most important. Weber's charm is mild, as quiet as his taps. He wasn't going to be a movie star or carry a Broadway show. His kind of art needed the concert stage.

And as much as the tap subculture that Weber belonged to needed Hines, it also needed to organize. A landmark tap summit at the Colorado Dance Festival in 1986 was a family reunion. Dancers from across the country converged on Boulder and Denver to celebrate the past and brainstorm about the future. Several participants, fired up, would start their own tap festivals back home, annual events in Boston, San Francisco, Houston, Chicago, St. Louis, and Portland, Oregon. At the Colorado tap festival in 1987, the International Tap Association was founded. (Honi Coles, Honorary Chairman. Gregory Hines, Honorary President. Marda Kirn and Sally Sommer and others, People Who Did the Actual Work.) Among various forms of advocacy, the ITA began publishing a newsletter with tap news, tap advice, listings and reports of tap events, articles on tap history, angry letters about tap controversies, and transcriptions of tap dancers interviewing tap dancers. The newsletter reflected the membership back to itself: several hundred people, spread across the country and the globe.

"That's another thing about tap dancers," Honi Coles offered during one of the first Colorado panel discussions, "There's no prejudice with us. With white, black, Oxford gray, pink, we have a togetherness that's not common in other fields." Steve Condos, the only white dancer on the panel, seconded the notion: "Tap dancers have a love, I can't explain it. They have a love for one another." This had always been true, to some extent, at least inside the stage door. But this togetherness didn't mean there was no prejudice. In addition to Coles and Condos, the panel included Jimmy Slyde, Eddie Brown, and Gregory Hines, who were performing and teaching at the festival. During a panel featuring Brenda Bufalino, Jane Goldberg, and Lynn Dally, someone in the audience—Terry Brock, a new member of the Jazz Tap Ensemble—asked why the women onstage weren't also teaching and performing.

On a panel the following day, Hines advised his fellow men to examine their own sexist attitudes and include women, because "tap dancing has come as far as it can go just on the strength of men's feet." During his performance that night, he stopped to asked women to join him. When Bufalino shouted back that she didn't have the right clothes, Hines offered her pants and shoes from his own wardrobe. The next year, the Colorado festival—whose original all-male lineup had been chosen by female organizers—included women as teachers and performers. Tap festival organizers ever after became conscious about diversity in gender and generation.

SOLE SISTERS

But the place of women in tap persisted as a question. One node of controversy was this matter of the right clothing. In her autobiography, Bufalino recounts fretting about what to wear when she was asked to fill in for Bunny Briggs on a bill with the Copasetics. Part of the problem was finding an outfit that would go with her Oxford shoes. Bufalino had become dissatisfied with the sound she could get from high-heeled pumps; she craved the bass notes of a wider heel, and yet felt she couldn't wear Oxfords with a dress. She ended up in a white tuxedo, a hardly unprecedented wardrobe choice, but there's more to the anecdote. Honi Coles asks her to dance a waltz to show her "feminine side," which she does but only to follow it, defiantly, with a fast Charlie Parker tune. The moment is a breakthrough, "probably the pivotal experience of my life." The reaction of Coles—who had once told her that women would never be as good as men—shifts from shock to fury to pride as people applaud. Everyone has to admit, finally, "that a woman can lay down the iron."

Bufalino felt she had something to prove. And she felt she had to dress more like a man to prove it. As she and the other young women were rediscovering the jazz tradition of tap, they asked their mentors why there hadn't been more female soloists. The answers they received weren't very satisfying: Chuck Green told Jane Goldberg that women had been discouraged from tapping because it was bad for their breasts. Might footwear have been a cause? Dianne Walker asked Sammy Davis, Jr., about the female dancers who wore flats. "Yeah, they could dance," Davis answered, "but the *women* wore heels."

During her second By Word of Foot festival in 1982, Goldberg presented a panel discussion that combined some of her young and white sisters with a few black women of an earlier generation. The result was less a disagreement than two parallel conversations. "There is no masculine and feminine rhythm," Bufalino asserted, and Tina Pratt, who had turned to shake dancing when tap went out, said, "Of course there are differences between men and women." After young Dorothy Wasserman argued that "people are used to watching women and listening to men," Pratt said she was quite happy to be watched. There was some consensus about women being less competitive than men, or competitive in a different way, the veterans asserting that while men were challenging one another on the street, women were busy in the rehearsal hall; the ladies did their stealing from the wings. When the question was posed whether shoe type made any difference to sound, all of the older women answered "No." All of the younger women answered "Yes."

For the younger participants, high heels weren't just high heels; they were symbols of patriarchal oppression, or at least a frivolous handicap. To wear low-heeled shoes, like men, was to level the playing field. In her book, Bufalino reports with satisfaction that soon after she started wearing low heels, Coles started judging any woman dancing in pumps as "not serious." Bufalino's tuxedo carried a similar meaning. She could remember the nightclubs where she thought she was doing art while the crowd yelled at her to "take it off." Wearing the tuxedo was a strategy for deemphasizing her sexuality so that her audience might pay attention to other things, such as the music she was making.

Bufalino discussed these issues in *Cantata and the Blues*, her autobiographical one-woman show of 1983. It was an outgrowth of solo programs she had been doing at the Blue Note jazz club on Monday nights. In monologue and song, she chafed at being forced to choose between jazz and classical music—which had both been part of her upbringing—and between being a woman and dancing like her male teachers. In the lyrics to "Too Tall, Too Small Blues," she lamented being always compared to Honi Coles. Few viewers, however, would have identified height as the salient point of contrast. The crucial difference was ease versus strain. Bufalino was a tap virtuoso, a highly versatile musician who had achieved that jazz benchmark, a recognizable sound—hers a glassy tone that sang against a strong floor of bass thumps. (And no tap dancer was more articulate about tap aesthetics.) But it could be difficult to hear that unless you closed your eyes. Her manner distracted, nervously wavering between hard-sell and pretentious, and the white mask she sometimes wore didn't help. Reviewers compared her to a powerhouse, to Ethel Merman. "While you can admire her—immensely—you can't love her," wrote Burt Supree in the *Voice*. Coles met audiences primed to adore an elderly black gentleman, a role he could play without effort, whereas Bufalino struggled against preconceptions of female performers over forty and not even her mastery projected comfort with herself. The internal forces that drove her to attempt things her mentor never would—to bring back tap when he was resigned to its demise—were likely the same forces that made her performances overwrought.

You could call that situation unfair. In a larger sense, there was something unfair, or ironic, about all such teacher-student comparisons. The women were *inviting* the men to upstage them. Katherine Kramer, a disciple of Bufalino and Ralph Brown, labeled the women of her generation the "Supermoms of Tap." To them fell the roles of nurturer and caretaker, at the same time that they were playing producer, administrator, and fund-raiser. Kramer wondered if, while wearing all of those hats, women were spending enough time and energy working on their own dancing. Several of the men required a great deal of caretaking: trips to the market, the doctor, the liquor store. All of them needed attention. Soon the men would be awarded grants, and they didn't fill out the applications themselves. At tap festivals, in classes given by the masters, it was usually the women who did most of the explaining, and the more feeble the masters grew, the more the women served as their "feet," demonstrating steps as the old men sat on stools and corrected impatiently.

Kramer also described the seductiveness of the men and how they attracted the women artistically and sexually. The men found the women attractive, too—attractive and unthreatening. For similar reasons, Bill Robinson had been happy to help Shirley Temple with the stair dance that he slapped Bill Bailey for attempting. Something in all of this helped make the tap revival possible—convincing the men to share what had once been stolen, motivating the women not just to take but to give.

Jane Goldberg, in her productions, continued to feature Cookie Cook, along with Buster Brown, Harold Cromer, Marion Coles, Leon Collins, and other elders. As she toured the country and Europe, old hoofers would emerge from the darkness of the theater as from the obscurity of the past. Their participation made for a surefire finale, but it could overwhelm the proceedings. At the 1984 premiere of *The Tapping Talk Show*, as soon as the goofy production had finished, a tap challenge took over: the older men in Goldberg's show, plus Honi Coles, battling younger men led by Gregory Hines. At the end, Hines bowed down to Coles, calling him what Coles had called Bubbles at By Word of Foot: the "winner and still champ." Sally Sommer, in the *Voice*, devoted two sentences to Goldberg's show and three columns to the much more exciting aftermath. Goldberg felt like the Invisible Woman.

Partially in response, she organized an all-women show. She had always included other women, even representatives of a category that did seem just about invisible at the time: the Female African-American Tap Dancer. For her new show, *Sole Sisters* (1985), she invited, among others, two more veterans. Mable Lee, born in Atlanta in 1921, had been a chorus line dancer at the Apollo, a cheesecake cover girl for *Ebony* in 1947, and a singer in more than a hundred "soundies." She put her shoes back on for Goldberg's By Word of Foot. Harriet Browne, born in Chicago a decade later, had given up dancing in the sixties, only to pick it up again fifteen years later at the instigation of a dance troupe director who had heard about the old lady down the block who could tap. Now Browne became known for her sand dance, which was especially fast. Both women proved that male elders had no monopoly on seasoned charisma. Browne was friendly and wry, a little bewildered by the attention. Lee was irrepressible, a woman who handled the problem of aging by ignoring it, delivering bumps and grinds in the total conviction that she was still a sexpot.

Brenda Bufalino was the only tap virtuoso in *Sole Sisters*, but virtuosity wasn't the point. In the show's 1986 version, its silly premise had Goldberg pining for an Astaire, yet what she found, via Browne's wise-talking fairy godmother and such numbers as "Post-Partum Blues," was a sister-hood of mutual support, a sorority Copasetics. The noncompetitive ethos prevailed into the postshow open jam, except when Gregory Hines took his turn. Over the years, Goldberg argued with her friend about many things, but if they had a core disagreement, it was about the challenge. As sincere as Hines was about inviting everyone to the tap party, in his mind there was a back room where the serious business was transacted. To Goldberg, a never-ending chain of title matches sounded more like sport than art. "My idea of winning," she later wrote, "was if everybody won."

For Goldberg, the heart of the matter was "sensibility": personality, humor. Like Robinson and Bubbles, she talked while she tapped, but she brought the topics up to date. In *Sole Sisters*, while banging a pot with a whisk, she cited a *Newsweek* cover story about women her age having a better chance of being the victim of a terrorist attack than they did of getting married. In another show, she and Sarah Safford traded steps and talked about their sex lives, giggling about the taste of semen. Goldberg would talk about how tap was supposed to be a happy dance but she had been doing it for years and was still depressed—a funny line that was funnier when delivered by a zaftig woman in a flouncy dress whose feet were knocking out a chipper rhythm. The tapping helped regulate her comic timing. Her act was amusing, wacky, and, in its self-deprecating messiness, endearing.

In 1986, *Sole Sisters* ran concurrently with the Jazz Tap Ensemble and Gregory Hines. Reviewing both, Marcia Siegel called the first black and intimate; the second, white and Hollywood and "for the millions." But only Hines was of Hollywood. Only he, the figurehead of black and intimate, had a mass following. *Sole Sisters* and the Jazz Tap Ensemble were part of the same family, two directions in which the Hoofers' Club legacy was being taken. Goldberg's shows were nonprofit vaudeville; Jazz Tap Ensemble was concert tap. In the *Voice*, Sally Sommer praised the Sole Sisters for proving that women could do it. "Technically, they've got their feet together. And they're prime for serious choreographic challenges." And tap choreography, in the serious sense that Sommer meant, was a zone in which the younger generation had a shot at doing what John Bubbles had told Jane Goldberg to do: surpass him.

17

CHOREOGRAPHY
AND THE COMPANY MODEL

If tap choreography meant the sequencing of steps, it went at least as far back as minstrelsy. Ned Wayburn and other Broadway dance directors had worked out spatial patterns for large groups of tappers, while the class acts had refined the precision of small ones. In films, Astaire had achieved a pinnacle of imagination and musicality. His dances had a shape and ideas that he developed as a composer or a poet does. Some expressed character or told a story. So, less enduringly, did Paul Draper's work. But Astaire and Draper kept their dances brief and confined themselves to solos and duets. Some of the great black acts expanded into trios and quartets, but they rarely strayed beyond unison or call-and-response, and they nearly always defaulted to serial solos. Fundamentally, there was the solo, the challenge dance, or the chorus line. The possibilities of sustaining a choreographic structure involving more dancers and greater compositional sophistication remained largely unexplored.

Moreover, at the heights of tap artistry in the jazz tradition, there was a strong suspicion of choreography. "Having a choreographer tell me what to do would ruin everything," Baby Laurence said. "I wouldn't be able to improvise or interpret the music, and I couldn't express my-

self." The identification of the dancer with the dance was so tight that
the idea that one could express oneself, or something larger than oneself,
by interpreting another person's creation—the way an actor approaches
a role, or a musician regards a composition—was almost entirely foreign.
It was foreign the way ballet was foreign, and for most of the hoofers, ballet
represented an abdication of freedom. (The possible freedom in escaping
the self was not considered.) All the best tap dancers of old had fashioned
routines for themselves, but they tended to be individualists, with little
interest in dancing routines made by somebody else or in making routines for somebody else to dance. The history of imitation and the allot-
ment of credit had not encouraged many to think differently.

Modern dance had its own tradition of the individual voice. Martha
Graham, to choose the greatest example, had created her own movement language in the thirties. Other modern choreographers were
expected, in some measure, to do the same. Graham worked out her
language on her own body, then taught it to others, and this was also
part of the model: the establishment of a company of dancers, trained in
the choreographer's methods and style, who serve both as the material of
her creations and the storehouse. Belonging to a company could function
as an apprenticeship, both for dancers and for future choreographers. Graham emerged out of the company of Ruth St. Denis and Ted Shawn, and
from her troupe branched off the great and very different dancemakers
Merce Cunningham and Paul Taylor, from whose companies branched
off other companies, and so on. Choreographic styles could be combed
for creative thefts and family relations. Although the choreographer was,
until he or she retired from dancing, usually the star dancer, the company
model marked a shift in emphasis from the performer to the choreographer and the work. A company built up a repertory that could be maintained or revived as dancers came and went, dances that might last beyond
the death of the choreographer. In the eighties, it was this model that
young tap dancers attempted to adopt. Choreography and companies,
they believed, were necessary for tap's survival.

Paul Draper had made the argument back in 1963, positing the need
for institutions and "a framework in which student dancers may envis-
age themselves." (A decade later, he told Jane Goldberg that he should
have been the one to form a tap company, but that he was too selfish.)

"Tap must be perceived as an art form," Brenda Bufalino wrote in 1989, "one that can be choreographed, performed in ensemble, notated, and put in repertory like other dance forms. Otherwise, it is in danger of dying out again." And: "If we do not have thriving companies, what is there for the young dancer to hope for? The aspiring tap dancer has only one hope at present: that is to be a star soloist. This single aspiration will eventually be a deterrent." Bufalino admired how the founders of modern dance had started on the same stages as tap dancers, and had, through years of poverty and struggle, created an alternative system of venues and funding, cultivating audiences with a taste for their kind of art.

Jack Cole recalled that when he practiced tap at Denishawn, the home base of Ruth St. Denis and Ted Shawn, St. Denis called a meeting to announce that "the temple" had been "defiled." In 1937, when tap still had the upper hand, Shawn had vilified it as an invention of the devil. After tap went into decline, though, it was treated more as a childish thing to be left behind. Many of the foremost choreographers of the latter half of the century studied tap in their youth. Before Merce Cunningham perplexed and enthralled audiences with his difficult dances and the auditorium-emptying soundscores his collaborators developed in complete independence, he was a teenaged tap dancer inspired by Astaire and the Nicholas Brothers. Though his extraordinary choreography severed sound from motion, you could find a residue of tap in the brisk footwork and vivifying rhythmic sense, but only if you were searching for it.

In the seventies, Twyla Tharp was the choreographer of the moment. Her *Bix Pieces* (1971), one of a series of her dances to early jazz, included a spoken lecture-demonstration that recalled, with humorous hatred, her childhood studies in tap. Yet Tharp states in her autobiography that she found inspiration for *The Fugue* (1970), a wild-seeming yet Bach-rigorous dance originally performed by three women in boots, when she saw *Tap Happening* with Arlene Croce. "Their taps," she writes, "forced my attention to the integration of sound and movement." Tharp's style, with its loose-swung torso and fancy feet, found a way to rescue jazz dance from "jazz dance," a way to recapture spontaneity, straight-faced humor, rhythmic subtlety, and cool without abandoning intelligence. And when, for *Push Comes to Shove*, her hit ballet of 1976, Tharp faced the task of imparting some of that style to Mikhail Baryshnikov, one of her methods was to have the Russian classicist watch old films of black tap dancers.

Tharp's work offered useful precedents for choreographers interested in doing something with tap. Her "crossover" ballets—calling a truce between modern and ballet, infusing classical steps with vernacular style and vice versa—were a sign of blurring boundaries between high and low. The 1960s postmodern movement out of which Tharp emerged had questioned most dance virtues. "No to spectacle, no to virtuosity" began Yvonne Rainer's 1965 manifesto of renunciation, and dances made by Rainer and her colleagues concentrated on everyday movements such as walking. The effect for tap was to prime dance audiences to pay attention to what might appear ordinary and to see function as form. At the same time, the ascetic experiments left many people hungry for skill and musicality, especially if these pleasures could be snuck in under the cover of unjustly disregarded black culture. It was into this world that young choreographers were attempting to transplant tap.

Gail Conrad was in at the beginning of the company-making trend, though she never quite belonged to the tap festival family. She used tap to underline points of drama or character in postmodern theater. The child of a ballroom dance duo, she took tap and ballroom lessons from her mother, then classes at the Cunningham school as a young adult. She was drawn to avant-garde theater troupes such as Mabou Mines and Richard Foreman's Ontological-Hysteric Theater, with whom she began to perform. This was around 1975, at the height of tap nostalgia, and when actors (the future Wooster Group) learned that Conrad could tap, they asked her for lessons. Teaching them, she taught herself. She also took private instruction from Cookie Cook, after being introduced to him by her neighbor Jane Goldberg. "Cookie fell into my life like a gift from the gods," Conrad told me. "All the finesse in my technique was Cookie's doing." She starting tapping on street corners and the Staten Island Ferry, taking along an accordionist who played sambas or music from Fellini films. Eclecticism was her delight.

For *Travelers: A Tap Dance/Epic*, Conrad strung together Latin American songs into a collection of animated postcards, an hour-long production that was something new for tap in 1978. Because she chose performers more for their stage presence than for their technical prowess, the technical level of her company ranged from Conrad's own miscellaneous competence down to beginner level. Yet the amateurishness jibed with a purposeful putting-on-a-show pretense. It was Conrad's imagistic theatrical sense but mainly her ballroom-derived carriage and line that earned her the approbation of Arlene Croce in *The New Yorker*. For Croce, Conrad was the sole exception, the point of contrast in her article about the young white women and their "low-primate stuff." Croce's blessing could jump-start a career. In Conrad's two-hour *Wave* (1981), an allegorical-satirical "tap-dance melodrama," the living room of a suburban family was inundated by waves, two panels on wheels like cutouts from a Hokusai, but this disaster left domestic rituals virtually unaffected. To convey this persistence of routine, Conrad used routines of tap. She used silent-movie pantomime and a stomping-match argument à la Astaire and Rogers. A solo for the mother combined a clipped quality in the tapping with florid arms to suggest an elegant control freak, a fairly complex character. The music roamed from Kurt Weill and Tchaikovsky to salsa and Dave Brubeck jazz to grab for a variety of moods.

Conrad wanted to tell "choreographic stories that you could hear as well as see." Among her tap contemporaries, she was probably the most inventive in making designs in space, and the most successful in conveying character. Rhythmically, her choreography was notably less intricate. Croce compared her favorably to Astaire: whole-body rather than just-the-feet. But to the ears of other critics now accustomed to judging tap in relation to Chuck Green, Conrad's tapping seemed unsophisticated. (That's how it sounds on video.) Tap for Conrad was a tool, a metaphor. Even Croce came to find too little dancing in Conrad's narrative pieces, "too little of which depended on the features of tap," and eventually concluded that what Conrad was trying to do with tap probably wasn't possible. Conrad's interests drew her away from the art of Cookie Cook. Unable to attract Broadway producers and tired of the administrative toil of her company, she disbanded it in 1985.

———

The company founded by Linda Sohl-Donnell was more along the lines of the Jazz Tap Ensemble. In fact, she was the dancer who took the place of Camden Richman when Richman retired, eventually to become a sushi chef. At Ohio State in 1971, Sohl-Donnell learned that tap was a step-child and that her dance-career aspirations might better be directed toward modern. She studied with Lynn Dally, and like Dally, she relocated to Southern California, where she soon formed a modern-dance troupe. In 1979, she had her epiphany at a UCLA concert featuring Honi Coles, the Nicholas Brothers, Sandman Sims, and Foster Johnson. "I became fascinated with what, to me, was a new art form," she would recall. "I knew I had to do it."

Sohl-Donnell read in the program bios that Johnson taught, and so it was Johnson, with his white Afro, whom she asked for lessons. After the first few classes, he told her to stop paying him, and over two years of intense if unsystematic instruction, he didn't tell her what he had told the *Los Angeles Times* before that UCLA concert:

> There has never been a white tap dancer that could reach the level of the best colored dancers. Never. And there have been some good white dancers. But they don't have it. They don't come up in the environment. They can steal steps or learn the steps or buy the routine, but you can't buy rhythm. Rhythm is a part of you because you've grown up in an environment where electricity is just part of the way of life. You have to live it to get it.

When Johnson and Sohl-Donnell performed together, she executed what he had choreographed while he improvised around her. After he died in 1981, she kept his dances alive. Sohl-Donnell next took classes from Eddie Brown, whose idiosyncratic accenting made her feel like a beginner all over again. After her first session with Honi Coles, Coles asked, "Will that do it for you?" but once it was clear that she wanted more, he gave it. "The training wasn't just learning steps," she told me. "It was about history, about music." The lessons in the rented studio weren't necessarily more important than the lessons over drinks afterward. "Eventually Honi told me, 'I don't know why you want another lesson. You've got more steps than anybody I know. You just need to go in a room and figure out what you're going to do with it.'"

She started choreographing tap pieces for her company, which she soon renamed Rhapsody in Taps, and she found tap constricting. "In modern, you can leap, jump, spin, roll," she recalled. "In tap, every time the foot hits the floor it better fit into the pattern." Her method was to choreograph first, then find a musician to compose or arrange; her music was always live. She was, of all the female tappers of her generation, the most successful in transplanting the articulate, lyrical upper body of a modern dancer onto high-level tap technique. Her sound was reminiscent of Coles's, and with her abundance of steps she could ably avoid cliché. Some of her works were traditional, such as *Drum Thunder* (1991), a challenge dance on pedestals, and she collaborated with top-notch jazz musicians such as Louie Bellson, an Ellington-alum drummer who said he thought like a tap dancer when he played. But she also combined the techniques of her mentors with odd meters, koto, and berimbau. In *Piru Bole* (1988), a duet with a tabla player, she ingeniously matched the pitched drumming and rhythmic syllables of Indian music. In 1999, after traveling to Bali, she made *Nusantara,* a forty-five-minute piece with a gamelan orchestra.

Though capably constructed, these weren't works of the highest originality, invention, or poetry. The cool presence of Eddie Brown, a guest artist until his death in 1992, pointed up the company's lackluster proficiency. (Bob Carroll, the troupe's improvising virtuoso, was in the tradition of his mentor, Louis DaPron: a schlumpy guy with great feet.) Rhapsody in Taps toured, but it was primarily a local troupe. With NEA and local grants, Sohl-Donnell managed to self-produce an annual performance in Los Angeles for three decades. In the mid-eighties, along with her first husband—who, like her second one, happened to be black— she went into debt producing events that brought together the tap masters of both coasts. These were some of the only shows where you could see Leonard Reed, Eddie Brown, and Louis DaPron on the same stage with Sandman Sims, Jimmy Slyde, and Leon Collins. While Rhapsody in Taps represented the present, Reed, as emcee, demonstrated how a septuagenarian could handle backward Over the Tops and nerve wings, swinging his Charleston legs violently. Sticking it to the young, he quipped, "This is me doing it tonight, them doing it tomorrow night."

Tap is music: that's what all the young tap choreographers insisted. But not all in the way of Anita Feldman. Growing up outside Chicago, she had been exposed to the teaching of the black hoofer Jimmy Payne, but at the University of Illinois in the early seventies she switched over, by necessity, to modern dance. The dramatic, emotive style taught at the college didn't appeal to her, yet the concept of choreography as an intellectual pursuit did. While seeking a master's degree at Columbia University, she served as an assistant to Robert Dunn, whose classes, a decade earlier, had helped foster the creation of convention-questioning postmodern dance. (Dunn, too, had once been a professional tap dancer, as a child in Oklahoma.) At the same time, Feldman honed her tap skills by studying with Brenda Bufalino and Steve Condos. When, in the early eighties, Feldman began trying choreography, she commissioned a composer to write her a score. Though based on songs by Thelonious Monk, it was only tangentially related to jazz. The dancer played twelve beats against the percussionist's seven, and tapped one rhythm with the right foot while tapping another with the left.

Feldman was interested in contemporary musical composition. In 1984, Steve Reich, whose compositions were ubiquitous and à la mode in postmodern dance, allowed her to treat his *Clapping Music* as a tap score. In Reich's piece, one performer repeatedly claps a twelve-count rhythmic cell based on an African bell pattern, as another performer, starting in unison with the first, shifts the pattern by an eighth note until the two performers are again in synch. Feldman had a percussionist hold down the base pattern as she circled him, tapping and clapping the shifting part, her movements growing more elaborate as she repeated the phrase. Her adoption of such minimalist methods gained her entry into the "new music" world, with its festivals and venues. Her performances were art school exercises, but they could sound closer to African practice than anything done by the Hoofers.

What Feldman came to patent as the Tap Dance Instrument was actually a collection of instruments. There were four hexagonal platforms made of oak and fir, each about the size of a café table, each with its own distinct timbre. One was bisected by scalar slats like a marimba, and there were also two smaller, diamond-shaped modules of pinging brass. All the parts could be used independently, fitted together, or spread across the stage as stepping-stones, islands of resonance. The instrument was a variation on the shingle, the platform, the portable tap mat. It was a drum to dance upon, funded by an NEA grant. In *Hexa* (1988), Feldman and two other dancers shared the instrument and a looping phrase composed by Lois V. Vierk. The performers' cyclical supplanting of one another gave the music-making a visual dimension, with the crowding adding a hint of interpersonal drama. Fed into the dance's machine, a dancing-school staple like hop-shuffle-hop got converted into a minimalist rhythmic cell. In *Landings* (1989), a duet with the percussionist Gary Schall, Feldman resembled an intent hopscotch player as she ingeniously spread tap technique across the instrument's surface. As Schall's long-sticked mallets darted between her legs, the line between musician and dancer blurred further.

These carefully constructed compositions had a sportive air, and over years of performing them, Feldman and her dancers gradually relaxed. This gradual process was part of the point of repertory, and it wasn't so far from the years of repetition that perfected the Berry Brothers' act. Like a vaudevillian, Feldman became best known for her gimmick, the Instrument, yet dance critics were respectfully admiring of her craftsmanship. Feldman was successful in earning grants and commissions, and in the eighties and early nineties—but only until then—that was one way to be a working tap dancer.

Though Heather Cornell grew up in Toronto, her path paralleled that of her American contemporaries: the tap classes as a kid, the drift into modern dance in college. When her teachers at York University told her to improvise, she felt she had no vocabulary to improvise with; improvising with jazz musicians in the music department made more sense, but her instructors disapproved, insisting that she ignore the music, set herself free from it. After Cornell moved to New York to study at the Cunningham studio, Peggy Spina, a Cunningham student who would run an all-female tap company of her own, directed her to the classes of Cookie Cook. "In ten seconds, I thought, Aha! This is what I was looking for. Music in Dance. Interchangeable."

Cornell learned from the masters—"time in the studio was such a small part of it"—and would come to value how they didn't break things down, how she had to figure it out for herself. She performed with the Jazz Tap Ensemble and Gail Conrad, picking up ideas. Her own company, Manhattan Tap, came together haphazardly, in 1985. Messing around with Shelley Oliver, Tony Scopino (the lead comic of Conrad's troupe), and Jamie Cunneen, she had assembled a fifteen-minute a cappella piece. Reviews of it were good enough to garner them a manager, who swiftly booked them into a festival in New York. When the manager asked them if they had a show, they said yes and made one. Their most successful dances were clever updates of traditional numbers: *Slipped Disc*, a sand dance for four; *Chair-O-Kee*, a complicated and yet comical take on the Copasetics' chair dance. Their programs interspersed improvisation and choreography, solos and group work. From the beginning, they performed with a live jazz trio, musicians with a New York edge who were more collaborators than accompanists. Starting out in modern-dance venues, the company also helped return tap to jazz clubs, as when they played the Village Gate for a series of Mondays in 1989 and 1990.

Dancing together, the chipper quartet could achieve a tight (if sometimes brightly vanilla) unison even while executing phrases as syncopated and intricate as those in a solo by Buster Brown or Cookie Cook. Some of the numbers were put together by those men, and Manhattan Tap invited them, along with Eddie Brown and Steve Condos, onstage as guest artists. This was one of many signals that Manhattan Tap saw itself as an extension of their tradition. "It was like magic being onstage with the old guys," Cornell told me. "We would work so hard. Do everything we knew. And then Cookie would come onstage, flip his hat in the air, miss his head, and the audience was in love with him. We used to ask each other, How long does it take to learn simplicity?"

In 1991, Tony Scopino died at the age of thirty-three—not of drink or drugs but as a casualty of the AIDS epidemic. Cornell assumed the post of artistic director and led a cohort of younger dancers. Collaborating with the renowned jazz bassist Ray Brown, she nervously informed him that her company had fallen apart and that she was bringing in new members. Brown told her, "I do that all the time. Keeps things fresh." (Brown taught her some Groundhog steps, which she put into "Gumbo Hump," the tap-friendly composition he let her use.) Through the nineties, Manhattan Tap served as an apprenticeship program rather like one of the big bands in which Brown had spent his early career: an impressive list of dancers got exposed to Cornell's process and the musicians and the guest masters, then moved on to solo careers or to form companies of their own.

Willowy and Waspy, Cornell grew into a soloist of fine-drawn musicality. Her stage persona was girlish at the wrists and in modestly shrugging shoulders, but there was an undergirding of steel. The tone of her concerts stayed informal, admitting no conflict between serious music-making and jokey interludes. The patent aim was conversation; that was the point of dancing with others. In a potentially noisy medium, Cornell was after quieter pleasures, such as good company, and her shows were the best at maintaining the spirit of the old guys. "The true intent of the work," Cornell once explained, "is to get to the place where the music is playing you." In the music of South America, Africa, and the Caribbean, tap was a new instrument, which gave Cornell and her dancers territory to explore that her mentors hadn't. Considering herself a musician, she wanted to get on the music circuits, but she had trouble convincing music producers. Like George M. Cohan or Astaire, she didn't like being considered just a tap dancer. The label got in her way.

Brenda Bufalino had a vision of tap as music. She had laid the groundwork by training a cadre of dancers, and on July 4, 1986, at a centennial celebration of the Statue of Liberty, her American Tap Dance Orchestra debuted. In the early days, she sometimes stood on a platform and played conductor. She dressed her dancers in tuxedos, the uniform of symphony musicians. But along with these outward shows, Bufalino divided her group into smaller groups, like the trumpet and saxophone sections of a big band, which could work in call-and-response or relay or canon or could combine separate rhythmic phrases into one big rhythm. Of course, two sections of tap dancers can't make use of the timbral and tonal contrast available between a section of trumpets and a section of saxophones, or even between two sections of drums. So the trick is to exploit the possibilities for differentiation—loud and soft, busy and spare, bass and treble—to design phrases that stay distinct yet mesh. For this, Bufalino had a rare gift.

She labeled what she did "counterpoint" or "fugue," and though a music theorist might have found her use of those terms imprecise, they conveyed the idea of rhythmically independent lines acting in concert. At its best, this interlocking catalyzed a chemical reaction of rhythm that a soloist could never equal. Bufalino tended to introduce her rhythmic phrases one at a time, breaking the structure down before building it up. The additive process trained her audience's ears and also gave the dances some drama; group unison arrived with the force of sudden clarity. Although the choreography had recognizable hallmarks—active hips, feet scuttling sideways—it seemed to incorporate most of tap history, drawing upon movement from associated vernaculars with a historian's punctiliousness. It was the most complex choreography yet executed by a group of tap dancers.

The music was mainly jazz, frequently in the form of artfully woven medleys. The musical arrangements were hers: "To me," she asserted, "that is the voice, how you arrange your material." Solos, duets, and trios varied the format. Bufalino sought to increase visual interest with all manner of floor patterns and turning bodies, but these often looked perfunctory, and though she drilled for exactitude of timing, aural balance, and tone, she didn't strive for corresponding visual precision. The concentration and proximity required to hold the rhythmic parts together restricted the spatial options. Bufalino's 1987 treatment of "Haitian Fight Song" by Charles Mingus—a composer with whom she was temperamentally and compositionally aligned—generated high intensity, and in *Touch, Turn, Return* (1989), the interpenetrating rhythms and rows of dancers built up an elemental power. In *Flying Turtles* (1990), the dancers swirling around in counterpoint resembled flocks of birds snapping into formation. Curling their torsos in Afro-Cuban contractions and swooping their arms, they suggested winged creatures and also tap dancers doing wings. This was Bufalino's choreography at its most visually convincing.

And yet the ungainliness remained, and it was compounded by the problem of affect. Serious works like *Touch, Turn, Return* seemed to demand something other than tap's traditional amiability: an impersonality, expression through the steps rather than through the face. The dancers seldom found it, and they couldn't look to Bufalino for help. Even by traditional standards, the ensemble suffered from a deficit of charm and a surfeit of effort. Their technically assured tapping often seemed hampered and diminished by personality, rather than enhanced. Their solos could be shapely, and a few members—especially the sparkplug dance captain, Barbara Duffy—could truly improvise. But Bufalino's disciples would dance their hearts out, and then Honi Coles, too frail to dance anymore, would sit on a stool and sing and remind the audience what was missing. In her own solos, Bufalino still sang terribly, grinned tensely, and composed, on the spot, conglomerations of rhythms and tones gorgeous enough to stand with those Coles used to compose. The American Tap Dance Orchestra was obviously her child.

Bufalino's most ambitious endeavor was *American Landscape*, an evening-length suite of songs by Hoagy Carmichael. First presented in 1990 and expanded over the years, it opened with the dancers stamping in counterpoint while wearing stylized buffalo headdresses, and it ended with a Native American circle dance that brilliantly segued through several meters, as if through several eras, into "The Riverboat Shuffle." In between came *Flying Turtles* and an overstuffed collection of trios, duets, and mostly solos, signature turns built around jump-rope tap or cartwheels. While the frame indicated an attempt to make nature poetry out of an urban art form, the contents were an all-tap variety show. *Gertrude's Nose, a Tap Dance Oratorio*, which debuted in 1996, stuck more firmly in the pastoral, and its mode was bolder, relying on nothing but the sonorities of taps, chirpy vocalizing, and Bufalino's own mediocre nature poems. Jennifer Dunning's kind criticism in the *Times* that the program was "confusingly unsettled in tone" could have applied to any of Bufalino's shows. A program note asserted that "the usual personality of a tap dancer is consumed by the character and the theme," a worthy goal as yet unattained. The note proclaimed "the distance between the artist and the art itself eliminated," but the artist was still getting in the way.

As the tap companies were laboring to expand ideas of tap, critics applauded the effort, if not always the execution. The most common critical charge was that the ensemble work came at the sacrifice of individuality. Reviewers, pining for the masters they had quickly come to love, regularly complained about a blandness, a homogeneity, sometimes characterized as "genderless" or "desexualized," sometimes as "feminized." Almost always, they singled out solos, rewarding tricks and showboating. Bufalino complained that the critics were nostalgic, determined to hold the form in the past. She charged that since the critics didn't have a vocabulary to discuss tap, they wrote only about personality and costumes. And reviewers did write a lot about personality and costumes: these things are hard to look past. (Especially her personality. And the costumes were often bad, as if unflattering attire were the only way to get people to listen.) But the mixed reviews accurately reflected the tough bind that tap companies were in. How to create a company style without losing the singular character of the masters? How to excise the corniness and low audience expectations still evident in the masters' manner without discarding charm or, worse, faking it?

If that wasn't tough enough, the company directors had other critics to please: the masters. Leonard Reed never tired of telling Linda Sohl-Donnell that people were not going to sit through a whole program of nothing but tap. "It's like kissing a girl for an hour," he once explained. "You can't just stand there and make love. You've got to find some food to eat and you go back and love her again." He held to that opinion, yet he came to the Rhapsody in Taps show every year. He also told Sohl-Donnell that if she was going to tap, she should just tap and not mix in other forms. And yet when she premiered her tap-and-tabla duet, Reed was the first in the audience to stand up and applaud. Sohl-Donnell remembered thinking, "I have permission." Brenda Bufalino had made a career out of defying the advice of Honi Coles, yet she also craved his approval. Early in the history of the American Tap Dance Orchestra, Coles attended rehearsals. For days, Bufalino recalled, Coles sat and listened to the counterrhythms. And then he came to her and said he understood: "We couldn't have done this because we didn't think this way."

Though program credits rarely indicated as much, the choreography that the elders provided for the companies was almost all collaborative. Eddie Brown, sober or not, would improvise beautiful phrases—because that was how he, or the little man in his head, thought—some of which Linda Sohl-Donnell, who had written the grant applications to fund this process, would teach to her company in set form. "Sometimes, I would impose some shaping," she told me. "Once I turned profile on a repeat. He liked that." As Brown had trouble remembering his own creations, Sohl-Donnell developed cues to spring his improvisations. In between solos, he sat on a stool; in between numbers, he napped in the wings. After Sohl-Donnell noticed that Brown, normally a one-spot dancer, was incorporating more traveling, she suggested that he might have been taking ideas from her. "Heh, heh," he responded. "You may be right about that."

When Brown choreographed for Manhattan Tap, Heather Cornell did the shaping, as she did for the Brown called Buster. The choreography with Buster's name on it packaged some of his steps nicely, but it was the man who mattered. He had no compunction about sitting out a chorus and just standing in the middle of the stage as the dance continued around him. He was more at home improvising a solo or rehashing his jokes, and even then he stopped whenever he felt like it. The company directors would allot him or Steve Condos or Bunny Briggs fifteen minutes and they might take forty-five. "When you get old," Buster would announce with disarming candor, "you can get away with anything."

Conglomerations, a piece that Honi Coles was commissioned to choreograph at the Colorado Dance Festival in 1989 with the assistance of Brenda Bufalino, was, in her opinion, "not such a good dance," though it had a lot of his ideas in it. None of the old masters, she thought, ever became choreographers. "They could make a little dance."

When Rhapsody in Taps won an NEA grant, in 1990, to invite Gregory Hines to choreograph, the process involved Sohl-Donnell "following him around the studio as he improvised, trying to catch certain chunks of material and hang on to them." Surprisingly, a decent dance emerged, though it would be hard to say that seeing Hines's steps done in unison by five women of middling stage presence constituted an advance in the art. "Groove," which Hines made for the Jazz Tap Ensemble

in 1998, came out similarly: a collection of his steps and rhythmic pro-
clivities set to smooth jazz.

When Jazz Tap Ensemble received an NEA grant to work with
Jimmy Slyde, Lynn Dally and one of her dancers spent a few days in
Boston with the master. He gave them some steps and some ideas about
how to put them together, and then he left to play golf. From this material, Dally, her dancers, and her musical director, all back in Los Angeles,
assembled a suite of solos, duets, and ensemble portions, all set to some
of Slyde's favorite standards. Periodically, the group sent videotapes of
the work in progress to the choreographer, who replied with terse notes.
The dance that resulted, amazingly, was a near-ideal balance between
set choreography and opportunities for improvisation. Its simple spatial
ideas rose gently out of musical transitions. A repository of the Slyde
style, *Interplay* still allowed room for the styles of the dancers performing
it; it raised theirs toward his. With talented improvisers, the piece could
work wonders.

The dancer who accompanied Lynn Dally on her sessions with Slyde
was Derick Grant, a young black man from Boston. That was in 1995,
five years after Dally had started up an apprentice program precisely to
develop such young dancers. Throughout the eighties, however, skin in
Grant's tonal range was hard to find in the group photos of tap companies. And that was the kind of detail that a grant panel in the 1980s was
likely to notice. Rhapsody in Taps was told it was not diverse enough,
even though Eddie Brown was prominently featured and most of the
musicians were black. Manhattan Tap and the American Tap Dance
Orchestra heard similar complaints. "Lots of places wanted to book us
for Black History Month," Linda Sohl-Donnell recalled. "And they would
ask me, can you put in some black students?" Jazz Tap Ensemble's agent
made comparable suggestions. Weren't there any young black tap dancers
interested in dancing for very little money and taking direction from a
middle-aged white woman?

Weren't there any young blacks interested in tap at all? Didn't anyone
want to grow up to be Gregory Hines? Tap's movie star was still determined to use his fame to promote the art. PBS's *Great Performances: Dance*

in America series had started in 1976, as both cause and effect of the dance boom, but it had not yet devoted an episode to tap. Aired in March of 1989, the one Hines designed was, according to his narration, a picture of "tap dance *now*, what's happening today." Accordingly, he included tap companies (American Tap Dance Orchestra, Manhattan Tap), and this was the largest audience they would ever have. There were the masters— Bunny, Jimmy, Sandman, Buster—but there was also Fred Strickler tapping contemplatively to a chamber orchestra playing Samuel Barber. There was the Philadelphia hoofer LaVaughn Robinson with his protégée Germaine Ingram, a young black lawyer. There were other women— Camden Richman, Dianne Walker, and the Eleanor Powell emulator Jennifer Lane—cordoned off in their own section and introduced by Hines half-incredulously exclaiming "Women in tap!"

Sandman Sims played his ornery self. (It was the same role he would soon play on several episodes of *The Cosby Show*, the era's most popular representation of black life.) A running joke in which he tried to loosen Hines's taps dramatized a genuine argument about style. Hines challenged a video double of himself. He luxuriated in the tonal gradations of the stage wood. He spoke of the smiling he was forced to do as a child, sharing that it wasn't until he was in his late thirties that he discovered a "naturalistic expression." The women talked about the confict between wanting to hit the floor as their male mentors did or dance like ladies, a conversation immediately followed by Hines saying, "Tap dancers always like to challenge each other. It's just part of the tradition."

But the emotional through-line of the program connected Hines, the elders, and the only other person allowed to join them in challenge: a shy fifteen-year-old named Savion Glover. "I get very emotional when I see Savion with these men," Hines explained. "It's not so much that I see myself. It's just that I see an experience I had with these men." It was Glover, in a sweatshirt and a painter's cap worn sideways, who was given the closing spot, Glover who was introduced with the phrase "the tradition lives on," Glover who improvised a cappella, tossing together quoted steps from his elders exclaimed at a higher pitch and his own astonishingly fast rattling, Glover who tapped up and down the stage stairs, as Hines did, finishing with a backflip into a split, as Hines had not, Glover who stole the show. And not just the show.

18

BLACK AND BLUE ON BROADWAY

During Gregory Hines's PBS tap special, Hinton Battle and Gregg Burge were introduced as "Broadway's Best." This didn't speak too well of tap on Broadway. With their wispy rhythms and ballet-based circus tricks, the affable duo exhibited a shallowness that regrettably remained traditional in theaters near Times Square. But the labeling was also odd, considering that the special also included the most successful tap dancer on Broadway. Not Gregory Hines. Tommy Tune.

He was Texan and tall, absurdly tall for a dancer, six feet six. Inside this tall person was a small one trying to get out. An inner child was the only interiority he ever appeared to reveal. Tune had learned his tap and ballet in a dancing school, and he was a young adult when he arrived in New York, in 1962. As soon as he discovered that no casting director was interested in tap, he squirreled his shoes away. He slouched through shows as a chorus boy before becoming part of Michael Bennett's team. Tune stood out, stood above, built for eccentric parts that weren't so common anymore. He was chosen for character roles in the old-timey film musical *Hello, Dolly!* (1969) and the twenties pastiche *The Boyfriend* (1971). Called in by Bennett to help choreograph *Seesaw* (1973), Tune came up with a tap number. He also performed in the show, as a version of himself, the gay choreographer, bringing down the house on a giant white staircase and earning his first of nine Tony Awards. From that point onward, tap stayed in his act, but it was as a director-choreographer that his career thrived. Though Tune was four years older than Bennett (who would die of AIDS in 1987), he was Bennett's heir, or the closest Broadway had.

First conceived as a revival of the 1927 Gershwin musical *Funny Face*, Tune's 1983 *My One and Only* ended up instead as a grab bag of Gershwin tunes threaded together with a new story as silly as the original but more knowing. The songs weren't served particularly well by this arrangement, but tap on Broadway was. Not so much in the routines Tune choreographed, though they were diverting enough, with such gimmicks as glow-in-the-dark canes. Nor did the benefit lie in the starring role for Tune, though it was good to have another leading man who could tap. The chief advantage was a new part for a black fairy godfather, a part made for Honi Coles—written for him, to be precise. Tune was a fan. The new story sent Tune's hayseed hero to Harlem, where Coles's character, Mr. Magix, counseled him to "ease into it." When Tune broke into Maxie Fords like a stretched Gene Kelly, Coles was forced to sigh, rise from his chair, and demonstrate. The duet he guided Tune through—one he had made with Jazz Tap Ensemble's Camden Richman—was as simple as Chaplin's dance with the bread rolls, mostly a matter of lifting toes and setting them back down. And yet it never failed to earn at least one encore, "a rare reminder," as Frank Rich wrote in the *Times*, "of how less can be more in a big musical."

The white leading man with the aw-shucks manner, singing Gerswhin songs and taking a research trip to Harlem—there was something very It's Getting Dark on Old Broadway about *My One and Only*'s new plot. In other numbers, Tune backed himself with a tuxedoed male chorus, as Astaire had, except this one was all-black. Tune's tap style was itself very 1920s, rooted in twenties syncopations and the Charleston. His small store of steps and rhythms fit with Gershwin's music and nothing much younger. In rehearsals, Coles kept pressing him to be more nonchalant—no, *more* nonchalant, every *more* meaning *do less*. Their duet staged that process, and this was the key difference between *My One and*

Only and the era it invoked: what Harlem was shown to supply. Instead of hot, there was cool. Instead of abandon, there was restraint. Instead of a minstrel mask, there was Honi Coles with his air of noblesse oblige, not something to be refined but refinement itself.

And instead of the simplifying fictions of the credits for *Gentlemen Prefer Blondes* in 1949, the *My One and Only* program acknowledged the "special material" Coles had contributed. Accepting a Tony Award, the seventy-year-old publicly thanked Father Time; later, in private, he told Brenda Bufalino that he wished he had won while he could still dance. After two years, Coles joined the national tour and exposed audiences around the country to the pleasure and lesson of his style. In his memoir, Tune tells of a Saturday matinee in Grand Rapids when Coles uncharacteristically failed to deliver his lines. Tune looked to the conductor, who skipped to the song. Coles went through the dance, perfectly, but signaled to Tune that he wanted to avoid the usual encore. He had suffered a stroke onstage, and his dancing days really were over.

TAP DANCE KIDS

My One and Only wasn't the only Broadway show interested in Honi Coles. The tap patriarch was also offered a cameo as the dead grandfather in *The Tap Dance Kid*. The offer wasn't especially flattering, since only a few years before, in a TV after-school special based on the same book, Coles had played the much larger role of the living uncle. The part of the uncle on Broadway, however, had already been given to the neophyte tap dancer Hinton Battle, fresh from his Tony-winning prancing in *Sophisticated Ladies*. Coles chose *My One and Only*.

The Tap Dance Kid took its story from *Nobody's Family Is Going to Change*, a charmingly frank children's book by Louise Fitzhugh, the author of *Harriet the Spy*. Published in 1974, the book presented a black family of the upper middle class—private schools, white maid—in which the son dreamed of becoming a tap dancer like his mother's brother and her deceased father. The boy's father, a lawyer, considered that aspiration unacceptable, and this attitude toward tap—that it was shameful, regressive, and sissy—was entirely plausible for the seventies. The story of a kid who's gotta dance, despite the strictures of his stodgy parents, was also a stock theatrical plot. This did not escape the attention of the team who adapted the book into a musical in 1983.

Serving as choreographer was Danny Daniels, the man who had premiered the Tap Dance Concerto back in 1952. His career as a choreographer had emerged from the limbo of TV specials with the 1981 film *Pennies from Heaven*, an honest-to-god MGM musical, albeit one that set the fantasy of Depression-era films against the harsh realities the fantasy was meant to escape. The characters lip-synched to period recordings, and the numbers that Daniels devised tweaked movie-musical conventions, raising the sexual subtext to the surface. Though tap was mainly used for period accuracy and rimshot punctuation, there was more of it than there had been in a movie for years. The steps were standard, yet to see a wonderfully sleazy Christopher Walken (once a student of Daniels) slink through them in a bar-top striptease was to see them anew. Unfortunately, the film flopped.

The tap tradition from which *Pennies from Heaven* drew was the one Daniels understood. In the late seventies, sensing renewed interest in tap at his Santa Monica dance studio, he had assembled a tap history concert, based on his own knowledge and his son's reading of *Jazz Dance*. Beginning with the Irish fleeing the Potato Famine for the Five Points, where they ran into freed slaves who had been denied their drums, it found room for minstrelsy, Juba, and tap on roller skates, and it culminated in what Daniels saw as the final elevation of the form, the blending with ballet in his own youth. Although Daniels described tap as "jazz music done with the feet" and "an improvisational art," he liked to compare tap to ragtime, buried, then dug up (and enjoying a fad following its use in the 1973 film *The Sting*)—an analogy that lodged tap in the past as a period dance. Meaning well, he taped for the New York Public Library a series of video interviews with tap dancers he knew: Hal LeRoy, Fred Kelly, Louis DaPron, old men who couldn't agree on terminology yet danced together just fine. In the videos, the guests teach Daniels, who is incredulous that anyone might have learned tap outside of a dance studio, and who exposes his own astonishing ignorance of black tap dancers. Fayard Nicholas, his only black guest, seems the only intersection between black tap and Daniels's world. In an interview with Jane

Goldberg in 1984, Daniels stated his view of tap's racial origins flat out: "It isn't black. It's Irish." Then he suggested that Honi Coles, new to him, "dances the way I dance" and that Coles must have learned from a Lancashire clog dancer when he was young.

These were the publicly expressed opinions of the man picked to choreograph the first musical about the black upper middle class, a show about blacks coming to terms with their heritage. For the mother's family, Daniels put together a basic soft shoe, and for "Fabulous Feet," an I-May-Be-Poor-but-I've-Got-Rhythm number, Daniels dared a tiny passage with three different rhythmic phrases going at once. Mainly, his rhythms were square. The father's vision of tap as a humiliation was answered implicitly by the boy's perception of tap as something beautiful, and by the boy's sense that during his big audition, he is guided by ancestors—figures resembling Fred and Ginger, Gene Kelly, and Bojangles. This was a sickly sweet variant of Gregory Hines's vision of the men who made him, with the cast of *That's Entertainment* substituted for the Hoofers and the Copasetics. The show acquired a slightly different charge on the national tour, when Harold Nicholas played the grandfather-ghost. But *The Tap Dance Kid* was a dream of old Hollywood and Broadway, the dream of a kid who wants to grow up to be not Hines, or even Harold Nicholas, but Hinton Battle.

Casting the show posed a problem. "At the first meeting," Daniels told me, "I asked the producers, 'Where are you going to get the black kids? Black kids don't tap anymore.' The producers said, 'No, all black kids tap.' So we put out a call for young black kid tap dancers. Nobody showed up." A tap boot camp was established in which aspiring boys were drilled for many months. The role was given to Alfonso Ribeiro, who left after six months to join the cast of the TV show *Silver Spoons*. Five other boys eventually made it through camp to play the kid.

Ribeiro became enough of a celebrity to market his own how-to-dance book, but what it taught wasn't tap. It taught the kind of dancing that excited kids his age. Out of the nightclubs of Northern California and the block parties of the Bronx, popping and locking and breaking had been picked up by the mainstream media, most prominently in films where break dancing served the populist function tap once had. Other continuities were easy to spot, from cardboard shingles and challenge dances bounded by a circle to flash moves, legomania, and subtler physical echoes. B-boys, like tap dancers, loved breaks, and they inspired DJs to extend those percussive pockets. The eye-catching style of their Bronx breakdowns attracted outside attention before rap, the more packagable commodity, eclipsed the dancing. And where minstrels were once known as "science niggas," rappers were said to be "droppin' science." When Honi Coles grumbled that he'd seen it all before, he really had. But nothing in *The Tap Dance Kid* was half as creative as the inventions of the best B-boys, and the young weren't likely to sense the connections.

Ribeiro also appeared in a music-video-style Pepsi commercial, playing the child counterpart to Michael Jackson. This was a famous commercial, because Michael Jackson was the most famous entertainer in the world. The obvious ties between Jackson's dancing and tap were the least significant: the routines that he and his brothers had been taught to give their Vegas appearances some adult appeal. A tap number with the Nicholas Brothers on the Jacksons' TV show in 1977 is a shallow exercise in showman versatility, lacking the groove that made Jackson's dancing to his own music so thrilling. Jackson was the apotheosis of Cholly Atkins's Motown, an appropriator on the order of Sammy Davis, drawing from James Brown's super-bad swivels (which drew from tap) and the snap of popping. He took his gliding Moonwalk not from Bill Bailey but from the *Soul Train* locker Jeffrey Daniel, yet he also cribbed from Astaire and Fosse, and Astaire via Fosse. Except perhaps for his toe-tip perching, the King of Pop had shed the overt links to tap, and what kid could recognize the hidden ones?

I was a kid then. I took break-dancing lessons, memorized all the moves from Jackson's videos, and hugely envied Alfonso Ribeiro. Tap, which I also enjoyed, seemed entirely removed. In *The Tap Dance Kid*, Ribeiro and his successors gestured toward the present with a little popping and the Moonwalk. It was a TV commercial for *The Tap Dance Kid* directed by Michael Peters, the choreographer of the most seminal Jackson videos, that many credited with keeping the show alive after tepid reviews. But most of the Tap Dance Kids themselves couldn't see tap as relevant and drifted into other pursuits. It took one of their own to make them see it differently.

THE SPONGE

Savion Glover was born in 1973 in Newark, a poor black-majority city still scarred by the riots six years earlier. He was the youngest of three brothers, each with a different father but all raised together by their mother, Yvette. She knew that Savion was going to be special, because God had told her so. Just before giving birth to her third child, she asked God for a name and saw a vision of a blackboard upon which the hand of God was writing the word *Savior*. That seemed a little blasphemous, even if divinely inspired, so in her mind she added a small stroke to the last letter and coined a name for her son. This is how she would tell the story to Savion's biographer, Bruce Weber, in the mid-nineties, when it would seem a fitting tale of origin for the young man widely considered the Savior of Tap, the messiah prophesied in the Book of Jerry Ames.

He grew up around music. Yvette was a gospel and jazz singer, and her parents were musicians. Before he could walk, Glover was banging on his mother's pots and walls and body, testing the tones of colanders and teakettles and putting on shows with his brothers. When the boy was four and a half, Yvette enrolled him in drum classes, only to have the teacher reject him as too advanced and forward him to the Newark Community School of the Arts. When Savion was six, Yvette's manager enlisted him as the drummer of a kids' band that played jazz in parks and schools. One day in 1982, the band performed at a Manhattan dance studio run by Maurice Hines and the jazz dancer Frank Hatchett. Two things happened that day, independently: Yvette Glover decided to sign her boys up for tap class, and Savion Glover was first exposed to Chuck Green and Lon Chaney. Fascinated by rhythms like none he'd heard before, the kid followed the big men into their dressing room, where Chaney explained how he had been a drummer before he devoted himself to tap. He complimented the boy on his drum work and suggested he try hoofing.

Once Glover started, he didn't stop. Walking down the street, waiting for the bus, in the shower: the tapping never ceased. This tapping wasn't Chaney-style; they didn't teach that at Hines-Hatchett. But from classes there, Glover moved into the *Tap Dance Kid* workshop and onto the stage of the Minskoff Theatre in September 1984. Eight shows a week, for some three hundred performances, the eleven-year-old incarnated Danny Daniels's idea of a tap dancer and followed Hinton Battle's model of how to please an audience. Doing splits in ruby sequins, Glover looked completely in his element. "I didn't really feel like I was performing," he would recall. "That was *my* life up there." His life: picked up by a chauffeur in the morning, who drove him to the Professional Children's School, to the theater, and back home to Newark—a life not so different from that of the Hines Kids or the Nicholas Kids before them.

Meanwhile, Leon Collins had died of cancer. On his deathbed, the Boston master had raised himself up to look in the face of his student Dianne Walker and tell her what his older sister had told him on her deathbed: "You dance for me." Walker got her first chance in 1985, when she replaced her mentor at the International Festival of Tip Tap in Rome, doing his "Flight of the Bumblebee" on a bill that brought together the Copasetics and the Hoofers on neutral turf. The producers wanted some kids in the show, so Walker brought three boys she had been teaching in Roxbury and had trained to mimic Chuck Green, Sandman Sims, and Bunny Briggs for a *No Maps on My Taps* concert. The producers also wanted girls, so Walker summoned two of them from the school that Paul and Arlene Kennedy, offspring of the Boston dancer-turned-teacher Mildred Kennedy, had established in Los Angeles. Since *The Tap Dance Kid* was closing, the current Kid was invited as well.

Walker had been thinking that tap, the kind she had learned from Collins, needed a kid. Compared to the other children, Glover had been minimally exposed to that tradition, yet it was immediately clear to Walker that he was the One. While the other kids played, Glover never left the rehearsal hall. He never left the adults. A boy wanting male role models found an abundance of them, dapper, confident, dazzlingly talented and warmhearted men, a dozen fairy godfathers. He already had a mother, and Walker already had children, but while her own children mocked her propensity to talk at great length, she could talk tap as long as she liked with the boy. Soon he was calling her Aunt Dianne. Everyone began referring to him as the Sponge.

THE KID IN FRONT

In the days of the Apollo, such a child would have had ample opportunity to absorb the lessons of his art. Those days were gone. Yet Glover was offered a chance almost as good. It came from two Argentine designers-turned-producers who specialized in sprucing up neglected music-and-dance traditions. Beginning with tango, Claudio Segovia and Héctor Orezzoli had moved on to flamenco, and now, with *Black and Blue*, they were attempting to resurrect the between-the-wars European revues that had starred American blacks. They hired three belting blues divas, and for dancing, they signed up some of the Hoofers, a tapping chorus choreographed by Henry LeTang, and one of LeTang's young pupils, Savion Glover.

This *revue noire* opened in 1985, in Paris, where the revue tradition had never really died. (LeTang couldn't believe it when people came backstage to meet the *choreographer*; that had never happened to him in America.) Scheduled for eight weeks, the show was held over for six months, six months during which Glover spent all his time with Jimmy Slyde and Lon Chaney and Buster Brown. Offstage, Chaney taught the kid to box and to understand tap as a fight, "against the history, against Broadway." Onstage, the twelve-year-old danced a duet with the seventy-nine-year-old George Hillman, still a Charlestoning man of high kicks and low bends. With Robinsonian grace, Hillman demonstrated a stair dance. Glover countered with splits. This dynamic was repeated in the finale, when groupings of the cast cycled through as Glover stayed out front and tapped along with all of them. He was the inexhaustible youth, the inheritor. He also joined the Hoofers' Line, watching and participating in the successive solos of the Track, learning how each man built off of the final phrase of the man before him. "This is nothing like what I was taught in dance class," Glover remembered thinking. "I saw it wasn't about pleasing the audience; it was about expressing yourself." To a child's mind, it had to be one or the other.

Although Segovia and Orezzoli's previous productions had been surprise successes in New York, it took until 1989 for *Black and Blue* to open on Broadway. In the interim, it acquired three more choreographers: Fayard Nicholas, Cholly Atkins, and the Savoy swing dancer

Frankie Manning. In Paris, Dianne Walker had danced in the chorus, years older and several sizes larger than the average chorus girl; in New York, she became assistant choreographer and swapped a LeTang soft-shoe trio for one of Atkins's devising. Set to Eubie Blake's "Memories of You," from *Blackbirds of 1930* (where it was sung by a mammy on a plantation), the number was the most sophisticated routine in the production, a trio that coyly shifted its orientation as a female model might angle her shoulders. Easing her way through the number's slow intricacies, Walker demonstrated why she had already earned the moniker "Lady Di." She was prim, delicate. At the end of the show, she joined the Hoofers' Line in a gown, the sole woman up there with the old men, a lady who could hoof.

Fayard Nicholas contributed a bouncy, flirty confection glazed with his trademark steps and circling wrists. LeTang's ensemble routines were the least distinguished, one number easily confused with another despite effects with curtains and lights. LeTang was a master of convention who had pumped out hundreds, maybe thousands, of similar routines. His dances had a mass-produced look—two measures of this, two measures of that—and he pandered to a fixed idea, cemented by decades of success, of what an audience could understand. During one rehearsal, Dianne Walker caught LeTang dancing in the Hoofer style, "and he let you know he could." That style, he told her, "never made me no money." *Black and Blue* earned him his third Tony nomination and his first win. It was a long time coming since his first credited show, the failed 1952 revival of the 1921 *Shuffle Along*.

Some of the young dancers in the chorus had stronger claims to lineage than the usual Broadway gypsies. Bernard Manners, whose feathery elegance came across in an Astaire-like shadow dance, had been performing as the youngest member of the Hoofers since the mid-seventies. Ivery Wheeler and Van "The Man" Porter had been trained in Vegas by Maceo Anderson, one of the original Four Step Brothers. Deborah Mitchell had stumbled upon the Copasetics in 1979. Bubba Gaines bequeathed to her the jump-rope tap he had learned from his Three Dukes partner James "Hutch" Hudson. Gaines told Mitchell that before Hudson overdosed on heroin, he had vowed to return. "But he never told me that it would be as a girl." Ted Levy's mother had been a Dyerette at

Chicago's Club DeLisa, and his father had forced him into classes at Sammy Dyer's studio. During the jam session after a Jane Goldberg production in 1985, Levy so impressed Cookie Cook that Cook dragged the attention stealer off the stage. Dianne Walker was also in that show, and Levy showed up at her hotel room carrying a TV and a VCR so that they might bond over tap videos till morning. He had the flair to do Fayard Nicholas steps justice, and along with Manners, he earned a place on the Hoofers' Line.

Nothing more than dancers in shirtsleeves and fedoras accompanying one another with a perpetual paddle and roll, the Hoofers' Line presented tap at its purest. In solos, Jimmy Slyde gave a slippery lesson in swing, and Bunny Briggs offered instruction in how to tap to a creamy ballad: posing prettily, softly tripling the time, pausing and diving in again. Though the stars of *Black and Blue* were the blues singers, the Hoofers were put up on a pedestal and honored. Walker had also convinced the producers to hire more children so that they might learn as Glover had. She brought the two girls from the Kennedy school in Los Angeles, Cyd Glover (no relation) and Dormeshia Sumbry. LeTang devised a stair dance for them and Savion to "Rhythm Is Our Business," placing that boast back in the mouths of black children. Walker made sure that all the kids paid attention, including Savion's understudy, Tarik Winston, and those who substituted later. "There was a war," Winston told me, "about who could get the older people's love."

Black and Blue was visibly about generations. Because Slyde and Briggs were the only hoofers given numbers to themselves, some critics read the show as a twilight of the gods, a last hooray. Because Glover stayed out front in the finale, other reviewers found a more hopeful message: A child shall lead them.

TAP: THE MOVIE

In 1989, the man out front was still Gregory Hines. That year, while *Black and Blue* was on the boards and just before Hines's PBS special aired, Tri-Star Pictures released a feature film with Hines as the star, a movie titled *Tap*. The director and writer was Nick Castle, Jr., the son of the man who had sent the Nicholas Brothers running up columns.

Hines is Max Washington, a cat burglar who's also the heir apparent of a family of tap dancers. He's a man who has abandoned his vocation and patrimony and has applied his agility to a life of crime. The film opens in his cell at Sing-Sing. We see the convict and we hear the voice of his late father in a memory of a childhood appearance on *The Ed Sullivan Show*. With dripping water to keep time, Max inflicts his resentment on a board and on the walls of his cell, spurts of rhythm gathering into a roll. A sweating, shirtless, angry black felon: even after *White Nights*, this was a new image for a tap dancer, a far cry from Astaire in the guardhouse or Bojangles traipsing down penitentiary stairs. Having served his time, Max is released, and the rest of the film offers him a choice: to continue his life of crime or to return to the righteous path of his father, and his father's dance studio, and the woman who runs it, Max's ex-girlfriend and former dance partner, Amy.

The dance studio has three floors, and the top one is the hoofers' domain, a sepia-tinted realm where old men play cards and reminisce about the glory days and nobody counts 5-6-7-8. These elders are Jimmy Slyde, Bunny Briggs, Steve Condos, Arthur Duncan, Harold Nicholas, and Sandman Sims. Amy's father is Sammy Davis, Jr. Max's homecoming quickly turns into a challenge dance, with each of the has-beens proving he's still got it, a scene that is the film's core of integrity. It was Hines's mission to give these men their due. They essentially play themselves, saying things they had said to Hines over the years. Davis is a jewel-less and broken-down Sammy, what he might have become had he done nothing but tap. And Hines, of course, is acting out a version of his own story, the tap prodigy who came of age as the work was drying up. Photos of him as a child performer, like the historical photos of tap dancers tiling the third-floor walls and scrolled in a slide show over the film's end credits, are bits of actuality sewn into the fictional fabric to authenticate it. The fiction is unconvincing—*Tap* is a mediocre film— but the real bits are valuable.

The question of "the real stuff," of the difference between a hoofer and an ordinary tap dancer, is a plot point. Trying to endear himself to Amy, Max auditions for the national tour of a *42nd Street*–like show she's

helping to cast. Vying for a solo, he tries to impress the director by offering him an improvisation in the Gregory Hines style. The director wants
to see the number as choreographed, as other dancers have performed it
over a long and successful run. This is how Broadway shows normally
function, but the scene is played as a humiliation. As Max seethes through
the time steps he's just called "bullshit" and "not even tap dancing," the
smarmy, craven, white director coaxes from him a smile, only to dismiss
him as the wrong type. Max's response is to throw the director to the
floor and scream into his face, "*You* smile! *You* smile!" The racial overtones are left to ring. Later, Max speaks with shame about how his father
took everything and came up smiling.

There's no suggestion that another path exists, no hint of Hines's
own experience on Broadway, much less of modern-dance venues and
tap companies. The closest the film approaches that side of tap's present
is a performance by Amy's students, her Shim-Sham Girls. The venue, a
Times Square nightclub packed with tap fans, had no real-life counterpart, but the Shim-Sham Girls were as actual as the tap patriarchs. The
Hollywood debut of Jane Goldberg, Dianne Walker, and Dorothy
Wasserman spans about a minute of screen time. (Frances Nealy, the
quartet's venerable fourth member, had been in films before, as a maid,
most recently in *Ghostbusters*.) The Broadway director's snap judgment
that only Wasserman, the blonde, might make it into one of his shows is
all too realistic. Suzanne Douglass, the woman who plays Amy, was not
a tap dancer but a beautiful and appealing actress who trained for the
film with Henry LeTang.

LeTang's coaching succeeded, especially during a rooftop scene in
which Amy and Max rekindle their romance by piecing together their
old "Black Fred and Ginger" routine. The number itself is no rival to
any Astaire-Rogers number, but there's a crackle of "Hard to Handle"
chemistry, and the casual approach, sidling up to the romantic plane
while mocking it a touch, suggests how tapped romance might work in
a less formal era. The aftermath implied by the Astaire-Rogers dances is
made explicit in *Tap* with steamy PG-13 sex. This is no improvement,
but such scenes were important to Hines, as he repeatedly told readers of
Ebony, important to his sense of responsibility about portraying a black
man on film in full.

The young man playing Amy's son was most definitely a tap dancer. For Savion Glover to treat Hines as a surrogate father was not an acting challenge. Their offscreen relationship was as much about attending family barbecues and Knicks games as about trading steps. In *Tap*, Glover is a believable teenager, sullen, bouncing his basketball. Taking over Amy's class after losing a bet, he teaches the other kids to tap cleanly, making the girls giggle and proving to the sole boy in the class—to any boy who watched the film—that tapping isn't just for girls. Since the rest of the movie, with its preponderance of men, made the same point, the more important suggestion was that tap wasn't just for the middle-aged and elderly. Not long afterward, Glover began appearing on *Sesame Street*, tapping in a baseball cap turned sideways. By 1991, he was a regular on the children's program, a celebrity recognized on the street by younger kids who wore their baseball caps sideways in imitation. *Tap* was another stage of Glover's apprenticeship. During much of the filming, Glover hovered near the elders, hugging the wall. "Get over here," said Sammy Davis one day. "You belong at the table."

Between Hines and Glover, *Tap* made tap seem current. And yet the plot focused on a different method of achieving that goal, a plan pushed by Sammy Davis's character to join tap with its enemy—the rock music that Sandman's character blames for killing the art—by hooking up tap shoes to electronics. The film's production team borrowed a system already developed by a dancer named Alfred Desio. A little man, light, loose, and dexterous with no technical weakness to disguise, Desio had attached electronic pickups to his soles and fed the signal into a synthesizer. *Tap* failed to demonstrate all the possibilities of this TapTronics system, but even Desio's own use didn't rise above gimmickry. Watching a man play with his electronic toys could be fun, and the space-age sounds put a twist on tap's eternal intrigue—How is he making those noises with his feet?—but the technology wasn't sensitive enough to capture nuances of touch, and the preprogrammed sequences of video-game bleeps were poor substitutes for music of the shoes. In film, where any sound could be dubbed, the system was particularly absurd. And in *Tap*, presented as the future and redemption of the art form, it was a travesty.

In making *Tap*, a backstager crossed with a gangster flick, Castle was clearly reaching back to the movies his father had made. There's a big

dancing-in-the-streets production number on a building site, where Max
teaches everybody how to steal rhythms from the sounds of the city, but
this is neither plausible nor transporting as fantasy, and it's much more a
construction of editing than of choreography. *Tap* lacks the old magic
and know-how. Castle hadn't inherited them, and it was unclear whether
anyone else had. Still, the future of tap *was* in the film. That's him
bouncing a basketball.

TAP GETS ITS DAY

What with *Tap* and *Black and Blue* and the *Dance in America* special, 1989
was quite a year for tap. After Hines and Glover and some elders and
the Jazz Tap Ensemble all played Carnegie Hall, on the first all-tap bill
there since the blacklisting of Paul Draper, Anna Kisselgoff, the chief
dance critic of the *Times*, deemed the event to have "confirmed the art
form's rebirth." Brenda Bufalino was also on the program and that same
year her American Tap Dance Orchestra converted a hair salon into
Woodpecker's, a studio with the kind of floor that hoofers dream about,
and a home for the company that was also a home for tap. Reviewing an
event there a few years hence, a concert by Ted Levy with Hines and
Glover and Slyde, Kisselgoff would declare, "It is no exaggeration to say
that the best dancing in America today comes from tap dancers."

In 1989, one could even find tap on MTV. In three of the music
videos for her album *Forever Your Girl*, videos that could claim much
credit for the album's number one position, the cheerleader-turned-
choreographer Paula Abdul burst into tap. There was an a cappella solo, a
call-and-response with her boys, a duet with a rapping cartoon cat. The
nod toward Gene Kelly and his cartoon mouse, along with a multitude
of the Maxie Fords he loved, paid tribute to the movie musicals that had
inspired Abdul to make up dances, but the videos looked of-the-moment,
for better and worse, chopped up by almost as many cuts as there were
steps. Abdul's inclusion of tap was another suggestion that the dance might
have currency among the young.

Finally, 1989 was the year that Congress gave tap its day. The idea
had been proposed by the Tap America Project, an advocacy group con-

sisting of three tireless tap dancers. Choosing as their target May 25, the date most widely accepted as Bill Robinson's birthday, Tap America lobbied Congressman John Conyers and Senator Alfonse D'Amato, and put on a press conference with the stars of *Tap*. Explaining his motivations, Representative Conyers said, "By golly, there ought to be a law to make everyone love tap dancing."

Congress couldn't mandate affection, but the official date did mean that in May, as in the Black History Month of February, tap dancers were likely to secure at least one gig. The annual celebration in New York, at which the tap community honored its own, became paradigmatic. The Tap Extravaganza, they called it. A once-a-year, make-the-most-of-it event, it always ran long: three, four, five hours. As Traci Mann, one of the tap enthusiasts who organized each event, explained, "Everyone we knew was onstage." Every year, a boilerplate proclamation by the mayor was read out loud, or one by the borough president, or both, along with the committee-written text of each of the awards. Thank-you speeches could extend indefinitely, especially if, as in the third year, twenty-four people received honors. Technical snafus were routine. The first awards went to the Copasetics and the Hoofers, but the committee worked its way around to including Paul Draper, Gene Kelly, and the Rockettes.

Amid the amateurishness, the salient fact was abundance, the active participation of four or five generations, a living history of the art. Buster Brown grooving like a much younger man, Jane Goldberg doing the steps of Cookie Cook while complaining about her depression, Savion Glover battering the floor in untied shoes, rattling away until someone told him to stop: such displays of continuity and vitality were now commonplace, almost to be taken for granted. Only in the honoring of the recent dead, their names declaimed from the stage or shouted out from the audience, was there an explanation for the urgency behind each Extravaganza. Everyone they knew had to be onstage because so much time had been lost and because time was running out.

19

YOUNG AGAIN

A hoofer could envy how Steve Condos made his exit. It happened in France, at the Biennale de la Danse in Lyons. The theme for 1990 was "An American Story," and the lineup for the tap concert included Jimmy Slyde, the Nicholas Brothers, the Jazz Tap Ensemble, and Savion Glover. Condos, a month away from his seventy-third birthday, danced generously through two sets. He was the life of the afterparty on Saturday night, playing piano for sing-alongs, and when a Sunday matinee was added, he gave as much as ever. He croaked his song "Ain't Nothing but a Hoofer" and he tapped, totally absorbed and with surpassing beauty, to "You Must Believe in Spring," a wistful French ballad about seasonal death and rebirth. Even on video, the performance comes across as extraordinary. Condos walked offstage dripping, out of breath, aglow, saying that he felt as if he could dance forever as he went into his changing area and closed the curtain. His friends heard a crash, the sound of a large man hitting the floor. Someone tried mouth-to-mouth. Emergency doctors arrived. The show went on, and at the end, all the dancers save one returned to the stage for the Shim Sham, half of them aware of what had happened, half not. Only after Shave and a Haircut did the announcement come: Steve Condos had died of heart failure.

"He died with his tap shoes on," the newspapers said. Three months later, his colleagues honored him with a benefit concert for a scholarship fund in his name. The concert was a celebration, a tap wake hosted by the half-paralyzed Honi Coles. Condos appeared on video and in the steps of a protégé, thirteen years old and black, named Marshall Davis, Jr. That kid (no relation to Sammy) opened the proceedings, Jimmy Slyde closed them, and twenty other tappers took turns in between. More crammed the stage for the Shim Sham. It seemed to some a one-of-a-kind event, but events like it became all too regular in the nineties, a defining feature of the decade. The shape and tone held fast as half of the participants crossed over from doing the eulogizing to being eulogized. Ralph Brown died a month after Condos. The next year it was Cookie Cook. Then Eddie Brown. Then Honi Coles. Lon Chaney, 1995. Bubba Gaines and Chuck Green, 1997. Peg Leg Bates, 1998. Harold Nicholas, 2000.

Astaire had died in 1987, his place in the world's cultural memory secure, but it was in reading the obituary that same year of the Hollywood tap choreographer Louis DaPron that one of DaPron's students realized that her teacher's stories had died with him. That student, Rusty Frank, set out to find and record other stories before it was too late. Thirty tap dancers made it into *Tap!*, the book of interviews she published in 1990. Compared to *Jazz Dance* (which was reissued in 1994, after a long period out of print, with a preface by Brenda Bufalino explaining how it had become the tap bible), *Tap!* was cursory. But the later book included much that the earlier one had missed, and in places, the newer contradicted the older, the same dancers telling the same stories differently a few decades on. At the bottom of each interview, Frank printed the date she had conducted it, and in a few cases—Willie Covan, Hermes Pan—this date was followed by another, mere months later, after which the subject was no longer available for interviews.

Nineteen ninety was also the year that the world lost Sammy Davis, Jr. He succumbed to throat cancer at the age of sixty-five. Davis was alive for his tribute, an event honoring his sixty years in showbiz that was filmed for television shortly before his death. There were, as might be expected, not many tappers in the procession of performing stars, but the only time the honoree rose up out of his ringside seat to perform himself was when a choked-up Gregory Hines shared his love by laying down iron. Here was a challenge that Davis could not lose. After a few teasing trades, Hines sank to his knees and kissed the shoes of his idol. Later, at the funeral, Hines spoke of having seen Davis one last time: on his deathbed the older man, unable to speak, mimed passing the younger man a basketball. The younger man mimed catching it.

This was symbolic, in the sense that it commemorated something that had already happened. Hines had caught the ball a long while back. In fact, he had started passing it to someone else, and enactments of that passing became a standard climax for tap events. Hines would do his thing and then at some point he would call up Savion Glover, who would trade with him until Hines mimed defeat. In case anyone missed the message, Hines used every public opportunity, every interview, to offer sports analogies of succession and talk up Savion as the future of tap. And if you wanted to see what he meant, from April 1992 through September 1993, you could find their ritual on a Broadway stage eight times a week.

JAMMING ON BROADWAY

Jelly's Last Jam took nine years to reach that stage. The producers had difficulty finding a black writer interested in tackling the complicated character of the New Orleans composer-pianist Jelly Roll Morton, a compound of such outsized talent and braggadocio that his claim to have invented jazz can neither be credited nor entirely dismissed. The producers found their writer, and a director, in George C. Wolfe, who had gained attention for satirizing black stereotypes in his 1985 play *The Colored Museum*. By the time Wolfe's take on Morton debuted in Los Angeles, Gregory Hines had dropped out. He was uneasy about embodying a figure who had become, in Wolfe's treatment, a light-skinned black racist facing damnation for denying his roots. When Hines signed back on, Wolfe gained a bankable leading man and a performer with the charm to make an antihero palatable, a Gene Kelly for his black Pal Joey. Hines, however, also came with a problem: How was the rise and fall of a great piano player to be portrayed by a tap dancer?

The answer was to use tap as metaphor—not just for the piano playing, which Hines could simulate, but for Morton's creative energies and frustrations and the African origins of jazz and the suppressed drum. Wolfe framed the story as a musical morality play in which Morton, recently deceased, is forced by a Death figure called the Chimney Man to face his past. In *The Colored Museum*, Wolfe had mocked the vapid reassurance of the dancing in all-black musicals, and in interviews he disparaged "cultural strip mining, where you don't go down through the dirt to get the jewel, you just scoop down and put it on top." In *Jelly's Last Jam*, the dirt is color and caste. It's the defensive snobbery that leads Wolfe's Morton to say, "Ain't no Coon stock in this Creole." Wolfe's script condemns Morton for this—for being a messenger who thought he was the message, and above all for his failure to honor those who came before. That was a judgment that Hines, honorer of elders, could get behind. He could also draw on family history: his mother's father had refused to attend her wedding because the man she was marrying—the soon-to-be Dad of Hines, Hines, and Dad—was dark-skinned. *Eubie!* and *Sophisticated Ladies*, the productions that had launched Hines's comeback, were exactly the kinds of revues that Wolfe was repudiating, but Hines's adult career had been a search for ways "to be real," to escape the forced smiles of his childhood. This show furthered that project. It even had a sex scene, as explicit and comically athletic as Hines could want.

Playing Young Jelly Roll was Savion Glover. In one early number, the older Jelly Roll taught the younger how to find his song in the sounds of the street. Amid vendors' cries ("Roots! Roots!") and the percussion of pots and pans, Hines led Glover into a challenge dance, their call-and-response at once dramatizing the growth of the artist and generating the excitement of a showstopping number. Neither in the improvisations nor in the unison sections, choreographed by Hines and Ted Levy, did the two Jellys confine themselves to period style. The choreography was loaded with Hines's pet steps, which he also traded with the chorus in the irresistible instructional number "That's How You Jazz." The second act was more innovative. Alone, passed over by musical fashion, Hines sat on a chair, venting his discontent in irregular fits of tap. Then Young Jelly appeared in half-light, laying down a time step over which old Jelly could improvise his groove back. Wolfe didn't shy away from minstrelsy: the first-act closer had Morton calling his darker best friend a nigger before selling himself as Doctor Jazz backed by a chorus in blackface. But tap represented something else in the show, something like what the Chimney Man called "the black soil from which this rhythm was born." Roots.

Jelly's Last Jam was hailed as a breakthrough. Reviewers who knew little about Morton dutifully expressed outrage at the racism; more knowledgeable critics saved their outrage for Wolfe's polemical distortions. Wolfe had taken Morton's tall tale of inventing jazz and treated it as a sin, but this exaggerated reaction to an exaggeration made for an engaging few hours of theater. Wolfe had an obsession about class within color, yet he knew how to turn his thoughts into fluid stagecraft, and he saw Hines's gift as a tap dancer as a gift not to be wasted. The title role, for all of its reductive psychology, was the best part Hines ever had. This time he won the Tony.

As for the contest embedded in every performance, the one between the forty-six-year-old hoofer and the eighteen-year-old, "winning was never in question." That's how Hines described his chances for *The New Yorker*, though he remembered one occasion when he thought he saw an opening. Glover came in tired after a night of partying:

> We get out on the stage, and we're doing it, but I can see he's not a hundred per cent. I do my first step and he does a step. I pull something out, and I riff on it, so that even the people onstage are going, "Ooh, ooh." So now he blinks a couple of times, like a rhino that hadn't seen me and now he's spotted me. Now he reaches for something very interesting. But it's still not, you know, there. I spin. I go up on both of my toes, and I just stay there, and I come down with a flourish. And now I can see his nostrils flaring and his eyebrows wrinkling. His lips come out pouting like they do, and he does an amazing step—he spins around, goes up on *one* toe, and then he hops on the toe to some kind of percussive thing that pissed me off. And when he did that a roar went up like it was a bullfight. The people onstage started laughing, because they knew I thought I had him.

THE REAL DEAL

Glover was happy enough outdoing Hines at each performance of *Jelly's Last Jam*, but after the two shows each Wednesday, he would head over to the jam session run by Jimmy Slyde and dance until two in the morning. At a small club called La Cave would be Chuck Green and Buster Brown and the hefty encouragement of Lon Chaney. Slyde had initiated the sessions to give younger dancers opportunities to practice with a band in front of an audience. He didn't think of himself as a teacher; he preferred the term "nudge." He taught by example and did much of his nudging through tap koans that could sound like platitudes but would work in the minds of his pupils like slow-release pills or time bombs. Lessons about the dance resonated as lessons about life. "You've got to fall," he'd say, "and you've got to learn how to get up, gracefully. Like you never fell." Continually, Slyde invoked the names of past dancers and the recent dead. "What we're doing," he said, "has been done before." Younger dancers began thinking of themselves as enrolled in the University of La Cave. Glover was the star student.

Yet Glover the improviser had also been dabbling in choreography. The nonprofit organizations Dancing in the Streets and Dance Umbrella commissioned him to set a dance on twenty-eight kids, an ensemble piece he called *New Tap Generation(s)*. The NEA funded his next work, which he called *The Real Deal*. Glover split his kids into two groups to make a point. The first danced to "Anything Goes," running through the Broadway clichés that Glover had learned in *The Tap Dance Kid*; the second tapped to hip-hop, still in three-and-a-break patterns but hitting harder and forgetting about their arms. Glover came out dribbling a basketball to make a speech suggesting that the first group should get together with the second. The result wasn't amalgamation. The first group conformed to the second's style. They got wise to the Real Deal. This is how Glover expected the New Tap Generation(s) to behave.

He gathered together a company, a crew, and gave it a chest-thumping name: Real Tap Skills. The members were his age and younger, drawn mostly from workshops and classes he was teaching. To them he was a star but also a peer. He made tap a young person's game, and his serious devotion to the art could inspire serious devotion. Jimmy Tate, who had preceded Glover as the Tap Dance Kid, was brought in as Glover's understudy for *Jelly's*, and rediscovered him in rehearsal: "I had no idea it was possible to get that good," Tate recalled. Tate, and others like him, started practicing a lot harder.

Around this time, Glover acquired Rastafarian dreadlocks and a scraggly beard, so that when he appeared at the Delacorte Theater in Central Park in August 1994, the young man who had always been described in the press as skinny earned the adjective "hulking." He and his crew were joined by Drummin' Two Deep, a duo of bucket drummers that Glover had met outside the Minskoff Theatre. They all treated the Shakespeare in the Park set as their street corner. Along with the new look came a new style. When pressed to supply a label for it, Glover offered "young" or "raw." He spoke about slang, about steps that had no official names. It was a heavy style: heavy in the heels, heavy on bass. It reflected the music in his Walkman, the groove and flow of hip-hop anthems by Public Enemy or Eric B. & Rakim. The normally inverse ratio between volume and speed no longer applied to him: he could dance faster and louder at once, without having to raise his feet higher off the floor. Though his speediest steps—an in-place duck-waddle that sounded like an endless press roll—tended to monopolize attention, one of his most characteristic moves was a simple slapping of the ground with the ball of a foot: the whack of a bucket drummer by other means. Glover wasn't concerned with appearing graceful. Following his notion of expressing himself rather than entertaining, he was as absorbed in his rhythms as Steve Condos had been. Yet Glover's physical force, combined with his look, especially in an age of gangsta rap, made the intensity of his search read as aggressive. He had renounced flips and splits, but at the end of the show, he improvised a cannonball jump into the theater's moat. Real Tap Skills and Drummin' Two Deep jumped in after him, ready to follow their leader wherever he chose to go.

BRING IN THE NOISE

The Delacorte program was a tryout. George C. Wolfe, now the director of the Public Theater, wanted to create a project for Glover. What would you like to do? he asked the dancer. "I just want to bring in the noise," Glover replied, "I just want to bring in the funk." To Wolfe, this suggested a title, one with meaningless apostrophes and a subtitle. *Bring in 'da Noise, Bring in 'da Funk: A Tap/Rap Discourse on the Staying Power of the Beat*, the Savion Glover vehicle that emerged in the fall of 1995, was in many ways a throwback, a racial pageant, an all-black musical that told the history of Africans in America one more time. The novelty here was to tell that story through tap and to merge it with a history of the dance, braiding the narratives into a fable about a mystical force called 'da Beat.

In the discourse of *Noise/Funk*—conveyed through the rapping of Reg E. Gaines, lyrics rendered by Ann Duquesnay, historical facts and figures projected on the backdrop, and the dancing of Glover and four of his friends—'da Beat arrived on the slave ships from Africa and persisted even when drums were outlawed. Tap derived from that thwarted impulse, a way of making "som'thin' from nuthin'"—much like drawing music from pots and pans, as demonstrated by Drummin' Two Deep. (Much like, for that matter, the "music in the tin pan" sung about by a blackface character in T. D. Rice's 1839 *Bone Squash*.) Racial oppression threatened to destroy 'da Beat. A scene of a buck dancer up on a cotton bale ended in his being lynched; a scene of a hopeful young father migrating to Chicago was followed by a vision of industrial hell; a scene of the good times after the factory workday was interrupted by a race riot. Then came more insidious threats: appropriation, assimilation. A scene of a Harlem Renaissance cabaret, with tuxedoed dancers Charlestoning and a chanteuse singing "I got the beat / You got the beat / The whole world has got the beat," careened into a blinding flash and a berserk scream. End of Act One.

The first section of Act Two, titled "Where's the Beat?," focused more narrowly on tap, tracking the attempts of a character called the Kid to break into Hollywood. On a studio lot, the Kid met a successful duo named Grin and Flash, who twirled their wrists, slid into splits, and advised the Kid to "Give 'em flash / Give 'em style / And big, big, big, big, big, big smile." Then he ran into Uncle Huck-a-Buck, who tapped up and down stairs, danced with a curly-headed doll, and sang "Who the hell cares if I acts de fool / When I takes a swim in my swimming pool?" Disgusted by these sellouts but rejected in turn by the jazz hipsters on

Central Avenue, the Kid ended up selling out himself, following the motto of the tap apostates: "No Beat, Just Flash." At this point, *Noise/Funk* abandoned tap history—had no more use for it—and rolled through the postwar decades of black history in four vignettes of life on a Harlem street corner, all summed up in the lyric "Ain't never gonna change." The present was represented by a sketch in which four young blacks—a B-boy, a student, a businessman, and a soldier—each tried and failed to hail a taxi. The show closed out with the young hoofers, dressed for the street corner, passing rhythms around with the bucket drummers, and explaining in voice-over how tap saved them from lives of crime.

That was the trajectory of *Noise/Funk*—except that, directly after the tap-in-Hollywood section, an ahistorical episode was inserted, a solo for Glover. With his back to the audience, he faced a triptych of mirrors and danced to a tape of his own voice, an interior monologue that was part memoir, part manifesto. "Hollywood, they didn't want us," said the voice. "They wanted to be, like, entertained." But Chuck Green and Jimmy Slyde, they were different: "They was educating, not entertaining." They were hoofing, or "dancin' from the waist down . . . People think tap dancin' is arms and legs and this big ol' smile. Naw, it's raw. It's rhythms. It's us. It's ours." As the voice described four of Glover's mentors— Green, Slyde, Lon Chaney, and Buster Brown—Glover sampled their signature steps, and as the voice recalled the experience of *Black and Blue*, how "their steps started changing my style," Glover demonstrated how his style changed their steps, accelerated them, turned up the volume. During this imitation dance, the voice contrasted "hitting," or express- ing oneself, with classroom tap: "That's not even tap dancing . . . I don't see how people would want to see that old school or, like, old style of tap dancin' when they know there's some real hittin' goin' on."

The monologue was rickety with internal contradictions. It drew a hard distinction between entertaining and educating, but praised Brown for being a real showman; it defined hoofing as raw and from the waist down, but admired Slyde as "mad smooth." Glover could combine rev- erence for his elders with contempt for the old ways and an adolescent arrogance—he told *The New Yorker* that tap "will probably go some- where now we got young hands in here." But the show's agenda was more Manichaean. It tried, incoherently, to expose a moral gulf between the audience-pleasing behavior of the Nicholas Brothers and the audience-pleasing behavior of the young hoofers, who perched on their toe-tips more frequently than the Nicholas Brothers ever had and adhered furiously to the LeTang Principle of Repetition.

Like *Jelly's Last Jam*, *Noise/Funk* reserved its arrows for those it perceived to be race traitors. Wolfe didn't need to invent resentment: the bitterness provoked by the Nicholas Brothers' Hollywood colony lifestyle and the way they made a point of never calling their dancing "hoofing," the conflicted feelings about Bill Robinson. The wounded pride of the Kid, rejected by Hollywood, could have been that of Jimmy Slyde. (It was curious, however, considering Wolfe's preoccupation with color, that no distinction was made between coal-black Robinson and light-skinned tappers such the Nicholas Brothers—or Hines and Glover. Even today, there are dark-skinned hoofers who will tell you that the light ones got famous because of their complexions.) Wolfe said that *Noise/Funk* wasn't attacking Bill Robinson but rather examining the stereotyped persona Robinson was forced to adopt, yet coming from the man who put a line like "Don't worry 'bout me playin' the shiftless fella / I got lots of money and a fine high yella" into the mouth of Uncle Huck-a-Buck, this was disingenuous. Wolfe could speak intelligently about the tap dancer's smile as one of the signs of safety that American culture requires blacks to wear, yet the show's satire was far too snide and self-righteous to get under the minstrel mask.

At a Princeton theater conference a year after *Noise/Funk* opened, August Wilson, the country's leading black playwright, told a largely white audience about "two distinct and parallel traditions in black art: art that is conceived and designed to entertain white society, and art that feeds the spirit and celebrates the life of black America." The first tradition, Wilson explained, began with slaves performing for their masters and led from Harlem Renaissance blacks performing for white audiences to the "crossover" artists of today; the second tradition stemmed from inside the slave quarters and led from the Black Power movement to Wilson's own work (which, he did not say, had been mostly supported by white institutions). Wilson's lecture and *Noise/Funk* both belonged to a third tradition, one that attempted to separate the other two absolutely and strictly—an impossible or necessarily falsifying project, since the two traditions, though real, were inextricably interwoven, interdependent, and often indistinguishable.

Even so, *Noise/Funk* did realize Wolfe's initial concept: Savion Glover as a repository of rhythms that could express history, rhythms that *contained* history. While the reference-riffing of Reg E. Gaines tried to rack up points by name-dropping black cultural figures, Glover's choreography, in its wordless eloquence, conveyed the resilience of African-Americans in a form at once symbolic and physical.

In the Middle Passage section, Glover sat alone, swaying as if in the hull of a slave ship. Slowly he rose, tracing semicircles on the floor with his feet, tentative scrapings that widened into whooshes and finally broke into a cascade of taps, defiant and mournful: an exile's lament. Four field hands appeared, each executing a different slow and rhythmic stylization of hard labor. Incorporating the semicircle scrape, they inherited it, building up a collective counterpoint that erupted into a double-time stomp, all hands clapping, with soloists taking turns in the middle of a juba circle, slicing up the field with wings. It was a Saturday night's release, an emancipation of energy that could chill a slave owner's blood. The dance that followed was the one of a buck dancer (Baakari Wilder, long-faced, long-armed, and long on soul) tapping the rural blues on a board balanced atop a cotton bale; his dance swaggered sweetly, which made it all the more horrifying when his neck twisted in an imaginary noose, his feet spasmed, and he went still. As the father heading north, Glover conveyed the hopes of a generation, mimicking the click-clack of a train with his skittering riff-walks. A machine dance suggested the influence of industrial sounds upon tap along with the dehumanizing effects of factory work. The "Quitting Time" strut reveled in the loose-fitting grace of black vernacular dance—men exchanging slack-fingered handshakes and watching the girls go by.

The choreography for the second act, like everything else about the second act, was weaker. Sending up the Nicholas Brothers, the young hoofers couldn't match the period style, much less hyperbolize it. (The loving imitation that Glover had offered to Harold and Fayard when the Kennedy Center honored the brothers in 1991 had been closer to the mark.) The big-armed wings Glover used to symbolize the Kid's betrayal of 'da Beat were, for the show's polemical purposes, too close to those that riddled the later "hitting" of the cast in contemporary garb. But Glover's evocation of the Harlem Blackout was powerful—a line of dancers, ready to riot, ratcheting up tension with fake-out accents against the low ostinato of a heel relentlessly dropping and patience running out. And in the 1980s vignette, he managed to sneak in the style of Gregory Hines, otherwise excluded by his crossover status. While the text treated gaiety as hypocrisy and only anger as real, Glover's pleasure in his dancing could not be repressed.

Noise/Funk could not account for the mentors Glover honored. It could not account for Glover. The distortions required to tell the history of tap without the Irish and white dancers and women were bound to disfigure it. But even the metaphor was faulty. Tap isn't som'thin' from nuthin'; it is something from something, what Africans brought and what Europeans brought and how cultures in conflict changed one another. It isn't just what was stolen, but what was shared.

When Robert Brustein, in his New Republic argument against the show's "victimology," asserted that "tap dancing was one of the very few expressions of American culture that knew no racial divisions" and that "the early black entertainers were generally free of racial resentment," he made it easy for Wolfe to respond with indisputable facts about double standards. Brustein would've done better to quote Buster Brown, who was given moral authority in Noise/Funk's own scheme. Brown wasn't free of racial resentment—how could he have been?—but he could say similar things without sounding like someone yearning for the days before blacks got uppity. "Tap dancing and show business as a whole," Brown once said, "has done a lot towards getting rid of this black or white thing. The dancers enjoy one another. They don't see color. They hear tap."

FUNK U

At the Public Theater and when it transferred to Broadway, Noise/Funk was showered with honors. Reviewers lauded it for the best dancing in years and for energy that could revitalize the American musical and make it young again. (As it happened, Noise/Funk was overshadowed by

Rent, the rock-and-AIDS version of *La Bohème* with the ads that read, "Tap dancing sucks.") Some critics objected to the glib satire, but everyone praised Glover. Even *New York*'s dyspeptic John Simon, who thought that *Noise/Funk* had too much tap in it, conceded that Glover took the form to new heights.

It was important that Glover tapped to hip-hop. As he pointed out, one reason tap had grown marginal was that dancers were tapping to one kind of music and partying to another. Gregory Hines had done some of the catching up, but only with Glover was tap once again strongly connected with the music of the young. At the same time, the young star was never comfortable with the labels "rap tap" or "hip-hop tap." As far as he was concerned, what he did was hoofing, the art of the men whose tradition he took responsibility for carrying forward. Glover often struggled to explain that "bringing in the noise" was about excellence, not volume, and that "hitting" was about clarity and expressive phrasing, not about how hard you struck the floor. "People think I dance angry," he told *The New Yorker*, "but I'm reachin' for a different tone." Meanwhile, the promotional materials for *Noise/Funk* peddled statistics of damage, such as how many tap shoes and drumsticks the cast burned through. Evidence of destruction was thought to appeal to the young.

Glover already did that. More and more young people responded to the invitation to come as they were, yet the impulse to copy him was so potent that even peculiar mannerisms, such as his habit of gripping a pant leg as a bronco rider grips a saddle, were reproduced. Use of the body grew more functional. A floor-directed gaze, an ever-deepening slouch, and involuntary twitches of the forearm indicated that the dancer was reserving all of his or her attention for improvisation. Would-be hoofers favored the model of shoe that Glover did, the Capezio K360, bulked up the way he liked it. (The spread of other habits could be smelled, a reek of cannabis wafting out of the *Noise/Funk* dressing rooms and sometimes into the theater.)

The cast of *Noise/Funk* had been drawn from Glover's longtime associates—Jimmy Tate and Dulé Hill from *The Tap Dance Kid*, Baakari Wilder and Vincent Bingham from Real Tap Skills. The understudies came from the same circle, connected to Glover's tap family or biologically related to him. As the run of *Noise/Funk* extended, though, and preparations for a national tour began, it became necessary to widen the pool. Glover left the show in July 1997, feuding with the producers, and didn't return until the final performances in January 1999. He didn't go on tour. In his absence, it became even more imperative to find young black men who could tap, or to teach them. The show established a training program, run by a well-versed alum of *Black and Blue* and *Jelly's Last Jam*, Ted Levy, that drilled young men in tap and tap history (the kind espoused by the show). Officially, it was named the New York Shakespeare Festival Tap Insitute, but everyone called it Funk University.

"It was like being reborn," Derick Grant told me about the Funk U experience. "Being a young black man, because of the generation gap, there was not much communication with our elders. *Noise/Funk* breastfed us that." Jason Samuels Smith, the mixed-race child of New York jazz dance teachers, described Funk U as a substitute for college: "It taught me about my own history. Made me want to despise my education. It taught me about not forgetting where it came from, who to give homage. If you don't pay homage, you're disgracing."

However disrespectful they may have appeared, the young hoofers shared with Glover a reverence for their elders and a reverence for tradition. Their sense of history, however, could be blinkered. "I love Savion," Harold Nicholas told *The Washington Post*, "but he's got to learn to think for himself." Fayard, who always bristled at the *flash* label, suggested that if George Wolfe had been white, the NAACP might have picketed the show. Among several letters of protest in the International Tap Association newsletter, Jerry Ames, whose name was so often left out in lists of the Original Hoofers, praised Glover but found his limiting definitions "gratuitous," insisting that tap was "no one's exclusive domain." Josh Hilberman, a white dancer who had studied with the old masters and befriended them and performed on the same stages, wrote to *The New Republic* about "misplaced black nationalism" in *Noise/Funk*. "It is lonely and cold as a white dancer in the '90s just as it was lonely and cold for a black dancer in the '30s."

Jane Goldberg sent the ITA newsletter a rambling journal entry. She was thrilled by the artistry of *Noise/Funk*, but she found the show's tap history simplistic as simplistic as the counterargument she conveyed from the choreographer of *The Tap Dance Kid*. "Only a nitwit would think that African Americans invented tap," said Danny Daniels. "They didn't even own shoes when they got here." The ugliness made Goldberg wax nostalgic: "In the seventies, we were so innocent. Thinking we could change the world with tap integration." When newly informed strangers now asked her if she knew that tap had started when drums were taken away from slaves, she sighed. But she already had a response to the questions of ownership. It had been in her act for a decade. You wanna know who started tap? she would ask. It was the Jews, *her* ancestors, waiting for Moses in the sands of Sinai, stepping on unleavened bread.

Even before *Noise/Funk*, Brenda Bufalino had been raising concerns about tap going backward. The idealization of the street corner drove her nuts. Don't let the dance dry out in a studio, she said, but tap sounds so much better on a nice floor. She looked wryly upon the surge of testosterone, upon men returning to the form once they smelled money. She worried that sophistication and subtlety would be stomped out. "If we revert to flash, and only the street corner, we're in trouble," she told me in 2001, "because the audience will tire of it again. It'll be yet again another trend."

BARE CHESTS AND BOOTS

As *Noise/Funk* was in development, another tap show was running on the concept of a small cast of men, a relish for making noise, and an aesthetic described by its creator-star as raw. This show also made a point of repudiating Broadway and Hollywood style. "Real Tap" was its preliminary title, but it was under the name of *Tap Dogs* that the production found global success and longevity far surpassing that of *Noise/Funk*.

Dein Perry, the creator of this tap juggernaut, hailed from Newcastle, Australia, a coal-mining and steelmaking town. American dancers had been visiting the area since minstrel days, and it was well within Hollywood's reach, yet during Perry's childhood in the late sixties and seventies, tap was largely a memory, preserved in old films. Perry's teacher, a paymaster at a local tube factory, gave classes in his garage. He taught a masculine style, discouraged his boys from taking ballet, and trained all his students hard for competitions. Perry was a champ, but he quit to drive trucks for his truck-driving father until seeing Gregory Hines on TV changed his mind. He moved to Sydney, where he spent years as a chorus dancer in Australian productions of American musicals, *42nd Street* and the like. With funds from the Australia Council for the Arts, he made a video for television in which he and his mates danced in Blundstone boots. To paraphrase Gene Kelly, how does a truck driver from Newcastle tap? Maybe like this.

In *Tap Dogs*, the show that stemmed from the video, the men dressed in ripped jeans and flannel shirts, or in jeans cut off at mid-thigh and no shirt at all. In work boots tipped with steel, they hammered a set that resembled a construction site. In volume, the show resembled a rock concert, and so it was received. One number resurrected the effect of showing dancing only from the shins down; the macho twist was to have a dancer appear to urinate. Another routine spewed welder's sparks in mock ejaculations. The men tapped together on electronic footpads, and electronics allowed Perry to tap with himself. The only conversational moment came between an older dancer and the youngest, their traded phrases growing longer until the kid was soloing. Most solos were slots for tricks. Most rhythmic phrases went *rattle, rattle, bang!* Yet top-dog posturing was overwhelmed by male bonding. Perry said that the show was about "being yourself," and indeed the lads seemed at ease, even if being themselves meant conforming to recognizable types.

Underneath the bluster, the show was conservative, derivative, loaded with ideas lifted from Hollywood musicals. Perry's younger brother reported on how he and Dein had studied videos of Gregory Hines frame by frame. When *Tap Dogs* toured the United States, Hines, that advocate for tap volume, praised Perry for building tap up. The American must have been surprised at what he had inspired. Much of the critical response, especially in Britain, split along class lines, with reviewers sneering at the antipodean barbarians or applauding a return to tap's proletarian origins. In the United States, much criticism that compared *Tap Dogs* to *Noise/Funk* played up the similarities of volume and virility rather than the differences of race, lineage, and artistry. The stated ambition of *Tap Dogs* was commercial—employment for Perry and his mates. It worked. By 1997, there were four companies touring the globe simultaneously; by 2000, there were eight. In 1998, Perry created *Steel City—Tap Dogs* with a bigger budget and a gigantic set. At the opening ceremonies of the 2000 Sydney Olympic Games, in a segment choreographed by him, hundreds of dancers banged their feet on aluminum tap boards as an emblem of Australian culture.

Also in 2000 came *Bootmen*, a semiautobiographical feature film written and directed by Perry. It's an astonishingly comprehensive collection of movie clichés. Among the borrowings from *Tap* is a conflict between a shallow choreographer and a rebel hero who gets in trouble for improvising. The hero's brother, who knocks up the hero's girlfriend before getting killed by a rival thief, leaves him the quasi-magical gift of tap shoes that hook up to amplifiers. The only extended dance number comes in the final two minutes, and it's cruder than *Tap Dogs*. Nevertheless, the movie is remarkably successful in one sense. Though the boys have to defend themselves against slurs, the world created by the film is one in which it's assumed that Australian steelworkers could love to tap. The preponderance of unoriginal ideas helps familiarize that counterintuitive notion. You could call that Dein Perry's larger achievement.

Noise/Funk was a Broadway breakthrough. *Tap Dogs* was a prosperous franchise. The success of *Riverdance* was closer to world domination. Multiple touring troupes of the show brought it to tens of millions. Many millions more saw it on TV. It wasn't a dance show. It was an industry.

Yet the initial spark was similar, the revitalization of a percussive dance tradition. In the case of *Riverdance*, the shock was greater because Irish dance was closer to fossilized. At least since the establishment of the Irish Dancing Commission in 1929, a nationalist undertaking under the body-fearing influence of the Catholic Church, Irish step dancing had been standardized, shackled by a set of rules as rigid as the arm position those rules mandated. In Ireland and in Irish America, step dancing became a discipline children were forced to study so that they might express the cultural heritage of their no-longer-dancing parents. Rather than a social pastime or an expressive art, Irish step dancing turned into an activity largely confined to beauty-pageant recitals and competitions, an in-group ritual left behind in adulthood and, for many, a source of shame or at least embarrassment.

Which is why the appearance of Irish dancers before millions of television viewers for the Eurovision Song Contest in 1994 came as such a surprise. "Riverdance" was an interval act, filling time while the judges tabulated scores. A fetching lass did a springy slip jig—so far, so ordinary, except for the brevity of her skirt. Then drums boomed, and a cocky fellow in a satin shirt bounded across the stage, floating on a froth of quick taps. There was something of a bullfighter in the set of his shoulders, a bullfighter who shimmied. The lass went so far as to caress him. Behind them, a line of black-clad dancers held their arms stiffly as they scissor-kicked in unison and beat out rhythms with the precision of the Rockettes. The performance was, relatively speaking, sexy. It wasn't embarrassed. To many, it embodied Irish cultural pride in a time of economic resurgence, and the ecstatic response spurred the producers to expand the seven-minute act into a full-length production.

Michael Flatley and Jean Butler, the cocky fellow and his partner, were both second-generation Irish-Americans. Flatley, thirty-six in 1994, had grown up short, shy, and poor in a tough Chicago neighborhood. For him, dancing was fighting, and he ascended the web of Irish dance championships until, at age seventeen, he became the first American to win the World Championship in Ireland. Trophies didn't pay the rent, though, so he followed his father into the plumbing business. The Chieftains, a revered traditional Irish band, brought him along to Carnegie Hall and the Hollywood Bowl, but after each triumph he returned to digging ditches. You couldn't make a living as an Irish dancer. Not until *Riverdance.*

Flatley was fast. In 1989, he earned a place in the Guinness Book of Records, clocking in at a scarcely credible twenty-eight taps per second. He took a maverick pride in casting off "eight hundred years of Irish repression." Yet his "loosening"—he raised his arms!—only showed how tight his style remained: physically tight, rhythmically narrow. It was his attitude that made the difference—not just his habit of appearing bare-chested in leather pants, but his projection of his own high self-regard and an energy that was, as he described it, "below the waist but above the knees."

Riverdance benefited from his stage presence, but it also easily survived his departure following a contract dispute. The producers didn't hide their opinion that Irish dance alone couldn't sustain an audience's attention for two hours. They were likely right about Irish dance as they conceived it: a formula of the same rhythms and climaxes surrounded by dry ice and a movie-trailer voice-over that made New Age garbage out of Celtic mythology. Bill Whelan's score herded the dancers down the same few paths. But it might have been to give the dancing a fighting chance against the score, as well as to control a variable product, that the decision was made to dance to recorded taps.

Another way the producers hedged was to bring in other, somehow related dance traditions: flamenco, balleticized Russian folk dance. A tap segment was at least justified by a migration-to-America theme. At first, the producers hired three Europeans of African descent who offered up their idea of American tap: the easiest-to-fake stuff skimmed off of Astaire and Nicholas Brothers movies. Then the producers hired Tarik Winston, a young veteran of *The Tap Dance Kid* and *Black and Blue* who had worked with the Nicholas Brothers directly. The new concept was a blacks versus Irish street-corner challenge. Winston choreographed the number with Colin Dunne, the Birmingham-born champion who replaced Flatley. "It was my chance," Winston told me. "I was thinking about Lon Chaney and Chuck Green and all the people who taught me, trying to get all of that into six to eight minutes."

"Trading Taps" opened with him and his friend Danny Wooten casually trading phrases with each other and an insipid saxophonist. Before long, they were joined by Dunne and two of his ramrod-straight buddies. The competition wasn't quite fair, since the Irish had reels to match their motions while the Americans had to swing against music that didn't. Playfully, the Americans mocked the Irish style, and vice versa, though this wasn't a fair comparison, either. (The Irish style was far easier to mock.) Winston spun across the stage on his toe-tips, Dunne answered by clapping his airborne feet together, Winston ran up a wall and flipped, and then he leapfrogged Wooten into splits. The number concluded with handshakes and hugs. They were all winners: the number never failed to prompt a standing ovation. None of this represented with much accuracy what must have been exchanged in the dives of Five Points, but the spirit of the exchange wasn't all fairy-tale. Follow it with the race riot from *Noise/Funk* and you would have a picture truer to history than either show approached.

Winston inserted into his contract a guarantee that his segment would always be performed without dubbing. His foot music was live, and his smile was sincere. He wanted to make friends. He asked the girls in the show to teach him drills. Trading taps was part of his tradition. "I could see how far the Irish dancing went back," he told me. "You see, they was step dancing before the Africans. In America, the Irish slaves and the Africans, they were both minorities, mixing together. It just looked logical to me." This attitude did not make Winston popular with his friends in *Noise/Funk*. But then, to Winston, *Noise/Funk* seemed like a cult. "I couldn't be in *Noise/Funk*," he told me. "I'm a *tap dancer*. It would be like asking Harold Nicholas to be in *Noise/Funk*. I would've had to grow dreadlocks." When *Riverdance* sold out Radio City Music Hall, a venue six times as large as *Noise/Funk*'s, Winston couldn't resist gloating. He was careful to recount for me the praise he received from the Nicholas Brothers and from Jimmy Slyde, who came backstage with the validating phrase "I *heard* you." Winston felt that something essential to the art of his mentors was being neglected. He believed that tap, under Savion Glover's influence, was growing too selfish, too self-serious. He thought it was losing the style and the class of the men who had taught him and Glover both.

Winston dreamed of a tap production on the order of *Riverdance*, but he had little hope that tap dancers could muster the necessary cooperation. "No one comes together because everyone wants to be the best." The international success of *Riverdance* did seem to demonstrate the universal appeal of rhythm (along with the universal appeal of the hokey and the hackneyed). The post-*Riverdance* spectacles of Michael Flatley—*Lord of the Dance*, *Feet of Flames*, ever more spectacular, expensive, and absurd—appeared to offer the same lessons. Soon, Flatley earned another entry in the Guinness book: highest-paid dancer, $1.6 million per week. He sold out arenas as if he were a rock star, a step dancer with groupies. Tap's dorkier cousin had made good, and these extravaganzas, along with *Tap Dogs*, suggested the possibility—threw down the challenge that tap might become commercial again.

ORDINARY TAPPERS

In the meantime, as a dozen or so young blacks cycled through "Trading Taps," *Riverdance* provided a few American tap dancers with the most regular gigs available. The nonprofit, concert-dance model, by contrast, was looking less and less viable. In 1994, Congress had loudly slashed the budget for the NEA, which, under pressure, discontinued its grants for individual artists (with some exceptions for writers and musicians). Tap dancers weren't making the kind of art that offended Jesse Helms, but those grants had been a key source of capital. And just as it became harder for tap companies and choreographers to get funding, it also became harder for them to get bookings. "Theaters wanted bolder productions, not subtle concert work," Linda Sohl-Donnell told me. "Presenters started asking how many men were in the company." Anita Feldman, creator of subtle concert work and the Tap Dance Instrument, disbanded her company and retired into teaching. Manhattan Tap converted to a per-project basis—sophisticated projects, but not many of them. And in the fall of 1995, Woodpecker's, the home of the American Tap Dance Orchestra, was forced to close. Rising rent was a problem, but also the debt incurred from a protracted court battle over a worker's compensation policy. A press release insisted that the closing of Woodpecker's wouldn't be the end of the orchestra, yet it turned out to be the beginning of the end. Within a few years, Brenda Bufalino would be a solo artist who choreographed mostly for youth ensembles that didn't have to pay dancers. (Electronic looping allowed her to do counterpoint with herself.) The financial pinch was felt across the dance world, but while other dance forms had developed institutional support structures that could adapt, concert tap had not.

Jane Goldberg, suffering from knee pain, suffered also from feeling passed over. There were no more articles about how she saved tap, and now not even the tap festivals seemed that interested in hiring her. Her old friend Gregory Hines told the *Los Angeles Times* that the seventies and the eighties had been the revival and that *Noise/Funk* was the renaissance. He told her to be happy, as he was, about the "natural succession," the lineage that Glover had reestablished. "We," Goldberg once explained to me, referring to the white women of her generation, "we were the unnatural succession." When, she quipped, were young black men going to take care of them?

Savion Glover, who had no trouble finding bookings, started another company. He called this one Not Your Ordinary Tappers. Its first job, in 1997, was the opening sequence for ABC's *Monday Night Football*. ABC also gave Glover his own TV special, *Savion Glover's NuYork*. His company appeared in the special, doing a number with a title—"Swing a Little Funk into Gang Gang"—that described itself and the whole program. Later, the group served as Glover's posse in a silly, gangsta-style tap showdown with the rapper then named Puff Daddy. (This was a retread of Glover's recent cameo in a Puff Daddy video, a significant bit of cross-marketing considering that Puff Daddy's album was number one.) *Savion Glover's NuYork* was a sequence of music videos demonstrating that Glover's tapping could mingle with contemporary music: reggae-inflected hip-hop, rap-injected R&B. It could express the sentiments of Puff Daddy's ode to conspicuous consumption or those of a Harlem church service. Though the situations were manufactured, they weren't false: Glover really did have that kind of cultural range. The best number paired him with Stevie Wonder, who told a starstruck Glover, "I can see you." Dance for the blind: I thought it was just a metaphor.

Glover's next TV special was filmed at the White House. Introducing his young guest as "the greatest tap dancer of all time," President Bill Clinton laughed in amazement. Glover, looking sharp in his dreadlocks, dark suit, beard, and no socks, made a fine ambassador. He danced without musical accompaniment, humming to help America hear the melody in his footwork. He gave a gracious speech thanking his hosts and mentors and explaining how tap is fun but also a serious discipline, able to express sadness, anger, thoughtfulness, and exuberance. The five serious young people of his troupe tapped out advanced phrases in unison. And then came Jimmy Slyde, swinging with a swinging band: Jimmy Slyde on national television, Jimmy Slyde at the White House, gazed upon by a smitten Savion Glover, who had brought him there.

Glover's shows were now concerts, more in the jazz than in the modern-dance sense. A jazz band played, mostly improvising on jazz standards, which is mostly what Glover and his dancers did, too. It was natural, if still unusual, for a jazz critic such as the esteemed Gary Giddins to review *Savion Glover/Downtown*, in 1999, as a jazz concert, and rate Glover as "one of the most inventive, stimulating jazz players in years." Dance critics tended to signal more unease with Glover's introversion. His cagey attitude toward his audience had something to do with the politics of *Noise/Funk*, a discomfort with the role of entertainer. Mostly, his attention was simply elsewhere: listening to the musicians, listening to his feet. His dances were musical compositions, and their variety was musical. Some personality emerged in the solos of the other dancers—in the as yet small space between their styles and his—but all of the group numbers were ordinary compared to what Glover did alone. He could dance allusively—Gregory Hines spoke of the complicated pleasure of seeing Glover quote Hines's steps at a speed Hines could only dream of—but Glover was less and less interested in weaving together old steps or even in coining his own. He was a man after a sound.

BRING IN THE LADIES

Like Hines before him, Glover traveled with his own heavily miked floor, and at the end of a show, he would open that floor to tap dancers in the house. Twenty years before, when Jane Goldberg had made this a feature of her concerts, it had been like opening the door of a closet long in disuse: forgotten items tumbled out. Now, an eager army of the young pounced onstage, evidence in every way of Glover's influence. They carried their bodies as he did and tried to address the floor with the same attack. But in other, important senses, they didn't all look like Glover. Some of them, for instance, were women.

There was even a woman in the group. It wasn't Dormeshia Sumbry, who had shared the Broadway experience of *Black and Blue*. ("Eight shows a week," she told me, "all I did was sit in the wings and take notes.") More recently, with the Jazz Tap Ensemble, Sumbry had honed her skills, learning to loosen her perfectionist tendencies enough to improvise. (To what level can be seen in a hilarious piece of footage from 1998. Gregory Hines is in challenge mode, trading manly steps with the slick Ensemble member Mark Mendonca while Sumbry hugs the back of the stage. After a while, Hines minces over to the wallflower and kids her timidity. She responds by striking a ladylike pose and then proceeding to repeat everything the men have done, better than they did it, mocking 'em every step. Hines falls to the floor in defeat.) Near the end of the Broadway run of *Noise/Funk*, Glover invited her to join the cast, finding a place for her in the show by disguising her in drag.

But the woman he invited to join his company had been tapping for only two years. Her name was Ayodele Casel, and though she had been born in the Bronx, she had spent much of her childhood in her mother's country, Puerto Rico. At the end of high school, she developed an obsession with Astaire-Rogers films, an interest her friends found bizarre. While she was studying acting at New York University, an acquaintance introduced her to another tap dancer, who suggested they practice together. Casel had never imagined anyone could tap as this young man did. He took her to tap jams, explaining, to her astonishment, that the dancers were improvising. He practiced with her once a week for a year. Then the young man, Baakari Wilder, invited her to a show he was in called *Bring in 'da Noise*. "When I saw it," said Casel, "it changed my life. I knew it was what I wanted to do." The lack of roles for a female hoofer did not discourage her. She practiced anyway, hours every day. She attended *Noise/Funk* so many times that the cast started letting her watch from the wings. Ted Levy allowed her to join the Funk University program. At jam sessions, she wondered why she was one of the only women to brave the floor when the floor got hot. Then she got a call from Glover. (This is how it worked with him: there was no audition; you got a call.) Casel's second job as a tap dancer was the *Monday Night Football* gig.

That she was the only girl, and also pretty, with a feisty cool, meant that Casel was going to attract attention, even if Glover hadn't placed her center stage. Dubbed the Funk Princess, she made the cover of *The Village Voice*. The accompanying article, by Itabari Njeri, didn't say much about her, but it juxtaposed her ascent against the historical neglect of black female hoofers, "the forgotten mothers of tap dance." Njeri cited a recent exhibition at the Philadelphia Folklore Project called "Plenty of Good Women Dancers," which cast light on Alice Whitman, Jeni Le-Gon, Louise Madison, and others, questioning why they weren't better known. The exhibition's curator, Deborah Kodish, charged that black women had been actively excluded from the tap revival—that black men and white women, in bed together, had kept black women out.

That theory would seem to ignore the participation of Marion Coles, Harriet Browne, and Frances Nealy in Jane Goldberg's shows and the fact that the young black female hoofers in the article (including Dormeshia Sumbry) had been hired and promoted by the white women supposedly doing the excluding. Why black women hadn't played a larger role in the tap revival was something that neither Kodish nor Njeri could adequately explain, but the article did reveal the poignant fact that young black women's knowledge of their predecessors didn't extend back much further than Dianne Walker. Dismayed by her own ignorance, Casel sought out Jeni LeGon, that onetime partner of Bill Robinson, and tracked her down in Canada, where, fed up with American racism, she had emigrated in the late sixties. The Funk Princess found in the Sepia Cinderella a kindred spirit, a girl playing with the boys because she didn't see why she shouldn't. Yet when Casel asked LeGon if she, as a black woman, had ever felt overshadowed, the older dancer's answer— "I was just happy to dance"—dissatisfied her. LeGon was a woman who showed no compunction in telling reporters about how Fred Astaire was a racist for ignoring her during the filming of *Easter Parade*, but "I was just happy to dance" could sound weak-willed to a young woman who hadn't yet been required to adjust her dreams.

Back in New York, Casel presented her own well-received show, *Ayo!* After that, she says, Savion Glover wasn't so nice in rehearsals anymore. "The other guys saw it, and were extra nice to me, but they didn't say anything to Savion." Casel stopped dancing for two years.

OPEN STYLE, CLOSED STYLE

When journalists asked Glover how it felt to bear the burden of perpetuating the tap tradition, he would say that he was passing the responsibility on to Cartier Williams, a protégé sixteen years younger. This handover was premature. Glover still had the ball and he seemed conflicted about what to do with it. On the one hand, he was a populist who called for tap to be in arenas, on TV, and in the movies. "I'm on a mission to brainwash an entire generation," he told *60 Minutes*. In *Savion: My Life in Tap*, an excellent young-adult picture book released in 2000, he said his goal was to put tap in "its proper place" at last. On the other hand, Glover was sensitive to any suggestion of "the dance" being treated with less than total seriousness. He was careful about whom he let in the circle, the Hoofers' Club of his approval. Gregory Hines's mantra—put on a pair of tap shoes and you're in—was not Glover's. "I'm not going to give anyone the feeling, like, come on in, yeah, it's open," he told the *Los Angeles Times*. Yet when Gia Kourlas of *Time Out New York* asked him if *Riverdance* and *Tap Dogs* were bringing tap down, he responded that those shows were all "contributions to the art form," because when people see them, "then they want to see more. Or they want to see the real thing."

Perhaps it would be more precise to say not that Glover was conflicted but that he saw no contradiction between wanting tap to become popular again—as popular as it had been in the thirties and forties—and wanting the tap that became popular to be his kind. Around the time Glover was born, Stanley Brown, the vaudevillian who ran the dance studio where Jimmy Slyde learned to slide, had articulated the common wisdom of black show business to Jane Goldberg. He distinguished between a closed style, which dancers performed for each other, and an open style, which got you a paycheck. Glover, who had been told all his life that whatever he did was great, defied that received knowledge. "I'm a tap dancer," he said, unashamedly, with no desire to be anything more, no implication that anything more might be required of him. He tapped as he wanted and expected everyone to listen.

———

This was the Savion Glover I found at the turn of this century kissing the shoes of Buster Brown. Usually, the mood at a Swing 46 jam session reflected Buster's if-you-can-walk-you-can-tap spirit, all those different types of people bringing their version of tap to the indoor picnic. When Glover slumped into the club, the mood shifted, the collective body language registering that the reigning champ had entered the building. Gregory Hines remained the bigger celebrity, the more beloved figure. Yet Hines was always pointing to Glover.

At Swing 46, Glover's influence was palpable. Technically, he had raised the bar, so that the average dancer tapped with a speed and complexity previously indicative of the exceptional. Stylistically, he was the dominant model, which meant fewer canned smiles and clichéd arms, and more disregard of the body. Indeed, some of the technical advancement stemmed directly from the demotion of physical presentation: mental energy concentrated in the feet, and physical exploits that a previous generation might have rejected as too awkward-looking—inside-out wings, tip-of-the-toe steps transferred to tip-of-the-heel—were now fair game. That pursuing such feats seemed to be the only goal was, however, a marker of how Glover's influence was diverging from his own practice. As their idol drilled deeper into sound, the young acolytes topped each other with stunts. Where in Glover's dancing you could sense the many predecessors who fed into his style, too much of the dancing of Glover's clones gave off no resonance beyond that of Glover himself. The kids weren't just stealing Glover's steps; they were skipping some.

But there was something else happening at Swing 46, one more twist in tap history. If the tradition surviving there was American, it wasn't exclusively American any longer. There were dancers from Europe, Australia, Brazil. Nearly half the participants were Japanese. And these international dancers weren't just joining in for the Shim Sham. Among them were some of the best tappers, the most distinctive. An American art had gone abroad, and it had come back home altered. People from other countries, other cultures, had honored the tap tradition by making it their own.

PART VI

AN AMERICAN TRADITION, A GLOBAL ART

An art can survive simply because its traditions survive, its practices continue. This kind of ritual survival is best accomplished in a society that remains static, and that is culturally homogenous. The survival of a work in a rapidly changing society, on the other hand, depends not only on whether it is handed down to us unmutilated, but on its ability to adapt to changing conditions of reception, on its capacity, when its original social function has been destroyed or altered beyond recognition, to create or inspire new kinds of significance that allow its vitality full play.

—CHARLES ROSEN, "The Future of Music," 2001

20

DANSE À CLAQUETTES, STEPTANZ, SAPATEADO, タップダンス

n 1977, when Jimmy Slyde was queried by the authors of *The Book of Tap* about the future of his art, he looked to Europe, where he had been teaching and performing. "Everybody there wants to tap dance," he said. "They really identify with American art and culture . . . the individual creativeness . . . the Europeans want to make up for the lack of respect that has been shown here. They want to make sure that tap dancing finds its proper niche in history. They appreciate it because they take the time to." In the dialect of Jimmy Slyde, "taking time" was a phrase of deep import.

This enthusiasm for the American art of tap, and the identification with it, wasn't happening only in Europe, though. It was happening all over the world. It had started before tap was called tap, as American dancers beginning with the minstrels took American percussive dance abroad; when tap was at the core of American popular culture, the movies had spread it farther. In each locale—in this chapter, I'll fly over a few—it found, as Slyde would say, a different niche in history. Tap

Opposite page: Kazu Kumagai in front of the Brooklyn Bridge, 2013 revealed something about each place, and each place revealed something about tap.

AMERICANS IN PARIS

American tap dancers had always found appreciative audiences across the Atlantic. African-American tap dancers in particular, like African-American entertainers in general, found in Europe a level of respect that was rarer back home. They didn't escape racial prejudice altogether. There were instances, especially in England, of black performers being denied accommodations or being insulted, often by traveling Americans. But European stereotypes of blackness largely worked in their favor as performers, making them exotic and in demand. Juba was celebrated as a "genuine nigger" but also as a "genius." In the thirties, when Buddy Bradley immigrated to London, he had to put up with asides about how "dancing is as natural to a darkie as breathing" in articles about his great success as a dance director, but he also had the success and the credit.

The entire careers of some American tappers transpired in Europe. The career of Louis Douglas exemplified how black dancers could be received there. A Philadelphia-born contemporary of Bill Robinson, he served his childhood apprenticeship in England and Germany. By 1910, he was on his own, crisscrossing Europe on the variety circuit, usually as the only black performer on a bill. Promoters called him *König der Negertänze*, King of the Nigger Dances. A Danish critic remarked that one expected niggers to be good dancers, but this one was special, musical, combining grotesque humor with technical virtuosity. In London, Douglas was "an established favourite." In Paris, he played on the same bills as Mistinguett and Maurice Chevalier, and there, in 1925, he made history as the choreographer and lead dancer for *La Revue Nègre*.

This was the production that transformed Josephine Baker from a St. Louis kid who crossed her eyes comically in *Shuffle Along* into a chic black Venus. Baker and Douglas were both clowns. She did her cheerful bump-and-grind topless only at the insistence of a French producer and only for the final number, a colonialist fantasy called "La Danse Sauvage." But it was that final number that French audiences found threatening and tantalizing, the end of civilization or an escape from civilization's dead end. Although French critics considered Douglas amusing, he didn't incite what Baker did—*le tumulte noir*, a rage for the Charleston and the Black Bottom, hers most of all. Unerotic, Douglas's tapping was of inherently less interest to the French.

The most intelligent, condescending response to *La Revue Nègre* came from the Russian émigré André Levinson, who attempted to draw from the production "the essential characteristics of Negro dance." This he did by sharply contrasting Negro dance with classical ballet. Ballet, he noted, is silent. It's an exclusively visual expression of music. Negro dancing, by contrast, conflates sight and sound; the dancer is a musical instrument. Where the ballet dancer seeks the illusion of flight, the tap dancer pounds his weight into the floor, pursuing rhythms. Levinson considered such rhythmic fantasy "an innate gift, not a conscious art—a gift that has become more or less atrophied in the cultivated human being."

Here was primitivism in its most cultivated form. To say that "the undeniable rhythmic superiority of these Negro dancers is nothing less than an adjunct of their irrepressible animality" is one way to handle undeniable superiority. Levinson could not consider the Negro dancer an artist because he did not consider rhythm to be art. Art required something to happen between the beats, something visual. Thus Levinson could make an exception of Josephine Baker, whose personality, he wrote, "transcended the character of her dance." He could turn her into a symbol, whereas black tap dancers disappointed him as "mere professionals." He found it ironic that Europeans doing the Charleston were, from his point of view, regressing toward the primitive, while the black tap dancers were moving—progressing, on his scale—toward softness and subtlety. Levinson did not know that he was watching the soft shoe, a refinement that had nothing to do with the black dancers' recent exposure to Europe.

Levinson only gestured at what many French commentators cried out against: the supposed moral contagion of black dance. When *La Revue Nègre* played in Berlin, the German critics also wrote about animals and the black conquest of civilization. They wrote about speed and rhythm devouring harmony. But they had as much to say about Douglas and his "Paganini virtuosity of the feet" as about Baker and her behind.

They marveled at the way, in Douglas's number "Les Pieds Qui Parlent," he danced his voyage from New York to Europe: sounding out the stormy seas, the railroad, a horse race. "Mister Douglas is a genius," wrote the great theater critic Alfred Polgar. "He dances entire biographies . . . His feet are a phenomenon of language. They can persuade you of whatever he wants . . . Nothing like this has been heard before, which is to say, seen." Maybe not in Berlin.

In 1930, a cameo in the German film *Einbrecher* preserved some of Douglas's art. As an entertainer at a *Negerball*, a mixed-race cabaret with a jungle decor and images of apes, Douglas is handsome in a tuxedo, debonair but humble. While sampling traditional steps, he's graceful: a class act. In the 1931 German film *Niemandsland*, he's once again a cabaret artist, a tap dancer named Joe Smile. His act is a stair dance, similar in outline to Robinson's though much more eccentric. Set during the First World War, the film introduces five soldiers—one each from Britain, France, and Germany, plus a Polish Jew, and Joe Smile as a recruit for the French colonial army—and throws them together in a cellar between enemy lines, in the no-man's-land of the title. Only Joe speaks everyone's language. He laughs at their nationalist arguments and mocks the din of incoming shells with the sounds he makes with his feet. *Niemandsland* is a pacifist movie, and its moral center is a black tap dancer. No wonder the Nazis would try to destroy all copies of the film.

Douglas seems to have spent most of the thirties in France, sometimes touring with a mixed-race troupe. Years before, by marrying the daughter of the composer Will Marion Cook, he had wed into the royalty of African-American show business, and the connection had brought him back to America periodically. When he staged dances for the 1927 Ethel Waters revue *Africana*, the black critic for *The Pittsburgh Courier* found Waters "distinctly racial" and Douglas "absolutely foreign." As war loomed again in the late thirties, Douglas returned to America, appeared in a few unsuccessful revues, and directed a for-the-people troupe founded by Langston Hughes. In his country of origin, Douglas was mostly unknown and archaic. His death from illness in 1941 was barely acknowledged.

———

Throughout the thirties, you could find reports in the black press about tap dancers who toured overseas and stayed for years. As one dispatch from Paris about the Five Hot Shots explained, "Good tap dancing, so commonplace in America, is rare here." That group's circuit extended past Europe, through Egypt to India, Singapore, China, and Japan before hopping to Hawaii and the West Coast. The seventeen-year-old Mackey Twins, Sam and Jim, followed the route in reverse, and in a series of articles for the *Baltimore Afro-American*, the twins' white manager, Irene West, recounted the trouble caused by all the young ladies attracted to her boys and by the American servicemen who objected. Langston Hughes caught the Mackey act in Shanghai, and he found them talented, "uneducated colored boys trying to get some fun out of life." When West returned home, the twins chose to stay in Paris, and when the war came, she lost touch with them, it seems for good: a common story. After the war, damaged Europe remained a refuge. The Four Step Brothers played the Lido in Paris for a year as Les Step Brothers, 4 Merveilles Noires, then toured other countries hungry for black marvels. Harold Nicholas spent the years 1958 to 1964 in France, where he transformed himself into a soigné nightclub single, recorded two albums, and married a Frenchwoman.

When Jimmy Slyde first toured Europe in 1966, he was moved by the respect shown him there as a jazz musician. So when he was invited to appear in a French documentary, he was happy to accept. The film was called *L'Aventure du Jazz* (1972), and it was directed by Louis Panassié. (This was the son of Hugues Panassié, who, in 1934, had written one of the first books of jazz criticism, a book that in taking jazz seriously helped not just Europe but America do the same.) A tour of France as a live counterpart to screenings of the film led to more jobs. In 1974, Slyde recorded a tap album in Paris—further confirmation for him of the superiority of the European outlook. (He wouldn't allow it to be sold in the United States.) Except for visits home to his mother, he stayed in France for the next half-dozen years.

Among those most affected by seeing him perform was a Parisian named Sarah Petronio. She wasn't a native. Her parents were Sephardic Jews from Burma who fled during World War II to India, where Sarah was born. When she was nineteen, her family emigrated to Brooklyn, where she married an American. She loved jazz and tap, but when a friend took her along to a Jerry Ames class, she wasn't impressed. When she and her husband moved to Paris in 1968, the tap she discovered there was even less to her liking. Tap in France was a recreational activity, a music-hall novelty you could learn in a few lessons. In one studio, she found the students dancing with their necks craned up, tapping by number from instructions on the ceiling. On a trip to New York, she investigated Henry LeTang, but his graduated routines also struck her as overregimented and impersonal. Already, she was teaching *les claquettes américaines* in Paris. Practicing alone, she tried to find a sound she wasn't sure existed. And then, in 1974, she went to see *L'Aventure du Jazz*, and during the intermission, the sound danced onstage in the form of Jimmy Slyde. She asked him to be her "guru."

A young white woman learned from an old black man, and the seventies tap renaissance came to France. This apprenticeship was not overregimented. Months passed before Slyde first called her, more months before he dropped by her studio. "He never arrived when he was expected," she would recall, and he left "when least expected." If Petronio asked a question, Slyde answered with another. The most definite thing he told her was not to dance like him. Instead, he invited her to dance *with* him, improvising a conversation together, along with a band. She also began working solo in Paris jazz clubs, and, still teaching, she established the American Center of Paris as "le temple du claquettes."

They called their duets "It's About Time." Unlike Honi Coles and Brenda Bufalino, the two members of this odd couple danced at the same cool temperature. Yet Petronio had listened to Slyde's counsel: she had her own style, kin to his yet distinct. Musically, it was alive with pauses and rhythmic displacements. Digging in, throwing her body around and bobbing her head, she looked at once like someone dancing to make rhythms and like someone dancing to the rhythms she was making. When she tossed in a high kick as a sop to Folies Bergère expectations, the irony in the gesture was apparent, but her cool-cat attitude could verge on affectation. The saving grace was playfulness—with other dancers, with musicians. She invited her audiences in close.

For five years in the nineties, Petronio lived in America, teaching in Chicago and dancing in South Side jazz clubs where hers was often the only white face. But she was part of the American tap festival circuit from its beginning, adopted as a flat-shoed sister by Brenda Bufalino and Lynn Dally even while her French short-shorts attracted feminist flack. A Parisian when in America, she brought a cosmopolitan flavor to tap shows stateside. An American when in Paris, she could feel isolated. But in France she stayed. Her daughter, Leela, was raised among tap dancers. When she grew up, she had no trouble adapting her mother's dancing to the hip-hop of her own generation (French hip-hop—more overtly intellectual, less overtly angry). Yet when Leela dances with her mother, it's obvious that she is part of a lineage, a lineage that is now international.

AUF DEUTSCH

In Europe, as in America, the films of Busby Berkeley, Astaire-Rogers, Eleanor Powell, and Shirley Temple packed dancing studios in the thirties. Powell's films were especially popular in Germany. To the National Socialists, the popularity of such films was an embarrassment. Minister of Propaganda Joseph Goebbels took it as a challenge. The premier German film studio, Universum Film AG (Ufa), produced its own Hollywood-style musicals and developed its own tap-dancing stars, with varying success. Gradually, Nazi authorities choked off the American competition, until, in 1939, they banned it outright.

Carmen Lahrmann, who dubbed Shirley Temple's voice into German and then attempted to duplicate her in German-made films, wasn't much of a dancer, and she had no Bill Robinson. The German public did not warm to her, but it did to Marika Rökk. Rökk's parents were German-speaking Hungarians. She had learned her craft on the international circuit, first in Paris with the Gertrude Hoffman Girls and then in New York at Ned Wayburn's school. Rökk's lunges, acrobatics, and multiple, if sometimes wobbly, turns bespoke a training like Eleanor Powell's, but her tapping could be clunkier, closer to the style of Ruby Keeler. She tossed her legs around with more force than either American and molded her face into a wider array of pouting, lip biting, and eyebrow raising. She was an Austro-Hungarian Betty Grable, flirtatious, feisty, and ultimately accommodating. Her characters tended to give up their artistic ambitions for married contentment. "Women Are Dangerous" was one of her songs, but she wasn't threatening—not to men, nor to the Nazi regime.

Rökk's films—more than a dozen between *Leichte Kavallerie* in 1935 and *Die Frau Meiner Träume* in 1944—were escapist fare, morale builders treasured by the German public during the Depression and wartime for the same reasons that Americans treasured their own musicals then. "I don't need millions," sang Rökk in 1939, "I only need your love and music." The increasing lavishness of the films—*Die Frau Meiner Träume*, in color, ends with a fifteen-minute Ziegfeld-style finale flitting all over the Axis—was a show of German capability, even though much of the German film industry's greatest talent was in exile, immeasurably enriching the culture of the enemy. To an American, the dance numbers seem tamer and less imaginative than their Hollywood models in almost every respect. Rökk taps across the tops of pianos and up and down staircases and in front of a mass of bare-legged chorus girls without ever touching the extravagance of a Busby Berkeley number. In her memoirs, Rökk confessed to stealing steps from Powell films. She added little that an American tap dancer would want to steal back. Her ballroom squires merely twirled and framed her. She had no Astaire, no Kelly, and neither did Germany. The Third Reich put forth no male tap stars, and Ufa employed no choreographer of comparable artistry.

That the precision tapping of ensembles such as the Gertrude Hoffman Girls resembled military drills had long been a truism of theatrical criticism. The similarity between the marching of the Girls troupe in the 1939 film *Wir Tanzen Um die Welt* (*We Dance Around the World*) and the Nazi pageantry already glorified in *Triumph of the Will* was even clearer. Such orderly expression of group discipline fit easily into Fascist aesthetics of spectacle and power, maintaining the idealization of physical culture in cuter uniforms and sparkly boots. Same with the borrowings from Busby Berkeley. As propaganda, the Nazi musicals tended to be less overt than Ann Miller's tapping to "Victory Polka." You could argue—as penitent German film scholars later did—that less overt meant more insidious. Goebbels said that the best propaganda was the kind not recognized as propaganda.

Nevertheless, the American origins of tap dance required some explaining. Like jazz, tap trailed associations with Weimar decadence, blacks, and Jews. Herbert John's 1940 *Steptanz im Selbstunterricht (Teach Yourself to Tap)* admitted that tap came from America, but insisted that the dance was not purely American. No, it had roots in old Nordic fishermen's dances and the Bavarian *Schuhplattler*, and it did not have "anything to do with Niggers." An official manual, released by the Reichstheaterkammer the following year, argued that tap was a universal impulse that each culture develops in its own way. "Today we also have German tap"—not "Americanized Nigger rhythms" but a dance expressing the German character and emphasizing melody instead of jazz syncopation. In 1941, the *Deutsche Tanzzeitschrift* went so far as to present a purely German story for the origin of tap: something about how young men, sitting around bored while girls spun fabric, began to tap their feet in rhythm. There were German tap dancers who didn't buy any of this, who didn't buy into the Nazi ideology at all. They emigrated or lay low. Jazz was never banned outright, but it was subversive. Jazz musicians and enthusiasts were co-opted or sent to the front or even to concentration camps. Tap dancers were likewise always in danger: of using the wrong music, of having the wrong style. It's likely that the best German tap dancers did not make it into films.

The career of Evelyn Künneke fell between the official and the banned. The daughter of the operetta composer Eduard Künneke, she was another young German inspired by Eleanor Powell—and also by Charles Jenkins, an American tap dancer performing at Berlin's Wintergarten. She was fifteen. Jenkins was twenty-two. She got pregnant. They got hitched. But Jenkins was not just American. He was Jewish, as was Künneke's maternal grandmother. Jenkins took their daughter back to his own country, and Künneke never saw them again. She continued her career in Germany, tapping in nightclubs under the Americanized name Evelyn King. During the war, she reverted to Künneke and had a hit song. Her tap number with a giant Sally Rand feather fan in the 1942 film *Karneval der Liebe* is more imitation Powell, but Goebbels considered the number un–German and had it cut. In 1944, while Künneke was performing for the troops, her comment that the Red Army might

triumph got her arrested, and she survived only through the interven-
tion of fans in the SS.

In her autobiography, Künneke tells of meeting Adolf Hitler in
1938, at the premiere of one of her father's operettas. Der Führer wanted
to talk about tap. As a movie buff, he considered himself a connoisseur.
Tap, he told her during a twenty-minute discourse, was "cheering, fresh,
and precise," dashing in a military sense. The highest exemplar of the
form, in his opinion, was Astaire. Presumably, Hitler was aware that he
shared a country of origin with Astaire's father but not that the dancer's
paternal grandparents were Jewish.

During the war, Astaire's films were forbidden. Hitler enjoyed them
in private. After the war, Germans greeted the movies with enthusiasm.
Evelyn Künneke's postwar career sputtered until the seventies, when,
rediscovered by the filmmaker Rainer Werner Fassbinder, she emerged
as an exemplar of prewar cabaret and a gay icon. Marika Rökk, sullied
by her association with the Nazis, pleaded naïveté and was making
movies again by 1948, tapping less and less. (Her later films are marvelous
kitsch: look for *Bühne Frei für Marika*, in which she plays a bored Martian
who visits the African jungle.) By the mid-fifties, she faced stiff competition from a younger, Italian-born singer, the multitalented, multilingual Caterina Valente. On a 1964 episode of the American variety show
Hollywood Palace, Valente jammed with four great jazz drummers, not
exactly trading but keeping up in a manner it's hard to imagine Rökk
matching. The jazz feeling is only intermittent in the German musical
films Valente made in the fifties, but a couple of those films included John
Bubbles. In *Liebe, Tanz und 1000 Schlager* (1955), the Father of Rhythm
Tap makes an appearance as a blithe spirit, an expatriate vaudevillian.
Bubbles was playing himself again; he spent much of the fifties in
Germany. In the film, he taps as he serves drinks. He holds his tray
steady, but his fellow Americans Jackson, James, and Carnell spin theirs:
that was their trademark, tapping while twirling trays. German film
gave these particular black dancers a specialty spot that Hollywood never
did. Carnell Lyons stayed in Germany, ekeing out a living as a soloist on
military bases and eventually touring Japan with his East German contortionist girlfriend.

In the late seventies, when the work dried up altogether, Lyons began to teach—in Berlin, and as demand rose, in workshops across the country. After class, he would invite students to bring their sleeping bags to his apartment and stay up late hearing stories and sampling his exile's library of tap footage. All of a sudden, there were people deeply interested in what Lyons had to offer. The tap revival had spread. In Germany, as in America, a split developed between those excited by Broadway and old Hollywood and those inspired by the movies of Gregory Hines and the tradition that Hines represented and revealed. Members of the second camp began to invite leading American figures to teach in Germany. In 1987, when Nürnberg first experienced Brenda Bufalino, a few of Lyons's students brought in their master from Berlin to vet her. Bufalino's treatment of a tune by Lyons's schoolmate Charlie Parker earned his quick endorsement. "She's a genius," he exclaimed. "She comes from Honi Coles."

For a few American teachers, a trip to Germany became a yearly ritual, sometimes the most reliable gig on the calendar. On Sam Weber's initial visit, he found his students very serious. Most were musically literate, yet they had trouble swinging. "Their aesthetic was: the more even, the more equally loud, the better. Like the teeth on a comb." It wasn't long before German enthusiasts moved from attending workshops with visiting Americans to attending tap festivals in America. Tap festivals soon sprouted on German soil. One measure of interest was the turnout for the Tap-o-Mania event that the American expatriate Ray Lynch organized in Stuttgart in 1998: nearly seven thousand participants tapping together in a train station.

If, at the height of his success in the forties and early fifties, you had told Carnell Lyons that his act would live on into the twenty-first century in the form of two Germans, he would have found your humor odd. But it was two of Lyons's German students—the bald and lanky Kurt Albert and his compact partner, Klaus Bleis—who resurrected the art of tapping while spinning trays. Rather than an exact copy, "Tap and Tray" was new wine in old bottles. The sight of these Germans in blue serge suits honoring outmoded conventions of black showbiz was comical, but it wasn't ridiculous. Their droll demeanor suggested that they were in on the joke, mostly. Rhythmically, they could have passed any blindfold test. "I never thought of being a dancer," recalled Albert. "I wanted to make that rhythm and make it look cool."

Many Germans latched onto the idea of the tap dancer as musician and let the body follow. For Sebastian Weber, much of the initial appeal of tap was that he could "be a dancer and not have to stand up straight and move my arm nicely." In 1989, as a teenaged exchange student passing through Boston, he stumbled upon the tap elders. More trips to the United States followed, and at La Cave, he came under the spell of Chuck Green, who took him on as a disciple, passing down steps on kitchen linoleum and stories interrupted by sudden slumber. To Weber, being invited into Green's life felt like being given the key to "a second world parallel to the one you know." One day, Green informed Weber that Weber had his own style. Back home in Germany, he founded Tapshot, a jazz combo. Twice, he toured with Buster Brown, trading taps with a hero sixty years older and two feet shorter. Weber is an intelligent musician with a near-total lack of physical grace. His productions can be conceptual—European-style *Tanztheater* with incisive grooves. He feels that the absence of a German tap tradition—to him, Germany doesn't have one—leaves him with greater creative freedom. His work is "absolutely not American" and at the same time "absolutely connected to the heritage of Chuck and Buster."

BEHIND THE CURTAIN

Born in Soviet Georgia, Alexander Ivashkevich was studying acting in Ukraine when, like any boy in Kalamazoo, he saw an Astaire film and fell in love with tap. This was in the late seventies, and he could find no one to teach him. Eight years later, after he had established himself as an actor in Estonia, he saw some tap in the Russian movie *Winter Evening in Gagry* and, inspired again, tried again to find a teacher. This time, he managed to track down Yuri Gusakov, a retired Russian tap dancer, who told him, "You cannot dance." Ivashkevich collected video clips—the Nicholas Brothers, *The Cotton Club*—and struggled to teach himself. Then, in 1992, "from God," the American Tap Dance Orchestra arrived in Estonia on a State Department–sponsored tour of Eastern Europe.

Ivashkevich's English vocabulary consisted of "yes, no, and Coca-Cola." He came to the ATDO workshop with tap shoes he had constructed himself. His mind harbored a thousand questions, and he could ask none. Through a friend with slightly better English, he requested more lessons, and Barbara Duffy offered him free instruction if he came to New York. The American embassy in Estonia provided him a plane ticket. Someone stole his money. Someone gave him a cat to deliver. In New York, after each class at Woodpecker's, Duffy would write him pedagogical notes, which the Russian friends he was staying with would translate in the evening. In this fashion, Ivashkevich learned, and when he returned to Estonia, he opened a dancing school that he named Dufftap, after his teacher. Without giving American hoofers much competition, he became the best tap dancer in Estonia, soon to be surpassed by his students. They believe as he does that "tap dance is freedom."

In the memoirs of the Russian choreographer Bronislava Nijinska, sister of Vaslav Nijinsky, she recalls receiving her very first dance lessons, in the early 1890s, from the black American tap dancers her father brought home from the Nizhny Novgorod *café chantant* where he worked. The men spread sand on a plank to teach her, and she was as much fascinated by their diamond pinkie rings as by their rhythms. Russian steps were a key ingredient in the repertoire of the black Americans Greenlee and Drayton when they arrived in the Soviet Union in 1926 with *The Chocolate Kiddies*, an offshoot of a Sissle and Blake revue. The Soviet filmmaker Dziga Vertov included a few seconds of *The Chocolate Kiddies* in his *One-Sixth of the World*, where his sandwiching of the snippets between images of Africans toiling in the fields and images of the furred bourgeoisie would seem to suggest the capitalist exploitation of blacks. The Soviet critic Vladimir Blum complained that the *Chocolate Kiddies* troupe wasn't even Negro, since it included mulattos, and dismissed the show as an orgy that perverted the unfortunate race. But he praised the cast as masters of their craft, carefree as children: "These people have rhythm, and contemporary European music could learn something from them."

Blum's critique touched both sides of the Soviet ideological response to tap and jazz: they could be disparaged as decadent, bourgeois, and

immoral, or they could be defended as the folk expression of the oppressed black proletariat. The popularity of tap and jazz in the Soviet
Union escaped either explanation, but in the wild oscillations of Soviet
policy, the folk defense proved enduringly effective. A blending of tap
with local folk forms happened both naturally and intentionally, as political cover. Leonid Utesov, a Jew from Odessa and the most popular
Soviet musician of the thirties, at one point declared that both jazz and
tap had been invented by street musicians at Jewish weddings in his
rough-and-tumble hometown. This was a joke, one that mocked—while
seeming to indulge—the Soviet propensity for claiming foreign imports
as homegrown inventions. Similarly, Utesov could sneak in the suspect
music his audience craved under the disguise of parody. He was a clown,
and his theatricalized jazz, and the tap that went with it, was a jolly assault
on decorum. Utesov marked seeing *The Chocolate Kiddies* as a seminal moment: the musicians didn't get the standing ovations, he noticed; the tap
dancers did.

It was in the role of a Crimean shepherd that Utesov starred in the
first Soviet musical, the 1934 farce *The Jolly Fellows*. His sidekick was
played by Lyubov Orlova, the socialist Cinderella of a cherished series
of musicals directed by her husband, Grigoriy Aleksandrov. On a trip
to Hollywood, Aleksandrov had been inspired by the work of Busby
Berkeley and had resolved to make Soviet-style musicals, ideologically
correct entertainments. In Aleksandrov's *Circus* (1936), Orlova plays an
American who flees a lynch mob after giving birth to a baby with a
black father; only in the Soviet Union does she find love and acceptance.
Orlova was a bright-eyed beauty, an operetta singer, a comedian, and no
dancer. When her character emerges from the top of a cannon in a flapper dress, the syllables she sings are nonsense—"Diggy, diggy, do!"—and
the noises she makes with her feet are even less articulate. As propaganda,
Circus wasn't anywhere near as reprehensible as the musicals that idealized the murderous collective farms. (In place of dance numbers came
choreographed harvesting; instead of Tiller Girls, there were girls tilling.)
Yet *Circus* did demonstrate how tap's joyful associations might be co-opted
for a legitimizing myth.

During the Second World War, the alliance with America allowed
for a limited importation of American films. (Marika Rökk films were

also treated as treasured booty by Soviet troops.) When *Sun Valley Serenade*, released in the United States in 1941, arrived in the Soviet Union in 1944, it was embraced by jazz fans for the Glenn Miller songs and by tap dancers for the Nicholas Brothers' rendition of "Chattanooga Choo Choo." In isolation, the film assumed an outsized importance. The Gusakov Brothers, Yuri and Boris, made a career of dancing to songs from *Sun Valley Serenade*. They had begun their study of tap as teenagers in 1937, when their father was sent to a labor camp, and they studied with a Polish dancer who claimed to have been to Hollywood, but much of their technique derived from this single film.

After the war came another ideological crackdown. Jazz musicians were censured, arrested, sent to Siberia. With the orchestra of that wily kitsch king Utesov, the Gusakovs danced a number called "American Puppets," demonstrating the corruptibility of the American electoral system to a boogie-woogie beat. Folk routines remained a refuge. Hence the sombreros that the Gusakovs wear in their most famous tap dance: a mostly unison Mexican waltz in the 1956 film *Carnival Night*. The film is about workers who put on a show in defiance of an uptight bureaucrat, a plot that gave extra pleasure in the Soviet Union. The movie would be aired on Soviet television every New Year, serving a function like that of *It's a Wonderful Life* in America. The Gusakovs are stiffer than the Condos Brothers, and despite the Latin tinge, their foot rhythms are so even, they could be German. Still, like the nutty jazz and warm-hearted festivities that surround them, their tapping signified play. In a later movie, the Gusakovs dance to jazz—a compilation of riffs built on the skeleton of "Chattanooga Choo Choo." They tap in sweaters and fur hats upon a block of ice, and even without the hints in the mise-en-scène, you might suspect that the dancers were Russian, just not that the year was 1968. Tap was no longer ideologically dangerous, but neither was it current. Rock and roll, its popularity stoked by official disapproval, had taken over.

Ignored, tap could return as nostalgia, which it did in the film *Winter Evening in Gagry*. Released in 1985, the same year as *White Nights*, this Soviet film is not a Cold War drama. America doesn't even get a mention. But the movie does concern a tap dancer, famous back in the fifties and now forgotten in a present of synthesizers and rock ballet. Divorced and alone, he watches a TV program that commemorates him as one of the honored dead. When he calls to protest, a producer offers to revive his signature number, but the old man replies that there aren't any tap dancers left to dance it. The one pupil who approaches him has no talent. This is not a Hollywood musical. The protagonist dies, and the film concludes in equivocal melancholy. Before that, however, we have seen the old man's Rosebud moment, a flashback to when his daughter joined his act one winter evening at a Black Sea resort. We have seen his signature routine—essentially, a solo version of the Gusakov Brothers' Mexican number—and another glimpse of him in his prime, tapping between drums à la Astaire. The tapping in *Winter Evening* is bland, the music awful, yet the film is affecting. It's touching that a Soviet film could express nostalgia for Soviet tap, a sense of loss about something that looks from the outside like an inferior substitute. It may have been inferior, but it was theirs.

Vladimir Kirsanov, who choreographed the tap sequences for the film, liked to quote his teacher, Vladimir Zernov, who compared tap to an old prostitute, loved by all but not respected. Kirsanov began his studies with Zernov at the State Circus School in 1965. When Konstantin Nevretdinov attended the Circus School in the early eighties, Kirsanov was his teacher. Watching American musicals at the State Film Fund, young Nevretdinov became convinced that to learn American tap he would have to go to America. "But I was impatient," he explained to me. "I wanted to amaze now." So, using his acrobatic skills, he painstakingly taught himself to tap upside down, on his hands. During the years when tap in America was transforming into a concert form, tap in Russia lived on in the circus.

It was only after the collapse of the Soviet Union that a tap festival sprang up. The first Moscow Tap Parade, in 1993, brought in Jerry Ames, whose American career had been nearly nonexistent for a decade. It also brought back Michael Kushner-Gusakov, who had performed as a Gusakov Brother and who had moved to New York. With "Tap on Hands" Nevretdinov, Kushner-Gusakov opened the Russian School of American Tap Dance in Moscow. By the 2002 Moscow Tap Parade, the organizers were clued in enough to invite Brenda Bufalino, Sarah Petronio, Tap and Tray, and Savion Glover. The Americans marveled at the profusion of the Russian acts, all the old-fashioned routines set to taped and antiquated music. (They took special delight in Oleko Abdullaev, who kept the secret of his four-legged tap dance hidden underneath his shiny black trench coat.) The Russians were equally amazed by Savion Glover and his twenty-minute improvisation. It wasn't long before Vasily Sedykh, exactly Glover's age, was mimicking Glover's style and fashion sense. A reporter for *Moskovskij Komsomolets* asked Vladimir Kirsanov what Russians needed to learn if they were to dance like Glover. His answer: "Freedom."

THE SOUND OF JAPANESE SANDALS

Tap may have first arrived in Japan on the black ships of Commodore Perry. In the course of persuading the Japanese to open trade with the United States in 1854, Perry invited the Japanese delegation to a banquet on his flagship. There, aboard the steam frigate *Powhatan*, Perry's sailors put on a minstrel show. The official account doesn't mention dancing, but Japanese sketches capture the blackface performers: banjo players, Tambo and Bones, two dancers with legs extended hip-high. The playbill for one of several subsequent Ethiopian concerts in Japanese ports advertises a pas de deux, and it seems improbable that a portrayal of "Plantation Niggas of the South" would neglect a breakdown. About the actual black crewmen noted in the record, little is known, except the remark of an Anglican missionary that their dancing pleased his children.

After such a portentous beginning, further reports of tap in Japan are hard to uncover, even through the 1920s, when jazz took over Japanese dance halls. Tap surfaced in musical revues, mostly in the world-conquering form of girl troupes. George Hori, who learned tap while working as a dishwasher in Los Angeles, trained such a troupe and opened what seems to have been the first tap studio in Tokyo, in 1932. He wrote a manual that stressed speed and pep, characterizing tap as an attempt to "reflect that alert spirit that personifies America and American progress." Since tap shoes were scarce, some students wore wooden sandals, or *geta*, studded with rivets.

Since tap was an American art, Japanese-American entertainers were perceived to have an edge on authenticity. Born in Hawaii, Alice Fumiko Kawahata grew up in Los Angeles. Supposedly another pupil of Bill Robinson, she was best known for wrapping a leg behind her neck while standing. In Japan, she became a recording star, a popular icon for "modern girls" and "modern boys." In 1933, at the age of seventeen, she wrote, choreographed, and starred in the inaugural revue of the Nippon Gejiko theater, Tokyo's answer to Radio City. No copies of her 1935 Japanese film *Back Alley Symphony* would survive the war, yet some of her recordings did—her taps are clear and simple. By 1939, she had married and retired. Nakagawa Saburo, a student of George Hori, took off for America at the age of seventeen. Interviewed by the Associated Press in 1935, he explained how he had found his inspiration to tap from American films and the best rhythms in the New York subway. His favorite dancer was Astaire: "He's got the Japanese personality." One Nakagawa film survives, *Whispering Sidewalks*, the musical he made upon returning to Japan in 1936. In a tux and a fedora, he looks slim, attractive, and very young. His knock-kneed tapping lunges in the direction of off-rhythms like someone trying to be Astaire.

The question of imitation was an especially vexed one for Japanese tap dancers, as it was for Japanese jazz musicians. The stereotype of the Japanese as a nation of imitators has a historical basis in centuries of borrowing from China and Korea, followed by a national project of catch-up with the West after those black ships appeared. In traditional Japanese aesthetics, "school" was valued over the individual; artistry was a trade in which apprentice disciples became masters by copying a previous master exactly. Japanese jazz musicians felt these pressures, recognizing analogues in the jazz tradition of imitation, while at the same time understanding that in jazz, imitation is never enough. Japanese tap dancers took longer to catch on.

After Pearl Harbor, of course, imitating Americans could get you in trouble. Nakagawa was questioned by army officials, who suggested that he might be an American spy using tap as Morse code (an idea that had also occurred to the writers of a sketch for Eleanor Powell in the 1936 revue *At Home Abroad*, an idea repeated in her 1942 movie *Ship Ahoy*). Japanese tap dancers did replace American nomenclature with numbers and code. A shuffle became "#1"; a flap, "#2." The ball of the foot, they called *tsuma*, "wife"; the heel, *otto*, "husband."

(In the United States, it was being of Japanese descent that could get you imprisoned. The Japanese-American tap dancer Dorothy Takahashi managed to stay on the big-time vaudeville circuits through the war. Her Chinese-American partner, Paul Wing, had learned his first steps in Palo Alto, from one of those proverbial colored newspaper boys. As Toy and Wing, the Asian-American duo studied with Willie Covan and Steve Condos. After Pearl Harbor, they were careful to tell the press that they were American-born, of Chinese descent, Americans who did American dances. Almost all of that was true. Wing joined the U.S. Army and fought in Europe. Toy performed with her sister. Her parents spent the war in an internment camp in Utah.)

Under the American occupation, American culture came out in the open again. Resident GIs and the American jazz musicians who traveled to Japan to entertain them brought a wave of interest in jazz that even after it subsided left a subculture of connoisseurs unsurpassed anywhere else in the world. But in contrast to the many American jazz musicians who toured Japan, only a few American tap dancers visited, and those only briefly. The principal influence on Japanese dancers remained American movies.

It was the films of Astaire that inspired the Nakano Brothers. Born in 1935 and 1937, Keisuke and Shouzo were movie-mad kids. By 1953, they were entertaining on the military base circuit. A photo from the following year shows the teenagers in straw boaters, their hands splayed in white gloves, their O-shaped mouths outlined in white against blackened faces. The juvenile pop star Chiemi Eri, who could look like a Mouseketeer and sing American hits in thickly accented but credible imitations of American artists, folded the brothers into her stage and television appearances. This made them the best-known tap dancers in Japan. If performing in America was the highest validation, then the Nakanos acquired the shiniest credential available in 1959: they worked in Vegas and befriended Sammy. Through the sixties, they were a regular feature of Japanese television and American-derived stage musicals.

When Kaoru Tomita started taking tap as a teenager in 1983, she was taught numbered steps fixed into set patterns. The steps were inherited; creating new ones was unheard of. You studied with one teacher, whom you could not surpass; attempting to study with more than one teacher could get you expelled by both. Since Tomita was also a jazz drummer, the idea that she couldn't shift accents struck her as absurd. So in 1987, she made her pilgrimage to New York, where she discovered not only that rhythmic variation was allowed but that exact copying was not. Returning to Japan, she founded an all-female tap company and spread the idea of tap as a "free, unrestricted" form. Tomita was far from alone. Many Japanese tap dancers her age and younger, taking advantage of a strong yen against the dollar, made study trips to America. Over the next two decades, Japanese visitors would be among the most patient and dedicated students, the most faithful attendees of jam sessions, the most reliable company members. Few stayed for good, and many carried their knowledge home to Japan, where National Tap Dance Day was first celebrated in 1991. Decade by decade, performances dominated by the Nakano Brothers and musical theater tap gradually gave way to styles more closely matching those you could find at New York's Tap Extravaganza the same year.

In the sixties, the parents of Hideyuki Higuchi had performed as a comic duo for American soldiers. Their son grew up in the family dance studio, but as a teenager he yearned to tap to his kind of music. Gregory Hines in *White Nights* (1985) revealed that it could be done. At one of Hines's performances in Japan, Higuchi responded to the call for hoofers in the house, and an impressed Hines directed him to Henry LeTang. Higuchi's time in New York coincided with Jimmy Slyde's jam sessions at La Cave, where the other dancers pushed the Japanese kid to find his own style. "In New York," he told me, "I found out what it is to be me." Back in Japan, he adopted a stage name, Hideboh, and gave his style a copyrighted label, Funk-a-Step. While his bounce recalled Buster Brown, his flopping bleached forelock did not. In attire and dance design, Hideboh's first ensemble, the Stripes, resembled a boy band, slickly choreographed to a backbeat. Some of that slickness stuck to the leader's solos, but he could also escape it, and play music with his feet.

The New York sojourn of Kazu Kumagai, born in 1977, coincided with *Noise/Funk*, a show in which he found young men his own age expressing themselves in a language he understood. At one of Glover's workshops, Kumagai danced well enough to get an invitation to join

Funk University. For months, he drilled tap all day long and wondered what he—not American, not black—was doing. His teachers presented him with a graduation certificate and a T-shirt printed with the words "Sole Brother." They gave him an audition, informed him he was hired, and put him into rehearsals, but Kumagai never performed in *Noise/Funk*. The management blamed visa difficulties, though everyone knew the less-easily-fixed problem. As Glover explained it to a colleague, "Kazu can get a taxi."

Demoralized, Kumagai considered giving up. He felt a question hanging over him: Could a Japanese man understand tap? And another question that had never occurred to him before: What did it mean to be Japanese? Encouraged by Gregory Hines, he sat in with musicians at progressive jazz clubs not usually welcoming to tap dancers. "I started realizing that tap dancing is a universal language," he told me. "The musicians and I, we understood each other." Kumagai did not become a Japanese Savion Glover, though there are certainly heavy traces of that model in his physicality and phrasing, an intense ebb and flow of energy in place of steps. Kumagai is a musician with a sense of drama, a style that persuasively communicates who he is and how he feels.

Is that style Japanese? Kumagai isn't sure. Other Japanese hoofers, especially while in America, have tried incorporating traditionally Japanese elements and have mostly turned them into gimmicks. In Japan, for the 2003 remake of the blind-samurai film *Zatoichi*, the Stripes tapped in *geta* sandals, in a scene that looks as though a Tokyo production of *Noise/Funk*, outfitted in Japanese robes, has been plugged into a Bollywood finale. Kaoru Tomita contends that differences in Japanese versus English speech rhythms transfer to the feet, but I can't hear them. I can say that for all the anxiety that Japanese dancers feel about being outside of Americanness, they also are at a further remove from the polarizing history of black and white. Although their hip-hop affectations can come off as silly or just wrong, they tend to appear less self-conscious than white Americans; the aesthetic of the cool seems not to chafe as much, so some of them grow into it faster.

In 2003, when the second tour of *Noise/Funk* brought Savion Glover to Japan for the first time, the tap king unsurprisingly spawned imitators. I visited Tokyo then and detected a rash of misunderstanding about "hitting," perhaps most obviously in the Boxmen, three young hopefuls who brought in the noise by tapping inside waist-high wooden boxes and crashing them down on the beat. Yet it was one of the Boxmen, in dreadlocks, who told me that Glover had opened their ears to subtlety. In the wake of Glover's visit, the tap scene grew stronger, offering more frequent jam sessions and producing more dancers comfortable with improvisation. Kumagai performs regularly with Japanese jazz musicians in clubs. He has his own company of dancers, and he and other Japanese tap dancers sell CDs and DVDs and appear on TV. Japan has its own tap festivals and holds National Tap Dance Day celebrations larger than those in America. Tap is flourishing in Japan, but Kumagai has a complaint: "The younger generation doesn't realize that tap existed before *Noise/Funk*."

SMALL WORLD

In 1987, when the International Tap Association was founded at the Colorado Dance Festival, the adjective was mostly aspirational. By the turn of the millennium, it was fully justified, not just because tap had spread around the world but because tap dancers around the world were now connected to one another. At annual gatherings such as the Royal Dutch Tap Dance Human Rhythm Festival or the Tapmotif Rhythm Summit on the Greek island of Lefkada or the two unrelated tap festivals in Helsinki, the students were international and so was the performing faculty, composed of many of the same dancers who hopped from festival to festival in the United States. If you drew a family tree linking those professionals to their teachers and models, the lines would branch back to few nodes: the mostly men who served as the tap elders of the eighties and nineties and the mostly women who helped pass on their tradition.

Barcelona is now one of tap's most vibrant hubs. In Catalonia, tap carried the appeal of not being flamenco—of not being Spanish—and perhaps that's why it was there that a community of tap dancers began to bud following the death of Franco in 1975. From 1988 on, the Catalonian city of Reus had its own tap festival, but this was tap at several removes from American models. Recognizing something different in the movie *Tap* sent tiny Guillem Alonso to New York in 1991, at age eighteen. He studied with Brenda Bufalino and Savion Glover. He improvised for Jimmy Slyde at La Cave and performed with the American Tap Dance Orchestra and Manhattan Tap. Back home, he started his own jam session and his own company. When he worked with older Catalonian tappers, you could sense a difference, as between someone who's lived in the country where a language is spoken versus someone who's picked up a few phrases from other nonnative speakers. Alonso taps to swing as idiomatically as he does to Spanish guitar. It was with Manhattan Tap that he learned a dance inspired by Harriet Browne, the out-of-retirement sand dancer. The sand dance he developed for himself begins in near darkness, with a spotlight illuminating a pouring ribbon of sand that Alonso shakes into a misty sine wave. To the scouring of traditional sand dancing, Alonso appends spins, slides, chugs, Charleston, and Michael Jackson moves. He gives the dance shape and humor. The best sand dancer in the world, perhaps ever, is from Barcelona.

In Asia, tap has spread to Taiwan, where over the past decade the modern-dance ensemble Danceworks has converted into a tap company. Its leaders study in New York and Tokyo and, since 2005, invite their Japanese and American teachers to an annual tap festival in Taipei. Their style resembles that of their mentors, whose productions theirs surpass in high-tech computer graphics. Their enthusiasm hasn't quite hopped over to mainland China, where tap arrived in the thirties via movies and lived in Shanghai jazz clubs before dying out with the Communist takeover. (When I spent a summer in Beijing in 1998, the only tap I noticed was my own. On a bet from my stepfather, I scraped across the concrete of Tiananmen Square. The police paid no more attention to me than they did to the peeing child I passed.) Tours of *Riverdance*, beginning in 2003, spread the assumption that tap was Irish. Much smaller tours of top American hoofers in 2008 and 2011 may have begun the work of clarification. Hong Kong, still culturally separate, got its own tap festival in 2010.

Australia, which had developed its own globally popular brand in *Tap Dogs*, now also has Grant Swift, a former boxer and stripper from

New Zealand whose bullyboy bulk makes the Tap Dogs look effete. He taught himself from videotapes of the Nicholas Brothers and Gregory Hines, and he reacted to his first tape of Savion Glover as to a vision of the future. He feels that "blacks taken to America started all the cool shit that's gone around the world." The all-white dancers of Swift Rhythm Hoofers chanted "In 1739 they stole the drum from the Africans" while doing West African dance in tap shoes and slapping their chests like Maori warriors. After traveling to New York, where he grew to revere Brenda Bufalino, Swift was inspired to take on the mission of bringing home the world-class teachers and information not easily available to him when he was starting out. Where he is rough-edged, his student Thomas Wadelton can do anything the kids in America can, and has won cutting contests in Chicago and New York. Not yet twenty at the L.A. Tap Fest in 2011, he reproduced the routine Baby Laurence did on TV in 1967, note for note and letter-perfect, inhabiting Laurence's grizzled cool with his own boyish charm.

In Latin America, tap has a smaller presence. In the 1940s, Liber Scal cribbed from Hollywood movies and billed himself as an American dancer named Fred Murphy, playing a comic Negro who tapped on roller skates to "Tico Tico." Working out his own methodology, he became the principal tap pedagogue of Buenos Aires, and after visiting the Colorado Dance Festival in 1992, he initiated International Tap Dance Day celebrations back home. More recently, Argentines who've studied in New York have introduced a rift between the *zapateador*, the aurally focused specialist, and the *ballarin de tap*, the musical comedy dancer who taps a bit. So far, the only Argentines to have achieved recognition in America are Martin and Facundo Lombard, Giacometti-gaunt twins born in 1977 who grew up performing hip-hop on TV. In New York in the late nineties—they were regulars at Swing 46—they grafted Savion Glover footwork onto what they call "free expression," but tap is only part of their success in touring shows and films such as *Step Up 3D*.

Brazil is a more interesting case. Tap arrived there in American movies and with American performers flying down to Rio and its casinos. These imports from the rich North were popular enough, but the country had its own wealth of rhythms and its own potent hybrids of Europe and Africa. It didn't need jazz to ignite a dance craze. In the south, there was the *chula*, a percussive Portuguese challenge dance; in the north, there was the *xaxado*, a sand-shuffling dance performed in sandals, quite similar to the Essence. While these folk traditions were never as widely popular in Brazil as tap was in the United States, they form part of an explanation for why there were no major Brazilian imitators of Astaire or Eleanor Powell. In populist musical films, dance numbers were constructed out of Brazilian materials. Brazil exported Carmen Miranda to the United States, where she sometimes danced with a Nicholas Brother on either side. With such abundance underfoot, why buy from abroad?

Curiosity, for one. Or elective affinity. All along, there were isolated autodidacts and expatriates, Australians and Italians as well as Americans black and white who opened studios to teach *sapateado*. A few students made it to the United States and hooked into the revival there. Steven Harper, one of the leaders of the Brazilian scene, grew up in Switzerland and studied in New York before moving to where people loved his dancing and beautiful women took him to the beach. By the nineties, Brazil had its own tap festivals to which it could invite Jimmy Slyde. The Americans told the Brazilians to make tap their own, but the Brazilians didn't need to be told. Some Brazilians stress a hip-swaying, feathered flamboyance, an overt sexiness that expresses the difference, they say, between tap and tap *dancing*. Others treat tap technique as one percussive element among many, the feet an equal partner with body slaps and mouth sounds in the assembly of polyrhythms. Along with bossa nova, samba, and other Brazilian styles that have long fed into jazz, Brazilian tap dancers bring *maracatu*, *baião*, *frevo*: a huge reservoir of grooves and vernacular movements to go with them. Brazil has its own imbricated history of black and white, but a North American can't help but notice that almost all Brazilian tap dancers are light-skinned—a class division, perhaps. Among the more distinctive is Valéria Pinheiro, a Brazilian Jane Goldberg who learned *xaxado* from her farmer father and spent much of the eighties traveling her vast country, particularly the heavily African northeast, to learn from old masters. Her carnivalesque productions are excavations of the African diaspora, and her technique, which she calls *"sapateadu brasileiro,"* doesn't borrow much more from tap than the shoes. Brazil also now has young hoofers as technically adept as their American peers. You might not guess they're Brazilian.

Could Canadian tap differ from American tap? In the days of vaudeville, the cities of Canada were on the upper loop of U.S. circuits, and had been since minstrel days. The best Canadian-born tap dancers gravitated across the border: Montreal's Johnny Coy, in the forties, in search of Hollywood glory; Toronto's Heather Cornell, in the eighties, in search of Merce Cunningham, only to find Cookie Cook. William Orlowski, born outside Toronto in 1952, acquired his obsession with tap via Astaire films beamed from TV stations in Buffalo. In the classes of a retired vaudevillian, he became the kind of postwar kid who never stopped practicing tap, then the kind of postwar young man who realized no one was hiring tap dancers anymore. On yearly trips to New York in the seventies, he took a few classes with the Copasetics and Jane Goldberg, but he came to the conclusion that their style wasn't his. Back in Toronto, he opened a tap-only dance studio he called the Hoofers' Club. Then, at twenty-five, he formed a tap company, audaciously naming it the National Tap Dance Company of Canada. He choreographed evocations of Astaire, a restrained ensemble piece to Bach, full-length narratives with original scores—dozens of works over the next decade. A collection of Paul Draper's writings had been published in 1977, and it resonated with Orlowski. Reaching Draper by cold call, the young Canadian procured a mentor. Draper taught Orlowski his solos "Political Speech" and "Sonata for Tap Dancer," transferring a legacy almost no one in America seemed to want. Draper came to Toronto to appraise Orlowski's company, and in approving ended up creating a piece set to drumming and E. E. Cummings poems.

Until Orlowski went solo in 1990, the National Tap Dance Company of Canada performed with symphony orchestras across the country. You could almost have called it the company that Draper had meant to found. In the States, it did pops concerts with the eminent conductor Erich Kunzel and once appeared with the National Symphony at the

Kennedy Center, and yet Orlowski and his company reaped little attention in the American press. They remain almost entirely unknown among American tap dancers. Orlowski took no part in the American tap festivals. Before Draper's death in 1996, mentor and disciple spoke ruefully about how tap had come full circle, from the street back to the street. By Orlowski's lights, tap today is "classless" and insular. "If that's the only thing you are going to present," he told me, "it will die a quick death."

In 2009, Orlowski did attend the Vancouver International Tap Festival, then celebrating its tenth anniversary with a Canadians in Tap conference. Also present was Heather Cornell, who after a long American career with Manhattan Tap now desired to be identified as Canadian. Her new ensemble, CanTap, featured several fine young Canadians who made their living in the United States. Their tap dance with hockey sticks, though clever, hardly constituted a distinctly national version of the art.

How about tap's parental regions? When American tappers teach in Africa, they often report back that Africans are exceptionally quick studies. Yet among the many aspects of African-American culture admired and adapted by Africans, tap seems not to figure much: more evidence, perhaps, that the dance is American, rather than African. South Africa offers tentative exceptions. Black vaudeville troupes of the thirties and forties, with names such as De Pitch Black Follies, modeled their tap routines on those in Hollywood movies; the tap duo Jubilation and Nice was compared with the Nicholas Brothers. One origin story for the gumboot dance developed by black South African miners in the 1890s involves a visit by blackface minstrels. Tap dancers outside of Africa now regularly borrow from that dance's stomps and boot slaps.

In the United Kingdom, the tap revival has only recently taken off. This is intriguing, considering the continual circulative connection with America. Films from the thirties capture music-hall acts demonstrating tap techniques and trends that lag only a step or two behind vaudeville and Broadway. In Jack Buchanan, a Scot, Britain had a man-about-town who drawled in song and dance. He was no Astaire, but he tapped, as did Jessie Matthews, Britain's darling of between-the-wars musical films. They learned from Buddy Bradley.

After the Second World War, such influences waned. The Clark Brothers, a Philadelphia act immortalized in the shoddy 1948 all-black revue film *Killer Diller*, chose the British variety circuit over the dwindling American one and made a living through men's clubs, cruise ships, stag nights, and the odd TV variety show, dropping names of performers they had worked with in America. Though they could boast prominent British entertainers among their brush-up students, they seem not to have inspired anyone in their line. For a long time, neither did Will Gaines, a Detroit bebop hoofer who came over with the USO in the sixties and stayed. While he admitted to having stolen from Teddy Hale, Gaines had scrapped Hale's elegant upper body for a freewheeling, ankle-shaking approach. He was also comfortable dancing entirely free, without a set song structure or meter, as he did regularly in the nineties with the free-jazz guitarist Derek Bailey. Their 1994 album *Rappin & Tappin* captures the improbable interaction of Gaines's percussive noodling, his jokes ("I'm sweating but it won't rub off"), and Bailey's whistling overtones and spooky dissonances.

Mostly, British tap curdled into a chintzy gesture that cycled in and out of fashion in West End musicals, a geriatric dance of game-show hosts whose highlight reels featured unequal challenge matches against Sammy Davis, Jr. It was a dancing-school style regimented by syllabi and accreditation: well scrubbed, bouncy, much closer to Lancashire clogging than to jazz, and to an American, rather weak tea. Visits in the early eighties by the *No Maps on My Taps* crew, Honi Coles with Brenda Bufalino, and the Jazz Tap Ensemble stirred some interest, but the closest equivalent to a tap revival came later through fans of the Lindy Hop: a transplanted Dutchman named Tobias Tak and a scholar of Harlem dance history named Terry Monaghan. At a Monaghan-produced show in 2002, a generational gap yawned between Will Gaines and the twenty-year-old Junior Laniyan, a black Londoner who had taken classes with Tak, studied the models in Tak's video collection, and was developing a lithe improvisational style of his own. Soon, Laniyan had a company, a mixed-race outfit called About Time. By the time Savion

Glover finally performed in London, in 2007, Laniyan had a monthly tap jam going, one eventually situated at the storied jazz club Ronnie Scott's. The scene resembled Swing 46: white, black, disproportionately Japanese.

Some of Monaghan's shows also included Seosamh O'Neachtain, a young and unschooled *sean-nós* dancer out of Galway and a strong representative of a neglected style under revival. Ireland was still dominated by *Riverdance* and Michael Flatley. Yet while Flatley's *Lord of the Dance* was playing at Radio City Music Hall in 1997, a member of the cast, a juvenile champion named James Devine, bought a ticket to see *Noise/Funk* and came away dissatisfied with the Flatley model. Devine already had speed: a year later he would break Flatley's taps-per-second record. What he took from Glover was a more flexible technique—sinking into his heels, digging into his own tradition. In Devine's 2006 touring show *Tapeire*, he rejected the canned spectacle of *Riverdance* for an informal jam session among musicians. In emulating the dreadlocked American, the Irishman in a ponytail restored something to Irish step dancing; he stole something back.

INTERNATIONAL IN NEW YORK

As much as tap was proliferating globally in the eighties and nineties, New York was still its center. New York was still where the most ambitious tap dancers came to study. It was where they met one another.

As a child performer in a small town in northeastern France, Olivia Rosencrantz was captivated by the tap in *The Cotton Club* and struggled to find teachers. At age twenty, in 1988, she moved to New York, where she was attracted to Brenda Bufalino's work by its European qualities; "it had thoughts behind it." Mari Fujibayashi was from Kyoto, where she grew up imitating MGM musicals. She auditioned for the American Tap Dance Orchestra on a whim, in red high heels. Rosencrantz and Fujibayashi both joined ATDO in 1991 and stayed for five years, before moving on to Manhattan Tap and forming a duo called Tapage. In 1999, when a French orchestra asked them to perform Morton Gould's

Tap Dance Concerto, they countered with "Sensemayá," by the Mexican composer Silvestre Revueltas. Based on a poem about an Afro-Cuban snake-killing ritual, "Sensemayá" is an ominous composition, with a creeping bass-line ostinato in 7/8 slashed by machete swipes of brass and passages of 11/16. In spare tap phrases complicated by close canon, Rosencrantz and Fujibayashi stalked through the imaginary brush with the bass line, stopped to follow something with their eyes, and waved their arms high in stylized alarm. Sinuous, they were the snake; taut, they were the hunter. More significantly, they were not tap dancers, not themselves. The occlusion of personality that had always eluded their mentor was not impossible. Bufalino had indicated a path that less encumbered tap dancers might follow farther.

While some international dancers mingled in American tap companies, more converged under the wing of Jimmy Slyde at La Cave. Herbin Van Cayseele's story was the most colorful. Born of African descent in French Guiana, he was one of eight children raised largely by his grandmother, a *voudon* herbalist. At age eight, he was "marked," possessed by the Yoruban gods Exu and Shango. But at age nine, Tamango—as he was then called—was wrested from his grandmother's world and shipped off to live in Paris with a strict father he didn't know. Salvation came in the form of Michel Van Cayseele, a baron who lived in the same building, along with his mother and her sixteen Persian cats. The baron eventually adopted the boy, and it was he who noticed that the kid went into something like a tap dance whenever he finished a painting. Maybe that woman tap-dancing on television could help.

By now, Tamango was twenty-one. If he had walked into any tap class besides that of Jimmy Slyde's French disciple, Sarah Petronio, he might have never become a tap dancer. "It was not especially about dance," he would recall. "It was about musicians, and this life of jamming." Within a year, he had fallen in with a group of buskers called the Over Excited. On a coin toss, they chose New York instead of Rio. Jane Goldberg took him to his first New York tap jam and let him crash at her apartment. Heather Cornell invited him to apprentice with Manhattan Tap, but he wasn't one for learning routines. La Cave was much more his style, and it became his principal school. The sessions he began to run on Sunday nights at an East Village dive called Deanna's were much more open-ended. Songs lasted twenty minutes or more; solos blended into duos or trios. Deanna's was about the younger generation experimenting, about them challenging one another all night long. It was Van Cayselle and his immigrant pals—his French friend Roxane, his Austrian friend Max—jamming until the place burned down.

In the mid-to-late nineties, Van Cayselle's appearance afforded him opportunities that his lighter-skinned *amis* did not share. He suffered through a tour of *Riverdance*, but he was much more at home dancing in clubs as a kind of impresario of the African diaspora, combining his tap improvisations with a stiltwalker from the Ivory Coast, a Brazilian *capoeirista*, hip-hop dancers, and an equally diverse band of musicians. Urban Tap, his name for this troupe, was a pun on his French name, though by 1998 he was calling himself only Tamango. His sensibility wasn't urban in the sense that Savion Glover's was. "I'm not a teenager," he told *Time Out New York*. "Anger is not my thing." His dancing was— and is—upright, loose, and liquid. Most of the action happens from the hips down, but the placid upper half can only be described as elegant. He has a winning smile and a muscled torso, once featured in a Madonna video. His chest is often bare, and with his trademark feathered pants, he suggests a satyr hoofed in metal. His tapping is articulate, supple. Though there are kids at every tap festival who could whip him in a cutting contest, his technique is sufficient. It's the total package that inspires judgments like that of Anna Kisselgoff in the *Times*: "One is tempted to call him the best dancer of any kind around."

That was in 1999, when Tamango was no longer a secret of clubgoers. His tours ranged much wider than the tap festival circuit, his global vision gaining him entry into the ever-expanding category of world music. Though his shows integrate high-tech sound and video, they are ultimately jam sessions like those he ran at Deanna's. His aim, he has said, is to conjure a dream, a trance. He brings a secular skeptic like me closer to that state when he eschews words; even in a voice as deep and seductive as his, mumbo-jumbo phrases raise barriers. Dancing barefoot on an amplified platform, Tamango convincingly cuts to tap's essence like few others.

When Roxane Semadeni was eight years old, she too was marked. At a jazz festival not far from her hometown of Toulon, she encountered Bunny Briggs. Enthralled, she approached the magic man after the show and he taught her a time step, that first tap seed. The following year, she witnessed Jimmy Slyde. This was in 1980, and for the decade that followed, tap played little role in her life. She went in for gymnastics and cross-country running, yet the initial exposure left an imprint. When Semadeni was twenty, she took a tap workshop with Heather Cornell and decided to try New York. Once in America, she made up for lost time, practicing eight hours a day. Like Tamango, she was invited to apprentice with Manhattan Tap, and, like him, she found that company life didn't suit her. The two francophones busked on the street together, attended the University of La Cave, and joined the hoofer family. Jimmy Slyde bought Semadeni dinners and a winter coat. He gave her a stage name: Roxane Butterfly.

In the flared pants she favors, Butterfly resembles a fashionable runner, cantered slightly forward, a line stretching through her chest and neck toward the finish. There's a continual lope to her motion, hips in play, the top of her head tracing rolling hills. Her feet blur, seeming never to pause even though her heavy syncopations mean she's pausing all the time, very briefly. Her slow settings don't get much use. She has some of Slyde's way of sketching loops on a stage, her limbs nearly tangling before they squeeze-slip free. Her signature move is a spin she leans into backward, revolving and revolving as she stirs in complications both rhythmic and visual.

In the late nineties, Butterfly did a stint with the Jazz Tap Ensemble, but clubs such as La Cave and Deanna's were her true habitat, and she sat in with musicians wherever she went. Few women behaved so boldly, and hoping to change that, Butterfly founded an all-female collective called BeauteeZ'n the Beat. A group of women musicians and dancers improvising powerfully sent a powerful message, one that Butterfly needlessly underlined with blunt text. For her next project, she piled on

New Age doggerel and self-congratulatory sentiments about not choosing a single identity, her clumsy words again trivializing something the dance and music were expressing more profoundly. Butterfly was turning, musically, to her Mediterranean roots—to her Moroccan mother and the sounds she had heard growing up in Marseilles. This was part of her ceaseless, successful project to prove that there is no such thing as "tap-dance music." Her Mediterranean heritage came out through her dancing as naturally as her quotations of Jimmy Slyde; one influence flowed into the other, as they had in life. Fluid construction was increasingly a strength of Butterfly's shows and of the rhythmically cogent choreography that helped her avoid the ruts into which her improvising inevitably strayed. Her technique is prodigious, and she is always pushing at the edges of her abilities. Though she was one of the most prominent and acclaimed tap dancers in New York, one of the best at winning grants and awards and at creating opportunities for herself and other tap dancers, Butterfly migrated back to Europe in 2008. There she could travel freely as a citizen and spread the art of her American mentors. Her Jimmy Slyde Institute is located in Barcelona.

Growing up in Vienna, Max Pollak dug jazz, played the drums, and was enchanted by tap in American movies. In his early teens, he found a few teachers who had studied with Carnell Lyons, that tray-spinning Kansas City paddle-and-roller based in Berlin. Later, he studied with Lyons himself. During Pollak's first trip to America, in 1991, he answered a newspaper advertisement announcing auditions for Manhattan Tap. Heather Cornell offered him an apprenticeship, and he took it, sold by the chance to work with the jazz bassist Ray Brown. Pollak stayed with the company until 1997, simultaneously studying drumming and composition at Mannes College, jazz at the New School, and tap with Jimmy Slyde and the other elders at the University of La Cave. At Deanna's with Butterfly and Tamango, he experimented, and everywhere he asked questions. There were few more diligent students of tap and its history, a fact that his Manhattan Tap colleagues once affectionately honored with a practical joke. Before a performance, they told Pollak that the great Scratch Johnson of Scritch, Scratch, and Scrotch was in the audience, then watched the Austrian frantically scramble to learn Scratch's famous dance, complete with its beard-scratching break. Only after the show did they let drop that Johnson did not exist. (Buster Brown liked the joke so much he incorporated the Scratch break into his classes, telling his credulous pupils about his days with Johnson. Thus is tap history made.)

Soon the ace pupil discovered a new subject. Through Heather Cornell and a class with the Latin percussionist Bobby Sanabria, Pollak discovered *clave*. Spanish for "keystone," *clave* is the foundation of Afro-Cuban music, the asymmetrical, African-derived rhythmic time line into which all the other rhythms must lock. Afro-Cuban rhythms—like the clave that Sidney Lanier had unknowingly transcribed from juba patting in 1880—entered the DNA of jazz in New Orleans and recrossed with successive crazes in Latin dance music. Tap dancers played around with a "Latin feel," and from the other direction, mambo dancers at the Palladium nightclub in the fifties tapped in *clave* because *clave* was second nature to them. But Pollak attempted something else. Methodically, he taught himself how to spread Afro-Cuban polyrhythms—two or three separate and interlocking rhythmic lines—across his body and feet. Clapping, slapping, tapping, he turned himself into an entire Afro-Cuban drum section. This was like rubbing your stomach while patting your head, but in different rhythms and while simultaneously playing a complex syncopation with your feet, singing in Spanish or Yoruba, and making the whole thing fuse as music and dance.

At first, it looked a little awkward—on Pollak and then on the dancers he taught the technique he called Rumbatap. And there was an additional awkwardness. Respectful scholar that he was, Pollak didn't just immerse himself in the music but also in the culture that produced it, taking research trips to Cuba and learning from *rumberos*. This wasn't ballroom rumba. It was the Afro-Cuban kind, and Pollak's dancing took more than the folkloric movements. The vision of an Austrian fellow with a goatee invoking African spirits gave off different resonances than when Tamango expressed the faith of his grandmother, even when Pollak did it in Tamango's shows.

Musically, Pollak's performances are wholly convincing. He can be witty, and his mind-bending, body-punishing virtuosity can make you laugh in astonishment. Composers now write suites and concerti for him. His experiments in narrative, crossing Cuban *orishas* with the Finnish epic *Kalevala*, have been less persuasive, mainly because they require a kind of acting that's outside the abilities of most current tap dancers. But tricky Bulgarian rhythms, dances counted in eleven, New Orleans second-line marches—these he can pull off. Whether or not you believe in plugging into divine forces, when his rhythms intermesh, they're hard to resist. The kicker to the joke in his doing the Shim Sham in *clave* is how neatly "Shave and a Haircut" fits.

Increasingly, it appears that ancestry and upbringing aren't any more essential to Rumbatap than they are to jazz tap. The most stalwart member of Pollak's company is Chikako Iwahori, from Japan, a woman whose training took her from the Nakano Brothers through Savion Glover and Manhattan Tap. Pollak teaches his method across the global tap festival circuit, and his influence can be felt in a shift toward more communal music-making. Appropriation hardly seems the right label when Pollak has made a habit of returning to Cuba like a tap Santa Claus, bearing loads of tap shoes. He's taught Rumbatap to members of one of Cuba's most venerable musical institutions, Los Muñequitos de Matanzas, who now regularly include it in their performances. When Pollak dances Rumbatap with them, they are the ones who look a bit awkward, but also—in their sparkliest outfits and tap shoes—very happy. Pollak gave tap to them, and now it's theirs, too.

"It's us, it's ours." So Savion Glover defined hoofing in *Noise/Funk*. The night that Max Pollak first saw the show, the Austrian immigrant answered with a shout: "That's not true!" Glover's definition excluded Pollak, who had dedicated his life to the tradition of Jimmy Slyde. Slyde was proud of his international protégés and Glover. No one was more supportive of Tamango and Roxane Butterfly and Pollak than the gruff-looking teddy bear Lon Chaney. At Swing 46, Buster Brown always introduced tappers from Japan or Brazil with a pleased note of wonder in his voice.

The chief danger of diffusion is dilution. And in some parts of the world, at various times, the tap that spread was awfully thin. Among today's non-American tap dancers, you can find plenty of funny accents and comical mishearings. The Telephone game is an international party line now. Yet rather than degeneration, the main impression is of a resilient tradition and a more capacious pool of talent. It's significant that tap festivals around the world are now inviting, as masters, dancers who are not American, and not because these festivals can't afford ones who are. It ain't where you're from, it's the way that you do it.

21

WHERE'S THE DANCE?

One night at the New York City Tap Festival in 2002, Savion Glover was upset. He wasn't scheduled to perform, but he was in the audience and would likely have been invited onstage even if he hadn't been making a ruckus. "Where are we?" he asked once he had the floor, sounding lost as he looked around with bloodshot eyes. Dancers waiting to do the Shim Sham filled the tense silence with mollifying murmurs. "Where's *the dance*?" Glover clarified, vehemently and vaguely expressing his disapproval of what he had seen at the festival. "I don't know everything," he continued. "I know a little something, though." Without further words, he did Steve Condos, Chuck Green, Lon Chaney, Gregory Hines. He did Savion Glover. His imitation dance was a retracing of steps, the steps that led to him. It was the tap gospel according to Glover, and when it ended, the festival director spoke with deference and relief. "*That's* where we are, Savion."

Certainly, one way of answering Glover's question would be to follow his career. At the 2003 festival, he and Gregory Hines were scheduled to do one of their passing-the-mantle rituals, but it was announced that Hines had been "called away by Hollywood." It turned out that what had called Hines away was actually cancer, and a few months later he was dead. This is not how it was supposed to happen, cut down at fifty-seven. Hines was supposed to age into an old master. Tap had lost its leading man, its spokesperson, its head of the family. Glover had lost a father figure, and the mantle was now wholly his.

For Glover's next touring concert, he took a title from Hines, *Improvography*, and wore a photo of him around his neck. He informed interviewers that his purpose was to be an entertainer from a line of entertainers. He even sang—mostly standards introduced by Astaire in likably unassuming approximations. In the first half of the program, which was almost completely improvised, sweat streamed from his beard as he led a quartet of veteran jazz musicians. The second half showcased his choreography for his new company, Ti Dii: routines to recorded pop. As before, Glover group numbers after Glover solo improvisation came as a letdown. It's difficult to imagine him reviving one of these dances; he seems not to conceive of any of his compositions as lasting, and no piece he's made since *Noise/Funk* has matched its metaphorical resonance. Yet amid the tight unison and swapping of positions, it was sometimes hard to distinguish between the improvised and the preset. This was interesting. Even as multiple dancers fell into the same groove, their synchronicity appeared serendipitous: improvography for more than one.

All seven members of Ti Dii were younger than their boss. Half were women; nearly half were white. (Andrew Nemr, light-skinned and of Lebanese descent, had been a member of Glover's first company, but exiled since *Noise/Funk*.) That seemed a sign. Other messages came in the form of *Hooferz Club*, a self-produced album on which Glover fit his tap life onto a gangsta-rap template, viciously bragging about murdering phonies in tap showdowns. Along with the dick-waving came expressions of love for "the dance" (personified as a woman in need of protection), an insistence on "the basics," and hip-hop invocations of ancestors. On *Hooferz Club 2*, he spoke directly to the departed Hines, pledging to preserve the dead man's legacy. Glover had denounced the first tour of *Noise/Funk*, in which he had not participated, as "corrupted," and he spoke of the 2002 tour, in which he starred, as a mission to get out "the information." More than ever, his interviews were marked by calls for purity. "Too much experimenting will lead to the artform's downfall," he told the *Houston Chronicle*. To Jane Goldberg in *Dance Magazine*, he complained about guys from New Zealand and gymnastic tap; "you don't mix bananas with macaroni and cheese and yams." Glover now acknowledged the visual appeal of the Nicholas Brothers, but he made clear that his ambition for tap was to have people "hear it as music rather than see it as dance." He allowed experimentation only when "experimentation is in the music."

For *Classical Savion*, which premiered in 2005, he danced to Vivaldi, Bach, Mendelssohn, and other classical composers, accompanied by a chamber orchestra. This was not Paul Draper, whom John Martin had praised for choosing tap "as a medium for art rather than hoofing." Nor was it someone following the score of Morton Gould's Tap Dance Concerto, about which the composer had insisted, "The important point is that this isn't hoofing." No, this was Savion Glover, son of the hoofers, improvising to European concert music in his own hoofer style. Wearing a tuxedo, he wiggled his head pompously or mocked ballet, as Hines used to: defensive antics not nearly as witty as his rhythms. Yet he treated the music with absolute seriousness, doubling the notes, layering on his own, coming forward as a soloist or blending in as much as was possible for the star of the show. Early in the first run, Glover seemed to be finding his way, falling back on familiar rhythms. Later, it became clearer how he had internalized compositional form—not just rhythmically, but melodically, thematically. He found where his anachronistic syncopations fit, where *he* fit in the music.

Still, the final number in *Classical Savion* was more indicative of his artistic direction. His jazz band joined him onstage, and as the bass player endlessly vamped, Glover repeated the same step dozens of times before taking exploratory flight. It was an approach with roots in the sixties jazz of the late John Coltrane, whom Glover was now always citing as a musical and spiritual model: a faithful apprentice so fixed on mastering tradition that he broke orbit, pushing boundaries of density and duration on a course that many fans did not want to follow. Glover was now regularly playing with Coltrane's peers. It's hard to say which was more affecting, his schoolboy delight or their amazed pride, like that of men meeting a son they didn't know they had. On the title song of *Who*

Used to Dance, an album by the masterly singer Abbey Lincoln, Glover's sensitive obligato could make you wonder why there wasn't more tap on jazz recordings; his beats on the Prince song "Joint 2 Joint" made a fair argument for tap on pop tracks. But Glover was best live, often in a purely musical setting, conversing with musicians of the highest caliber in a venue that raised no expectations of a dance show. When he played jazz clubs, it wasn't just on Mondays.

In dance venues, he struggled with the regular expectation of novelty. *Visions of a Bible* (2005) had a spare concept—just Glover and a gospel singer—that he filled with the spirit rejoicing, and *SoLo in TIME* (2009), while applying little thought to the notion of including flamenco musicians, was nevertheless engaging. But when Glover attempted to broaden visual appeal in one half of *Invitation to a Dancer* (2007), the results were cringeworthy: by the modern and ballet dancers he invited, Glover exposed how miserably little he knew about modern and ballet. Half of *SoLE PoWER* (2010) involved Japanese tap dancers and booty-shaking rap-video girls in a daft Afro-futurist fantasy that turned the Copasetics' chair dance into a strip-club routine. These group efforts in making tap accessible exhibited either contempt for entertainment or a severely impoverished idea of it.

The other part of *Invitation* introduced Glover's preferred mode, where his heart was. He called it Bare Soundz: himself and one or two other hoofers sharing miked platforms. They were drummers on amplified shingles, attuned to one another like a jazz trio, switching seamlessly between choreography and improv, between solo and backup, between one groove and the next. The most attuned was Marshall Davis, Jr., the self-effacing student of Steve Condos whose development of Condos rudiments could draw out of slammed feet a quiet soulfulness. Glover's dancing, instead of separating into breath-length phrases, could run like an engine, with him finessing the throttle for rate and pitch. Other times, he worried a rhythm like a loose tooth. It was these qualities that led Alastair Macaulay, in a 2010 *Times* review, to deem Glover "tedious" and unmusical, a "mindlessly dull" virtuoso on a "private trip."

In 2011, I saw Glover work an audience at the newly resurgent Apollo into a frenzy, and the Robinson-style staircases he used for *STePz* in 2013 released his playful exuberance. Steps, in the dance-terminology sense, still shook free from his stocked library, voluntary and involuntary allusions to the departed. "It's prayer," he said, and in his stripped-down mode, the stage was a shrine, often bedecked with blown-up photos of dead tap masters. Tap for him was perpetual elegy, or communion. "Nothing is going to change," he kept saying, in dance and in pronouncements religious in their conservatism. "Nothing is ever going to be the same," he kept saying, because those fathers and uncles were gone. In his 2014 *Om*, surrounded by candles and other theatrically hokey distractions, while dancing to the chants of various creeds, Glover broke through to a new level of virtuosity, astonishing even for him. Tapping with unprecedented speed and force, he nevertheless could sustain multiple lines of tone. But most unbelievable was the intensity: frightening, at times painful. (Many people walked out in the middle.) The sound was huge, deep, what he had long been drilling for. The man for whom tap was religion had drummed and driven it into a spiritual art, mystical, inhuman, out of this world.

However insular and inwardly focused, Glover couldn't help but share his love. He remained ubiquitous in his mission to spread the word. In New York City alone, he appeared in venues of just about every size and kind. He tapped on TV, too: award shows, tributes, commercials. In 2000, he had a featured role in Spike Lee's film *Bamboozled*, a scattershot satire in which a black television executive spitefully produces a minstrel show only to see it become a cultural fad. The film seemed to support the idea that tap was second only to comedy among arts still saddled with the legacy of minstrelsy. (In 2005, the black comedian Dave Chapelle, speaking of his decision to leave his hit TV show, would famously draw a metaphorical distinction between "dancing" and "shuffling.") Glover's role in *Bamboozled*, written for him, was that of a street hoofer who's picked up some things from "Slyde and Chaney" and who agrees to appear in blackface "as long as the hoofing is real." At the climactic moment when he refuses to "play himself" and goes on without corking up, he opens his dance of authenticity with the rudiments of Steve Condos.

In *Bojangles*, a hack biopic of Bill Robinson made for Showtime in 2001, Glover played an absolutely Glover-like young usurper to Gregory Hines's Hines-like Bojangles. Glover's next film was *Happy Feet* (2006), an animated environmentalist fable about penguins who express themselves through song. Mumble is a tone-deaf misfit among them who becomes a hero by expressing himself through his feet (a habit never called "tap dancing"). His voice is Elijah Wood's, but his sounds—and also, through motion-capture technology, his movements— are Glover's. Curiously, it works: an animated penguin moves like Glover, incidentally revealing how much Glover normally moves like a penguin.

The situation wasn't exactly a retread of the splicing of Cholly Atkins's tap sounds onto the image of a white dancer. Glover got credit. (Though the credit, as John Rockwell pointed out in the *Times*, was buried.) And for Glover, being heard and not seen wasn't so objectionable. *Happy Feet* was a blockbuster, and Glover told *The Washington Post* he was unreservedly pleased that "someone wanted tap dance." He expressed his hope that the film might operate on American culture as Shirley Temple films had and spark a "resurgence in the dance." That, of course, was what Glover had already done, though the nature of his success—the Savion-as-savior line, combined with his habit of speaking of himself and a decreasing few as "the Last HooFeRz Standing"— tended to cast everyone else in shadow.

THE FESTIVAL CUL-DE-SAC

Another way to answer the question Glover posed that night in 2002 would be to look around him. Where's the dance? Right then it was at Tap City, the New York City Tap Festival, founded the previous year. What Atlanta and Helsinki had, tap's supposed capital finally had as well. In the days since Jane Goldberg's By Word of Foot and the summits in Colorado, the tap festival—one to three weeks of classes and panel discussions, culminating in a performance or two—had taken over as tap's primary institution. It was a sign of the times when, in

2001, Tony Waag converted Brenda Bufalino's American Tap Dance Orchestra, which had been essentially dormant since 1996, into the American Tap Dance Foundation, an organization centered on youth education and on producing an annual tap festival.

Festivals are the new circuit. A revered teacher such as Dianne Walker can hop from one to the next, May through September. Younger hoofers bounce around the globe. The festivals are good at administering intense doses of instruction and inspiration. Their default performance mode—a sampler—is good for displaying variety, for tacitly demonstrating the range of people attracted to the art, and for showing how an improviser can handle a song and what a choreographer can say briefly. But there's rarely room for anyone to expand or develop art that doesn't fit into a variety format. And the drive to excellence regularly collides with a mandate to be inclusive. The principal audience for these performances seems to be other tap dancers, and too often the shows seem designed to keep it that way.

Those limitations would be less worrisome if the festivals weren't so dominant. The American Tap Dance Foundation, experimenting with other formats and a small-town touring show, has had some small success, artistic rather than commercial. Its American Tap Dance Center, which opened in 2010, is a tiny, hard-won toehold of New York real estate, useful but very far from dreams of a tap equivalent to the School of American Ballet or Jazz at Lincoln Center. The Chicago Human Rhythm Project, founded in 1990 by Lane Alexander, is the longest running of the festivals and the most robust. Slowly, it has been expanding into a year-round institution, organizing a series of concerts and touring shows. In 2007, it sent a group to China.

The name of the tap festival in Austin is Soul to Sole. It is run by Tapestry Dance Company, which was founded by Acia Gray and Deirdre Strand in 1989. Currently the nation's lone year-round tap company with salaried members, Tapestry has developed a local presence and some excellent dancers, but although it has toured extensively (recently to China), it has yet to gain much national attention. Of the nationally known troupes of the eighties, only the Jazz Tap Ensemble lasted into the new millennium, and only as a pickup company. The level of talent was higher than ever, but it didn't hold together. The company model seems less sustainable than it once was, less relevant perhaps. That trend can be tracked across other dance forms—evidence of larger shifts in the financing and presentation of the performing arts. But especially for young tap dancers, who have grown up on the festival circuit at a remove from the world of concert dance, the building and maintaining of a company may not appear worth the effort. Similarly, Brenda Bufalino's goal of creating a tap repertory—of making tap an art with a history and future of *works* rather than of steps and dancers—remains mostly unfulfilled. Along with the Shim Sham and the B.S. Chorus, students may learn a Copasetics routine, yet there's a great distance between that and, say, *Swan Lake*.

IMAGINING TAP

Although the success of *Noise/Funk*, *Tap Dogs*, and even *Riverdance* seemed to hold out the possibility of tap returning to the for-profit marketplace, after *Noise/Funk* Broadway reverted. When period-appropriate, revivals included tap. There were crafty, capable choreographers—Kathleen Marshall, Casey Nicholaw, Jerry Mitchell, Warren Carlyle, and the savviest, Susan Stroman—but their conception of tap was mainly restricted to evocations of Broadway's faded glory.

Derick Grant came from a different tradition. Born the same year as Savion Glover, he grew up in his aunt's Roxbury dancing studio and was one of the kids brought to Rome for the 1984 event at which Glover became the One. After that, though, Grant drifted into the adolescent pursuits of his Boston buddies. It wasn't until the early nineties that the Jazz Tap Ensemble's apprentice program pulled him back in. In footage from that time, he's ebullient, a sunny heir to Jimmy Slyde. Glover hired him as the first understudy for *Noise/Funk*, and when Glover dropped out of the first national tour, Grant took over the lead. After the show closed, he told me, "it was like recovering from a meteor smash." Tap was back on top, except that it wasn't. Through the Jazz Tap Ensemble and teaching, Grant met and reconnected with tap dancers he wasn't supposed to respect but did. Tired of waiting around for someone to hire him, he found a producer—a real estate agent whom his friend Aaron Tolson had met on a tour of *Riverdance*—to book Chicago's Harris Theater for a four-week run of his own *Imagine Tap!* in 2006.

There were eight soloists and an eight-member ensemble, a fair sampling of the best hoofers Grant's age and younger. Five were white; six were women. *Imagine Tap!* was a revue, a string of scenarios: the doll who comes to life (Ayodele Casel), kids goofing off in detention. In structure and in spirit, it harked back to *Black and Blue*. One number directly alluded to that show's "Butter and Egg Man," with three men in chefwear vying for the attention of a female singer. An homage to flash acts, this routine took all the acrobatics, the whole scale of dancing that *Noise/Funk* treated with scorn, and presented it without quotation marks, as part of a hoofer's natural idiom. During the opening number, as dancers in tailcoats revolved in Busby Berkeley kaleidoscopes and pulled trenches, a bunch of guys in basketball jerseys slid in looking like the cast of *Noise/Funk*, there to sweep away the sellouts. But Grant had no such intention. Jerseys mingled with tails, and bringing in the funk did not preclude trenches, properly pulled. A number Grant called "the whole show in a nutshell" made use of Ray Hesselink, a dancer in the Tommy Tune line and the clearest possible representative of the tap *Noise/Funk* had rejected. While Tolson, a black dancer playing a homeboy humiliated in a basketball game, hammered out his frustration, Grant sent Hesselink in to save the day with a smile: Happy Tap and Angry Tap reconciled.

Though *Imagine Tap!* was weakened by some nice-guy muddle, its generosity was cheering. And though the show revealed and suffered from its creators' theatrical inexperience, it also strongly suggested possibilities, drawing from a broader tradition to access a wider expressive range without sacrificing technical advancements and contemporary style. Where Broadway tradition gave the chorus line the simplest choreography, Grant could trust his ensemble with much of his smartest material. The cast, all children of the festivals, found acting more of a challenge. They weren't Broadway babies dying to get into a show;

they were hoofers searching for a commercially viable format. That search continues.

NEW TAP GENERATION(S)

Much of the impetus behind *Imagine Tap!* came from Grant's awareness of all the underused, underrecognized talent around him. He himself is a compelling soloist, deeply versed in tradition, a big man of athletic delicacy who sets himself off-balance to force invention. But he also seems like a team player, and in *Imagine Tap!*, he ceded the next-to-closing spot to a dancer five years his junior. Once a sloppy fifteen-year-old substitute in *Noise/Funk*, Jason Samuels Smith had since driven himself with a punishing work ethic. As a video-game samurai in *Imagine Tap!*'s twist on the hoofer-as-gunslinger conceit, he riddled to shreds every prior usage of machine-gun metaphors. A hard-hitting attack is the most obvious sign of Glover in him, yet Smith makes more of a display of rhythm. He devises devious challenges for his feet: steps turned inside out, unnatural activity along odd edges. It was indicative of both his attitude and his abilities that he once honored Peg Leg Bates by locking one leg as if it were wooden and then adapting all his own crazy footwork to that condition: it was devotion expressed through difficulty. Looking to footage of past masters for style as well as sound, he reincorporated such connective tissue as the high-pressure slide. The suaveness that results, poised against the pounding exertion, contributes to a brutal charm that Smith acknowledges with a sly, goateed grin.

A fearsome soloist, Smith has also emerged as a tap missionary and a leader, roles indicated in the name of his first company, Anybody Can Get It. In 2003, he co-founded a now-thriving tap festival in Los Angeles. The following year, he starred in *Tap Heat*, a short film without dialogue or much intelligence. In it, Smith is a dreadlocked tap outlaw investigated by a policeman of tap orthodoxy: Arthur Duncan, grown white-haired since the cancellation of *The Lawrence Welk Show*. Their challenge dance ends in mutual acceptance and cross-fades into a big production number choreographed by Danny Daniels to the corniest possible arrangement of "I Got Rhythm." Inclusiveness so anodyne may inspire longings for *Noise/Funk*'s narrow-minded fervor, but a similar routine for the Jerry Lewis Telethon won Smith the first Emmy for tap choreography since Astaire. Smith's gifts found better use in *India Jazz Suites*, a concert and then a series of tours and a documentary, all with Pandit Chitresh Das, a senior master of the Indian percussive dance *kathak*; the mutual respect communicated through challenge dancing honored two traditions. As a dancer, Smith keeps maturing, his perverse innovations settling into naturalness as he pushes the envelope somewhere else. As a choreographer, he's yet to show much imagination. But he's attracted attention from television producers and nonprofit dance presenters. On the international tap festival circuit, Smith is king, the obvious model for dozens of Brazilians and Japanese.

Younger Americans nip at his heels. Take Joseph Wiggan. Born in 1986 as the youngest of seven children in South Central L.A., Wiggan got a first-class tap education at the school of Paul and Arlene Kennedy and then as an apprentice with the Jazz Tap Ensemble and in a kind of postgraduate study with Smith. One of the Three Chefs in *Imagine Tap!*, Wiggan handles Smith's mind-boggling footwork with a gentler touch and more through-the-body finesse, his albatross arms swooping snow angels into the air while his feet whisper. His musicality and his courtesy summon the ghost of Chuck Green. Lately he has been touring with Cirque du Soleil.

Jared Grimes, another *Imagine Tap!* chef, was three in 1986, when his mother gave him his first tap lessons. At age twelve, he joined the North Carolina Youth Tap Ensemble, a superior outfit that supplied him with solid training and a ticket into the tap festivals. Grimes is always setting off untested pyrotechnics, insane stuff that leaves tap experts happily bewildered. Also a hip-hop dancer, he's accustomed to popping the beat through all parts of his body. He's a musician who has tapped with the Jazz at Lincoln Center Orchestra—a coup, since today's few big bands use hoofers about as frequently as symphony orchestras do—but he is far from reluctant to put on a show. His stated role model is Sammy Davis, Jr. So goes the new wave: dancers who find no contradiction between the hoofer tradition and all-round entertaining. The misalignment between Grimes's tap mastery and his mediocre singing and comedy skills—unfortunately also typical of this new wave—underscores the rarity of a Sammy Davis or a Gregory Hines. Still, in 2013 and 2014, Grimes was on Broadway, stopping the show with tap in the next-to-closing spot of *After Midnight*, a Cotton Club–style revue. The format was a throwback; Grimes's tapping was not.

Kendrick Jones II, born into the postindustrial decay of Flint, Michigan, in 1985, answered one of Hines's end-of-show invitations at age fourteen and found an advocate in his idol. Jones slimmed as he grew and learned to handle his long stems more in the manner of Honi Coles. He has baby-faced good looks, and he can swing to bring the house down. In *Stairway to Paradise*, a short-run 2007 anthology of Broadway revues, his solo spot was "Doin' the New Low Down," a stair dance, and he managed to channel Bojangles while staying entirely himself, suggesting the style of 1928 through his own steps. That's one mark of a living tradition.

Another is Dormeshia Sumbry-Edwards. The bright little girl in *Black and Blue*, the young lady in drag outdancing the boys in *Noise/Funk*: she is now a grown woman, married, a mother of three. In the 2003 tour of *Noise/Funk*, she danced as a woman, providing audiences with the rare pleasure of watching Savion Glover meet his match. In *Imagine Tap!*, she played a woman in a business suit waiting for the subway, tapping out her discontent, and then, as the number blossomed into an MGM fantasy sequence with hints of "Too Darn Hot" in the score, turning red-hot momma to beat Ann Miller. This wasn't satire. This was outclassing. Sumbry-Edwards has all the poise and posture, the regal or sassy positioning of arms and shoulders, to make a movie queen envious. But she also has technical chops, rhythmic acumen, and an in-the-bones access to the whole of the tap tradition that no Hollywood lady ever had, and probably no Harlem lady, either. When she is fully inspired, she is like Jimmy Slyde or Astaire—sound and motion in the same dance impulse. Her "Flight of the Bumblebee" is obviously a tour de force, but the greater marvel is how she burns into a ballad. Laser-precise with tap needlepoint or rapid-fire chisel blows, she delivers astonishments with an air of suffering no fools.

And she does it in high heels. Sumbry-Edwards has reclaimed the taboo footwear for women of her generation and younger, who are less likely to see pumps as handicaps than as instruments of feminine expression. In truth, it is only in Sumbry-Edwards's high-heel dancing that I sense no restriction or loss. A class she offered in high-heel technique, provocatively called "Mastering Femininity in Tap," prompted e-mail objections from Jane Goldberg, who lamented a step backward for feminism. But the young women see themselves as Third Wave. The heels are an option, as are flats; they're part of an array of choices that encompass hard-hitting aggression, coquetry, and asexuality. There was something liberating about how, in Jason Samuels Smith's 2009 show *Charlie's Angels*, three women (Sumbry-Edwards, Michelle Dorrance, and Chloé Arnold) could pose in lingerie like Farrah Fawcett while tapping out note-for-note renditions of steeplechase solos on Charlie Parker recordings. Though it's a strain to see the progress in Arnold's Syncopated Ladies, endorsed by Beyoncé for the female empowerment of pushing their sexiness in bustiers, today's female tap dancers unquestionably enjoy more stylistic range, more freedom, than their male counterparts. Everything that men do is open to women, while the reverse does not hold. (The fear of sissiness that pervaded *Jazz Dance* in the sixties is no longer overt, yet conceptions of masculinity continue to be narrower in tap than in other dance forms.) For this change, credit goes to the Supermoms of Tap, mothers whom the young women, quick to venerate deceased grandfathers, are prone to overlook.

I could write much more about the post-Glover generations. There are many more striking dancers I could describe, more all the time. As in sports, each generation breaks the records of the preceding ones, because technique is progressive. Art is not, and when the youngsters imitate the old guard, they get the steps, but often not the style. Watching them in their own accelerated mode, I sometimes lose track of the groove. In admitting this, I am probably dating myself, though it is a complaint I hear echoed by the best tap dancers my age and older, such as Dormeshia Sumbry-Edwards.

Few of the young have shown much promise as choreographers. The exception is Michelle Dorrance, a stringy, pale tomboy from North

Carolina. The daughter of a ballerina and a soccer coach, she has the kind of tap skills that prompted Ted Levy, the head teacher of Funk University, to compare her favorably with an old black man. For much of the past decade, it was hard to find a tap company or project that didn't include her, from Glover's Ti Dii to *Imagine Tap!*. At once dorky and hip, she could pull off the sexy poses and the kick-ass footwork in *Charlie's Angels* but also twist her gangling limbs into a knockabout comedy of splayed and quick-sinking knees. At its best, her choreography lays bare emotions hidden in the mechanics of tap technique, revealing how swiveling ankles expose tender parts. It takes tap's darker emotions and makes them visible for people who can't necessarily hear them in the shadings of percussion. Dorrance has shown some aptitude for larger-scale composition and has earned recognition in the world of contemporary dance. Her *Blues Project*, a collaboration with Sumbry-Edwards and Derick Grant, was an unforced celebration of confluent traditions and interracial friendship that also alluded to the pressures to divide. It raised hopes that tap dancers might free themselves from their past without forgetting it.

Some tap dancers have benefited from the recent explosion of interest in dance among producers of TV competitions. But for now, those producers' ignorance of (or disregard for) how to present tap—to begin with, by hiring tap-cognizant sound engineers and providing appropriate flooring—has meant that tap loses more than other forms in the translation to TV. Though it gestated through competition, it can't compete. Even the best hoofers—Glover, Samuels Smith, Sumbry-Edwards—haven't registered. The trouble that lesser tap dancers have had competing in these shows is partly an outcome of the unequal way the competitions are structured, but their struggle is also a sign of how separate tap has become from other kinds of dance. It remains peripheral to contemporary popular culture, and its place in more specialized zones is far from secure.

HISTORY

When I got back into tap, I often practiced at a place called Fazil's. Founded in 1935, in a different location under the name Michael's, Fazil's was a ramshackle, if-those-floors-could-talk kind of spot: the real-life site of the true hoofer's studio in Gregory Hines's *Tap*, the Copasetics' home base in *Great Feats of Feet*, the place where Fred Astaire invites Judy Garland to rehearse in *Easter Parade*. In 2009, its building was demolished to make way for new construction. Hoofers saved pieces of the floor as if they were pieces of the Tree of Hope. For years afterward, there was an empty lot where the building used to be.

The Copasetics are all gone, as are all of Buster Brown's peers. The women who brought them out of semiretirement haven't really taken their place. For that and other reasons—above all, the hole left by Gregory Hines—tap these days can feel young. It can seem curiously immature, even though Savion Glover is over forty, even though the art form is at least as old as the U.S.A.

The young are serious students of that history, though what history mostly means to them is footage: the compilations of video clips from movies, TV variety shows, documentaries, and concerts that tappers of Glover's generation and after grew up swapping and studying. *This* is their repertory. This is their usable past. Accordingly, the most significant historical development of the last decade or so has been the spread of the Internet. More and more, tap history lives on YouTube. For me, this development has been thrilling in the sudden appearance of a new dancer or an old clip I had searched for in vain, if also maddening when footage that had cost me much effort or money to acquire was instantly available to all. The last point is important: available to all, anywhere in the world. The practice of stealing steps, now wired and wireless, is less geographically determined than ever. Or, to put it another way, the models widely available for study are no longer restricted by mass-market distribution channels or by access to private collections. A kid can search out Baby Laurence even though Laurence made no movies—can study Dormeshia Sumbry-Edwards even if she never strikes it big.

Of course, the technology introduces challenges of intellectual copyright and compensation, as well as new threats of a digital age in which copies swamp originals. YouTube comment boards—dominated by don't-make-them-like-that-anymore grumbling, if not by fetishists who tag videos with phrases like "womans tap shoe metal makes me hard"—are no substitute for person-to-person transmission. As ever, exposure is only the beginning. But tap dancers abroad already report beneficial effects: better and more plentiful sources producing higher-quality reproductions and responses. Many of the students who flock to international tap festivals do so to learn from the heroes they've discovered online.

You, reader, can instantly access much of the footage I've described in this book. If you haven't already, go ahead and search. But I also suggest that you go witness some tap in person. It still lives in jam sessions. Circa 2000, if you attended Buster Brown's tap jam at Swing 46, you would find a pubescent prodigy named Michela Marino Lerman. From 2009 into the present, you could find her at the New York jazz club Smalls, hosting her own jam. "Who's got their shoes on?" she asked, as Buster used to, and opened the floor to everyone while also trying to convince skeptical young musicians that it's possible to play jazz at the highest level with one's feet. Some of the old Swing 46 gang was there, many of them no better or worse, just older. Dancers too young to have attended Buster's jam were developing their own styles. Half the participants still came from East Asia, but where a camcorder once might have started a fight, recording by smartphone was now commonplace. Video of the jam was broadcast, via Web feed, all over the world: the sound and image of dancers crowding for the Shim Sham in this basement club, not far from where Juba once jigged.

Like Swing 46, Smalls was a site of tradition. What transpired there was a continuation of what had transpired at La Cave, at the Purple Manor, on the pavement in front of Minton's, in the alley behind the Apollo, on the street corners of Philadelphia and Chicago, and in the Hoofers' Club. It was a continuation, probably, of what had taken place in Pete Williams's Five Points saloon and on the shingles of Catharine Market.

I didn't know about all that when I started this book. I didn't know how far back it went. I thought I knew what tap was: a fun activity from my childhood, a hobby of my adulthood, a way to fantasize that I was Fred Astaire. When I started to discover the vastness of what I hadn't known about tap, it was chastening. There was a lot I thought I knew but didn't know about the history of my country.

Throughout that history, tap has periodically been pronounced dead, a fate it shares with most enduring arts. Pundits issued death certificates for jazz every time jazz changed: when it evolved from a fabulously multisourced folk art to a massively popular, nearly universal form, and then again after that popularity faded and the variety encompassed by the word *jazz* grew and grew. But new jazz musicians keep extending its history. Likewise with ballet, which might have begun in the courts of Europe but has been transformed, again and again, in different places and circumstances. Compared with today's popular culture or the Old Masters' art in museums, jazz and ballet are both marginal. But compared with tap, both ballet and "America's classical music" are established, with well-funded institutions and a thick body of professional and amateur scholarship bestowing cultural respect. Tap is much poorer, scrappier, more vulnerable. Tap might be less burdened by the weight of its past, simply because while some parts—especially the Hollywood part—are widely and disproportionately familiar, so much else isn't. Or maybe, at this late date, perpetual history lessons are required for audiences to be able to process tap properly.

In any case, examining the whole of that history—as much of it as can be found—has consequences. Encountering any tap dancer, I am now ultrasensitive to influences: aware of distinctions between allusion, imitation, and originality; clued into stolen steps and what's been done with them. For me, every tap dance is an imitation dance, even if all the dancer is doing is his or her own jig. What Hines said he was, and what Glover still insists he is—a dancer in a lineage—that is how I see and hear them. But my perception is also affected by my awareness of those who came after them, and also by branches Glover seldom acknowledges. I see them as part of the whole motley family tree.

Sometimes I am disappointed or exasperated or bored by tap dancers. Why can't they use their bodies with fuller and more articulate expressiveness and coordination, as in other forms of dance? Why can't they be more poetically suggestive and structurally sophisticated, as in other forms of choreography? And from the aural side, isn't a tap dancer's tiny tonal range an awful limitation? How can they sing properly with such an instrument? So many of the questions arise from the central category confusion of music and dance. Tap is so simple, and so complex. Its glory flows from its meager means: a pair of feet, usually within a pair of shoes. The history, if you know it, colors the questions, but it doesn't make them go away. For that, you have to catch a great tap dancer and open your eyes and ears.

NOTES

Abbreviations Used

HTC: Harvard Theater Collection

IJS: Interview transcripts for *Jazz Dance*, Marshall Stearns Collection, Institute of Jazz Studies, Rutgers University

IJSOH: Jazz Oral History Project, Institute for Jazz Studies, Rutgers University

ITAN: International Tap Association Newsletter

JD: Marshall and Jean Stearns, *Jazz Dance* (Schirmer Books, 1979)

JOH: Jazz Oral History Program Collection, Archives Center, National Museum of American History, Smithsonian Institution

NYPL: New York Public Library for the Performing Arts

RF: Rusty E. Frank, *Tap!: The Greatest Tap Dance Stars and Their Stories, 1900–1955* (William Morrow, 1990)

Opening Act

4 *"What the eye sees"*: Paul Draper, "Look or Listen?," *Dance*, March 1962.
6 *"the jazzman's true academy"*: Ralph Ellison, *Shadow and Act* (Vintage, 1995), p. 268.
9 *"He was a little guy"*: Buster Brown, interview by Dianne Walker, February 8, 1997, NYPL.
10 *"easy living"*: "Closing the Gap," *ITAN* 10, no. 2 (July–August 1999), p. 8.

10 *"We had tried to imitate them"*: Kurt Albert and Klaus Bleis, "The Buster Brown Story," *ITAN* 13, no. 2 (Fall 2002), p. 25.

11 *"They had certain places"*: Buster Brown, interview by Dianne Walker.

12 *"After that, everything just fell"*: Kurt Albert and Klaus Bleis, "The Buster Brown Story," *ITAN*, Fall 2002, p. 27.

12 *"You could dance"*: Buster Brown, interview by Dianne Walker.

13 *"the biggest highlight"*: Melba Huber, "Gotta Go Tap Dancing," *ITAN* 13, no. 2 (Fall 2002), p. 24.

15 *"I could close my eyes"*: *About Tap* (directed by George Nierenberg, 1985).

15 *"When you're dancing"*: "Closing the Gap," *ITAN* 10, no. 1 (July–August 1999), p. 30.

15 *"They look like they're coming"*: Ibid., p. 11.

1. Stealing Steps

20 *"It was a simple thing"*: Leonard Reed, interview by Fred Strickler, March 27, 1997, NYPL.

20 *"The whole club would join us"*: JD, p. 196.

20 *"I never got any money"*: Leonard Reed, interview by Fred Strickler.

21 *"old films"*: *Leonard Reed's Revenge of the Shim Sham* (Rusty E. Frank Presentation, 2002), DVD.

21 *"I knew how to come up with"*: Leonard Reed, interview by Fred Strickler, February 11, 1997.

21 *"There was always dancin"*: RF, p. 42.

23 *One of those novices*: JD, p. 174.

23 *Bubbles would say*: The New Yorker, August 26, 1967.

23 *"You can take whatever you stole"*: RF, p. 97.

23 *"That was affectionately called"*: RF, p. 42.

24 *"One night I started practicing"*: JD, p. 213.

24 *"I invented that step"*: JD, p. 215.

24 *"You can't copyright"*: IJS. Interviewing people for *Jazz Dance*, Marshall Stearns asked questions while Jean Stearns (who told me this in 2009) took down the answers in shorthand, which she then expanded into typewritten transcripts that don't always match the quotes in the printed book. For certain facts and phrasings, I chose the transcript version.

25 *Some described tests*: ITAN, January–February 1996, p. 3.

25 *"Maybe I didn't do"*: Danny Daniels History of American Tap: Hal LeRoy, 1978, NYPL.

2. Original Steps

28 *"the jigginest fellow"*: Federal Writers' Project, *Slave Narratives*, XVI, part 4, p. 34.

29 *"There is, without doubt"*: Richard Jobson, *The Golden Trade* . . . (Speight & Walpole, 1623), pp. 105–108.

30 *"One would be apt to say"*: Michel Adanson, *A Voyage to Senegal, the Isle of Goree, and the River Gambia* (J. Nourse, 1759), p. 308.

30 *"With crooked knees"*: Jobson, *Golden Trade*, pp. 105–108.

30 *was said to have no bones*: Robert Farris Thompson, *African Art in Motion* (Berkeley: University of California Press, 1974), p. 252.

30 *"The Negroes do not dance a step"*: Adanson, *Voyage to Senegal*, p. 149.

31 *"creates within himself"*: Thompson, *African Art in Motion*, p. 262.

31 *could follow three or four rhythms*: Peggy Harper, "Dance in Nigeria," *Ethnomusicology* 13, no. 2 (May 1969), p. 290.

31 *"metronome sense"*: Richard Alan Waterman, "African Influence on the Music of the Americas," in *Acculturation in the Americas*, ed. Sol Tax (University of Chicago Press, 1952), p. 213.

32 *"stamp on the ground"*: Thompson, *African Art in Motion*, p. 32.

32 *"To do difficult tasks"*: Robert Farris Thompson, *African Arts* 7, no. 1 (Autumn 1973), p. 41.

33 *"Breaking the beat"*: Robert Farris Thompson, "Coming Down the Body Line," in *Dancing Between Two Worlds*, ed. C. Daniel Dawson (Ragged Edge Press, 1991), p. 8.

33 *executing the ancestors' steps*: Thompson, *African Art in Motion*, p. 28.

34 *"the moving thing"*: W. G. Raffe, *Dictionary of the Dance* (A. S. Barnes, 1964), p. 247.

34 *morris dance*: John Forrest's *The History of Morris Dancing, 1458–1750* (University of Toronto Press, 1999) is fearsomely empirical in identifying the many layers of origins and the bidirectional flow of imitation and parody among social classes. No scholarship of equivalent rigor exists for the jig or the hornpipe.

35 *The first uses*: George S. Emmerson, "The Hornpipe," *Folk Music Journal* 2, no. 1 (1970), pp. 12–34.

35 *basic equipment*: J. S. Bratton, "Dancing a Hornpipe in Fetters," *Folk Music Journal* 6, no. 1 (1990), pp. 65–82.

35 *"The country lads"*: William Hone, *The Table Book* (William Tegg, 1827), p. 553.

36 *According to oral history*: Pat Tracey, "The East Lancashire Tradition," *English Dance and Song* 23, no. 2 (1959), pp. 39–41.

36 *"quick, well-timed clatter"*: Edwin Waugh, *Sketches of Lancashire Life and Localities* (Whitaker and Co., 1855), p. 190.

36 *"Persons in Clogs"*: Ibid., p. 4.

36 *"Twopenny hops"*: Henry Mayhew, *London Labor and London Poor*, vol. 1 (George Woolfalk & Son, 1851), p. 12.

36 *"clog-hornpipe"*: Pierce Egan, *Boxiana*, vol. 2 (Sherwood, Jones, and Co., 1824), p. 332.

36 *tighter-fitting clogs*: Julian Pillings, "The Lancashire Clog Dance," *Folk Music Journal* 1, no. 3 (1967), p. 159.

37 *dance in early Gaelic texts*: See Breandán Breathnach, *Folk Music and Dances of Ireland* (Ossian Publications, 1996), pp. 35–45.

37 *accounts of traveling Englishmen*: See Helen Brennan, *The Story of Irish Dance* (Roberts Rinehart, 1999), pp. 15–28.

37 *"An Irishman may be said to love"*: Thomas Crofton Croker, *Legends of the Lakes*, vol. 2 (John Ebers and Co., 1829).

37 *"of all the amusements"*: William Carleton, "The Country Dancing-Master," *Irish Penny Journal*, August 29, 1840, pp. 69–71.

37 *Exhibitions of mastery*: See Croker and Carleton.

38 *"dance on a plate"*: Brennan, *Story of Irish Dance*, p. 80.

38 *influence of the dancing masters*: Ibid., pp. 64–72.

40 *Catholic Irish occupied a position*: See David R. Roediger, *Wages of Whiteness* (Verso, 1999); Noel Ignatiev, *How the Irish Became White* (Routledge, 1995); David T. Gleeson, *The Irish in the South, 1815–1877* (University of North Carolina Press, 2001).

40 *"We often at sea"*: Thomas Phillips, *A Journal of a Voyage Made in the Hannibal of London* (For John Walthoe, 1732), p. 230.

42 *Caribbean accounts*: See *After Africa*, ed. Roger D. Abrahams and John F. Szwed (Yale University Press, 1983).

42 *"strange indecent attitudes"*: George Pinckard, *Notes on the West Indies* (Longman, Hurst, Rees, and Orme, 1806), vol. 1, pp. 263–68.

42 *dances that made it to Europe*: For instance, the African-derived and once notorious zarabanda and chacona became the sedate sarabande and chaconne. See Ned Sublette, *Cuba and Its Music* (Chicago Review Press, 2004).

42 *One Sunday in 1739*: See *Stono: Documenting and Interpreting a Southern Slave Revolt* (University of South Carolina Press, 2005).

43 *churchmen objecting*: Morgan Godwyn, *The Negro's and Indians Advocate* (Printed for the author by J.D., 1680), pp. 32–33; see also Dena J. Epstein, *Sinful Tunes and Spirituals* (University of Illinois Press, 2003).

43 *"astonishing agility"*: J.F.D. Smyth, *A Tour in the United States of America* (Dublin: Printed by J. Perrin, 1774), pp. 27–28.

43 *"irregular and grotesque"*: Nicholas Cresswell, *The Journal of Nicholas Cresswell, 1774–1777* (Lincoln McVeagh/The Dial Press, 1924), pp. 18–19.

44 *Separate scholars*: See Philip D. Morgan, *Slave Counterpoint* (University of North Carolina Press, 1998), p. 586.

44 *"distorting their frames"*: John Pierpont, *Journal*, MS, Pierpont Morgan Library, New York, quoted in Epstein, *Sinful Tunes*, p. 84.

44 *"mania" for dancing*: Moreau de Saint-Méry, *Moureau de Saint-Méry's American Journey* (Doubleday, 1947), p. 60.

44 *so did their white masters*: see Kate Van Winkle Keller, *Dance and Its Music in America, 1528–1789* (Pendragon Press, 2007).

45 *"impudent" Irishmen*: *Virginia Gazette,* August 17, 1739.

45 *"He values himself"*: *Virginia Gazette*, December 1, 1774.

45 *Thomas Jefferson's younger brother*: *Memoirs of a Monticello Slave* (University of North Carolina Press, 1951), 50. See also: Phillip Fithian, *Journals and Letters* (University of Virginia Press, 1968), pp. 61–62.

45 *"cut-out jig"*: See Keller, pp. 141, 180–83. Though European observers compared dance with French and Tuscan forms, its structure more closely resembles that of Afro-Caribbean forms such as the chica or calenda.

45 *"bacchanalian"*: Cresswell, *Journal*, pp. 52–53.

45 *a Glasgow songbook*: See Keller, *Dance and Its Music*, p. 183.

45 *"originally borrowed"*: Andrew Burnaby, *Travels Through the Middle Settlements of North America in the Years 1759 and 1760* (A. Wessels, 1904), p. 57.

46 *William Turner*: See Keller, *Dance and Its Music*, pp. 329–38, 354–55.

46 *a young John Adams*: John Adams, *Diary and Autobiography of John Adams* (Atheneum, 1964), p. 172.

46 *distressed informant*: *Boston Evening Post*, January 14, 1740.

46 *"Most fatiguing"*: William Bentley, *The Diary of William Bentley, D.D.,* vol. 4 (Essex Institute, 1914), p. 457.

47 *The evidence is shaky*: See Shane White, *Somewhat More Independent* (University of Georgia Press, 2012), pp. 95–106.

47 Satanstoe: James Fenimore Cooper, *The Novels of James Fenimore Cooper: Satanstoe* (D. Appleton, 1880), pp. 73–75.

47 Market Book: Thomas F. De Voe, *The Market Book*, vol. 1 (Burt Franklin, 1969), pp. 344–45.

48 *Northup described*: Solomon Northup, *Twelve Years a Slave* (Louisiana State University Press, 1968), p. 137.

48 *"If you wish to look"*: Ibid., p. 166.

49 *"They seem never to have known a care"*: Francis Parkman, *Journals* (Harper and Brothers, 1947), p. 483.

49 *"the happiest of the human race"*: William B. Smith, "The Persimmon Tree and the Beer Dance," *Farmer's Register* 6 (April 1838), pp. 58–61.

49 *"the most effective means"*: Frederick Douglass, *My Bondage and My Freedom* (Miller, Orton, and Mulligan, 1855), p. 310.

49 *"we'd dance long as"*: James Campbell, interview in George P. Rawick, ed., *The American Slave*, series 2, vol. 16 (Westport, CT: Greenwood, 1972), Ohio section, p. 20.

50 *"Might whip us"*: Charles Grandy, interview in Charles L. Perdue, Jr., Thomas E. Barden, and Robert K. Phillips, eds., *Weevils in the Wheat* (University of Virginia Press, 1976), p. 119.

50 *"placid bosom"*: Northup, *Twelve Years*, p. 167.

50 *"Molly move like the handsaw"*: William B. Smith, "Persimmon Tree," p. 60.

50 *corn shuckings*: See Roger D. Abrahams, *Singing the Master* (Pantheon, 1992).

51 *1914 memoir*: John Allen Wyeth, *With Sabre and Scalpel* (Harper, 1914).

51 *a platform for public events*: Nancy Williams in Perdue et al., eds., *Weevils*, p. 318.

51 *Yet Isaac Williams*: Isaac Williams, *Sunshine and Shadow of Slave Life* (Evening News Printing, 1885), p. 62.

51 *"Setting the Floor"*: Fannie Berry in Perdue et al., *Weevils*, p. 50.

51 *Touring the South*: Frederick Law Olmsted, *Journeys and Explorations in the Cotton Kingdom*, vol. 2 (Sampson Low, 1861), p. 73.

51 *A Rhode Island man*: Lewis Paine, *Six Years in a Georgia Prison* (Bela Marsh, 1852), p.179.

52 *"Us slaves watched white folks' parties"*: *JD*, p. 22.

53 *Samuel Mordecai*: Samuel Mordecai, *Virginia, Especially Richmond* (George M. West, 1856), p. 311.

53 *"the attitude and the language"*: Northup, *Twelve Years*, p. 138.

53 *ripe matter*: See chapter four of Shane White, *Stylin'* (Cornell University Press, 1998).

53 *"a joke of no ordinary magnitude"*: *Pennsylvania Gazette*, reprinted in *Freedom's Journal*, March 14, 1828.

53 *"If the big white folks dance"*: *New York Enquirer*, December 9, 1828.

53 *"a remarkable taste in distorting"*: Robert Waln, *The Hermit in America* (Philadelphia, 1819).

53 *Sylvia Dubois*: *Sylvia Dubois: A Biografy* (Oxford University Press, 1988), p. 60.

54 *"tote herself"*: Hannah Crasson, interview in Rawick, *American Slave*, vol. 14, p. 191.

54 *"easy careless manner"*: See Keller, *Dance and Its Music*, p. 332.

54 *water on their heads*: Mary Armstrong, a house slave in St. Louis, reported in her Federal Writers' Project interview that dancing with water on her head was her mistress's idea.

54 *"sinking"*: John Fanning Watson, *Methodist Error* (D. and E. Fenton, 1819), p. 63.

54 *"as substitute for the dance"*: Charles Lyell, *A Second Visit to the United States*, vol. 1 (Harper and Brothers, 1849), p. 270.

55 *"the remains of some old idol"*: Laura M. Towne, *Letters and Diary* (Riverside Press, 1912), p. 20.

55 *"flippin' yo' arms"*: Fannie Berry in Perdue et al., *Weevils*, p. 49.

55 *other former slaves*: See the Federal Writers' Project interviews of Liza Jones and William Adams.

55 *one 1841 story*: J.F.H. Claiborne, "A Trip Through the Piney Woods," in *Mississippi Historical Society Publications*, vol. 9, p. 535.

55 *early-nineteenth-century New York ballrooms*: See Washington Irving, *Salmagundi*, January 24, 1807, p. 17.

55 *associated with French dancers*: See *The Memoirs of John Durang* (University of Pittsburgh Press, 1966), p. 11.

56 *Isaac Williams*: Isaac Williams, *Sunshine and Shadow*, pp. 61–62.

56 *a white Bostonian*: *The Boston Lyceum*, March 15, 1827.

56 *a Negro banjoist*: *Sketches and Eccentricities of Colonel David Crockett* (J&J Harper, 1833), pp. 37–40.

56 *New Jersey farmers*: *The Lay of the Scottish Fiddle* (For James Cawthorn, 1814), p. 71.

56 *terpischorean skill*: Irving, *Salmagundi*, January 24, 1807, p. 17.

56 *"undoubtedly of African origin"*: *The Lay*, p. 180.

56 *The sports Tom and Jerry*: Pierce Egan, *Life in London* (Cambridge University Press, 2011), pp. 286–90.

57 *"The jig . . . was an African dance"*: Henry William Ravenal, "Recollections of Southern Plantation Life," *Yale Review* 25 (June 1936), pp. 768–69.

57 *poor whites in Baltimore*: *The Sun*, November 23, 1939.

57 *amusingly rustic habits*: *The Madisonian*, December 24, 1840.

57 *Fragments of juba songs*: See William B. Smith.

57 *juba meant "giblets"*: Bessie Jones, *For the Ancestors* (University of Illinois Press, 1983), p. 45.

58 *friend of Edgar Allan Poe*: *The Complete Works of Edgar Allan Poe*, vol. 27 (G. D. Sproul, 1902), p. 22.

58 *explain syncopation*: Sidney Lanier, *The Science of English Verse* (C. Scribner's Sons, 1880), p. 189.

58 *white dandy*: Roediger, *Wages of Whiteness*, p. 99.

58 *po'bockorau*: Jerry Duke, *Clog Dance in the Appalachians* (printed by author, 1984), p. 27.

58 *Mobile Buck*: James Edwin Campbell, *Echoes from the Cabin and Elsewhere* (Donohue and Henneberry, 1895), p. 36.

58 *Jolly Old Uncle Buck*: Orland Kay Armstrong, *Old Massa's People* (Bobbs-Merrill, 1931), p. 261.

59 *One former house slave*: James Wiggins, interview in Federal Writers' Project, *Slave Narratives*, vol. 16, p. 243.

59 *"you know a nigger is jest a born"*: Dan Barton, interview in *Gumbo Ya-Ya* (Houghton Mifflin, 1945), p. 240.

59 *"celebrated jig dancer"*: Julia Morgan, *How It Was* (Publishing House Methodist Episcopal Church, South, 1892), p. 120.

60 *"Virginia 'break-down'"*: J.F.H. Claiborne, *Life and Correspondence of John A. Quitman*, vol. 1 (Harper and Brothers, 1860), p. 42.

60 *The next usages*: *Baltimore Patriot*, October 19, 1833.

60 *"a peculiarly American institution"*: Ed. James, *Jig, Clog, and Breakdown Dancing Made Easy* (printed by author, 1873), p. 1.

3. Imitation Dance

61 *"science niggas"*: *Spirit of the Times*, February 15, 1840.

62 *"a genius in the dancing line"*: P. T. Barnum, *The Life of P. T. Barnum* (Redfield, 1855), p. 210.

62 *"the little 'Wirginny Nigger'"*: *Morning Herald* (New York), July 18, 1840.

62 *"He could twist his feet"*: Noah M. Ludlow, *Dramatic Life As I Found It* (G. I. Jones and Company, 1880), p. 533.

62 *"little nigger Apollo"*: *New Orleans Picayune*, January 12, 1841.

62 *"He would walk around"*: James Thomas, *From Tennessee Slave to St. Louis Entrepreneur* (University of Missouri Press, 1984), p. 48.

62 *1841 playbill*: New Theater (Mobile), February 22, 1841. HTC, MS Thr 556 (348).

63 *a Mr. Tea*: *New York Journal*, April 9, 1767.

63 *Harlequin figures*: See John O'Brien, *Harlequin Britain* (Johns Hopkins University Press, 2004).

63 *grotesque*: See *The Grotesque Dancer on the Eighteenth-Century Stage* (University of Wisconsin Press, 2005).

63 *all the blackface*: See Dale Cockrell, *Demons of Disorder* (Cambridge University Press, 1997).

63 *Thomas Dartmouth Rice*: The best account of Rice is W. T. Lhamon, Jr.'s introduction to *Jump Jim Crow* (Harvard University Press, 2003).

64 *"A Virginia Breakdown"*: *Baltimore Patriot*, October 19, 1833.

64 *"Zip Coon"*: See Cockrell, *Demons of Disorder*.

65 *the word* coon: Roediger, *Wages of Whiteness*, p. 98.

65 *1842 playbill*: Printed in Bob Carlin, *The Birth of the Banjo* (McFarland, 2007), p. 61.

65 *"Dars musick"*: Nathan, p. 133.

65 *"knockin' de breff"*: Broadside (January 31, 1843), quoted in Frank Dumont, "The Golden Days of Minstrelsy," *The New York Clipper,* December 1914.

66 *illustration from 1859*: Bryant's Minstrels playbill of December 19, 1859, printed in Hans Nathan, *Dan Emmett and the Rise of Early Negro Minstrelsy* (University of Oklahoma Press, 1962), p. 233.

67 *"the oddities, peculiarities"*: Quoted in Robert Toll, *Blacking Up* (Oxford University Press, 1974), p. 30.

67 *"who urge the negroes"*: *Manchester Times,* June 10, 1843.

67 *"great fidelity"*: Ludlow, *Dramatic Life*, p. 332.

67 *"the negro character"*: James Gordon Bennett, *New York Herald*, April 27, 1837.

67 *"steal off to some negro hut"*: *The New York Clipper*, April 13, 1878.

68 *echo trickster figures*: See W. T. Lhamon, Jr., *Raising Cain* (Harvard University Press, 1998), pp. 181–85.

68 *"Knock Jim Crow"*: Bessie Jones and Bess Lomax Hawes, *Step It Down* (Harper and Row, 1972).

68 *borrowing from black street performers*: See Lhamon, *Jump Jim Crow*, p. 38.

68 *reported a police raid*: Daily Picayune, January 12, 1841.

68 *had already praised Diamond*: Daily Picayune, January 3, 1841.

69 *he handed coins to blacks*: Whip, January 21, 1843.

69 *setting of New Orleans*: E. P. Christy, founder of the successful and enduring Christy Minstrels, also claimed to have studied blacks in New Orleans. See *Christy's Plantation Melodies*, 4th ed. (Fischer and Brothers, 1854).

69 *"regular Ethiopian breakdowns"*: Picayune, June 24, 1845.

70 *an 1844 account*: Joseph N. Field, "The Death of Mike Fink" in *Humor of the Old Southwest* (University of Georgia Press, 1975).

70 *"rough frolics"*: T. B. Thorpe, "Reminiscences of the Mississippi," *Harper's New Monthly Magazine* 12 (1855).

70 *the tune of "Zip Coon"*: T. Alston Brown, "The Origin of Negro Minstrelsy," *The New York Clipper*, May–August 1913.

70 *the 1833 Davy Crockett story*: Sketches and Eccentricities, pp. 37–40. The author, Matthew St. Clair Clarke, might have been using the title of the popular song generically.

71 *"a very ignorant person"*: The New York Clipper, June 20, 1874.

71 *"If you turn your face away"*: Robert Cantwell, *Bluegrass Breakdown* (University of Illinois Press, 2003), p. 269.

72 *"as a counterfeit bill"*: Isaac Williams, *Sunshine and Shadow*, p. 61.

72 *denied minstrel authenticity*: Frances Anne Kemble, *Journals of a Residence on a Georgian Plantation in 1838–1839* (Harper and Brothers, 1863), p. 96.

72 *origin stories*: See particularly "Stephen C. Foster and Negro Minstrelsy," *The Atlantic Monthly*, November 1867.

72 *"Now my brodder niggers"*: Lhamon, *Jump Jim Crow*, p. 115.

73 *sublimated aggression*: See Lhamon, *Raising Cain*.

73 *against European culture*: See William J. Mahar, *Behind the Burnt Cork Mask* (University of Illinois Press, 1999).

73 *"jump, dance, and knock his heels"*: Quoted in Nathan, *Dan Emmett*, p. 115.

74 *"La Bayadere in Ole Kentuck"*: Playbill of National Theater, October 18, 1839, HTC, MS Thr 556 (348).

74 *"Pat Juba"*: Yankee Doodle, October 10, 1846.

74 *"bleaching process"*: New York Musical Review, December 7, 1854.

74 *"India rubber"*: The Semi-Weekly Eagle (Vermont), June 23, 1851.

75 *ease and grace*: Ibid.

75 *given it the name*: New York Herald, August 17, 1856.

75 *"a rude and untutored"*: The New York Clipper, May 22, 1858.

75 *A. M. Bininger*: Library of Congress, Prints and Photographs Division, LOT 10767.

76 *"oddest outré"*: Lowell Daily Citizen, April 24, 1865.

76 *"the most natural"*: Charleston Mercury, June 12, 1857.

76 *"Happy Uncle Tom"*: Frank Brower, *Black Diamond Songster* (Dick & Fitzgerald, 1863), pp. 5–8.

76 *a Massachusetts soldier*: Passages from the Life of Henry Warren Howe (Courier-Citizen Co., 1899), p. 91.

77 *"Jim Crow or Negro Car"*: Reprinted in *Liberator*, October 1, 1841.

77 *Emerson gave a lecture*: Liberator, August 15, 1845.

4. Dancing Juba for Eels

78 *"black boys who usually dance"*: "Sunday's Work," *New York Tattler*, October 22, 1841.

78 *an 1842 piece*: "Dancing for Eels," *Flash*, November 12, 1842.

78 *"some years ago"*: John Jay Brown, *American Angler's Guide* (D. Appleton and Co., 1876), pp. 275–76.

79 *a stance*: Robert Farris Thompson, "Kongo Influences on African American Artistic Culture," in *Africanisms in American Culture* (Indiana University Press, 2005).

79 *"those unheard of"*: National Theater Playbill, HTC, MS Thr 556 (348).

79 *Long Island niggers*: "De Long Island Nigger," *Emma Snow Song Book*, quoted in Nathan, *Dan Emmett*, p. 84.

80 *New York Board of Health*: *Statement of Facts Relative to the Late Fever Which Appeared in Bancker-Street and Its Vicinity* (Board of Health and Elam Bliss, 1821).

80 *"a great dancer"*: Quoted in Shane White, *Somewhat More Independent*, 179.

80 *"jumping about, twisting"*: Horace Lane, *The Wandering Boy* (Luther A. Pratt, 1839), p. 69.

80 *"Such fiddling and dancing"*: *An Account of Colonel Crockett's Tour to the North and Down East* (E. L. Carey and A. Hart, 1835), p. 48.

80 *"a knot of little"*: *Evening Tattler*, January 25, 1840.

81 *an illicit excursion*: Ned Buntline, *The Mysteries and Miseries of New York* (W. F. Burgess, 1848), pp. 89–91.

81 *Dickens's account*: Charles Dickens, *American Notes for General Circulation* (Baudry's European Library, 1848), pp. 111–12. Dickens sardonically names the establishment "Almack's," after the fancy London social club, but perhaps he, a fan of Pierce Egan, was also thinking of Egan's All-Max and its double shuffles.

82 *Juba's given name*: "The Rise and Fall of Burnt Cork," *The New York Clipper*, November 4, 1876, p. 255. Brown says there were two Jubas. The other may have been Lewis Davis, "alias Master Juber, a gentleman ob color . . . at present engaged . . . in dancing negro breakdowns": *New York Daily Express*, September 14, 1840.

82 *"little negro called 'Juba'"*: *New York Sporting Whip*, January 28, 1843.

82 *"the Original JOHN DIAMOND"*: *New York Herald*, July 8, 1844.

82 *circulated a letter*: Carlin, *Birth of the Banjo*, p. 105.

82 The Boston Post *scoffed*: See *Daily Picayune*, December 15, 1841.

83 *a clipping printed around 1875*: "The Negro Minstrels of the Nights Gone By," HTC, Clips Pers (Bryant, Dan).

83 *"the greatest dancer in the world"*: *Public Ledger* (Philadelphia), January 15, 1845.

84 *"No conception"*: Georgia Champions playbill, June 18, 1845, HTC, MS Thr 556 (454).

84 *"unquestionably the greatest"*: *Daily Evening Transcript* (Boston), September 2, 1845.

84 *skit about a rigged*: "Going for the Cup," described in Mahar, *Behind the Burnt Cork Mask*, pp. 158–62.

84 *King of the Negro Dancers*: *New York Herald*, January 28, 1848.

84 *possibly fighting*: Alston Brown, "Early History of Negro Minstrelsy," *The New York Clipper*, February 25, 1912.

84 *a playbill cameo*: HTC, Joseph N. Ireland scrapbook.

84 *Another illustration*: *Illustrated London News*, August 5, 1848.

84 *"The dancing of Juba"*: *Observer*, June 11, 1848.

85 *"Such mobility"*: *The Mirror and United Kingdom Magazine*, July 1848.

85 *"The most interesting part"*: *Manchester Guardian*, October 18, 1848.

85 *"a musician"*: *Illustrated London News*, May 8, 1848.

85 *"hear the exact time"*: *Sheffield and Rotherham Independent*, October 28, 1848.

85 *"a terrible clatter"*: *The Puppet-Show*, August 12, 1848.

86 *"the ease and grace"*: *Advertiser*, June 12, 1848.

87 *"Such energy"*: *Weekly Dispatch*, June 25, 1848.

87 *"as eccentric"*: *Era*, June 14, 1848.

87 *"an ideality"*: *Theatrical Times*, quoted in Marian Hannah Winter, "Juba and American Minstrelsy," *Dance Index* 6, no. 2 (February 1947), pp. 28–47.

87 *"jumping very fast"*: *Era*, August 4 and 11, 1850.

87 *Winter would call Juba*: Winter, " Juba and American Minstrelsy."

88 *a single anonymous article*: "Negro Minstrels and Their Dances," *New York Herald*, August 11, 1895.

89 *imitation dance*: With the Thayer's Minstrels in Boston, Edward Gray, known as the "Boston Rattler," did imitation dances of the same dancers but including one of Juba.

89 *According to the playbill*: Georgia Champions playbill, June 18, 1845, HTC, MS Thr 556 (454).

5. The American Clog

90 *"Barnum, with the enterprise"*: Thomas Low Nichols, *Forty Years of American Life* (John Maxwell and Company, 1864), p. 392.

91 *a letter to the sporting paper*: Quoted in James W. Cook, "Dancing Across the Color Line," *Common-place* 4, no. 1 (October 1, 2003).

91 *"in exaggerating the peculiarities"*: Frederick Douglass, *The North Star* (Rochester), June 29, 1849.

91 *recounting the origin*: Reprinted in *Atlanta Constitution*, January 19, 1885.

92 *"most laughable"*: *Quincy Daily Whig*, December 15, 1876.

92 *"The performer moves"*: Quoted in *JD*, p. 50.

92 *"combination of knee work"*: *Indianapolis Freeman*, February 8, 1913.

92 *"lie flat on his stomach"*: Sam Lucas, *New York Age*, August 15, 1915.

93 *"His mouth is his fortune"*: *Daily Nebraska Press*, May 2, 1874.

93 *"If they hate me"*: Flournoy Miller, quoted in *JD*, p. 51.

93 *"a caricature of Negro life"*: James Weldon Johnson, *Black Manhattan* (Da Capo, 1991), p. 93.

93 *"break down the ill-feeling"*: Tom Fletcher, *100 Years of the Negro in Show Business* (Da Capo, 1954), xvii.

94 *"A negro can play"*: *St. Louis Journal*, quoted in program for Callendar's Minstrels, Philadelphia, January 29, 1873, HTC.

95 *possibly apocryphal*: *Libertine*, June 15, 1842.

95 *put out an ad*: *The New York Clipper*, May 24, 1862.

95 *Naomi Porter*: *Daily Picayune*, June 2, 1862.

95 *male judges*: *The New York Clipper*, June 21, 1862.

95 *"trick heels"*: David K. Dempsey and Raymond P. Baldwin, *The Triumph and Trials of Lotta Crabtree* (Morrow, 1968), p. 134.

95 *died destitute*: *New York Times*, May 26, 1896.

96 *at her death*: *New York Times*, April 17, 1893.

96 *learned to jig:* Constance Rourke, *Troupers of the Gold Coast* (Harcourt, Brace, 1928), p. 137.

96 *swift rise of variety:* "Variety Shows," *New York Times,* April 9, 1876.

96 *"came from the negro":* *Washington Post,* May 24, 1891.

96 *"Challenge Dance":* reprinted in *This Grotesque Essence* (Louisiana State University Press, 1978), pp. 14–20. Originally published by Happy Hours Company in 1874, it had been in the repertory of Bryant's Minstrels, possibly in the same form, since 1857.

97 *clog dancing was brought:* Barney Fagan, "On with the Dance," unpublished manuscript, circa 1930, courtesy of Anthony Barrand.

97 *"Lancashire Clog Hornpipe":* Rhett Kraus, "Step Dancing on the Boston Stage," *Country Dance and Song* 22 (June 1992), p. 3.

98 *"for the ladies":* Harry Chapeau, interviewed in *Atlanta Daily Constitution,* November 25, 1879.

98 *"Stand erect":* J. H. Clifford, *Jig and Clog Dancing Without a Master* (T. H. Harrison and Co., 1864).

98 *"One must never stand":* Henry Tucker, *Clog Dancing Made Easy* (Robert M. De Witt, 1874).

98 *one Bowery professor:* *Washington Post,* February 3, 1889.

99 *pass around his clogs:* Douglas Gilbert, *American Vaudeville* (Dover, 1968), p. 24.

99 *under the stage:* "One of Minstrelsy's Vets," *Washington Post,* June 2, 1929.

99 *The title:* Wm. F. Bacon, *Complete Dancing Instructions for Light and Heavy, Genteel and Plantation Songs and Dances* (A. J. Fischer, 1871).

99 *Newcomb:* Bobby Newcomb, *Tambo: His Jokes and Funny Sayings* (Wehman Bros., 1882), p. 7.

99 *was so popular:* Michael Bennett Leavitt, *Fifty Years in Theatrical Management* (Broadway Publishing, 1912), p. 37.

99 *some other minstrels:* *The Critic,* January 27, 1870.

100 *screwing of pennies:* Ralph Keeler, "Three Years as a Negro Minstrel," *The Atlantic Monthly* 24 (July 1869), pp. 71–86.

100 *"stop-time":* Fagan, "On with the Dance."

100 *"market men":* *New York Dramatic Mirror,* August 6, 1898.

100 *"a refinement of the Essence," "greatest stylist":* Harland Dixon in *JD,* pp. 51–53.

101 *"habitually ridicule":* Fagan, "On with the Dance."

101 *"My style was original":* Harland Dixon file, IJS.

101 *An ad:* *New York Clipper,* July 14, 1896.

101 *Another Primrose and West poster:* Library of Congress, LC-USZ62-26103.

102 *"By watching Negroes":* Helen Ormsbee, "Pioneer of Broadway Syncopation," *New York Herald Tribune,* November 10, 1935. See also "First Rag-time Dancer," *Los Angeles Times,* June 9, 1902.

102 *One exception:* Lafcadio Hearn, "Levee Life," *Cincinnati Commercial,* March 17, 1876.

103 *"discordant tunes":* *New York Tribune,* December 26, 1893.

103 *"the greatest buck and wing":* *Los Angeles Times,* January 1, 1899.

103 *"not to be dreamed":* *Brooklyn Eagle,* June 20, 1895.

103 *"the dance of the stalwart":* Black America program, HTC, MS Thr 556 (250).

103 *One article:* *Boston Daily Globe,* July 21, 1985.

104 *"T'aint no use":* *The Age-Herald,* October 10, 1897. Reprinted from *New York Sun.*

104 *"chalk line walk":* Fletcher, *100 Years of the Negro,* p. 19.

104 *The name emerged*: "What a Cake Walk Is," *Kansas City Star,* March 9, 1892.

104 *1870s competitions*: "Colored High Jinks," *Morning Telegraph,* December 30, 1877,

104 *"The style"*: "Walking for Dat Cake," *New Haven Register,* February 27, 1879.

104 *"The white people"*: Quoted in Lynn Abbot and Doug Seroff, *Out of Sight* (University Press of Mississippi, 2002), p. 209.

105 *local contenders*: "Best Buck Dancer Here," *Kansas City Star,* October 4, 1896.

105 *after winning*: St. Louis Republic, March 5, 1892, p. 3.

105 *"fascinating combination"*: *Minneapolis Journal,* April 23, 1900.

105 *"simply clog dancing"*: *New York Tribune,* February 18, 1892.

105 *"Negroes call their clog"*: Rupert Hughes, "A Eulogy of Ragtime," *The Musical Record,* April 1, 1899, p. 158.

105 *"low antics"*: *Leavenworth Advocate,* April 4, 1890.

106 *"the beats corresponding"*: "The Father of Ragtime," *New York Times,* September 12, 1915. For another version, see *San Francisco Chronicle,* November 6, 1899.

106 *The same theory*: *Indianapolis Freeman,* December 23, 1911.

107 *"to compel the public"*: James Weldon Johnson, *Autobiography of an Ex-Colored Man* (Sherman, French, 1912), p. 102.

107 *"the great changes"*: "The Origin of Ragtime," *New York Times,* March 23, 1924.

107 *"It took a lot of concentration"*: JD, p. 206.

108 *"grim, backwoods humor"*: W. C. Handy, *Father of the Blues* (Da Capo, 1969), p. 184.

108 *carried a story*: *Topeka Weekly Call,* January 26, 1895.

109 *or so he would let be said*: Lincoln Barnett, "Fred Astaire," *Life,* August 25, 1941, p. 77. I can find no other source for this fact.

6. Big Time

115 *"In Boston"*: Jack Donahue, "Hoofing," *Saturday Evening Post,* September 14, 1929.

116 *"I didn't know"*: Bill Smith, *Vaudevillians* (Macmillan, 1976), p. 169.

117 *"The variety show"*: Bill Hartley, "In Vaudeville," *Everybody's Magazine* 13 (August 1905), p. 232.

117–118 *The order and composition*: George Gottlieb, "Psychology of the American Vaudeville Show from the Manager's Point of View," *Current Opinion* 60 (April 1916), pp. 257–58.

118 *"They have to establish"*: Gilbert Seldes, "The Damned Effrontery of the Two-a-Day," *Vanity Fair,* October 1922.

119 *carried a mat*: Gilbert, *American Vaudeville,* p. 164.

120 *"Nature helped me"*: Donahue, "Hoofing."

120 *packed more eccentric steps*: *Evening Times* (Pawtucket, RI), November 11, 1895.

120 *"the little darkies"*: I. S. Metcalf, *Plain Dealer,* September 28, 1917.

120 *"You started in a medicine show"*: JD, p. 63.

121 *"the pretty girls"*: JOH. Interview by Rusty Frank, February 27, 1993.

121 *"a comic, exaggerated," "put the yokels"*: JD, p. 65.

122 *"shake his head"*: JD, p. 70.

122 *"a great coon shouter"*: *Freeman,* February 11, 1911.

122 *"dancers who were so good"*: JD, p. 73.

122 *"eight minutes of footology"*: *Freeman,* September 19, 1914.

123 *"He came out"*: JD, p. 76.

123 *"Honolulu Pickaninny"*: *Rising Sun*, February 6, 1903.

124 *"Don't look disgusted"*: Quoted in Henry T. Sampson, *Blacks in Blackface* (Scarecrow Press, 2014), p. 663.

124 *boasting*: *Freeman*, November 19, 1910.

125 *"danciest"*: *Freeman*, March 23, 1912.

125 *"a good self-impersonator"*: *Freeman*, December 6, 1913.

125 *"twisting and turning"*: *Freeman*, August 5, 1916, p. 7.

125 *"I'm going to do it!"*: *JD*, p. 287. For Tack Annie, see James Haskins, *Bricktop* (Welcome Rain, 1999), pp. 31–32.

125 *"for exercise"*: *JD*, p. 85.

125 *two facts*: *Freeman*, July 7, 1904.

126 *best girl buck dancer*: *Freeman*, November 6, 1915.

126 *On a Friday afternoon*: *Freeman*, October 12, 1912.

126 *"The white people"*: *Freeman*, November 6, 1909.

127 *"He could imitate anything"*: *JD*, p. 175.

127 *"The stage is the only"*: Reprinted in *Fort Worth Morning Register*, October 17, 1901.

127 *"insurance"*: Joe Laurie, *Vaudeville* (New York: Henry Holt, 1953), pp. 56 and 203.

127 *"They had never seen"*: RF, p. 25.

128 *The only lessons*: Robert Dwan, "A Legend in His Own Feet," *Los Angeles Times*, July 26, 1981.

128 *"Everybody knew"*: Dwan. See also RF, p. 26.

129 *"You were doing it"*: *JD*, p. 270.

129 *"It was worth it"*: RF, p. 28.

129 *he would tell*: RF, pp. 28–29.

129 *partially verifiable*: "Too Hot for Bill," *Chicago Defender*, January 19, 1924.

130 *Primrose had inspired*: *Washington Post*, December 9, 1939.

130 *One of many accounts*: Jim Haskins and N. R. Mitgang, *Mr. Bojangles* (William Morrow, 1988), p. 37.

130 *according to his fellow performer*: Fletcher, *100 Years of the Negro*, p. 287.

131 *"I think he was cleaning his gun"*: St. Clair McKelway, "Bojangles-II," *The New Yorker*, October 13, 1934, p. 30.

131 *"The men, who are honest"*: *Denver Tribune*, May 14, 1912.

132 *"The negro gets a fair deal"*: *Duluth News-Tribune*, February 16, 1912.

132 *one of Cooper's later partners*: Eddie Hunter, in Haskins and Mitgang, *Mr. Bojangles*, p. 93.

132 *"Bo had that personality"*: Haskins and Mitgang, *Mr. Bojangles*, p. 94.

132 *"the most efficient"*: Curtis Mitchell, *The Dance*, June 1926.

133 *"That man was so sharp"*: Gary Giddins, *Satchmo* (Da Capo, 2001), p. 49.

133 *his wife once reported*: Haskins and Mitgang, *Mr. Bojangles*, p. 161.

133 *"I didn't like the idea"*: St. Clair McKelway, "Bojangles-I," *The New Yorker*, October 6, 1934, p. 28.

134 *Aiston Shoe Company*: Fletcher, *100 Years of the Negro*, p. 295; *New York Daily News*, April 23, 1946.

135 *"Indescribably liquid"*: Robert Benchley, *The New Yorker*, October 8, 1930.

135 *"the steady beat"*: *Chicago Daily News*, October 12, 1931.

136 *Dancers tell a story*: *JD*, p. 186. Pete Nugent told the Stearns this story at a meeting of the Copasetics Club in 1960. See IJS.

7. The Practical Art of Stage Dancing

137 *Lively Bootblack*: John McCabe, *George M. Cohan* (Da Capo, 1980), p. 26.

137 *"endurance dancer"*: Frederick Russell, "50 Years a Dancer," *American Dancer*, April 1938.

137 *"The only way"*: George M. Cohan, "The Practical Side of Dancing," *Saturday Evening Post*, May 21, 1910.

138 *"a general dancing rough-house"*: Quoted in Ethan Mordden, *Make Believe* (Oxford University Press, 1997), p. 9.

139 *"nigger dances"*: Quoted in Lewis Erenberg, *Steppin' Out* (Greenwood Press, 1981), p. 164.

139 *Frank Young*: *Kansas City Star*, March 13, 1904.

140 *"effects"*: Ned Wayburn, "Realizing Musical Shows," *New York Tribune*, February 9, 1913.

140 *writing about the Follies*: Edmund Wilson, "The Follies as an Institution," *American Earthquake* (Doubleday, 1958), pp. 50–51.

141 *"business, business"*: Siegfried Kracauer, "Girls und Krise," *Frankfurter Zeitung*, May 26, 1931.

141 *"expresses American syncopated rhythms"*: Ned Wayburn, *The Art of Stage Dancing* (Belvedere, 1980), p. 97.

142 *One story puts the plates*: RF, 175.

142 *To a writer*: "Dance Revolution in Musical Comedy," *New York Times*, September 6, 1925.

144 *"perfect rhythm"*: Peter Clark MacFarlane, "Clown and Superclown," *Everybody's Magazine*, 1914.

145 *"From then on"*: JD, p. 207.

145 *"sublime and grotesque"*: Heywood Broun, *New York World*, May 17, 1923.

145 *"as negroid"*: *New York Telegram*, May 18, 1923.

146 *"more fun to watch"*: Pete Nugent in JD, p. 200.

146 *"best all-round"*: Donahue, "Hoofing."

146 *a 1929 ad*: *New Yorker*, June 15, 1929, p. 52.

146 *"more clown than hoofer"*: Brooks Atkinson, *New York Times*, January 11, 1928.

146 *"the sharp sting"*: George White, "The Song and Dance Game," *The Dance*, January 1927, p. 15.

146 *black boy*: According to Willie Covan, the boy was Sonny Swinton, brother of *In Old Kentucky*'s Harry. IJS.

147 *"an adept stepper"*: *New York Times*, June 8, 1920.

147 *"He is one of those extraordinary persons"*: Alexander Woollcott, *New York Times*, October 8, 1919.

148 *"apparently impromptu"*: Sheppard Butler, *New York Times*, June 5, 1922.

148 *Woollcott was soon*: *New York World*, November 23, 1927.

148 *inserted tap*: Bob Thomas, *Fred Astaire* (St. Martins, 1984), p. 79.

8. It's Getting Dark on Old Broadway

150 *"the negro as he really is"*: Carl Van Vechten, *New York Press*, December 14, 1913.

150 *"the real nigger stuff"*: Van Vechten, "The Negro Theater," *In the Garret* (Knopf, 1920).

150 *"the greatest buck dancer"*: Sylvester Russell, *Freeman*, August 29, 1914.

150 *"a variety"*: Arthur Ruhl, *New York Tribune*, February 19, 1914.

151 *a classic showbiz tale:* See Robert Kimble and William Bolcom, *Reminiscing with Sissle and Blake* (Viking Press, 1973).

152 *"The first reportorial responsibility"*: Heywood Broun, *World*, November 28, 1922.

153 *"clog dancing"*: *World*, October 30, 1922.

153 *Miller once explained: JD*, p. 145.

154 *"dizzy hoofing"*: Jack Lait, *Variety*, August 26, 1921.

155 *"a broad smile": JD*, p. 144.

155 *called him perfect*: *Guardian*, December 27, 1928.

156 *"Broadway has no superior"*: Chappy Gardner, *Pittsburgh Courier*, November 3, 1928.

156 *"If I ever lost that bow": JD*, p. 89.

157 *"There was no step"*: Willie Bryant file, IJS.

157 *"A colored audience"*: *Baltimore Sun*, December 1931, quoted in Sampson, *Blacks in Blackface*, p. 68.

157 *"the first black man"*: Vernon Scott, *Sun-Sentinel*, October 6, 1985.

157 *Leslie Hope*: Bob Hope, *Have Tux, Will Travel* (Simon and Schuster, 1954), p. 38.

157 *"You don't have to see my feet"*: RF, p. 225.

158 *"lullaby hoofing"*: Percy Hammond, *New York Herald Tribune*, October 8, 1930.

158 *"reduced his act"*: Brooks Atkinson, *New York Times*, December 4, 1933.

158 *"Robinson was absolute tops": JD*, p. 187.

158 *"It's really very simple"*: Robert Benchley, *The New Yorker*, October 18, 1930, p. 34.

159 *"There are hundreds"*: *New York Times*, May 27, 1929.

159 *"gold-inlaid"*: McKelway, "Bojangles-I," p. 26.

160 *"all black men"*: *Chicago Defender*, October 11, 1930.

160 *"There are places"*: *New York Times*, July 18, 1922.

160 *"suffer from too much"*: Ashton Stevens, *Chicago Herald and Examiner*, March 31, 1924.

160 *"People who went"*: Kimble and Bolcom, *Reminiscing*, p. 181.

160 *"Colored folks"*: Jack Lait, *Variety*, August 26, 1921.

161 *The sharpest journalistic*: Salem Tutt Whitney, *Chicago Defender*, November 1, 1930.

161 *imitations of themselves*: This was more complex than he indicated, since Amos and Andy were modeled after Miller and Lyles, black artists working old minstrel conventions.

162 *1930 magazine advertisement*: *New Yorker*, September 27, 1930.

162 *Elsewhere*: Warren G. Harris, *The Other Marilyn* (Arbor House, 1985), p. 20.

163 *"marvelous, new, dirty"*: Cecil Beaton, *The Wandering Years* (Little, Brown, 1961), pp. 215–16.

163 *"but he made them": JD*, p. 165.

163 *photos of Bradley*: *The Dance*, September 1927 and January 1928.

163 *began hiring Bradley*: Michael Thornton, in his biography of Jessie Matthews (Hart-Davis, 1974), claims that Fred Astaire suggested to Matthews that she persuade Cochran to hire Bradley.

163 *prosperous Soho school*: See *Ebony*, July 1950.

164 *"a bad imitation"*: Richard Lockridge, *New York Sun*, October 23, 1930.

164 *"at the expense"*: Eric Walrond, *Opportunity*, November 1924.

164 *"Negro performers"*: Brooks Atkinson, *New York Times*, December 4, 1933.

164 *"When I see"*: Heywood Broun, *New York World*, October 30, 1934.

164 *"Regular darkie business"*: Robert Garland, *New York Telegram*, October 30, 1930.

165 *"They learn to dance"*: Edmund J. Kiefer, *New York Post*, February 5, 1929.

165 *"Negro dancing itself"*: John Martin, *New York Times*, July 8, 1928.

166 *"the primal freshness"*: Mary Austin, "Buck and Wing and Bill Robinson," *The Nation*, April 28, 1926.

166 *"in vaudeville chains"*: Alain Locke, *The Negro and His Music* (Arno Press, 1969), p. 134.

167 *"the status"*: Alain Locke, *The New Negro* (Albert and Charles Boni, 1925).

167 *"A safe and sane"*: *Chicago Defender*, December 22, 1928.

Interlude: The Color Line

169 *"white and Irish"*: Leonard Reed, interview by Fred Strickler, February 11, 1997.

170 *"I was standin' there"*: RF, p. 40.

171 *"You never have"*: *Baltimore Sun*, December 1931, quoted in Sampson, *Blacks in Blackface*, p. 68.

172 *"The audience was always"*: JD, p. 86.

9. Rhythm for Sale

175 *"The white man owned"*: *A Dancing Man* (video, directed by Dave Davidson, PBS, 1991).

175 *"I lived in a completely"*: JOH, interview by Rusty Frank, April 24, 1993.

176 *"I thought it was like a toenail"*: Ibid.

176 *"Momma, you can whip me"*: Ibid.

176 *after he kicked a sheriff's son*: *Dancing Man*.

177 *"All comedians had cork"*: JOH.

177 *"What do you dance, kid?"*: Ibid.

177 *"Not seventh heaven"*: Ibid.

178 *"One by one"*: George Tichenor, "Colored Lines," *Theatre Arts Monthly*, June 1930.

179 *"Negro dancing"*: Zora Neale Hurston, "Characteristics of Negro Expression," in *Negro: An Anthology* (Wishart, 1934), pp. 39–46.

180 *"The way you looked"*: *Dancing Man*.

180 *"Effortless steppers"*: Reprinted in *Chicago Defender*, January 13, 1923.

181 *"dovetailed"*: JD, p. 289.

181 *"footloose aristocrat"*: *New York Times*, May 27, 1932.

182 *Burns Mantle suggested*: *Daily News*, June 2, 1932.

182 *Theophilus Lewis proposed*: *New York Amsterdam News*, August 27, 1930.

182 *When he returned*: *Chicago Defender*, February 24, 1934.

182 *According to Rector's dance partner*: Ralph Cooper, *Amateur Night at the Apollo* (Harper-Collins, 1990), p. 44.

182 *convalescing*: *Chicago Defender*, October 19, 1940.

183 *"became as good"*: IJS.

183 *Colored Vaudeville Comedy Club*: *Chicago Defender*, November 29, 1924.

184 *it reopened*: *Afro-American*, October 17, 1925; *Chicago Defender,* December 19, 1925.

184 *announced officers*: *Pittsburgh Courier*, September 11, 1926.

184 *The first time*: Details from 1979 interview by George Nierenberg in ISJOH.

184 *"You don't dance"*: Ibid.

185 *"to fool the public"*: The New Yorker, August 26, 1967.

185 *Bubbles overheard*: ISJOH.

185 *Reviewers started reporting*: Chicago Tribune, September 28, 1921, and March 29, 1922.

185 *Soon he visited*: Bubbles dated this visit to 1921, but the club seems not to have existed until 1924. Buddy Bradley (*JD*, p. 215) recalled the new variations but not a date.

185 *"I didn't want 'em"*: The New Yorker, August 26, 1967.

186 *"thinking about"*: JD, p. 215.

186 *"That's what I added"*: ISJOH.

186 *These signal developments*: 1922 is the date Bubbles gave Marshall Stearns (IJS).

187 *proposed by later tap dancers*: The main proponent of this view, in many interviews, was Honi Coles.

188 *"I took the white boys' steps"*: The New Yorker, August 26, 1967.

188 *"I was everybody"*: ISJOH.

188 *"He played a lotta piano"*: Melody Maker, April–June 1954.

188 *The biggest applause*: Bernard Sobel, "Comedy Dancing," Dance, March 1947.

189 *one critic*: New York Dramatic Mirror, September 10, 1921.

189 *another critic*: New York Times, October 19, 1927.

189 *"tied the show"*: Variety, August 4, 1922.

190 *"going from the ridiculous"*: IJS.

190 *Green could still recount*: See "Buck & Bubbles and Their Act," Mura Dehn Papers, NYPL.

191 *"full of good dancers"*: ISJOH. According to Leonard Reed and Bill Bailey, Bubbles avoided the Hoofers' Club to avoid having to battle Harry Mays. Mays toured black and white vaudeville with the silver-voiced singer Danny Small. Their Buck-and-Bubbles-like act—songs, ukulele playing, and crossfire comedy, with a tap encore—played the Palace, in 1927, but split soon after. Small teamed up with his wife, while Mays confined his activities to the bar at the Band Box club, and in the obituaries that followed Small's death in 1935, his former partner is already a forgotten man.

191 *"We had lots and lots of time"*: ITAN 6, no. 5 (January–February 1996), p. 3.

193 *"Fayard was in everybody's way"*: Constance Valis Hill, Brotherhood in Rhythm (Oxford University Press, 2000), p. 47.

193 *"If I thought of something"*: Ibid., p. 49.

194 *"because we could show them"*: Ibid., p. 83.

196 *"most important"*: Reprinted in Afro-American, June 17, 1933.

196 *"magic feet"*: Defender, August 11, 1934.

196 *"the only rivals"*: Defender, June 23, 1934.

196 *Eddie Cantor affectionately spoke*: Defender, December 1, 1934.

196 *"ad lib song-and-dance"*: JD, p. 275.

198 *"Our trio had class"*: JD, p. 299.

199 *"you could close your eyes"*: Cooper, p. 138.

199 *"Correct Dress"*: Defender, June 8, 1935.

199 *As Gary*: JD, pp. 301–302.

199 *"Northern dilettantes"*: Richard Bruce Nugent, Gay Rebel of the Harlem Rennaissance (Duke University Press, 2002), p. 148.

200 *Nugent once said*: JD, p. 302.

200 *"I'm a tap dancer"*: JD, p. 301.

200 *For their 1933 debut*: ITAN 6, no. 5 (January–February 1996), p. 3.

201 *"flashy monopede"*: Courier, June 13, 1931.

201 *An ecstatic reviewer*: *Melody Maker*, June 17, 1932.

202 *Coles had been given*: Alan Kriegsman, *Washington Post*, August 16, 1980.

203 *"I felt I couldn't leave"*: *Masters of Tap* (Jolyon Wimhurst, dir., 1983).

203 *white dancers came around*: Honi Coles interview, video, WBGH, 1981.

204 *"bored, faintly annoyed"*: *New York Times* review of "Hot Rhythm," August 22, 1930.

204 *driving a taxi*: *Amsterdam News*, November 14, 1942.

205 *"a blond, pretty"*: Reprinted in *Afro-American*, May 11, 1935.

205 *Mabel claimed*: *Defender*, January 4, 1936.

205 *"She wasn't just a woman"*: Cheryl Willis, "African American Rhythm Tappers," in *Dancing Female* (Routledge, 2014).

205 *"the greatest of them all"*: IJS.

205 *"doing so much dancing"*: Germaine Ingram, *Works in Progress*, Philadelphia Folklore Project 18, no. 1 (Winter 2005).

205 *"I would take it,"*: RF, p. 127.

205 *"no bubs"*: RF, p. 120.

206 *A job offer*: *Defender*, November 16, 1935.

206 *influential gossip column*: Louella O. Parsons, *Milwaukee Sentinel*, December 13, 1934.

206 *"a child without race"*: *Defender*, January 10, 1935.

206 *Hoofers' Club*: RF, p. 126.

207 *"I want a man"*: Cholly Atkins, *Class Act* (Columbia University Press, 2001), p. 127.

207 *A crowd of hundreds*: *New York Times*, August 21 and October 24, 1934.

208 *The house chorus line*: Honi Coles, "The Dance," in *The Apollo Theater Story* (Apollo Operations, 1966).

208 *"Up in the balcony"*: Ted Fox, *Showtime at the Apollo* (Holt, Rinehart, 1983), p. 100.

211 *"Those Lindy Hoppers"*: JD, 331.

211 *"I'm not going in the pit"*: Stanley Dance, *The World of Earl Hines* (Da Capo, 1983), p. 71.

211 *started their own band*: It was a good one, with Red Allen, Hot Lips Page, and Shadow Wilson, among others.

212 *"The only time"*: Hill, *Brotherhood in Rhythm*, p. 137.

214 *"Let them kill"*: IJS.

214 *"no one"*: Arthur Pollak, *Brooklyn Eagle*, September 4, 1930.

214 *"like most darkies"*: *Judge*, November 15, 1930.

214 *"probably uttering"*: *The New Yorker*, May 16, 1931.

215 *"sweet sound"*: *New York Telegram*, January 16, 1933.

215 *in the same issue*: January 6, 1936.

215 *objected:* January 11, 1936.

216 *"refined her art"*: *New York Times*, January 31, 1936.

216 *"Maybe it comes natural"*: Hill, *Brotherhood*, p. 124.

217 *"good to see"*: *Wall Street Journal*, April 16, 1937.

218 *"After he learned"*: *George Gershwin Reader* (Oxford University Press, 2004), p. 223.

218 *giving "performances"*: Edward Jablonski, *Gershwin* (Da Capo, 1998), p. 286.

218 *interview in 1975*: Hatch-Billops collection, March 25, 1975.

218 *"Why he's—he's the black"*: Oscar Levant, *A Smattering of Ignorance* (Doubleday, 1940), pp. 179–80.

218 *"a humorous, dancing"*: *New York Times*, October 20, 1935.

218 *"clogging"*: Olin Downes, *New York Times*, October 11, 1935.

220 *"My ears could hear"*: Tony Thomas, *That's Dancing!* (Abrams, 1984), p. 129.

220 *"the rhythm boys' "*: *New York Times*, November 22, 1931.

220 *"the best dancers"*: JD, p. 192.

221 *"We nearly killed"*: Ibid., p. 193.

221 *"It got so"*: IJS.

221 *"Are there any faster"*: *Variety*, July 2, 1930.

222 *"I didn't hire him"*: Danny Daniels History of American Tap: Hal LeRoy.

223 *"the most stylish"*: *Life*, July 24, 1931.

223 *inquiring journalists*: Jane Goldberg, "John Bubbles: A Hoofer's Homage," *Village Voice*, December 4, 1978. Goldberg quotes Bubbles as saying "Ann Miller," but because of the time and location, he must have meant Marilyn.

223 *in his autobiography*: Fred Astaire, *Steps in Time* (Da Capo, 1982), pp. 49–50.

223 *private conversations*: Larry Billman, *Fred Astaire: A Bio-Bibliography* (Greenwood Press, 1997), p. xiii.

224 *Sometimes he would mention*: Sarah Giles, *Fred Astaire: His Friends Talk* (Doubleday, 1988), p. 69.

224 *Diana Vreeland*: Ibid., p. 5.

224 *"he might want to look"*: Howard Dietz, *Dancing in the Dark* (Quadrangle, 1974), p. 138.

224 *"John Bubbles was different"*: Bob Thomas, *Fred Astaire*, p. 42.

224 *"Bubbles and I"*: IJS.

224 *"like a library book"*: Todd Decker, *Music Makes Me* (University of California Press, 2011), p. 244.

224 *It was customary*: JD, p. 203.

225 *"strictly a sideline"*: Bob Thomas, *Fred Astaire*, p. 79.

225 *"Fred Astaire can dance"*: Quoted in Billman, *Fred Astaire*, p. 11.

225 *"The greatest tap dancer"*: *New Yorker*, November 29, 1930.

226 *"our most accomplished"*: *Life*, June 19, 1931.

226 *"outlaw style"*: Astaire, *Steps in Time*, p. 325.

10. How to Hoof in Hollywood

231 *"For the screen"*: Mary Mayer, "Talkies Turn Dance Tide," *Los Angeles Times*, November 2, 1930.

231 *"If you can walk in time"*: Alice L. Tildesley, "Dance Your Way into the Movies," publication unknown, December 1929.

231 *"America has gone"*: *New York Times*, August 20, 1930.

234 *the* Times *commented*: *New York Times*, January 23, 1927.

235 *"into the actual rhythmic"*: *New York Times*, July 22, 1928.

235 *"I never cared"*: Bob Pike and Dave Martin, *The Genius of Busby Berkeley* (CFS Books, 1973), p. 53.

238 *"Either the camera"*: John Winge, "How Astaire Works," *Film and Theatre Today*, January 1950, p. 8.

239 *"like writing music"*: Morton Eustis, "Fred Astaire," *Theatre Arts Monthly*, May 1937, p. 380.

239 *"You give your best"*: John Mueller, *Astaire Dancing* (Wing Books, 1991), p. 8.

240 *"master of the broken rhythm"*: Bob Thomas, *Fred Astaire*, p. 119.

240 *"became strictly black"*: RF, p. 77.

240 *"Fred and I"*: Bob Thomas, *Fred Astaire,* p. 120.

240 *The first time*: David Fantle and Tom Johnson, *Reel to Real* (Badger Books, 2009), p. 89.

240 *"dancing was transformed"*: Arlene Croce, *The Fred Astaire and Ginger Rogers Book* (Galahad Books, 1972), p. 8.

241 *"I used to do it"*: Mueller, *Astaire Dancing,* p. 16.

241 *One editor*: Eustis, "Fred Astaire," p. 9.

242 *"She sometimes threw"*: Croce, *The Fred Astaire and Ginger Rogers Book,* p. 88.

243 *"I couldn't get enough"*: Bob Shayne, "What Ever Happened to Tap Dancing," *Performing Arts: The Music Center Monthly* 2, no. 11 (1968).

243 *"You've got a little"*: Astaire, *Steps in Time,* p. 8.

246 *a story about George Gershwin*: *George Gershwin Reader,* pp. 235–36.

246 *more stereotyped scenario*: Mueller, *Astaire Dancing,* p. 109.

247 *"the first American"*: Barnett, "Fred Astaire," p. 78.

247 *"Every dance ought to"*: Eustis, "Fred Astaire," p. 381.

247 *"Tap dancing can be"*: *New York Times,* November 2, 1941.

248 *"rather specialized"*: Astaire, *Steps in Time,* p. 241.

248 *Do you tap?*: John Kobal, *People Will Talk* (New York: Knopf, 1986), p. 220.

248 *"like an algebra lesson"*: Tony Thomas, *That's Dancing!,* p. 254.

249 *"possibly the best"*: *Time,* December 5, 1932.

249 *By her own report*: Jerry Ames and Jim Siegelman, *The Book of Tap* (David McKay, 1977), p. xi.

249 *Chuck Green*: Interview by George Nierenberg, IJSOH. See also Guy Trebay, "Hoofing It," *Village Voice,* January 21, 1986.

249 *"There must be some"*: Kobal, *People Will Talk,* p. 221.

253 *"I would try to think"*: Ibid., p. 228.

253 *the papers quoted Robinson's*: *Chicago Daily Tribune,* December 6, 1934.

253 *same vaudeville bill*: Anthony Slide, *The Vaudevillians* (Arlington House, 1981), p. 18. She told the same story during a 1981 public interview by Robert Chatterton at the Variety Arts Theater in Los Angeles.

254 *"If she thought"*: Atkins, *Class Act,* p. 34.

254 *Robinson was not allowed*: Slide, *The Vaudevillians,* p. 124.

254 *Another time*: Galligan, David, "Eleanor Powell," *The Advocate,* June 11, 1981.

255 *"Let's get your feet attached"*: Shirley Temple, *Child Star* (McGraw-Hill, 1988), p. 92.

255 *dubbing her own taps*: Ibid., p. 129.

256 *"the perfect interracial love match"*: Donald Bogle, *Toms, Coons, Mulattoes, Mammies, and Bucks* (New York: Viking Press, 1973), p. 47.

256 *"the first interracial"*: Temple, *Child Star,* p. 98.

256 *"He was the happiest man"*: Mel Watkins, "That Vaudeville Style," *APF Reporter* 2, no. 6 (1979).

258 *raised hackles*: *Pittsburgh Courier,* February 20, 1937.

258 *Robinson's response*: Ibid., July 10, 1937. Sawyer became one of Hollywood's only female dance directors, at Fox, often teamed with Nick Castle.

259 *going to be redone*: *Amsterdam News,* March 27, 1943.

259 *High-profile negotiations*: See Thomas Cripps, *Slow Fade to Black* (Oxford University Press, 1993), pp. 376–78.

259 *"slinky sexy"*: *The New Yorker,* January 7, 1985.

260 *about their act*: *Life*, December 6, 1943.

261 *"The films had more meaning"*: IJSOH.

262 *"colored people"*: IJS.

262 *came upon an article*: *Dance*, February 1964.

263 *"Let me see you"*: Hill, *Brotherhood in Rhythm*, p. 177.

263 *"used his hands"*: Fantle and Johnson, *Reel to Real*, p. 84.

263 *"the whole body"*: RF, p. 72.

263 *"We were like inventors"*: Letter to Marshall Stearns, IJS.

264 *"Castle would say"*: IJS.

264 *"mostly just let them go"*: IJS.

265 *Fox didn't know*: Hill, *Brotherhood*, pp. 212–14.

268 *The Apollo Theater manager*: Jack Schiffman, *Harlem Heyday* (Prometheus Books, 1974), pp. 174–75.

268 *According to Warren*: RF, p. 161.

270 *According to LeGon*: *On Tap*, March–April 2001, p. 15.

274 *When Steve started improvising*: RF, pp. 107–109. Later, Condos also adapted to bebop, as the dancer for Woody Herman's Herd in 1944–46 and with Lennie Tristano's first trio.

274 *"I don't have it"*: RF, p. 209.

275 *"That was the first"*: Danny Daniels History of American Tap: Louis DaPron, 1978, NYPL.

276 *the taps would be dubbed*: "Robert Scheerer," *On Tap*, April–May–June 2005, p. 22.

276 *"You sure you haven't"*: RF, p. 209.

277 *"one of the great ones"*: *Baltimore Sun*, April 29, 1945.

277 *Match the music*: Interview with the author.

278 *"Buried on the campus"*: *Atlanta Constitution*, June 27, 1940.

278 *"People like to hear me"*: *New York Times*, April 30, 1950.

279 *"just average"*: *New York Times*, July 4, 1973.

281 *many choreographers*: RF, pp. 246–47.

282 *"you want to bang"*: Astaire, *Steps in Time*, p. 249.

283 *inspiration from records*: Decker, *Music Makes Me*, p. 44.

284 *"Some of them thought"*: Alvin Yudkoff, *Gene Kelly* (Backstage Books, 1999), p. 13.

284 *experts at stealing*: Clive Hirschhorn, *Gene Kelly* (W. H. Allen, 1974), p. 38.

284 *As Fred told*: RF, p. 177.

285 *the Snake Pit*: Yudkoff, *Gene Kelly*, p. 40.

285 *"At the time"*: Ibid., p.64.

285 *"After some scenes"*: Tony Thomas, *That's Dancing!*, p. 179.

286 *"A tap dancer who can"*: *New York Times*, June 8, 1941.

288 *"dancing, his time"*: Oscar Peterson, *A Jazz Odyssey* (Continuum, 2002).

289 *Almost nothing comparable*: In *You're My Everything* (1949), Dan Dailey does "Chattanooga Choo Choo" with two of the Berry Brothers, who play porters.

289 *"They thought they were looking"*: RF, p. 230.

291 *"from the waist up"*: RF, p. 151.

291 *"You can tell"*: Mindy Aloff, *Willamette Week*, 1979. Reprinted in *DanceView Times* 1, no. 3 (October 13, 2003).

291 *most underrated dancer*: Another candidate would be Eddie "Rochester" Anderson. Watch him squire a maid, Astaire-Rogers-style, in *Buck Benny Rides Again* (1940).

293 *Nelson saw himself*: *Dance*, May 1956, pp. 24–25.

294 *Pete Nugent claimed*: IJS.
294 *"The trend"*: *Dance*, February 1947, p. 14.

11. Before the Fall

297 *"Tap dancing is"*: Edwin Denby, *Dance Writings* (Knopf, 1986), p. 136.
298 *"Tap is the style"*: Walter Terry, *New York Herald Tribune*, August 31, 1941.
298 *"He does not think"*: John Martin, *New York Times*, October 28, 1934.
298 *Draper's ranking*: Irving Drutman, "18-Karat Hoofer," *Saturday Evening Post*, December 12, 1942.
299 *"to denominate him"*: *Washington Post*, March 25, 1941.
299 *"one of the major"*: Stark Young, *The New Republic*, March 30, 1942.
299 *"unique"*: John Martin, *New York Times*, October 28, 1934.
299 *"art—solacing"*: *Christian Science Monitor*, October 8, 1935.
299 *"into the realm"*: *Chicago Daily Tribune*, July 3, 1938.
299 *"a downpour of language"*: Mabel Dodge Luhan, *Intimate Memories: European Experiences* (Harcourt, Brace, 1935), p. 270.
299 *her son would suggest*: *The New Yorker*, January 7, 1939, p. 25.
300 *"I thought it would be a soft"*: *Christian Science Monitor*, October 8, 1935.
300 *"I wanted to do something"*: *Ballet Review* 5, no. 1 (1975–76).
300 *"the natural way"*: *PM*, December 24, 1946.
300 *an anonymous donor*: Leonard Lyons, *New York Post*, January 3, 1965.
300 *wrote a poem*: E. E. Cummings, *Complete Poems* (Liveright, 1994), p. 431.
300 *The exercise*: *Christian Science Monitor*, October 8, 1935.
300 *"style instead of speed"*: *New York Herald Tribune*, March 8, 1938.
301 *"the most available way"*: *Ballet Review* 5, no. 1 (1975–76).
301 *"It's not a case"*: *PM*, December 24, 1946.
302 *Wolcott Gibbs*: *The New Yorker*, January 8, 1955.
302 *Edwin Denby had faulted*: Denby, *Dance Writings*, pp. 187–88.
303 *someone called the cops*: See Adler's account in *It Ain't Necessarily So* (New York: Grove Press, 1987), p. 171, and "The Wayward Press: Greenwich Tea Party," *The New Yorker*, April 15, 1950.
304 *"beat them bowlegged"*: "Wayward Press," p. 114.
304 *"spouts the party-line"*: Adler, *It Ain't Necessarily So*, p. 165.
304 *American Legion would protest*: *New York Times*, July 22, 1955.
304 *John Martin congratulated*: *New York Times*, May 4, 1958.
305 *"His classes"*: Interview with the author.
305 *"There has never been"*: *Dance*, May 1952, p. 25.
305 *Draper had spoken*: *Christian Science Monitor*, October 8, 1935.
305 *"The important point"*: *New York Herald-Tribune*, July 11, 1954.
306 *Daniels posed*: "Tap Dance Concerto," *Dance*, March 1953.
306 *"as much like a ballet slipper"*: Interview with the author.
306 *John Martin*: *New York Times*, November 23, 1952.
306 *"Not every student"*: Paul Draper, *On Tap Dancing* (Marcel Decker, 1978), pp. 1–2.
306 *"A heavy-footed"*: Ibid., p. 87.
306 *"traditional belief"*: *Dance*, November 1959.

306 *"communicating something special"*: *Dance*, September 1956.

307 *"as an expression"*: *Dance*, August 1957.

307 *"He could do slaps"*: *Ballet Review* 5, no. 1 (1975–76).

307 *"an exceedingly fine artist"*: IJS.

307 *"It is entertainment"*: *Ballet Review* 5, no. 1 (1975–76).

307 *"He learned"*: IJS.

307 *"a very odd style"*: IJS.

307 *"no more sense"*: IJS.

307 *"saying things"*: IJS.

308 *"a man who did"*: Edwin Denby, *Looking at the Dance* (Horizon, 1968), p. 360.

308 *"I just don't feel"*: IJS.

309 *Jo Jones*: Jones could also throw a dancer if he felt like it. See "Bunny Briggs," *On Tap* 15, no. 3 (2004), p. 32.

309 *"show folks' dancer"*: *Defender*, September 5, 1942.

310 *"I called him Bravery"*: IJSOH.

310 *"When you watched"*: Atkins, *Class Act*, p. 124.

310 *"a motherfucker"*: Miles Davis, *Miles* (Simon and Schuster, 1989), p. 68.

310 *"was the show"*: Stan Britt, *Dexter Gordon* (Da Capo, 1989), p. 66.

310–311 *remembered playing*: Jane Goldberg, "A Drum Is a Tap Dancer," *Village Voice*, August 30, 1988.

311 *Pete Nugent*: JD, p. 303

311 *"This guy had absolutely"*: Atkins, *Class Act*, p. 81.

312 *"what they were known"*: Hill, *Brotherhood*, p. 225.

312 *"Can't you nigguhs"*: Dizzy Gillespie, *To Be, or Not . . . to Bop* (Doubleday, 1979), p. 223.

312 *"Jazz tap"*: IJS.

314 *Born to a Cleveland*: *Afro-American*, November 16, 1935.

314 *He once told a reporter*: Leonard Lyons, *Washington Post*, August 22, 1937.

314 *"transitional steps"*: JD, 349.

315 *"They was music"*: IJSOH.

315 *"Baby and Groundhog"*: Davis, *Miles*, p. 132.

315 *Baby Laurence later boasted*: George Wein, *Myself Among Others* (Da Capo, 2003), p. 242.

315 *in and out of jail*: *Amsterdam News*, January 18, 1958, claims that Hale had been jailed fourteen times.

315 *The trumpeter Chet Baker*: Chet Baker, *As Though I Had Wings* (St. Martin's, 1997), p. 85.

315 *deported on similar charges*: *Jet*, December 23, 1954.

315 *Leslie Uggams*: American Tap Dance Foundation gala, 1997.

316 *While strapped to a lie detector*: *Amsterdam News*, June 4, 1955.

316 *shot in the leg*: *Jet*, November 14 and December 5, 1957, and February 20, 1958.

316 *"If you weren't in"*: Davis, *Miles*, p. 133.

316 *According to Schiffman*: Jack Schiffman, *Uptown* (Cowles Book Company, 1971), p. 66.

317 *"a short, dumpy guy"*: IJS.

317 *"short and slovenly"*: IJS.

317 *probably Clarence Taylor*: *Pittsburgh Courier*, December 17, 1932, identified a Clarence "Groundhog" Taylor with the Whitman Sisters.

317 *in one interview*: IJS.

317 *"a boy who was always disappearing"*: JD, 342.

317 *federal entertainment tax*: New York Times, April 2, 22, and 25, and June 1, 1944; January 19, 1947.

318 *"No longer are routines"*: "Seymour Felix," The Dance, October 1927.

320 *"The chorus girl"*: Agnes De Mille, And Promenade Home (Little, Brown, 1956).

320 *"Bravura display"*: New York Times, December 19, 1943.

321 *"best hoofer"*: New York Times, May 24, 1940.

321 *"strives to convince"*: New York Times, July 21, 1942.

321 *"He uses taps"*: New York Times, August 16, 1942.

321 *"to be good"*: Dance, May 1946.

321 *had nothing to do*: Atkins, Class Act, pp. 90–91.

322 *"balletic flash stuff"*: RF, p. 269.

322 *In film from the early fifties*: Rock 'N' Roll Revue (Studio Films, 1955). Leonard Reed claimed to have written and directed the film.

322 *for educational television*: Camera Three, Season 10, Episode 18, "Over the Top to Bebop."

323 *struggled to get him*: IJS.

323 *"doing a white boys' act"*: Atkins, Class Act, p. 114.

324 *"Negro cast makes it"*: New York Times, September 13, 1942.

324 *Peg Leg Bates visited*: The New Yorker, November 20, 1943.

324 *Jimmy Smith*: Amsterdam News, October 31, 1942.

324 *began speculating*: In Amsterdam News, August 24, 1940, the leading candidates were Bill Bailey, Ralph Brown, and—Frank Schiffman's pick—the flash-in-the-pan Walter Green.

324 *earliest extant footage*: Rhythm and Blues Revue (Studio Films, 1955).

324 *"The nightclubs and theaters"*: IJS.

324 *While performing at Café Zanzibar*: Ebony, August 1950.

325 *"Suddenly God"*: Bill Bailey, "Why I'm Dancing Again," Negro Digest, September 1951.

325 *"When I leave this world"*: Defender, June 17, 1950. See also "Bunny Briggs: A Quality of Heart," On Tap 15, no. 2 (September–October 2004), p. 16.

325 *"the greatest thing"*: Panel Discussion at San Francisco Jazz Tap Festival, July 1987.

325 *"dressed like a gentleman"*: RF, p. 112.

325 *He had a step*: "Bunny Briggs: A Quality of Heart," p. 21.

326 *it came to him*: Briggs told this story at the By Word of Foot festival in 1980.

326 *It came to their attention*: IJS, Honi Coles and Pete Nugent files.

326 *Carnell Lyons*: Kurt Albert and Klaus Bleis, "A Tribute to Carnell Lyons," On Tap 12, no. 6 (March–April 2002), p. 11.

326 *"couldn't sell himself"*: Jesse Hamlin, San Francisco Chronicle, July 5, 1987.

326 *Barnet thought*: Charlie Barnet, Those Swinging Years (Da Capo, 1992), p. 114.

327 *Trading steps with the boys*: See Cheryl Willis, Tap Dance: Memories and Issues of African-American Women Tap Dancers . . . (PhD diss., Temple University, 1991).

328 *Cholly Atkins*: Atkins, Class Act, pp. 126–27.

329 *"His dancing is the same"*: New York Times, May 22, 1945.

329 *"We don't want to hear"*: Defender, November 1, 1941.

329 *"We call it Tom"*: Buster Brown, interview by Dianne Walker, NYPL.

329 *Robinson taking out a gun*: Haskins and Mitgang, Mr. Bojangles, pp. 218–21.

329 *newspaper accounts*: Atlanta Daily World, September 25, 1938. Soon after the incident, Fox dropped his contract.

329 *"He proved he was no Uncle Tom"*: Haskins and Mitgang, *Mr. Bojangles*, p. 201.

329 *his funeral*: *New York Times*, November 29, 1949; *New York Herald Tribune*, November 29, 1949.

330 *"everything just fell"*: Albert and Bleis, "The Buster Brown Story."

330 *"What happened"*: Hilda See, *Defender*, June 25, 1955; Ralph Mason, *Afro-American*, January 24, 1959.

12. The Break

333 *corny stories*: Haskins and Mitgang, *Mr. Bojangles*, p. 268.

333 *debut program*: Stephen Bourne, *Black in the British Frame* (Continuum, 2005), p. 60.

334 *first televised cabaret*: *Amsterdam News*, June 17, 1939.

335 *People came up to him*: *Dancing Man*.

336 *"I used more tap dancers"*: Ames and Siegelman, *Book of Tap*, p. 101.

336 *Louis DaPron*: Julie Wheelock, *Los Angeles Times*, September 2, 1984.

337 *"Ofay Femmes"*: Hilda See, *Defender*, October 14, 1955.

337 *"tap dance in the fifties"*: Billie Mahoney, *ITAN* 5, no. 6 (March–April 1995), p. 5.

337 *One night, Charlie Parker*: October 31, 1950.

337 *on a record with Moondog*: *Moondog* (Prestige Records, 1956).

338 *Cholly Atkins remembered*: Atkins, *Class Act*, p. 98.

338 *The footage of him*: *Toast of the Town*, January 22, 1950.

338 *barraged with letters*: See "The Wayward Press: Greenwich Tea Party."

338 *when Lincoln-Mercury dealers*: *Amsterdam News*, June 7, 1952.

340 *"indestructible constitution"*: *New York Times*, April 14, 1955.

340 *Bunny Briggs recalled*: Jane Goldberg, *Shoot Me While I'm Happy* (Woodshed Productions, 2008), p. 59.

340 *during a 1964 Christmas show*: IJSOH.

341 *"I didn't take chances"*: Interview with the author, May 6, 2004.

342 *"done more for the cause"*: *New York Times*, October 18, 1958.

343 *history of tap*: The tap history told in *Bell Telephone Hour*'s 1966 "The Song and Dance Man" fixed Lancashire clogging as the root, crediting Irish reels, Spanish zapateado, and German schuhplattler as influences on buck dancing, and putting the American Negro in the mix only as "a little of this, a little of that." Then the host, Donald O'Connor, danced with the Nicholas Brothers.

344 *went on a diet*: *New York Times*, June 16, 1961.

345 *"It didn't bother us"*: Interview with the author, August 28, 2002.

345 *"They said colored people"*: Ibid.

348 *One story*: Sammy Davis, Jr., *Sammy: An Autobiography* (Farrar, Straus and Giroux, 2000), pp. 57–60.

348 *"I've got to have them"*: *Playboy*, December 1966.

351 *"the most exciting Negro"*: Davis, *Sammy*, p. 195.

351 *"people weren't coming"*: Fox, *Showtime at the Apollo*, p. 176.

352 *opinions on index cards*: Frank Schiffman Apollo Theater Collection, National Museum of American History.

352 *"tap may be a vanishing art"*: *Amsterdam News*, November 21, 1964.

352 *He complained*: *Pittsburgh Courier*, January 30, 1965.

353 *He would offer*: Jacqui Malone, *Steppin' on the Blues* (University of Illinois Press, 1996), p. 118. See also Honi Coles interview, video, WBGH, 1981.

353 *teach them something nostalgic*: Atkins, *Class Act*, p. 161.

13. Continuation

354 *on their way home*: "Closing The Gap: Leroy Myers," *On Tap* 15, no. 3 (Winter 2004).

355 *"We communicated"*: David Hajdu, *Lush Life* (Farrar, Straus and Giroux, 1996), p. 118.

355 *"We had great times"*: Video interview of Buster Brown by Sebastian Weber, October 16, 2001.

356 *"of the kind that becomes legendary"*: *New Yorker*, July 21, 1962.

357 *Several witnesses*: Burt Goldbatt, *Newport Jazz Festival: An Illustrated History* (Dial Press, 1977), p. 95. The book reproduces a few frames that Goldblatt filmed with his 8mm camera—precious footage evidently lost.

357 *"If you get in there"*: "Bunny Briggs: A Quality of Heart," *On Tap* 15, no. 3 (2004). He applied the same strategy during an appearance on the Jack Paar show, August 1, 1962.

357 *Voice of America audio*: "Newport Jazz Festival, July 6, 1963," Voice of America Music Library Collection, Library of Congress.

357 *the jazz bassist Charles Mingus*: George Frazier, *Boston Sunday Herald*, July 8, 1967.

358 *"It was a daily prayer"*: IJSOH.

358 *"Chuck was having some problems"*: Buster Brown, interview by Sebastian Weber, 2001.

358 *"infallible pendulum rhythm"*: *New Yorker*, November 22, 1976.

359 *she accompanied the dancer*: Linda Dahl, *Morning Glory* (University of California Press, 2001), p. 254.

359 *Dannie Richmond*: Jane Goldberg, "Drum Is a Tap Dancer."

359 *The short* New Yorker *article*: February 20, 1960.

359 *grandiloquently polite letters*: IJS.

359 *traded Laurence milk*: Patrick O'Connor, "Tap Happening," *Dance*, August 1969, p. 42.

360 *claimed to have invented*: Elinor Rogosin, "Chatting with the Hoofers," *Eddy*, no. 8 (Spring 1976). Other times, he credited L. D. Jackson, a cellmate of his who had learned the steps from Carnell Lyons.

360 *"I've been waiting to battle"*: IJS.

360 *"It was not exactly"*: JS, p. 347.

360 *"Dancing jumped"*: JS, p. 345.

360 *"dancers have been persecuted"*: IJS.

361 *film made for educational television*: *A Concert of Sacred Music at Grace Cathedral* (directed by Ralph J. Gleason). Ellington also brought Briggs back onto *The Ed Sullivan Show*.

361 *"the American mentality"*: Jimmy Slyde, interview by Sally Sommer, August 2, 1996. NYPL.

361 *"Tap . . . is not a big ticket-selling"*: Interview with the author, May 4, 2004.

362 *He would stress that slides*: *About Tap*.

363 *one of their jokes*: JOH, April 27, 1993.

364 *"not merely the best"*: *New York Times*, December 27, 1968.

364 *"The most highly developed"*: JD, p. 358.

365 *They said the same of him*: Atkins, *Class Act*, pp. 138–42.

366 *"taken for granted"*: New Yorker, May 17, 1969.

367 *Out of a Ned Wayburn*: Jill Silverman, "Hoofers Are on Tap," *New York Times*, March 1980.

367 *"one of our two really indigenous"*: Dance, August 1963. Jay told the "pages and pages" story at the By Word of Foot festival in 1980.

367 *dismissed the tap dancing*: Dance, March 1963.

367 *"trying to show"*: Dance, February 1965.

367 *prescient proposal*: IJS.

368 *Jay wasn't the first*: The Russian émigrée Mura Dehn had been performing her own version of jazz dance since 1930. In the mid-fifties, she presented the occasional "Concert of Jazz Dance Theater" with James Berry, and filmed the invaluable documentary *The Spirit Moves*. Starting in 1960, she incorporated Baby Laurence, Buster Brown, and Chuck Green into Razzle Dazzle Scintillators concerts at community centers, and in 1968, she took Brown, Cookie Cook, and other hoofers on a State Department tour of Africa.

368 *prompting reviews*: New York Times, November 9, 1968.

368 *"like a big prize fight"*: Rogosin, "Chatting with the Hoofers."

368 *when he attended*: Stearns notes from June 3, 1963, IJS.

368 *"The real lovers"*: New York Times, December 21, 1963.   ·

369 *Buttonholing Dahdah*: Bob Dahdah, interview with the author, January 11, 2002.

369 *a flyer*: IJS.

369 *gigs in a Maryland mall*: Washington Post, March 4, 1969.

369 *Honi Coles had been announced*: Amsterdam News, April 5, 1969.

369 *"a veteran trouper"*: New York Times, August 1, 1967.

370 *inform interviewers*: Rogosin, "Chatting with the Hoofers."

370 *More plausibly*: New York Times, September 9, 1977; Los Angeles Times, September 20, 1985.

370 *he was inspired by Hal LeRoy*: IJS.

370 *that biography*: Interview with author, July 15, 2002. See also *Danny Daniels History of American Tap: Jerry Ames*.

370 *"token integration"*: O'Connor, "Tap Happening."

370 *"You may not think"*: New York, July 21, 1969.

371 *Walter Kerr*: New York Times, August 31, 1969.

371 *"some of the most gorgeous"*: June 29, 1969.

371 *When Draper attended*: Bob Dahdah, interview with the author.

371 *reels that remain*: Footage of film of *Tap Happening*, May 12, 1969. 20 min. NYPL.

371 *"the most skillful dancer"*: New York Post, July 30, 1969.

371 *Ames recalled*: Interview with the author.

14. Revival

376 *"I wanted to show"*: Ames and Siegelman, *Book of Tap*, p. 109.

376 *"a lost pleasure"*: New York Times, January 31, 1971.

376 *Clive Barnes confided*: New York Times, January 20, 1971.

376 *"If you do a musical"*: Ibid., p. 112.

377 *the ghosts were supposed to*: Ethan Mordden, *One More Kiss* (Palgrave Macmillan, 2003), p. 38.

377 *"Tap dancing on the stage"*: Quoted in John Anthony Gilvey, *Before the Parade Passes By* (New York: St. Martins, 2005), p. 248.

380 *The dancewear supplier Capezio*: *Wall Street Journal*, July 11, 1977.

380 *housewives and suburban fathers*: Don Kerwin, "Are You Ready for the Tap Boom," *Chicago Tribune*, October 22, 1972.

380 *"The worse the economy gets"*: *Newsweek*, April 7, 1975.

380 *"trying to salvage"*: Ames and Siegelman, *Book of Tap*, p. 26.

381 *"Why did tap die out?"*: Ibid., pp. 98 and 18.

381 *"The final challenge"*: Ibid., p. 115.

382 *"When my solo came"*: Interview with the author.

382 *"Each one of us"*: Green, IJSOH.

382 *A short documentary*: *Jazz Hoofer: The Legendary Baby Laurence* (directed by Bill Hancock, 1981).

15. Renaissance

383 *"tap dancing is a thing"*: "Newport Jazz Festival, July 6, 1973," Voice of America Music Library Collection, Library of Congress.

383 *nobody wants to see*: Brenda Bufalino, interview with the author, November 8, 2001.

384 *"You don't belong here"*: RF, p. 274.

384 *"I was built for it"*: Interview with the author.

384 *She was accused*: Brenda Bufalino, interview by Rusty Frank, April 21, 1993, JOH.

384 *"They used to stand"*: Steven Harper, "An Interview with Brenda Bufalino," *ITAN* 10, no. 4 (November–December 1999).

385 *"You have to give up rhythm"*: Interview with the author.

387 *her own 1978 concert*: "Singing, Swinging and Winging" (DVD, 1978), NYPL.

388 *she would recall:* Brenda Bufalino, *Tapping the Source* (Codhill Press, 2004), p. 58.

389 *"Somebody"*: Jane Goldberg, "It's All in the Feet," *Patriot Ledger*, April 24, 1974.

389 *her first instructional session*: Jane Goldberg, "Tap Festival," *Dancescope*, Autumn 1981.

390 *"You're dancing like"*: Goldberg, *Shoot Me*, p. 47.

390 *"That's what the time steps"*: Abby Wasserman, "Tap Dancing: A Rediscovered Art Form," *Washington Star*, January 6, 1979.

391 *The initial plan*: Interview with the author.

391 *The evening began*: *It's About Time*, videotape, NYPL.

391 *"Break down the doors"*: *New York Times*, February 26, 1978.

391 *Goldberg's next show*: *Shoot Me While I'm Happy*, videotape, NYPL.

392 *"a favorite aunt"*: Sally Sommer, "Tap Roots," *Village Voice*, March 19, 1979.

392 *film collection of Ernie Smith*: Now housed at the Smithsonian Institution. Also see "Talk of the Town," *The New Yorker*, November 25, 1961.

393 *"She Saved Tap Dancing"*: *Jewish Community Voice*, November 14, 1980.

393 *John Bubbles*: Goldberg, "A Hoofer's Homage."

393 *"interested in this idea"*: *By Word of Foot*, videotape, NYPL.

393 *Carroll noted*: Noël Carroll, *Dance*, January 1981.

394 *"This has got to change"*: Sally Sommer, "The Rhythm Method," *Village Voice*, October 29, 1980.

394 *"The greatest tap dancers"*: Sommer, "Tap Roots."

394 *Marcia Siegel*: "Where Up Meets Down," *New York*, March 26, 1979.

395 *"Those who study"*: *The New Yorker*, October 23, 1978.

396 *"That tap dancers"*: Goldberg, "Tap Festival."

396 *According to Bufalino*: Interview with the author.

396 *"You've put me in a funny spot"*: Honi Coles interview, video, WBGH, 1981.

397 *an adulatory profile*: Caila Abedon, "Still Dancing After All These Years," *New York*, May 21, 1978.

398 *Sandman Sims, a Hoofer*: Harold Cromer, interview with the author, 2006.

398 *"biographies, inescapably"*: Arlene Croce, "Doing the Old Low Down," *The New Yorker*, April 28, 1980.

398 *"Maybe they're not ready"*: Anne Levin, *Other Stages*, December 27, 1979.

399 *Dizzy Gillespie would remember*: David Wadsworth, "Bebop Hoofer Leon Collins," *ITAN* 8, no. 4 (November–December 1997).

399 *"It makes me disgusted"*: *Songs Unwritten: Leon Collins* (video documentary, directed by David Wadsworth, 1989).

399 *"It doesn't belong to us"*: Ibid.

399 *Collins was notably less generous*: Dianne Walker, interview with the author, January 17, 2002.

399 *"throw you to the wolves"*: Pam Raff, interview with the author, January 17, 2003.

400 *she was newly divorced*: Joan Hill, interview with the author, March 2004.

400 *The street corners*: Carolyn Clark, "Eddie Brown," *ITAN* 3, no. 4 (May–June 1992).

401 *In New York*: *Eddie Brown's Scientific Rhythm* (video documentary, directed by Sharon Arslanian, 1990).

401 *This meant visiting the home*: Maggie Lewis, "Reveille for Taps," *Christian Science Monitor*, January 2, 1980.

402 *"Is it in the box?"*: Heather Cornell, interview with the author, September 27, 2001.

402 *"It was more than just picking up steps"*: Lewis, "Reveille for Taps."

402 *"I like to get up"*: *Eddie Brown's Scientific Rhythm*.

402 *"And, like, I didn't have to see"*: Lewis, "Reveille for Taps."

402 *Dally's father*: Lynn Dally, interview with the author, 2001.

403 *"He had a white Afro"*: Fred Strickler, interview with the author, 2001.

403 *"the former tap dancer"*: *Pittsburgh Courier*, November 7, 1959.

403 *he would die*: Janice-Laureen Arkatov, *Los Angeles Times*, January 17, 1982.

404 *"a little overstarched"*: Croce, "Doing the Old Low Down."

405 *"You're supposed to be someone"*: Chuck Green, interview by Mura Dehn. NYPL.

406 *feeding Green walnuts*: George Nierenberg, interview with the author, 2006.

406 *"I like to talk about"*: IJSOH.

406 *traveling with Green posed challenges*: George Nierenberg, interview with the author, 2006.

407 *"I get in a trance"*: Transcript of 1986 Colorado Dance Festival panel discussion, *ITAN* 8, no. 2 (July–August 1997).

408 *"They mixed it in with our dancing"*: Sandman Sims, interview by Camille Billops, Hatch-Billops Collection.

408 *"genuine American invention"*: "Variety Shows," *New York Times*, April 9, 1876.

16. Lineage

410 *"natural rhythm"*: *Ebony*, April 1948.

410 *"So we went to his dressing room"*: Maurice Hines, interview with the author, June 29, 2007.

411 *TV footage*: See "The Hines Brothers" and "Music on Ice," NYPL.

411 *"Henry would insist"*: *Eye on Dance: Rhythm's the Name of the Game* (videotape, 1986), NYPL.

412 *"I wanted to be real"*: Dinitia Smith, "Jelly on a Roll," *New York*, June 8, 1992.

412 *He worked as a busboy*: Joyce Wadler, *Washington Post*, February 24, 1985.

412 *two men's-sensitivity groups*: Orde Coombs, *New York*, March 30, 1981.

413 *"It's no secret"*: *New York Times*, March 2, 1981.

413 *Long Island talent-show champion*: *Amsterdam News*, September 11, 1976.

413 *he knew almost no tap*: Sheryl Flatow, "Tap Happy," *Ballet News*, June 1985.

414 *tapped on the man's coffee table*: Pamela Sommers, *Washington Post*, February 12, 1989.

416 *"Sure, he was putting"*: Ibid.

417 *satisfied the eleven-year-old*: Hines commented on his floor during a press conference at the Woodpecker's Tap Dance Center, August 21, 1992. See also Sally Sommer, "Tap Happy," *Dance*, December 1988.

418 *The core of Weber's childhood*: Sam Weber, interview with the author, August 2001.

419 *"That's another thing"*: Transcription of 1986 Colorado Dance Festival panel discussion, *ITAN* 8, no. 3 (September–October 1997).

420 *Bufalino recounts fretting*: Bufalino, *Tapping the Source*, p. 72.

420 *"probably the pivotal experience"*: Bufalino, interview with the author.

420 *bad for their breasts*: Jane Goldberg, "Tapping into View," *Jazz*, Winter 1978.

421 *"Yeah, they could dance"*: Dianne Walker, interview with the author.

421 *"There is no masculine"*: *By Word of Foot II* (videotape), NYPL.

422 *"While you can admire her"*: Burt Supree, *Village Voice*, July 17, 1990.

422 *"Supermoms of Tap"*: Katherine Kramer, *ITAN* 3, no. 3 (September–October 1992).

423 *devoted two sentences*: Sally Sommer, *Village Voice*, April 3, 1984.

423 *the Invisible Woman*: Goldberg, *Shoot Me*, p. 187.

423 *pick it up again fifteen years later*: Rachel L. Swarns, *New York Times*, June 11, 1996.

424 *"My idea of winning"*: Goldberg, *Shoot Me*, p. 183.

424 *"for the millions"*: Marcia Siegel, *Christian Science Monitor*, November 6, 1986.

424 *"Technically, they've got their feet"*: *Village Voice*, November 11, 1986.

17. Choreography and the Company Model

425 *"Having a choreographer"*: *JD*, p. 341.

426 *"a framework"*: "Future for a Tap Company," *Dance*, May 1963.

427 *"Tap must be perceived"*: "Beyond the Solo," *ITAN* 1, no. 2 (February 1989).

427 *"the temple"*: Quoted in Jerome Delamater, *Dance in the Hollywood Musical* (UMI Research Press, 1988.)

427 *"Their taps"*: Twyla Tharp, *Push Comes to Shove* (Bantam Books, 1992), p. 135. The avant-garde was interested. Merce Cunningham, James Waring, and Yvonne Rainer all attended *Tap Happening*.

428 *one of her methods*: Marcia Siegel, *Howling Near Heaven* (St. Martin's, 2006), p. 107.

428 *"Cookie fell into my life"*: Gail Conrad, interview with the author, November 2008.

429 *ears of other critics*: Alan M. Kriegsman, *Washington Post*, March 5, 1983.

429 *"too little of which"*: *New Yorker*, January 28, 1985.

430 *learned that tap*: Linda Sohl-Donnell, interview with the author, June 21, 2001.

430 *"I became fascinated"*: Linda Sohl-Donnell, "A Los Angeles Inspiration," *ITAN* 5, no. 1 (May–June 1994).

430 *"There has never been"*: Sondra Lowell, *Los Angeles Times*, August 17, 1979.

432 *Growing up outside Chicago:* Anita Feldman, interview with the author, March 15, 2002.

432 *she commissioned a composer*: Anita Feldman, "Tap Scored," *ITAN* 1, no. 3 (Spring 1989).

432 *Tap Dance Instrument*: Anita Feldman, "The Tap Dance Instrument," *ITAN* 1, no. 2 (February 1989).

434 *"In ten seconds"*: Heather Cornell, interview with the author.

435 *"The true intent"*: "Closing the Gap," *On Tap* 18, no. 1 (Summer 2007).

436 *"To me"*: Brenda Bufalino, interview with the author.

438 *"It's like kissing a girl"*: "Closing the Gap," *On Tap* 11, no. 3 (September–October 2000).

438 *"I have permission"*: Linda Sohl-Donnell, interview with the author.

438 *"We couldn't have done this"*: Brenda Bufalino, interview with the author. Leslie Gaines told her that he did sometimes think that way, in the old days, but that the audience never would have accepted it.

439 *"Sometimes, I would impose"*: Linda Sohl-Donnell, interview with the author.

439 *"not such a good dance"*: Brenda Bufalino, interview with the author.

439 *"following him around"*: "Los Angeles Inspiration."

440 *"Lots of places"*: Linda Sohl-Donnell, interview with the author.

18. Black and Blue on Broadway

442 *Tune had learned*: Tommy Tune, *Footnotes* (Simon and Schuster, 1997).

443 *"a rare reminder"*: Frank Rich, *New York Times*, May 2, 1983.

443 *In rehearsals*: Tune, *Footnotes*, p. 197.

444 *he told Brenda Bufalino*: Bufalino, interview with the author.

444 *Tune tells of a Saturday matinee*: Tune, *Footnotes*, p. 197.

445 *a tap history concert*: Danny Daniels, interview with the author, June 2001.

446 *"It isn't black"*: Danny Daniels, interview by Jane Goldberg, *Footprint* 1, no. 2, (Fall 1984).

446 *"At the first meeting"*: Daniels, interview with the author.

447 *credited with keeping the show*: Samuel G. Freedman, *New York Times*, February 2, 1984.

448 *how she would tell the story*: Savion Glover and Bruce Weber, *Savion* (William Morrow, 2000), p. 40.

449 *"I didn't really feel"*: Ibid., p. 58.

449 *His life*: Geri Bain, "Savion Glover," *Dance Pages*, Spring 1985.

449 *"You dance for me"*: Dianne Walker, interview with the author.

450 *LeTang couldn't believe it*: Henry LeTang, interview with the author, December 20, 2001.

450 *"I saw it wasn't about pleasing"*: Glover and Weber, *Savion*, p. 58.

451 *"and he let you know"*: Dianne Walker, interview with the author.

451 *"But he never told me"*: Deborah Mitchell, interview with the author, August 25, 2003.

451 *Ted Levy's mother*: Ted Levy, interview with the author, 2001.

452 *"There was a war"*: Tarik Winston, interview with the author, April 1, 2009.

452 *some critics read the show*: Arlene Croce, *The New Yorker*, February 6, 1989.

452 *other reviewers*: Eva Resnikova, *The New Criterion*, April 1989.

455 *"Get over here"*: Dianne Walker, interview with the author.

456 *"confirmed the art form's rebirth"*: *New York Times*, September 20, 1989.

456 *"It is no exaggeration"*: *New York Times*, December 23, 1992.

456 *Tap America Project*: Nicola Daval and Carol Vaughn, "How We Got Our Day," *ITAN* 5, no. 1 (May–June 1994).

457 *"By golly"*: Jacqueline Trescott, *Washington Post*, September 15, 1988.

457 *"Everyone we knew"*: Traci Mann, interview with the author, January 15, 2002.

19. Young Again

458 *His friends heard a crash*: Sarah Petronio, interview with the author, March 2002.

461 *"cultural strip mining"*: Jon Pareles, *New York Times*, April 15, 1992.

461 *family history*: Dinitia Smith, *New York*, "Jelly on a Roll."

462 *"winning was never in question"*: John Lahr, "King Tap," *The New Yorker*, October 30, 1995.

464 *"I had no idea"*: Jimmy Tate, interview with the author, January 12, 2003.

464 *"hulking"*: Jennifer Dunning, *New York Times*, August 31, 1994.

469 *"victimology"*: Robert Brustein, *The New Republic*, March 4, 1996.

469 *"Tap dancing and show business"*: "Closing the Gap," *ITAN* 10, no. 1 (May–June 1999), p. 25.

471 *"It was like being reborn"*: Derick Grant, interview with the author, April 9, 2001.

471 *"It taught me"*: Jason Samuels Smith, interview with the author, March 2, 2001.

471 *"I love Savion"*: Pamela Sommers, *Washington Post*, June 9, 1996.

471 *if George Wolfe had been white*: *ITAN* 7, no. 3 (September–October 1996).

471 *"misplaced black nationalism"*: *The New Republic*, April 15, 1996.

472 *"Only a nitwit"*: *ITAN* 7, no. 3 (September–October 1996).

472 *"If we revert"*: Brenda Bufalino, interview with the author.

473 *"being yourself"*: Kevin Courtney, *Irish Times*, March 5, 1996.

473 *Perry's younger brother reported*: Nelson Presley, *Washington Times*, February 8, 1998.

475 *"eight hundred years"*: Michael Flatley with Douglas Thompson, *Lord of the Dance* (Touchstone, 2006), p. 103.

476 *"It was my chance"*: Tarik Winston, interview with the author.

478 *"Theaters wanted bolder"*: Linda Sohl-Donnell, interview with the author.

479 *Her old friend Gregory Hines*: Elaine Dutka, *Los Angeles Times*, March 12, 1998.

480 *"one of the most inventive"*: Gary Giddins, *Village Voice*, June 17, 1998.

481 *"Eight shows a week"*: Dormeshia Sumbry-Edwards, interview with the author, March 21, 2001.

481 *"When I saw it"*: Ayodele Casel, interview with the author, April 16, 2009.

482 *"the forgotten mothers"*: Itabari Njeri, *Village Voice*, July 28, 1998.

483 *"I'm not going to give anyone"*: Anne Midgette, *Los Angeles Times*, March 28, 2000.

483 *"contributions"*: Gia Kourlas, *Time Out New York*, December 2000.

20. Danse à Claquettes, Steptanz, Sapateado, タップダンス

487 *"Everybody there wants"*: Ames and Siegelman, *Book of Tap*, p. 121.

488 *"dancing is as natural"*: J. Murray Smith, *Royal Pictorial*, reprinted in *Defender*, September 1, 1934.

488 *The career of Louis Douglas*: Rainer E. Lotz, *Black People* (Lotz, 1997).

489 *"the essential characteristics"*: *André Levinson on Dance* (Wesleyan University Press, 1991), pp. 70–75.

490 *"Mister Douglas is a genius"*: Alfred Polgar, *Auswahl* (Rowohlt, 1968), pp. 282–83. My translation.

490 *"distinctly racial"*: *Pittsburgh Courier*, July 23, 1927.

491 *"good tap dancing"*: Edgar A. Wiggins, *Afro-American*, March 4, 1933.

491 *a series of articles*: Irene West, "The Dancing Twins," *Afro-American*, October 26, 1946.

491 *"uneducated colored boys"*: Langston Hughes, *I Wonder as I Wander* (Octagon, 1974), pp. 252–55.

492 *when a friend took her*: Sarah Petronio, interview with the author.

492 *"He never arrived"*: Melba Huber, *Dance Universe*, December 1, 2003.

494 *In her memoirs*: Marika Rökk, *Herz mit Paprika* (Heyne, 1976).

495 *a purely German story*: Esabe George, *Deutsche Tanzzeitschrift*, 1941.

495 *Jazz was never banned*: See Michael H. Kater, *Different Drummers* (Oxford University Press, 1992).

496 *"cheering, fresh, and precise"*: Evelyn Künneke, *Sing Evelyn Sing* (Rowohlt, 1982), p. 40. My translation.

496 *dancer's paternal grandparents*: Peter J. Levinson, *Puttin' On the Ritz* (St. Martin's, 2009), p. 1.

497 *"She's a genius"*: Kurt Albert, interview with the author.

497 *"Their aesthetic was"*: Sam Weber, interview with the author.

497 *"I never thought"*: Kurt Albert, interview with the author.

498 *"be a dancer"*: Sebastian Weber, interview with the author, July 4, 2009.

498 *"from God"*: Alexander Ivashkevich, interview with the author, July 24, 2001.

499 *"These people have rhythm"*: Vladimir Blum, "The Negro Operetta," *Zhizn' Iskusstva* (March 23, 1926), quoted in Sally Banes, *Writing Dancing in the Age of Postmodernism* (Wesleyan University Press, 1994), pp. 165–66.

500 *Leonid Utesov*: See S. Frederick Starr, *Red and Hot* (Oxford University Press, 1983). The black American Henry Scott, lured to the U.S.S.R with the promise of an education, became somewhat famous as a tap dancer with Alexander Tsfasman's orchestra in Moscow. See Aljean Harmetz, *New York Times*, November 5, 1989.

502 *"But I was impatient"*: Konstantin Nevretdinov, interview with the author, June 2001.

503 *on the black ships of Commodore Perry*: Victor Fell Yellin, "Mrs. Belmont, Matthew Perry, and the Japanese Minstrels," *American Music* 14, no. 3 (Autumn 1996), pp. 257–75.

504 *"He's got the Japanese personality"*: *Hartford Courant*, July 23, 1935.

505 *The Japanese-American tap dancer*: Dorothy Toy, interview with the author, March 2004. See also interviews with Toy and Wing in the 1994 revision of Rusty Frank's *Tap!*

505 *Kaoru Tomita*: Interview with the author, March 2003.

506 *"I found out what it is"*: Hideyuki Higuchi, interview with the author, March 2003.

506 *Kazu Kumagai*: Interview with the author, March 2003.

507 *"Kazu can get a taxi"*: Barbara Duffy, interview with the author.

509 *Guillem Alonso*: Interview with the author, September 15, 2001.

510 *"blacks taken to America"*: Grant Swift, interview with the author, e-mail correspondence, 2009.

511 *Steven Harper*: Interview with the author, July 12, 2001.

511 *Valéria Pinheiro*: Interview with the author, July 2, 2002.

512 *William Orlowski*: Interview with the author, August 21, 2009.

514 *The Clark Brothers*: Stephen Clark, *Living with Legends* (Bartham Press, 2000).

514 *Will Gaines*: *Guardian*, October 9, 1981.

514 *Junior Laniyan*: Interview with the author, e-mail correspondence, August 2009.

515 *"it had thoughts behind it"*: Olivia Rosencrantz, interview with the author, July 2002.

515 *Mari Fujibayashi*: Interview with the author, July 7, 2002.

516 *Herbin Van Cayseele's story*: Sally Sommer, "A Tapper Named Tamango," *Dance*, February 2001.

516 *"It was not especially about dance"*: Jennifer Dunning, *New York Times*, February 4, 2001.

517 *"I'm not a teenager"*: *Time Out New York*, May 1–8, 1996.

517 *"One is tempted"*: *New York Times*, December 26, 1999.

518 *Roxane Semadeni*: Interview with the author, July 2001.

519 *Max Pollak*: Interview with the author, July 2001.

519 *Before a performance*: Jeannie Hill, interview with the author, October 17, 2002.

521 *Chikako Iwahori*: Interview with the author, September 13, 2001.

521 *"That's not true"*: Max Pollak, interview with the author.

21. Where's the Dance?

524 *He informed interviewers*: Lola Ogunnaike, *New York Times*, December 29, 2003.

524 *"corrupted"*: Karen Campbell, *Boston Globe*, October 6, 2002.

524–525 *"Too much experimenting"*: Molly Glentzer, *Houston Chronicle*, December 22, 2002.

525 *"you don't mix bananas"*: Jane Goldberg, *Dance*, December 2002.

525 *"hear it as music"*: Jim Carnes, *Star Tribune* (Minneapolis), November 6, 2006.

525 *"experimentation is in the music"*: Goldberg, *Dance*, December 2002.

526 *"tedious"*: Alastair Macaulay, *New York Times*, June 22, 2010.

528 *John Rockwell pointed out*: *New York Times*, December 28, 2006.

528 *"someone wanted tap"*: Sarah Kaufman, *Washington Post*, December 17, 2006.

530 *mainly restricted to evocations*: The tapped death by electric chair in Stroman's 2010 production of *The Scottsboro Boys* is an exception.

530 *"it was like recovering"*: Derick Grant, interview with the author.

536 *compare her favorably*: Michelle Dorrance, interview with the author, January 12, 2002.

ACKNOWLEDGMENTS

For taking on a project of this size and scope, I have no one to blame but myself. For helping me complete it, however, I have many people to thank. The book began as a thesis project in the writing department of the School of the Arts at Columbia University, and I was highly fortunate in the encouragement and guidance I received from Richard Locke, Patty O'Toole, Honor Moore, Michael Scammell, Brenda Wineapple, and my fellow students. Lis Harris deserves special credit for first proposing that I should write about tap. All through the process, Michael Janeway was a model, a mentor, and a friend; my joy in seeing this book into print is darkened by my regret that I didn't finish in time to give him a copy.

I am thankful to the editors at several publications who allowed me to try out my ideas about tap on the job: Elizabeth Zimmer and Brian Parks at *The Village Voice*; Wendy Lesser at *The Threepenny Review*; Wendy Perron at *Dance Magazine*, Liesl Schillinger, Shauna Lyon, Yvette Siegert, and Katia Bachko at *The New Yorker*; Fletcher Roberts, Julie Bloom, Myra Forsberg, and Alastair Macaulay at *The New York Times*. Some of what I wrote for those publications also appears, in different form, in this book.

I am beholden to the staffs of the Schomburg Center for Research in Black Culture, the Hatch-Billops Collection, the Library of Congress, the Smithsonian Institution, the Academy of Dance on Film, the Museum of Television & Radio (now the Paley Center for Media), the Harvard Theatre Collection, and especially the fine people at the Institute of Jazz Studies at Rutgers University and the New York Public Library for the Performing Arts, where I spent countless hours. Norton Owen at Jacob's Pillow amazed me with his eagerness to assist. Stays at Blue Mountain Center, Yaddo, and the MacDowell Colony were of great help in the project's development. I thank Patsy Tarr and 2wice Arts Foundation for a grant.

The scholars Tony Barrand, Frank Cullen, Dale Cockrell, Stephen Johnson, W. T. Lhamon, Jr., William J. Mahar, and Keri Smith magnanimously responded to my queries and improved the book with their suggestions. Kate Draper opened up her father's archive. Hans-Joachim Schmidt sent me a CD of Teddy Hale on *The Eddie Condon Floor Show*. Mark Cantor gave me a precious copy of John Bubbles in *In and Out*. Norikoshi Takao was an important source about tap in Japan, as was Elizabeth Souritz about tap in Russia and Uwe Meusel about tap in Germany. Liber Scal and Alicia Batana graciously sent me much material on tap in Argentina. By granting me access during the early years of the New York City Tap Festival, Tony Waag sped up my tap education. Jane Goldberg was more open than I deserved with her exceptional archive and many frank conversations. Beyond accompanying me on spelunking trips in various libraries and contributing many finds from Germany, Kurt Albert was a steadfast companion in research, the only person I knew as interested in tap arcana as I was.

I am grateful to the many people who generously gave of their time and knowledge in interviews: Susan Abbot, Kurt Albert, Charon Aldredge, Lane Alexander, Guillem Alonso, Jerry Ames, Chloe Arnold, Bob Audy, Ofer Ben, Ira Bernstein, Klaus Bleis, Bunny Briggs, Brenda Bufalino, Roxane Butterfly, Ayodele Casel, Cintia Chamecki, Lorraine Condos, Gail Conrad, Heather Cornell, Skip Cunningham, Bob Dahdah, Lynn Dally, Danny Daniels, Christina Delius, Alfred Desio, Michelle Dorrance, Barbara Duffy, Arthur Duncan, Anita Feldman, Rod Ferrone, Claudio Figuera, Rusty Frank, Mari Fujibayashi, Melissa Giattino, Jane Goldberg, Susan Goldbetter, Derick Grant, Steven Harper, Higuchi Hideyuki, Josh Hilberman, Jeannie Hill, Joan Hill, Maurice Hines, Alexander Ivashkevitch, Chikako Iwahori, Marc Bamuthi Joseph, Rhythm Kaneko, Arlene Kennedy, Katharine Kramer, Kazu Kumagai, Jenny Lane, Junior Laniyan, Stefanie Larriere, Jeni LeGon, Michela Marino Lerman, Henry LeTang, Ted Levy, Jacqui Malone, Traci Mann, Thomas Marek, Cintia Martin, Uwe Meusel, Avi Miller, Deborah Mitchell, Margaret Morrison, Pia Neises, Miriam Nelson, Andrew Nemr, Konstantin Nevretdinov, George Nierenberg, William Orlowski, Denise Pennington-Sheerer, Sarah Petronio, Leela Petronio, Valéria Pinheiro, Max Pollak, Tina Pratt, Pam Raff, Leonard Reed, Robert Reed, LaVaughn Robinson, Olivia Rosencrantz, Sara Safford, Bob Sheerer, Jason Samuels Smith, Linda Sohl-Donnell, Prince Spencer, Peggy Spina, Jean Stearns, Fred Strickler, Shea Sullivan. Dormeshia Sumbry-Edwards, Jimmy Tate, Chance Taylor, Michael Tiranoff, Kaoru Tomita, Dorothy Toy, Tony Waag, Dianne Walker, Dorothy Wasserman, Sam Weber, Sebastian Weber, George Wein, Chester Whitmore, Baakari Wilder, Tarik Winston, Nicholas Young, Steve Zee. I apologize if I have left anyone out.

Robert Gottlieb honored me by soldiering through the manuscript in its most gargantuan form and offering sage advice. I am indebted to Judah Adashi, Jon Yaeger, and Apollinaire Scherr for their close readings and constant support. Commenting on more than one draft was the least of Julie Orringer's contribution. It's hard to imagine how I could have made it through without her.

As a rookie author, I was in excellent hands with Robert Cornfield for an agent. I am eternally grateful to Paul Elie for first championing the book at Farrar, Straus and Giroux. His counsel, spread across a long wait, was more crucial than he may know. Jeff Seroy (and his super-capable assistant, Steven Pfau) guided me through the final stretch with confidence-building poise and charm. I was further blessed by the heroic copyediting of

John McGhee, the proofreading of Judy Kiviat, Christopher Caines, and Susan Goldfarb, and the gorgeous design of Abby Kagan. It was a pleasure and a privilege to be photographed by Nancy Crampton.

To my parents I owe all, but my mother deserves special recognition for having put me into my first tap class and getting me to those that followed. As she once said about encouraging my habit of reading, she didn't know what monster she was creating. Ellen Blain, my wife, did know what she was getting into. Our marriage has hardly known a day when I was not working on this book or worrying about it—all that pressure, on top of the tapping that will, I'm afraid, persist past the book's publication. She endured everything with grace and love. She made it possible. Not even Fred with Ginger was as lucky as I am.

INDEX

Note: Unless otherwise identified, entries in italics are Broadway shows; entries in quotation marks are songs and/or dance numbers. Page numbers in italics indicate illustrations.

Woods, Tommy, 152
Woody, Charles, 197
Woollcott, Alexander, 145, 147, 148
Wooster Group, 428
Wooten, Danny, 476
World War I, *see* First World War
World War II, *see* Second World War
Worrell, Jennie, 95

"Yankee Doodle Dandy," 138, 288
Yankee Doodle Dandy (film), 236
Yates, Billie, 20
Yeah-Man, 181
Yes, I Can! (Davis), 348
Yes Sir, That's My Baby (film), 291
"Yes, We Have No Bananas," 188
Yoruban dancing, 32, 33, 41
You Can't Have Everything (film), 216, 267
You'll Never Get Rich (film), 282
"You Must Believe in Spring," 456
Young, Frank, 139

Young, Lester, 309
Young, Stark, 299
Young, Trummy, 33
Young People (film), 258
"You're Just a Little Nigger but You're Mine All Mine," 123

Zambia, 32
Zanuck, Darryl, 278
Zatoichi (film), 507
Zernov, Vladimir, 502
Ziegfeld, Florenz, 139–40, 143, 150, 183, 216, 222, 223, 249
Ziegfeld Follies, 139–41, 143–44, 146, 147, 149, 150, 152–53, 162, 164, 182, 189–90, 216, 222, 235, 245, 341
Ziegfeld Follies (film), 287
Zinn, Howard, 388
"Zip Coon," 64, 69, 70
Zukor, Adolph, 275
Zulu, 57

A NOTE ABOUT THE AUTHOR

Brian Seibert is a dance critic for *The New York Times* and a contributor to *The New Yorker*. Born and raised in Los Angeles, he lives in Brooklyn with his wife and daughter. This is his first book.